ALEXANDER S. SALLEY, JR.

The History of
Orangeburg County
South Carolina

FROM ITS FIRST SETTLEMENT TO THE
CLOSE OF THE REVOLUTIONARY WAR

by
A. S. Salley, Jr.
Member Southern History Association

HERITAGE BOOKS
2011

HERITAGE BOOKS
AN IMPRINT OF HERITAGE BOOKS, INC.

Books, CDs, and more—Worldwide

For our listing of thousands of titles see our website
at
www.HeritageBooks.com

A Facsimile Reprint
Published 2011 by
HERITAGE BOOKS, INC.
Publishing Division
100 Railroad Ave. #104
Westminster, Maryland 21157

Copyright © 1897 A. S. Salley, Jr.

Originally published
Orangeburg, S.C.:
R. Lewis Berry, Printer
1898

— Publisher's Notice —
In reprints such as this, it is often not possible to remove blemishes from the original. We feel the contents of this book warrant its reissue despite these blemishes and hope you will agree and read it with pleasure.

International Standard Book Numbers
Paperbound: 978-0-7884-0442-9
Clothbound: 978-0-7884-8677-7

TO

THE MEMORY

OF

MY GRANDFATHER,

THE LATE

DR. A. S. SALLEY,

AND

To the People of Orangeburg County,
AMONG WHOM HE LIVED ALL THE YEARS OF HIS LIFE, AND FOR
WHOM HE LABORED PROFESSIONALLY FOR OVER FIFTY
YEARS OF THAT LIFE, THIS VOLUME IS
RESPECTFULLY DEDICATED.

It is a remarkable fact that very many persons are prone to study the history of every other country, while totally neglecting that of their own country; and yet the study of local history is one of the most delightful of studies.

The State of South Carolina, in historic interest, stands among the very first of our States; but, nevertheless, the numerous valuable historical works on South Carolina have long since passed out of print because of the lack of interest manifested in them, and many people in this State to-day accept as history the false writings of uninformed partisan writers, and, what is worse, permit their children to be taught these falsehoods as truths.

Orangeburg County is rich in historic treasures, and although a few of these treasures have been collected and given to us in several works on South Carolina, they are still out of the reach of the average reader, on account of the scarcity of these works to-day. It is my purpose to present in these pages the various extracts pertaining to Orangeburg, from several of the works referred to above, and, in addition, to give much history of Orangeburg County that has never before been published, including the record of marriages, births and deaths, kept by Rev. John Ulrick Giessendanner and his successor, Rev. John Giessendanner, from 1737 to 1761.

Some may think that I have gone too much into detail, and that I have put in much that might have been left out; but this work is not prepared "for the use of schools", but according to the approved style of purely local histories, and I can only add, in the words of Dr. Ramsay, in his History of South Carolina, that, "Every day that minute local histories of these states are deferred is an injury to posterity, for by means thereof more of that knowledge which ought to be transmitted to them will be irrecoverably lost."

In preparing this work I have freely consulted, Ramsay's History of South Carolina and his History of the Revolution in South Carolina; three editions of Simms's History of South Carolina, his Geography of South Carolina, his South Carolina in the Revolutionary War, and his novel "The Forayers"; Howe's History of the Presbyterian Church in South Carolina; Dalcho's History of the Protestant Episcopal Church in South Carolina; Col. Henry Lee's Memoirs of the War in the Southern Department; Moultrie's Memoirs; Drayton's Memoirs; Drayton's View of South Carolina; Johnson's Traditions of the Revolution; O'Neall's Bench and Bar of South Carolina, and his Annals of of Newberry District; Carroll's Historical Collections of South Carolina; B. F. Perry's Sketches; Gibbes's Documentary Histories; Collections of the South Carolina Historical Society; Logan's History of the Upper Country of South Carolina; Mills's Statistics of South Carolina; Industrial Resources of South Carolina (Vol. III); Thomas's History of the South Carolina Military Academy; La Borde's History of the South Carolina College; Tarleton Brown's Memoirs; a pamphlet on the Formation of Judicial and Political Sub-Divisions in South Carolina, by J. P. Thomas, Jr.; a pamphlet entitled "The Names, as far as can be ascertained, of the Officers who served in the South Carolina Regiments on the Continental Establishment, of the Officers who served in the Militia, of what troops were upon the Continental Establishment, and what Militia Organizations served", by Gen. Wilmot G. De Saussure; the Statutes of South Carolina; the files of various old South Carolina newspapers in the Charleston Library, dating as far back as 1732; the public records in the offices of Register of Mesne Conveyance and Judge of Probate of Charleston, dating back to 1700; those in the office of the Secretary of State at Columbia, dating back to 1682; and numerous old deeds, grants, letters, &c. &c.

I have, perhaps, quoted rather freely from the "History of the German Settlements and of the Lutheran Church in North and South Carolina", by Rev. G. D. Bernheim, D. D.; but what Dr. Bernheim has written is too important to be left out of a work on Orangeburg. He has gone deeper into the history of one of the most important elements of our population, the German settlers, than any other of our historians; and if I had spent years in making researches, in the end, I could not have improved upon Dr. Bernheim's observations, although I have been able to make additions here and there to what he has written.

I am also under obligations, for valuable assistance, to Rev. A. E. Cornish, Librarian of the Episcopal Library in Charleston; Langdon Cheves, Esq., of Charleston; Henry F. Jennings, Esq., of Columbia; Mr. W. W. Culler, of Orangeburg County; Mr. Yates Snowden, of the *News and Courier;* and my grandfather, Mr. C. M. McMichael, of Orangeburg. From my grandfather, the late Dr. A. S. Salley, I also received valuable information and suggestions.

To my father, for his generous aid; and to all others

who lent their interest and sympathy, I beg to make my acknowledgments.

A. S. SALLEY, JR.

Orangeburg, S. C.,
April 1st, 1898.

INTRODUCTION.

There have existed in South Carolina various territorial divisions. There have been counties, parishes, townships, districts or precincts, election districts and judicial districts. Landgrave Joseph Morton became governor of South Carolina in 1682, and one of the first measures required of him was the division of the inhabited portion of the province into three counties. (Order of Proprietors, May 10, 1682.) Berkeley, embracing Charles Town, extended from Sewee on the North to Stono Creek on the South; beyond this to the northward was Craven County, and to the southward Colleton. Shortly afterwards Cartaret County was added to the number. This County included the country around Port Royal; later, about 1708, it was called Granville County.

The territory now embraced within Orangeburg County formed parts of Berkeley and Colleton. That part of Orangeburg East of the Edisto river, with the exception of a narrow strip along that river southward from a point a few miles below the city of Orangeburg, was in Berkeley County, and that part West of the Edisto, together with the above mentioned strip, was in Colleton. In 1704, an Act was passed creating parishes within the several counties. In Berkeley County six parishes were established, but none of them included any territory now embraced by Orangeburg County. In 1706 two parishes were established in Colleton County, but did not likewise include any of the territory now embraced by Orangeburg County.

In 1730, by royal authority, eleven townships were laid off in square plats on the sides of rivers in South Carolina, each containing 20,000 acres. They were designed to encourage settlements, and the plan was that each township should eventually become a parish. When their population increased to one hundred families, they were to have the right to send two members to the General Assembly. Of these eleven townships two were laid off on the Santee, (or more properly on the Congaree, a branch of the Santee, and the Santee), one on the Pon Pon, (Edisto), and one on the Savannah, opposite to the present site of Augusta. These were Amelia, so called probably after the Princess Amelia; the township that was at first called Congaree, but which was called Saxe-Gotha by Governor Broughton in 1736; the township that was at first called Edisto, but after its settlement by the Germans, Swiss and Dutch in 1735 was called Orangeburgh, presumably in honor of William of Orange; and New Windsor.

In 1765, the townships of Amelia and Orangeburgh were erected into St. Matthew's Parish by the following Act of the General Assembly of the Province of South Carolina: (Statutes of S. C., Vol. IV., page 230.)

(*No.* 944.) "AN ACT for establishing a Parish in Berkley County, by the name of St. Matthew, and for declaring the road therein mentioned to be a public road.

"WHEREAS, several inhabitants of the said county, by their petition to the General Assembly, have represented many inconveniences which they are under for want of having a parish laid out and established in the said county, contiguous to and including Amelia township, and prayed that a law may be passed for that purpose: we therefore humbly pray his most sacred Majesty that it may be enacted.

"I. *And be it enacted,* by the Honorable William Bull, Esq., Lieutenant Governor and Commander-in-chief in and over the Province of South Carolina, by and with the advice and consent of his Majesty's Council and the Commons House of Assembly of the said Province, and by the authority of the same, That immediately from and after the passing of this Act, a parish shall be laid out and established in Berkley county aforesaid, in the following manner, that is to say, by running a line from the plantation of Garrard Nelson on Santee River, inclusive, to the place where the new road leading from the plantation of Tacitus Galliard, Esq. to the road leading from Charlestown to Orangeburgh, intersects the line that divides the parish of St. George Dorchester from St. James Goose Creek, and from thence to continue on the said line until it intersects the Four Hole Creek the second time, thence following the said Creek till it intersects the south east bounds of Orangeburgh township, and from thence along the bounds of the said township to the southward, and where that line reaches Edisto River, up the course of the said river until the north west boundary of the said township, from the River a north east course along the line of the township until it joins the south west bounds of Amelia township, and from thence a north east course till it reaches Beaver Creek; and that the said parish shall hereafter be called and known by the name of St. Matthew, and the inhabitants thereof shall and may have, use, exercise and enjoy all the rights, privileges and immunities that the inhabitants of any other parish do or can use, exercise or enjoy by the laws of this Province.

"II. *And be it also enacted* by the authority aforesaid, That a church, chapel and parsonage house shall be built at such places within the bounds of the said parish, as the major part of the commissioners hereafter named, shall order and direct; and also, that a chapel shall be built at such place within the bounds of the said parish as the major part of the commissioners hereafter last named, shall order and direct.

"III. *And be it also enacted* by the authority aforesaid, That the rector or minister of the said parish for the time being, shall officiate in the said church and chapels alternately, and shall be elected and chosen in the same manner as the rectors or ministers of the several other parishes in this Province are elected and chosen, and shall have yearly paid to him and his successors forever, the same salary as is appointed for the rector or minister of any other parish in this Province, (the parishes of St. Philip and St. Michael excepted,) out of the fund appropriated or to be appropriated for payment of the salaries of the clergy in this Province: and the public treasurer for the time being is hereby authorized and required to pay the same, under the like penalties and forfeitures as for not paying the salaries due to the other rectors or ministers of the several other parishes in this Province; and the said rector or minister of the said parish shall have and enjoy all and every such privileges and advantages, and be under such rules, laws and restrictions, as the rectors or ministers of the other parishes in this Province have and enjoy, or are subject and liable unto.

"IV. *And be it enacted* by the authority aforesaid, That Colonel Moses Thompson, Col. William Thompson, William Heatly, Thomas Platt, Tacitus Galliard, Timothy Dargon, Robert Whitten. William Flud, John Burdell, Christopher Coullett and John Oliver, be, and they are hereby appointed, commissioners or supervisors for the building of the church, chapel and parsonage house in the said parish of St. Matthew, exclusive of that part of the parish called Orangeburgh Township; and that Christian Minnick. Gavin Powe. Captain Rowe, Colonel Chevillette and John Govan, or a majority of them, be, and they are hereby appointed, commissioners or supervisors for building the chapel in that part of the parish called Orangeburgh Township; and they, or the major part of them, are fully authorized and impowered to purchase a glebe for the said parish, and to take subscriptions, and to receive and gather, collect and sue for, all such sum and sums of money as any pious and well disposed person or persons shall give and contribute for the purposes aforesaid; and in case of the death, absence or refusing to act of any of the said commissioners, the church wardens and vestry of the said parish of St. Matthew, for the time being, shall and may nominate and appoint another person or persons to be commissioner or commissioners in the room or place of such so dead, absent or refusing to act, as to the said church wardens and vestry shall seem meet; which commissioner or commissioners so to be nominated and appointed, shall have the same powers and authority for putting this Act into execution, to all intents and purposes, as the commissioners herein named.

"V. *And be it also enacted* by the authority aforesaid, That the inhabitants of the said parish of St. Matthew, qualified by law for that purpose, shall choose and elect two members, and no more, to represent the said parish in General Assembly; any law, usage or custom to the contrary thereof in any wise notwithstanding: and that writs for the electing of members to serve in the General Assembly for the said parish, shall be issued in the same manner and at the same times as for the several other parishes in this Province, according to the directions in the Act intitled 'An Act to ascertain the manner and form of electing members to represent the inhabitants of this Province in the Commons House of Assembly, and to appoint who shall be deemed and adjudged capable of choosing or being chosen members of the said house.'

"VI. *And be it further enacted* by the authority aforesaid, That the new road leading from the ferry of Tacitus Galliard, Esquire, to the road leading from Charlestown to Orangeburgh, shall be, and it is hereby declared to be, a public road, and shall be worked upon and kept in repair by the inhabitants of each parish through which the said road runs, in the same manner as all the other public roads in this Province are; and that the commissioners herein before appointed shall also be commissioners of and for the said road, and all other roads in the said parish of St. Matthew, and shall have the same powers and authority as any other commissioners of the high roads in this Province have; and in case any of the said commissioners shall die or refuse to act, the remaining commissioners shall, from time to time, choose one or more commissioner or commissioners in the room of him or them so dying or refusing to act, and he or they so chosen shall have the same powers and authority as the said other commissioners.

"RAWLINS LOWNDES, *Speaker.*
"*In the Council Chamber, the 9th day of August, 1765.*
"*Assented to:* WM. BULL."

By order of the King's Privy Council, Governor Montagu published, in the *South Carolina Gazette* of Monday, February 29th, to Monday, March 7th, 1768, the following proclamation annulling the above act:
"South Carolina:

"By His Excellency the Right Honorable, Lord Charles Greville Montagu, Captain-General, and Governor in Chief, in and over the said Province, &c. &c.

"A PROCLAMATION.

"Whereas the Right Honorable the Earl of Sheburne, one of his Majesty's principal Secretaries of State, hath transmitted to me a minute of his Majesty in his most honorable Privy council, signifying, that an Act of the General Assembly of this Province, entitled, 'an Act for establishing a Parish in Berkley County by the Name of St. Matthew, and for declaring the road therein mentioned to be a public Road'; together with a Representation from the Lords Commissioners of Trade and Plantations thereupon, having been referred to a committee of his Majesty's most honourable Privy Council for Plantation Affairs; the said Lords of the Committee had reported as their Opinion to his Majesty that the said Act ought to be repealed; and his Majesty having taken the same into Consideration, was pleased by the Advice of his Privy Council, to declare his Disallowance of the said Act; And pursuant to his Majesty's Royal Pleasure thereupon expressed, the said Act was thereby Repealed, and declared Void and of none Effect: I HAVE THEREFORE issued this my Proclamation, hereby notifying the same, and requiring all Persons whom it may concern, to take Notice and govern themselves accordingly.

GIVEN under my hand, and the great seal of the said province, at CHARLES TOWN, this 29th day of February, Anno Domini one thousand seven hundred and sixty-eight, and in the eighth year of his Majesty's reign. "C. G. MONTAGU,

"By his Excellency's command, John Bull, Pro. Sec. God save the KING."

Notwithstanding this veto the General Assembly, in April following, re-enacted the same measure under the same title, with the same preamble; fixed the same boundaries, made the same conditions as to church, chapel and parsonage, and declared the same road mentioned in the former Act to be a public road. The only differences between the Act of 1768, which became permanent, and that of 1765, are to be found in the fourth and fifth sections of the Acts. In the fourth section of the Act of 1768 the following commissioners or supervisors were appointed for the building of the new church, chapel and parsonage house in the said parish of St. Matthew, exclusive of Orangeburgh Township: Benjamin Farrar, Col. William Thomson, William Heatly, Thomas Platt, Tacitus Gaillard, Thomas Sabb, John Bordell, John Caldwell, Robert Whitton, William Flood and John McNichol. For the building of a chapel in Orangeburgh Township the following commissioners were appointed: Gavin Pou, Captain Christopher Rowe, Samuel Rowe, William Young and Andrew Govan.

The fifth section differs from the same section of the former Act in that it provides for only one Representative in the Provincial Assembly instead of two, and further provides that the number of Representatives for St. James Goose Creek be reduced from four to three in consequence of this allowing of a Representative for St. Matthew's Parish. The Act is dated April 12th, 1768, and is signed by P. Manigault, Speaker, and assented to by Governor Montagu. (Stats. of S. C., Vol. IV., p. 298.)

In 1768 an Act was passed dividing the Province of South Carolina into seven judicial *districts* or *precincts*,*

---

*In 1767 (April 18th) the Legislature passed "An Act for granting to his Majesty the sum of Eighteen Thousand Pounds current money, to be paid for a general survey of this Province, and for appointing commissioners to enter into a written agreement with Tacitus Gaillard, Esq. and Mr. James Cook, for that purpose". (Stats. of S. C., Vol. IV., p. 262.) Whether this survey was made or not the records do not show, but James Cook did publish in 1771, a map of South Carolina which showed the boundaries of the districts laid off by the Act of 1768.

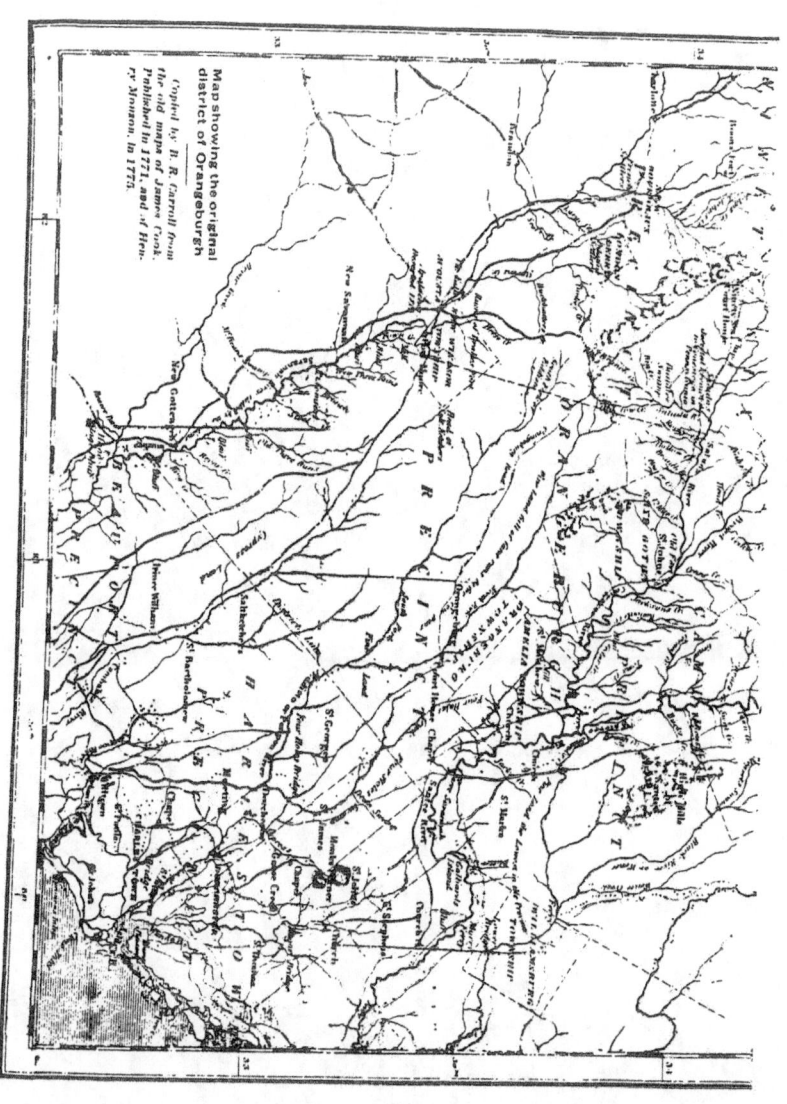

and authorizing the holding of Courts of General Sessions and Common Pleas therein, twice a year, to sit for six days, for the trial of causes criminal and civil arising within the same, "as nearly as may be, as the Justices of Assize and *Nisi Prius* do in Great Britain". The third of these districts was called the "District, or Precinct, of Orangeburgh", including "all places between Savannah, Santee, Congaree and Broad Rivers, the said line from Nelson's Ferry to Matthew's Bluff, and a direct line to be run from Silver Bluff, on Savannah River, to the mouth of Rocky Creek, on Saluda River, and thence in the same course to Broad River". It was not, however, until 1789 that these Courts were given complete and equal jurisdiction with the Courts at Charleston, and writs and process made returnable to them and not to the Court at Charleston. A Clerk and a Sheriff was allowed to each district. It will be observed that this, the original District of Orangeburgh, contained all of the present Counties of Orangeburg, Barnwell, Bamberg and Lexington, (and Calhoun "in futuro") and the larger part of Aiken. (All save the present townships of Shultz, Hammond, Gregg, Shaw and Ward.) It included the whole of the townships of Orangeburgh, Amelia and Saxe-Gotha, and a part of New Windsor.

In March, 1778, the Township of Orangeburgh was erected into a parish called Orange, by the following Act of the State Legislature: (Statutes of S. C., Vol. IV.. pp. 408-9.)

(*No.* 1072.) "AN ACT for dividing the Township of Orangeburgh from the Parish of St. Matthews, into a separate Parish, by the name of Orange Parish, and for the other purposes therein mentioned.

"WHEREAS, the inhabitants of Orangeburgh Township were, by an Act of the General Assembly passed on the twelfth day of April, in the year of our Lord one thousand seven hundred and sixty eight, included in the Parish of St. Matthew, whereby the said inhabitants have sustained many inconveniences, which still subsist; for remedy whereof,

"I. *Be it enacted* by his Excellency Rawlins Lowndes, Esq., President and Commander-in-chief in and over the State of South Carolina, by the honorable the Legislative Council and General Assembly of the said State, and by the authority of the same, That the dividing line between the district of Charlestown and Orangeburgh shall henceforth be the dividing line between the Township of Orangeburgh and the parishes of St. Matthew, St. John's Berkley county. St. James Goose Creek and St. George Dorchester; and from the said Charlestown district line the Four Hole Creek, as far as the line that divides Amelia Township and Orangeburgh District, following the said line to the north-west boundary line of the said Township, shall be the dividing line between St. Matthew's parish and the township of Orangeburgh; and that the inhabitants residing on and between the said Charlestown district line and the north-west bounding of Amelia township, and on and between the said district line and Santee River, be hereafter deemed and known in law to be the inhabitants of St. Matthew's Parish; and the inhabitants being and residing on and between the said Charlestown district line, and the north-west bounding line of Orangeburgh township, and between the Four Hole Creek and the line that divides the townships of Orangeburgh and Amelia, and Pon Pon River, be hereafter deemed and known in law to be the inhabitants of Orange Parish.

"II. *And be it further enacted* by the authority aforesaid, That the inhabitants of St. Matthew's Parish, being qualified as by law directed, shall choose three members to represent them in General Assembly: and the inhabitants of Orange Parish, qualified as aforesaid, shall choose three members to represent them in the General Assembly; and that writs for the election of members for the General Assembly shall be issued in the same manner and at the same time as writs have been and shall be issued for the other parishes and districts in this State.

"III. *And be it further enacted* by the authority aforesaid, That Thomas Wild, John Robinson, Henry Rickinbacker, James Carmichael, Jacob Woolf, Jr., Henry Felder, Jr., Andrew Frederick, John Clayton and Peter Moorer, Sr. be, and they are hereby appointed, commissioners for keeping in repair the Public Road from the above said north-west boundary line of Orangeburgh township to the place where the said road crosses Charlestown district line, and that they shall have the same powers and authorities as any other commissioners of the high roads in this State may or can exercise and enjoy; and in case any of the said commissioners shall die or refuse to act, the remaining commissioners shall from time to time choose one or more commissioner or commissioners, in the room of him or them so dying or refusing to act, and he or they so chosen, shall have the same power and authority as the other commissioners have; any law, usage or custom to the contrary notwithstanding.

"HUGH RUTLEDGE. *Speaker of the Legislative Council.*
"THOMAS BEE, *Speaker of the General Assembly.*
"*In the Council Chamber, the 16th day of March, 1778.*
"*Assented to:* RAWLINS LOWNDES."

The Constitution of 1778 provided that the whole State should, as soon as possible, be divided into dis-

---

The road referred to in the last section of the above Act is the road now known as the Bull Swamp road above Orangeburg, as Broughton Street in the city of Orangeburg, and as the old Charleston road below Orangeburg.

tricts and counties, and that County Courts should be established. Accordingly in 1783 (March 16th.) the Legislature, concluding that it was "necessary to divide this State into counties of a convenient size, in order to the establishment of courts of inferior jurisdiction",* passed "An Ordinance for appointing Commissioners in each of the Circuit Court Districts, for dividing the same into Counties". Under the Ordinance commissioners were appointed in each of the several districts and "empowered and directed to lay off and divide" their respective districts "into counties of a convenient size, of not more than forty miles square, unless where the number of inhabitants and situation of the lands" required some deviation; were required to "recommend a proper place as nearly central as possible in each of the said counties, for erecting court houses and goals", and were required to "make report thereof to the first session of the General Assembly", held after the last day of December following. The following were the commissioners appointed to divide Orangeburgh District: William Arthur, George Robinson, William Thomson, John Parkinson, George Rennarson, Charles Middleton and Uriah Goodwyn. They were "authorized and impowered at the public expense to employ surveyors", where they deemed it "absolutely necessary", "to fix and ascertain the boundary lines of each district or county respectively". (Stats. of S. C., Vol. IV., p. 561.)

Following this Ordinance, the Legislature, on March 12th, 1785, passed "An Act for laying off the several Counties therein mentioned, and appointing Commissioners to erect the Public Buildings". The following clause of the Act concerns Orangeburgh District: "The

---

*To be held once in every three months in each of the counties, to be presided over by seven Justices of the Peace. A Clerk and a Sheriff was allowed to each county.

ORANGEBURG COUNTY. 13

district of Orangeburgh shall be divided into four counties, viz: beginning at the boundary line of Charleston district, in Four Hole swamp, thence along the main branch to the head, from thence northwest 25° to Beaver creek, and thence along the same to the Congaree, thence down Santee to Neilson's ferry, thence along Charleston district line to the beginning, and shall be called by the name of Lewisburgh county; one other county, beginning at the corner of Lewisburgh county line, in the Four Hole swamp, thence along the said line to Beaver creek, thence southwest 54° to the road leading from Orangeburgh to Ninety-Six, in the fork of Edisto river, thence south to the head of Little Saltketcher, thence down the said Saltketcher to the district line, thence to the beginning, and shall be called by the name of Orange county; one other county, beginning at the mouth of Beaver creek, thence along the line of Orange county, thence southwest 54° to the road leading from Orangeburgh to Ninety-Six, thence along the road to the district line, thence along the said line to Saluda river, thence along Union county* line to Broad river, thence down the same and Congaree river to the beginning, and be called by the name of Lexington county; one other county, beginning on the Little Saltketcher swamp, at the corner of Orange county line, thence along the district line to Savannah river, thence up the same to the district line, thence along the said line to the south branch of Edisto, thence down the same to Tyler's ferry, thence a direct line to the Saltketchers, where the line of Beaufort district intersects, to Orange county line, thence south to the head of Little Saltketcher, thence down the same to the beginning, and shall be called Winton county". The justices of

---
*Of Ninety-Six District.

the several counties were authorized to erect and keep in good repair, within each of their respective counties. and at the charge of such county, "one good and convenient court-house, with necessary jury rooms, and one good and sufficient county gaol, of such materials, workmanship, size and dimensions", as they should order and appoint, "together with a pillory, whipping post and stocks". The justices were empowed "to purchase, or receive by donation, two acres of land whereon to erect the said county buildings, for the use of such county, and for no other use whatsoever". A failure on the part of the justices of the county to have erected and kept in good and sufficient repair, "a court house, prison, pillory and stocks" would subject every justice so failing to a fine of two hundred pounds. to be recovered by action of debt, one half to go to the treasurers for the time being, for the use of the county, and the other half to the person who should inform and sue for the same in the Court of Common Pleas. The justices were given full power "to levy and assess an annual tax on the taxable property of the several inhabitants within the respective counties, for building the court houses, prisons, pillories. whipping posts and stocks", and they were required to put the public buildings in the most convenient part of each county. (Stats. of S. C., Vol. IV., p. 661. et seq.)

In 1790 a convention of the people of South Carolina met in Columbia to establish a constitution for the government of the State conformably to the principles of the Constitution of the United States. The Constitution of 1790 was the work of that Convention. "It constituted the organic law of the State until 1865. It vested legislative authority in a Senate and a House of Representatives. Representation in the General Assembly was accorded to certain sub-divisions, which were called 'Election Districts.' These election districts comprised nearly all of the old parishes and many of the counties which had been laid off in 1785 for the County Court establishment. Those parts of the State in which County Courts had not been established retained for the most part their parish divisions for representative purposes, and in the other parts of the State the election districts corresponded in name and territory, in most instances, with the counties." The County of Lexington, however, was the Election District of Saxe-Gotha until 1852 when it was changed to the Election District of Lexington, and, in the course of time, the Election District of Winton became known as the Election District of Barnwell.

"When the Constitution of 1790 was adopted, it provided that the judicial power of the State should be vested in such Superior and Inferior Courts as the Legislature might establish. Accordingly, in 1791, an Act was passed to amend the Acts regulating the Circuit Courts in the State. This Act created two new Judicial Districts, namely: Pinckney and Washington, making in all nine districts, instead of seven as formerly. The Districts were laid off anew." Orangeburgh District "included all places between the Savannah, Santee, Congaree and Broad Rivers, the said line from Nelson's Ferry to Matthew's Bluff, and direct line to be run from Silver Bluff, on the Savannah River, to the mouth of Rocky Creek on Saluda River, and thence in the same courses to Broad River." It will be noticed that the district remained exactly the same as when first laid off in 1768.

"In 1798, an Act was passed to establish a uniform and more convenient system of judicature. This Act provided for the holding of District or Circuit Courts in many of the Counties of the State, and in those Districts of the State wherein County Courts had not been established. and provided for the arrangement of those Courts into several circuits or ridings. The twenty-four Districts created by this Act were known as Judicial Districts, in contradistinction to the Election Districts of the State. These Judicial Districts, in some instances, covered the same territory as the Election District." In others they differed. In Orangeburgh they differed. In some instances, although the Judicial and Election Districts were identical in territory, yet they had different names. Lexington District, for instance, was for many years represented in the Legislature as Saxe-Gotha. One of the Judicial Districts so created was Barnwell, which included "that part of the former District of Orangeburg as is included between South Edisto and Savannah Rivers". Orangeburgh District included all of the former District save Barnwell.

In 1804 Lexington County was cut off from Orangeburgh District and erected into Lexington District.

"The next changes to be noted were made by the Constitution of 1865. There had always been a struggle in the State to make the Judicial and Election Districts the same in fact as well as in name, and, as has been mentioned, the names of some of the Election Districts were changed to correspond with the Judicial Districts. The Constitution of 1865 nearly ended the contest, for by its provisions every Judicial District in the State. with one exception, was made an Election District". (This exception was in the case of the District of Charleston, the provision for that District being that it should "consist of two Election Districts, one comprising the Parishes of St. Philip's and St. Michael's, to be known as the Election District of Charleston, the other comprising the remainder of the Judicial District, to be known as the Election District of Berkeley.") "Under the authority of this Constitution, District Courts for each District were established with a certain limited jurisdiction. They lasted until the Constitution of 1868 was adopted. The number of Representatives, and the method of appointment, prescribed by the Constitution of 1865 were the same as provided in the Constitution of 1790 and in the amendments thereto. Until an apportionment should be made upon a new enumeration, it was provided that the representation of the several Election Districts should continue as heretofore.

"The Constitution of 1868 made all Judicial Districts Counties, and declared each County an Election District." (The old Election District of Berkeley was absorbed into Charleston County.)

In 1871 Aiken County was formed out of parts of the counties of Orangeburg, Edgefield, Lexington and Barnwell.

Having discussed the various political divisions and sub-divisions of Orangeburg County from the earliest time, next we discuss the history of the people of that County. But before proceeding, a word as to spelling. It will be observed that the apostrophe before the possessive "s" has been dropped in late years from the name St. Matthew's, and it is now written St. Matthews. The "h" has also been dropped from Orangeburgh in late years. For our purposes we shall use the "h" up to the year 1868 when the Districts were abolished and Counties established in their stead. Charleston will be spelt "Charlestown" whenever its Colonial or Revolutionary history is mentioned, as it was so spelt in Colonial and Revolutionary days. The spelling, capitalization, abbreviation and punctuation of all quoted matters will be given as in the original.

CHAPTER I.

THE FIRST SETTLERS.

Section 1. Who they were, and where they came from.

Probably the first settlement made by a white person in the territory now embraced by the County of Orangeburg was made on what is now known as Lyons Creek, in 1704, by Henry Sterling, who is supposed to have been an Indian trader. Prior to 1735 but few white inhabitants had settled in this section, and these were mostly English, Scotch and Irish.

Dr. Alexander Hewat, in his History of South Carolina, (Carroll's Historical Collections of S. C., Vol. I., p. 207.) says that in 1716, as a precaution against the incursions of the Yemassee Indians, a small fort was erected on the Congaree in Berkeley County; and the Journal of Council of January 20, 1720, says: "Since the Indian war have been obliged to maintain the following Garrisons—viz: at the Congarees 130 miles N from Charles Town a captain and 20 men" &c., &c. This fort was a little below the present site of Columbia, but on the opposite side of the river, as is shown by a map in the first volume of Carroll's Historical Collections of South Carolina.

In the tenth chapter of Logan's History of Upper South Carolina the following account is given of the establishment of this fort: "No direct mention is made in the State records of a traffic with the Cherokees, previous to the assumption of the management of the peltry trade by the public authorities of the province in 1716. In that year it is stated that goods had been sent up by order of the Assembly for their use. This was done in compliance with a sort of commercial treaty, formed at this period, with the Cherokees through the diplomacy, on the one side, of Col. James Moore, and of Charite Hayge, a distinguished conjurer and friend of the English, on the other. It was stipulated that there should be a regular exchange of goods and peltries between Charleston and the Nation. * * * * * *

"It was also agreed that a trading house and fort should be built the approaching fall, at a place known as the Congarees, the Conjurer promising to repair thither, at that time. with eighty warriors—one half of whom were to assist in cutting logs for the fort, and the other to carry the goods, expected to be brought up by the English that far, the remainder of the distance to the Cherokee towns.
* * * * * * * * *

"Though Fort Moore, and the one beyond the Savannah, were built in 1716, that at the Congarees, contrary to the agreement with Charite Hayge, was not erected till two years later. The reason assigned by the Board for deferring the work was, that the trading house and garrison at Savannah Town were sufficient for the trade until the Cherokees had concluded the war they were at that time waging with a branch of the Muscogees.

"Hewit remarks of this fort that with the others it was erected for the special purpose of defence and against the same dangers. If the records must be credited, however, it would appear that the Cherokees themselves requested that it should be built in view of their increasing traffic with the English; and it was in compliance with that request, and the enlarged demands of the trade, that in the summer of 1718 a body of men was sent up from Charleston to be employed in its construction.

"In August of that year, Capt. Charles Russell,* who, at the recommendation of the Board, had been appointed by the governor the first commandant of the fort, was ordered to proceed to the country, and there enlist the men who were to constitute its garrison as soon as it should be completed. Among those who were thus enlisted for this service, were Ralph Dayton, John Evans, and Edward Darlsley, the first soldiers who ever did duty in the old fort at the Congarees.

"We have before us an extract from the instructions given by the Board to one Dauge, an assistant agent among the Cherokees, in relation to the public work at Congarees:

"'You are to proceed at once to the Cherokee Nation, and, on your arrival, inform the Conjurer and other head-men that, in a month or six weeks, we shall have a settlement at the Congarees, to which place they may resort, and procure whatever goods they may need; that we would have built the fort earlier than this, if some of our people had not run away with the boat which had been prepared to carry up the men and implements necessary for its construction. Inform the Conjurer also, that we expect him to hasten down in order to meet at the Congarees with a supply of provisions, the train of pack horses, which is now on its way with the men and tools to be employed on the fort, and with a quantity of ammunition for the Cherokees.'

"In the fall of the previous year, 1717, the Board had said to a trader just setting off for the Nation: 'Acquaint Charite Hayge that our new Governor Johnson has arrived, and we will speedily fix a garri-

---

*A native of Massachusetts, but born of English parents who had settled in that province.

son and factory at the Congarees, whence the Cherokees may be supplied with arms and ammunition.'

"Samuel Kinsman was the head carpenter, who executed the work, and was paid nine pounds per month for his services. As this fortress was designed simply as a safeguard for the goods and other property belonging to the trade, accumulated here, it was of no more formidable construction than a common stockade inclosure.

"The name was derived from the Congaree Indians, in whose settlement it had been built. It stood on or near the site occupied, in after-years, by old Fort St. John's, a short distance above the mouth of Congaree Creek, near the present City of Columbia. Here was once the great centre of trade for the Catawbas, and Middle and Lower Cherokees. The Over-hills traded chiefly at Savannah Town.

* * * * * * * * *

"At this period, Savannah Town and the Congarees often presented scenes more boisterous and busy than many a commercial town of the present, with far more pretention in situation and trade. On their outskirts are encamped numerous caravans of pack-trains, with their roistering drivers, who are mostly mischievous boys. The smoke from a hundred camp-fires curl above the thick tops of the trees, and the woods resound with the neighing of horses, and the barking and howling of hungry Indian dogs. A large supply of goods has arrived from Charleston, and every pack-saddle came down from the Nation loaded with skins and furs, and these being now displayed to the best advantage, the work of barter begins.

"In the open air and in the trading-house are congregated a motley assembly of pack-horsemen, traders, hunters, squaws, children, soldiers, and stately Indian warriors—some silent and grave, seemingly uninterested in the scene; but the greater number loudly huxtering, and obstinately contending over their respective commodities in trade, in many barbarous tongues.

"The hunters from distant wilds want a supply of powder and ball, each squaw fancies some bright-colored fabric for a new petticoat or dress, while the warriors and old men eagerly demand guns, ammunition and blankets.

"The clamor begins, however, presently to subside, and at length the last bargain has been struck, and the goods and peltries have alike changed hands. The packs are once more made up; the goods for the Indian towns, and the skins for the market on the seaboard, and everything is again ready for the trail. The boys crack their whips, and with shouts and halloos that make the forests ring, the trains enter the narrow paths, and are soon far on their way, leaving the garrisons and agents of the posts to the dull monotony of the wilderness till their next visit."

About 1719 Richard Heatly, "of Berkley County planter," and his wife Mary,* moved from Cooper river to Santee, (within the present County of Orangeburg) and their son William is said to have been the first white child born in this section. Richard Heatly died a few years later, and his widow married Captain Charles Russell, J. P., commandant of the Congaree garrison. Captain Russell's family, together with the families of other members of the garrison, became permanent settlers in this section. Captain Russell died in 1737. He is mentioned in the Statutes of South Carolina for 1734 (Vol. III., p. 391) as captain of rangers, from which we infer that the fort had been

---

*They were married in the parish of St. Thomas and St. Denis in 1714.

abolished and rangers substituted in its stead. We find, as an item of the expenditures of the Province in 1736-7: "Mary Russell, widow, in full for her husband's services as agent, &c. 124 00 00"; from which we take it that from an Indian fighter Captain Russell became an Indian agent, and the following item on the same account probably refers also to him: "To so much allowed for the payment of two men who went up with Major Russell, to be lodged in the hands of the Treasurer, to be paid on proper application, at the rate of £20 per month each." On April 13, 1739, a grant of land was made to Mrs. Mary Russell, "wife of Charles Russell," in trust for her children. The land was situated at or near McCord's Ferry, between the Congaree and Wateree rivers, in Craven County, "over the Congaree" from Amelia Township. It was surveyed Decr. 10, 1741, by George Haig, Deputy Surveyor-General. Mrs. Russell died Jan. 5, 1754, and was buried at her plantation, and the Rev. John Giessendanner in recording her burial states that she had lived in the township (Amelia) twenty-six years.

About 1730 Moses Thomson, with his family and his connections, the Maxwells and Powells, moved into Amelia Township from Pennsylvania. Dr. Joseph Johnson, in his "Traditions of the Revolution", says that the Thomsons were Irish people from Pennsylvania. A member of this family, William Thomson, married Eugenia, daughter of Capt. Charles Russell, and John McCord, a member of another of the families early settled in this section, married her sister, Sophianisba Russell. From these three early Orangeburgh families, Russells, Thomsons and McCords, descended many people who have become prominent in the history of South Carolina. Among their descendants we find the names Thomson, McCord, Heatly, Hart, Taber, Rhett, Haskell, Cheves, Darby, Sinkler, Goodwyn,

Hayne, Michel, Stuart, and many others equally well known.

A leading spirit in this section about 1737 was Major Christian Motte. He is mentioned in old records of that day as being present at marriage ceremonies at Orangeburgh, and the Statutes show that he was, in 1738, an Inquirer and Collector of taxes for the parish of St. John's, Berkeley. He probably collected the taxes for the townships of Amelia and Orangeburgh, as those townships were nearest to St. John's. It is not likely that he remained in this section, as no records have been found to show that he became a permanent settler in this section, and an extract from the *South Carolina Gazette* of January 25—29, 1741, seems to indicate that he then lived in Charlestown. The extract referred to is an advertisement of a wonderful medicine that was "guaranteed to cure or no money taken", and reads as follows: "To be had of John Lax Indian Doctor at Col: Saunders plantation at Cypress swamp or of Major Christian Mote in Charles Town a Decoction" &c., &c. This name must not be confounded with Ft. Motte, for that place obtained its name from Col. Isaac Motte and his heroic wife, Rebecca, who were well known in Charlestown subsequent to this, and who owned a plantation in St. Matthew's Parish, the house of which was seized and garrisoned as a fort by the British during the Revolution, and hence the name Fort Motte.

Probably the first settler in the vicinity of where the present town of Orangeburg is located was John Hearn, (pronounced Harn) who lived just below where Orangeburg now stands as early as 1732. His plantation contained five hundred acres of land and embraced lands now or lately belonging to Messrs John H. Dukes, A. L. Dukes, G. W. Brunson, and Mrs. Mary Hughes. The following certificate of admeasurement,

which accompanies the plat to the above lands, is recorded in the office of the Secretary of State at Columbia.
"South Carolina.

"By virtue of a warrant from his Excellency, Robert Johnson, Esqr. Governor. &c., Bearing date the 28th, day of November 1732, and a precept thereon to me directed by James St. John Esqr. his Majesties Surveyor General of the said province of South Carolina bearing date the 18th, day of December 1732, I have admeasured and sett out unto John Hearne of Colleton County Planter a Plantation or Tract of Land Containing five Hundred acres where he now lives Situate in Colleton lying and being part of the land reserved for the Inhabitants within the Township of Edisto Butting and Bounding to the South Westward on pon pon river to the Northwest on twenty thousand acres of land laid out for the said Township to the Northeastward and Southeastward on land reserved for the Inhabitants of the said Township and hath such form and marks as are represented in the above delineated plat certified the twentieth Day of September anno domini 1733 Per me.
"George Haig Depty. Surveyor."

The following is a copy of the grant which was made to Mr. Hearn, of the lands so laid out:
"South Carolina.

"GEORGE THE SECOND by the grace of God of Great Brittain, France and Ireland King Defender of the Faith &c.

"TO ALL to whom these presents shall come Greeting, Know Ye that we of our special grace certain knowledge and meer motion Have given and granted and by the presents for Us Our Heirs and Successors Do give and grant unto Mr. John Hearn his Heirs and assigns all that parcel or tract of land containing five hundred acres situate lying and being in Colleton County in the province aforesaid butting and bounding to the South Westward on pon pon River to the North westward on twenty thousand acres of land laid out for the said Township to the North eastward and South eastward on land reserved for the Inhabitants of the said Township and hath such shape form and marks as appears by a plat thereof hereunto annexed together with all woods underwoods timber and timber Trees lakes ponds fishings waters water courses profits commodities appurtenances and hereditaments whatsoever thereunto belonging or in any wise appertaining together with privileges of hunting hawking and fowling in and upon the same and all mines and minerals whatsoever saving and reserving nevertheless to us our heirs and successors all white pine trees if any there should be found growing thereon and also saving and reserving to us our heirs and Successors one tenth part of mines of silver and gold onely TO HAVE AND TO HOLD the said tract of five hundred acres of land and all and singular other the premises hereby granted with the appurtenances unto the said John Hearn his heirs and assigns for ever an free and Common Soccage he the said John Hearn his heirs and assigns Yielding And Paying therefore unto us Our heirs and Successors or to our Receiver General for the time being or to his Deputy or Deputies for the time being Yearly that is to say on every twenty fifth day of March at the rate of three Shillings sterling or four shillings Proclamation money for every hundred acres and so in proportion according to the quantity of acres contained herein the same to grow due and be accounted for from the date hereof Provided Always and this present Grant is upon condition Nevertheless that he the said John Hearn his heirs and assigns shall and do within three years next after the date of these presents clear and cultivate at the rate of one acre for every five hundred acres of land and so in proportion according to the quantity of acres herein contained or build a dwelling House thereon, and keep a Stock of five head of cattle for every five hundred acres upon the same and in proportion for a greater or lesser quantity.

AND UPON CONDITION that if the said rent hereby reserved shall happen to be in arrear and unpaid for the space of three years from the time it became due and no distress can be found on the said lands tenements and hereditaments hereby granted that then and in such case the said lands tenements and hereditaments hereby granted and every part and parcel thereof shall revert to us Our heirs and Successors as fully and absolutely as if the same had never been granted.

"Given under the Great Seal of Our Said Province Witness Thomas Broughton Esqr. Our Lieutenant Governor of our said Province of South Carolina the twelfth day of May in the Eighth year of Our Reign and in the year of Our Lord One Thousand seven hundred and thirty-five.

"Thomas (Seal) Broughton."

"And hath thereunto annexed a plat Representing the same tract of land certified by James St. John Surveyr. Genl the 20th. September 1733.

Signed by the Honble. Thomas Broughton Esqr. Lieut. Govr. in Council.
J. Badenhop,
C. C."

The foregoing deed was recorded May 28th. 1735. In the *South Carolina Gazette* of June 25, 1753 this place is advertised for sale as follows:

"John Hearne's place is offered for sale. 500 acres lying & being in Colleton county; butting & bounding to S. W. on Ponpon River, N. W. on Edisto Township to N. E. & S. E. on lands reserved for the Inhabitants of said Township.

"100 acres in the limits of Orangeburgh Township, b. & b. to N. E. on lands laid out to John Strutzenecker, to N. W. on land belonging to John Hearne S. W. on Ponpon S. E. on land laid out to Henry Wuester, one town-lot N. 253."

Another of the early settlers of Orangeburgh Township was Henry Salley, who settled in the township about 1735, as will be seen by the following certificate of measurement for a grant of land, and a subsequent conveyance of the same:

"So. Carolina.

"Pursuant to a precept under the hand & seal of James St. John Esq His Majesty's Sur. Genl I have admeasured & laid out unto Henry Zaley a tract of Land in Orangeburgh Township in Berkeley County containing Two hundred acres Butting & Bounding to the S. W. on Pon Pon River to the N. E. on land not laid out; to the S. E. on land laid out unto Jacob Twyther & to the N. W. on land laid out to Barbara Hatcher & also one Town Lot in Orangeburgh, containing one half of an acre; Known on the grand plat of the s^d Town by the number one hundred & 68: Butting & Bounding to the S. W. on 165 laid out to Hans Deitricks Junr to the N. E. on a Street; to the S. E. on N 169 Laid out to Jacob Miller; to the N. W. on N 167. Land laid out to Henry Rickenbaker, & each hath such shape & marks as are represented by the above plat. Certified the 20 Sep^t 1735.

"Geo. Haig D. S."

It will be observed that in the foregoing certificate the name is given "Zaley," but that must have been the way Mr. Salley's German neighbors called it, for the name has always been Salley, and the following extract from a later deed of the same tract of land,

ALEXANDER S. SALLEY, M. D.

Born April 26th, 1818—Died April 1st, 1895.

from John Salley, Jr., to John Salley, Sen., clearly shows Mr. Haig to have been in error in beginning the name with the letter Z: "All that plantation or Tract of Land—Original Bounty—containing two Hundred acres Situate in (the former) Berkly County, & in Orangeburgh Township." * * * * * "The said Tract of Two Hundred acres of Land and Town Lott aforesaid, was Originally Granted to Henry Zaley (more properly Salley) on the Seventeenth day of September One thousand Seven Hundred and thirty Six" * * * * "Which said Tract of Land & Town Lott aforesaid Devolved in a Lineal Decent to the aforesaid John Salley, Junr as being Heir at Law to the said Tract of Land & Town Lott." This last deed was made August 26, 1790. As early as 1741 the name occurs on Giessendanner's record book spelt "Sähly", and a few years later the same authority records it "Sally"; but the name has obtained in Yorkshire, England, and vicinity, for centuries; and the bearers of the name have always spelt it as the bearers of it in Orangeburg spell it to-day—"Salley." The name Salley signifies "the field of sallows, and was so named undoubtedly", says Whitaker, in his History of the Deanery of Craven, "from real salix and leza ager". (Species of willow.) There is a village of the same name in the parish of Gisburne (in the Deanery of Craven) in Yorkshire.

For some years previous to 1735 John Peter Purry, a Swiss gentleman, had been trying to establish Swiss colonies in South Carolina, and had actually established one on the Savannah river at a place called Purrysburg. He gave such a glowing account of the country in a pamphlet, (See Carroll's Historical Collections of South Carolina, Vol. II.) which he freely distributed throughout Switzerland, Holland, North Germany and the Provinces of the Rhine, that a great many settlers were induced to come to Carolina. The first ship load for Orangeburgh Township arrived in Charlestown in July 1735, and immediately set out for the township on the Edisto, which was thereafter named Orangeburgh. The next year another installment of settlers arrived, and in 1737 a third arrived, bringing with them a Lutheran minister, the Rev. John Ulrick Giessendanner. Others arrived later. Dr. David Ramsay in his "History of South Carolina", page 11, says that the vessels which brought them over usually returned with loads of rice, and made profitable voyages. Rev. J. U. Giessendanner and his nephew and successor, Rev. John Giessendanner, kept a record of the marriage, baptismal and burial ceremonies performed by them, and from the burial record we are able to learn where many of these settlers came from in the old country. From Switzerland came Peter Hugg (Canton Bern, 1735); Anna, wife of Peter Roth; Rev. John U. Giessendanner and his wife; John Giessendanner, Jr.; Jacob Giessendanner; Hans Henry Felder (1735); Jacob Kuhnen and wife (1736); Ann, wife of Jacob Bossart; Melchior Ott (1735); Anna Negely, widow; Magdalena, wife of Hans Imdorff; Martin Kooner; Peter Moorer; Zibilla Wolf (Grisons); John Friday (1735); John Dietrick (1735); Barbara Fund; Henry Wurtzer (1735); Henry Horger; Jacob Stauber (Canton Zurich, 1750); Henry Haym and John Myers. From Germany came John George Barr; David Runtgenauer; Lewis Linder and Elias Snell (1735). From Holland came William Young. These are all whose places of nativity are given, but it is reasonable to presume that the many other settlers bearing the same family names as the above, came from the same places.

Besides the above there are many more names on the Giessendanner record that are unmistakably German; among them the names: Stroman, Stoudenmire. Shaumlöffel, Geiger, Holman, Hessy, Kuhn, Yutsey (Utsey), Yssenhut (Whisenhunt), Kreyter (Crider), Huber, Shuler, Rumph, Zimmerman, Rickenbacker, Köhler (Culler), Hungerbüller (Hungerpiller), Wannamaker, Amaker, Keller, Inabinet, Zeigler, Leysaht, Golson, Joyner, Ferstner, Tilly, Hartzog, Whetstone, Balziger, Brunzon, Stehely (Staley), Starekey (Sturkie), and Theus—names nearly all of which obtain in this section to-day.

There are many names to be found on the Giessendanner record that are evidently not German names. These settlers came in about the time of the German settlements or a little later. In some instances the Giessendanner record tells where the settler came from. This was the case with Gideon Jennings, who came in to Orangeburgh Township, with his wife and two sons, Philip and John, in 1736. In recording his death the Rev. Mr. Giessendanner states that he was an "Italian protestant," and in recording the death of his wife, Ursula, a few years later, he speaks of her as the "widow of Gideon Zanini alias Jennings". Whether Jennings is the English for Zanini, or whether Gideon Jennings was an Englishman who went to Italy, (seeing that he was a protestant) and there assumed the name Zanini and changed back to the English name Jennings upon resuming habitation among English people, or whether he changed his name to Jennings because he fancied that name, or for other cause, is only a matter of conjecture, but, at any rate, the Jennings family has long been a large and influential one in this section and members of it have intermarried with many of the oldest families in the County.

William Barrie, another of the early settlers, is recorded by Giessendanner as having been a native of

Scotland, and Seth Hatcher as a native of Virginia. The Larry, or Larey, family frequently mentioned by Giessendanner was an Irish family.* Other names not German to be found on the record are: Martin, Gardner, Bunch, Powell, Oliver, Brown, Curtis, Robinson, Robison, Barber, Bright, Weekly, Gibson, Barker, Sullivant, Haig, Holmes, McGraw, McFashion, Reece, Cheavy, Potts, Good, Fitzpatrick, Carter, Tate, Jones, Tap, Hickie, Smith, Gossling, Murphy, Clements, Whiteford, Hill, Mercier, Partridge, and Wright. Some of them have a decidedly Hibernian smack, others sound English, others Scotch, and one or two sound somewhat Frenchy. It is likely that some of these settlers came from the colonies to the northward, while others of them doubtless came from the lower parishes of South Carolina.

Another prominent man among the early settlers of Orangeburgh was John Chevillette, who had formerly been an officer under Frederick the Great—probably before Frederick became King of Prussia. That he had been a friend of that king is shown by the letters that that monarch wrote to him (which letters were long in possession of the late Mrs. William Gilmore Simms) telling him how to cultivate the vine to make wine in Carolina. Col. Chevillette married in Orangeburgh Township, in 1745, Mrs. Susannah Hepperditzel, a widow, by whom he had one son. John Chevillete, who married the widow of Donald Govan, and was the step-father of Eliza Govan,† who married Nash Roach, and not the father, as Trent puts it on page 96 of his Life of Simms.

The defeat of the revolutionary efforts in England and Scotland in behalf of Charles Edward, the "Young

---

*It was a descendant of this family that established the first newspaper in the District.

†The mother of Mrs. Wm. Gilmore Simms.

Pretender", in 1745, caused many of the defeated revolters to flee to America; and among these was Andrew Govan, who settled in Orangeburgh Township, where he and his descendants became prominent. The late Wm. Gilmore Simms used to relate a very pretty little tradition to the effect that the rebel Govan was condemned and about to be executed, when his friends wrecked the scaffold upon which he was about to be executed. In the fall of the scaffold Govan had a leg broken, but in the confusion he escaped and hid in a London sewer for a day or two, when he made his escape and embarked for America. John Govan was a kinsman who also came to Orangeburgh about the same time, but he afterwards moved to Granville County. Christopher, Henry and Samuel Rowe. and Gavin Pou were also Scotchmen who settled in Orangeburgh Township about 1740.

After the English conquest of Acadia (Nova Scotia) in 1755, it will be remembered that the French Acadians then captured were cruelly carried off and distributed among the British Colonies to the South. South Carolina got a portion of these Acadians, and some of these were settled in Orangeburgh, Amelia and Saxe-Gotha Townships, as we find in Volume IV., p. 72, of the Statutes of South Carolina, the following items of account showing that certain persons living in those townships had been paid for maintaining them:

"Stephen Crell, of Saxe-Gotha township, £54.00.00.
  Henry Gallman, " " 53.00.00.
  Henry Hertel, " " 24.00.00.
  Henry Serstrunk, " " 12.00.00.
  Henry Heartley, of Amelia " 26.00.00.
  William Heatly, " " 171.10.00.
Christopher Rowe, of Orangeburgh, (to be
    paid when duly certified.) 64.00.00."

The name Dukes occurs frequently in the Giessendanner record. (Sometimes it is written Dukes and sometimes Duke.) In Hotton's "List of Persons who went from Great Britain to the American Plantations," on p. 362, William Dukes is mentioned as having embarked from Barbadoes on the Barque *Adventure* for Carolina on April 7th, 1679. The Dukeses on the Giessendanner record are doubtless descendants of his. and the large and influential Dukes family now in Orangeburg County are undoubtedly the descendants of the persons mentioned by Giessendanner.

The lower section of the Province, which had been previously settled, also furnished a share of the settlers for Amelia and Orangeburgh Townships. Among these we find the names Porcher, Richardson, Sabb, Gaillard, and Huger—names which shed lustre on the early history of old St. Matthew's Parish.

Section 2. The German settlers of Orangeburgh Township; their church and their pastor.

The following account of the settling of Orangeburgh by the Germans and Swiss is given by Rev. George Howe, D. D., in his History of the Presbyterian Church in South Carolina, Vol. I., pp. 216 and 217: "A trader, Henry Sterling, had located himself, and obtained a grant of land on Lyon's Creek, in 1704. But it was not until 1735 that this portion of the province had any considerable number of whites. The arrival of the settlers who found their way thither is thus mentioned in the South Carolina Gazette, under date of July 26th:— 'On Sunday last arrived two hundred Palatines; most of them being poor, they were obliged to sell themselves and their children for their passage (which is six pistoles in gold per head) within a fortnight of the time of their arrival, or else

J. W. H. DUKES,
Mayor of Orangeburg,
1891—1898.

A. F. H. DUKES,
Member S. C. House of Representatives,
Orangeburg County, 1896—1898.

J. H. DUKES,
Sheriff Orangeburg County,
1892—1898.

W. HAMPTON DUKES,
Deputy Sheriff Orangeburg County,
1892—1898.

COL. D. E. DUKES,
Coroner Orangeburg County,
1888—1898.

ORANGEBURG COUNTY.

to pay one pistole more to be carried to Philadelphia. The most of them are farmers, and some tradesmen. About two hundred and twenty of the Switzers that have paid all their passages are now going up the Edisto to settle a township there. The government defrays them on their jurney, provides them provisions for one year, and gives them fifty acres ahead. The quantity of corn bought for them had made the price rise from fifteen shillings, as it was last week, to twenty shillings.'

"These persons became the first settlers in Orangeburg township, which had been laid out in a parrellelogram of fifteen miles by five on the North Edisto, and was called Orangeburg in honor of the Prince of Orange.* Germans of the [Lower] Palatinate settled in the township, but some portion of the settlers were from Switzerland, from the Cantons of Berne, Zurich, and the Grisons, and were Calvinists we suppose of the Helvetic confession, and Presbyterian in their views of Church government. Their minister, John Ulrich Giessendanner, came with them, and the register of marriages, baptisms, and burials, commenced by him in the German language, was continued by his nephew and successor, John Giessendanner, down to the year 1760. John Ulrich Giessendanner died in the year 1738. His nephew John, by the request of the congregation, went to Charleston for the purpose of 'obtaining orders' from Rev. Alexander Garden, the Bishop of London's commissary, but was persuaded by Major Christian Mote, whom he met, that he ought

---

*William Charles Henry Friso, who had married Anne, daughter of George II., in 1734;—afterwards William IV., "stadtholder, captain, and admiral-general of Zealand", and later "captain and admiral-general of the whole union, and stadtholder of the Seven Provinces." (Holland, Zealand, Friesland, Guelderland, Utrecht, Overyssel and Groningen.)

not to apply to him, but to other gentlemen to whom he would conduct him, who, if they found him qualified, would give him authority to preach. Major Mote made him acquainted with the Presbytery of South Carolina, who in 1738 gave him authority to preach the gospel among his German neighbors. This he continued to do, and thus kept up the Church of their fathers unchanged for a season, though he afterwards went to London and took Episcopal ordination. —(Journal of Upper House of Assembly, Vol. X., 1743 —1744.)"

Dr. Howe in Chapter II., pp. 250—251 further says: "In the same year 1743, the German and Swiss settlers of Orangeburg were interfered with in their religious worship by an attempt made by Rev. Bartholomew Zauberbuhler to oust their pastor, John Giessendanner. Mr. Zauberbuhler was himself a native of the canton of either St. Gall or Appenzel, one of the Protestant cantons of Switzerland, and was therefore in his own country an adherent of the Helvetic Confession, setting forth the doctrines of the Reformation as proclaimed by Zwingle, Bullinger and Calvin. He had been engaged in the settlement of a colony of Swiss Protestants in the newly-constituted township of New Windsor, opposite Augusta. He had resolved to seek Episcopal ordination, and had petitioned council that he might be sent to preach to the Germans in Orangeburg and on the Santee, and that he might receive a competent salary till such time as he could be consecrated by the Bishop of London, after which he proposed to visit Germany and to bring over others of his countrymen, 'it being a great encouragement to them to know that they may have the gospel not only on their passage, but after their arrival.' Council grants him £500 out of the township fund, provided he could obtain Commissary Garden's certificate of his qualifications for ordination. Armed now with a supposed authority from Governor Bull and Commissary Garden, he came into the pastoral charge of Giessendanner, and sought to expel him and occupy his place. A petition signed by about fourscore of the inhabitants of Orangeburg is spread out on the journals of the governor and council, detailing the facts, and praying for redress. Mr. Zauberbuhler was summoned by the governor, reprimanded for his interference, and curtailed of half the salary allowed him, unless he should bring over the foreign Protestants as he had stipulated. The petition is an interesting historic document, apologetic that their pastor is not *rectus in ecclesia*, according to the established religion of the province. It states that Mr. Giessendanner had been introduced in Charleston 'to an Asssembly of Presbytery, who, upon examination, furnished him with orders to preach'; that he hath done this in Dutch (German) constantly for the space of five years, to the inexpressible satisfaction of the congregation at Orangeburg; that 'two years ago, the petitioners being full sixty miles from any other place of worship, some of whom he had not been favored with a sermon for seven years, observing said Mr. John Giessendanner to be a man of learning, piety, and knowledge in the Holy Scriptures, prevailed on him to officiate in English every fortnight, which he hath since performed very articulate and intelligible, to the entire satisfaction of the English petitioners, and always behaves himself with sobriety, honesty, and justice, encouraging virtue and reproving vice.'—(MS. Records of Gov. and Council, March 6th, 1743, State Archives, Columbia.) This document reveals to us the existence and action of the Presbytery in Charleston in 1738, and is of interest otherwise. Mr. Giessendanner continued his ministry some time longer, until, to meet the state of things in this new country, he went to London in 1749, received Episcopal ordination, and returned in 1750 as a minister of the Episcopal church. His labors, both before and after this period, seem to have been assiduous, and his record of baptisms, marriages, and burials, yet preserved, shows that they extended over a wide track in the central portion of South Carolina. It is one among numerous other proofs of the absorbing nature of an ecclesiastical system established by law over a people the majority of whom are dissenters from it. Most of these settlers were probably Lutherans, but a portion must have been brought up under the Helvetic Confession and Heidelberg Catechism, and in their own land professed the Reformed or Calvinistic faith."

On page 494, Dr. Howe further says: "We have expressed our conviction on pp. 216, 217, that a portion of the original settlers of Orangeburg, those namely from certain cantons of Switzerland (and it may be true also of others), were of the Calvinistic or Reformed church, and Presbyterians. This is confirmed in part by the fact that 'there was a Presbyterian meeting house erected on Cattle's Creek, in 1778, and was called the Frederican church, after Andrew Frederick, who was its principal founder. Another of the same denomination was built at Turkey Hill'. 'There are,' say Drs. Jamieson and Shecut, writing 1808, 'two others of the same denomination in Lewisburgh'. 'The Presbyterians have supplies only from the upper country and the North Carolina Presbytery. From the want of preachers of their own denomination, the descendants of the old stock are falling either with the Baptists or Methodists, according to the neighborhood in which they live'.—(Statistical acct. of Orangeburg.—Ramsay, Vol. II., Appendix.)"

Dr. Howe is clearly in error on one point: The Rev.

John Ulrick Giessendanner did not come over with the settlers of 1735 as Dr. Howe makes it appear, but came over in 1737 as is shown by his register, which Dr. Howe mentions. Dr. Howe does not state that these ministers, Rev. John U. Giessendanner and his nephew, Rev. John Giessendanner, were Lutheran ministers, but it was, nevertheless, the case. Dr. Frederick Dalcho, who wrote at a much earlier period than Dr. Howe, in his History of the Protestant Episcopal Church in South Carolina, states, and upon good evidence, that these ministers and their congregations were Lutherans; and Rev. G. D. Bernheim, D. D., in his History of the German Settlements and the Lutheran Church in North and South Carolina, proves conclusively that such is the case, and that, while Rev. John Giessendanner, the younger, received ordination and a license to preach from the Charleston Presbytery, he continued to preach in Orangeburgh as a Lutheran minister until the time when he left for England to be ordained as an Episcopal Clergyman. Dr. Bernheim's account of the settling of Orangeburgh is undoubtedly the most authentic that has ever been written, and will therefore be given herewith: (p. 99.)

"*Section 10. The German and Swiss Colonists of Orangeburg, S. C., A. D. 1735.*

"The story of the settling of Orangeburg, South Carolina is a page in the history of that State which has never been fully written. The cause of this omission can scarcely be accounted for, as ample materials were within the reach of former historians. Certain outlines have been given, but nothing very satisfactory has been furnished.

"'The first white inhabitant who settled in this section of country was named Henry Sterling; his occupation, it is supposed, was that of a trader. He located himself on Lyon's Creek in the year 1704, and obtained a grant of a tract of land, at present in the possession of Colonel Russel P. McCord.' (*Mills*, p. 656.)

"'The next settlers were some three or four individuals, who located themselves at the Cowpens, northwesterly of the low country white settlements; these, and the Cherokee and Catawba Indians* were all the inhabitants who had preceded the Germans.' (*Mills*, p. 657.)

"The colonists of Orangeburg County and town were mostly German and Swiss, who came over from Europe in a large body, occupying several vessels, and even to the present day their descendants are easily recognized by their unmistakable German names, and are found to be the principal owners and occupants of the soil in this portion of South Carolina.

"The principal facts concerning the early history of these colonists are mainly derived from the Journals

---

*Lawson visited the Congaree section before any whites had settled there, and this is what he wrote: "The next morning Santee Jack told us we should reach the Indian (Congaree) settlement betimes that day. About noon we passed by several fair savannas, very rich and dry, seeing great copses of many acres that bore nothing but bushes about the bigness of box trees, which, in their season, afford great quantities of small black-berries, very pleasant fruit, and much like to our blue huckleberries that grow on heaths in England. Hardby the savannas we found the town, where we halted. There was not above one man left with the women, the rest being gone a hunting, for a feast. The women were very busily engaged in gaming. The names or grounds of it I could not learn, though I looked on above two hours. They kept count with a heap of Indian grains.

"When the play was ended the king's wife invited us into her cabin. The Indian kings always entertain travelers, either English or Indian, taking it as a great affront if they pass by their cabins. The town consists of not above a dozen houses—they having other straggling plantations up and down the country, and are seated upon a small branch of Santee River. Their place hath curious, dry marshes, and savannas adjoining to it, and would prove an exceeding fine range for cattle and hogs, if the English were seated thereon.

"These Indians are a small people, having lost much of their former numbers by intestine broils; but most by the small-pox. We found

of Council of the Province of South Carolina, as found in manuscript form in the office of the Secretary of State, as well as from the Church record-book, kept by their first pastors, the two Giessendanners, uncle and nephew, written in the German and English languages, which is still extant, and has been thoroughly examined by the writer; and as these additional facts are now presented for the first time, it is hoped that they may open new avenues, which will afford future historians of the State additional sources of research and information.

"That the German element of the Orangeburg colonists came partly from Switzerland, we learn from the records of the Giessendanners' church-book, as it was the custom of the younger Giessendanner to mention the place of nativity of all the deceased, in his records of each funeral of the early settlers; and as this emigration from that country to Orangeburg oc-

---

here good store of chinkapin-nuts, which they gather in winter, great quantities of, drying them, and keeping them in great baskets. Likewise hickerie-nuts, which they beat betwixt two great stones, then sift to thicken their venison broth therewith; the small shells precipitating to the bottom of the pot whilst the kernels, in form of flour, mixes with the liquor.

"The Congarees are kind and affable to the English; the queen being very kind—giving us what varieties her cabin afforded—loblolly made with Indian corn and dryed peaches. These Congarees have abundance of storks and cranes in their savannas. They take them before they can fly, and breed them as tame as dung-hill fowls. They had a tame crane at one of their cabins that was scarce less than six foot in height, his head being round with a shining crimson hue, which they all have.

"These are a very comely sort of Indians, there being a strange difference in the proportion and beauty of these heathen. The women here being as handsome as most I have met withal, being several five-fingered brunettos amongst them. These lasses stick not upon hand long, for they marry when very young, as at twelve or fourteen years of age.

"We saw at the king's cabin the strangest spectacle of antiquity I ever knew—it being an old Indian squaw, that, had I been to have guessed her age by her aspect, old Parr's head, the Welch Methusa-

curred only two or three years subsequent to the emigration of a former Swiss colony to Purysburg. S. C., it certainly requires no great stretch of the imagination to explain the causes which induced such a large number of emigrants from that country to locate themselves upon the fertile lands of South Carolina. which were described so glowingly by John Peter Purry and his associates.

"Let any one examine the pamphlets, as found in vol. ii of Carroll's Collections, which Mr. Purry published in reference to the Province of South Carolina. and which he freely distributed in his native country. in which the fertility of the soil, salubrity of the climate, excellency of government, safety of the colonists, opportunities of becoming wealthy, &c., &., are so highly extolled, and corroborated by the testimony of so many witnesses, and he will easily comprehend what the Switzers must have fancied that province to be. viz.: the El Dorado of America,—the second Palestine of the world.

"Mr. Purry's account of the excellency of South Carolina for safe and remunerative settlement went round, from mouth to mouth. in many a hamlet and cottage of the little mountain-girt country, losing

---

lem, was a face in swadling clouts to hers. Her skin hung in reaves like a bag of tripe; by a fair computation, one might have justly thought it would have contained three such carcasses as hers then was. From what I could gather she was considerably above one hundred years old, yet she smoked tobacco, and eat her victuals, to all appearances, as heartily as one of eighteen. At night we were laid in the king's cabin, where the queen and the old squaw pigged in with us.

"In the morning we rose before day, having hired a guide the over night to conduct us on our way. The queen got us a good breakfast before we left her; she had a young child which was much afflicted with the colic, for which she infused a root in water, held in a gourd; this she took in her mouth, and spurted it into the mouth of the infant, which gave it ease. After we had eaten, we set out for the Wateree Indians."

nothing by being told from one family to another; which, with the additional fact, that many had relatives and friends living in both the Carolinas, whom they possibly might meet again, soon fastened their affections upon that province, and induced them to leave the Fatherland, and make their future homes with some of their countrymen in America. Their little all of earthly goods or patrimony was soon disposed of; preparations for a long journey were quickly made, as advised by Mr. Purry in his pamphlet; the journey through North Germany towards some seaport was then undertaken; and, with other Germans added to their number, who joined their fortunes with them whilst passing through their country, they were soon rocked upon the bosom of the ocean, heading towards America, with the compass pointing to their expected haven, Charleston, South Carolina.

"These German and Swiss settlers did not all arrive in Orangeburg at the same time; the first colony came during the year 1735; another company arrived a year later, and it was not until 1737 that their first pastor, Rev. John Ulrich Giessendanner, Senior, came among them with another reinforcement of settlers; whilst Mills informs us that emigrants from Germany arrived in Orangeburg District as late as 1769, only a few years before the Revolution.*

"Like most of the early German settlers of America, these colonists came to Carolina not as 'gentlemen or traders', but as tillers of the soil, with the honest intention 'to earn their bread by the sweat of the brow', and their lands soon gave evidence of thrift and plenty, and they, by their industry and frugality, not only secured a competency and independence for

---

*This is probably true, as there are some German families that have long resided in Orangeburg, but whose names do not appear on the Giessendanner Record.

themselves and their children in this fertile portion of South Carolina, but many of them became blessed with abundance and wealth.

"From the records of Rev. Giessendanner we learn that there were also a considerable number of mechanics, as well as planters and farmers, among these colonists; and the results of this German colonization were extremely favorable to Orangeburg District, inasmuch as they remained there as permanent settlers, whilst many of their countrymen in other localities, such as Purysburg, &c., were compelled to leave their first-selected homes, on account of the want of health and of that great success which they had at first expected, but the Orangeburg settlers became a well-established and successful colony.

"It has been asserted that the German congregation established in Orangeburg among these settlers was Reformed, which is evidently a mistake, as any one may perceive from the following facts. On the one hand, it must be admitted that the Switzers came from the land where John Calvin labored, and where the Reformed religion prevails, but where there are also many Lutheran churches established. It is also admitted that the Giessendanners were natives of Switzerland, but it would be unsafe to conclude from these facts that the German congregation at Orangeburg, with all, or nearly all, of its members, and with their pastors, were Swiss Reformed or Calvinistic in their faith. On the other hand, although nothing positive is mentioned in the Record-book of the Church, concerning their distinctive religious belief. yet the presumptive evidence, even from this source of information, is sufficiently strong to conclude that this first religious society in Orangeburg was a Lutheran Church. The facts from which our conclusions are drawn are:

"*Firstly.*—Because a very strong element from Germany was mixed with their Swiss brethren in the early settling of this county, which, by still later accession of German colonists, appears to have become the predominating population, who were mostly Lutherans, and the presumption becomes strong that their church-organization was likewise Lutheran.

"*Secondly.*—It seems to have been a commonly admitted fact and the prevailing general impression of that time, when their second paster had become an ordained minister of the Church of England.

"*Thirdly.*—In examining their church records one will discover, through its entire pages, a recognition of the festivals of the Lutheran Church, as were commonly observed by the early Lutheran settlers.

"*Fourthly.*—In Dalcho's History of the Prot. Epis. Church in S. C., published in 1820, at the time when the son of the younger Giessendanner was still living *(see Mills' Statistics, p. 657, published as late as* 1826), it is most positively stated concerning his father, that 'he was a minister of the Lutheran Church.' (*Dalcho*, p. 333, *footnote.)* How could Dr. Dalcho have been mistaken when he had the records of the Episcopal Church in South Carolina before him; and in that denomination this was the prevailing impression, as was, doubtless, so created from Giessendanner's own statements in the bosom of which Church he passed the latter days of his life.

"*Fifthly.*—One of the churches which Giessendanner served before he became an Episcopal clergyman, located in Amelia Township, called St. Matthews, has never been any other than a Lutheran Church, and is still in connection with the Evangelical Lutheran Synod of South Carolina.

"*Sixthly.*—The Orangeburg colonists, after their paster departed from their faith, were served with Lutheran pastors entirely, numbering in all about seventeen ministers, and only for a short time a Reformed minister, Rev. Dr. Zübly, once labored there as a temporary supply.

"*Seventhly.*—In Dr. Hazelius' History of the American Lutheran Church, p. 64, we have the following testimony, gathered from the journal of the Ebenezer pastors, Bolzius and Gronau, found in Urlsperger's Nachrichten: 'Their journal of that time mentions among other things, that many Lutherans were settled in and about Orangeburg in South Carolina, and that their preacher resided in the village of Orangeburg.'

"It is to be hoped that all this testimony is satisfactory to every candid inquirer, that the first established Church of Orangeburg, S. C., which was likewise the *first* organized Lutheran Church in both the Carolinas, was none other than a *Lutheran* Church; that those early settlers from Germany and Switzerland were mostly, if not all, of the same denomination, and that Dr. Dalcho has published no falsehood by asserting that 'their paster was a minister of the Lutheran Church.'

"The first colony of German and Swiss emigrants who settled in Orangeburg village and its vicinity in 1735, as well as those who selected their homes in Amelia Township along Four-hole swamp and creek, did not bring their pastor with them; the Rev. John Ulrich Giessendanner did not arrive until the year 1737; he was an ordained minister and a native of Switzerland, and was the first and at the time, the only minister of the gospel in the village and District of Orangeburg; we infer this from Mills' Statistics, p. 657, stating that there were but four or five English settlers residing in the District before the Germans arrived, and these few would not likely have an English minister of their own to labor among them. We infer this, moreover, from the record of Giessendanner's marriages; the ceremony of one was performed in the English language during the first year of his ministry, with the following remark accompanying it: 'Major Motte having read the ceremony in the English language,' from which we conclude that at the time, October 24th, 1737, Rev. Giessendanner was still unacquainted with the English language, and that on this account he solicited the aid of Major Motte in the performance of a clerical duty. That there could have been no other minister of the gospel within reach of the parties, who did not reside in the village, otherwise they would not have employed Rev. G. to perform a ceremony under such embarrassing circumstances.

"Rev. J. U. Giessendanner came to this country with the third transportation of German and Swiss settlers for this fertile portion of South Carolina. In the same vessel also journeyed his future partner in life, who had resided at his home in Europe as housekeeper for twenty-six years, and to whom, on the 15th. of November, 1737, he was 'quietly married, in the presence of many witnesses, by Major Motte;' doubtless by him, as no minister of the gospel was within their reach, to which record he piously adds: 'May Jesus unite us closely in love, as well as all faithful married people, and cleanse and unite us with himself. Amen.' By this union he had no children, since both himself and his partner were 'well stricken in years'.

"The elder Giessendanner did not labor long among this people. Death soon ended his ministrations in Orangeburg, and we infer that he must have died about the close of the year 1738, since the records of his ministerial acts extend to the summer of that year, whilst these of his nephew commence with the close of the year 1739. Allowing the congregation time to make the necessary arrangement with the nephew, and he to have time to seek and obtain ordination, as we shall see hereafter, besides the inference drawn from the language of a certain petition, &c., we learn that during the fall of 1738, the Rev. John Ulrich Giessendanner, Sr., was called to his rest, and thus closed his earthly career.

"The congregations in Orangeburg village and District now looked about them for another servant of the Lord to labor among them in holy things, but the prospect of being soon supplied was not very encouraging. The Ebenezer pastors were the only Lutheran ministers in the South at that time, and they could not be spared from their arduous work in Georgia, and to expect a pastor to be sent them again from the Fatherland was attended with many difficulties. Another plan presented itself to them. The nephew of their first pastor, who had prepared himself for the ministry, was induced to seek ordination at the hands of some Protestant denomination, and take upon himself the charge of these vacant congregations in the place of his departed uncle.

"From the records of the Orangeburg Church we learn that their second pastor was also named John Ulrich Giessendanner, but he soon afterwards dropped his middle name, probably to distinguish him from his uncle, and so is he named in all the histories of South Carolina, which give any account of him.*

"Difficulties and sore trials soon attended Rev. John

---

*It appears from the German portion of the record book that he signed himself in some places "John Ulrick Giessendanner" and in others "Ulrick Giessendanner", and it was not until he returned from England that he invariably signed himself "John Giessendanner." See also Dalcho, p. 333.

Giessendanner's ministry; the Urlsperger Reports state, in vol. iii, p. 1079, that the town of Orangeburg was then, A. D. 1741, in a worse condition than Purysburg; that the people were leading very sinful lives, manifesting no traces of piety, and that between pastor and hearers there were constant misunderstandings. It is also stated that their lands were fertile, but, as they were far removed from Charleston, and had no communication with that city by water, they could not convert their produce into money, and on this account very little or no money was found among them. Dr. Hazelius likewise gives an unfavorable account of the state of religion in that community. On p. 64, he remarks: 'From one circumstance mentioned with particular reference to that congregation, we have to infer that the spiritual state of that church was by no means pleasing. A Mr. Kieffer, a Salzburg emigrant and member of the Ebenezer congregation, was living on the Carolina side of the Savannah River, whose mother-in-law resided at Orangeburg, whom he occasionally visited. On one occasion he remarked, after his return, to his minister, Pastor Bolzius, that the people at Orangeburg were manifesting no hunger and thirst after the word of God; he was therefore anxious that his mother-in-law should remove to his plantation, so that she might enjoy the opportunity of attending to the preaching of the word of God, which she greatly desired.' All this testimony, though in the main correct, needs, however, some explanation. and by referring to the Journals of Council for this province, in the office of the Secretary of State, we will soon discover the cause of such a state of things. The people had been but sparingly supplied with the preached word, the discipline of the Church had not been properly administered, and when the younger Giessendanner took charge of these congregations, and attempted to regulate matters a little, whilst the majority of the people sustained him in his efforts, a minority, who were rude and godless, became his bitter enemies, and were constantly at variance with him.

"This condition of Church affairs opened the way for the Zauberbühler difficulties, which are very minutely described in the Journals of Council of the Province of South Carolina, vol. 10, page 395, *et seq.*: the main facts of this troublesome affair were the following:

"During the year 1743, a Swiss minister of the gospel, formerly located along the Savannah River, at New Windsor, Purysburg, and other places, named Bartholomew Zauberbühler, very adroitly attempted to displace the Rev. John Giessendanner from his charge in Orangeburg, and make himself the pastor of those churches. He supposed that by becoming an ordained minister of the Episcopal Church, at that time the established church in the Province, he would have rights superior to the humble Lutheran pastor in charge at Orangeburg, and, as he supposed, have the law on his side in thus becoming the pastor himself. The records of his evil designs, which have long slumbered in oblivion in manuscript form on the shelves of the Statehouse at Columbia, are now brought to view, and read as follows:

"'Nov. 9th, 1742. Read the petition of Rev. B. Zauberbühler, showing that as there were a great many Germans at Orangeburg, Santee, and thereabouts, who are very desirous of having the word of God preached to them and their children, and who desire to be instructed in the true religion, humbly prays: That he may be sent to serve them and to be supported with a competent salary until he shall be able to take a voyage to England to be ordained by the Bishop of

London, and at the same time proposes to bring over with him a number of Germans, which he thinks may be as great a number as ever were brought at any time into this province, it being a great encouragement to them when they find that they may have the Gospel, not only on their voyage, but also after their arrival in this province, preached to them, &c.

"'Upon reading the said petition, it was the opinion of His Majesty's Council, that providing the petitioner do produce a certificate from the inhabitants of Orangeburg, as also a certificate from ye Ecclesiastical Commissary, Mr. Garden, of his qualifications to receive orders in the Church of England, and his engaging to go home to London to receive ordination, and after that to go to Germany to procure others of his countrymen to come over to settle in this province, that the sum of five hundred pounds currency be advanced him out of the township fund, in order to enable him to perform the same.'

"Journals of Council, vol. xi, pp. 74-76. Under date of Feb. 13th, 1743-44: 'Reconsidered the petition of Rev. Mr. Zauberbühler, which had been exhibited at this Board on the 10th day of November, 1743, praying that in consideration of the earnest desire of the inhabitants of Orangeburg, Santee, to have a person to preach the gospel to them in their own language, he is willing to perform that pastoral duty, but being as yet unordained, desires to be supported with a competent salary until he shall be able to take a voyage to England to be ordained, at which time he proposes to bring over a number of foreign Protestants to settle in this province, who are unwilling to come over for want of having the gospel preached to them in their voyage here. Whereupon it appearing by a former minute of Council, of the 10th of November last, that provided the petitioner shall produce a certificate from the inhabitants of Orangeburg of their desire to receive him as a preacher amongst them, and also a certificate from the Rev. Mr. Garden of his qualifications to receive orders, that then the sum of £500 current money be advanced him out of the township fund, in order to enable him to perform his voyage, and bring on the Protestants to settle here as he mentions. Whereupon the petitioner produced the following certificate from the Rev. Mr. Commissary Garden:

" 'South Carolina.
" 'These are to certify whom it may concern, and in particular the Rt. Rev. the Lord Bishop of London, that the bearer, Bartholomew Zauberbühler, a native of Appenzell in Switzerland, appears to me on creditable testimony to have resided in this Province for the space of seven years last past, and during that time to have been of good life and behavior as becometh a candidate for holy orders, &c., &c.,
" 'Signed,   Alexander Garden.
" 'February 13th, 1743.'

" 'On producing the said certificate his Excellency signed an order on the public Treasurer for the sum of £500, to be paid him on condition that the Treasurer take his written obligation to repay the said money upon his returning and settling in the Province, in case he does not bring over the Protestants he mentions.'

"The following counter-petition against Mr. Zauberbühler from the Orangeburg settlers is found in vol. xi of Journals of Council, pp. 139-143, and dated March 6th, 1743:

" 'Read the humble petition of the German and English inhabitants of Orangeburg and the adjoining plantations, showing to his Excellency, to whom it is directed, that the petitioners heartily congratulate his Excellency on his auspicious ascension to the government of this Province, hoping that by his judicious care and power not only their present grievances, but likewise all other misfortunes may evaporate and vanish. And ye said petitioneers humbly beg leave to acquaint ye Excellency, that above five years ago, the German minister happening to die, Mr. John Giessendanner, by the consent and approbation of your said German petitioners, went to Charlestown with the intention to make his application to the Rev. Mr. Alexander Garden, Commissary, to admit him into holy orders, to preach in German in this township; and when the said Mr. John Giessendanner came to Charlestown aforesaid, he accidentally met with one Major Christian Motte, who acquainted him that he ought not to trouble the said Rev. Alexander Garden with the affair, but to go with him to some certain gentlemen, who, if they found him sufficient, would directly give him orders according to his desire; upon which the said Mr. John Giessendanner, being then a stranger to the English method of proceeding in such cases, accompanied the said Major Christian Motte, and was by him introduced to an Assembly of the Presbytery, who, after examination, presented him with orders to preach, which he has since done in German constantly for the space of five years to the inexpressible satisfaction of the congregation at Orangeburg; and about two years ago your said English petitioners, being fully sixty miles from any other place of divine worship, some of whom had not been favored with an opportunity of hearing a sermon in the space of seven years, observing the said Mr. John Giessendanner to be a man of learning, piety, and knowledge in the Holy Scriptures, prevailed with him to officiate in preaching once every fortnight in

English, which he hath since performed very articulate and intelligible to the entire satisfaction of ye said English petitioners, and always behaves himself with sobriety, honesty, and justice, encouraging virtue and reproving vice.

"'And the said Mr. John Giessendanner lately observing great irregularities and disorders being committed almost every Sabbath day by some wicked persons in one part of the township, publicly reprimanded them for the same, which reproof so exasperated them that they threatened to kick the said Mr. John Giessendanner out of the church if he offered to preach there any more, and have lately sent for one Bartholomew Zauberbühler, a man who not long ago pretended to preach at Savannah town, but, as your said petitioners are informed, was soon obliged to leave that place and a very indecent character behind him. The last week he arrived at Orangeburg, and upon the last Sabbath, he, the said Bartholomew Zauberbühler and his wicked adherents associated together, and pretended that the said Bartholomew Zauberbühler had brought with him a power from the Hon. William Bull, Esq., late Lieutenant-Governor of this Province, his Majesty's Hon. Council, and the Rev. Mr. Alexander Garden, Commissary, an order to expel the said Mr. John Giessendanner from the church. and to preach there himself, and some of ye said petitioners demanded a sight of his said authority, but he refused to produce it, which occasioned great animosities and disorders in the congregation, and when the said Bartholomew Zauberbühler makes his second appearance at or near Orangeburg, which he declares shall be at ye expiration of three weeks, there will certainly be more disturbance and confusion than before, unless some powerful means be used to obstruct it.

"'Whereupon your said petitioners most humbly

ORANGEBURG COUNTY. 55

beg that your Excellency will be pleased to interpose with your authority, and direct the said Mr. Alexander Garden, if he hath given or granted any such orders, to countermand them, and to permit the said Mr. John Giessendanner still to officiate for them in divine service, free from any further disturbance or molestation, &c.

"'Signed by John Harn, and above forescore more subscribers.*

"'Ordered by Council that the consideration of this affair, and of the above petition, and those of Mr. Zauberbühler, be deferred until Mr. Zauberbühler's return from England, and that ye Clerk acquaint them therewith in writing.'

"Fortunately, however, Mr. Zauberbühler had not yet departed on his journey to England as the Council had supposed, but had been lurking for awhile in Orangeburg District, and as soon as he returned to Charleston he once more made his appearance upon the floor of the Council chamber.

"Journals of Council, Vol. XI, p. 143: 'Bartholomew Zauberbühler, being returned from Orangeburg Township, attended his Excellency in Council, and laid before him two written certificates from justices of ye peace there in his favor, and which were read, representing his sobriety and good behavior, whereupon Mr. Zauberbühler was by his Excellency directed to wait again on Rev. Mr. Garden, and to learn if he has any objections to his receiving orders in England, and to report the same.'

"Journals of Council, Vol. XI, p. 152: 'Bartholomew Zauberbühler attended his Excellency, the Governor, in Council, according to order, whom the Governor gave to understand that he had not acted well in the

---

*All efforts to find the original of this petition, with the names appended, have been unsuccessful.

exhibiting a certificate from the Township of Orangeburg, read at this Board on November 13th, 1742, seeing that under the notion of having an invitation to the ministry by the majority of that Township, there was, on the contrary, a later memorial laid before the Board, signed by near ninety of the inhabitants, and by far the majority of the Township, praying that Mr. Giessendanner, their present minister, might be continued to preach among them, and that Mr. Zauberbühler's going to preach in the said Township, and his design to be settled there as a minister, was not by their desire, on the contrary, had occasioned no small disturbance in the said Township. That his proceedings with the Lieutenant-Governor and Council in ye said affair had not been with that candor that might have been expected from one who designed to take on him holy orders, and that, therefore, he ought to be contented with at least one-half of what had been paid him by ye Treasurer, and return the other £250, or, at any rate, to procure a joint security of one residing in Charlestown that he would return the money in case he did not bring over the Protestants mentioned, but that if he did bring them over the whole £500 should be allowed him; whereupon Mr. Zauberbühler withdrew.'

"After this action of the Governor and Council we read nothing more of Mr. Zauberbühler in the Journals of Council, and the Rev. John Giessendanner was permitted to continue his labor as pastor in Orangeburg without further molestation.

"The historical facts deduced from the above State papers are the following:

"That the Rev. John Ulrick Giessendanner, Sr., who was the first pastor at Orangeburg, departed this life during the close of the year 1738, having labored there but little more than one year.

"That his nephew, the Rev. John Giessendanner, became his successor some time during the year 1739, and that he was 'a man of learning, piety, and knowledge in the Holy Scriptures'; he was probably educated for the ministry, but left Europe before he had been ordained; that, although a Lutheran in his religious persuasion, as we learn from other documents, he applied for ordination at the hands of any Protestant ministry who were empowered to impart the desired authority, there being at that time no Lutheran Synod in all the American colonies. That he was ordained by the Charleston Presbytery is certain, but that he was not a Presbyterian in faith is evident also, else he would not have endeavored first to obtain ordination at the hands of the Protestant Episcopal authority, and only changed his purpose of becoming Episcopally ordained at the suggestions of Major Christian Motte, and doubtless to avoid an expensive and wearisome voyage to Europe, which he would have been obliged to undertake had he insisted upon obtaining the requisite authority to preach the gospel and administer the sacraments either in the Lutheran or Episcopal Church.

"That the first Orangeburg Church must have been built some time before the above-mentioned petition was written, A. D. 1743, as it is therein spoken of, as being then in existence.

"That Rev. John Giessendanner labored faithfully as a good servant of his Master, even bringing enmity upon himself for reproving vice; likewise, that he preached in the German and English languages.

"That the country in the vacinity of Orangeburg must have been sadly deficient at that time in the enjoyment of the usual means of grace, as many persons were living sixty miles from any other church, some having not heard a sermon preached for seven years;

need we wonder at the irregularities in faith and conduct manifested in those days.

"That Rev. Giessendanner must have had a considerable congregation, inasmuch as the petition drawn up in his defence was signed by nearly ninety male persons, who were either all members of his congregation, or mostly so, and the remainder his friends and adherents.

"That Rev. Bartholomew Zauberbühler must have sadly degenerated in the latter period of his ministerial life, as the Ebenezer pastors give us a very favorable account of him several years previous in the Urlsperger Reports, when he first came to this country.

"Rev. Giessendanner was affectionately remembered by the Church in Europe. Rev. Bolzius, in the Urlsperger Reports, Vol. III, p. 875, states: 'I also wrote a letter to-day to young Mr. Giessendanner, the present minister in Orangeburg, informing him that a donation of about nine guilders had been collected for him in Switzerland, of which a respectable merchant in Zurich writes, that as old Mr. Giessendanner had died, this amount should be paid over to his nephew. Also, that we will send him, as soon as possible, those books collected for him in Switzerland, which are sent in the chest for us, and which has not yet arrived.

"'I would have been pleased to have sent him this money sooner had any safe opportunity presented itself. I entreated him, likewise, to write to me occasionally, and inform me of the transactions of the departed Giessendanner, which may be of great service to him.

"The name Giessendanner occurs in several other paragraphs of the same Reports, but only in connection with the books and money above-mentioned; but nothing further is said concerning himself and his ministry, or that of his predecessor. He was probably prevented from imparting the desired information on account of the want of communication between Ebenezer and Orangeburg.

"Rev. John Giessendanner labored ten years as a Lutheran minister, after which, in 1749, he went to London to receive Episcopal ordination* at the hands of Rev. Dr. Sherlock,† Bishop of London. The reasons for making this change in his Church relationship are not known; however, it is presumable that, as he was then the only Lutheran pastor in South Carolina, he preferred to enjoy a more intimate connection with some ministerial organization than the one that was then afforded him in the bosom of his own Church; and although the Ebenezer pastors were also then laboring in the South, nevertheless they were somewhat distantly removed from him, and dwelling in another Province. He doubtless also had his fears that some other Zauberbühler difficulty might harass him again, and thus, by taking this step, he would have all legal preferences in his favor, as the Church of England was then virtually the established Church of the Province.

"He was united in marriage to Miss Barbara Hug, and became the father of several children, one of whom, a son named Henry, born July 3d, 1742, was still living in 1826, as he is mentioned in 'Mills' Statistics;' and his widow spent the close of her life with one of her children residing in Georgia.

"Henry Giessendanner was married to Miss Elizabeth Rumpf, February 25th, 1767; he recorded the birth of but one child, Elizabeth, in his father's church-book.

---

*Ordained Deacon Aug. 27, and Priest Sept. 24, 1749.—Dalcho, p. 333.

†Gen. D. F. Jamison once had a prayer book that Dr. Sherlock had presented to Rev. Mr. Giessendanner.

though he may have had more children, whose names were not entered there. This record-book likewise informs us that Rev. John Giessendanner had a brother and sister living in Orangeburg, named George and Elizabeth (afterwards married to a Mr. Krieh), and that the whole family were natives of Switzerland; hence also the money sent Rev. Giessendanner came from this country, as mentioned in the Urlsperger Reports. This concludes the history of the Giessendanner family, as far as it is necessary for our purpose, and until recently it was not known that these two pastors were the first Lutheran ministers that labored in South Carolina—even their very names had become almost obliterated in the annals of the Lutheran Church. Dr. Dalcho yet adds this information, that Rev. John Giessendanner departed this life during the year 1761.*

"The Orangeburg settlers at first clustered together near the banks of the Edisto River, and built their dwellings near each other in the form of a small town, supposing that the adjacent stream would be advantageous in forming an outlet for them to Charleston, in the transportation of lumber to market. A year later other German emigrants arrived, who located themselves on lands adjoining their predecessors, and thus this tide of immigration continued until the entire district became mostly colonized with German and Swiss emigrants. The present town of Orangeburg is located very near the spot where this original German village once stood. In this village the first Lutheran church in the Carolinas was erected,† and

---

*His will is dated March 5, 1761; probated July 24, 1761.—Probate Court Records, Charleston County, p. 124.

†The late Mr. John Lucas doubted that Rev. John Giessendanner had a church building before going to England, but was of opinion that the congregation had some place of assembly. The record book does not say, but I think the evidence is strong the other way.

there also the first Lutheran pastor of this congregation lived and died; his nephew and successor, as is supposed by some of the present inhabitants, had his home several miles from the village, where he died and was buried.*

"Some half a mile from the centre of the present town, of Orangeburg and towards the Edisto River there is a graveyard, which presents the appearance of having been a long time in use for the interment of the dead, and where the entombed generations of the present day are silently slumbering with those of the past. It is still styled *'the old graveyard,'* although there are many new-made graves to be seen in it; and here, doubtless, repose the remains of the first Lutheran pastor in the Carolinas.

"During the evening twilight of autumn the writer visited this hallowed spot, in order to commune with the dead; the seared and faded leaves of October overhanging his head or rustling beneath his feet; the peculiar sighing sound of the winds of autumn, passing through the foliage of the Southern long-leaved pine trees, produced Nature's sad and fitting requiem for the dead. He sought for records of the past upon some dilapidated tombstone, but his search was unavailing, and, like the fallen leaves of many years past, even these mementos of a former age were no longer visible.

"What lessons of the vanity of all human greatness, namely: the power of wealth, the pride of family, the pleasures and gayeties of life! All end at last in the grave—all alike blend in one common dust.

"Around this place, with the old church edifice very near it, the former village stood; they are both thus

---

*Mr. Lucas said his wife was also buried there, but it is more likely that she was buried in Georgia, where Dr. Bernheim says she "spent the close of her life".

described by a correspondent: 'The Orangeburg church was built of wood and clay, in much the same manner as chimneys are when made of clay; the old graveyard is still used as a burial-ground common to all: and the site of the church is still plainly seen—it is in the village, and was at that day in the centre of it. I have learned this likewise from an old gentleman who remembers hearing his father saying this as above. It fell to ruins at the time of the Revolution; but the spot has never been built upon since that day, and is now known as 'the old churchyard.' This church was the one used by the Rev. John Giessendanner as an Episcopal church, and no doubt used likewise by him at first as a Lutheran church; its dimensions were—say thirty by fifty feet.'

"The time when the old church edifice was erected is now no longer known, and can only be a matter of conjecture; however, it is possible that this event occurred during the elder Giessendanner's ministry—the records do not positively state this to have been the case, nevertheless several indications are given which make it very probable that this was the time.

"It became changed into an Episcopal house of worship in 1749, when the pastor, the younger Giessendanner, took orders in the Church of England, as he continued to labor there to the close of his life. At the time this change was effected, the congregation numbered 107 communicants, and on Whitsunday following 21 persons more were admitted to the Lord's Supper.

"In concluding the history of this congregation, we would simply add, that after Rev. Giessendanner's death nothing further is known concerning it until 1768, when a new Episcopal chapel was ordered to be erected, and the Rev. Paul Turquand preached there in connection with another congregation.

"During the Revolutionary War, Rev. Turquand was absent,* and labored in the valley of the Mississippi, but returned in 1788, when he resumed his labors in Orangeburg, and died the following year; since then no trace is left of the history of the church and its congregation.

"The present Episcopal Church in the town of Orangeburg is of recent organization, and their house of worship is comparatively new, indicating that the old church edifice, the still later erected chapel, and the former congregation have long since become entirely extinct.

"The existing Lutheran church and congregation in Orangeburg are of a still more recent date; both the organization and church edifice have no historical connection with the past, made up of material in membership who have become citizens of the place not many years ago."

It is evident, from an inspection of the Giessendanner record, that Rev. Mr. Giessendanner regular served the townships of Orangeburgh and Amelia, after his return from England, as Episcopal minister, and that he also held services occasionally in Saxe-Gotha Township. In Saxe-Gotha he usually held services at the house of Mrs. Elizabeth Haig, afterwards Mrs. Elizabeth Mercier. From 1749 to 1756 the services for Amelia Township were held at the houses of Mrs. Mary Russell, William Martin, Moses Thomson, Capt. William Heatly, Ann and Charles Russell. In 1757 the services were held in a chapel, which had probably just been built, and the late Mr. Lucas wrote: "I am under the impression that Amelia Chapel was in the neighborhood of the above persons' habitations for we see that no service was held in any of their

---

*He was here during a part of the time, as will be shown later.

houses after the Chapel was built." It seems that after the erection of St. Matthew's Parish in 1765, and the subsequent employment, in 1766, of Rev. Paul Turquand as minister of the Parish, that this chapel went by the name of "the old church." (Minutes of the Vestry, 1767.) At a later date another chapel was built in Amelia Township* near Mr. Campbell's and still later another was built at "Bellville," the plantation of the Thomsons.†

The late Mr. John Lucas made extensive researches into the history of the old church and grave-yard above referred to by Dr. Bernheim, and as what he has written on the subject will be of interest to many, I will h re give it:

"The original plan of Orangeburg‡ shows that the old grave-yard, now known as the village grave yard, and used as such by all denominations in common for both white and black without leave or hindrance, being free to all, was at the time the original plat was made, then known as the church yard, and as such was so marked on the plat.

"This said old grave yard now in use and corresponding as to situation as per plat annexed is situated on the East side of the Bull Swamp Road, North of the street marked as Russell Street on plat, which is the

---

*"Agreed that the Revd. Mr. Turquand provide a Folio Bible & a Common Prayer Book for the use of the Chappel".—Minutes of Vestry, July 6, 1769.

†"Agreed that a chappel be built at Belvelle that the old church neer half way swamp be repaired Also the Chappel neer Campbells be repair'd that Subscriptions be made for each respectively and that service be perform'd in each alternately".—Minutes of Vestry, April 17th, 1786.

‡Mr. Samuel P. Jones had a copy of this plan made from the original in the office of the Secretary of State, from this Judge Glover made a copy and from Judge Glover's copy Mr. Lucas made a copy which is now in the record book of the Church of the Redeemer in Orangeburg.

THE OLD GIESSENDANNER CHURCHYARD.
From Photo by O. B. Rosenger, Orangeburg, S. C., 1898.

same street as that on which the present brick Court House now stands say —— feet. There is a lot between the grave yard and the Bull Swamp Road* which corresponds with the space marked for public square. This said lot is now owned by the Town Council of Orangeburg.

"The old Court House of wood and jail of brick occupied the second square North of the said street on which the new Court House now stands. The jail was destroyed & another built.† The Court House still stands having had many changes and uses. First as a church for first one and then another denomination, a masonic Lodge, black-smiths's shop, and it is at this present time in good order and repair, & is owned and used as a residence by Mr. John Marchant. This said square (C. H. & Jail) is on the West side of the Bull Swamp Road or street known on map as Broughton street. There is no other grave yard nor has there been any other known in this village except this one & those recently opened by the Methodist ch., Lutheran, & Baptist and not as yet used for burials.‡ The Catholic, Presbyterian & this Episcopal Church of the the Redeemer has grounds in use not older than 10 to 12 years.

"Tradition, as well as facts, has marked this old village grave yard as the grave yard and the spot on which stood the Prot. Epc. Church known in the Book of Record of the Revd Jno. Giessendanner as the Church & Churchyard of Orangeburgh and in which he officiated.

"There is a mound of earth on the South end which

---

*Which lot has since been filled with graves, mostly of negroes.
†Upon the site where the First Baptist Church now stands.
‡The Methodist and Lutheran church-yards were never used as burial grounds.

marks the spot on which the church stood. Many old persons recollect hearing this called the Episcopal Church yd. & show this mound as the spot on which the church stood. Mr. Peter Rowe, an old gentleman near 86 years old, says he remembers his father's pointing out this yard & mound as the Church & church-yard of this Book of Record by Jno. Giessendanner's church, and said it was built of wood & clay in same manner as chimnies are done. I, J. Lucas, have examined the foundation & think it must have been built in some such manner as described, as no signs of brick I found, & should think it to be about 30 by 60 feet. The mound I cannot account for except it must have been used as a raised earth floor having some sort of foundation to keep in the earth so raised. Dr. Wm Rowe remembers his grandfather Jacob Rickenbaker aged —— years & now dead —— years to say that this was the Episcopal church & church yard as per Book of Record. He also remembers & so does Capt. John C. Rowe and also D. Rowe a bell which belonged to this Church of Giessendanner to be in possession of their grandfather & father also. From them and through the Rev. Dr. J. W. Tayler I learn that this bell was borrowed from Mr. —— Rowe by Mr. Wm. Murrowe who kept a hotel for use therein. Mrs. Caroline Gramling, formerly his* widow says Mr. Edward Spencer who married her sister's daughter got it from her first husband and hung it in a window at the Methodist Church from which it fell and was broken so as to be useless. It lay for many years where it fell. Mr. James Harley remembers seeing it so lying in a broken condition & thinks it was made away with by a blacksmith. Mrs. Gramling (maiden name Stroman.) says she remem-

---

*Mr. Murrowe's.

bers that the said grave yard was the Episcopal church yard and that it went by that name. Her father told her the bell was never hung owing to a brake in the holding part or head.

"Mrs. J. W. Taylor, an old lady, wife of the Rev. J. W. Taylor, remembers that this ground was known as the Episcopal churchyard. Her family was Episcopal. There are relics of the former Episcopal Church in the shape of Prayer books, &c. Mrs. Arant, an old lady, now living has her mother's Prayer book. (Engh). The said Mrs. Arant was born in 1776 & was baptized in the Protestant Episcopal Church. Mr. & Mrs. Christopher Rowe were her sponsors. Mr. Donald Rowe and also his brother, Capt. Jno. C. Rowe, remember hearing their grandfather Jacob Rickenbacker say that this was the grave yard and the spot on which was built the Episcopal Church of this Record of the Revd J. Giessendanner. The said Jacob Rickenbacker was the son of the first Rickenbacker that came to this country from Germany. The lands owned by their fathers are still in the possession of the Rowe family, situated by and near this village in which the family live as their fathers did before them. Other families are still living in and on the same places as their forefathers before the Revolution. This district was changed but slightly in many instances of family names & residences.

"In the grave yard of Orangeburgh Church of this Record as above were buried Michael Christopher Rowe and his wife and many of his family after him. Mr. Peter Rowe has also informed me that he remembers the bell mentioned before, and that he was born before Michael Christopher Rowe died and that numbers of the members of families still continue to use this grave yard as the place for family burials & as the ancient place of rest of their forefathers.

"The Revd J. W. Taylor of the Protestant Episcopal Church, and assistant minister of this Church of the Redeemer in Orangeburg, was buried in this old village church yard. His obituary was written by the Rev. D. X. Lafar, of the Presbyterian Church, and who for some time was the Paster of the Presbyterian Church of Orangeburg, in which he calls the grave yard 'The Old Church Yard.'

"Capt V. de V. Jamison, a brother of Gen'l D. F. Jamison, said to me that his brother, Gen'l D. F. Jamison, had, & and perhaps still has, in his possession a prayer book belonging to the late Revd John Giessendanner which was presented to him by the Bishop of London.

"The Amelia Chapel, it is believed, was situated somewhere near the plantation of Mrs. Mary Russell. Its exact location may be yet discovered. The Chapel ordered to be built by an act passed April 12, 1768, (See Dalcho's Church History) in that part of the Parish called Orangeburg Township was never built, no evidence remains that it was.*

"From the close of Dalcho's History service Episcopal was very seldom held here & few and far between until about the year 1848, at which time Rev. R. D. Shindler became a missionary at this place & resided in this village.   *   *   *   *   *   *   *

---

*There is very strong evidence that it was built. From the minutes of the vestry of St. Matthew's Parish we learn that at a meeting of the vestry and wardens held at the parish church, October 10, 1770, it was "agreed that when Mr. Turquand receives the above he do purchase a Folio Bible & quarto common Prayer Book for the use of the chappel at Orangeburgh". And Mr. Lucas himself stated that Mrs. Arant had a prayer book used by her mother at Orangeburgh, and that Mrs. Arant herself was baptized in the Protestant Episcopal Church, and that she was born in 1776; which was eight years after 1768. Again, my grandmother, Mrs. A. S. Salley, tells me that she remembers a part of an old church standing in the old church yard when she was a small girl, which was about 1835.

"John Lucas, Sec. & Treas. of the Church of the Redeemer, Octo. 31, 1866."

It is singular how much the descendants of the first settlers of Orangeburg have neglected this old grave yard in which the bones of their ancestors lie buried, and in which stood the first Lutheran church in the Carolinas, and likewise the first Episcopal church in Orangeburg, and in which also stood the Episcopal chapel that succeeded the old church. As an instance of this indifference, it is related by Ex-Governor Perry in his "Sketches," p. 113, that when Hon. A. P. Butler was a young man he went to Orangeburg with an idea of locating there. He put up at a little tavern, and finding it quite chilly, he ordered the negro boy who waited in the house to bring him some lightwood. The boy went out and in a few minutes returned with an armful of grave markers. "Where did you get those?", asked Mr. Butler. "Pull 'em up out de grave yahd", answered the negro. Mr. Butler thereupon decided that he would not locate among people who had so little reverence for the dead, and went elsewhere.

Section 3. The settlement of Saxe-Gotha; the condition of the settlers; their spiritual advantages and disadvantages.

When Orangeburgh District was formed in 1768 Saxe-Gotha Township, now Lexington County, was included in that district; so that in giving the history of Orangeburgh District it is proper to include the history of Saxe-Gotha Township up to the time when it was separated from Orangeburgh District and was included in Lexington District.

In 1730, it will be remembered, eleven townships were laid off on the banks of rivers in South Carolina, and of these eleven townships two were laid off on the Santee. Or, more properly, on the Congaree, a branch of the Santee, and the Santee. These were Amelia and the township which up to 1736 was called Congaree Township, but which in that year was called Saxe-Gotha by Governor Broughton.

It is possible that there were a few unsettled traders and members of the former garrisons of the Congaree fort settled in this township previous to 1736. The following account of the settling of Saxe-Gotha Township is taken from Rev. G. D. Bernheim's History of the German Settlements in the Carolinas; Section 11: (p. 126.)

"In Mills' Statistics of South Carolina, page 611, we have the following statement in reference to Lexington District (now County): 'This District, when first settled, was merged in Orangeburg precincts. A parish and township were laid out in about the year 1750, and named Saxe-Gotha, in compliment to the first settlers of the country, who came from that part of Germany.'

"An entirely different statement may be found on pages 25 and 26 of Dr. Hazelius' History of the American Lutheran Church; from which we learn that the name Saxe-Gotha originated in Queen Anne's time, and that the first settlers of that county 'came from the neighborhood of the Rhine, Baden, and Würtemberg,' kingdoms considerably removed from Saxe-Gotha.

"But from the Journals of Council, in the office of the Secretary of the State, the date of the settlement of Saxe-Gotha by Germans is unmistakably fixed to be 1737, and that few, if any, of the first settlers of that county came from Saxe-Gotha.

"Council Journal, vol. viii, p. 69: 'May 26th, 1742. —Petition of John Casper Gallier and family, John

Casper Gieger and family, John Shalling and family, Abraham Gieger and family, Jacob Liver and family, Julius Gredig and family, Caspar Fry and family, Conrad and Caspar Küntzler (now Kinsler), John Jacob Bieman and family, Herrman Gieger and family, Elizabeth Shalling and family, showing that, as they arrived and settled in his Majesty's Township of Saxe-Gotha, even since the year 1737, and received his Majesty's most gracious bounty of provisions and warrants for lands in Saxe-Gotha Township, but that they could not find in what office they are, therefore they humbly pray his Honor, the Lieutenant-Governor, and his Majesty's honorable Council, that they would be pleased to order that search may be made,' &c., &c.

"Again, under date 1744, 'John Jacob Gieger arrived seven years ago, is now married, and prays for one hundred acres of land over against Santee River, opposite Saxe-Gotha, where he has already begun to clear ground and almost finished a house. Granted'. Subtract seven years from 1744, and we have again the date 1737, the time of the first settlement of that township by Germans.

"From the above reliable source of information we evidently perceive that Mills' statement is entirely incorrect, and that Saxe-Gotha Township was laid out and received its name long before the year 1750, as it is spoken of in the Journals of Council as early as 1742, as being then a township and known by the name Saxe-Gotha, and may have been so called, according to Dr. Hazelius' statement, during Queen Anne's time, previous to the year 1714, the time of her Majesty's death. However, the Council Journals likewise prove the Doctor to have been mistaken in stating that these lands were wrested from the *Germans*, for they settled there, and their descendants are there still, occupying the very lands which their forefathers had received by warrant from the king of England, showing conclusively that, inasmuch as their titles came directly to them from the first legal authority, these lands had not yet passed into other hands.

"But it is possible that, as in the State of New York, the benevolent Queen Anne did make grants of land for church and school purposes in Saxe-Gotha Township, which, however, could not be occupied at the time, as the settlements in South Carolina had then not been extended so far inland; the Indians were still in possession of that portion of the province, and the grants and good intentions of the Queen were eventually lost sight of and forgotten. Afterwards, when the Germans did actually locate themselves in Saxe-Gotha, new warrants were issued and secured to them by the authority of the then ruling sovereign, his Majesty George II.

"Independent of the actual account and dates of the settling of this township, we have before us the general rule that 'Westward the star of empire takes its way,' and that the farther westward or inland the settlements were made, the later will be the dates of such settlements. This is the result of natural causes, and admits of no exceptions to the well-known rule: the first settlers of America necessarily located themselves along the seashore, afterwards a little more inland, whilst the aborigines, living in the forest, gradually receded from the march of civilization; then further encroaches were made upon their territory, and so on, gradually, until the Appalachian chain of mountains was reached. After the Revolutionary War even the mountains formed no barrier to the settlements of the whites, and thus, in a short time, nearly all of America became populated, even beyond the valley of the Mississippi.

"Orangeburg, South Carolina, was settled by Germans in 1735; Saxe-Gotha, further inland, of necessity was settled still later; hence common sense will admit of no date of permanent settlement earlier than, or even as early as, that period of time.

"Saxe-Gotha comprised nearly all that portion of territory embraced at present in Lexington County, it is not many years since the name was changed, in honor of the battle of Lexington, Massachusetts, by an act of legislature, which was a most unfortunate exchange of names, being less euphonic, very inappropriate, and altogether unhistorical.* Give us back the the old name, and may the citizens of old Saxe-Gotha, in South Carolina, never be ashamed of their German names and German extraction.

"How the name originated, as applied to this township, it is impossible to state. It certainly was not so called in compliment to the Germans who settled there, as they came from a different section of Germany; it is possible that the name, 'Saxe-Gotha', was applied to this scope of territory during Queen Anne's reign, as intimated by Dr. Hazelius, and thus, even by name, it was to be distinguished as a future home for German emigrants.

"The following record of this settlement is made in the Urlsperger Reports, vol. iii, p. 1791: 'Wednesday, December 2d. 1741. We had heard nothing before of Saxe-Gotha in America, but we have just received the intelligence that such a town (township) is laid out in South Carolina, twenty-five German miles (100 Engglish miles) from Charlestown, on the road which passes through Orangeburg, and settled with German people. Doubtless the majority of them were German Reformed, as they have a Reformed minister among them, with whose character we are not yet acquaint-

---
*Nor was the honor ever appreciated by the people of Massachusetts.

ed'. This minister was the Rev. Christian Theus, of whom we shall say more hereafter. He commenced his labors in Saxe-Gotha as early as 1739.

"The Geiger families and their neighbors were not compelled to remain a long time as isolated settlers in their new homes; the name Saxe-Gotha sounded so agreeably familiar to the ears of the Germans that they flocked in numbers to this Germany in America.

"Besides, a certain German, named Hans Jacob Riemensperger, contracted with the government to bring over a number of Swiss settlers, many of whom he located in this township, as we learn from Urlsperger, vol. iii, p. 1808, and from the Journals of Council, on several different pages. In addition to these settlers, this same Riemensperger, in company with a Mr. Haeg, brought a number of orphan children to Saxe-Gotha, for which service to the province, as well as for the boarding of the children, they brought in their accounts to the Council for payment. Vol. viii, pp. 69 and 70."

The following extract from the *South Carolina Gazette* of November 13th, 1736, should settle the question as to how this township got its name, and set at rest the differences in statements given by various South Carolina historians on this point:

"His Honour the Lieut:Governour* having been desired to visit the Townships of Amelia Orangeburgh & Saxe-Gotha. so named by his Honour, & before known by the name of Congaree Township, in order to settle some Inconveniences complained of by the Inhabitants of those Townships, did after the adjournment of the General Assembly & when the Business of the Council was dispatched, set out for the said Townships on the 19 October, settling all matters to the entire satisfaction of the inhabitants & re-

---
*Broughton.

turned in good Health to his seat at the Mulberry on the 3d November."

As Broughton did not become Lieutenant-Governor of South Carolina until 1735, the theory advanced by some historians that the township received its name in Queen Anne's time is fallacious. The paragraph from the *South Carolina Gazette* given above should settle the point as to how Saxe-Gotha Township got its name, but just why Governor Broughton should have given it that name is a point yet to be decided.

Dr. Bernheim, on p. 131 of his history, writing of the settlement of Redemptioners, says: "Some of our best and most useful settlers in the South were persons, who, too poor to pay their passage-money across the ocean, were sold by the captains of the vessels, that brought them to America, to any one of the settlers who felt inclined to secure their labor. The price for which they were sold in Carolina was usually from five to six pounds, sterling money, and both men and women were thus alike sold to service; and then, by hard labor, which extended over a period of from three to five years, they eventually redeemed themselves from this species of servitude.

"The advantages of such an arrangement to them and to their adopted colony were, upon the whole, important and salutary.

"1. Our infant colonies stood in need of a useful population which would prove a defence to the country in case of the execution of the continued threatenings of a Spanish invasion, and the sudden attack of hostile Indians.

"2. Besides, labor was greatly needed for the cultivation of the virgin soil, and these poor Germans— many of them excellent farmers, some of them useful artisans, and all of them hard-working people—furnished this labor, and at very cheap rates.

"3. The country also needed permanent settlers who would become habituated to the soil and climate, who would learn to love their adopted country, by being compelled to remain until they had fully tested all the advantages of the same; these the Redemptioners abundantly supplied in their own persons.

"4. Nor were the advantages to *them* of slight importance. They had nothing to risk in the shape of property, as they possessed nothing of this world's goods, and thus they never became a prey to those landsharks which often despoil the less sagacious immigrants of much of the possessions which they brought with them to America.

"5. Besides, they were the poorer class of people at home in Europe, and would always have remained in this condition, had such an arrangement not existed: but now they enjoyed the flattering prospect of receiving competency and wealth at some future day.

"6. Then again, their servitude became their apprenticeship in America; in the meantime they learned the English language, they became acquainted with the laws and customs of the new country, they discovered by silent observation what would in future be to their advantage, and thus in every way did they become qualified by sagacity, industry, and economy, for their new and independent sphere of life.

"Yet it must be confessed that they had to endure many hardships; often were they rigously treated by their ship captains; ill and insufficiently fed on their voyage across the ocean, and on shore before they were purchased for their services; exposed publicly for sale as the African slave: often treated harshly by their masters who purchased them, and compelled to labor in the broiling sun of a southern climate, and many, by disease and death, frequently closed their short earthly career.

"However, when our country had become sufficiently populated, the government interposed and put an end to this kind of servitude, on account of the severity of the lot of these unfortunate laborers, and thus abandoned this source of colonization. In confirmation of these facts, the following extracts will furnish abundant proof, and are herewith submitted:

"Journals of Councils, vol. xiv, p. 37, January 24th, 1744: 'Read the petition of a considerable number of Protestant Palatines, most humbly showing that the poor petitioners have been on board the St. Andrew's, Captain Brown commander, these twenty-six weeks past, and there is as yet no likelihood for them to get free of her, because there are none of us yet who have purchased their service; they therefore humbly pray his Excellency and Honors that they may find so much favor as to their passages that a sum equivalent to discharge the same be raised by the government, for which they promise to join in a bond to repay the same within the term of three years, with lawful interest; and that if any of them shall not be able to pay the above sum within that time, that the government in that case shall have full power to dispose of them and their families as they shall think proper, &c. Ordered to make investigations, and report.'

"Vol. xiv, pp. 62 and 63: 'Several Protestant Palatines, who arrived hither on Captain Brown's ship, and whose services have not as yet been purchased, sent a complaint, by their interpreter, to the governor, that the said Captain Brown had often withheld their diet from them on board his ship, and that they had been several days without meat or drink; particularly that last Friday they were the whole day without any, the least sustenance, and had been the like for several days before, and not only they, but all the rest of the Germans that still remain on board Captain Brown's ship.

"'Captain Brown being sent for and interrogated whether he had used those foreigners in the manner they had represented, answered, that if they had asked him for food in their language he would not have understood them.

"'His Excellency ordered the captain's steward to be sent for, who attended accordingly, and the original contract between Captain Brown and those Palatines in Holland was also sent for and laid before the Board, which being read and the particular species of of diet that was allowed for every day of the week specified, his Excellency asked, in particular, if the said Germans had been fed last Friday in the manner contracted for?

"'The steward replied that the Germans would sometimes reserve the taking of diet on certain days in order to have double allowance another. But his Excellency gave Captain Brown to understand that as he was by virtue of his contract bound to maintain those foreigners till they were disposed of, if any should die for want while aboard his ship, he must answer for their lives; after which they withdrew.'

"The accounts of the trials and hardships of these persons, as narrated in the Urlsperger Reports, are entirely too numerous to be inserted in these pages: those who feel inclined to search for themselves are referred to the volume and page of those Reports. where they can find all they desire to know concerning the Redemptioners. Vol. i, p. 10; vol. ii, pp. 2472, 2482, 2508. How the Redemptioners conducted themselves can be learned from vol. ii, pp. 2193, 2200, 2213, 2221, 2404, 2413.*

* * * * * * * * *

---

*Copies of the Urlsperger Reports can be seen in the library of Newberry College, or in the Astor Library, New York City.

"The following extracts indicate that many such servants were sold and located in Saxe-Gotha, and after their legal discharge from servitude they obtained the king's bounty and tracts of land, the same as other settlers.

"Journal of Council, vol. xi, p. 486: 'Petition of John Wolfe and wife, natives of Berne, Switzerland, too poor to pay passage-money, entered into the service of Anthony Stack, of Saxe-Gotha, for three years, being now discharged from service, prays for his quota of land and bounty-money. Granted, on evidence of his written legal discharge.'

"Vol. xi, pp. 142 and 143: 'Fullix Smid, of Switzerland, servant of David Hent, lately deceased, discharged by his executors, applied for and received 150 acres of land and bounty in Saxe-Gotha.'

"It is useless to multiply instances, which could easily be done; these extracts will fully show the correctness of all the foregoing statements, and that Saxe-Gotha, with many other settlements, received her full share of this class of useful settlers, who proved to have been upon the whole a great benefit to their adopted country.

"During the period that intervened between the years 1744 and 1750, Saxe-Gotha received a large influx of population, and much of the available land of that township was then occupied. The vessel which bore them across the ocean was the ship St. Andrew, Captain Brown, commander, who doubtless treated his paying passengers well, although he acted so unfeelingly to those who were to be sold for their passage-money. Mention is likewise made of a Captain Ham, who brought other German settlers to South Carolina, but whose passengers chiefly located themselves in Orangeburg, whilst others settled in Saxe-Gotha.

"All these German colonists came mostly from those

provinces bordering on the Rhine, such as Switzerland, Baden, the Palatinate, and Würtemberg. They excelled as tillers of the soil, and were accustomed to the culture of the vine, and thus they constituted the very class of people which did become greatly serviceable to the prosperity of Carolina, but whose influence upon the physical welfare of their adopted county has been as yet little noticed by the various historians of the South.

"The Saxe–Gothans were fortunate and blessed in obtaining the services of a pious and faithful pastor; all the records extant speak in the strongest terms of praise concerning him, but, at the same time, all agree in stating that he had a hard life of it, that he was not appreciated, that he was often persecuted for righteousness' sake, and this treatment he received at the hands of the very people for whose good he labored and prayed. Two years after the first settlers set foot upon the soil of Saxe–Gotha, the Rev. Christian Theus arrived and labored in their midst; and as these settlers were not neglected in the administration of the means of grace, which unfortunately was the case with many others of the early colonists, they really had no excuse for their conduct, and should have treated their pastor in the most friendly manner.

"Dr. Muhlenberg's journal, published in the Evangelical Review, vol. i, p. 540, contains the following statement:

"'October 22, 1774. This afternoon I had an acceptable visit from the Reformed minister, the Rev. Theus, of the Congarees (Congaree River), in South Carolina. 120 miles from Charleston. His brother Theus, a painter, lately deceased, received me as a stranger most kindly into his house, when, thirty-two years ago, I travelled through here on my journey from Savannah to Philadelphia, and afforded me an opportunity to preach on Sunday to the then yet few German families. The Lord requite his love in eternity! The aforesaid pastor, Theus, came with his parents into this country from Switzerland as a *candidatus theologiæ*, was examined and ordained by the Reverend English Presbyterian Ministerium, and since 1739 has performed the duties of the ministerial office in the scattered country congregations among the German Reformed and Lutheran inhabitants, and has conducted himself with the propriety and fidelity due his station, according to the testimony of capable witnesses. We had agreeable conversation, and he promised me a written account of church matters in these country congregations, which, moreover, he is best able to furnish, having lived longest in this country, and being an erudite man.'

"It is to be regretted that this '*written account of church matters*', if Dr. Muhlenberg ever received it, has never been published; what interesting material it could now furnish the Church, which must forever be buried in oblivion!

"The Doctor continues: 'He also furnished me with a more detailed description of the sect mentioned October 5th, the members living near him. At a certain time he came unexpectedly into their meeting, and found Jacob Weber contending that he was God, and the said Smith Peter (or Peter Schmidt) insisting that he himself was Christ, and that the unconverted members must be healed through his stripes. Pastor Theus, opposing such blasphemy, the leaders became enraged and threatened his life, and counselled with the rabble whether to drown or hang him. He escaped, however, from their hands, fled to the river, and fortunately found a negro with his canoe at the shore. sprang into it, and was conveyed across.'

"Here we have the impartial testimony of Rev. Dr.

Muhlenberg, gathered from 'capable witnesses', of the parentage, ordination, date of ministry in Saxe-Gotha, piety and learning of the Rev. Christian Theus, up to the period immediately preceding the Revolution. This brief narrative, coming from such a source, is not only entitled to our entire credit, but speaks as much of that devoted man of God as though a volume were written to perpetuate his name and memory.

"Rev. Theus lived to be an aged man, for we discover his name in the list of members of the '*Corpus Evangelicum*', and present at every meeting of that body until the year 1789,* the last meeting of which the records are still extant. How much longer he was spared to do good we know not; but from the dates which are in our possession, he had at that time been half a century in the ministry of his Savior.

"His resting-place is still pointed out to the stranger, and is located in a field along the state road, between Columbia and Sandy Run, about eight miles from Columbia. It is the only grave that can still be seen there, and tradition says that his dwelling was located not far from that graveyard. Mr. Abraham Geiger, now also in eternity, erected the tombsome, at his own expense, at the head of Rev. Theus' grave, to

---

*This fact seems not to have been taken cognizance of by the Provincial Assembly in 1756, for on the 27th of January of that year, an Act was passed for paying the ministers of the several parishes in South Carolina, and in the third section of that Act the following provision occurs: "Whereas, the inhabitants of the Congrees, and the inhabitants of the Waterees, have never had any minister of the gospel to preach and perform divine service among them, *Be it therefore enacted* by the authority aforesaid, that the public treasurer of this Province for the time being shall pay to such minister of the gospel of the established church as shall statedly preach and perform divine service at Saxegotha, or such other centrical place in the Congrees as the commissioners hereinafter named shall direct, and six times a year at least, at the most populous places within forty miles of the same, the sum of seven hundred pounds current money per annum".
—Stats. of S. C., Vol. IV., p. 21.

perpetuate his memory. Had Mr. Geiger not performed this labor of love, the church and the world would never even have known where the first pastor of Saxe-Gotha, the contemporary of Giessendanner, Bolzius and Gronau, had been laid down to rest. The inscription is now much defaced by the hand of time, and can scarcely be deciphered; nevertheless, we are thankful for this much, and would wish that we could gather similar mementoes of the resting places of all of the first German ministers in the South.* The inscription reads as follows:

"'This stone points out where the remains of Rev. Christian Theus lie. This faithful divine labored through a long life as a faithful servant in his Master's vineyard, and the reward which he received from many for his labor was ingratitude.'

"Rev. J. B. Anthony, one of the late pastors of Sandy Run Lutheran Church, adds yet this information, published in the Lutheran Observer, A. D. 1858: 'Among the octogenarians of this vicinity we have not been able to learn much more of Mr. Theus than the rude stone, now standing in a vast cotton-field, records. Few now living recollect to have seen him. No records of those early times are known to exist.† The small school-house, which is said to have stood near his grave, has long since disappeared. A few other graves are said to be here, but as no stones can be found in this sandy section to place at the head and foot, lightwood knots are frequently substituted by the poor, hence, when these decay, there is nothing left to mark the place.'

---

*The burial places of the two Giessendanners are unknown. It is, however, reasonable to suppose that they were buried in the old Episcopal church yard.

†The name of Christian Theus occurs several times in the Giessendanner record.

"The spiritual and moral condition of the Saxe-Gothans is not very highly extolled in the Urlsperger Reports. Rev. Bolzius, who gives us the account, may have been somewhat prejudiced, inasmuch as his Ebenezer colony had lost some runaway white servants, who probably concealed themselves in the neighborhood of the Congaree River, and in several pages of his diary he berates both the Saxe-Gothans and the government of South Carolina that they were not returned; thus, perhaps, his human feelings were too much enlisted on the side of prejudice and interest whilst speaking of these people. We insert the following extract:

"Urlsperger Reports, vol. iv, p. 672: 'Wednesday, April 25, 1750.—The German Evangelical Lutheran inhabitants of Congaree, in South Carolina, which new settlement has been named Saxe-Gotha, had besought me, several months ago, to come to them and preach for them, and administer the Lord's Supper. I sent them books suitable for the edification of adults and the instruction of children, and wrote them that my circumstances did not permit me to make so long a journey. Now I have received another letter, in which the former request is renewed, and in which they likewise beseech me to assist them in the erection of a church and in obtaining a pastor. They have a congregation of about 280 souls, who could attend church if the house of worship were erected in the midst of their plantations.

"'The Reformed have received 500 pounds, Carolina currency, from the government, which amounts to something more than 500 guilders, for the building of a church, but no one is interested for the Lutherans, unless I would do something in their behalf. They live with the Reformed in great disunion, at which I showed my displeasure in my former letter. A few families have removed from this place among them, who might have supported themselves very well here; afterwards three adult youths were persuaded to leave their service here, and two (white) servants ran away, all of whom are harbored in the Congaree settlement. The citizens themselves, as a Carolina minister once wrote me, lived disorderly among each other, and estimate their Reformed minister very low. I have no heart for this people. If they were truly concerned about God's word, then so many unworthy people would not have located in their midst, as there are other places where good land and subsistence may be obtained.

"In this very letter they inform me that they have built both a saw-mill and a grist-mill, and expect to build more of the kind. Why then should they be unable to erect a house of worship if they were sincerely in earnest?'

"The above record in Bolzius' diary, published in the Urlsperger Reports, is in strict accordance with the testimony of Dr. Hazelius on the Weberites—which sect arose some ten years later,—with Dr. Muhlenberg's account, with the inscription on the tombstone on Rev. Theus, and with several living witnesses, who were contemporaries with many old citizens of a former day, whose narratives they still well remember.

"Whilst many of the Saxe-Gothans were not devoid of blame, and deserved censure in those days, there were others whose life and conduct were praiseworthy, and others who were devotedly pious, and who were anxious to enjoy the blessings of the means of grace, and it is sad that Rev. Bolzius permitted his feelings of interest for his own colony to cause him to act so unfriendly toward this people, and to send no kind word of encouragement to them, when they besought him to visit them and break to their hungry souls the bread of life. Who knows what good he might have accomplished by a friendly visit? Who knows what future evil, *e. g.*, that Weber heresy, he might have been the instrument of preventing? Besides all this, he, a minister of the Gospel and of like persuasion with these people, had no right to withhold his influence and sympathy from *two hundred and eighty souls*, (we are surprised at so large a number) who extended such a Macedonian call to him, and besought him twice to interest himself in their behalf in procuring a minister for them, who were almost as sheep without a shepherd. Who could calculate the influence the Lutheran Church would have exerted in those regions, had this large congregation been properly cared for, and supplied with the means of grace? Besides, had Rev. Bolzius been instrumental in securing a pious and efficient pastor for them at that early period, and this pastor, laboring side by side with Rev. Theus, how much that faithful servant's hands would have been strengthened, and how much good seed might have been sown, springing up to everlasting life, which would have entirely changed the spiritual and moral condition of this people. Deprive men of the Gospel and the Sacraments, take away or refuse to give them the benign influences of Christianity, and we need not be astonished at 'disorderly living' and heresy in doctrine.

* * * * * * * * *

"The present citizens of old Saxe-Gotha, now Lexington County, are an entirely different people; their forefathers could not prevent unworthy settlers from locating themselves among them. Many of those depraved men met an untimely death in the war with the Cherokees; a few perished miserably at the hand of administrative justice; others were cut off by disease and an early death; whilst a number moved to other parts of the country. It is exceedingly doubtful whether many of those reprobates left their descendants behind them in Saxe-Gotha, as all traces of Weber and Schmidt have entirely disappeared.

"We have seen that Rev. Theus came to the Congaree settlement in the year 1739. In what building he first preached is unknown, but arrangements were soon made for the erection of a church. As early as 1744-5 John Jacob Riemensperger petitioned the government of South Carolina to do something toward the erection of churches and school-houses for the German settlers in various localities; otherwise they would continue to do what many had done heretofore, move with their families to Pennsylvania, where all these advantages could be enjoyed. That the government entered into such arrangement we have already seen from the Urlsperger Reports, for five hundred pounds currency was donated for the building of a German Reformed Church, which, we presume, had been completed at that time, A. D. 1750, and the people were enjoying the means of grace in their new house of worship. Tradition informs us that this German church stood near the spot where the remains of Rev. Theus are deposited, but it has long since been no more. We now turn to an ancient map of South Carolina, originally published in 1771 and 1775, and recently reprinted in 'Carroll's Collections'. Near the Congaree River, a short distance below the confluence of the Saluda and Broad Rivers, and in the township of Saxe-Gotha, a church is laid down, bearing the name St. John's. This substantiates all the abovementioned records and traditions, gives us the exact locality of that church, which, in the proper proportion of distances, would be the very spot where the grave of Rev. Theus can still be seen, and furnishes, furthermore, the name by which that church was known. This house of God must have been destroyed during the Revolutionary War, as all traces of the same after that period appear to have been lost; it is not mentioned in the general act of incorporation of all the German churches, passed by the legislature of South Carolina in 1788.

"During the years 1759 and 1760, the people of Saxe-Gotha suffered greatly from the ravages of the Cherokee war. During the time that the French and English were at war with each other in the colonies of America, which however did not reach as far South as the Carolinas; the French instigated the Cherokee Indians to make war upon the peaceful settlers of the two Carolinas, who murdered the white inhabitants at midnight, whilst they were wrapped in their peaceful slumbers, and committed atrocities at which humanity shudders. The Congaree and Fork settlements were then mostly exposed to the fearful inroads of the savages, as but few settlers were living further in the interior than the Germans were at that time. Bolzius informs us, that many were compelled to take refuge among the Germans at Ebenezer and Savannah, whilst others fled for safety to Charleston, Purysburg, and other places, until those Indian hostilities were ended, and peace and security was again restored."*

On pp. 168-69 of his book, Dr. Bernheim makes this significant remark: "The Newberry County Germans

---

*It appears from certain passages in the Giessendanner record that the inhabitants of Orangeburgh Township also had some fears of Indian outrages, and that many of them collected together in forts or block-houses; (See baptismal entrys Nos. 611, 616, 617, 624.) and that at least one German citizen of Orangeburgh Township, John Whetstone, Jr., served in the expedition against the Cherokees. (See No. 105 on burial list.)

were mostly all descendants from the original German settlers in Saxe-Gotha Township, with an occasional addition from the German settlements of North Carolina and Virginia." Dr. Bernheim should have placed Orangeburgh Township along with Saxe-Gotha. An examination of the Giessendanner record will show that many of the names thereon obtain in Newberry and Saluda counties to-day.

During the Revolutionary War many of the Hessian hirelings of the British army deserted and became permanent settlers in this country. Dr. Bernheim says, p. 174: "Among these Hessian deserters was one who afterwards became a Lutheran minister in South Carolina, named John Yost Mütze, known better as Rev. J. Y. Meetze, and whose history was obtained from one of his sons. He deserted near Charleston at the time the British army was besieging that city from the other side of Ashley River; he was pursued some thirty miles, but finally made his escape over Bacon's bridge, where he was safe within the American lines. He located himself in Saxe-Gotha Township, now Lexington County, six miles above the present county-seat, and became the forefather of a large and influential family in that section of the country. The following tablet inscription marks the spot where his remains now repose:

"'Sacred to the memory of the Rev. J. Y. Meetze, who departed this life May 7th, 1833, aged 76 years, 5 months, and 5 days.'"

Section 4. The settlers of Barnwell.

That portion of Orangeburgh District, afterwards embraced in Barnwell District, also received a share of the German settlers, as Dr. Bernheim says, by the breaking up of the Dutch colony on James Island, the gradual absorption of the unsuccessful German and Swiss colony at Purysburg, and the influx of other German settlers from Orangeburg County."

The same section also received many settlers from Virginia. In this connection the following extract from "Memoirs of Tarleton Brown," p. 3, will be of interest: "Flattering inducements being held forth to settlers in the rich region of South Carolina contiguous to the Savannah River, and my uncle, Bartlet Brown, having already moved, and settled himself two miles above Matthew's Bluff, on the Savannah River; my father brought out some negroes, and left them with his brother to make a crop; and in 1769, a year afterwards, my father and family, consisting of eleven persons, emigrated to this country and settled on Brier's Creek, opposite to Burton's Ferry. We found the country in the vicinity very thinly inhabited. Our own shelter for several weeks to protect us from the weather was a bark tent, which served for our use until we could erect a rude dwelling of logs."

General Johnson Hagood is authority for the statement that Tarleton Brown probably has more descendants in Barnwell County to-day than any other man who ever lived in that county. Among the other natives of Virginia, early settled in the same section, were the Wright and Erwin families.

CHAPTER II.

THE GIESSENDANNER RECORD.

Almost every South Carolina historian who has mentioned Orangeburg has spoken of the Giessendanner Church record-book, but Dr. Bernheim is the only writer who has gone beyond a mere mention of the fact that this record-book existed. What Dr. Bernheim has said of this interesting work has already been given in these pages.

After the death of Rev. John Giessendanner in 1761, his son Henry came into possession of the book, and a few scattering records were made by him. After his death the book fell into the hands of his second wife, who, previous to her marriage to Henry Giessendanner, was the widow Larey; and through her it fell into the hands of her son, Daniel Larey. Daniel Larey left it to his daughter, Mrs. M. B. Treadwell, of Orangeburg. Mrs. Treadwell, after keeping it for many years, turned it over to the late Mr. John Lucas, Senior Warden of the Church of the Redeemer (Episcopal) at Orangeburg, and Mr. Lucas, after making a copy of it, turned it over to the Diocese of South Carolina, and it was deposited in the Episcopal Library in the small building in the rear of St. Stephen's Chapel, on Anson Street in Charleston. It was there that the writer first saw the book, and copied it by permission of Rev. A. R. Mitchell, Secretary of the Diocese of South Carolina. Since then Bishop Capers has had the book returned to Mrs. Treadwell at her request.

The book appears to have been an ordinary, but substantial, blank book, over which Rev. John Giessendanner, or some subsequent keeper of the book, had stretched a raw-hide binding and sewed it on with thick, twisted, white chord. It is in a very dilapidated condition; some of the pages being torn in half, and numerous pages have been lost.

It is evident that the first Giessendanner, who began to keep the record in the fall of 1737, and kept it until his death, the latter part of 1738, kept it in a different book; for when his nephew began to keep the record in 1739 he says that the record kept by his uncle has been copied from the old book into the new, and after giving the record kept by his uncle, he begins his own record. The record kept by the elder Giessendanner and most of that kept by the younger before his trip to England for ordination was written in German, and the records here given for that period are from translated notes made by Dr. Bernheim, and others, for Mr. Lucas; and possibly some of them were made by Henry Giessendanner, as the papers appear to be of different ages, (some appear to be very old) and in different handwritings.*

The parts, preserved and translated, of those records kept up to the time when the younger Giessendanner went to England are very meagre and scattering, but those kept after his return are very complete. It is doubtful if there was a church record-book kept in the Province at that time, that is as complete.

The younger Giessendanner started to keep all of the records of marriages, births, and deaths in one book and divided the book equally into three parts and kept the marriages in the first part, the births in the second part and the deaths in the third part. His record before his departure for England only covered

---

*I have heard that Dr. Bachman translated some of the German records into English for Mr. Lucas.

a few pages in each part. After his return from England he continued with the record, but the record of one part usually took up more than its allotted space, so that he would have to run it over a few pages beyond the record of the next part and continue it therefrom. On this account it requires some patience to get the records straight.

I give the record as nearly like the original as I can, with the style of spelling, punctuation and abbreviations unchanged. The following is the imperfect translation of the incomplete record kept in German by Rev. John Ulrick Giessendanner, and by Rev. John Giessendanner before his departure for England:

"Catalogus Conjugatorum.

"This Book contains the names of all those who were Married and Baptized by me in Orangeburgh in Public as well as in Private & herein accurately Recorded.
"John Ulrick Giessendanner.
"Minister."

"Anno 1740.

"This Book should be carefully preserved that those who may wish to know of their family may find it in the Book of Record."—John Giessendanner, the younger. Then follows a quotation from Genesis 2 Chap. 18 v. "And the Lord said it is not good for man to be alone I will make a help meet for Him"; then follows another passage from 128 Psalm and another from Hebrews 13. 4.

"Here follows a Register, or List of such persons as were married and joined together in matrimony by my predecessor & Uncle, deceased, and now in Heaven. This register is copied from the old Book into this new one—word for word accurately—as he wrote and kept it."

Anno–1737–

1stly. I have on 24 Oct° by request of Major Motte— & two Englishmen—who are Majors—and at their own Risk and Responsibility Married in the house of Mrs Price a widow—in the Village of Beystein—a Possession of the English Crown. Joseph Russel to Mrs. Margaret Russel. Her maiden name was Price. The Major read the marriage service in English in my presence.

2d 3 Novr Was publicly married & joined together in Matrimony Simon Sanger to Miss Barbara Strowmann.

3dly Nov. 15 I John Ulrick Giessendanner got married—in presence of many witnesses—to my house keeper who for 26 years served in our house & who from affection and to escape family troubles followed me over the ocean—& to prevent & obviate any cause offence or scandel I married her. privately. Major Motte read the marriage service. May Jesus unite us closely in love, as well as all faithful married people, and cleanse and unite us with himself. Amen.

[4] 26 Jany 1738 Married—Jacob Pruncen to Miss Barbara Fusters Lawful daughter of Johannes Fusters.

[5] 31 Jany 1738 Following Persons married Peter Grimmer to Dorothea Huber Lawful daughter of Johannes Huber—In Zimmermanns Daughters house.

[6] Elias Schnell—son of Henry Schnell to Anna Barbara Meyer—John Meyer daughter.

[7] 24 Feby John Shaumlöffel to Anna Maria widow of Nicolas Dirr.

[8] 12 April. I have married in presence of English & German witnesses—after 3 times publishing the Banns & in presence of the congregation of our Church Christian Meyers—Johannes Meyers' Lawful son to Rebecca Young—William Youngs daughter from Holland—Johannes Myers from Switzerland.

No 9. John —— in Amelia Township, Miss Nessa Wolf.

The foregoing is all of the elder Giessendanner's record that is given. The following is the younger Giessendanner's record:

Anno 1740.

Jay 1st On New Year Day ——

By 3 Public publishments of Banns, at 3 different Places—and after Service was over—The following got married that day—

1s John Jacob Meyer a lawful son of Mr. Henry Meyer—To Miss Anna Bustrin. (Buser.)

2d Privately, Mr. Conrad Alder to Mrs. Anna Burgin, widow, in Her own House—Her former Husband was Henry Rickenbaker—after the Banns hath been 3 times published.

3—Privately in Her own house in presence of several witnesses—Jacob Pier Hans Fridig and Jacob Kuhn—The following two persons were married—Mr. Benedict Koller to Magdalina Springin—Mr. Johannes Springin's lawful daughter.

(4) 3 Jany that is on Thursday after 3 times publ. publicly in a large congregation, Banns, Mr. Richard Horsfort & Miss Barbara Diedrick, that is Mr. John Diedrick's lawful daughter.

(5) The 14 Jany. at sun set in Mr. Henry Schnell's house after 3 times publication in German; & once in English language Mr. Benjamin Carter in Amelia Township to Rebecca Murphy.

(6) The 3d Feby. The following persons were after Publication John Julius Tapp son of Christian Tapp to Anna B. Hergersperger widow—maiden name Kesebirnger.

(7) (This entry is obliterated.)

8. Thomas Joyner and Faithy Carse In Amelia.

9. Joseph Ratford and Eugenia Carse In Amelia.

10. Lewis Montier, and N. N.
11, Joseph Greiter to Susanna Shuler.
12, Mathias Keller to Maria Handshy.
13, Henry Rickenbacker to Anna Diel.
14. Jacob Wannamaker to Susan Shuler.
(16)* Anno 1740, Thursday 10, Decbr. married after usual publication, Hans in the Village† to Magdalene Piercy maiden name Bush.
(17) Jacob Wolf to Veronica Fluhbacker, widow, & daughter of Hans Domin.
(18) (This entry is obliterated.)
(19) January 12 on Tuesday, married Kilian Abecklin to Maria Schwartz. Witness, Hans Freydigs, & Christian Schwartz. published 2 times.
(20) Joseph Cuttier to Maria Sahly, Witness Hans Diedrick jun. Hans Freydig, Henry Wurtz, and Joseph Robison.
‡Thursday 14, April married (after two times publishing) private Joseph Hasforts, nickname Cooper.**
(21) William Smith to Abigail Shannon, Witness Richard Hasford, Thos. Morys, James Merrimans, John Jennings etc.
(22) Wednesday 1, July Married in Capt. Harn's house, John Hamelton to Catharine Myers, widow etc.
(23) Anno 1741. Thursday 3 Septbr. in Mr. John Hearns, Esqr's house married†† ("See book")‡‡
(24) Tuesday 19, Novbr. married privat after once publishing Christ. Schwartz to Elizabeth Fusterin. widow, in presence of Kilian Abecklin, John Fuster and 2 children.
(25) Sunday 22 Decbr. private. once publish. Ed-

---
*There was no No. 15 in the book. †The groom seems not to have had a surname. ‡Not numbered. **Woman's name not given.
††Obliterated. ‡‡In Mr. Lucas's copy, now the property of the Church of the Redeemer, is the rest of this entry, as follows: "James Pendarvis to Catherine Rumph witness John Hearn John Pearson John Hammelton John Diedricks John Danners Robert Whitefords".

ORANGEBURG COUNTY. 97

ward Gibson to Susanna Schwartz, Witness Christian & Joseph Schwartz & John Souderecker.

(26) Tuesday 31st Decbr. private married in Amelia Township, Joseph Lyons to Barbara Gartman, widow. witness Benjamin Carter.

(27) Wednesday 1. Jany in Amelia Township, married Joseph Joyner to Miles Jackson. ("see book") Witness John Hammelton, John Fairchild, Richard Hasfort, William Martius, Thomas Jackson.

(28) On Sunday 25. April married John Pearson to Mary ―― Witness John Hearns, Adin Frogat & Jacob Wannamaker, etc.

(29) Thursday 18. May married publicly Christian York to Miss Barbara Heym Witness Henry Wurtz, Henry Straumann, Hans Roth, Peter Hurger.

(30) Thursday 25,. married privately. Peter Grieffous to Anna Otto, witness Peter Hurger, & Jacob Kuhner.

(31) Sunday 18. (July) married John Jacob Straumann to Anna Margaretta Schaumlöffel Witness, Henry Wurtz, Henry Straumann, Peter Hurger, & Hans in the village.

(32) Monday 6$\underline{th}$ fallmonth (Sept.) married John Atkinson to Sarah Carter. Witness Joseph Lyons. Miles Jackson, Lewis York Chris Stean.

Anno 1742.

(33) Thursday 12. Sumer month (October) married Hans Georg Henry Hess. to Miss Catharina Magdalena Shuler. Witness, Peter Hurger. Michael Larry. Valentia Justus Elias Schnell.

(34) Tuesday 30 Winter month (November) married John Inabnet to Miss Marguretta Negly Witness― Hans Danner. Simon Sanger―Wardz Henry Strowmann & Isaac Otto.

1745*

―――

*For several years the marriage records are lost.

(100) 13 Novbr. got married Joseph Abraham Schwerdt to M$\underline{rs}$ Elizabeth Souderecker Witness Georg sen, & Jacob Giessendanner.

(101) 1745/6 Monday 13 Jany, married Johann Chevillette to Mrs. Susanna Hepperditzel, Witness, Joseph Robinson. ——

1746/7 Saturday 7 Feby

Philip Jennings & Elizabeth Late Hasfort Witness— Joseph Hasforts, Frogat, Brand Pendarvis & Lucas Wolf. ——

Thursday 19 Feby married Thos. Jones to Elizabeth Davis, Witness, Samuel Wright Capt. Thompson etc.

Ditto Melchior Ott to Mrs. Anna Barbara Zangerin Witness, Peter Maurer, Sr. & Henry & Jacob Friger, Hans Huber, Henry & Jacob Straumann.

Febry 24, Martin Kooner to Mary Joyner. Witness Nathan Joiner, Ja's Cars, Francis Kooner.

A. D. 1739

(1) Dec. 25, The following children were Baptized: Johannes Stetzel, son of George & Maria-Linden Stetzel. Sponsors John Diedrick & Miss Barbara Hueden. Born Octob 27, 1739.

(2) Anna Hugin—Legitimate ch of Theodore Hugin & Magdalin Balmarin—Spons. Johannes Dolch, & Sn$\underline{s}$ Barbara Heinein formerly Hoeffertin—Mrs. Agnes Diebuebdin formerly Ininjlin—Born on the 12 of Nov. 1739.

(3) Margaret Whetstein, Mr. Johannes Whetstein & Mrs. Anna Freauenfaederin's legitimate son. Spons. Jacob Bruel Mrs Margaret Bruel formerly Miss Bringolt & Mrs. Susannah Hepperdittel—formerly Mrs Acker. Born July 8. 1739.

A. D. 1740.

[4] On the first day of January was baptized Mar-

garet Kollerin—child of Mr Benedict Koller & Mrs. Magdalin Springen. Spons Mr. Jacob Thieren & Mrs Regina Krichen formerly Mrs. Brant Mrs Margretta Frydigin formerly Miss Bolleriu—was Born 14 Nov. 1739.

(5) In Mr Henry Rickenbacker's house privately baptized—on the 7 March—Henry Rickenbacker child of Henry Rickenbacker & Mrs Anna Deul. Spons Joseph Robinson—Anna Margerett ——* & others.

(6) On Sunday 25. April—by baptism admitted into the church Margaretta Legt child of Henry Hauscig & his wife Spons—Margretta Bachrden. & Magdelin Acker.

(7) Monday 26 April—Privately Baptized Edward Freeman Shnellgrove. L son of Freeman Shnellgrove & his wife Spons Peter Horger—Johannes Wettstein Anna Wettstein.

(8) April 27 Tuesday was baptized Regina Barbara Legt child of Mr. Christopher Rowe & His wife. Spons Henry Sneller, John Bruderer, Regina Jutsig & Miss Barbara Honig.

(9) 3 of May Publicly Baptizen William Siceceals, Brand Pendarvis & Mrs Anna Ro.

A. D. 1741.

(10) On the Easter Sunday—were baptized in presence of the whole congregation John Meyer. Legitimate child of Hans Jacob Meyer & Anna Buester—Spons—John Frittstein & Ulrick Buester & Mrs Barbara Horsfort, formerly Miss Diedricks.

(11) On the Sunday 24 May was Bt Hans Henry Strauman Legit child of Mr. Henry Strauman & Mrs. Catharin Strauman formerly Miss Horger in presence of Spons. Mr. Simon Saenger, Verona Freydig.

(12) On Sunday 31 May was Baptz Johannes Wett-

*Obliterated.

stein. Legit child of Mr. Johannes Wettstein & Anna Wettstein formerly Miss Fraeuenfelder Spons—Mr. Johanness Acker—Hans Jacob Meyer & Anna Barbara Laessig formerly Miss Kesselringer.

(13) On Sunday 5 July was Bapt$\underline{d}$ William Robinson. Legit child of Mr. Robinson & wife. Spons—Mr Hans Danners, David Rumpfer Elizabeth Rothig— according to the rules of the Church of England & Book of Common Prayer.

(14) Monday 14 Sept—was Baptized Privately Anna Maria Margretta Diedricks—Leg child of Mr. Johannes Diedricks & His Wife—Spons Henry Wuertzer Peter Hurger, Margret Koenig, formerly Hessig—& Margretta, Laehryig—formerly Bodenerig.

(15) 21 Sept Monday evening Privately Baptized Robert Pue Legt child Mr. Gavin Pue & wife—Spons— Michael Christopher Rowe, John Lucy Wolff & Sertina Wolff.

(16) 27 Sept on Sunday—was Publicly in the English Language Bapt$\underline{d}$ John Jones—Leg child of Mr. John Jones & wife Spons. John Pearson Richard Hasfords & Barbara Hasford.

(17) Oct^o 15. On Thanksgiving day Baptized on Barnard Elliott's Plantation. Elizabeth Linder, Legt child Mr. Ludwig Linder & wife—Spons. Mr. Ulrick Giessendanner Elizabeth Reigchig.

(18) Dec$\underline{r}$ 30 was baptized by me in Amelia Township Privately William Harrys Legt child William Harrys and Mary Brood Spons. Elias Teat Benjamin Carter & Rebecca Carter.

(19) Ibiden — — In same Place

On Thursday 31 dec$\underline{r}$ 1741 Baptiz William Weekly Leg child Thomas Weekly & His wife Spon—Freeman Shnellgrove W Cammel & Mrs Cammel.

Anno 1741/2 On Sunday 25 April by Baptisen admitted into the church Margaretta Legt child of Henry Hauscig and his wife Spons Margretta Bachrgen & Magdalena Acker.

Monday 26 April Privately Baptized Edward Freeman Snellgrove Leg$^{\underline{m}}$ son of Freeman Snellgrove and his wife Spons Peter Hogan Johanna Wettstein and Anna Wettstein.

April 27 Tuesday was baptized Regina Barbara Leg^{mt} child of Mr Michael Christopher Row and his wife—Sponsors Henry Sneller, John Bruderer Regina Iutsey Miss Barbara Honig

3$^{\underline{d}}$ May Publicly Baptized William Leg$^{\underline{t}}$ child of Jacob Wanneumacker & his wife Sponsors William Siddal, Brand Pendarvis and Mrs Anna Row

Anno 1742.

June 25 on Sunday. I Baptized. Henry my own Leg. child. Ulrick Giessendanner & my wife Barbara formerly Miss Hugg. Spons-Mr. Henry Wurtz. Michael 1... gry Anna Rohrig formerly Miss Diedricks which child came to light on Saturday afternoon June 1742. In the Sign of the Twins.

At the Same time Baptized Hans Michael Legt child of Re . . . vs & his wife Feldgnig Spons. Hans Imdorff, Michael Barry & Regenia Kuchin.

On Sunday 5 July. Jacob Danner son of Hans Danner and Barbara his wife, was Baptisen Spons; Hurger & Michael.

1743.

Sunday, The 19 Haymonth (July) is baptized in the Ch Bottes a child called Christian, lawful child, Mr. Henry Faussen & his wife Anna Maria (by witness) John Julius Tappier. Christian Roth & Maria Christianna his wife

Sunday the 11th Fallmonth (Sept.) is admitted by baptism to the holy Communion in the Church Bottes. Maria Elizabeth, lawful child of Mr Jacob Strauman

& his wife Anna Margareth, by witness Henry Wurtz & Maria Elizabeth Shaumlöffel & Mrs Barbara Zangerig.

Sunday 14 April 1745 is baptized in the Church Bottes—Elizabeth, lawful child, Mr Henry Giessendanner, & his wife Barbara, maiden name Hurger. Witness are Johann Chevillette. Mrs. Barbara Zangerin, maiden name Straumann & Mrs Margareth Inabinet, maiden name Negely. The child was born Sunday morning about one hour before day the 27 day of January 1744/5 in the syn of the Ram.

Anno 1745 The 21st August is baptized in the Church Bottes, Henry, lawful Child, Mr. Henry Faust, & Anna Maria (witness, Henry Heim. Joseph Krauter & Anna Roth, his wife.

Anno 1745 The 29 fallmonth is baptized in the Church Bottes*

Augt. 17. (1746.)

Admitted to the holy Communion in the presence of the Congregation the following infants, Maria, lawful daughter of Mathias & Maria Keller, (Witness) Henry Reichmann & wife Mrs Anna Maria Markly & Mrs. Elizabeth Reich.

Ditto as above.

Anna lawful daughter of John & Anna Eberly, (Witness) Louis Reich & Mrs. Anna Margaretha Beltzer.

Decbr 14/46

Benedict lawful son of Benedict Kollers and his wife Magdalena (Witness) Isaac Hotto, Bartholome Spring & his wife Margaretha.

Ditto Decbr 25/46

John lawful son of Mr. Georg Hessys and his lawful wife Anna Catharina (Witness) Michael Christopher Row, Nicolas Shuler & Mrs Anna Rickenbackerin. & Mrs Magdalena of the village.

---

*Name not given.

Jany. 1/47.
Joseph, lawful son of Joseph Kreuter & his wife Susannah (Witness) Jacob Porter. Joseph Huber, & Mrs. Elizabeth Rothin & Mrs Anna Elizabeth Biegelmann.

Febry 1/7 Samuel (lawful son of Samuel Davis & his wife Salome (Witness) Michael Christopher Row Abraham Yssenhut & Mrs Verena Wurtzer.

D$\underline{o}$ Margaretha lawful daughter of Louis Reichen & his wife Elizabeth (Witness) Jacob Giessendanner & Mrs Agnes Giessendanner & Mrs Margaretha Row.

Febry 3. At Mr. Thomas Jones's House. Thomas, son of John Jones, and Hannah his wife, Deceased, he was before lawfully baptized by private Baptism by ─────── at Stono was now only signed with the sign of the Cross (Witness) Eugenia Jones, & George Pou.

Feby 3 1747 In the House of M$\underline{r}$ Thomas Jones. Eugenia daughter of John Jones and Hannah his wife deceased. Goss, Joseph Jones, Patience Faure & Eugenia Faure.

Ditto. In Domo Predicti
Thomas son of Peter and Ann Grieffous: Goss, John Jones Eugenia Jones and Thomas Jones.

March 1$\underline{st}$ In the house of Mr Thomas Fort, John son of Leonhard and Sarah Warnedow Goss John Fitz Mrs Lammons and for want of another the mother

March 8$\underline{th}$ Frederick Son of John & Ann Wolf: Goss Henry Woortzer, Thomas Wolf Agnesia W. late widow of Lewis York deceased.

Ditto Isham Peter Frant. son of Thomas and Ann Maria Eberhard: Goss: Peter Moorer Junr Francis Kooner and Jgft Dorothea Weistine

1747 March 15$\underline{th}$ Samuel, son of Joseph and Margaret Grieffous. Goss Michael Christopher Row Peter Hottow and Ursula Pendarvis

Ditto.

Baptized March 15 Carl & Anna Hotto Lawfull son ————————— Sponsors Joseph Buph & wife Anna Maria Cuttier and Jacob Rickenbaker

Ditto.

Magdalena & Regel Lachrie Lawful Daughter Sponsors. Johann in the old field Mrs Barbara Giessendanner and Mrs Magdalena Koller

March 20 1747 Baptized Baldhasar lawful Child of Mr John Inabnet and his wife Margaret Born March 12th Spons Hans Balsiger. Hans of the Village Mrs Verona Wartzer

1747

Thursday 14 April Baptized in Henry Schnell house Catharina Magdalene, Adam & Margaretta Schnell lawful Child Spons George Kotgen & Jacob Giessendanner Miss Magdalene Horger and Mrs Catharina Wanamaker

1747 Tuesday April 14 Baptized in the House of Henry Schnell, Henry son of Jacob & Catharina Wanamaker Spons. Henry Schnell Senr & Johannes and Mrs Margaretta Schnell.

Ditto—Catharina Barbara George and Christina Barbara Kotgein lawful daughter Sponsors Henry Schnell & Barbara Schnell & Jacob and Catharina Wannamaker

Ditto—Henry son of John & Esther Jones. Goss, Henry Schnell Senr Henry Horger Junr Adam Snell and Barbara Lyons

Sunday 19 April at Holy Easter Baptized Anna Christine Barbara Nicolas and Christine Lawful daughter Sponsors Jacob Kuhnen Mrs. Anna Rickenbacker & Mrs Barbara Heim

1747. Sunday the 28 Haymonth (July) is baptized in the Church Bottes. Johannes lawful child Mr Jo-

hann Ulrick Giessendanner & wife Barbara maiden name Hugg (Witness) Johannes Amaker Geo Giessendanner & Mrs Regel Larey, maiden name Kochin. The child was born Friday morning about 2 hours by day the first day in May Anno prodicte in the syn Twins-Sept 2ᵈ 1747
Baptized John son of Thomas and Eugenia Jones. Sponsors John and Mary ——— John Wood*
1747 Sept William. Son of William and Mary Harris, Goss John Gusseand Barbara & Peter Hook Magdalen Hook Barbara Giessendanner†
Nov. 15 1747 Recᵈ into Christ Church Abraham son of Abraham and Mary Yessenhoot: Goss Jacob Rumph Peter Hugg & Anna Dattwyler Born Sept 29
——————*

1748

April 24 Baptized John son of Brand and Arketta Pendarvis, Goss Michael C Rowe Lucas Wolf Ann Rose

On Wednesday August 3 1748 Baptized George Henry son of Leopold Clausand W. A his wife Goss Henry Snell Senʳ George Giessendanner Junr̲ Phillipina Regina Yutzy and Fritchman.

1748 August 25 Baptized one child name, Susannah Mr Joseph & Susannah Kreiter s lawful daughter Sponsors Jacob Roth, Hans Balziger & Susannah Huber & Mrs. Susannah Fryday

Ditto John son of Phillip & Elizabeth Jennings Sponsors Goss. John Jennings Hasford and Abraham Ursella Pendarvis-

1748 September 25ᵗʰ Baptized Felder; born Sept 8 son of Henry and Maria Elizabeth uxorsegas sponsors Jacob Giessendanner, Jacob & Lovisia Horger.

*This entry was on the inside cover of the book, and may not be correct as to dates.
†This is a detached entry, but belongs here, evidently.

Oct̊ 2 Johann Matthias Petri et Anna uxorsejus Sponsors Henrick Wartzer Joseph Kreider Barbara Giessendanner and Agnes Giessendanner

Oct̊ 9— Baptized Johann Jacob Henreick and Catharina Strawmann uxoris ejus Sponsors Henrick Wartzer Michael Row Elizabeth Roth & Margaretha Row

This closes up the record kept by Rev. John Giessendanner before his departure for England. The following list, made out in English in the handwriting of Rev. John Giessendanner, is recorded in the book; and was doubtless made out by him shortly after he returned from England, as it is evident from the position it occupies in the book that it was made out at an early day, as the recording preceeding it caught up with it; thus placing it in the midst of the record of births kept in English after his return from England. By comparing it with the translated record, already given, of the marriages performed by Rev. John Giessendanner before his trip to England, it will be seen that it is made up from those records. It contains some marriages not given in the German record—probably because the pages containing the record (in German) of those particular marriages have been lost. At any rate this list, translated as it was by the Rev. John Giessendanner himself, is a valuable supplement to the translated record already given:

A List of all those; who have been maryed by me John Giessendanner. V. D. M.

1 Mr. John Chevillette Esqr. Jan: 13th 1745/6. To Susannah Hepperditzel. Widow.
2 George Giessendanner Jun.. To Agnes Diedrich. Widow.
3 Jacob Wolf. 1740. 10th Decbr To Veronica Tommen. Widow.
4 Jacob Wolf.... To Appollonia Shuler.

ORANGEBURG COUNTY. 107

5 Hans im Dorff 1740. 10$\underline{th}$ Dec$\underline{br}$ To Magdalene Pieren. widow.
6 Jacob Wannenmacher...To Catharina Shuler.
7 John Kitchin...To Barbara Pfund. widow.
8 Samuel Davis To Salome Fuster.
9 Henry Felder 1747. Dec$\underline{r}$ 15. To Mary Elizabeth Shaumlöffel
10 John Fairy 1743. Febr: 5$\underline{th}$ To Ann Yssenhut....
11 Christian Thwartz 1741. To Elizabeth Fuster. widow. Nov. 19$\underline{th}$
12 John Simmons... To Catherina Zorn, widow.
13 John Fuster... To Sirrah Hatcher.
14 John Cleaton....To Sirrah Fuster. widow.
15 James Pendarvis 1741..To Catherina Rumph. Sept$\underline{br}$ 3$\underline{d}$
16 John Pearson 1742...To Mary Raiford. April 25$\underline{th}$.
17 John Hammilton 1741..To Catherina Myers, Widow. July 1$\underline{st}$
18 Thomas Puckridge...To Catherina Pfund.
19 Jacob Roth....To Catharina Ygly. widow.
20 George Gatz....To Barbara N. widow
21 Hans Jacob Strauman 1748. To Ann Margareth Shaumlöffel July 18$\underline{th}$
22 Hans Jacob Myer 1740. To Ann Buser. January 1$\underline{st}$......
23 Hans Jacob Gyger...To Margaret Shuler. widow
24 Jacob Horger...To Lovisia Shaumloffel.
25 Peter Moorer Jun....To Margaret Larry.
26 Hans Giegelman....To Ann Elizabeth Shuler
27 John Jubb.....To Eve Catherine Shuler.
28 Antony Ernst.....To Ann Barbara Gyger.
29 Melchior Ott 1746/7. Febr. 19$\underline{th}$ To Ann Barbara Zangin.
30 Henry Strauman 1740. April 1$\underline{st}$ To Catharina Horger.

31. Christian York 1742. May 18th To Barbara Heym.
32. Joh: Julius Tapp 1740. Febr: 3d To Ann Barbara Hergersperger, widow.
33. Georg Adam Ernst.... To Ann Barbara Tapp. widow.
34. Hans in Abnit 1742 Nov. 30th To Margaret Nägely.
35. Henry Rickenbacher.... To Ann Diel.
36. Hans George. Hessy 1742. Oct 12th To Catharina Margaret Shuler.
37. Joseph Deramas.... To Ann Pfund.
38. Peter Grieffous. 1742. May 25th To Anna Hottow.
39. Leonhard Warnedow.... To Sirrah Hottow.
40. Charles Hottow.... To Ann Tshudy
41. Benedict Koller 1740. Jany. 1st... To Magdalene Spring.
42. Michael Larry.... To Regula Koch.
43. Peter Hottow..... To Margaret Barbara Shuler.
44. Joseph Kreüter.... To Susannah Shuler.
45. Andrew in Abnit.... To Mary Nägely.
46. Conrad Alder 1740. January 1st.. To Ann Rickenbacker, Widow.
47. Richard Hasfort 1740. Jany. 3d To Barbara Diedrick.
48. Benjamin Carter 1740 Jany: 14th To Rebecca Murphy, widow.
49. Thomas Joyner.... To Faithy Carse.
50. Joseph Ratford.... To Eugenia Carse.
51. Lewis Montier.... To M. Biddys.
52. Matthias Keller.... To Mary Handsby.
53. Joseph Lyons. 1740/1. Jany: 4th To Susannah Grim. widow.
54. Joseph Lyons. 1741. Dec. 31.... To Barbara Gartman.
55. Killian Abeclin 1740/1.—To Mary Schwartz January 12th

ORANGEBURG COUNTY. 109

56. Joseph Cuttier 1741. March 27th To Ann Mary Sähly.
57. William Smith 1741. April 14th To Abigal Shannon.
58. Evard Gibson 1741.. Dec. 22d—To Susannah Schwartz.
59. ———* Joyner 1741/2. Jany. 6th To Miles Jackson.
60. (Was on the top edge of the page and has worn off.)
61. Joh: Abraham Schwardtfeger 1745. To Elizabeth Souderecker, widow. Dec. 27th
62. Phillip Jennings 1746/7. Febr. 7th. To Elizabeth, late Hasfort
63. Thomas Jones 1746/7. Febr: 19th To Elizabeth Davis......
64. Martin Koonen 1746/7. Febr: 24th To Mary Joyner. February 24th
65. Hans Adam Shnell...To Margaret Yootzy.
66. Elias Shnell....To M. Fritchman.
67. Bernhard Schnell...To N. Shuler.
68. Charles Kitchen...To Eugenia Megrew.
69. John Middleton....To Sirrah Goodby.
70. Samuel Hudson 1746. July. To Margaret Maxwell, widow.
71. Nathan Joyner....To Winifred N.
72. John Sullivan....To N. Snellgrove.
73. William Hickey...To Rebecca Gant.
74. Thomas Eberhard...To Mary Moor.
75. Paul Bunch 1748. April 28th To Amy Winigum.
76. Christian Theus....To N. N..
77. Brand Pendarvis To Ursetta Jennings.
78. Joseph Cooper To Margaret N.
79. Hans George Shlappy...To Magdalene Huber.

*Torn out.

80. Daniel Geltzer....To Margaret Brick, widow.
81. Hans Eberly....To Ann Marckly.
82. John Kannady 1747. Sept 29th To Mary Godfrey.
83. Jonathan Brimstone...To Martha Pickings....
84. Samuel Pickings...To N. Patton.
85. George Flutt....To N. Pickings
86. Francis Lamons....To N. N.
87. Flowers Michill February 1st.. To Elizabeth Warren 1747/8.
88. William Gray....To Ann Shaw.
89. Samuel Gandy March 14...To Rosina Zellwegerin.
90. William Clement January 28th. To Mary Callyhon. widow, 1747.
91. James Dean......To Dina Even.
92. William Weanright.....To Hannah Williams, widow.
93. Daniel Deruraseux March.14th To Olivia Wood.
94. Jacob Rumph 1748. May 19th To Ann Dattwyler.
95. Solomon Witham July 29th 1744..To Francis Merryan.
96. John Robinson....To Isbell Butcher.
97. Henry Sally Junr. To Magdalena Huber
98. Jacob Koonen 1748. Septemb 1st. To Catharina Negely.
99. Francis Koonen 1748. Sept: 1st. To Ann Maria Hagin.
100. John Fitch January 16th 1748/9 . . To Ann Holmes.
101. Daniel Shyder......To Elizabeth Richard.

Here follows the record of marriages which Rev. John Giessendanner kept after his return from England, where he had been ordained as an Episcopal minister. This record was kept in English. That kept before his voyage to England was all kept in German, as already stated.

At the head of each of the five pages containing the entries from 6 to 24 is written "A List of Persons marryed per Jn⁰ Giessendanner. V. D. M."; at the head of each of the remaining seven pages containing the entries from 25 to 69 is written "Register of Marriages per John Giessendanner. V. D. M.":

A list of Persons marryed in the Church of Orangeburgh and on Sundry other places since my return from England according to the Liturgy of the Church of England and the Form prescribed in the Book of Common Prayer

Per
    J. Giessendanner
      Minister of Orangeburgh and
      Amelia Townships.

List of Persons
1750. On Monday, May 14th. 1750 was marryed and joined together by Banns.

(1.) Jacob Frank and Sarah Flood, widow, both living down this river.

Being present: John Chevillette, Esq., Michael Christopher Rowe, Peter and Joseph Grieffous, etc. etc.

(2.) On Monday, May 21st. In the Congree Garrison by Banns:

William Berry and Mary King, widow, both in Saxa-Gotha Township: Present Archibald Campbell, Esq.. Herman Gyger, Henry Gallman, etc. etc.

(3.) On Tuesday, June 5th In the Church of Orangeburgh by Ditto: Jacob Morff and Christina Hessy, both of this Township: Being present: Michael Christopher Rowe. Hans George Hessy.

(4.) On Monday, June 11th In ye Church of Orangeburgh by Ditto. David Griffith and Hannah Middleton, both of Berkly County. Being present: Michael Christopher Rowe, Henry Strowman, John Chevillette. Esq.

(5.) On Sunday, June 17th. In the Presence of the Congregation in the Church of Orangeburgh, by Ditto: Jacob Stauber and Miss ———* of this Township.

(6.) On Sunday, June 24th. In the Church of Orangeburgh in presence of the Congregation—By Banns: John Frederick Ot and Magdalene Wechter, late wife of George Wechter, deceased, both living in Amelia Township.

(7.) On Thursday June 28th. In the House of these married Person by Ditto: Casper Kuhn and Anna Barbara Ernst, late wife of George Adam Ernst, of this Township, deceased; Being present: Valentine Yutzy, John Fritchman, John Friday Junr etc. etc.

(8.) On Wednesday, July 11th. In the Church of Orangeburgh By Ditto: Robert Andrews of Saxa-Gotha Township, and Mary Carney of Amelia Township. Being present: John McCord, Sam'l Bright. Robert Seawright etc. etc.

(9.) On Thursday, July 19th. In ye Church of Orangeburgh By Ditto: Joseph Markis and Ann Pickings. both living down this River: Being present: Joseph Griffis, David Jackson.

(10.) On Tuesday August 7th In the Church 'o Ditto. By Ditto John Frederick Huber and Barbara Kreyter. both of this Township: Being present Martin Binsky, John Friday Senr· et Junr· Henry Heym.

(11.) On Saturday, September 22nd. In ye Church of Orangeburgh. By Banns. Miles Riley and Elizabeth Weekly. widow of Thomas Weekly, of Amelia Township. deceased. Being present: William Cammel, William Cooper. Caspar Ott.

(12.) On Wednesday, October 3rd. In the Church 'o

---

*Name obliterated.

Ditto. By Ditto. William Heart of the Congrees & Sirrah Young of Edistoe Fork. Being present Adin Frogat, William Young etc. etc.

(13.) On Thursday, December 6th. In the Church of Orangeburgh. By Ditto: William Mecket & Ann Roth of this Township: Being present Henry Haym, George Giessendanner, Junr. Charles Hottow etc. etc.

(14.) On Monday, Dec. 24th. in the Church of Orangeburgh, by Ditto: Henry Wetstine & Barbara, widow of Hans Ulrick Morff, deceased, both of this Township: Being present, Henry Haym, Caspar Kuhn, Peter Moorer, Junr. etc. etc.

1751

(15.) On Tuesday, February 5th. at the house of Mrs. Mary Russell in Amelia, by Licence, John McCord of Saxa-Gotha & Sophinisba Russell of Amelia Township, Being present Samuel Bright, Charles and John Russell.

(16.) On Tuesday April 2nd. In Orangeburgh Church By Banns Peter Murer, Junr. To Magdalene Horguer; Both of this Township, Being present Valentine Yutzy, Samuel Suther, etc.

(17.) On Tuesday April 30th. in Ditto. By Ditto. John Harresperger To Elizabeth Frichman, both of this Township. Being present Nicolas Shewler, Conrad Yutzy, Jacob Ott etc. etc.

(18.) On Tuesday, May 28th. In Ditto. By Ditto. Robert Lammon to Barbara, widow of Jacob Brunzon, deceased. Both living upon Edistoe River. Being present Michael Christopher Rowe, Joseph Griffous, Samuel Davis.

(19.) On Thursday September 5th. In Ditto. By Ditto. James Lewis to Esther, widow of John Jones, late of Amelia Township. Deceased. Being present Robert Gossling, Christian Minnick, Michael Christopher Rowe, etc. etc.

(20.) On Thursday, September 26th. In Orangeburgh Church, Freeman Snellgrove of Amelia Township to Ann Jenkins, widow, Being present: Miles Riley, John Fairy, Joseph Duke.
1752.

(21.) On Sunday, February 2nd. In Ditto. By Ditto. Peter Roth to Agnes, late widow of George Giessendanner, Deceased. In presence of the Congregation.

(22.) On Sunday, February 23rd. In Ditto. By Ditto. Christopher Stehely to Elizabeth, widow of Christian Schwarz, Deceased. In presence of the Congregation.

(23.) On Friday December 27th. 1751. In Ditto. By Ditto. Gotlieb Ebert to Anna Amacher. Being present: Henry Wartzer, Martin Binsky, Michael Larry, etc.

(24.) On Tuesday, March 31st. In Ditto. By Ditto. Emanuel Miller to Mary, widow of Andrew Inabnet, of this Township, Deceased. Being present: Henry Wartzer, Henry Rickenbaker, etc. etc.

(25.) On Tuesday June 9th. 1752. In Orangeburgh Church. By Banns: Henry Crummy to Magdalene Zorn; both of Orangeburgh Township. Being present: William Barrie, Henry Felder, Luke Patrick.

(26.) On Tuesday, July 2nd. 1752. In Orangeburgh Church. By Banns: William Young of Edisto Fork to Mary Linder, below Orangeburgh Township: Being present: Michael Christopher Rowe, Johanes Wolfe, Lewis Linder.

(27.) On Monday, July 13, In Amelia at the house of Mr. William Martin: By Banns. Thomas Cryer and Elizabeth Powell; both of Amelia Township; Being present John McCord, Charles Russell, William Thompson.

(28.) On Tuesday July 21st. In Orangeburgh Church.

ORANGEBURG COUNTY. 115

By Banns. Jacob Kooner. Sen![?] and Anna, late widow of Martin Tshudy. deceased, both of Orangeburgh Township. Being present: Henry Wartzer, —— Inderabnet, Ulrick Reber etc. etc.

(29.) On Tuesday September 26th. In Orangeburgh Church. By Banns. John Nicolas Shuler to Verena Hoggin.

(30.) John Heller to Esther Ott.

(31.) John Frederick Ulmer to Mary Barbara Shuler; all of Orangeburg Township. Being present: John Miller, Henry Rickenbaker, Lewis Golsen, etc.

(32.) On Tuesday October 3rd. In Orangeburgh Church. By Banns. John William Leysath to Ursula Giessendanner, of this Township: Being present: Henry Wartzer, Jacob Ott, Peter Roth, etc. etc.

(33.) On Tuesday December 19th. In Ditto. By Ditto. Lewis Golsen to Elizabeth Stehely.

(34.) Caspar Oth to Mary Stehely. All of Orangeburgh Township. Being present: Benedict Koller, Joseph Kryter, Henry Horger, Junr.

(35.) On Tuesday December 26th. In Ditto. By Ditto. Christopher Monheim to Catharine Fry; both lately arrived from Germany in Orangeburgh Township. Being present: John Shaumlöffel. John Friday, Jun. Jacob Roth.

1753.

(36.) On Sunday, March 25th. In Ditto. By Ditto. George Frederick Knobel to Elizabeth Fichter, both lately come into this Township from Germany: Being present: Henry Felder, Barnard Snell, Jacob Giessendanner.

(37.) On Tuesday, April 10th. At the house of Moses Thompson, Esqr. In Amelia. By Ditto. Thomas Ballew to Ann Cox. Being present: Moses and William Thompson, Thomas Courtonne.

(38.) On Thursday, April 12th. In Orangeburgh

Church Marryed by Banns. George Jacob Kurner to Ann Catharina Larrywecht, widow, both lately arrived in this Province from Germany. Being present: Michael Christopher Rowe, Ulrick Raber.

(39.) On Tuesday, April 24th. In Ditto. By Banns. Henry Mell to Mary Catharina, widow of Isaac Huttow, late of Orangeburgh Township, deceased.

(40.) Bernard Zeigler to Anne Mary Wedlin, widow, both lately come in from Germany. Both couples in presence of John Amacher, Senr., Frederick Huber, John William Leysaht, etc.

(41.) On Tuesday June 7th. In Ditto. James Elerson to Elizabeth Elerson; both near Orangeburgh Township. Being present: Henry Crummy, Michael Larry, The Banns been published at Orangeburgh May 27th; et 31st., June 3d.

(42.) On Tuesday September 4th. In Ditto. Joseph Huber to Elizabeth Horrmutt.

(43.) John Valentin Kranick to Anna Mary Heckler. All of Orangeburgh Township. Being present: Lewis Golson, Martin Binsky, Lewis Kern, etc.

(44.) On Tuesday September 27th. In Ditto. By Banns. Edward Brady to Rachael Whiteford of Amelia. Present: William Powell, John Burdell, etc.

(45.) On Thursday at the house of John Eberly. Marryed October 11th. By Banns.

John Grossman to Margaret Stephen; both of Berkeley County. Being present: Lewis Linder, John Eberly, etc.

(46.) On Sunday, November 4th. In Orangeburgh Church. By Banns. Christopher Miller to Angelia Zeigler, widow. In presence of the Congregation.

1754

(47.) On Tuesday, February 12th. Joyned into the Holy State of matrimony at the house of Simon

Theus, commonly called Monk's Corner, in St. John's Parish, by virtue of Licence derected to me, Simon Theus of the said Parish to Elizabeth Mackey of Amelia Township. Present: John Lloyd, Robert Rawlins, Clerk of the Crown. etc. etc.

(48.) On Tuesday, February 19th. In Orangeburgh Church. By Banns. Jacob Beck to Brigitta Smith, both of Amelia Township. Present: Christopher Rowe, John Friday, Senr. & Junr.

(49.) On Sunday, March 10th. In Amelia. At the house of Charles Russell. By Banns. Christian Reichart to Catharina Peterman; both of Amelia Township. In presence of the Congregation.

(50.) On Thursday, March 14th. In Orangeburgh Church. By Banns. Daniel Linder to Sarah Hill of Berkeley County. Present: James Tilly, Alexander McCord, John Burdell, etc., etc.

(51.) On Monday, April 9th. In Orangeburgh Church. Marryed By Banns. Henry Young of Edisto Fork to Ann Hill of Orangeburgh Township. Present: John Burdell, David Hall, etc., etc.

(52.) On Sunday, May 12th. In Amelia. By Banns. Benjamin Spurlock to Mary Elizabeth Smitzer, both of Amelia Township. Present: Moses Thompson, John Chevillette, John Lloyd, etc.

(53.) On Tuesday, July 16th. In Orangeburgh Church. By Banns. Conrad Yutzy to Magdalene Warner; both of Orangeburgh Township. Present: Henry Snell, Senr. & Junr., Christopher Rowe, etc., etc.

(54.) On Tuesday, August 6th. In Orangeburgh Church. By Banns. John Henry Shilling to Ann Margaret McLennen; both of Orangeburgh Township. Present: Henry Rickenbaker, Henry Mell, Sam Suther.

(55.) On Tuesday, August 20th. In Ditto. By Banns. James Taylor to Elizabeth, late widow of William

Barrie; both of Orangeburgh Township. Present: Henry Felder, Henry Crummy. etc., etc.

(56.) On Thursday, August 22d. In Amelia. By Licence. Charles Russell to Ann Dargan; both of Amelia Township. Present: John McCord, John Lloyd etc. etc.

(57.) On Sunday, October 27th. In Orangeburgh Church. By Banns. Marryed: Emanuel Mineor to Rachel Hatcher, both of Edistoe Fork. Present: The Congregation, Samuel Suther,* David Hall, &c.

(58.) On Tuesday, December 3d. In Ditto. By

---

*From the History of Rowan County, North Carolina, by Rev. Jethro Rumple, the following sketch is taken: "Rev. Samuel Suther was one of the early German Reformed ministers in Guilford, Rowan and Cabarrus. In the journal of Gov. Tryon for 1768, he relates that while he was at Major Phifer's in Mecklenburg (now Cabarrus) on Sunday, the 12st of July, he 'heard Mr. Luther, a Dutch minister, preach.' No doubt this is a misprint for Mr. Suther, since there is no evidence that such a minister as Luther was here, and there is evidence of the presence of a Rev. Mr. Suther. He was sent out from the old country to preach to the German Reformed people in the Carolinas, and was pastor of the Guilford charge during the Revolutionary war. Mr. Suther was a man of learning, and an uncompromising patriot during the struggle for American freedom. His residence was a mile from the battle ground of the Regulators in Alamance, May 16th, 1771. During the Revolution he was an outspoken patriot, and so obnoxious to the tories that he was often compelled to hide himself from their vengence. It is said that there was but one single tory in his entire charge. Capt. Weitzell, a member of Mr. Suther's church, commanded a company in the battle of Guilford Court House that was made up of members of the Reformed Church. The records of Lower Stone Church mention Samuel Suther as its pastor in 1782, and that he had removed thither from Guilford County. This was in the days of tory ravages, when Col. David Fanning and his troop of marauders struck terror into the region that extends from Guilford to Cumberland county. As he had many enemies around him, he found it expedient to remove to a more peaceful region. The date of his death and the place of his burial are unknown to the writer. There are a number of families by the name of Suther residing in and near Concord." This is probably the same Samuel Suther mentioned by Giessendanner, and he probably sojourned awhile in Orangeburgh before receiving his license to preach in this country.

Banns. Jacob Ott to Margaret Fichtner, both of Orangeburgh Township. Present: Henry Wartzer, Adam Snell, George Hessy, &c. &c.

(59.) On Thursday, December 19th. In Ditto. By Banns. John Gibson to Margaret Fludd, both below Orangeburgh Township. Present: David Hall.

(60.) On Sunday, December 22nd. In Ditto. By Banns. Jacob Dirr of Amelia and Eva Catharina Keyser of Orangeburgh Township. Present: John Frederick Huber, & Henry Felder, &c.

(61.) On Monday, December 23rd. In Ditto. By Banns. John Joyner, Junr. to Naomy Bunch, both of Amelia Township. Present: Henry Snell, Senr., Christopher Rowe, etc.

1755.

(62.) On Monday, February 17th. In Ditto. By a Licence directed to me. Josiah Evans to Margaret Larkins, of Prince Frederick Parish. Present: James Tilly, Senr. & Junr.

(63.) On Tuesday, February 18th. In Ditto. By Banns. Barnard Hertzog to Anne Mary, late widow of Warner Ulmer, of Orangeburgh Township. Present: Col: John Chevillette, Henry Wartzer, &c.

(64.) On Thursday, August 14th. at the house of Capt. John Lloyd in Amelia Township, Marryed—By Licence; William Thompson to Eugenia Russell, both of the Township aforesaid. Present: John McCord, Edward Barwicke, &c.

(65.) On Sunday, August 24th. In Orangeburgh Church. By Banns: John George Hayner to Eva Catharina Barrin; both of Orangeburgh Township. Present: Jacob Giessendanner, Henry Felder, &c.

(66.) On Monday, December 29th. In Ditto. By Ditto. John Ofill to Elizabeth Rice, both of the Saltketchers in Colleton County. Present: Isham Clayton, Samuel Pickings, &c.

1756.

(67.) On Tuesday, January 27th. In Orangeburgh Church. By Ditto. John Jacob Wymer to Anne Diedrick, both of Orangeburgh Township. Present: Samuel Suther, John Jennings. &c.

(68.) On Monday, February 2nd. In Ditto. By Ditto. John Anding to Margaret, late widow of Rudolph Brunner, both living below Orangeburgh Township in Berkly County. Present: Henry Wurtzer, Lewis Linder, John Aberly, &c.

(69.) On Sunday, February 15th. In Ditto. By Banns. James Clatworthy to Mary, Widow of ——— Rush. Present: Joseph Wood, &c.

The remainder of the marriage record kept by Rev. John Giessendanner is lost from the book, but several fragmentary records were entered by later custodians of the book, as follows:

"John Pou to Elizabeth Giessendanner Boath of Orangeburgh Township."*

"Henry Giessendanner and Elizabeth Rumph Maryed the 25 Day of february 1767

"Henry Gissendaner"

"Henry Gissendanner & Mary Larry Marryed the 21 January 1796."†

The following is also recorded among the later items: "Jacob Kooney Come to me to Live With me th 26 of Septr 1771 and Movd a Way again the 16 of November 1771." What that meant is not explained.

Following the record in English of marriages, is the record in English of the baptisms performed by Rev. John Giessendanner after his return from England. At the head of each of the thirteen pages containing the entries from 11 to 97 is written. "A list of Children

---

*No date given. †Second wife—she was a widow.

baptized per J. Giessendanner. V. D. M."; at the head of each of the forty-two pages containing the entries from 98 to 422 is written, "Register Book of Baptisms per Jnº Giessendanner. V. D. M."; at the head of each of the four pages containing the entries from 423 to 482 is written, "Register of Christenings by John Giessendanner. V. D. M."; and at the head of each of the remaining twenty-five pages containing the entries from 483 to 639 is written, "Register of Births & Christenings by John Giessendanner V. D. M." The following is the baptismal record:

A List of Children Baptized by me in the Church of Orangeburgh and in Sundry other places Since my return from England according to the Liturgy of the Church of England and the forms prescribed in the Book of Common Prayer

John Giessendanner
Minister of the Church in and of
Orangeburgh Township and
Amelia Township-

1749-50.

(10.)* On Sunday, March 18th. 1749-50. Received publick Baptism in the Church of Orangeburgh Joseph, son of James and Marget Tilly; born ———. Goss: Joseph Robinson, Brand Pendarvis, and ———

On Sunday, April 1st:

(11.) Christian, son of John and Margaret Inabnet; born March the 17th. a. c. Susceptr. Hans Jacob Stroman, Henry Wetzstine, and Mrs Mary Inabnet.

(12.) On Sunday, April 8th. in Amelia Township at the house of Mrs. Mary Russell: Charles, son of William and Mary Elizabeth Heatly; born November 15th. 1749. Susceptr: John McCord, Charles Russell, Miss Sophia Russell.

---

*From 1 to 10 lost.

Eôdem Die eodemg Locô:
(13.) William, son of William and Martha Evans; Seven months old. Susceptr. Freeman Snellgrove, and as no others could be got, the parents themselves.
Eôdem Die eodemg Loco:
(14.) Powel, son of Ditto. Susceptr. Thomas Powel and the parents.
Eôdem Die et Loco:
(15.) John, son of Thomas and Elizabeth Barker; born October 2nd. 1749. Susceptr. Samuel Bright and the mother.
Eôdem Die et Loco:
(16.) Josias, son of an unknown father and Mary Gibson; born June 20th. 1746. Susceptr. Hopert Gibson.
(17.) On Easter Monday, April 16th. 1750. Received public baptism in the Church of Orangeburgh, Ann Appollonia, daughter of Jacob and Ann Appollonia Wolf; born March 19th. a. c. Susceptr. Nicolas Shuler, Mrs. Barbara Jennings, Ann Elizabeth Giegelman.
Eôdem Die et Loco.
(18.) Margaret, daughter of Nicolas and Regula Larry; born March 27th. a. c. Susceptr. John Jennings, Mary Regina Philippina Yutzy, Catharina Kuhnen.
(19.) At the Congrees in the house of Mrs. Elizabeth Haig on Saturday May 19th. Edward, son of Edward and Obedience McGrae; born August 5th. 1746. Susceptr. Thomas McFashon, Herman Gyger, Isabel Potts.
Eôdem Loco.
(20.) Sunday May 20th. Naomy, daughter of Nicolas and Naomy Fritz; born March 19th. 1748. Susceptr. Solomon Holmes, Sirah Snelling, no more.
Eôdem Die et Loco.
(21.) Elizabeth, daughter of the parents aforesaid:

ORANGEBURG COUNTY.

born March 19th. 1744. Susceptr. Henry Snelling, and the mother of the baptized, no more.

Eôdem Die et Loco.

(22.) Grace, daughter of Hugh and Mary Murphy; born May 10th. 1749. Susceptr. Henry Snelling, Sirah Snelling, Ann Ginnoway.

(23.) At the Congrees in the house of Mrs. Elizabeth Haig on Sunday, May 20th. 1750, Gabriel, son of Andrew and Rebecca Clements; born December 25th. 1749. Susceptr. Marget Reece, no more.

Eôdem Die et Loco.

(24.) Sirah, daughter of Thomas and Ann Cheavy; born April 23rd. a. c. Susceptr. Solomon Holmes, Elizabeth Good and the mother.

In the Church of Orangeburgh.

(25.) On Whit Sunday June 3rd., Mary, daughter of Joseph and Mary Grieffous; born April 12th. a. c. Susceptr. Adin Frogat, Mrs. Maria Catharina Ottow, Mrs. Ann Grieffous.

Eôdem Die et Loco.

(26.) Ann, daughter of John and Barbara Potts; born May 8th. a. c. Susceptr. Isaac Ottow, Mrs. Ann Ottow, Elizabeth Tshudy.

(27.) On Sunday, June 10th. In Amelia Township at the house of Mrs. Mary Russell; Mary, daughter of James and Elizabeth Carter; born 4th. January 1749. Susceptr. Henry and Mary Carter, Elizabeth Tate.

Eôdem Die et Loco.

(28.) Mary, daughter of John and Esther Jones; born 20th. October 1748. Susceptr. Conrad and Mary Halman, Elizabeth Lap.

Eôdem Die et Loco.

(29.) Margaret, daughter of William and Rebecca Hickie; born 19th. November 1747. Susceptr. Robert Gossling, Esther Jones and Mary Whitford.

(30.) In Amelia Township at the house of Mrs. Mary Russell, on Sunday, June 10th. 1750; John, son of Henry and Mary Carter; born in December 1747. Susceptr. James Carter, James Barker and Elizabeth Carter.

Eôdem Die et Locô.

(31.) Margaret, daughter of John and Mary Sullivant; born 15th. June 1749. Susceptr. William Evans, Martha Evans, and Mary Sullivant.

Eôdem Die et Locô.

(32.) Winified and Martha, daughters of Thomas and Sarah Powel.

(33.) Winifred born in May 1747, Martha born in April 1750. Susceptr. for both: James Carter, Martha Evans and Sarah Powel.

In the Church of Orangeburgh.

(34.) On Sunday June 17th.

David, son of David and Ann Rumph; born April 1st. a. c. Susceptr. Jacob Rumph, William Beary, Barbara. wife of John Jennings.

Eôdem Die et Locô.

(35.) Elizabeth, daughter of Adam and Margaret Snell; born March 10th. a. c. Susceptr. John Fritchman, Lovisa, wife of Jacob Horger, and Magdaline Werner.

Ibidem.

(36.) On Sunday July 1st.

Johannes, son of Abraham and Mary Issenhut; born May 31st. a. c. Susceptr. Peter Hug, John Inabnet. Agnes, wife of George Giessendanner, Junr.

In the Church of Orangeburgh.

(37.) On Sunday, July 1st.

Ann, daughter of Seth and Susannah Hatcher; born April 24th. a. c. Susceptr. Michael and Regula Larry. Anna Angelia, wife of Ulrich Raber.

(38.) In Amelia at the house of Mrs. Mary Russell.

ORANGEBURG COUNTY. 125

On Sunday July 8th. Elizabeth, daughter of Robert and Elizabeth Gossling; born February 1st. 1745. Susceptr. William Evans. Elizabeth, wife of Thomas Barber, and Elizabeth, widow of Thomas Weekly.
Eôdem Die et Locô.
(39.) George, son of Robert and Elizabeth Gossling aforesaid; born May 13th. a. c. Susceptr. Moses Thompson, Thomas Powel, and Mary, wife of Robert Whitford.
(40.) On Sunday, August 19th. In the Church of Orangeburgh. Leonard, son of Leonard and Sirrah Warnedow; born January 15th. 1749/50. Susceptr. Isaac Hottow, William Cooper, and Sirrah his wife.
Eôdem Die et Locô.
(41.) Sirrah, daughter of John and Sirrah Clayton; born April 30th. a. c. Susceptr. William Pendarvis, Sirrah, wife of William Cooper, and Mary, wife of David Rumph.
Eôdem Die et Locô.
(42.) Johannes, son of Henry and Ann Rickenbacker, born ―――――. Susceptr. John Inabinet, John Harrisperger, and Catharina Diel.
In the Church of Orangeburgh.
(43.) On Sunday, September 16th. Anna, daughter of Jacob and Anna Rumph; born August 26th. a. c. Susceptr. George Giessendanner, Junr., Mary, wife of Hans Balsiger and Anna, wife of Joseph Robinson.
Eôdem Locô.
(44.) On Sunday September 30th.
Maria, daughter of Andrew and Mary Inabnet; born July 27th. a. c. Susceptr. Caspar Negely, Maria Stehely and Anna Amacher.
Eôdem Locô.
(45.) On Sunday, October 28th. Isaac, son of Jacob and Barbara Brunzon; born ―――――. Susceptr. Abraham Yssenhut, Samuel Davis, and ――― wife of Elias Snell.

Eôdem Die et Loco.

(46.) William, son of Joseph and Margaret Cooper; born September 13th. a. c. Susceptr. William Cooper and Sirrah, his wife, and John Wolf.

(47.) On Sunday November 11th. At the house of Mrs. Russell in Amelia Township, Thomas, son of Peter and Mary Oliver; born in October last. Susceptr. Robert and Mary Whitford, Joseph Ferstner.

(48.) Also: John, son of John and Regania Tittleby; born in October last. Susceptr. David Merkly, Joseph Ferstner, Mary Ann, wife of Conrad Halmann.

(49.) In the Church of Orangeburgh. On Sunday, November 18th. John, son of Luke and Mary Patrick of Edistoe Fork; born October 20th. a. c. Susceptr. William Barry, Jacob Rumph, and Ann, his wife.

Eôdem Die et Loco.

(50.) Elizabeth, daughter of Thomas and Catharina Puckridge; born September 21st. a. c. Susceptr. William Barry, Ann, wife of Henry Rickenbacker, and Ann, wife of John Deramus.

Eôdem Loco.

(51.) On Sunday. November 25th. George, son of Jacob and Barbara Bowmann; born September 15th. a. c. Susceptr. George Giessendanner, Junr., Jacob Rumph and Ann, his wife.

Eôdem Loco.

(52.) On Sunday, December 2nd. Hans George, son of John and Susannah Frydie; born November 29th. a. c. Susceptr. John Inabnet, George Giessendanner, Senr., and Anna Angelia, wife of Ulrich Reber.

Eôdem Loco.

(53.) On Sunday, December 16th. Catharina, daughter of Henry and Catharina Strowman: born November a. c. Susceptr. Jacob Giegelman. Ann Elizabeth, wife of John Giegelman, and Ann, wife of Henry Rickenbacker.

ORANGEBURG COUNTY.

Eôdem Die et Loco.
(54.) Ann Margaret, daughter of Peter and Ann Griffous; born October 14th. a. c. Susceptr. Joseph Griffous and*
1751.
(55.) In the Church of Orangeburgh. On Sunday, January 20th. Hans Heinrich, son of Joseph and Ann Koch; born November 28th. last. Susceptr. Henry Wetstine, Hans Negely and Regula, wife of Michael Larry.
Eôdem Die et Loco.
(56.) Isaac, son of Peter and Margaret Barbara Hottow; born December 4th. last. Susceptr. Isaac Hottow, Charles Hottow and Ann Margaret, wife of George Shuler.
(57.) On Sunday, January 27th. Abraham, son of Johnathan and Martha Brunson; born March 26th. 1749. Susceptr. Isaac Gleaton, Abraham Yssenhut, and Sirrah Hardman.
(58.) On Sunday, February 3rd. Eva Maria, daughter of Werner and Anna Maria Ulmer; born December 28th. last. Susceptr. Hans George Shuler, Senr., Anna Maria, wife of John Shaumlöffel, and Esther Ott.
(59.) On Sunday, February 17th. William, son of John and Eva Catharina Jubb; born December 19th. last. Susceptr. Abraham Hasfort, William Pendarvis, Anna Elizabeth, wife of John Giegelman.
(70.)† On Sunday, June 2nd. In Orangeburgh Church. Thomas, son of Joseph and Margaret Duke; born 4th. September last. Susceptr. David Rumph, Ulrich Roth, Sertina, wife of Brand Pendarvis.
(71.) On Monday, June 17th. John Ulrich, son of Peter and Ann Roth; born 12th. of this instant. Sus-

---

*Other names obliterated.
†From 60 to 69, inclusive, lost from the book.

ceptr. John Giessendanner, George Giessendanner, Junr., Elizabeth Roth, widow.

On Sunday, June 30th. In Ditto.

(72.) Rachel, daughter of John and Rachel Brunzon; born December 1746. Susceptr. Joseph Couture, Mary, his wife, Ann, wife of Joseph Griffith.

Eôdem Die et Locô.

(73.) Alexander, son of John and Rachel Brunzon; born in March 1749. Susceptr. Joseph Griffith and Ann, his wife, and John Elders.

Eôdem Die et Locô.

(74.) Sirrah, daughter of John and Rachel Brunzon; born in January last. Susceptr. William Pendarvis. Ann, wife of Joseph Griffith, Mary, wife of Joseph Couture.

(75.) On Sunday, July 14th. In Amelia Township. Catharina, daughter of John and Mary Morrison; born the 13th. May last. Susceptr. William Thompson. Rebeccah Thompson, Eugenia Russell.

(76.) On Sunday, September 8th. In Amelia Township. James William, son of William and Mary Elizabeth Heatly; born July 27th. last. Susceptr. John Russell, William Thompson, Eugenia Russell.

Eôdem Die et Locô.

(77.) John Henry, son of Joseph and Mary Festner; born in August last. Susceptr. Nicolas Durr, Henry Whetstone, Eleanor, wife of John Whetstone.

Eôdem Die.

(78.) William, son of Garret and Agnesia Fitz Patrick; born March 27th. last. Susceptr. Robert Rogers, John Fouquett, and Ann Mary, his wife.

(79.) On Sunday, September 15th. In Orangeburgh Church. Peter, son of Johannes and Elizabeth Wolf; born August 28th. last. Susceptr. John Giessendanner, Hans Imdorff, and Magdalena, his wife.

Eôdem Die et Locô.

(80.) Mary. daughter of Gavin and Margaret Pou; born August 3rd. last. Susceptr. Lucas Wolf, Elizabeth, wife of Philip Jennings, and Margaret, wife of Joseph Cooper.

(81.) On Sunday, October 27th. 1751. In Orangeburgh Church. John, son of David and Mary Jackson; born October 4th. curr. Susceptr. Peter and Joseph Griffith, Maria Catharina, wife of Isaac Hottow.

(82.) On Sunday, November 3rd. In Ditto. Hans Henry, son of William and Anna Meekel; born October 3rd last. Susceptr. Ulrich Roth, Henry Haym and Barbara, his wife.

Eôdem Die et Locô.

(83.) Hans Ulrick, son of Felix and Margaret Morff; born April 10th. last. Susceptr. John Giessendanner, John Heller, Margaret, wife of Peter Larry.

Eôdem Die et Locô.

(84.) Margaret, daughter of Barnard and Susanna Elizabeth Shnell; born May 15th. last. Susceptr. Jacob Roth, Barbara, wife of Henry Haym, and Margaret, wife of Adam Shnell.

(85.) On Sunday, December 1st. Samuel, son of John and Margaret Inabnet; born October 24th. last. Susceptr. Samuel Suther, John Friday, Junr., Mary, wife of John Balziger.

Eôdem Die et Locô.

(86.) Maria. daughter of Michael Christopher and Margaret Rowe; born October 25th. last. Susceptr. John and Barbara Giessendanner, Isaac Hottow. Susanna Barbara Giessendanner.

(87.) On Sunday December 15th. 1751. In Orangeburgh Church. Jacob, son of Thomas and Anna Maria Eberhardt; born November 26th. last. Susceptr. Jacob Giessendanner, Jacob Ott. Magdalena Werner.

(88.) On Sunday, December 29th. Elizabeth, daughter of John and Elizabeth Burdell; born October 29th

1750. Susceptr. Peter Faure and Sarah, his wife, Barbara, wife of John Jennings.
Eôdem Die et Locô.
(89.) Mary, daughter of David and Mary Rumph: born August 16th. 1751. Susceptr. Brand Pendarvis, Ann, wife of Joseph Robinson, Ann, wife of Jacob Rumph.
1752.
(90.) January 1st., John, son of Henry and Mary Elizabeth Felder; born December 12th. 1751. Susceptr. Jacob Rumph, Jacob Giessendanner, Anna Margaret, wife of Jacob Strowman.
On Sunday, January 12th. In Amelia.
(91.) Rosina, daughter of John and Regina Tittily: born January 6th. 1752. Susceptr. David and Rosina Markly, Ann Mary Festner.
Eôdem Die et Locô.
(92.) Charles, son of John and Sophianisba McCord: born November 7th. 1751. Susceptr. Charles Russell. John and Rachel Lloyd.
(93.) On Sunday, January 12th. In Amelia.
Rachel Elizabeth, daughter of John and Rachel Lloyd; born October 9th. 1751. Susceptr. Charles Russell, Eugenia Russell, Mary Elizabeth, wife of William Heatly.
On Sunday, February 2nd. In Orangeburgh Church.
(94.) Johann Nicolas, son of Hans George and Catharina Hessy; born* Susceptr. John Heller, Nicolas Shuler, Margaret, wife of Christopher Rowe.
(95.) On Sunday, February 23rd. Rebekar, daughter of Samuel and Willoughby Fox; born September 11th. 1751. Susceptr. John Burdell, Mary Fox, Elizabeth, wife of William Barrie.

---

*No date given.

On Sunday, March 8th. In Amelia.
(96.) John, son of Joseph and Miles Joyner; born the 15th of July 1750. Susceptr. John Russell, Joseph Jackson. and Mary Jackson.
On Sunday, March 15th. In Orangeburgh Church.
(97.) Sarah, daughter of Leonard and Sarah Warnedow; born* Susceptr.†
(98.) April 13th. Baptized. Catharina, daughter of Joseph and Anne Deramus; born 12th. of February last. Susceptr. William Bonnell, Barbara Pund. widow, and Catharina, wife of Thomas Prickridge.
(99.) On Sunday, April 26th. In Orangeburgh Church. Benjamin, son of Brand and Sertina Pendarvis; born February 9th last. Susceptr. Gavin Pou, Samuel Suther, Sarah, wife of William Cooper.
(100.) On Sunday May 10th. In Amelia. Elizabeth, daughter of Thomas and Elizabeth Barker; born March 17th. last. Susceptr. John Russell, Elizabeth, wife of Miles Riley, and Mary Cammel.
On Sunday May 17th. In Amelia Church.
(101.) Maria Catharina, daughter of Martin Stoudenmeyer and Anna, his wife; born February 8th. last. Susceptr. Frederick Huber, Mary Catharina, wife of Elias Snell, and Maria Catharina, wife of Isaac Hottow.
(102.) On Sunday, June 21st. In Ditto. Johannes, son of Adam and Margaret Snell; born March the 28th. last. Susceptr. John Harrisperger, Henry and Mary Elizabeth Felder.
June 21st. Baptized in Orangeburgh Church.
(103.) Johannes, Son of Richard & Mary Busk; Born May 2d last:
Suscept.r David Rumph, Brand Pendarvis, and Sertina, his wife...

---

*No date given. †None given.

(104.) On Sunday June 28th   In Ditto.
James, Son of John & Christina Fairy; Born Dec.r 29th 1751. Suscept.r Joseph Griffith, Seth Hatcher, Christina Fairy.

(105.) On Sunday July 12th In Amelia at the House of Mary Russell.
John, Son of Morris & Phibbe OHearn; Born March 17th. 1752. Suscept.r
Caspar Brown, John Elders Sen. Mary, wife of Conrad Holman.

Eôdem Die et Locô.

(106.) Priscilla, Daughter of Thomas & Frances Curtis; Born Septemb.r 23.d 1751.
Suscept.r William Thompson, Ann Cox, & Phible, wife of Morris OHearn.....

(107.) On Monday July 13th In Amelia at the House of William Martin.
Samuel, Son of Thomas & Faithful Joyner; born January 13th 1752. Suscept.r John Gardner, James Cape, Agnes Joyner.

Eôdem Die et Locô.

(108.) Elizabeth, Daughter of Thomas & Faithful Joyner; born Sept.r 17th 1749. Suscept.r James Cape, Agnes Joyner, Elizabeth Frances.

(109.) July 13th Baptized. In Amelia at the House of William Martin.
Mary, Daughter of Paul & Naomi Bunch; born July 71th. 1750. and

(110.) Elizabeth, their Daughter; born April 17th 1752. Suscept.r for both: Joseph Joyner, Winifred Joyner, Mary Bunch.

(111.) On Sunday July 26th In Orangeburgh Church.
Mary=Elizabeth, Daughter of Jacob & Ann=Apollonia Wolf; born May 29th 1752. Suscept.r John George Hessy, Ann Diedrick, Ann Wolf.

ORANGEBURG COUNTY. 133

Eôdem Die et Locô.
(112.) Elizabeth. Daughter of William & Bellinder Booth; born July 6th. 1752. Susceptr Henry Felder, Mary, wife of Joseph Griffice, Magdalene Werner.
(113.) On Sunday August 2d ... In Ditto.
Jacob, Son of Jacob & Anna Rumph; born July 9th. 1752. Susceptr John Friday Jun. Abraham Yssenhut, Barbara, wife of Jacob Bowman.
(114.) On Sunday August 9th In Amelia.
John, Son of Patrick & Ann Railly; born July 12th. 1752. Susceptr Conrad Holman, Garret Fitz Patrick, & Mary, wife of Robert Whitford.
(115.) August 16th. Baptized In Orangeburgh Church.
Michael, Son of Michael & Regula Larry; Born July 8th. 1752. Susceptr. John Giessendanner, Samuel Suther, Margaret, wife of Michael Christopher Row.
(116.) On Sunday August 30th...... In Ditto.
John, Son of John & Sirrah Clayton; born October 25th 1751. Susceptr Luke Partrick, Brand Pendarvis, & Sirrah, wife of Peter Faure.
(117.) On Sunday Septembr 24th.. In Amelia.
Mary, Daughter of Henry & Mary Carter; Born August 10th. 1750. Sureties: Joseph Clarry, Elizabeth Lapp, & Mary=Ann, wife of Conrad Holman.
Eôdem Die et Locô.
(118.) Joseph, Son of the Parents aforesaid: Born April 13th 1752. Sureties: Joseph Clarry, Charles Russell, Elizabeth Jones.
(119.) On Sunday Octobr 22d In Orangeburgh Church.
Verena=Maria, Daughter of Wenner & Ann=Mary Ulmer; born August 29th. 1752. Susceptr John Friday Jun. Verena, wife of Nicholas Shuler. & Anna=Maria, wife of Nicholas Durr.
(120.) On Sunday Octobr 29th.. In Ditto.
Antony, Son of Joseph & Ann Robinson; born Au-

gust 23ᵈ 1752. Susceptʳ John Jennings, Henry Crummy, & Sarah. wife of William Cooper.

(121.) On Sunday Octobʳ 29ᵗʰ. Baptized in Orang. Church.

Elizabeth, Daughter of Joseph & Margaret Cooper: born in August last. Susceptʳ Jacob Wolf, Ann Wolf, & Margaret, wife of Gavin Pou.

(122.) On Sunday Novembʳ 12ᵗʰ In Amelia.

Mary, Daughter of Michael & Mary..Magdalene Looser; born Septʳ 3ᵈ 1752. Susceptʳ George..Ulrick Carich, Mary„Ann, wife of Conrad Halman, & Mary= Regina Tittely.

Eôdem Die et Locô.

(123.) Frederica, Daughter of Martin & Magdalena Poutchmouth; born Octobʳ 23ᵈ 1752. Susceptʳ Valentine Shoemaker, & Lorothea Shoemaker, & Mary=Ann, wife of Conrad Halman.

(124.) On Tuesday Novʳ 14ᵗʰ Administered private Baptism at the House of Peter Larry in Presence of the said Peter Larry, Peter Negely. Hans Negely etc. to

Hans Jacob, Son of Jacob & Catharina Koonen: Born Octobʳ 1ˢᵗ 1752.

(125.) On Sunday Novʳ 19ᵗʰ. In Orangeburgh Church.

William, Son of Joseph & Margaret Grieffous; born Octobʳ 2ᵈ 1752. Susceptʳ Christian Roth, Peter Grieffous, wife of Elias, Mary=Catharina.

Eôdem Die et Locô:

(126.) Susannah, Daughter of John & Barbara Giessendanner; Born Thursday night Octobʳ 26ᵗʰ 1752. Susceptʳ John=William Leysaht & Ursula, his wife. Margaret, wife of Michael Christopher Row.

(127.) Baptized in Orangeburgh Church. On Thursday, November 23ʳᵈ·· Luke, son of Luke and Mary

Partrick, born ——— 1752. Susceptr. Peter Faure.*
Rebecca, wife of Christian Minnick.
On Sunday, December 3rd.
(128.) Johann Henry, son of Samuel and Elizabeth Suther; born October 2nd. 1752. Susceptr. John Harrisperger, Henry Rickenbacker, and Anna, his wife.
On Sunday, December 10th. In Amelia.
(129.) Absolom, son of John and Agnes Griffen; born September 21st. 1748. Sureties: Nathan Joyner and Winifred, his wife, and Mary Ann, wife of Conrad Halman.
Eôdem Die et Locô.
(130.) Choice, daughter of John and Agnes Griffen, born January 3rd. 1750. Susceptr. John William Leysaht, Mary Ann, wife of Conrad Holman, and Winifred, wife of Nathan Joyner.
Eôdem Die et Locô.
(131.) Charles. son of Nathan and Winifred Joyner; born September 27th. 1751. Susceptr. John Griffen, Gideon Bunch, and Elizabeth Makkie.
(132.) On Sunday, December 17th. In Orangeburgh Church. Anne, daughter of Jacob and Ann Catharina Wannamaker; born May 31st. 1752. Susceptr. Hans George Shuler, Senr., and Catharina, his wife, and Mary Margaret Sknyder, widow.
(133.) Baptized in Orangeburgh Church, on Sunday, December 24th. William, son of James and Margaret Tilly; born October 9th. 1752. Susceptr. William Barrie. William Cooper, and Margaret, wife of Christopher Rowe.
On Christmas Day. December 25th.
(134.) Henry. son of Peter and Margaret Barbara Hottow. born ————— 175—. Susceptr. Henry Sally. Junr., Isaac Hottow. Susannah Youn.

---

*Next name obliterated.

1753.

(135.) On Sunday, February 4th. Johann. Caspar, son of John Caspar and Anna Barbara Mintz; born January 26th. 1753. Susceptr. John Friday, Senr:, John Friday, Junr., and Susannah, his wife.
Eôdem Die et Locô.
(136.) Margaret. Daughter of Gottlieb & Anne Ebert; born January 21st. 1753. Susceptr. John Amacher Junr., Margaret, wife of Peter Larry, & Margaret, wife of Ulrick Stereky.
On Sunday February 11th In Amelia.
(137.) Catharina. Margaret. Daughter of Thomas & Margaret Crommelich; born Febr 9th 1753. Susceptr Mathew & Margaret Sreferet, & Catharine Ax.
On Sunday, Febr 18th In Orangeburgh Church.
(138.) Isaac and Jacob, Twins, Sons of Abraham & Mary Yssenhut; born Decembr 26th 1752. Susceptr for Isaac: Henry & Mary„Elizabeth Felder, and Hans Balziger.
(139.) Susceptr for Jacob: Jacob Rumph, Joseph Duke, & Mary, wife of Hans Balziger.
On Sunday February 18th 1753. In Orang: Church.
(140.) Catharina, Daughter of John & Catharina Miller; born January 3d 1753. Susceptr John Giessendanner, Verena, wife of Henry Wurtzer and Elizabeth, wife of John Harrisperger.
Eôdem Die et Locô.
(141.) Theodor, Son of Nicolas & Mary Dirr; born January 20th 1753. Susceptr Theodoris Fichtner, Adam Snell, & Barbara, wife of Henry Snell Senr.
Eôdem Die et Locô.
(142.) John, Son of Emanuel & Mary Miller; born January 15th 1753, Susceptr John Inabnet. John Harrisperger, & Elizabeth, wife of Samuel Suther.
On Sunday February 25th In Ditto.
(143.) Christian, Son of Barnard & Susannah..

ORANGEBURG COUNTY. 137

Elizabeth Snell; born Dec.r 20th 1752. Susceptr Michael Christopher Row, John Anding, & Elizabeth, wife of Samuel Suther.
Eôdem Die et Locô.
(144.) Joseph, son of Robert and Frances Ellison; born January 8th 1753. Susceptr Jacob Giessendanner, Martin Sally, & Elizabeth Ellison.
On Sunday March 25th In Ditto.
(145.) William, son of John & Sarah Clayton; born Decembr 18th 1752. Susceptr John Kays, John Logan, & Elizabeth, wife of Samuel Suther.
Baptized In Orangeburgh Ohurch.
(146.) On Sunday March 25th
Gideon, son of Philip & Elizabeth Jennings; born Febr 17th. 1753. Susceptr Jacob Rumph, John Clayton, & Barbara, wife of John Jennings.
On Sunday, April 1st. In Ditto.
(147.) Johannes, Son of Joseph & Anna Koch; born March 17th. 1753. Susceptr John Harrisperger, John Amacher Jun. & Margaret, wife of Peter Larry Sen.
On Sunday April 8th In Amelia.
(148.) Mary, Daughter of William & Mary.. Elizabeth Heatly; born March 3d 1753. Susceptr James Courtonne, Rachel, wife of John Lloyd, and Rebecca Thompson.
Eôdem Die et Locô.
(149.) Barbara, Daughter of William & Barbara Tash; born March 5th. 1753. Susceptr Frederick Burckhard Margaret, wife of Henry Kaun, & Barbara Burkhard.
(150.) On Tuesday April 10th. At the House of Moses Thompson, Esqr In Amelia.
George, Son of William Vance Deceased, & Sarah, his wife; born November 8th. 1751. Susceptr Moses Thompson Esqr , William Thompson. Rebecca Thompson.
(151.) Baptized .... In Orangeburgh Church.

On Easter „Sunday April 22ᵈ ....

Bernhard=David, Son of John..Jacob & Christiana..
Barbara Hungerbuller; born Decr 24tʰ 1752. Suscepr
Bernhard Zeigler, David Kuntzenauer, & Ana..Margaret Barrin ....

Eôdem Die et Locô:.

(152.) Anne, Daughter of Henry Jun. and Magdalene
Sally; born Decr 16tʰ. 1752. Susceptr Martin Sally.
Anne, wife of Jacob Kuhnen Sen. & Christina, wife of
Nicholas Yonn.

Eôdem Die et Locô.

(153.) Zibilla..Catharina, Daughter of Conrad &
Mary=Elizabeth Hungerbuller; born Febr 1ˢᵗ 1753.
Susceptr Henry Shilling, Zibilla..Catharina Petrin. &
Catharina Barrin..........

(154.) On Sunday April 29tʰ... In Ditto.

Joseph, Son of Joseph & Martha Wood; born January 20tʰ. 1753. Susceptr John Giessendanner, John
William Leysaht, & Susannah„Barbara Giessendanner.

Eôdem Die et Locô.

(155.) Grace, Daughter of William & Sarah Heart:
born March 19tʰ 1753. Susceptr Martin Sally, Elizabeth, wife of William Barrie, & Rebeccah, wife of
Christian Minnick.

Eôdem Die et Locô:

(156.) Sarah, Daughter of Joseph & Margaret Duke:
born March 15tʰ 1753. Susceptr Peter Faure, and
Sarah, his wife, & Elizabeth, wife of Samuel Suther.

(157.) Baptized....   In Amelia.

On Sunday May 20tʰ

Mary„ Daughter of John & Mary Sullivan: born
January 27tʰ. 1752. Susceptr. Robert Gossling, Mary.
wife of Robert Whitford, and Elizabeth, wife of
Thomas Barker.

Eôdem Die et Locô:

(158.) Charles Fouquett, Son of Archibald Campbell & Eugenia, his wife, dec^d born Novr. 4th. 1751. Suscept^r John Fouquett Esqr James Bently & Susannah, his wife.

(159.) On Sunday May 27th In Orangeburgh Church. Lydia, Daughter of David & Mary Jackson; born March 4th 1753. Suscept^r William Cooper & Sarah, his wife, & Margaret, wife of Joseph Griffice

(160.) On Whitsunday June 10th. In Orang: Church. Ann=Catharina, Daughter of Barnard & Apollonia Lebennder, born May 27th. 1753. Suscept^r John & Ann..Catharina Simmons, & Catharina Funtzius, widow.

Eôdem Die et Locô:

(161.) Elizabeth..Barbara, Daughter of Elias & Mary..Catharina Snell; born May 10th 1753. Suscept^r Frederick Huber, & Anna..Barbara, his wife, & Elizabeth, wife of John Harrisperger.

(162.) Baptized..... In Orangeburgh Church. On Whit Sunday June 10th... John Henry; Son of Charles & Ann Hottow; born May 26th 1753.. Suscept^r Henry Mill; Jacob Tshudy, Margaret McLannon.

(163.) On Sunday June 17th... In Amelia. Mary..Ann, Daughter of Conrad & Mary..Ann Halman; born May 14th. 1753. Suscept^r Caspar Brown. Maria, wife of Joseph Festner, and Regina, wife of John Willis......

(164.) On Sunday June 14th. In Orangeburgh Church. John, Son of John & Elizabeth Burdell; born March 17th. 1753. Suscept^r Christopher Row, Jno William Leysaht, & Margaret, wife of Christ^r Row.

(165.) On Sunday July 8th. In Amelia. Mary. Daughter of John & Agnes Griffen; born

April 21st. 1753. Susceptr Caspar Brown, Brigitta Smith, & Mary, wife of Martin Pontchmouth.

(166.) On Sunday July 29th In Orangeburgh Church. William, Son of William & Mary Young; Born May 19th. 1753. Susceptr John Giessendanner, Lewis Linder, & Mary..Magdalene, his wife.

(167.) On Sunday August 12th. In Amelia. Mary..Margaret, Daughter of Matthew & Margaret Sigfritt; born June 10th 1753. Susceptr Thomas Gumble, Margaret & Mary..Ann Sigfritt.

(168.) Baptized.... In Orangebr. Church. On Sunday August 19th. ... Elizabeth, Daughter of Henry & Ann Rickenbacher: born July 3d 1753. Susceptr Henry Shilling, Elizabeth, wife of John Harrisperger, & Catharina, wife of Hans George Hessy.

(169.) On Sunday Septr 16th. In Saxagotha Township. Margaret, Daughter of Peter & Elizabeth Mercier, born July 25th. 1753. Susceptr William & Esther Seawright, Elizabeth Mercier...

Eôdem Die et Locô:
(170.) William, Son of Alexr & Margaret McGrue: born April 24th 1752. Susceptr Alexander & Mary Fraser, Mary McGrue.

(171.) On Sunday Septr 23d In Orangeburgh Chrch. Johannes, Son of John William & Ursula Leysaht: born Septr 2d 1753. Susceptr John & Barbara Giessendanner, Michl Christopher Rowe.

(172.) On Sunday Septr 30th... In Ditto. Johannes, Son of John Jun. and Susannah Fridig: born Septr 9th 1753. Susceptr Ulrick Raber, John Balziger Sen: and Margaret, wife of Christopher Row.

Eôdem Die et Locô.
(173.) Elizabeth, Daughter of John & Eva..Cathari-

na Jubb; born February 13th 1753. Susceptr * Mary, wife of Joseph Couton, & Catharina, wife of George Hessy.....
Baptized...... at the House of John Eberly.
(174.) On Thursday Octobr 11th.. Susannah, Daughter of John & Ann Eberly; born in August 1753. Susceptr Eberhardt & Ann Kirchner, & Mary..Magdalene, wife of Lewis Linder.
On Sunday Octobr 21st In Orangeburgh Church.
(175.) Frederick, Son of Henry & Mary..Elizabeth Felder; born Septembr 1st 1753. Susceptr Frederick Huber, Nicholas Shuler, & Barbara, wife of John Jennings.
Eôdem Die et Locô.
(176.) John=Frederick, Son of Nicholas & Verena Shuler; born Septembr 8th 1753. Susceptr Frederick Ulmer, Francis Koonen, & Ann..Mary, wife of Warner Ulmer.
Eôdem Die et Locô.
(177.) Elizabeth, Daughter of Lewis & Mary=Barbara Roth; born Octobr 12th 1753. Susceptr Jacob Giessendanner, Elizabeth, wife of Samuel Suther, & Ann Apollonia, wife of Jacob Wolfe.
On Sunday Octobr 28th...... In Ditto.
(178.) Robert, Son of Gavin & Margaret Pou; born Septembr 11th 1753. Susceptr Christopher Rowe, John Logan, Barbara, wife of John Jennings.
On Sunday Novembr 4th..... In Ditto.
(179.) Mary..Elizabeth, Daughter of Lewis & Catharina..Elizabeth Kern; born Octr 6th 1753. Susceptr Frederick Huber, Margaret, widow of Jacob Gyger, & Anna..Elizabeth. wife of John Giegelman.
Baptized .... In Orangeburgh Church.

*First name obliterated.

(180.) On Sunday Novembr 25th Elizabeth, Daughter of John & Barbara Platt; born October 28th 1753——— Susceptr Ulrick Roth, Ann. wife of William Meckel, & Ann, wife of Peter Griffith. On Sunday December 9th In Amelia.

(181.) Lydia, Daughter of Thomas & Elizabeth Cryer; born May 2d 1753. Susceptr Garret Fitz=Patrick. Ann, wife of Thomas Raily, & Priscilla, wife of William Martin.

Eôdem Die et Locô.

(182.) Margaret..Catharina, Daughter of Valentine & Margaret Shoemaker; born Novembr 10th 1753. Susceptr Jacob Whideman, Margaret Myer and Ann Myer.

Eôdem Die et Locô.

(183.) Ann..Margaret, Daughter of Michael & Ann.. Mary Smith; born Septembr 7th 1753. Susceptr John Myer, Barbara, wife of Henry Whetstone. & Ann..Margaret Darweta.

(184.) On Tuesday Decembr 11th Administered private Baptism at the House of Mary Stehely to Margaret, Daughter of Caspar & Mary Oth; born Septr 29th 1753. Present: Melchior Oth, Joseph Kryter. John Negely etc. etc.

(185.) On Friday Decembr 14th Administered private Baptism at the House of Henry Stareky to Ann. Daughter of sd Henry & Elizabeth Stareky; born Novembr 28th 1753. Present: Haym, Peter Negely.

(186.) On Wednesday Decembr 26th. 1753. In Oraneb. Church. Baptized

Zibilla, Daughter of Barnard & Anne..Mary Ziegler: born Decr 10th 1753. Susceptr Joseph & Elizabeth Huber, & Zibilla Funtzius....

Eôdem Die et Locô:

(187.) Mary..Margaret, Daughter of Hans..George & Rosina Russel: born Octobr 25th 1753. Susceptr Peter

ORANGEBURG COUNTY. 143

& Margaret..Barbara Hottow, & Mary, wife of Abraham Yssenhut.
(188.) On Sunday Decembr 30th.... In Ditto. Susannah, Daughter of James & Elizabeth Carter; born August 29th 1753. Susceptr David Hall, Margaret, wife of Christopher Rowe, & Barbara, wife of John Jennings.
1754
(189.) January 1st............ In Ditto. John, son of John..Peter & Magdalene Tondel; born Novembr 30th 1753. Susceptr John..Veronica Anding, & Frederick Huber.
(190.) On Sunday January 13th..., In Ditto. Hans Ulrick, Son of Christian & Elizabeth Roth; born January 5th 1754. Susceptr Hans Roth, Ulrick Roth, & Ann, wife of Charles Hottow........
Eôdem Die et Locô:
(191.) Margaret, Daughter of John & Margaret Inabnet; born January 2d 1754. Susceptr Caspar Negely, Magdalene, wife of Hans Imdorff, and Magdalene Hugg, widow...
(192.) Baptized..... In Orangeburgh Church.
On Sunday February 3d...
Jacob, Son of Jacob & Mary=Susannah Herlan; born January 29th 1754. Susceptr Joseph & Susannah Kryter & John Mintz.
Eôdem Die et Locô:
(193.) Margaret..Barbara, Daughter of George..Frederick & Elizabeth Knobel; born December 18th 1753.
..... Susceptr Nicolas Dirr. Barbara Egly, & Margaret Fichtner.....
(194.) On Sunday February 10th ... In Amelia.
Mary, Daughter of John & Sophinisba McCord; born Decembr 11th 1753: Susceptr William & Mary..Elizabeth Heatly. & Rachel, wife of John Lloyd.
Eôdem Die et Locô:

(195.) Mary..Elizabeth, Daughter of John & Regina Tittily; born January 3ᵈ 1754. Susceptʳ Jacob Peck. Mary..Ann, wife of Conrad Halman, & Brigitta Smith.
(196.) On Sunday February 17th. In Orangeburgh Church.
Abraham, Son of Abraham & Susannah La Puis: born February 2ᵈ 1754. Susceptʳ Henry Haym, Joseph Huber & Elizabeth, his wife.
Eôdem Die et Locô:
(197.) John..Christopher, Son of Caspar Andrery & Sophia..Elizabeth Hannicke; born February 16th 1754. Susceptʳ John Giessendanner, Christopher Row, & Verena, wife of Henry Wurtzer.
Eôdem Die et Locô.
(198.) Catharina=Barbara, Daughter of Stephen & Mary..Ann Whitman; born Febʳ 3ᵈ 1754. Susceptʳ John Friday Jun. Catharina, wife of Henry Stroman. & Barbara, wife of Frederick Huber.
(199.) Baptized.... In Orangeburgh Church.
On Sunday February 17th
Mary=Catharina, Daughter of Wenner & Ann..Mary Ulmer; born January 9th 1754. Susceptʳ George Hessy, Mary, wife of Nicolas Dirr, & Catharina Barrin.
(200.) On Friday February 22ᵈ Administered private Baptism at the House of Hans Imboden to Ulrick, Son of the said Hans & Catharina Imboden; born January 25th 1754. Present Peter Negely, Joseph Koch, &c. &c.
(201.) On Sunday March 10th In Amelia.
Garret, Son of Garret & Agnesia Fitz-Patrick; born Novembʳ 9th 1753. Susceptʳ John..Frederick Ox. William Ballentine, & Mary..Ann, wife of Conrad Halman.
Eôdem Die et Locô:
(202.) Rosina, Daughter of John..Conrad & Juliana Huber; born ———— 1754...

ORANGEBURG COUNTY.   145

Suscept<u>r</u> Joseph Festner, Rosina Marky, & Margaret Konig.
(203.) Eôdem Die et Locô:*
(204.) On Sunday March 17th   In Orangeburgh Church.
Ann, Daughter of John & Esther Heller; born January 1st 1754. Suscept<u>r</u> Peter Roth, Magdalene, wife of Peter Murer Jun.. & Catharina, wife of Hans..George Hessy....
(205.) Baptized....   In Orangeburgh Church.
On Sunday March 24th
Peter..Herman, Son of Henry & Magdalene Crummy; born Feb<u>r</u> 2d 1754. Suscept<u>r</u> Hans Imdorf, Henry & Mary..Elizabeth Felder...
(206.) On Wednesday April 3d At the House of — — — — — Mr. Daniel Shyder.
John, Son of the s<u>d</u> Daniel & Elizabeth Shyder; born March 20th 1754. Suscept<u>r</u> John Giessendanner, John Baker, & Susannah=Barbara, wife of George Giessendanner.
(207.) On Sunday April 7th.. In Amelia.
Mary, Daughter of Samuel Bly & Margaret Beck; born March 1st 1754. Suscept= Peter Beck, Mary,, Ann, wife of Conrad Halman, & Mary, wife of Robert Whitford...
Eôdem Die et Locô:
(208.) Anna, Daughter of Henry & Margaret Koone; born March 8th 1754. Suscept= Jacob Wideman, Anna, widow of Hans Whetstone, & Barbara, wife of Henry Whetstone.
(209.) On Thursday April 11th In Orageburgh Church. Hans=Emanuel, Son of John,,Martin and Ann,,Margaret Hossleiter; born March 18th 1754. Sus-

---

*This whole entry has been erased from the book, or else was never put in.

cept= Emanuel Miller, John & Elizabeth Harrisperger.
(210.) On Easter,,Sunday April 14th Baptized.
In Orangeburgh Church.
George,,Adam, Son of John,,Frederick & Mary,,Barbara Ulmer; born March 20th 1754. Susceptr Nicolas Shuler, George Hessy, & Julianna, wife of Henry Snell Jun.
Eôdem Die et Locô:
(211.) Mary,,Elizabeth, Daughter of John & Elizabeth Waber; born March 24th 1754. Suscep= Nicolas Waber Jun, Anna,,Maria, wife of Nicolas Waber, Sen,, & Eve,,Elizabeth Hertzog /
Eôdem Die et Locô:
(212.) Mary,,Elizabeth, Daughter of Jacob & Anna Bress; born March 1st 1754.. Suscept Hans=George Rintz, Ann,,Mary, wife of Bernhard Ziegler, & Elizabeth Myer....
Eôdem Die et Locô:
(213.) Anna,,Catharina, Daughter of George & Catharina Ulrick; born January 26th 1754. Suscep= Ulrick & Angelia Raber, & Anna,,Catharina, wife of George,, Jacob Kurner.
(214.) On Tuesday April 23d .. In Charles Town.
At the House of Jnọ Frederick Shroder.
Christina,,Dorothea, Daughter of the sd Jnọ Frederick & Dorothea Shroder; born April 13th 1754. Suscep= John Kelly, Christina, wife of Christopher Nuffer, & Margaret, wife of John Kelly.
(215.) Baptized: At the House of Thomas Pendarvis near the Four Holes.
On Friday April 26th
David,,Frederick, Son of John & Ann,,Margaret Windlee; born February 18th 1754. Susceptr David Rumph, Hannah, wife of Thomas Pendarvis, & ———
Eôdem Die et Locô:
(216.) Sarah, Daughter of David & Mary Rumph;

born May 7th 1753. Susceptr Abraham Pendarvis & Ann,,Margaret, wife of John Windlee.

(217.) On Sunday May 5th In Orangeburgh Church. Regina, Daughter of Michael & Regula Larry; born March 18th 1754. Susceptr Ulrick Roth, Susannah, wife of John Friday Jun= & Ann, wife of Joseph Deramus.

(218.) On Sunday May 12th - - In Amelia. Mary, Daughter of John & Mary Morrisson; born Novembr 3d 1754. Suscept William Ballentine, Ann, wife of Duncan McIntire, & Barbara Burkhardt.

Eôdem Die et Locô:

(219.) Eugenia, Daughter of William & Eleanor Ballentine; born May 1st 1754. Suscep= Moses Thompson; Eugenia Russell, & Mary, wife of John Morrisson.

(220.) Baptized........ At Amelia.

On Sunday May 12th John=Conrad, Son of Michael & Magdalene Looser: born March 1st 1754. Suscep= Conrad Halman, John Tittely, & Brigitta, wife of Jacob Peck.

Eôdem Die et Locô:

(221.) Hans=Michael, Son of Christopher & Ann,, Mary Kimmler; born April 12th 1754. Suscept Michael Kirril & Mary,,Margaret, his wife, & Thomas Grimlock.

Eôdem Die et Locô:

(222.) Christopher, Son of Michael & Magdalene Kirril; born May 12th 1754. Suscept Christopher & Ann,,Mary Keller, & Thomas Grimlock.

(223.) On Sunday May 26th In Orangeburgh Church. Mary, Daughter of Thomas & Mary Eberhardt; born March 22d 1754. Suscept= John Amacher Jun,, Mary Cammel & Margaret, wife of Michael Christopher Rowe.

(224.) On Sunday June 9th... In Amelia,, Benjamin, Son of Henry & Mary Carter; born April

13th 1754. Susceptr Alexander Tate, Robert Carter, & Mary, widow of Robert Whitford.

Eôdem Die et Locô:

(225.) Robert, Son of Thomas Hails & Eleanor, his wife deceas'd; born Octobr 28th 1753: Susceptr Alexander Tate, William & Elizabeth McNicols.

(226.) Baptized..... In Amelia.

On Sunday June 9th

Margaret, Daughter of Alexander & Isabell Tate: born Septembr 26th 1753. Suscep= Henry Carter, Catharina McNicols, & Elizabeth Vance=

(227.) On Sunday July 7th In Orangeburgh Church.

Jacob, Son of Hans,,George & Catharina Hessy; born June 15th 1754. Susceptr Jacob Rumph, John Heller & Mary,,Barbara, wife of Frederick Ulmer.

(228.) On Sunday July 14th. In Amelia at the House of Capt. William Heatly administered public Baptism to Harry, a negro,,Child, belonging to Timothy Darigan.

(229.) Thomas, belonging to

(230.) Robert, belonging to

Suscep: for the Three: Timothy Darigan, Thomas, a Baptized Negro, belonging to the sd Timothy Darigan, Nancy, a baptized negro,,woman, belong. to Nelly, a Ditto belong. to

(231.) On Sunday July 28th In Orangeburgh Church.

John, Son of Henry & Catharina Strowmann; born July 7th 1754: Susceptr John Giessendanner. John Ott, & Barbara Egly.

(232.) On Sunday August 25th... In Ditto.

Samuel, Son of Leonhard & Sarah Warnedow: born Febr 15th 1754. Suscep= Jacob Koonen, Isaac Hottow, & Ann, wife of Peter Griffice.

(233.) Baptized ... In Orangeburgh Church.

On Sunday Septembr 1st

Ann=Margaret, Daughter of Elias & Mary=Catharina

ORANGEBURG COUNTY. 149

Snell; born August 13th 1754. Susceptr John Fritchman, Ann,,Margaret, wife of George Shuler Sen, & Mary,,Margaret Shnyder, in the Room of Barbara. wife of Henry Snell Sen=

(234.) On Sunday Septembr 22d... In Ditto. Johann,,Adam, Son of Adam & Margaret Snell; born August 24th. 1754. Suscept Jacob Whideman, Henry Snell Jun,, & Juliana, his wife.....

Eôdem Die et Locô:

(235.) Jacob, Son of Johannes & Elizabeth Wolf; born June 18th 1754. Suscept Jacob Koonen, Sen,, Francis Koonen, & Magdalene, wife of Hans Imdorff.

(236.) On Sunday Septembr 29th... In Ditto. John, Son of Joseph & Margaret Griffice; born July 17th 1754. Susceptr Rudy Harrisperger, Joseph & Mary Coutier.

Eôdem Die et Locô:

(237.) John, Son of Mark Chatterton, late of the Wateree deceasd & Ann, his wife; born June 28th 1754. Suscept Jacob Toomer, Joseph Griffice, & Ann, wife of William Meckel.

Eôdem Die et Locô:

(238.) Frances, Daughter of Seth & Susannah Hatcher; born Decembr 25th 1751. Susceptr Peter Griffice, Catharina, wife of John Jubb & Hannah Wolf.

Eôdem Die et Locô:

(239.) Mary, Daughter of Seth & Susannah Hatcher; born April 4th 1754. Suscept Ulrick Roth, Elizabeth, wife of Samuel Suther, & Margaret, wife of Gavin Pou.

(240.) Baptized... at Saxagotha .. at the House of Mrs Elizabeth Mercier.

On Sunday October 6th.

Martha,,Ann, Daughter of Nathaniel & Ann Partridge; born March 1st 1754. Suscep= John & Mary Pearson, & Mary, wife of William Hay.

Eôdem Die et Locô:

(241.) Nathaniel, Son of Nathaniel & Ann Partridge: born January 15th 1751. Suscept= John & Mary Pearson &c...

Eôdem Die et Loco:

(242.) Martha, Daughter of John & Mary Pearson: born Novr 7th 1754. Suscep= John Handasyd, Ann, wife of Nathaniel Partridge & Mary, wife of William Hay.

Eôdem Die et Locô:

(243.) John, Son of Henry & Sarah Snelling; born April 2d 1754: Suscep„ John Handasyd, Richard Jackson, Mary Gill....

(244.) James, Son of James & Mary Danly; born Septembr 22d 1753. Suscept= Frederick O'Neal, Richard Jackson, & Dorcas, wife of Benjamin Eberhardt.

Eôdem Die et Locô:

(245.) Isabell, Daughter of Benjamin & Dorcas Eberhardt; born Septembr 8th Suscep= Hugh & Esther Leviston, & Margaret, wife of Alexander McGrue.

Eôdem Die et Locô:

(246.) Rose, Daughter of James & Mary Danly; born Septembr 10th 1751. Suscep= Richard Jackson, Eugenia Gibson & Ann Hyde.

(247.) Baptized..... In Orangeburgh Church. on Sunday Octobr 20th

Abraham, Son of Jacob & Ann Rumph; born Septembr 27th 1754. Suscep= Abraham Rumph, John Balziger Jun= Susannah=Barbara Giessendanner.

(248.) On Saturday Octobr 26th. Administered private Baptism at the House of Peter Murer to a Sick Infant viz. John, Son of Peter Murer Jun„ & Magdalene, his wife; born August 4th 1754. Present: John & Jacob Giegelman &c.

ORANGEBURG COUNTY. 151

(249.) On Sunday Decembr 1st In Orangeburgh Church.
Jacob, Son of Francis & Mary Koonen; born Octobr 27th 1754 :||: Suscep,, John Friday Sen,, John Wolf in the Room of Jacob Koonen Sen,, & Anne, wife of Jacob Rumph in the Room of Verona, wife of Jnº Nicolas Shuler...
Eôdem Die et Locô:
(250.) John=Frederick, Son of Christopher & Angelia Miller; born Septembr 4th 1754 ·|. Suscept= Jnº Frederick Huber, Andrew Frederick, & Magdalene, wife of Peter Sondel..........
(251.) On Sunday Decembr 15th In Orangeburgh Church.
Maria, Daughter of Abraham & Mary Yssenhut; born Octobr 3d 1754. Suscep= Henry & Mary=Elizabeth Felder, & Margaret, wife of Christopher Rowe.
(252.) On Sunday Decembr 22d. In Ditto. John= Jacob, Son of John,,Caspar & Anna,,Barbara Mintz; born Decembr 4th 1754. Suscept Lewis & Catharina,, Elizabeth Kern, & Michael Smith.
(253.) On Christmas,,Day Decembr 25th In Ditto. Johannes, Son of John & Ann,,Margaret Myer; born Novembr 16th 1754. Suscep·· Jacob & Anna Wideman, & Melchoir Smith.
(254.) Baptized .... In Orangeburgh Church.
On Thursday Decembr 26th
Ulrick, Son of Henry & Elizabeth Stareky; born ——— 1754. Suscep= Peter Larry, Ulrick Stareky Jun,, & Anna Hug.
(255.) On Sunday Decembr 29th .... In Ditto.
Benjamin, Son of Joseph & Martha Wood; born Octobr 14th 1754. Suscep= Ulrick & Angelia Raber, & Lewis Linder.....
Eôdem Die et Locô:
(256.) Sarah, Daughter of Thomas & Hannah Pen-

darvis; born Novembr 1st 1754 :||: Suscep= Abraham Hasfort, Sertina, wife of Brand Pendarvis, & Barbara, wife of John Jennings.

Eôdem Die et Locô:

(257.) Daniel, Son of Daniel & Sarah Linder; born Novembr 3d 1754. Suscep= Lewis & Mary,,Magdalene Linder, & James Tilly Sen...

1755.

(258.) On Sunday February 2d .. In Ditto.

Maria=Regina. Daughter of George,,Frederick & Elizabeth Knobel; born Decembr 28th 1754= Suscept John,,Adam & Regina Witt, & Mary, wife of Nicolas Dirr....

(259.) On Sunday Febr 16th.. In Ditto.

Mary,,Catharina, Daughter of Joseph & Anne Deramus; born Decembr 22d 1754. Suscep= John & Mary Balziger, & Catharina, wife of Hans,,George Hessy.

(260.) On Monday Febr 17th... In Ditto.

Peter, Son of William & Sarah Brunson; born Decembr 28th 1854. Josiah & Margaret Evans & William Cantey.

(261.) Baptized .... In Orangeburgh Church.

On Sunday March 2d

Mary, Daughter of Philip & Elizabeth Jennings; born Decembr 31st 1754. Suscep= Gavin & Margaret Pou, & Barbara, wife of John Jennings.

(262.) On Sunday March 16th -- In Ditto ——

Joseph, Son of Adam & Ann,,Margaret Evinger; born March 2d 1755. Suscep= Joseph Huber, John Friday Sen= & Susannah, wife of John Friday Jun=

Eôdem Die et Locô:

(263.) *Son of Jacob & Apollonia Wolf; born† 175— Suscep,, John Jennings, Lewis Roth & Margaret. wife of Christopher Rowe.

---

*Name obliterated. †Date obliterated.

ORANGEBURG COUNTY.

Eòdem Die et Locô:

(264.) Elizabeth, Daughter of Conrad & Magdalene Yutzy: born Decembr 26th 1754. Suscep= John Fritchman, Elizabeth, wife of John Harrisperger, & Catharina, wife of George Hessy.

(265.) On Easter„Sunday March 30th.. In Ditto.
Elizabeth, Daughter of Barnard & Susannah„Elizabeth Snell; born ——— 175- Suscep= Elias Snell, Barbara, wife of Jnọ Frederick Huber, & Ann„Margaret Snyder, widow.

(266.) On Easter„Monday March 31st
John„Adam, Son of Caspar & Anna„Maria Kuhn; born August 12th 1754. Suscep„ John & Susannah Friday, & Adam Snell.

(267.) Baptized ..... In Orangeburgh Church.
On Sunday April 6th
Issom; Son of John & Sarah Clayton; born Novembr 14th 1754. Suscep„ Philip & Elizabeth Jennings, & Joseph Griffice.....

Eòdem Die et Locô:

(268.) Rebecca, Daughter of Henry & Ann Young; born Febr 16th 1755. Suscep„ John Kays, Rebecca, wife of Christian Minnick, & Sarah, wife of Willm Cooper.

(269.) On Sunday April 13th In Amelia.
Patty, Daughter of Francis & Mary James; born March 13th 1755. Suscep„ John Dargan, Dorcas Dargan & Ann Dargan.

Eòdem Die et Locô:

(270.) Mary, Daughter of Edward & Margaret Barwick. born March 30th 1755. Suscep„ William Thompson; Eugenia Russell & Margaret McNicols.

Eòdem Die et Locô:

(271.) Elizabeth, Daughter of William & Mary„ Elizabeth Heatly; born February 28th 1755. Suscep„

William & Deborah Sabb, & Marion, wife of John Fouquett......

(272.) On Sunday April 20th In Orangeburgh Church.

Magdalene, Daughter of Emanuel & Mary Miller; born February 21st 1755. Suscep., Lewis Golson, Mary Stehely |:widow:| & Anna Negely.

(273.) On Sunday April 27th.. In Ditto.

Martin, Son of Peter & Margaret,,Barbara Hottow; born April 1st 1755. Suscep= Martin Sally, Henry Shilling, & Ann Diedrick.

Baptized... In Orangeburgh Church.

(274.) On Sunday April 27th

Anne, Daughter of Joseph & Susannah Kryter; born August 31st 1754. Suscept= John Negely, Barbara Negely & Anna Hug....

(275.) On Whit,,Sunday May 18th - - In Ditto.

Catharina=Margaret. Daughter of Conrad & Mary,, Elizabeth Hungerbuller; born 19th April 1755. Suscep,, Lewis Kern, Anne,,Catharina Funtius. & Ann,, Catharina Barrin.

(276.) On Wednesday May 28th...In Ditto.

Jane, a Bastard Child of Mary, Daughter of Samuel Fox; born Octobr 15th 1754. Suscept= John Gibson. Willoughby, wife of Samuel Fox & Margaret, wife of Joseph Griffice.

(277.) On Sunday June 1st..... In Ditto.

Lewis, Son of Luke & Mary Patrick; born May 2d 1755. Suscept. Michael Christopher Rowe, Brand & Sertina Pendarvis.....

(278.) On Sunday June 15th.... In Ditto.

Catharina, Daughter of John,,Nicholas & Verena Shuler; born May 8th 1755. Suscept. Henry Rickenbacher, Catharina, wife of George Hessy, & Mary, wife of Francis Koonen.

(279.) On Sunday June 22d.... In Ditto.

Samuel, Son of Henry & Mary,,Elizabeth Felder; born June 5th 1755. Suscept Samuel Suther, John Inabnet, & Anne, wife of Henry Rickenbacher.

(280.) Baptized ...... In Amelia.
On Sunday July 13th
Mary,,Ann, Daughter of Nathan & Winifred Joyner; born Novembr 1st 1754. Suscept William Martin, Mary Whitford |: widow| & Mary Ratford.

(281.) On Sunday July 20th In Orangeburgh Church.
John,,Peter, Son of Henry Snell Jun,, & Juliana, his wife; born June 24th. 1755. Suscept Jno. Peter Beck: Jno. Frederick Ulmer, & Margaret, wife of Adam Snell.

(282.) On Sunday July 27th .. In Ditto.
John,,Frederick, Son of Jacob & Joanna Hegler, born May 23d 1755. Suscept John & Ann,,Margaret Myer, & Jno. Frederick Myer.

(283.) On Sunday August 10th (In Amelia)
Robert, Son of Willian & Mary Walling, born February 22d 1751. Suscept William Ballintine, Robert & Ann Stewart.

Eódem Die et Locô:
(284.) Administered private Baptism to Joseph, Son of Jeremiah & Catharina Strother; born March 6th 1755. Present: Moses Thomson Esqr William Ballintine &c.

(285.) On Sunday August 17th in Orangeb,, Church Hans,,Barnard,, Son of Jno Jacob & Christina.,Barbara Hungerbiller; born June 5th 1755. Suscept John Waber, Barnard & Anne,,Mary Zeigler.

(286.) Baptized .... In Orangeburgh Church.
On Sunday August 31st
George=Alexander, Son of Joseph & Barbara Duke; born June 21st 1755. Suscept Christopher Monheim, & Mary,,Catharina, wife of Henry Mell.

(287.) On Sunday Septembr 14th ... In Amelia.

David, Son of James Lewis deceas'd, & Esther his wife; born August 9th 1755. Suscept Peter Oliver, William Ballintine & Barbara Burckhard.

Eôdem Die et Locô:

(288.) John, Son of John & Eugenia Millis; born July 21st 1755. Suscept Edward & Margaret Barwick. and Thomas Barwick.

(289.) On Sunday Septembr 21st In Orangebrg Church.

George,,Henry, Son of John=Peter & Magdalene Sondel; born August 7th 1755. Suscept George,,Jacob & Ann,,Catharina Kurner. & Henry Felder...

(290.) On Sunday Octobr 5th.... In Ditto....

Philip, Son of Gavin & Margaret Pou; born August 17th 1755. Suscept Philip Jennings, Joseph Cooper & Hannah Wolf.

Eodem Die et Locô:

(291.) *Son of Joseph & Mary Coutier; born†

(292.) On Sunday Octobr 26th - - - - In Ditto.

Henry, Son of Adam & Barbara Frölich; born April 9th 1755. Suscept Henry Heym, Henry Stareky & Anne Hug.

(293.) Baptized .... In Orangeburgh Church On Sunday October 26th

Susannah, Daughter of the Revd John Giessendanner, & Barbara his wife; born Sunday Octobr 5th 1755. Suscept Jacob Giessendanner, Elizabeth, wife of Samuel Suther & Anne Hug.

(294.) On Sunday November 2d In Ditto.

William, Son of John & Rachel Brunzon; born April 3d 1753, and their Daughter

(295.) Elizabeth; born Decembr 28th. 1754.

Suscept for the two: Thomas Edwards, Samuel Suther, & Rachel, wife of Michael Larry.

---

*No name given †Nothing else given.

(296.) On Sunday Novembr 16th.. In Ditto John,,Jacob, Son of Bernhard & Anne,,Mary Ziegler; born Septembr 23d 1755. Suscept John Friday Jun,, & Susannah, his wife. & Jn⁰ Jacob Hungerbiller.

Eôdem Die et Locô:
(297.) Margaret, Daughter of Jacob & Catharina Koonen; born Octobr 24th 1755. Suscept Peter Roth, Mary, wife of Hans Balziger Sen,, & Anne, wife of Jacob Rumph.

Eôdem Die et Locô:
(298.) Mary,,Catharina, Daughter of John & Elizabeth Waber; born Septembr 9th 1755. Suscept Barnard Hartzog, Lewis & Catharina,,Elizabeth Kern.

(299.) On Monday Novembr. 17th Receiv'd private Baptism at the House of the Rev. John Giessendanner a Sick Infant brought thither, named - - -
Mary, Daughter of John & Barbara Platt; born Octobr 24th 1755. Present, Ann, wife of Charles Hottow &c.

The aforementioned Infant, viz:
Mary, Daughter of John & Barbara Platt, which had receiv'd private Baptism on Monday Novembr 17th last, was presented in the Church of Orangeburgh, where it was receiv'd according to the due & prescribed order of the Church on Sunday Novembr 30th Suscept Jacob Tshudy, Anne, wife of Jacob Koonen Sen,, & Susannah Yonn.

(300.) On Monday Decembr 1st Administered private Baptism at the House of Caspar Oth in Orangebr. Township to Hans,,George. Son of the said Caspar & Mary Oth; born June 4th 1755. Present: John & Rudolff Harrisperger, John Fritchman, John Horguer &c.

(301.) On Sunday Decembr 21st In Orangeb,, Church Jacob. Son, of Jacob & Margaret Ott: born August 14th 1755. Suscep,, John Heller, Jacob Giessendanner. & Barbara Ygly.· · ·

(302.) On Monday Decembr 29th In Ditto
William, Son of John & Elizabeth Ofill: born February 20th 1750. Suscep: Isham Clayton, Samuel & Anne Pickings——
Eôdem Die et Locô:
(303.) John, Son of the said John & Elizabeth Ofill; born in August 1753. Suscep= Joseph Chambers, William Mitchel, & Elizabeth, wife of Thomas Barker.
Eôdem Die et Locô:
(304.) Thomas, Son of Thomas & Elizabeth Barker: born Septembr 15th 1755. Suscep., Isham Clayton, Joseph Chambers, & Hannah Wolfe.
(305.) Baptized... In Orangeb,, Church.
1756.
On Thursday January 1st
Margaret, Daughter of Henry Sally Jun,, & Magdalene, his wife; born March 14th. 1754. Surets Peter & Margaret Larry & Barbara Negely.
(306.) On Sunday January 11th . . In Amelia
Charles, Son of Charles & Ann Russell; born Decembr 3d 1755. Surets= John Lloyd, John Dargan, & Dorcas, wife of Benjamin Milner.
(307.) On Sunday January 18th. In Orangeb,, Church
Henry, Son of Henry & Magdalene Crummy; born Decembr 25th 1755. Suret= Henry Wurtzer, Henry Felder, & Magdalene, wife of Hans Indorff........
(308.) On Sunday January 25th In Orangeb,,·Church
Charles, Son of Charles & Anne Hottow; born ——— 1755. Suscep,, Henry Rowe, Jacob Hottow, & Anne. wife of Peter Griffith.
Eôdem Die et Locô:
(309.) Eve,,Catharina, Daughter of Christopher & Catharina Monheim: born Decembr 25th 1755. Suret,, Jno George & Eve,,Catharina Hayner, & Eve,,Catharina Hirter......
(310.) On Monday February 2d In Orangeb,, Church

Lewis, Son of Peter & Christina Kramer; born August 19th 1755. Suret,, Lewis Linder, John Aberly, & Margaret, wife of John Anding.
(311.) Baptized at the House of Elizabeth Mercier in Saxegotha
On Sunday February 22^d
John, Son of James & Mary Danly, born Decemb,, 5th 1755. Suret,, Jos & Mary Evans &c. - - -
Eòdem Die et Locô:
(312.) John, Son of Benjamin & Dorcas Aifred; born August 27th 1755. Suret: Alexander & Margaret McGrue, & Charles Middleton.......
Eòdem Die et Locô:
(313.) John, Son of*
Eòdem Die et Locô:
(314.) Malachy, Son of Thomas & Race Howell; born May 20th 1755.
Eòdem Die et Locô:
(315.) Thomas, Son of Thomas & Sarah Hodge; born April 1st 1753. Suscep,, Charles Middleton, Anne Danly &c.
Eòdem Die et Locô:
(315.)† Burril, Son of Caspar & Naomy Foust; born January 11th 1756. Suscep,, John Parks, Henry & Anne Hartel...
Eòdem Die et Locô:
(316.) William, Son of James & Mary,,Anne Berry, born March 30th 1755.
Eòdem Die et Locô:
(317.) Sarah, Daughter of John & Mary Lane; born Novr 23^d 1755.
Eòdem Die et Locô:
(318.) Sarah, Daughter of Gilbert & Elizabeth Gib-

---

*Remainder of this entry was either erased or left out.
†Two entries numbered 315.

son; born June 21$\underline{st}$ 1755. Suret,, William Brown. &c.

(319.) Baptized... In Orangeb,, Church On Sunday February 29$\underline{th}$ Jonathan Riggs, Son of Peter & Mary Wood; born March 7$\underline{th}$ 1755. Suret,, Gavin & Margaret Pou, & Peter Griffith......

(320.) On Tuesday Night March 2$\underline{d}$ Administered private Baptism at the House of Lewis Golsen in Orangeburgh Township to a Sick Infant viz,, John,, Caspar, Son of the said Lewis & Elizabeth Golsen: born February 11$\underline{th}$ 1756. Present. John Caspar Stareky, Ulrick Stareky &c....

(321.) On Sunday March 7$\underline{th}$. In Orangeburgh Church
Caspar, Son of John & Margaret Inabnet; born February 21$\underline{st}$ 1756. Suret: Caspar Negely, Henry Felder, & Susannah,,Barbara, wife of George Giessendanner.
.....

Eôdem Die et Locô:
(322.) Hans,,George, Son of Lewis & Mary,,Barbara Roth; born ————— 1756. Suret: John & Susannah Frydig, & Hans Indorff

Eôdem Die et Locô:
(323.) Christian, Son of Christian & Elizabeth Roth. born February 19$\underline{th}$ 1756. Suret: Jacob Roth, Isaac Hottow, & Barbara; wife of John Platt

Eôdem Die et Locô:
(324.) Salome, Daughter of Hans,,George & Rosina Russel; born Decembr 21$\underline{st}$ 1755. Suret= Samuel Suther, Angelia, wife of Ulrick Raber. & Mary,,Elizabeth, wife of Henry Felder.

(325.) Baptized... In Orangeburgh Church On Sunday March 21st
Elizabeth,,Barbara, Daughter of Lewis & Catharina,, Elizabeth Kern: born February 17$\underline{th}$ 1756. John &

ORANGEBURG COUNTY.

Elizabeth Waber, & Barbara, wife of Jn̊ Frederick Huber......
Eôdem Die et Locô:
(326.) Mary,,Catharina, Daughter of Stephen & Mary,,Ann Whitman; born February 9th 1756. Suret= Hans,,George & Mary,,Catharina Usman, & Magdalene Usman........
(327.) On Sunday March 28th In Orangeb,, Church George. Son of James & Margaret Tilly; born Novembr 28th 1755. Suscep,, Jacob Giessendanner, George Shuler, & Margaret Barr....
(328.) On Easter,,Sunday April 18th.. In Orang,, Church Jacob, Son of Jacob & Anne Whideman; born March 22d 1756. Suret,, Ulrick Booser, Jacob Annis, & Anne,,Margaret Whetstone ———
Eôdem Die et Locô:
(329.) Hans,,Peter, Son of Andrew & Margaret Frederick; born March 16th 1756. Suret,, Jn̊ Peter & Magdalene Sondel, & Jacob Kearn
Eôdem Die et Loco:
(330.) Mary,,Elizabeth, Daughter of Barnard & Mary,,Apollonia Lebennder; born January 14th 1756. Suret., Henry & Mary,,Elizabeth Felder, & Margaret, wife of Andrew Frederick ———
Baptized.... In Orangeb,, Church
(331.) On Easter,,Sunday April 18th.
Nicholas, Son of George & Catharina Ulrick; born February 26th 1756. Suret,, Rudolff Harrisperger, Nicholas Zorn, & Catharina, wife of John Simmons.

(332.) On Easter,,Monday April 19th In Ditto,
Paul, Son of Lewis & Frances Patrick; born March 2d 1756: Suret: Samuel Suther, Luke Patrick, & Sarah Cooper, widow....
Eôdem Die et Locô:
(333.) John,,Michael, Son of John,,Martin & Anne,,

Margaret Hossleiter; born March 17th 1756.
Suret,, Johannes Wolf, Caspar & Mary Ott———

(334.) On Saturday May 1st In Amelia,, at the House of Mr Charles Russell...

Joseph, Son of John & Rachel Lloyd; born February 19th 1756. Suret,, William Thomson, Joseph Russell, & Anne, wife of Charles Russell.

(335.) On Sunday May 23d - - In Orangeb., Church Elizabeth, Daughter of Benedict & Magdalene Koller; born April 3d 1756. Suret,, Henry & Verena Wurtzer, & Barbara, wife of the Revd John Giessendanner...

(336.) On Thursday May 27th... In Ditto Anne, Daughter of Francis & Mary Koonen; born May 14th 1756. Suret: Jacob Koonen, Anne, wife of Jacob Rumph, and Anne Hug.....

(337.) On Tuesday June 15th Administered private Baptism at the House of John,,Valentin Kranich in Orangeburgh Township to a Sick Infant, viz:

John,,Peter, Son of the said John,,Valentin & Anne,, Mary Kranich; born June 6th 1756. Present: Peter Moorer Sen,, John Giegelman &c.

(338.) On Sunday June 20th. In Orangeb,, Church Jacob, Son of Samuel & Elizabeth Suther; born 3d Day of June. 1756. Suret: Henry Wurtzer, Jacob Giessendañer, & Barbara, wife of the Revd Jno Giessendañer.

Eôdém Die et Locô:

(339.) Mary,,Magdalene, Daughter of Jno Frederick & Mary-Barbara Ulmer; born 25. April. 1756. Suret,. John,,George Hayner, Catharina, wife of George Hessy, & Mary,,Barbara Ulmer........

(340.) On Sunday July 11th In Amelia...

Eugenia, Daughter of William & Eugenia Thomson; born June 25th 1756. Suret,. Moses Thomson Jun,, Rachel, wife of Capt John Lloyd, & Eugenia, wife of James Baird.

ORANGEBURG COUNTY.

(341.) On Sunday July 25.. In Orangeburgh Church —Thomas, Son of John & Elizabeth Burdell; born March 3d 1756. Suret. Adam Snell, Conrad & Magdalene Yutzy..........

(342.) On Sunday August 1st In Orangeburgh Church John, Son of Elias & Mary,,Catharina Snell; born July 10th 1756. Suret: John Frichman, John Harrisperger, & Anne,,Margaret Snyder, widow.

(343.) On Sunday August 8th At Saxagotha in the House of Mrs Elizabeth Mercier
Hugh, Son of*

(344.) Baptized... In Orangeburgh Church On Sunday August 15th
John,,Theodore, Son of Barnard & Anne,,Mary Hartzog; born July 3d 1756. Suret,, John & Elizabeth Waber, & Theodore Fichtner....

(345.) On Sunday August 22d .. In Amelia
Rachel. Daughter of Henry & Mary Carter: born February 8th 1756. Suret., Robert & Elizabeth Twiddie, & Mary Whitford, widow.

(346.) On Sunday August 29th In Orangeb., Church Jonathan, Son of Joseph & Martha Wood: born July 14th 1756. Suscep,. Luke Patrick, Lewis Patrick, & Susannah,,Barbara Giessendanner.

(347.) On Sunday Septembr 12th In Amelia
William, Son of William & Rachel Hickie; born Septembr 10th 1754. Suret., Thomas Bamrick. Caspar Brown & Rachel Gant.....

(348.) On Saturday Septembr 18th .. Administered private Baptism at my own House to
Alexander, Son of John & Judith Tennison: born July 22d 1756. (the said John Tennison being then on his Journey from Georgia to the Northward)...

---

*The remainder of this entry was either erased, or was never put down.

(349.) On Sunday September 19th In Orangeb„ Church John„Conrad, Son of Caspar & Anna„Maria Kuhn; born April 16th 1756. Suret.. Hans„Ulrick Dantzler, Conrad Hungerbiller, & Christina„Barbara, wife of John Jacob Hungerbiller....

(350.) On Sunday September 26th In Orangeb„ Church Thomas, Son of Leonhard & Sarah Warnedow; born 12th May 1756. Suret,, Jacob Hottow, Abraham Hasfort & Margaret, wife of Joseph Griffice...

(351.) Baptized.. In Orangeburgh Church On Sunday September 26th..
Mary„Catharina, Daughter of Frederick & Elizabeth Strubel; born August 15. 1756. Suret., Lewis & Catharina„Elizabeth Kern, & Anne Mary, wife of Nicolas Waber Sen...

(352.) On Sunday October 3d In Orangeb„ Church —Anne„Catharina, Daughter of Henry & Anne Rickenbacker; born August 10th 1756. Suret. Nicholas Dill, Barbara, wife of John Jennings, & Anne, wife of John Caspar Stereky........

(353.) On Sunday October 24th.. In Orangeb„ Church
Hannah, Daughter of Nicholas Waber Jun„ and Maria„Barbara, his wife; born 24th September 1756. Suret„ John & Elizabeth Waber, & Elizabeth, wife of Frederick Strubel.......

(354.) On Sunday Octobr 31st In Orangeb„ Church Margaret, Daughter of Philip & Elizabeth Jennings; born October 9th 1756. Suret„ John & Barbara Jennings, & Susannah„Barbara Giessendanner.

Eôdem Die et Locô:
(355.) Rachel, Daughter of Joseph & Margaret Cooper; born August 14th 1756. Suret. Abraham Hasfort, Mary, wife of Joseph Coutier, & Regina, alias Rachel Rowe.

ORANGEBURG COUNTY.

(356.) On Sunday Novembr 21st In Orangeb,, Church Hans,,Ulrick, Son of Nicholas Dirr late deceas'd, & Mary, his wife; born Novembr 2d 1756. Suret. Revd John Giesssendanner, John & Elizabeth Giegelman...

(357.) On Sunday Novembr 28th In Orangeb,, Church Anne, Daughter of Catharina, wife of Thomas Puckridge, but a considerable Time Since cohabiting with William Pendarvis, who desired Baptism for the said Child as his; born Octobr 4th 1756. Suret: Brand Pendarvis, Margaret, wife of Christr Rowe & Anne, wife of Joseph Deramus.

(358.) On Tuesday Novembr 30th Administred private Baptism to a Sick Infant, brought to my House by the Parents, viz: Jacob, son of Henry & Catharina Strowman, born Novembr 17th 1756.

(359.) On Sunday December 5th. In Orangeb., Church Hans,,Henry, Son of Martin & Margaret Kemler; born Octobr 21st 1756. Suret,, Hans and Margaret Dantzler, & Henry Dantzler......

(360.) On Sunday Decemb 12th In Amelia Garret. Son of Garret & Agnesia Fitz,,Patrick; born Decembr 15th 1755. Suret. John Morrison, Duncan McIntire, & Anne Jones.

(361.) On Sunday Decembr 19th In Orangeb,, Church Susannah, Daughter of Jacob & Mary,,Sasannah Herlan; born November 30th 1756. Suret: Lewis & Mary,, Barbara Roth, & Catharina, wife of Jacob Koonen....

(362.) On Tuesday Decemb..21st Administred Baptism to a Sick Infant, born this 21st Decemb. 1756. viz: Anne,,Margaret, Daughter of Jacob & Anne Wymer.... at the House of Peter Roth....

(363.) On Christmas,,Day Decembr 25th In Orangeb,, Church Anne,,Mary, Daughter of John & Elizabeth Harrisperger; born ——————— 1756. Suret,, Rudolff Herrisperger, Anne, wife of Henry Rickenbacker, & Mary,,Catharina, wife of Elias Snell.

(364.) On Sunday Decembr 26th In Orangeb,, Church Henry, Son of Henry & Anne Young; born Novembr 28th 1756. Suret. John Wolf Sen, Luke Patrick, & Regina,,Barbara Rowe....

Eôdem Die et Locô:

(365.) Mary, Daughter of William & Mary Young; born Novr 3d 1756. Suret. James Tilly Sen,,, Barbara, wife of John Jennings, & Susannah,,Barbara Giessendanner...

(366.) Baptized... In Orangeburgh Church On Sunday Decembr 26th Mary, Daughter of Henry & Mary Jordan; born Decembr 7.th 1756. Suret., Peter & Anne Griffith, & Elizabeth, wife of Joseph Thornton....

Eôdem Die et Locô:

(367.) Thomas, Son of Thomas & Hannah Pendarvis; born September 23d 1756. Suret., Peter Faure, William Pendarvis, & Catharina, wife of Thomas Puckridge.

1757

(368.) January 1st... In Orangeb,. Church Ulrick, Son of Ulrick & Eve.,Mary Brunner; born Decemb,, 17th 1756. Suret,, Jacob Ott, Rudolff Herrisperger, & Christina, wife of Nicholas Yonn.

Eôdem Die et Locô:

(369.) Anne,,Margaret, Daughter of John & Eva,, Catharina Jubb; born April 28th 1756. Suret: Henry & Anne,,Margaret Shilling, & Margaret Gyger, widow.

(370.) On Sunday January 2d .. In Orangeb., Church

Samuel, Son of Daniel & Sarah Linder; born July 28th 1756. Suret.. Jacob Giessendanner, Christopher Rowe. and Elizabeth Linder.....

Eôdem Die et Locô:

(371.) Martha, born November 20th 1752.

(372.) Susannah, born March 26th 1754.

ORANGEBURG COUNTY.

(373.) Rebeccah, born August 15th 1756. Those three the Daughters of Jonathan & Martha Brunzon: Suret for the three: Daniel & Sarah Linder, Isaac Hottow, Samuel Brunson, Mary Brunson & Margaret, wife of Joseph Griffice...

(374.) On Tuesday January 4th... In Orangeb,, Church
Zachariah, Son of William & Agnes Aldridge; born 18th January 1754. Suret: Abraham Hasfort, Peter & Sarah Faure.

(375.) Baptized.... In Orangeburgh Church
Sarah, Daughter of William & Agnes Aldridge; born 14th July 1755. Suret: Anne Faure & Anna,,Maria Kemlerin, & Isaac Hottow....

Eôdem Die et Locô:

(376.) Henry, a Mulatto,,Bastard of Aña,.Maria Kemlerin; born in March 1755. Suret,, Peter Faure, William & Agnes Aldridge......

(377.) On Sunday January 16th In Orangeb,, Church John,,George,,Melchior, Son of John,,Caspar & Anna.,Barbara Mintz; born January 4th 1757. Suret,, John Friday Jun: Melchior Smith, & Anne,,Margaret Tyner.......

(378.) On Monday January 17th In Orangeb,, Church James, Son of John & Sarah Clayton; born ——— 1756. Suret: Peter Faure. Anne Faure & Isham Clayton......

(379.) On Wednesday January 19th At the House of John Aberly below Orangeburgh Township John,, Nicholas, Son of John & Margaret Anding; born Novembr 27th 1756. Suret,, John Aberly, Nicholas & Margaret Noe.....

Eôdem Die et Locô:

(380.) Catharine,,Margaret. Daughter of John & Anne Aberly: born Decembr 31st 1756. Suret,, Revd

John Giessendanner, Margaret, wife of John Anding, & Margaret, wife of Nicholas Noe....

(381.) On Wednesday January 26th At the House of Frederick Thore at the Four Holes....

Anne, Daughter of David & Mary Rumph; born Decemb,, 27th. 1755. Suret: Thomas & Hannah Pendarvis, & Anna, wife of Frederick Hoggs....

(396.)* Baptized.... In Orangeburgh Church On Sunday February 27th

John,,Martin, Son of George,,Frederick & Elizabeth Knobel; born January 18th 1757. Suret: Martin Egly. Barnard & Anne,,Mary Hertzog....

Eôdem Die et Locô:

(397.) John,,George, Son of John.,George & Eve.. Catharina Hayner; born January 26th 1757. Suret,. Conrad Hungerbiller, Hans Ulmer, & Anne,,Margaret Barrin.

Eôdem Die et Locô:

(398.) Catharina, Daughter of Henry Snell Jun., & Juliana, his wife; born February 2d 1757. Suret: Henry Snell Sen,,, Catharina, his wife, & Anne, wife of Jacob Whideman.

(399.) On Monday February 28th At the House of Moses Thomson Esqr.. In Amelia....

Katherine, Daughter of Bryan White. & Katherine, his wife, deceas'd; born January 30th 1757. Suret: Peter & Katherine Burns, & Elizabeth McFarlen......

(400.) On Sunday March 6th In Orangeburgh Church Anne,,Elizabeth, Daughter of Martin & Susannah Sally; born 19th January. 1757. Suret: John Sally. Mary, wife of Luke Patrick, & Christina, wife of Nicholas Yonn....

(401.) On Monday Night March 7th Administred

---

*From 381 to 396 lost.

ORANGEBURG COUNTY. 169

private Baptism at the House of Adam Snell in Orangeburgh Township to a Sick Infant, viz: Magdalene, Daughter of said Adam & Margaret Snell; born February 10th 1757. Present: Henry & Jacob Horger, Peter Murer Jun. — — — — — —

(402.) Wednesday March 9th Administred private Baptis'm at the House of Peter Murer in Orangeb,, to John,,Henry, Son of the said Peter Murer Jun., & Magdalene, his wife, born December 26th 1756....
.....

(403.) Eôdem Die et Locô:
Maria,,Magdalene, Daughter of Henry Horger, Junior, & Catharina, his wife, born October 20th 1756: Present: Adam Snell, John & Jacob Giegelman &c.

(404.) On Sunday March 13th. In Amelia Chappel—Mary, Daughter of Charles & Anne Russel; born ——— ——— 1757. Suret: William & Eugenia Thomson, & Katherine Dargan....
Eôdem Die et Locô:

(405.) Frances, Daughter of John & Sarah Hope; born April 2d 1754. Suret: John Burdell, Marion, wife of John Fouquett & Mary,,Ann, wife of Conrad Halman.

(406.) On Sunday March 27th In Orangeburgh Church Samuel, Son of Jacob & Apollonia Wolf; born February 16th 1757. Suret., John Wolf Sen,, John & Anne,,Elizabeth Giegelman......

(407.) On Sunday April 3d :. In Amelia Chappel John, Son of John & Sophinisba McCord; born January 26th 1757. Suret: John Russell, Robert and Elizabeth Twiddie......

(408.) On Thursday April 7th. In Orangeburgh Church John, Son of Abraham & Mary Yssenhut; born March 1st 1757. Suret.. Barnard Lebennder, John & Margaret Inabnet......

(409.) Baptized... In Orangeburgh Church

On Easter„Sunday April 10th.
Henry, Son of Jacob & Anna Wannenmaker; born March 27th. 1756. Suret: Jacob Hottow, John Roth Jun. & Anna„Magdalena Tapp....

(410.) On Sunday May 1st.. In Orangeb„ Church. James, Son of John„James & Anne. Shoolegre, born January 10th 1757. Suret: Henry Felder, James & Elizabeth Taylor...

(411.) On Sunday May 15th. In Orangeb. Church Abraham, Son of Henry & Mary„Elizabeth Felder; born March 28th 1757. Suret: Abraham Yssenhoot, Barnard Lebennder, & Margaret, wife of John Inabnet.......

(412.) On Assension„Day May 19th In Orangeb„ Church Johannes, Son of Joseph & Susannah Kryter; born in February 1757. Suret: John Stehely, John Friday Jun.. & Barbara, wife of Frederick Huber..

Eôdem Die et Locô:

(413.) Susannah, Daughter of Jacob & Ann Rumph, born May 1st 1757. Suret: Abraham Yssenhut, Anne, wife of Joseph Deramus, & Susannah„Barbara Giessendañer.

(414.) On Whit„Sunday May 29th In Orangeb„ Church William, Son of John & Phibbie Mitchel; born Octobr 10th 1755. Suret: William Bowers, Lewis Netman, & Elizabeth Funtzius.

(415.) On Sunday June 12th In Amelia Chappel.
David, Son of David & Mary Jackson; born April 11th 1757. Suret: John Burdell, Valchtine Shoemaker, & Mary„Ann. wife of Conrad Halman.

(416.) Baptized... In Amelia Chappel.
On Sunday June 12th.
Anne, Daughter of David & Mary Jackson; born July 22d 1755. Suret: John Burdell, Mary„Ann, wife of Conrad Halman, Dorothy, wife of Valentine Shoemaker.......

On Sunday July 3ᵈ In Orangeb„ Church..
(417.) Elizabeth & ⎱ Daughters of Thomas & Sarah
(418.) Anne   ⎰ Lovelies: Elizabeth born 15ᵗʰ
February. 1757. Anne born 2ᵈ July 1754. Sureties for both: Edward Nicks, Mary, wife of Willᵐ Durberville, & Elizabeth, wife of Joseph Thornton.

Eôdem Die et Locô:
(419.) Elizabeth, Daughter of William & Sarah Hunter; born 2ᵈ November 1755. Suret: Lewis Patrick, Mary, wife of Peter Wood, & Mary, wife of William Durberville.....

(420.) On Sunday July 17ᵗʰ In Orangeb„ Church John„Henry, Son of Jnᵒ Nicholas & Verena Shuler; born 6ᵗʰ June 1757. Suret„ Henry Felder; Martin & Zibilla„Catharina Egly..

Eôdem Die et Locô:
(421.) Barbara, Daughter of Adam Frölich deceased, & Rarbara, his late wife; born June 17ᵗʰ 1757. Suret: John Roth, Junior, Rachel Rowe, & Barbara, wife of the Rev. John Giessendanner.

Eôdem Die et Locô:
(422.) Elizabeth„Barbara, Daughter of John & Elizabeth Waber; born June 9ᵗʰ 1757. Suret.. Nicholas & Maria„Barbara, wife of Frederick Strubel... ———

(423.) Baptized... At the House lately possess'd by Willᵐ Mᶜ Nichol, near Amelia Township
On Thursday August 4ᵗʰ
Elizabeth, Daughter of William & Elizabeth McNichol; born April 28ᵗʰ 1757. Suret. Thomas Hails, Mary MᶜGowan, & Margaret, wife of John MᶜGowan.

(424.) On Monday August 15ᵗʰ — — — — —
Stephen, Son of William & Sarah Hart; born January 6ᵗʰ 1757. Suret„ Luke & Mary Patrick, & Revᵈ John Giessendanner......

(425.) On Sunday August 28ᵗʰ In Orangeb„ Church Martha, Daughter of John & Margaret Gibson; born

Decembr 16th 1756. Suret: George Fox, Rachel, wife Michael Larry, & Willoughby Fox, widow.

Eôdem Die et Locô:

(426.) Elizabeth, Daughter of William & Mary Dann; born March 18th 1757. Suret: Thomas Lywick, & Willoughby Fox, widow.....

(427.) On Tuesday Septembr 30th Administred private Baptism in my own House in Orangeburgh, to

Maria, Daughter of Caspar & Mary Oth; born April 8th 1757. Present. Lewis Golsen, Peter Stehely &c.

(428.) On Sunday Octobr 9th In Amelia Chappel Thomas, Son of John & Anne Millis; born June 10th 1757. Suret,, Alexander & Isabell Tate, & William Thomson.

Eôdem Die et Locô:

(429.) Joseph, Son of Conrad & Mary,, Anne Halman; born Septemb,, 8th 1757. Suret: Caspar Brown, Joseph Festner, & Regina, wife of Adam Willis...

(430.) Baptized... In Orangeburgh Church

On Sunday Octobr 23d

Anna, Daughter of Jno Henry & Anne,, Margaret Shilling; born Septembr .. 1757. Suret: Peter Griffith, Anne, wife of Henry Rickenbacker, & Mary,, Catharina, wife of Henry Mell...

(431.) On Sunday Novembr 6th. In Orangeb,, Church George,, Riggs, Son of Peter & Mary Wood; born December 4th 1751. Suret.. Joseph Griffith, Henry Sally Jun,, & Elizabeth, wife of Joseph Thornton.

(432.) On Sunday Novembr 13th. In Amelia Chappel Mary, Daughter of William & Eugenia Thomson; born Octobr 3d 1757. Suret: Joseph Russel, Rachel. wife of Capt John Lloyd. & Katherine, wife of Timothy Dargan.

(433.) On Sunday Novembr 20th In Orangeburgh Church—John,, Lewis. Son of Caspar & Ana,, Maria

ORANGEBURG COUNTY. 173

Kuhn; born Septemb$\underline{r}$ 24$\underline{th}$ 1757. Suret: Lewis & Elizabeth Golsen & Peter Stehely.

Eôdem Die et Locô:

(434.) Hans,,Caspar; Son of Barnard & Anne,,Mary Ziegler; born Septemb$\underline{r}$ 28$\underline{th}$ 1757. Suret: Conrad Hungerbiller, Caspar Kuhn & Anne,,Margaret Barrin.

Eôdem Die et Locô:

(435.) John,,Jacob, Son of Conrad & Maria,,Elizabeth Hungerbiller; born Septemb$\underline{r}$ 3$\underline{d}$ 1757. Suret: Barnard Ziegler, Jacob and Christina,,Barbara Hungerbiller.....

Eôdem Die et Locô:

(436.) John,,Jacob, Son of Abraham & Susannah Du Puis; born Octob$\underline{r}$ 23$\underline{d}$ 1757. Suret: John Giegelman, Jacob and Mary,,Susañah Herlan......

Eôdem Die et Locô:

(437.) Mary,,Elizabeth, Daughter of John & Susañah Friday; born Octob$\underline{r}$ 9$\underline{th}$ 1757. Suret,, Lewis & Mary,, Barbara Roth, & Elizabeth, wife of John Harrisperger.

(438.) Baptized... In Orangeburgh Church On Sunday Novemb$\underline{r}$ 20$\underline{th}$ Magdalene, Daughter of Barnard & Susañah,,Elizabeth Snell; born Septemb 16$\underline{th}$ 1757. Suret:.. Frederick Hoff, Mary,,Catharina, wife of Elias Snell, & Eve,, Catharina, wife of John,,George Hayner.

(439.) On Sunday Decemb$\underline{r}$ 11$\underline{th}$ In Amelia Chappel Margaret, Daughter of Samuel Bly & Margaret Beck; born Novemb$\underline{r}$ 5$\underline{th}$ 1757. Suret: Caspar Brown, Mary,, Anne, wife of Conrad Halman & Mary Whiteford, widow.

(440.) John, Son of Barnard & Mary,,Apollonia Lebennder; born Octob$\underline{r}$ 16$\underline{th}$ 1757. Suret: Frederick Huber. Abraham & Mary Yssenhut- Baptized.. On Sunday, Christmas,,Day. Decemb$\underline{r}$ 25$\underline{th}$ 1757....

(441.) On Wednesday Decembr 28th... Baptized
(442.) Mary and Lydia, both the Daughters of Thomas & Lucretia Oisins; Mary born Decembr 28th 1751. Lydia born Octobr 6th 1757. Suret for both: John & Margaret Gibson, & Willoughby Fox, widow....

1758:)

On Saturday January 7th. .... Baptized
At the House of Colonel Richardson in St Mark's Parish, Craven County
(32.) Thirty„two Children.....
(475.) On Sunday February 5th In Orangeb„ Church Barbara, Daughter of Henry & Magdalene Crummy; born Decembr 26th 1757. Suret: John Wolf Sen„ Margaret Koller, & Barbara, wife of John Jennings.
(476.) On Monday February 13th In Orangeburgh Church William, Son of Joseph & Mary Dewidd; born March 7th 1757. Suret: Charles Strother, John Thomas, & Anne, wife of John Taylor...
(477.) Friday March 3d Administred private Baptism at the House of John Giegelman in Orangeburgh to Mary„Elizabeth, Daughter of John & Anna„Elizabeth Giegelman; born February 6th 1758. Present: Valentine Kronick, Jacob Giegelman &c.
(478.) On Sunday March 5th. In Orangeb.. Church Abraham, Son of Joseph & Margaret Griffice; born January 19th 1758. Suscept: Andrew Govan, John Wolf Sen, & Susañah„Barbara Giessendanner.
(479.) Eôdem Die et Locô:
Patty, Daughter of John & Barbara Platt; born ———————— 175—. Suret: Charles Hottow, Mary„ Katherine, wife of Henry Mell. & Margaret, wife of Samuel Densmore.
(480.) On Easter„Sunday March 26th. In Orangeb., Church

– – – Daughter of Jacob & Anna Wideman; born February 26th 1758. Suret: Rudolph & Elizabeth Theiler, & Anne,,Mary, wife of Caspar Kuhn....

(481.) On Easter,,Monday March 27th In Orangeb,, Church Susannah, Daughter of Joseph & Barbara Duke; born ——————— 175—. Suret:*

(482.) On Sunday April 16th. In Orangeb,, Church Anna, Daughter of Jacob & Catharina Koonen; born March 31st 1758. Suret: Francis Koonen, Anna, wife of Joseph Deramus, & Barbara Harrisperger, widow.

(483.) Baptized..... In Orangeburgh Church On Sunday April 23d

John,,Jacob, Son of Jacob & Johanna Hegler; born March 13th. 1758. Suret: John & Margaret Myer, & Frederick Myer.

Eôdem Die et Locô:

(484.) Isaac, Son of Charles & Anne Hottow; born 23d of March 1758. Suret: Isaac Hottow, Simon Yonn, and Margaret Dietrick.

Eôdem Die et Locô:

(485.) Margaret, Daughter of Jacob & Dorothy Tshudy; born March 21st 1758. Suret: Henry Bossart, Margaret Koller, & Mary,,Catharina Tshudy......

(486.) On the Fast Day Wednesday May 17th. In Orangeb,, Church John,,Frederick, Son of Lewis & Catharina,,Elizabeth Kern; born March 9th 1758: Suret: Melchior Smith, Frederick & Barbara Huber.

Eôdem Die et Locô:

(487.) Abraham, Son of John & Sarah Clayton; born April 11th 1758. Suret: Isham Clayton, Abraham Hasfort, Barbara Harrisperger, widow.

(488.) On Sunday May 21st.... In Amelia Chappel William, Son of Thomas & Jane Platt; born Decembr

---
*Left out.

22ᵈ 1757. Suret: Moses & Jane Thomson. & John Thomson.

Eôdem Die et Locô:

(489.) Sarah, Daughter of William & Mary Thomson; born December 21ˢᵗ 1757. Suret: Moses & Jane Thomson, Jane Beard, widow.

Eôdem Die et Locô:

(490.) Martha, Daughter of Thomas & Anne Powel; born, Octobr 12th 1757. Suret: William Thomson. Sarah Powel & Anne Powel.

(491.) Thursday May 18th Administred private Baptis'm in my own House to

Catharina, Daughter of Henry & Catharina Horger. born March 25th 1758. Present Valentine Yutzy &c. ——— ———.

(492.) On Sunday May 28th. In Orangeburgh Church George,,Lewis; Son of Adam & Anna,,Margaret—Evinger; born May 4th 1758. Suret: Johannes Wolf. George,,Lewis & Mary,,Barbara Roth...

(493.) On Sunday June 11th.. In Amelia Chappel Rachel, Daughter of Edward & Rachel Brady, born March 6th 1758. Suret: William McNicol, Mary McGowan, & Sarah Thomson...

(494.) On Sunday June 18th .... In Orangeburgh Church Margaret, Daughter of George & Eva,,Catharina Hayner; born May 5th 1758. Suret: Adam & Anne,, Margaret Snell & Mary,,Elizabeth Strowman.

Eôdem Die et Locô:

(495.) Anna,,Catharina, Daughter of Henry Snell Senr & Catharina, his wife, deceased; born in May 1758. Suret: Adam Snell, Juliana, wife of Henry Snell Junr & Anna,,Catharina Barrin.

(496.) On Sunday June 25th In Orangeb.. Church Mary,,Magdalene, Daughter of Jacob & Anna Wan-

ORANGEBURG COUNTY. 177

nenmaker; born October 4th 1757. Suret: Jacob Roth,* Barbara Frölich. widow, & Mary. wife of Abraham Yssenhut.

(497.) On Sunday July 9th In Amelia Chappel. Jacob, Son of Garret & Agnesia Fitz,,Patrick; born February 9th 1758. Suret: John McColloch, George McColloch & Lydia McColloch.

(498.) Baptized...... In Orangeburgh Church On Sunday July 23d Peter Son of John & Margaret Inabnet; born July 6th 1758. Suret: George Giessendanner, Abraham Yssenhut, & Mary.,Elizabeth. wife of Henry Felder.

Eôdem Die et Locô:
(499.) Seth, Son of Seth Hatcher deceas'd & Susannah, his wife; born April 23d 1757. Suret: Nicholas & —— Susannah.,Elizabeth Zorn, & Henry Zorn...

Eôdem Die et Locô:
(500.) Elizabeth. Daughter of Christian & Elizabeth Roth; born June 3d 1758. Suret= Jacob Roth, Catharine, wife of Uirick Roth, & Mary,,Catharina Tshudy.
.....
Eôdem Die et Locô:
(501.) Anna,,Margaret. Daughter of Henry & Appollonia Dentzler: born May 29th 1758. Suret: Hans., Henry Dentzler, Margaret, wife of Hans.,Ulrick Dentzler, & Anna, wife of Jacob Wideman...... .

---

*South Carolina Gazette, May 9th, 1768: "On Thursday the 26th of May instant will be sold by public vendue, at the plantation of the late Jacob Roth, deceased, in Orangeburgh Township, All the said plantation, with the Standing crop thereon, three very good plantation slaves, and two children; the stock of cattle, horses, hogs, household furniture, plantation tools, and all other articles belonging to said estate. The conditions will be made known on the day of sale.

"All persons having any demands against the said estate, are desired to bring them in properly attested; and all those indebted, to make payment by the above day to.
"John Herrisperger, } Executors."
"Henry Rekenbacher, }

(502.) On Sunday July 30th. In Orangeburgh Church, John,,Jacob. Son of John.,Frederick & Mary,,Barbara Ulmer; born July 3d 1758. Suret: Jacob Giessendañer, & Jacob & Margaret Ott.

(503.) On Sunday August 27th In Orangeb,, Church John, Son of Ulrick & Eva,,Maria Brunner; born Augt 4th 1758. Suret: John Miller, Nicholas Yonn, & Elizabeth, wife of John Herrisperger.....

Eôdem Die et Locô:

(504.) Jacob, Son of Andrew & Margaret Frederick: born June 20th 1758. Suret: Peter Shoeman, Peter & Margaret Dirr.

(505.) Baptized...In Orangeburgh Church On Sunday August 27th.

Anna, Daughter of Emanuel & Mary Miller; born August 5th 1758. Suret: John Stehely, Anna Negely, & Elizabeth, wife of John Herrisperger.

Eôdem Die et Locô:

(506.) Sarah, Daughter of Adam & Anne,,Margaret Snell; born July 16th 1758. Suret: Barnard Ziegler, Mary,,Elizabeth, wife of Conrad Hungerbiller, & Catharine Herter...

(507.) On Sunday Septembr. 3d . In Orangeburgh Church Susannah, Daughter of John & Elizabeth Burdell; born July 4th 1758. Suret: Lewis Ulmer, Elizabeth Tilly, & Mrs Hawskin, widow.

(508.) On Sunday Septembr 10th In Amelia Chappel Jane, Daughter of Thomas & Fanny Curtise; born Febr 7th 1757. Suret: John & Fanny Millis, and Katherine Ballintine....

(509.) On Thursday Septembr 14th. In Oranegb.. Church. Anna, Daughter of Leonard & Sarah Warnedow; born March 10th 1758. Surets: Charles & Anna Hottow and Anna Kays..

(510.) On Sunday Septembr. 17th In Orangeb,. Church Anna, Daughter of Joseph & Anna Cook; born

August 14th. 1758. Suret: Jacob Yssler, Rachel, wife of Michael Larry & Barbara Frölich, widow.
Eôdem Die et Locô:
(511.) Elizabeth. Daughter of John & Anne,,Margaret Myer, born August 2d 1758. Suret: Frederick Myer, Lovisa, wife of Jacob Horger, & Verena, wife of Jno Nicholas Shuler.
(512.) Baptized in Orangeburgh Church.......
On Sunday Septembr 17th
Elizabeth. Daughter of John,,Peter & Magdalene Sondel: born June 8th 1758. Suret: Peter Shoeman. Ann,,Catharina. wife of George.,Jacob Kurner, & Ann= Mary=Catharina, wife of Ulrick Roth....
(513.) On Sunday Octobr 1st Baptized at a House upon the High.,Hills in St Mark's Parish, where performed Divine Service.......
(514.) Two Children.
(515.) On Tuesday Octobr 3d At the House of Col. Richard Richardson in St Mark's Parish.......
Ezekiah.,Cantey. Son of the said Richard Richardson & N. his wife: born Sepr 28th 1758. Suret: Josiah Cantey, Miss N. Richardson, & Richard Richardson Jun.....
Eôdem Die et Locô:
near Amelia
(516.) Margaret, Daughter of John & Margaret McGowan: born 15th Septr 1758. Suret: George McNichols* & his wife & Katharine Flood......
(517.) On Sunday Octobr 8th In Amelia Chappel. Moses. Son of Jeremiah & Katherine Strother: born August 8th 1758= Suret: Jeremiah Strother, Swen & Elizabeth Themboro. ——— ——— ———

---

*The will of one George McNichols, recorded in the office of Judge of Probate, Charleston, is dated 1753, and is to be found on page 143, of the book for that period.

Eôdem Die et Locô:

(518.) Margaret, Daughter of Richard & Mary Baldridge; born August 31st 1758. Suret- - John Thomson, Sarah Thomson, & Elizabeth Vance.

(519.) Baptized..... In my House On Saturday Octobr 14th James, Son of Isham & Anne Clayton; born Septembr 5th 1758. Suret: Peter Faure, Lewis Netman & Mary Faure.....

(520.) On Sunday Octobr 15th. In Amelia Chappel. Rachel, Daughter of William & Jane Newton; born Septr 11th 1758. Suret: William McNichol, Elizabeth, wife of William Heatly, & Mary,,Anne, Wife of John Fouquet.....

(521.) On Sunday Octobr 22d In Orangeburgh Church Anne,,Katharine, Daughter of Nicholas & Susannah,,Elizabeth Zorn; born Septr 23d 1758. Suret= Henry Zorn, Eva,,Katharine Pfuntzius, widow, & Anna,,Maria,,Catharina, wife of Ulrick Roth..

(522.) On Saturday Novembr 4th At the House of John Aberly below Orangeburgh Township Anna,. Barbara, Daughter of John & Margaret Anding; born Septr 8th 1758. Suret= Frederick and Barbara Huber. & Barbara, wife of Peter Shoeman.

Eôdem Die et Locô:

(523.) Anna,,Barbara, Daughter of Peter & Barbara Shoeman; born in Decembr 1757. Suret: George Drechsler, Margaret, wife of John Anding, & Anne Aberly.

Eôdem Die et Locô:

(524.) Anna,,Margaret, Daughter of Peter and Katharine Dirr; born January 20th 1758.. Suret: Peter & Barbara Shoeman. & Margaret, wife of John Anding....

(525.) Baptized... In Amelia Chappel

ORANGEBURG COUNTY. 181

On Sunday Novembr 12th
Rachel, Daughter of William & Mary,,Elizabeth Heatly; born August 24th 1758. Surets Cole John Chevillette, Anne, wife of James Courtonne, & Rachel, wife of John Lloyd ....
Eôdem Die et Locô:
(526.) Jeremiah, Son of Randal & Rachel McCarthey; born Septembr 23d 1758. Surets Cornelius Thys, Garret & Agnesia Fitz Patrick.
Eôdem Die et Locô:
(527.) Rachel, Daughter of William & Rebecca Hickie; born Octobr 28th 1758.
Surets. Joseph Gant, Anne, wife of Robert Gossling, & Rachel wife of Randal McCarthey.....
(528.) On Monday Novembr 27th Administred private Baptis'm in my House to
John, Son of Jacob & Lovisa Horger; born Octobr 28th 1758. Present: John Myer, John Ott &c.
(529.) On Sunday Decembr 10th. In Amelia Chappel*
(530.) Eôdem Die et Locô:†
(531.) On Sunday Decembr 17th.
Baptized ..... In Orangeb,. Church
Jacob, Son of Martin & Margaret,,Barbara Kemler; born Novembr 1st 1758: Suret.. Jacob Morff,‡ Conrad Hungerbiller & Barbara Dentzler.....
(532.) On Sunday Decembr 24th In Orangeb,, Church Catharina,,Elizabeth, Daughter of Lewis and Mary,, Barbara Roth; born Decembr. 1758. Suret.. Lewis & Elizabeth Golsen, & Catharina, wife of Hans,,George Hessy.
(533.) On Sunday Decembr 31st In Orangeb,, Church--

---

*Rest left out. †Left blank.
‡The will of Jacob Morff, "of Saxe-Gotha" Township, is dated October, 1762, and is recorded in the office of Judge of Probate, Charleston, on page 220, of the book covering that year.

Susannah, Daughter of Daniel & Sarah— Linder; born Octob.r 30th 1758. Surets John Thomson, Elizabeth Tilly, Susannah Tilly.......
Eôdem Die et Locô:
(534.) Sarah, Daughter of Martin & Susañah Sally: born March 13th 1758. Surets Joseph Coutier Jun.. Mary Coutier & Anna Yonn..
Eôdem Die et Locô:
(535.) Mary, Daughter of Jno Herman & Elizabeth Crummy; born Febr. 2d 1753. Suret: Henry and Mary„Elizabeth Felder, & Martha. wife of Joseph Wood.
1759.
January 15th.
(536.) Charles, Son of Barnard & Martha Linsey: born Febr. 18th 1756. Suret: Thomas Farles, Frederick & Anna Hougs..
(537.) Baptized... January 15th
Elisha, Son of Frederick & Anna Hougs; born Septembr. 5th 1758. Suret. Barnard & Martha Lindsay. Thomas Farles...
Eôdem Die:
(538.) Benjamin & ⎫ both the Sons of Bartilot and
(539.) William   ⎭ Katherine Brown; Benjamin born January 27th 1756; William born Octobr. 5th 1757. Surets for both: Henry Rowe. William Dewidd &c.
(540.) On Sunday ...... In Orangeb., Church
——— Daughter of Jacob & Margaret Ott: born ——— 175— Surets*
(541.) On Wednesday Febr. 7th.. In Orangeb.. Church Christopher. Son of Henry & Anna Rowe: born January 20th 1759. Surets Andrew & Rachel Govan. John Giessendanner...

---

*None given.

ORANGEBURG COUNTY. 183

(542.) On Sunday Feb. 18th... In Orangeburgh Church
Elizabeth,,Barbara, Daughter of George and Catharina Waber; born January 21st 1759. Surets Nicholas & Barbara Waber, & Elizabeth Waber, widow..
Eôdem Die et Locô:
(543.) John,,Theodore, Son of George,,Frederick & Elizabeth Knobel; born Jan. 10th 1759. Surets Theodore Fichtner, Frederick Ulmer, & Anna,,Maria Hertzog...
(544.) On Sunday March 4th. In Orangeb,, Church Samuel, Son of James & Judith Nicks; born January 30th 1757. Surets Nathainiel & Mary—Watson, & Jacob Hottow.
(545.) Baptized..... In Orangeburgh Church On Sunday March 4th.
Jane, Daughter of Nathaniel & Mary Watson; born Octobr 9th 1758. Surets Frederick Huber, Jacob Hottow, & Margaret, wife of Sam! Densmore.
(546.) On Sunday March 11th. In Amelia Chappel.
James, Son of Samuel & Mary Carney; born April 5th 1758. Surets Arthur Carney, Moses Thomson |: Taylor | & Mary.,Ann, wife of Conrad Halman.
(547.) On Tuesday March 13th Administred private Baptis'm at the House of Jacob Stroman in Orangeburgh Township to
Anna,,Margaret, Daughter of the said Jacob & Eva,,. Catharina Stroman; born Novembr 3d 1758. Present: John Shaumloffel &c.....
(548.) On Sunday March 25th In Orangeb,, Church John,,Lewis, Son of Lewis & Elizabeth Golsan; born February 9th 1759. Surets John and Barbara Giessendanner. John Harrisperger...
Eôdem Die et Locô:
(549.) Hans,,Jacob, Son of John,,Caspar & Anna,,

Barbara Mintz; born March 12th 1759. Surets John
& Elizabeth Giegelman & Jacob Giegelman.
(550.) On Sunday April 1st. In Orangeb,, Church.
Lewis, Son of Lewis & Frances Patrick; born Septr
17th 1758. Surets John Clayton. Henry Zorn, & Anna, wife of Joseph Deramas...
Eôdem Die et Locô:
(551.) John, Son of William Pendarvis. & Catharina,
wife of Thomas Puckridge; born Febr 22d 1759. Surets Joseph Deramas, Jacob Fund, & Mary, wife of
Abraham Yssenhoot.......
(552.) Baptized.... In Amelia Chappel
On Sunday April 8th.
Anna, Daughter of William & Deborah Sabb; born
February 2d 1759. Surets William & Mary,,Elizabeth Heatly; & Anna Jones.....
Eôdem Die et Locô:
(553.) William, Son of Thomas & Mary Eberhardt;
born January 29th 1759. Surets. William & Rebecca
Mitchel &c..........
(554.) On Easter,,Day, April 15th. In Orangeb,.
Church Hans,,George, Son of Francis & Mary Koonen:
born March 21st. 1759. Surets 'George Balziger. Jacob Rumph, Catharine. wife of Jacob Koonen.
Eôdem Die et Locô:
(555.) Eva,,Catharina. Daughter of Adam & Anna..
Barbara Rupp; born January 3d 1759. Surets. Martin Zimerman, Eva,,Catharina. wife of George Hayner,
& Eva,. Elizabeth Hertzog.......
Eôdem Die et Locô:
(556.) Lucretia, Daughter of Joseph & Sarah Clemmons; born May 1st 1758. Surets Henry Sally Jun.
.. Christina, wife of Nicholas Youn, & N. wife of
Henry Sally Sen.
Eôdem Die et Locô:

(557.) ———————— Daughter of Joseph & Mary Coutier; born*
(558.) On Sunday April 22ᵈ In Orangeb,, Church Peter, Son of Henry & Mary,,Elizabeth Felder; born April 2ᵈ 1759. Suretˢ John & Barbara Giessendañer, Jacob Giessendañer.
(559.) Baptized.... In Orangeb,, Church On Sunday May 6ᵗʰ. Rebecca, Daughter of James and Frances—Grant; born April 6ᵗʰ 1759. Suretˢ John & Barbara Giessendanner, & Barbara, wife of John Jennings.
(560.) On Sunday May 13ᵗʰ. In Amelia Chappel Jane, Daughter of Thomas & Jane Platt; born March 3ᵈ 1759. Suretˢ Moses and Jane Thomson, & Moses Thomson Junior.....
Eôdem Die et Locô:
(561.) David, Son of John† & Sophinisba MᶜCord; born March 12ᵗʰ 1759. Suretˢ William Thomson, John Russell, & Rachel, wife of John Lloyd.....
(562.) On Sunday May 20ᵗʰ In Orangeb.. Church Hans,,Paul. Son of John,,Martin and Anna,,Margaret Hossleiter; born April 7ᵗʰ 1759. Suretˢ Francis & Mary Koonen, & Kilian Grissert....
(563.) On Sunday May 27ᵗʰ In Orangeb,, Church Agnes, Daughter of Henry & Esther Volckart; born May 18ᵗʰ 1759. Suretˢ Frederick Huber, Agnes Huber, & Verena, wife of Henry Würtzer.....
(564.) On Friday June 1ˢᵗ Administred private Baptism at the House of Jacob Herlan in Orangeburgh Township to a Sick Infant, viz: Johannes, Son

---

*Rest left out.
†The *S. C. Gazette*, of Monday, August 29, 1768, contains the following advertisement of Sophonisba McCord, Administratrix, and Charles McCord, Administrator: "To be sold, at public Auction, on Monday, the 12th day of September next (if a fair day) if not the next fair day following: All the personal estate of Capt. John McCord, late of St. Mark's Parish, deceased," &c.

of the said Jacob & Mary,,Susannah Herlan; born May 20th 1759. Present: Anna Koller. NB: This Child recover'd, and was receiv'd according to the Order of the Church on Sunday July 22d 1759. Surets Nicholas Yonn, John Stehely, Anna Koller.

(565.) Baptized... In Orangeburgh Church On Whit Sunday June 3d
Daniel, Son of John,,Nicholas & Verena Shuler; born April 25th 1759. Surets Daniel Shuler, John & Margaret Myer....

(566.) On Monday June 4th Administred private Baptis'm in my House to
Frederick, Son of Peter & Magdalene Murer; born April 5th 1759. Present: John & Ulrick Oth...

(567.) On Monday June 4th In Orangeb,, Church Thomas, Son of Henry & Anne Young; born April 13th 1759. Surets Gavin Pou, John,,Lewis Wolf, & Elizabeth Tilly........

Eôdem Die et Locô:
(568.) Rachel, Daughter of John Crummy deceas'd and Elizabeth, his late wife; born March 2d 1757... Surets Henry & Magdalene Crummy, & Margaret, wife of Joseph Griffith......

(569.) On Sunday June 10th. In Amelia Chappel Mary, Daughter of William & Frances Flood; born March 33d 1759. Surets James Flood, Catharine Flood & Mary Hammelton....

Eôdem Die et Locô:
(570.) Mary,,Elizabeth, Daughter of Alexander and Anne Boy; born April 28th 1759. Surets John Foust. Anna,,Margaret Dentzler, & Anna Smith.

(571.) On Sunday July 1st In Orangeb,, Church Catharina, Daughter of Joseph & Margaret Cooper: born May 17th 1759. Surets William Pou, Margaret, wife of Gavin Pou. & Barbara, wife of John Jennings.

ORANGEBURG COUNTY.

(584.)* Baptized..... In Orangeburgh Church On Sunday August 19th.

Elijah, Son of John Crummy deceas'd, & and Elizabeth, his late wife; born March 5th 1755. Surets Henry Crummy, Peter Sandel & Mary Inabnet——

(585.) On Sunday August 26th In Orangeb,, Church Mary,,Elizabeth, Daughter of Caspar & Mary Oth; born August 4th 1759. Surets John Oth, Mary,,Elizabeth Stroman, & Mary, Wife of Francis Koonen.

(586.) On Thursday Septembr 13th In Orangeb,, Church James, a Bastard,,Child of Elizabeth Crossby; born May 28th 1759. Surets Peter Faure, Isham & Anna Clayton.

(587.) On Sunday Octobr 21st. In Orangeb,, Church Joseph, Son of George Hessy and Catharina, his wife; born August 24th 1759. Surets. Joseph Deramas, Jacob Weimer, & Verena, wife of Nicholas Shuler.

Eôdem Die et Locô:

(588.) Anna, Daughter of John & Barbara Giessendanner; born Monday Septembr 10th 1759. Surets Christopher Rowe, Rachel, wife of Andrew Govan, and Barbara, wife of John Jennings: Born between 9 & 10 o'clock.

Eôdem Die et Locô:

(589.) Anna, Daughter of Ulrick & Margaret Stereky born Septr 12th 1759. Surets John Stereky, Anna Koller, and Catharina, wife of Jacob Koonen.........

Eôdem Die et Locô:

(590.) Regina, Daughter of Jacob & Apollonia Wolf; born Septr 6th 1759. Surets. Frederick Huber, &c.

(591.) Baptized ... In Orangeburgh Church. On Sunday Novembr 18th.

John.,Frederick, Son of Henry & Juliaña Snell; born

---

*From 572 to 583, inclusive, lost.

Septr 23^d 1759. Suret^s. Frederick Hoff, Philip Wagner & Mary Duboy..........

Eôdem Die et Locô:

(592.) Jacob, Son of Adam & Anne,,Margaret Snell; born Septr 21st 1759. Suret^s Peter Murer, Ulrick & Anne,,Mary=Catharina Roth....

Eôdem Die et Locô:

(593.) Catharina,,Margaret, Daughter of John,,Peter & Magdalene Sondel; born Septr 28th 1759. Suret^s. Ulrick & Anne,,Mary,,Catharina Roth, & Maria, wife of Andrew Frederick.

(594.) On Sunday Novemb^r 25th In Orangeb,, Church Anna,,Margaret, Daughter of Jacob and Christina,, Barbara Hungerbiller; born August 26th 1759. Suret^s Caspar & Anna,, Maria Kuhn, and Margaret, wife of Joseph Huber.

(595.) On Sunday Decemb^r 16th In Orangeb,, Church David, Son of Jacob & Anna Rumph; born Novemb^r 10th. 1759. Suret^s Henry Felder, Francis Koonen, & Catharina. wife of Jacob Koonen....

(596.) On Christmas,,Day Decemb^r 25th. In Orangeb,, Church Susannah, Daughter of George & Susañah,,Barbara Ulrick; born Novemb^r 27th 1759. Suret^s. John & and Barbara Giessendanner, & Ursula Leysath —

(597.) Baptized.... In Orangeb,, Church.

On Christmas,,Day Decemb^r 25th

Eva,,Catharina, Daughter of Bernhard and Anne,, Mary Ziegler; born —————— 1759, Suret^s*

(598.) On Wednesday Decemb^r 26th. In Orangeb,, Church Joseph, Son of Thomas & Hannah Pendarvis; born Septemb^r 3^d 1759. Suret^s. Philip Jennings, Brand Pendarvis, & Mary, wife of Henry Jordan — —

1760.

January 1st.. In Orangeburgh Church

---
*None given.

(599.) Susannah, Daughter of John & Eva.,Catharina Jubb; born May 24th 1759. Surets Conrad Kryter, Susañah Kryter, widow, & Apollonia, wife of Jacob Wolf.

(600.) Sunday January 6th In Orangeb,, Church Jane, Daughter of John & Sarah Clayton; born Novembr 19th 1759. Surets Henry Felder, Mary Faure, & Catharine Simons........

(601.) Eôdem Die et Locô: Margaret, a Bastard,,Child of Margaret, Daughter of Hans Imboden; born Decembr 28th 1759. Surets Nicholas & Christina Yonn, & Margaret Snyder.

(602.) On Sunday Febr 3d In Orangeburgh Church. Rebeccah. Daughter of Joseph & Barbara Dukes; born Septr 12th 1759. Surets Henry Felder, Hannah, wife of Jonathan Johnson, & Mary, Wife of Jacob Fund.

(603.) On Saturday Febr 2d At the House of Benedict Koller John,,Ulrick, Son of Benedict & Magdalene Koller born Jan. 30th 1760. Surets Revd John Giessendanner, &c.

(604.) Baptized / Sunday Febr 10th In Orangeburgh Church John,,Jacob, Son of Jno Henry & Ann,,Margaret Shilling; born January 5th 1760. Suretss.. Charles & Jacob Hottow, & Zibilla,,Catharina, wife of Martin Egly.

On Monday Febr 11th. Administred private Baptis'm

(605.) To Reuben ⎫ the three Children of Reuben
(606.) Mary ⎬ and Elizabeth Roberts; Reuben
(607.) Solomon ⎭ born Octobr 14th 1756. Mary born January 4th. 1758. Solomon born 23d January 1760...

Eôdem Die... Administred private Baptism

(608.) To Henry and ⎧ both the Sons of James &
(609.) William ⎨ Mary Scytes; Henry born Febr 15th 1757. William born Decembr 10th 1758.

(610.) Eodem Die... Administred private Baptis'm to Archibald, Son of Charles & Lucy Scytes; born January 1st 1760........

(611.) On Wednesday Febr 13th Administred private Baptis'm in Capt Rowe's Fort to
Elizabeth, Daughter of Henry & Anna,,Catharina Horger; born Decembr 25th 1759. Present: Peter Roth, Henry Rickenbacker.........

(612.) On Sunday Febr 17th In Orangeburgh Church Daniel, Son of Conrad & Magdalene Yutzy; born Novembr 8th 1759. Surets Daniel Shuler & Mary.. Barbara, his wife, & George Hertzog.......

(613.) On Sunday Febr 24th In Orangeb,, Church Anna, Daughter of Jacob & Dorothy Tshudy; born Febr 17th 1760. Surets Simon Yonn, Margaret, wife of Jacob Hottow, & Anna, wife of Charles Hottow.

Tuesday Febr 26th Administred private Baptis'm to

(614.) Peter and ⎫ Sons of George & Mary Cornwell:
(615.) Billander ⎭ Peter born July 11th 1757. Billander born January 24th 1759.

(616.) On Saturday March 8th at John Oth's Fort Jacob, Son of Ulrick & Eve.,Mary Brunner; born ———— 1760. Surets Lewis Golsen, John Stehely. for Jacob Rumph. & Barbara, wife of John Giessendañer

(617.) Eôdem Die et Locô: Administred private Baptism to
Jacob, Son of Jacob & Anne.,Margaret Giegelman: born Febr 23d 1760. Present: John Giegelman &c.

———————

(618.) On Sunday March 2d In Orangeb.. Church James, Son of John & Barbara Platt: born Febr 26th 1760. Surets Samuel Suther. Henry Rickenbacker, & Anna. wife of Jacob Bussart.

(619.) On Sunday March 9th In Amelia Chappel

ORANGEBURG COUNTY. 191

Thomas, Son of Thomas & Elizabeth Cryer; born Septr. 11th. 1759. Suret^s Thomas & Anne Powel. and Agnes Joyner.....

Eôdem Die et Locô:

(620.) Deborah, Daughter of Thomas & Anne Powel; born Jan^r 17th 1760. Suret^s. Thomas & Elizabeth Cryer & John Powel.....

(621.) On Monday March 24th In Orangeb., Church Josiah, Son of William and Rebeccah Cantey, of St Mark's Parish; born Jan^r 20th 1760. Suret^s. William Sims, James & Elizabeth Brunson.........

(622.) Baptized... In Amelia Chappel On Sunday April 13th .....
William, Son of Edward & Elizabeth Guphill; born Novr 1st 1759. Suret^s. John and Joseph Collins and Ann Guphill.....

Eôdem Die et Locô:

(623.) Catharine, Daughter of Willm & Catharine Strother; born Feb^r 28th 1760. Suret^s. John Davis, Dorcas Milner and Elizabeth Dargan......

(624.) On Thursday April 17th In John & Ulrick Oths Fort
Elizabeth, Daughter of Ulrick & Barbara Oth; born April 9th 1760. Suret^s. John Oth, Barbara, wife of John Giessendañer, & Elizabeth Giessendanner.

(625.) On Sunday April 20th In Orangeburgh Church Johannes, Son of Jacob & Anna Wideman; born March 1st 1760. Suret^s John and Barbara Giessendanner and Peter Murer........

(626.) Eôdem Die et Locô: Administred private Baptism to Elizabeth. Daughter of Samuel & Elizabeth Suther; born April 5th 1760. Present: Frederick Huber.

(627.) On Sunday May 18.th In Orangeburgh Church Ulrick, Son of Charles & Anna Hottow; born May 7th

1760. Surets. William Wañenmacker, Christian and Elizabeth Roth..........

Eôdem Die et Locô:

(628.) Anna, Daughter of Jacob and Anna Wannenmacher; born March 5th 1760. Surets Jacob Bowman, Anna, wife of Charles Hottow, and Anna, wife of Joseph Deramas....

(629.) Baptized... In Orangeb,, Church On Whit,,Sunday May 25th.

Anna, Daughter of Henry and Apollonia, Dentzler; born April 15th 1760. Surets Ulrick Bruñer, Margaret, wife of Jacob Ott, & Margaret, wife of John Myer....

(630.) On Sunday June 8th. In Amelia Chappel Helena, Daughter of Garret and Agnesia Fitz,,Patrick: born*

(631.) On Tuesday June 10th Administred privat Baptis'm in my House to John,,Jacob, Son of John and Charlotte Roberts; born May 23d 1760.†

(632.) On Sunday June 15th In Orangeb,, Church Maria,,Barbara, Daughter of Hans,,George and Catharina Waber; born May 23d 1760. Surets Conrad Baumgartner, Anna,,Maria, Wife of Barnard‡ and Barbara, wife of Nicholas Waber.

(633.) On Sunday June 29th **
 John, Son of John and ††
—————— 1760. Surets ‡‡

(634.) On Sunday August 10th Baptized in Amelia Chappel Jane,,Margaret, Daughter of Thomas and Isabel Murray; born May 13th 1760. Surets Moses Thomson Esqr Sarah Thomson, and Elizabeth wife of Robert Twiddie.

(635.) On Sunday August 17th. In Orangeb,. Church Anna,,Margaret, Daughter of Martin and Mar-

---
*Rest left out. †Rest left out. ‡Name torn off. **Other words torn off. ††Other name torn off. ‡‡Rest gone.

ORANGEBURG COUNTY. 193

garet„Barbara Kemler; born July 4th 1760—Surets Barnard Ziegler. Appollonia, wife of Henry Dentzler, and Anna„Margaret Myer......

(636.) On Sunday Septembr 7th. In Orangeb„ Church Isham, Son of Isham* and Anne Clayton; born May 10th. 1760. Surets Henry Felder, Tobias and Mary Hertzog........
Eôdem Die et Locô:

(637.) Anne, Daughter of Henry and Magdalene Crummy; born April 15th 1760. Surets Henry Zorn, Sarah Crummy and Catharine Simmons......

(638.) On Sunday Septembr 14th. In Amelia Chappel Andrew. Son of William and Mary„Elizabeth Heatly; born August 14th 1760. Surets Jerome Courtonne. Willm Sabb, and Rachel, wife of John Lloyd.
Eôdem Die et Locô:

(639.) William, Son of Samuel & Mary Carney; born Decr 22d 1759. Surets John Mitchel, John Johnson, Mary Fitz Patrick.

(640.) †and Agnes Jackson; born‡
On Easter day April 7 1751 Baptized in Orangeburgh Church Maria, Daughter of Richard & Elizabeth Hainsworth Born Feby 17 Last. Spon Michael Christopher Row, Margaret His wife, Christiana wife wife of Jacob Morff.**

Here the record of births kept by Rev. John Giessendanner ends, as the few remaining records made by him have been lost from the book. The following records were made by subsequent custodians of the book:

---

*The *Gazette of the State of South Carolina*, in February, 1778, announced the death of Isham Clayton at Orangeburgh.
†First name torn off. ‡Rest torn off. **"Omitted in the regular account of Children Baptized."—Mr. Lucas's copy.

"Elizabeth Giessendanner the Daughter of Henry & Elizabeth Gissendanner Born July the 10- 1783."

"Elizabeth Giessendanner the Daughter of Daniel Giessendanner and Ann Giessendanner born December 21, 1791. Henry"

The following is the burial record kept by Mr. Giessendanner after his return from England:

A List of Persons deceased and buried in the Township of Orangeburgh Per J Giessendanner Minister of the Township—
1749—50

(1.) On Sunday the 25th of Februy was entered and buried in the Church yard at Orangeburgh the Body of Dorothy Moorer wife of Peter Moorer Junr. She died the day before after a Fortnights Illness Aged —

(2.) On Thursday April the 19th Eodem Locô was entered and Buried the Body of Anna Magdalena, Daughter of Ulrick and Anna,,Angelia Raber: She died after ten Days Illness: Aged 2 year. 7½ months.

(3.) On Tuesday Augst 14th Eodem Loco was entered and buried the Body of one who went by the name of William Little, or William Little Williams. He died at Mr. Joseph Robinsons Aged about 70 years.

(4.) On Sunday September 9th eodem Locô was entered and buried the Body of Jacob Stauber, a native of Canton Zürich in Switzerland Inhabitant of Orangeburgh for about 7 months, who died after 9 dys Illness on Saturday Sept 8th a. c. (aged 44 years Left A Wife)

A List of Persons deceased and buried

(5.) On Saturday November 10th 1750 was enterred & buried in the Church yard of Orangeburgh at a numerous Attendance of People the Body of Peter Hugg, one of the first and principal settlers of this Township where he had been a Liver with his Family these 15 years past. He was born in Switzerland Canton Bern, September n. s. 26th 1696 and dyed on Thursday night November 8th 1750 much lamented by his wife and children, and all that knew him.

(6.) On Monday Novembr 26th eodem Locô was entered and buried the Body of John Niclaus Hessy son of Hans George & Catherine Hessy of this Township He dyed the day before after two months Illness Aged 19 months

(7.) On Friday Novembr 30th was unfortunately drowned in Santee River Swamp whether he was gone hunting after Cattle in Company with Several others and afterwards was buried in the woods the Body of ———————— Andrew Inabnet Aged about 27 years, a Liver in this Township. His unfortunate death being a deplorable loss to his wife and 3 small children.

(8.) On Monday Decembr 3d was entered and buried the Body of an Infant baptized the Day before named Hans George son of John & Susannah Fridig He dyed the night before and was buried in his Father's Plantation Aged 4 Days.

A List of Persons deceased and buryed

(9.) On Wednesday January 2d 1750/1.

Was entered in the Church yard of Orangeburgh the Body of Ann Barbara wife of Caspar Kuhn of this Township. She dyed after one Days Illness on Monday night Decembr 31st Aged ————

(10.) On Thursday March 7th was entered (at the Plantation of the Father of the deceased) the Body of Hans Jacob son of Henry & Catherina Strowmann of this Township Aged 2 years and about 6 months.

(11.) On Saturday March 30th was entered in the church yard of Orangeburgh the Body of Gideon Jennings an old Protestant Italian Liver in this Township these 14 years past. who died the day before, his Age unknown.

(12.) On Monday August 12th was enterred in the Church yard of Orangeburgh the Body of Anne Roth, wife of Peter Roth, Miller and Carpenter: She was born in Switzerland June 4th 1722, n. s. and died the day before her Burial having been confined to her bed since her Delivery for the space of nine weeks. Ætat: 29 years and some weeks— 1751.

(13) On Thursday Augst the 29th was enterred the Body of George Giessendanner Junr. who was born in Switzerland 17 July n. s. 1723 and dyed on Tuesday night August 27th 1751. After 11 Days confinement in Bed and a consumptive lingering Ailment of several years Aged 28 years and some weeks, ———

(14.) On Monday Octobr 28th was enterred the Body of Anna wife of John Wolf, A Liver in Orangebr. Town.

(15.) On Friday January 3d 1752 was enterred at the Plantation of Capt. James Tilly the Body of Daughter of the sd James Tilly and Margaret his wife; She was born Octobr 3d 1737. and died on Thursday January 2d 1752. After 3 days Illness—Aged 14 years and 3 months.
1752

(16:) On Tuesday January 28th was entered in the Church yard of Orangeburgh the Body of Hugh McCoy= He was unfortunately kickt of his Horse on Sunday evening Jan 26th as he was mounting the same, of which after much Anguish and Pain he died on Munday night Janr 27th.

(17.) On Thursday Feb. 20th was enterred the Body of Maria Daughter of Christopher & Margaret Row after some weeks Illness: Aged 3 Mo. 29 days—

(18.) On Sunday May 24th 1752 was enterred in the Church yard of Orangeburgh the Body of Regina. wife of Jacob Kuhnen Senr. a native of Switzerland and settled in this Township in the year 1736. She dyed after a lingering Illness of one month in the 74th year of her age, and had lived with her above named Husband in wedlock 52 years

(19.) On Munday August 17th was buryed the Body of Isaac Hottow, a Settler in this Township for several years past, who died suddenly on Saturday August 15th on the edge of the Path as he was going home and was found and taken up dead between. his Home and the Town of Orangeburgh, no mark of any Fall or violence done him could be seen on his Body. He left a wife and 7 children. four of which are marryed. He was aged 57 years and buryed at his own Plantation.

(20.) At the Same Time and Place, and into the same Grave was enterred the Grand child of the said Isaac Hottow named Susannah Daughter of Charles & Ann Hottow, who died on Monday August 17th in the morning after a Fortnights Illness. aged one year—

21 { On Wednesday Septr 27th was buryed at the Plantation of the late Isaac Hottow de'cd the Body of Catharine Daughter of Peter and Ann Griffice of this Township. She died the Day before being Septr 26 after two days Illness aged 3 years and about 9 months.

1753

Register of Buryals in Orangeburgh Township J. G.

(22.) On Thursday March 29th 1753 was buryed at the Plantation of Joseph Kryter the Body of Daughter of said Joseph Kryter and Sarah his wife: She dyed of a cough Ætat.

(23) On Sunday July 15th was enterred in the Church yard of Orangeburgh the Body of Margaret daughter of Michael & Regula Larry; She died after a lingering Illness of nigh a Twelvemonth atat 3 years 3 months—

(24) On Monday Septr 24th was enterred in the Church yard of Orangeburgh the Body of*

(25) On Saturday Octob^r 27th 1753 was enterred in the Church yard of Orangeburgh the Body of William son of Joseph & Margaret Grieffous died Octob^r 26th Atat 1 year 24 Days

(26) On Monday Decemb^r 17th 1753 was enterred at the Plantation of Henry Starcky the Body of Ann daughter of the said Hy & Elizabeth Starcky died Octb^r 16th Atat 18 days.

(27) On Wednesday Jany 2^d 1754 was enterred at the Plantation whereon Joseph Kock now lives the Body of– Hans Heinrich, Son of the said Joseph & Ann Kock died Decemb^r 31. 1753. Atat 3 years 3 weeks.

Register of Buryings ——— Orangeburgh Township.
1754.

(28) On Saturday January 5th died and on Sunday Jany 6th was enterred at the Plantation of Mrs. Mary Russel in Amelia Township, the Body of the said Mary Russel, who lived in the s^d Township nigh 26 years, and died aged about 55 years—after 4 Days Illness — — — — — — — — —

(29) On Monday Febry 4th died and the following day was enterred in the church yard of Orangeburgh the Body of John Ulrick son of Peter Roth & Ann his late wife deceas'd who died after a lingering Illness of some months; aged 2 years & upwards of 7 months.

(30) On Monday March 11th was enterred at the Plantation of Wm Barrie the Body of s^d. Wm Barrie, a native from Scotland but a Liver in Orangeburgh Township for many years. He dyed after a lingering Illness of several months on Sunday March 10 Ætat=

(31) On Wednesday July 10th died & the day follow-

---

*Name not given.

ing was enterred at the Plantation whereon Jacob Bossart then lived. the Body of Ann wife of the said Jacob Bossart some Time agoe arrived from Switzerland, in this Province She died after three weeks Illness aged nigh 60 years.

(32) On Saturday August 3d died after three weeks Illness and on Sunday August 4th was enterred at the Plantation of John Friday Jur the Body of Zibella daughter of Barnard & Ann=Mary Ziegler, aged 7 months 3 weeks

The remainder of the burial record which now follows was not copied from the original, but from a copy of the original, made by the late Mr. John Lucas, Warden of the Church of the Redeemer in Orangeburg. His copying was not as precise as to details as the foregoing, but is correct as to the substance of the entries:

Page 8.

Register o Buryings Orangeburgh Town ship 1754

No. 33 On Saturday Octo 19 died and on Sunday Octo 20 was Enterred at the Plantation of Henry Stroman the Body of Catharina Barbara, Daughter of Stephen & Mary ann Whitman aged 8½ months.

34 On Friday Novm 29 died / having unfortunately and as was generally judged by an unhappy accident shot himself whilst he thought to fire at deer—David Runtgenauer a Foreigner from Germany, and late servant of Capt James Tilly and was Enterred at the plantation of Christopher Monheim on Saturday Nov 30 aged unknown

35 On Thursday Decr 12th died of a lingering Illness, attended with apoplectick Fits and on Friday Decmr 13 was Enterred at the Plantation of John George Barr in Orangeburgh Towuship the body of

the said John George Barr a native of Germany aged 48 years 2½ months

36 On Saturday Dec$\underline{m}$ 21th died after having been afflicted with a tedious Illness of almost 84 years, and on Sunday Decr 22$\underline{d}$ was Enterred in the Church Yard of Orangeburgh the Body of Christian Huber, son of Hans Huber of Orangeburgh Township aged 30 years &

1755

37 On monday March 24th died after 14 days Illness and on wednesday March 26. 1755 was Enterred in the Church yard of Orangeburgh the Body of Susannah Daughter of John and Barbara Giessendanner aged 2 years 5 months

38 On Thursday Augt 21th died after four weeks Illness and on Friday august 22 was Enterred in the Church Yard of Orangeburgh the Body of Mary Elizabeth, daughter of John and Susannah Fridig of Orangeburgh Township aged 6 years and 5 months.

Register of Buryings. Orangeburgh Township
———— Page 9. ————

1755.

N$\underline{o}$ 39 On Tuesday August 26th died after some months Illness and on Wednesday August 27 was Enterred in the Church Yard of Orangeburgh The body of Ann Margaret daughter of Elias and Mary Catharine Snell of Orangeburgh Township Aged about 26 years—

40 On Thursday Augt 28. died after a tedious and most painful Disorder of Nigh Seven years and on Friday August 29th was Enterred at the plantation of Henry Rickenbacker in Orangeburgh Township the body of Catharine Dill a maid aged about 26 years.

41 On Thursday Oct$\underline{o}$ 23^d died after a long disorder and a few days confinement in Bed and on Friday

Oct⁰ 24 was Enterred at the Plantation of Melchior Ott, a native of Switzerland who settled in the said Township in the year 1735 aged about 57 years

1756

42 On monday Jany 19th died after a long disorder and one days confinement in Bed and on Wednesday Jany 21st was Enterred at the plantation of John Spring in Orangeburgh Township The Body of Margaret wife of the said John Spring aged about 73 years.

43 On Saturday morning January 31st died after Thirteen days Illness and on Sunday Feby 1 was Enterred in the Church Yard of Orangeburgh the Body of Barbara wife of Henry Snell—Senior of Orangeburgh Township aged about 72 years

Register of Buryings Orangeburgh Township

—— Page 10 ——

1756

44 On Sunday Feby 8th died of a painful disorder and on Monday Feby 9th was Enterred at the Plantation of Joseph Robinson in Orangeburgh Township the body of Anne, wife of the said Joseph Robinson aged about.

45 On Wednesday April 14th died after one months Illness and on Thursday April 15th was enterred in the Church Yard of Orangeburgh the body of Jacob Kuhnen senior a native of Switzerland who settled in Orangeburgh Township in the year 1736 aged about 83 years

46 On Thursday June 17th died after a lingering Illness of nigh a Twelve month and on Friday June 18th was Enterred in the Church Yard of Orangeburgh the Body of Abraham Son of Jacob and Anne Rumph aged one year 8 months & 20 days

47 On Sunday July 4th died after some months Illness and on Monday July 5 was Enterred in the

Church Yard of Orangeburgh the Body of John Balziger—Senior—of the said Township of Orangeburgh—Anno atat 59 years 9 months & 9 days

48 On Wednesday Sept 8th died after Eight days Illness and on Thursday Sept 9th was Enterred in my absence at the plantation of Martin Kooner in Orangeburgh Township the Body of Hans Jacob, son of Jacob and Catharina Kooner of the Township aforesaid aged 4 years wanting 22 days

49 On Friday Sept 17th died and on Saturday Sept 18th was Enterred in the Church Yard of Orangeburgh the Body of Ursula, widow of Gideon Zanini |alias| Jennings late of Orangeburgh Deceased aged Sixty seven Years.

Page 11
1756

50 On Monday Sept 19th died and on Tuesday Sept 20th was Enterred in the Church yard of Orangeburgh the Body of Lewis son of Luke and Mary Patrick of Orangeburgh aged 16 months 18 days

51 On Sunday Sept 26 died and on Monday Sept 27 was Enterred at the Plantation whereon the deceased then lived the Body of Seth Hatcher of Edisto Fork a native of Virginia aged about 70 years

52 On Tuesday Octo 5th died of the bloody Flux and on Wednesday Octo 6th was Enterred at the Plantation of John Harrisperger in Orangeburgh the Body of Nicholas Dirr of said Township aged 35 years a Carpenter & Millwright.

53 On Monday Octo 11th died of the Bloody Flux

54 Peter and on Tuesday Octo 12 died of the Same disorder Jacob both the sons of Johannes and Elizabeth Wolf of Orangeburgh who were both Enterred in the plantation of the said Johannes Wolf on Wednesday Octo 13th Peter aged 5 years & 1 month 13 days. Jacob aged 2 years 3 months and 22 days.

55 On Tuesday Oct⁰ 12 died of the Bloody flux and on Wednesday Oct⁰ 13 was Enterred at the Plantation of Francis Kooner in Orangeburgh the Body of Jacob son of the said Francis and Mary Kooner aged two years wanting 15 days

56 On Friday Oct⁰ 15th died and on Saturday Oct⁰ 16 was Enterred on the plantation of John Martin Hossleiter of Orangeburgh Township the Body of Hans Emanuel son of the said John Martin and Anne Margaret Hossleiter aged 2 years 7 months

Register of Buryings Orangeburgh Township 1756.

57 On Saturday Oct⁰ 16 died and on Sunday Oct⁰ 17 was Enterred at the plantation of Jacob Herlan in Orangeburgh Township the body of Mary Catharina Daughter of the said Jacob & Mary Susannah Herlan aged 11 years wanting 2 months

58 On Friday Evening Dec^m 3^d died after Ten weeks Confinement in Bed and on Sunday Decr 5th was Enterred in the Church yard of Orangeburgh the Body of Magdalene late widow of Peter Hugg of Orangeburgh deceased aged 59 years wanting 22 days.

59 On Sunday night Dec^m 26 1756 died & on monday Dec^m 27 was Enterred at the Plantation of Peter Roth in Orangeburgh the Body of an Infant named Anne Margaret, daughter of Jacob & Anne Wymer aged 6 days

1757

60 On Saturday Jany 8th died & on Monday Jany 10th was Enterred in the Church yard of Orangeburgh the Body of Elizabeth, widow of Henry Hessy deceased aged almost 79 years--

61 On Sunday Jany 16 died & on monday Jany 17 was enterred in the Plantation whereon Henry Sterckey lives in Orangeburgh Township the Body of

Elizabeth wife to the said Henry Sterckey aged 3— years

62 On Friday morning Feby 4th died & on Saturday Evening Feby 6th was Enterred at the plantation of William Howell the Body of the said William Howell a settler for many years over Santee or Congaree River in Craven County aged ——

Register of Buryings Orangeburgh Township
1757

63 On Tuesday night March 15th died in child Bed and on Thursday March 17th was Enterred in the Church yard of Orangeburgh the Body of Margaret wife of Adam Snell aged about 26 years

64 On Wednesday April 27th died of a lingering Illness Illness and on Thursday April 28th was enterred in the plantation of Jacob Strowman of Orangeburgh Township the Body of Margaret wife of the said Jacob Strowman aged 36 years & 3 days

65 On Wednesday June 8th died & on Thursday June 9th was Enterred in the Church Yard of Orangeburgh the Body of William, son of John & Phibbie Mitchel, lately come from the Northward aged 20. mo.

(66) On Wednesday August 31st died after nine days Illness and on Thursday Septr 1st was entered in the church yard of Orangeburgh the Body of Magdalena wife of Hans Imdorff of Orangeburgh a native of Switzerland aged about 70 years

(67) On Saturday Novm 19th died & on Tuesday Nov 22 was Enterred in the church yard of Orangeburgh the Body of Susannah wife of Hans Huber of Orangeburgh aged about seventy years.

(68) On Sunday Novr 27th died in child Bed & on Monday Novr 28 was Enterred on the plantation of Abraham Dupuis in Orangeburgh the Body of Susan-

nah wife of the said Abraham Dupuis aged 37 Years, 9 mo.

(69) On Thursday Dec<u>r</u> 1<u>st</u> was Enterred in the church yard of Orangeburgh the Body of Evan Reece a settler on the North side of Congree River who died at the house of Luke Patrick in Orangeburgh on Tuesday Nov<u>r</u> 30<u>th</u> then being on his Journey to Georgia

Register of Buryings   Orangeburgh Township 1758.

(70) On Tuesday Jany 13 1758 died of a lingering Illness and on Sunday January 15<u>th</u> was Enterred in the Church yard of Orangeburgh the Body of Elizabeth wife of Joseph Huber of the said Township aged about 29 years

(71) On Thursday night Feby 22 died and on Saturday Feby. 4 was Enterred in the plantation of Martin Koonen in Orangeburgh Township the Body of Barbara wife of the said Martin Koonen aged about 67 years—

(72) On Thursday March 9<u>th</u> died and on Saturday March 11 was Enterred on the plantation of Melchior Otte of Orangeburgh Township the Body of the said Melchior Otte a native of Switzerland aged about 60 years.

(73) On Saturday night March 11<u>th</u> died of a pleurisy and on Monday March 13<u>th</u> was Enterred on the plantation of John Harrisperger in Orangeburgh the Body of his brother Rudolph Harrisperger aged 27½ years.

(74) On Tuesday March 14<u>th</u> died and on Wednesday the 15<u>th</u> was Enterred in the church yard of Orangeburgh the Body of Anna Negely widow a native of Switzerland aged

(75) On Friday morning March 17<u>th</u> died in child Bed, and on Saturday March 18<u>th</u> was Enterred in the

Church yard of Orangeburgh the body of Barbara wife of the Revd John Giessendanner aged 33 years 3½ months

(76) In the same cophin with her was laid and buried in the same grave her little Infant born last Tuesday March 14th having been baptized on Wednesday and named George died on Thursday night March 16th 1758.

Register of Buryings Orangeburgh Township.
1758

(77) On Saturday March 25 1758 died after ten days Illness and on Sunday March 26 was Enterred in the church yard of Orangeburgh the Body of Agnes wife of Peter Roth of Orangeburgh aged —— years

(78) On Saturday April 1st died after six days Illness at the house of Mr Henry Wurtzer in Orangeburgh and on Monday April 3d was Enterred in the church yard of Orangeburgh the Body of Regina Philippina wife of Valentine Yutzy below Orangeburgh Township aged about 40 years.

(79) On Monday April 3d died of an apoplectic Fit and on Tuesday April 4th was enterred on the plantation of John Harrisperger in Orangeburgh the Body of Mary Catharina wife of John Kitelman of Orangeburgh aged almost 60 years

(80) On Monday April 3d 1758 died after Three days Illness and on Tuesday April 4th was enterred on the Plantation of Joseph Kryter in Orangeburgh the body of the said Joseph Kryter aged —— years

(81) On Monday April 3d after Eight days Illness and on Wednesday April 5th was Enterred in the church yard of Orangeburgh the Body of Lewis Linder a native from Germany and Planter below Orangeburgh Township He died at the house of the Revd John Giessendanner aged about 50 years

ORANGEBURG COUNTY. 207

Register of Buryings Orangeburgh Township
1758
(82) Sunday April 23ᵈ died after 9 days Illness and on Tuesday April 25th was Enterred in the Church yard of Orangeburgh the Body of Jacob Friday Junior of Orangeburgh aforesaid aged Thirty years

(83) On Thursday April 27 after 9 days Illness and on Friday April 28 was Enterred on the plantation of John Friday where the deceased died the Body of Sarah Elders wife of John Elders, Senʳ aged ——— years ———

(84) On Wednesday May 3ᵈ died in child bed & on Friday May the 5th was interred in the Church yard of Orangeburgh the Body of Catharina wife of Henry Snell, Senior* aged —— years

(85) On Friday May 19th died and on Saturday May 20 was interred on the Plantation of John Shaumlöffel in Orangeburgh Township ——————— wife of the said John Shaumlöffel aged ———————

(86) On Wednesday June 28th died Suddenly and on Thursday June 29th was Enterred on the plantation of Martin Koonen in Orangeburgh the Body of the said Martin Kooner Senior a native of Switzerland aged ———

(87) On Saturday July 15th was unfortunately drowned in an Indigo vat and on Sunday July 16 was interred on the Plantation of Henry Haym in Orangeburgh the Body of Barbara daughter of Adam Frolick deceased & Barbara his wife aged almost 13 mo—

(88) Thursday Novʳ 30th 1758 died after a long and lingering disorder and on Friday Evening Decʳ 1ˢᵗ was enterred in Orangeburgh Church yard the Body of

---

*The will of Henry Snell, who lived "near Orangeburgh Township", is dated 1760, and is recorded in the office of the Judge of Probate, Charleston County, on page 234 of the book for that period.

Anne wife of John Jacob Wymer of Orangeburgh aged about 23 years

1758

(89) Thursday Dec<u>r</u> 21<u>st</u> died after 15 days Illness and on Friday Dec<u>r</u> 22 was enterred on the plantation of Peter Murer in Orangeburgh Township the Body of the said Peter Murer Senior a native of Switzerland aged almost 75 years.

1759

(90) On Thursday Feby 22 died after some days Illness and on Friday Feby 23 was enterred in Church yard of Orangeburgh the Body of Zibilla Wolf widow a native of the Grisons County in Switzerland aged 73 years

(91) On Monday March 5<u>th</u> died after about three weeks Illness and on Tuesday March 6<u>th</u> was enterred in the church yard of Orangeburgh the Body of Michael Larry of Orangeburgh, Blacksmith aged about 34 years.

(92) On Wednesday evening March 21, 1759 died after Eleven days Illness and on Friday March 23<u>d</u> was enterred on the plantation of the late Melchior Otte late of Orangeburgh deceased the body of Barbara, widow of said Melchior Otte, aged 50 years—

(93) On Wednesday April 11<u>th</u> died after some days Illness and on Thursday April 12<u>th</u> was interred in the church yard of Orangeburgh the body of Elias Snell a native of Germany but residing in, So. Ca since the year 1735 aged almost 40 years—

Register of Buryings Orangeburgh Township
1759

(94) On Tuesday April 24<u>th</u> died and on Wednesday April 25<u>th</u> was interred on the plantation whereon Emanuel Miller now lives the Body of Mary Daughter of Andrew Inabnet deceased and Mary his late wife Aged 8 years 9 mo

(95) On Tuesday May 15 died and the day after was interred on the plantation of John Caspar Mintz The Body of John Jacob son of the said John Casper Mintz and Anna Barbara his wife aged 4 years 5 mo 21 days

(96) On Friday May 25 died & the day after was interred on the plantation of John Casper Mintz the Body of John George Melchior son of John Casper Mintz and Anna Barbara his wife aged 2 years $4\frac{1}{2}$ mo

(97) On Monday June 18th died of an apoplectick Fit and the day after was interred in the Church yard of Orangeburgh the Body of John Friday Senr a native of Switzerland and a settler in this Township since the year 1735 aged about 69 years

(98) On Thursday June 21st died after a lingering Illness and the day after was interred in the Church yard of Orangeburgh the Body of John Dietrick a native of Switzerland and a settler in this Township since the year 1735 Aged about 73 years

(99) On Wednesday June 27th died after three days sickness and on Friday June 29 was interred on the plantation of Nicholas Yonn in Orangeburgh the body of Anna Barbara daughter of the said Nicolas Yonn and Christina Yonn aged 15 years 6 mo–

Register of Buryings Orangeburgh Township 1759

(100) On Friday July 20th died after nine days Illness and the day after was interred in the plantation of Nicholas Yonn in Orangeburgh Township the Body of Nicholas son of the said Nicholas & Christina Yonn aged almost 8 years.

(101) On Thursday Morning August 16th died after 8 days Illness and the day after was interred in the Church yard of Orangeburgh the Body of Capt Jacob

Giessendanner He was born in Switzerland Jany 25/1727 Therefore aged 32 years 6 mo 3 weeks

(102) On Friday August 31$\underline{st}$ died after a lingering Illness of above a Twelvemonth and the day after was interred on the plantation of Henry Rickenbacker of Orangeburgh the Body of Anna, mother to the said Henry Rickenbacker and wife of Conrad Alder aged 63 years 11 mo

(103) On Saturday Sept 29$\underline{th}$ died and the day after was enterred in the Church yard of Orangeburgh the Body of Barbara Kitchen |alias| Fund widow a native of Switzerland aged ——

(104) On Sunday Nov$\underline{m}$ 25 died after a few days Illness and the day after was interred in the Church yard of Orangeburgh the Body of Henry Wurtzer a native of Switzerland and a settler in Orangeburgh since 1735 aged 55 years & some months

1760

Register of Buryings Orangebg T. Ship

(105) On Friday Jany 11$\underline{th}$ 1760 died and one day after his return from the Cherokee Expedition and the day after was interred on the plantation of the Late John Whetstone Senr deceased the Body of John Whetstone Junr son of the above aged about

(106) On Tuesday Jany 15 died and the day after was enterred in the Church yard of Orangeburgh the Body of Elizabeth Daughter of Adam Snell and his wife deceased aged almost 10 years—

(107) On Friday Feby 1$\underline{st}$ died in Child Bed and the day after was interred in the Church yard of Orangeburgh the Body of Magdalene, wife of Benedict Koller aged —— years

(108) On Tuesday Feby 5th died and the day after was interred in the church yard of Orangeburgh the Body of John Ulrick son of Benedict Koller & Magdalene his wife deceased Aged 7 days

(109) On Thursday Feby 14th died & the day after was interred in the Church yard of Orangeburgh the Body Henry Horguer Senr a native of Switzerland Aged about 89 years—

(110) On Monday Feby 25th died & the day after was interred in the Church yard of Orangeburgh the Body of Magdalene wife of Henry Sally Junr aged ——

Register of Buryings Orangeburgh T. S.

1760

(111) On Tuesday Feby 26th died of a pleuritic disorder & the day after was interred in the Church yard of Orangeburgh the Body of George Ulrick aged about 28 years

(112) On Wednesday Feby 27th died & the day after was interred on the plantation of Casper Foust in Orangeburgh the Body of ————— wife of Frederick Purly Shoemaker aged ——— years

(113) On Thursday March 6 died after nine days Illness & the day after was interred on his own plantation in Orangeburgh the Body of Henry Haym, a native of Switzerland aged about 60 years

(114) On Friday March 7th died after a pleuritic disorder of 8 days & the day after was interred on the plantation of Ulrick Oth the Body of Francis Kooner Aged 35 years

(115) On Tuesday March 11 died after Five days Illness, and the day after was entered on his own plantation in Orangeburgh the Body of Kilian Gussert aged ——— years

(116) On Wednesday March 12th died after 9 days Illness and the day after was interred in the plantation of John Ulrick Oth the Body of Catharine wife of Jacob Kooner aged ——— years

(117) On Thursday March 13th died & the day after was interred in the above plantation the Body of

John, son of Johannes & Elizabeth Wolf aged 15 years 3 months and 13 days, was sick 11 days

Register of Buryings Orangeburgh Township 1760

(140)* On Saturday June 21ˢᵗ died of the small pox† and the day after was interred in Church yard of Orangeburgh the Body of Mary Magdalene. Daughter of Jacob & Anna Wannenmaker, aged 2 years & 8 months

(141) On Thursday June 26ᵗʰ died of the small pox and the day after was interred in the Church yard of Orangeburgh The body of Anna, daughter of the above Wannenmaker and Anna his wife aged 3 months 3 weeks

(142) On Thursday July 29 died and the day after was enterred in the church yard of Orangeburgh the Body of Regina Daughter of Jacob and A —— Wolf aged 10 months

(143) On Friday August 1ˢᵗ died ——————— was interred in the Church ———————————— ———————— the Body‡

A List of Persons Deceased and Buryed in the Churchyard of Orangeburgh ——
1760
No**
144

(145) On Wednesday Octº 15ᵗʰ died & the day after was interred on the Plantation of Ulrick Brunner in Orangeburgh Township the Body of John, son of the said Ulrick Brunner and Eva Maria his wife aged 2 months 11 days

(146) On Saturday Octº 18ᵗʰ died & the day after

---

*From No. 117 to No. 140 in record lost.

†That there was any difference of opinion as to whether this was small pox or "aggravated chicken pox", the record saith not.

‡Other words torn off. **The entry torn off.

was interred on the plantation of Lewis Roth in Orangeburgh Township the Body of Catharina Elizabeth daughter of said Lewis Roth and Mary Barbara his wife aged 22 months

(147) On Sunday Oct^{o} 19th died the day after was interred on the plantation of Capt William Seawright at Beaver Creek the Body of the said William Seawright aged between 50 and 60 years

(148) Novr 7 died and the day after ———— was interred in the Church Yard*

The subsequent burial records are missing, but there could not have been many numbers after 148, as Rev. John Giessendanner died early in 1761.

The following is the record as to communions, kept by Rev. John Giessendanner after his return from England:

The number of all those who have received The Holly Communion on Easter and Monday in the Church of Orangeburgh according to the Form and use of the Church of England.†

On Sunday April 15 the following

1 Michael Christopher Row
3 John Futchman and his wife
4 Mary Margareth Shnyder
5 Barbara Jennings
6 Agnes Giessendanner
8 Wenner Ulmer, and his wife
10 John Frederick & George Lewis Ulmer
12 Nicholas Durr & His wife
14 George Giessendanner Senr & wife
16 Hans Fryding Junr & his wife
18 Hans George Hessey and his wife

---

*The part of the page containing the balance of this record is torn off and lost.

†The year of this record is not given, but 1750 was undoubtedly the date.

19 Verona Wurtzer
20 Miss Catharina Diel
22 Henry Heym, and his wife
23 Magdalene Hug
24 Ann Negely widow
25 Magdalene Imdorff
27 Hans and Joseph Huber
28 Hans Amacker
29 Elizabeth Hessy widow.
30 Ann Mary Faust widow
31 Miss, Ursula Giessendanner
33 Jacob & Regina Kuhnen
35 Hans Inabnet and his wife
37 Caspar Nagely George Shuler
38 Henry Rickenbacker
40 Henry Strauman and His wife
42 John Chevillette and his wife
43 Elizabeth Roth —widow—
44 Veronica Anding
45 Ann Barbara Snell
46 Mary Stehely J$\underline{r}$
47 Barbara Giessendanner
49 Felix Morff and His wife
51 Francis Kuhner, and old Jennings
52 Jacob Stauber

On Monday April 16$\underline{th}$ the following
Hans Imdorff and Mary Inabnet
Ann Barbara Ernst and Ann Rumph
Apollonia and Zibilla Wolf
Miss Barbara Kryter
Susanna Huber
Hans Fridig Senr and his wife.
Mary Stehely Sen

On Easter 1753 Had 107. one hundred and seven communicants all from Germany—Michael Larry—provided the wine for the Sacrament for Easter 1753.

Note:—George Giessendanner provided the Sacrement Wine for Whitsuntide

Received on Whitsunday June 3ᵈ the following new Communicants after proper instruction viz

John Nicholas Herter

John Barr,	Ann Margret Myer
John Dentzler,	Anna,,Catharina Mell
Isaac Hottow,	Anna Barbara Young
Jacob Foust,	Agnes Huber
Henry Stroman,	Christina Hossleiter
Conrad Kryter,	Elizabeth Kays
John Faust,	Eva Eliz^{bth} Hertzog
Henry Dentzler,	Mary Elizabeth Stroman

Anna Barbara wife of Henry Dentzler
Margaret wife of Jacob Hottow
Mary Tshudy (In all 20)

On Easterday 1758 the following children were confirmed and admitted to the Lord's Ch.

1 Nicolas Dill
2 Ottinaries Dantzler
3 Rachel Rowe
4 Maria Inabinet
5 Veronica Hirsch
6 Maria Magdalena Shnell
7 Anna Weigne
8 Anna Koller
9 Mary Robinson
10 Barbara Ulmer

The following is a rather unique piece of latinizing, by the reverend old gentleman: "1748 Sept. 25, Baptizetus est born Sept. 8th· H. H. & Marie Elizabethe uxaris urgis Suscept: Jacob Giessendanner. & Jacob & Louisa Horger."*

The following bit of humor is also culled from the pages of the Giessendanner book: "Information: Put a Miller, a Weaver and a Taylor in a bag and shake

---

*Meant for the record of baptism of a son of Hans Henry and Mary Elizabeth Felder.

them and the first that Comes out will be a thief or an honest man."

The Rev. John Giessendanner's will is dated March 5th, 1761, and was proved July 24th, 1761,* so that he must have died sometime between those dates.

---

*See page 124, Judge of Probate's book, Charleston County, for that year.

CHAPTER III.

THE COLONIAL PERIOD.

*Section 1. Pioneer Life in Orangeburgh.**

The early settlers of that section of South Carolina that was erected into Orangeburgh District in 1768, had many trials and hardships to undergo, such as all settlers in a new and unbroken country have to contend with. The country was infested with wild beasts, birds, and reptiles that were a constant menace either to the settlers or their agricultural interests; savage Indians were all about them, and frequently gave them much trouble; and, the seat of all government being at Charlestown, no officers of the law resided among them save the Rangers and a few justices of the peace, and from the number of advertisements that appeared in the *South Carolina Gazette* from time to time, it would seem that the chief duty of the justices of the peace in those early days was the advertising of stray animals picked up.† There were

---

*Or, Roughing it on the Edisto.

†*South Carolina Gazette*, March 26, 1753: "A Stray'd bay mare near 14 hands high, with some saddle spots, branded on the mounting shoulder 3 M in one, and on the mounting buttock A S, taken up by *Joseph Wood* below *Orangeburgh*. The owner may have her again, making proper application to
"*Christian Minnick*, J. P."

In the *Gazette* of April 11, to 18, 1768, "Lewis Golsay" (Golsan), "J. P.", advertises: "John Staley informs of a yellow bay gelding" &c., and "Elizabeth Golsin, of a small pyde heffer" &c.; and on May 9, 1768, "Lewis Golsan, J. P.", advertises a stray horse picked up by Adam Whetstone. Again in the *Gazette* of July 4, 1768, "Lewis Golsan, J. P.", advertises "a stray horse picked up by John Amacker; two bull stags picked up by Jacob Kooney", and "a stray horse picked up

no courts of law in that section, but criminals had to be carried to Charlestown for trial, and the result of this was that few criminals were brought to trial for crimes committed in that section. But, fortunately, these people were a quiet, industrious people and crimes among them were few. This lack of proper criminal courts of trial led to what is known as "Regulation", in the upper country of South Carolina, in the period just prior to the Revolution, but there is no evidence to show that "Regulation" played any con-

---

by James Newton".

In the *Gazette* of Monday, July 11, 1768, Moses Thomson, J. P., advertised "a stray mare picked up by Moses Curtis".

In the *Gazette* of Monday, August 8, 1768, several stray horses are advertised by "William Thomson, J. P., Amelia, July 28, 1768", as "picked up" by John Switman, Richard Switman, Ebenbard Steventir, and Major Lloyd.

In the *Gazette* of Monday, Sept. 5, 1768, "Lewis Gonsan, J. P.", advertised strays "picked up" by Adam Brickel, Peter Imboden, John Starley, and Valentine Cronich. Golsan also advertised strays "picked up" by Joseph Cook and Henry Boshard, in the *Gazette* of Oct. 10, 1768.

In the *Gazette* of Thursday, January 26, 1769, Jacob Rumph advertised two hogs that he had taken up at Orangeburgh, and John Fairchild advertised a stray horse that had been "picked up" by Solomon Wood of the "Forks of the Edisto".

In the *Gazette* of March 23, 1769, William Thomson, T. M., of Amelia, advertised stray horses "picked up" by Henry Whetstone and George Kubler.

In the *S. C. Gazette and Country Journal* of June 13, 1769, Philip Pearson, J. P., of Saxe–Gotha, gives notice of a number of stray animals "picked up".

From the *South Carolina and American General Gazette* for Friday, May 12th, to Friday, May 19th 1775, page 2: [Charleston Library.]

"John Salley, senr. informs me of a *bright bay Gelding*, twelve hands high, five years old, a star on his forehead, branded on the mounting buttock S [], a trotter; also a *bay Mare*, near twelve hands high, four years old, branded on the mounting shoulder I ⊰, a trotter; also a *strawberry roan Mare*, near thirteen hands high, six years old, branded on the mounting shoulder and buttock B. R. The owners may prove their property within six months, at Orangeburgh, before
"Samuel Rowe."

siderable part in Orangeburgh District; though we do find the following notice in the *South Carolina Gazette* of March 16th, 1769:

"In Council, 13th March 1769. It having appeared to his Excellency, and the Board, that Benjamin Farrar, and Barnabas Arthur, Eqrs. Justices of the Peace for this Province, had been instrumental in formenting and increasing the Disorders that prevailed among the People who stiled themselves REGULATORS in the Back Country: His Excellency, by the Advice of the Council was pleased to strike their Names out of the Commission of the Peace." Farrar and Arthur were both prominent citizens of Saxe-Gotha Township. While the chief seat of "Regulation" was higher up in the State, still there were some disturbances in Saxe-Gotha and Amelia Townships, hardly in Orangeburgh Township, or the section between the North Edisto and Savannah rivers.

The condition of the country embraced by the present county of Barnwell is given by Tarleton Brown in his "Memoirs". About the same conditions existed in the other parts of Orangeburgh District, so some extracts from the "Memoirs" will be given here. After stating that he had moved to South Carolina from Virginia with his parents and settled on Brier Creek, opposite to Burton's Ferry, in 1769, he goes on thus: "Having cleared a piece of land, we planted, and found the soil to be exceedingly fertile in the river swamp, producing abundant crops. The country was literally infested with wild beasts, which were very annoying to the inhabitants—killing the stock and destroying the crops—and were so bold, daring, and ravenous, that they would come into our yards, and before our doors take our sheep and poultry. Indeed, it was dangerous to venture out at night beyond the precincts of our yards unarmed. We used every device to exterminate them, and ultimately effected our object by setting traps and poisoned bait.

"The forest abounded with all kinds of game, particularly deer and turkeys—the former were almost as gentle as cattle. I have seen fifty together, in a day's ride in the woods. The latter were innumerable, and so very fat that I have often run them down on horseback. The range for cattle was excellent; it was a very common thing to see two hundred in a gang in the large ponds. In any month in the year beeves in the finest order for butchering might be obtained from the forest. It was customary then to have large pens or enclosures for cattle under the particular charge or direction of some person or persons; I was informed by one of those who kept a pen at King Creek, that there had been marked that spring seven hundred calves. Our produce for market was beef, pork, staves, and shingles. There was but little corn planted in that section then; and, indeed, there was scarcely any inducement to plant more than sufficed for our own consumption, there being but few mills in the country, and consequently very little demand for the article.

"From the fact of the new and unsettled state of the country, it may readily be inferred that the roads were very inferior; in truth, they were not much better than common bridle paths; and I feel confident in asserting that there were not, in the whole Barnwell District,* any conveyances superior to carts of common wood slides. There were a great many wild horses running at large in the forest when we first settled in the district, a number of which were caught and sold by various individuals, who pursued exclusively the business for a livelihood."

---

*It was not Barnwell District at that time, but a part of Orangeburgh District.

ORANGEBURG COUNTY.

The writer tells us of the cow-pens, situated in various parts of the district. One of these pens was situated upon the present Middlepen creek, and was the middle pen of the cattle raisers for a certain territory, and hence the name of the stream. Another of these pens was owned by Capt. John Salley, the writer's great great grand-father, but the family tradition has always been that it was his own pen, as he had thousands of acres of land and many cattle; and Mr. Brown speaks of it* as "Capt. Salley's 'Cowpens'"—doubtless a collection of pens at one spot. It is said that the spot on Dean Swamp whereon this pen stood is still so fertile as to show a marked difference between the crops planted there and those all around.

What Mr. Brown has said about the wild beasts in this section is confirmed by the traditions of many old people hereabouts. One old gentleman of this county relates that his elders have often told him of the troubles the early settlers had with beasts of prey. The settlers had to build their cow-pens and sheep folds and poultry houses very near their dwelling houses, and had to keep their firearms constantly loaded and primed in order to protect their stock. The same old gentleman tells of an old wolf trap that was built in the Limestone section before the Revolution, and which was still to be seen ten or fifteen years ago, though there are now no traces of it left. It was built by digging a large, grave-shaped hole in the ground about ten or twelve feet deep. Then the walls of this pit were secured by means of a snug fitting pen of notched poles built from the bottom of the pit to a level with the surface, so as to prevent a wolf from scratching his way out. A board was then nicely balanced lengthwise over the pit, and a piece

---
*"Memoirs", page 12.

of fresh meat suspended over one end of the board, so that if a wolf walked out on the board to try to get the meat he was dumped into the pit, from which he was unable to escape, and where he was killed by the hunters soon thereafter. It was usually the custom to drag a piece of fresh meat about through the woods for several miles, and finally to drag it to the wolf trap, so that wolves might follow the trail and be led into the snare. The same old gentleman remembers going to the trap when quite small and seeing some of his neighbors kill a wolf.*

Bear were also plentiful in this section in the days of the pioneer, and occasionally one is to be met with to-day in the Edisto river swamp. Mr. Benjamin Culler,† grand-father of Mr. W. W. Culler of this county, once killed a large bear in a hand to hand encounter. It was near his home in the Limestone section. He was stooping over a spring when suddenly a little dog he had with him sprang, apparently much frightened, into the spring beside him and splashed the water all over him. This caused Mr. Culler to straighten up suddenly, and just as he did so a large bear clasped the little dog in his embrace. Quick as thought Mr. Culler grabbed old bruin by the long hair on the back of his head, and drawing his hunting knife, gave him

---

*He was also present at the killing of the last wolf killed in this section, which was about 1839 or 1840. It was killed by William Robinson on the plantation of his father, Joseph Robinson, on Limestone. He shot it twice and broke both of its fore legs, but in spite of its crippled condition it managed to turn back every dog that came within reach of it. A short time before that a lone wolf had made its appearance on Great Branch, and "Jack" McMichael got a shot at it and wounded it, but did not bag it. But as it was never seen in that section afterwards, it was supposed that it died of its wounds. In each or these instances the wolf had played havoc with the sheep about it before being brought to earth.

†Or Collar, as it was then spelled.

a few swift stabs under the foreshoulder and laid him low. He weighed 370 or 380 pounds.

The early settlers of Orangeburgh doubtless found some buffaloes roaming the forests about them, for there are old salt licks to be seen in this section to-day that are still called "buffalo licks." It is doubtful though if there were ever many buffaloes in this section of South Carolina, as the topography of the country was not suited to them, and it is more than likely that deer, bear, wild horses and the small animals did most of the licking at the salt licks of this section, notwithstanding the fact that the buffalo has received the credit of producing these mosquito farms of to-day.

The beaver was also to be found in this section in the days of our first settlers, and, although it has been long over a century since he passed out of our territory, he has left his impress* behind him. There were one or more Beaver creeks and Beaver dams in the old District of Orangeburgh.

Mr. W. W. Culler also gives a description of a very unique dwelling house that was built about 1750, or earlier, by his great grand-father, Benedict Köller, on the lands that had been granted him by the government, and which lands are still in possession of the Culler family. The last wall of this house was torn down by Mr. Culler himself about 1835, and he remembers perfectly well how it was constructed. It was about 16 x 20 feet. The sides were built by putting up in line eight fat lightwood posts, with eight or nine feet clear the ground, about two feet apart. Each post had a groove cut in the sides facing the neighboring posts. These grooves ran the entire length of the posts. The spaces between the posts were filled in by sliding into these grooves a wicker

---
*And perhaps his imprint.

work of small twigs made somewhat as stick baskets are made. The ends of the house were built up in the same manner, save that a space was left for a door. The outside wall was then plastered over with a plaster made of red clay and the inside was quite smooth and nice looking when plastered with a plaster made of native lime. The floor was made by hewing small logs flat on the upper and under sides and laying them together as a floor is laid, and then putting on a finishing touch with an adz. The roof was made of the same material and then sodded. The door was made of the same sort of boards joined together by wrought nails which Köller himself had made by hand at his own forge. The hinges were made of dogwood, and very ingeniously arranged so that the door might swing on them, very much as our modern iron gates revolve on an iron rod. Beneath this structure was a cellar, which has only been filed up in the last decade. With such a house as that the settler could defy the elements, the wild beasts and the savage Indians.

A number of notes, extracted from the Statutes of South Carolina, the columns of the old *Gazettes*, and other authorities, that bear on matters and people in the section embraced within this work, will be reproduced here, as they give some insight into the condition of affairs in this section in colonial days, and familiarize us with the names of many of the families then living here:

The Statutes of South Carolina* show that on April 21, 1753, the Provincial legislature appointed commissioners "To build a Bridge over the pond in the Four Holes Swamp, commonly called Gibbe's pond, and to lay out, make and keep in repair, a road from the said bridge, as convenient as may be, into the Orangeburgh

---

*Vol. IV, page 5.

old road, from the head of the path leading from Dorchester to Izard's Cow-pen."* The "old road" here spoken of was opened in 1737† by an act of the Council establishing "a road from the head of the path that leads from Dorchester to Capt. Izard's Cowpens to the Township of Orangeburgh."

The follow described plantation was offered for sale in the *South Carolina Gazette* of June 18, 1753: "A Plantation at Orangeburgh, containing 250 acres, esteemed the best Land in that Township, on which one Lary now dwells, bounding N. E. on said Lary's Land, S. E. on Hans Spring's and Henry Fousts; and a Town-Lot in the said Township, No. 32."‡

On May 11, 1754, an Act was passed "for vesting the Ferry over Savanna river, at the Garrison of Fort Moore, in New Windsor, in John Stewart of New Windsor, his executors, administrators and assigns, for the term therein mentioned; and for establishing a Ferry over Santee river, in the township of Saxe-Gotha, from the land of Martin Fridig, on the South side, to the opposite landing on the North side, of the said river, and for vesting the same in the said Martin Fridig, his executors, administrators and assigns, for the term therein mentioned."**

---

*On April 7, 1770, an Act was passed "for repealing an Act entitled 'An Act for appointing Commissioners to build a Bridge over the Pond in the Four Hole Swamp, commonly called Gibbes' Pond, and to lay out and make and keep in repair a road to and from the said bridge, as convenient as may be, into the Orangeburgh old road, from the head of the said path leading from Dorchester to Izard's Cowpen'; and for authorizing and empowering the Board of Commissioners of the Roads for the parish of St. George Dorchester, to lay out and make and keep in repair the road mentioned in the said Act".—Stats. of S. C., Vol. IV, page 322.

†The "Old Charleston Road." ‡Lot No. 32 on the original plan of Orangeburgh was a lot near the river. **Stats. of S. C., Vol. IV, page 13.

The *South Carolina Gazette* of May 21st, 1754, contains a notice from William and Thomas Sabb, of Amelia Township; and the *Gazette* of May 28th, 1754, advertises 1700 acres of land "on Edisto opposite Orangeburgh Township."

On April 13th, 1756, the Legislature passed "An Act for laying out, making and keeping in repair a Road from the bridge commonly called Minnick's bridge, to the 15 mile post on the road leading from Orangeburgh township to Charlestown, and for rebuilding the said bridge and keeping the same in repair."*

On the schedule of provincial expenses for the year 1758† the following items concerned citizens of Orangeburgh:

"To Henry Gallman, on several orders for provisions and carriage of stores,‡	3292 12 09
"To John and Henry Gallman, for provisions,	361 13 06
"To William Seawright, for carriage of stores, £30; and on an order of Philip Puhl's, for provisions, £180	210 00 00
"To Barnard Snell, on Lewis Coleson's order, for horse hire,	10 00 00
"To Isham Clayton, for driving cattle,	6 00 00
"To John Geissendanner, for slaves executed,	200 00 00
"To Jacob Rumph," [constable, for fees on trial of slaves]	"9 07 06
"Elizabeth Mercier," [provisions]	"26 05 00"

On the schedule for 1760** the following items concern us:

---

*Stats. of S. C., Vol. IV, page 30. †Stats. of S. C., Vol. IV, page 63. ‡To frontier forts. **Stats. of S. C., Vol. IV, page 137 et seq.

ORANGEBURG COUNTY.

"To Henry Gallman, on an order of John Conrade Geiger, for the carriage of stores to the Congrees, 27 00 00

"To Henry Gallman, for the carriage of stores to Fort Prince George, 670 00 00

Christopher Rowe, Henry Gallman, Conrade Holman and Gavin Pou were all paid for carrying presents to the Indians, while John Fairchild received compensation for entertaining Indians.

On the schedule of expenses from January 1st, 1762, to December 31st, 1763,* the following items are of interest:

"Moses Thomson", [for holding an inquest] "15 00 00
"Henry Gallman", [for entertainment of Indians] "59 05 03
"Conrad Hallman, ditto, 19 03 04
"To Elias Houser, Cherokee keeper, 57 00 00
"William Thompson," [for conveying prisoners to jail] "10 00 10"

On the schedule for 1764† we find:
"To Godfrey Dreyer, for sundries supplied Fort William Henry and other Forts, 295 04 10
"Peter Bull, or Phul, for flour, for the Orangeburg militia, £6 00 00
"Christian Minnick, for a steer, 10 00 00
"Jacob Wolf, for two hogs, 8 00 00
"Henry Richenbacer, for carrying on a hue and cry,‡ 4 07 06"

From the schedule for 1766** we cull:
"William Thomson," [for repairs to Fort Prince George] "16 10 00

---

*Stats. of S. C., Vol. IV, page 198 et seq. †Stats. of S. C., Vol. IV, page 223 et seq. ‡Doubtless as a warning of the approach of hostile Indians. **Stats. of S. C., Vol. IV, page 248 et seq.

"John Fairchild, for surveying 20,000
acres of land for the Chickesaw
Indians,   184 03 04
"To Christopher Rowe, for provisions
for a scout,   £21 17 06
"Henry Gussendenner, for constable's
fees,   25 00 00"

On April 12th, 1768, the Legislature passed "An Act for establishing and making public a road to lead from Orangeburgh to Saludy, and from thence to Bush and Rayburn's Creeks, and for appointing Commissioners for the same; and also for establishing and making public a Ferry over Saludy river, and vesting the same in Samuel Kelly and John Millhouse, their Executors, Administrators and Assignees, for the term therein mentioned".*

From the *Gazette* of May 9, 1768, we extract: "The Grand Jurors of the body of the province of South Carolina presents" * * * * "as a grievance that Thomas Bond, a J. P. of Amelia Township, is a person unworthy of that dignity; on information of Moses Kirkland. When these presentments were taken into consideration process was issued requiring Bond to come in, plead to, and answer the presentment." The same paper, mentioning the prisoners at the Charles-Town Court, remarks: "Thomas Owen, Jun. convicted of wilfully burning the house of Anthony Distoe, pleaded his Majesty's pardon." Distoe, or Duesto, was of Orangeburgh District.†

The *Gazette* of Monday, July 11th, 1768, contains this notice:

"I do hereby forwarn all persons not to credit my

---

*Stats. of S. C., Vol. IV, page 302.   *S. C. Gazette*, April 11, to 18, 1768.   †See O'Neall's Bench and Bar, Vol. II, page 343.

Wife,* or any other person, on my account, without a written order from under my hand.
"Christopher Wise.
"St. Matthew's Parish, July 2d, 1768."

The *Gazette* of July 18th, 1768, contains the following advertisement: "A Plantation or Tract of Land, containing 187 acres, situate in Amelia Township" * * * "late the property of Robert Stewart, and sold under execution by
"ROGER PINCKNEY, Provost-Marshal."

On April 7th, 1770, an Act was passed by the Legislature,† for establishing a road "from Orangeburgh Bridge to Indian Head.‡

On the same day an Act was passed "for stamping and issuing the sum of Seventy Thousand Pounds, for defraying the expence of building the several Court Houses and Goals appointed to be built in the several Districts in this Province", under the Act of 1768, creating the seven Districts, or Precincts. The late Judge T. W. Glover stated, in some notes prepared by him, that the Orangeburgh District jail was built in the village of Orangeburgh in 1772; and Dr. Joseph Johnson, in his "Traditions of the Revolution", says that Col. William Thomson was the first Sheriff of the District, and that he assumed the duties of the office in June 1772.

The following notice is taken from the South Carolina *Gazette* of January 23rd, 1775:
"South Carolina.
"November Assizes, 1774.
"*Whereas* at a Court of General Sessions of the

---

*Not very complimentary to his wife. †Stats. of S. C., Vol. IV, page 318. ‡The Ninety-Six Road.

Peace, Oyer and Terminer, Assize, and General Goal-Delivery, begun and holden at Orangeburgh, for the District of Orangeburgh, on Saturday the 5th Day of November, 1774,

   Charles Heatley,
   George Hales,
   James Baldrick
   Thomas Newman, and
   Daniel Kelly,

Being duly summoned, and returned, to serve as Grand Jurors; and John Newman, Melchior Smith, Gersham Kelly, Peter Corbin, Sadrick Parler, George Robinson, and Richard Barklow, As Petit Jurors, made Default, and were noted for Non Appearance:

This is to give notice.

That the former will be fined in the Sum of Ten Pounds and the latter in the Sum of Five Pounds Proclamation-Money of America, each, unless they shall make good and sufficient Excuses, upon Oath, for ther Non Appearance, by the third Tuesday in May next.

     "James Caldwell,* D. C. C. & P."

The following similar notice also appeared in the *Gazette* during February 1775:

"South Carolina,

"Orangeburgh District.

"Whereas at a Court of Common Pleas, begun and holden at Orangeburgh, on Tuesday the 8th Day of November 1774, William Tucker, Wm Heatley, Sen., George Hales, Henry Young, and George Freeman, Sen., Being duly summoned and returned to serve as Jurors at the said Court, made Default, and were noted for Non-Appearance.

---

*James Caldwell was, it seems, at that time acting as District Clerk for both Orangeburgh and Ninety-Six Districts.

"This is to give notice.

"That they will be fined in the Sum of Five Pounds, Proclamation-money of America each, unless they shall make good and sufficient Excuses upon Oath, for their Non-Appearance, and transmit the same to the Pleas-Office, in Charles Town, on or before the First Tuesday in April next.

"Peter Bonnetheau* C. C. & P."

From the *Gazette* of April 3rd, 1775, the following notice is taken:
"South Carolina,
"In the Court of Common Pleas.

"February Term
"Their Honours the Judges, Chose their Circuits, which are as follows; viz. April Assizes, Southern Circuit:

Justices { Honorable the Chief Justice
         { Mr. Justice Cossett.

Orangeburgh District, at Orangeburgh, Wednesday April 5th. Clerk { Peter Bonnetheau.

Section 2. *Indian Troubles.*

In the *South Carolina Gazette* of April 14th, 1748, Governor Glen published a proclamation announcing that "George Haig, Justice of the Peace," had been carried off† by "French Indians from the Congarees or new township of Saxa-Gotha";‡ and in consequence there-

---

*Peter Bonnetheau was Clerk of the Court of Common Pleas at Charlestown and civil processes for all the districts were returned at Charlestown.

†They captured Haig and his servant, but the servant escaped.

‡In the *South Carolina Gazette* of January 8, 1754, Mrs. Elizabeth Mercier advertised as "Executor of George Haig", and stated that she was "late" his wife. In the *Gazette* of July 2, 1753, Patrick Brown and Thomas Corker, "who survived George Haig", advertised for James Gill.

of he recommended that Council provide for two small troops of horse and for building a fort "at the Congarees." From this it would seem that the fort established at the Congarees in 1718 had long since been abandoned. It is quite likely that after the fears of Yemassee incursions had blown over that the fort was abandoned, and that Captain Russell and his men were employed as rangers, for in the "Contingency" account for 1734*, the following item appears: "To the Rangers under Captain Russell, four hundred and five pounds seventeen shillings. 405 17 00." Captain Russell died in 1737, and by his death his rangers were probably broken up. At any rate it appears that a fort called St. John's was built near the site of the old fort at the Congarees, and that troops were organized in this section in accordance with Governor Glen's suggestion, and that in the course of ten years there were several regiments instead of two troops. Col. Moses Thomson was, about 1750, commander of the "Township battalion", that is, the provincial forces of the region southwest of the Santee, and outside of the old parishes. William Thomson was a captain of Rangers,† 175··—1759. For his services in the Cherokee war, 1759, he was promoted major, and the Assembly, in the Act of July 31st, 1760, voted him £275. He is spoken of by Hewat‡ as "Major Thomson,"** and the *South Carolina Gazette* of September 27th, 1760, says: "Our 7 companies of Rangers are to be completed to full numbers and W^m. Thomson, Esq., being appointed Major Commandant of the whole, they will soon be equal to a Regiment of Light Horse." He afterwards commanded the "Township battalion", and was made col-

---

*Statutes of S. C., Vol. III, page 391. †Frontier mounted police.
‡Carroll's Historical Collections of South Carolina, Vol. I, page 465.
**Also Statutes of S. C., Vol. IV, page 127.

onel in 1765.* Tacitus Gaillard was also a colonel,† but his commission was revoked by the Governor in 1769. Peter Mercier, whose will was made in 1754, and proved in 1755, declares himself therein‡ to have been "Lieutenant in one of the three Independent companies." John Chevillette, the same who had been an officer under Prince Frederick of Prussia, commanded a battalion of provincial malitia,** and Wm. Gilmore Simms says, in "The Forayers," p. 264, that Christopher Rowe was commissioned captain,†† in 1755, in "Colonel John Chevillette's regiment of foot", and that his commission was then (1855) extant.‡‡ Captain Christian Minnick is mentioned in the *South Carolina Gazette* of March 23rd, 1752; John Lloyd is called Captain by Giessendanner and Major in the *Gazette* of August 8th, 1768, and James Tilly, Jacob Giessendanner and Christopher Rowe are all spoken of as captains by Giessendanner.

These malitia officers and rangers were kept quite busy from about the time of the carrying off of Haig, until the close of the Cherokee war in 1761, for, says Logan,§ "from 1749, to the close of Col. Grant's campaign, in 1761, embracing a period of more than ten years, there was not a settlement in this portion of the province that was not exposed to the inroads of hostile savages, and at their hands became the not unfrequent scene of bloody tragedies and domestic ruin."

About 1750, Herman Gieger, who has already been mentioned as one of the first settlers of Saxe-Gotha

---

S. C. Gazette and Country Journal, July 12, 1774; *S. C. Gazette*, Jan. 23, 1775; *S. C. G. & C. J.*, Jan. 17, 1775; Moultrie's Momoirs, Vol. I, page 17. †*S. C. Gazette* Feb. 23, 1769. ‡See book for that year, page 290, office of Probate Judge, Charleston. **Stats. of S. C., Vol. IV, pages 118 and 127. ††See also Statutes of S. C., Vol. IV, page 299. ‡‡In Simms's possession. §History of the Upper Country of South Carolina.

Township, was living at the Congarees and carrying on trade with the Indians.

"On one occasion," says Logan, p. 302, "he had been employed, it seems, by the provincial authorities in Charleston, to go, in company with a member of the Board of Indian Trade, to the Cherokee Nation, in search of the precious metals, which were supposed to exist in inexhaustible abundance in that mountainous region. Having set out, and reached in safety one of the middle towns, they there discovered several of their friendly *settlement* Indians in the hands of a party of hostile Canadian savages, who had captured them near Charleston, and were carrying them prisoners to their towns in the north."

Gieger's pity was aroused, and, at the head of a body of traders, he succeeded in rescuing the friendly Indians, but this act of kindness afterwards cost him his life.

The following summer, having set out for the Catawba Nation, in company with a half-breed, they were intercepted and captured by several of the very party of Canada Indians from whom Geiger had rescued the friendly Indians a year before, by whom he was carried toward the Great Lakes, and finally murdered.*

On the 7th day of May, 1751, Mrs. Mary Gould, or Cloud, appeared at the house of Martin Friday, at the Congarees, severely wounded, and reported to Capt. Daniel Sellider, of the Saxe-Gotha company, that on Saturday, the fourth, two Savannah Indians had come to her house, situated about half way between the Congarees and Savannah Town, and, after partaking of her husband's hospitality, had suddenly arisen in

---

*In the *South Carolina Gazette* of June 18th, 1753, John and Henry Gallman advertised for the creditors of "Herman Geiger, of Saxe-Gotha, deceased".

the dead of night and murdered her husband, and her two children, and a young white man who was living with them, and had dangerously wounded her and left her for dead. It is also recorded that Mrs. Gould died of her wounds soon after.

About the same time Stephen Crell, of Saxe-Gotha, informed Governor Glen that a gang of Indians had been killing "horses, *mares,* and cattle" at the Congarees, and in the more northern settlements, after which they went to the house of John Gieger, and carried off his negro boy. Two women, who were the only members of the family at home at the time, tried to save the boy, but were threatened with death by the savages.

In 1754 the Cherokees of the up-country committed several murders, and sacked several stores; whereupon the frontier settlers hastily assembled, and fortified themselves at Ninety-Six, the Congarees and other convenient points. But it was not until 1759 that the Cherokees made any serious outbreak.

Shortly after the breaking out of Cherokee hostilities in 1759, Dr. Hewat says:* "The Governor† set out for Congarees, the place of general rendezvous for the militia, and about one hundred and forty miles distant from Charlestown, where he mustered in all about one thousand four hundred men." From the Congarees Governor Lyttleton marched his little army against the Cherokees in the Northwestern part of the province, but before shedding much blood he succeeded in arranging terms of peace with them.

The rejoicings on account of the peace were scarcely over when the news arrived of a fresh outbreak of hostilities. General Amherst, the British Command-

---

*History of South Carolina, pages 445 and 446 of Carroll's Collections, Vol. I. †Lyttleton.

er-in-Chief in America, was then appealed to, and he sent a battalion of Highlanders, and four companies of the Royal Scots, under command of Colonel Montgomery, afterwards Earl of Eglinton, to South Carolina, where he landed in April, 1760; but as the conquest of Canada was the grand object of the year's campaign in America, he had orders to strike a sudden blow for the relief of Carolina, and return to head-quarters at Albany without loss of time. Hewat says, p. 455: "Several gentlemen of fortune, excited by a laudable zeal for the safety of their country, formed themselves into a company of volunteers, and joined the army. The whole force of the province was collected, and ordered to rendezvous at Congarees".

* * * * * * *

"A few weeks after his arrival Colonel Montgomery marched to the Congarees, where he was joined by the internal strength of the province, and immediately set out for the Cherokee country." In this expedition the Indians were defeated, but not quelled, and so soon as Colonel Montgomery retired from their country they immediately resumed hostilities. They captured and killed most of the garrison at Fort Loudon, and had designs on Fort Prince George. "In consequence of which", says Hewat, p. 465, "orders were given to Major Thompson, who commanded the militia on the frontier, to throw in provisions for ten weeks into that fort, and warn the commanding officer of his danger."

The British authorities next sent Col. Grant to the aid of South Carolina, and he, with the assistance of the provincial militia under Colonel Arthur Middleton, succeeded in finally defeating and overthrowing the Indians; but the chief glory in this last expedition belonged to the provincial militia. and it is greatly to be regretted that the names of the militia men from the townships of Amelia, Saxe-Gotha and Orangeburgh cannot be here given. Some of them are known, but the majority are not.

The people of Orangeburgh Township had, at least, some of the scare of the Indian warfare of this period, for from the Giessendanner record we learn that several forts* existed in the Township, and from the wording of the record we are led to believe that the inhabitants assembled in these forts with their families in times of Indian troubles.

On the Schedule† of the expenses of the Indian warfare the following items concern us: William Thomson, a cart; Conrad Holman, corn and straw; "To the following persons, for Colonel John Chevillette's battalion", &c; Michael Snyder, flour; Elizabeth Mercier, English peas, and corn; Michael Lightner, hire of a mare; Rev. Mr. John Giessendanner, for hire of a horse 7 days; Christopher Minnick, for cattle; Henry "Rinchenbackor," flour, peas and hogs; "Nicholas Shooler", for a steer; Godfrey Dreyer, flour; "Conrad Holman, for entertaining the Governor and several others, ... 55 00 00;" Michael Christopher Rowe, 30 13 00; Moses Thomson, for a steer; Jacob Rumph, cart hire; Christopher Rowe, for cattle; Jacob Fridig; David Fridig; and Henry Whetstone, wagon hire; "To pay the battalion of Colonel John Chevillette, (as the muster roll of the said battalion was settled by a committee of the Assembly,) 13,109 12 08"; "To Major William Thompson, a gratuity for his services, 275 00 00". Other Orangeburgh names are on the statement, as having furnished provisions, hired wagons, pastured cattle and rendered various other services for which they received pay from the public treasurer.

---

* "Block houses", no doubt. †Stats. of S. C., Vol. IV, July 31, 1760.

Section 3. Heresy in the "Dutch Fork".

In the section devoted to the settling of Saxe-Gotha Township some mention has been made of the Weber, or Weaver, "heresy." The following interesting account of that trouble, which culminated in 1760, is taken from Dr. Bernheim's history, p. 195 et seq.:

"In Saxe-Gotha Township, Lexington County, South Carolina, and 'in the neighborhood of what is now called Younginer's Ferry', there originated a sect among the Swiss and German settlers, who were called Weberites. Their heresy was of so revolting a nature, that it would be desirable to pass it by in silence, if it could be done without doing injustice to a faithful and correct narration of historical facts.

"Rev. Dr. Hazelius give us a brief sketch of the doings of these Weberites in his American Lutheran Church, p. 103; and the Rev. Dr. Muhlenberg has also furnished us a more extended account of them in his journal, translated and published in vol. i of the Evangelical Review, dating their transactions as having occurred in the year 1760; nevertheless, the origin of this sect must have taken place some time before, as that is the date of the culmination of their heresy into the crime, which brought their leader to suffer the just penalty of the law.

"Dr. Muhlenberg's account is as follows: 'Mr. Strobel, the son-in-law of Rev. Mr. Martin, a wealthy tanner, sent for me in a chaise, to convey me out of town to dine with him. He told me, among other things, a remarkable history of an abominable sect, which had arisen among the Germans in South Carolina, A. D. 1760-1, and had some similarity with Knipperdolling and Jan Van Leiden. They committed murders, on which account one of them, named Jacob Weber, who called himself a god, and slew a person, was hanged. Their founder is said to have been Peter Schmidt. The sect originated at Saluda Fork, about one hundred miles from Charleston (125 or 130 miles).

"'Jacob Weber was a Swiss. He first became an exhorter, then he advanced himself still farther, but before his end he came to his senses, and saw his error.

"'The people in the country, in general, grew up without schools and instruction. Occasionally a self-taught (auto-didacter) minister may labor for awhile amongst them, yet it continues only a short time. The people are wild, and continue to grow wilder, for what does it profit them to hear a sermon every four, six, or twelve weeks, if in early youth the foundation of Divine Truth had not been laid? The aforesaid sect had so far obtained the supremacy that several families united with it for fear of their lives; numbers of both sexes went about uncovered and naked, and practiced the most abominable wantonness. One of them pretended to be God the Father, another the Son, and a third the Holy Spirit; and the pretended Father, having quarrelled with the Son, repudiated the pretended Son, chained him in the forest, declared him to be Satan, and finally gathered his gang, who beat and trampled on the poor man until he died; he is reported also to have killed the pretended Holy Ghost in bed. A report of these circumstances having reached the authorities in Charleston, the malitia were ordered to arrest the pretended deity, when he was tried, condemned, and executed upon the gallows.

"'The English inhabitants scoffed about it, and said the Germans had nothing to fear, their Devil having been killed, and their God having been hanged. Such are the fruits of not inculcating the doctrine of Divine Truth early in youth, and of leaving man to himself. Rom. I: 21-32. This sect spread from South to North

Carolina, thence to Maryland and Virginia, among the German and English population, and has likewise left some seed of this heresy in Charleston. Upon this gross Satanic tragedy a more subtle temptation followed. Quakers, Anabaptists, &c., spread themselves in the country regions around, and appear to be better suited to the circumstances of the land at this time.

"'October 9th. To-day I received the original copy of a letter dictated by Jacob Weber in prison before his death, for the benefit of his children, which reads as follows:

"'"*Jacob Weber's Confession.*

"'"April 16th, 1761, being imprisoned and ironed, it occurred to me and the jailor to transmit to my beloved children a sketch of my mournful life. I, Jacob Weber, was born in Switzerland, in Canton Zurich, in the county of Knomauer, in the parish of Stifferschweil, and was raised and educated in the Reformed Church. In the fourteenth year of my age I journeyed with my brother to South Carolina, leaving my parents; and soon after my arrival I lost my brother by death. Thus I was forsaken of man, and without father or mother. But God had compassion on me amid much trouble and sorrow. He planted the fear of the Lord in my heart, so that I had more pleasure in the Lord, in godliness, and the Word of God, than in the world. I was often troubled about my salvation when I reflected how strict an account God would require, that I must enter into judgment, and know not how it would result. Although God drew me with his grace, I found also the reverse in my corrupt nature, which was excited with the love of the world, viz., of riches, honors, and an easy life.

"'"Mankind love a social life, and as the Lord drew me back in many wonderful ways, I came, therefore, nearer to him; notwithstanding I always attended to my religious services and prayer, but with a heart cold and averted from God. Through such exercises of the heart I arrived at a knowledge of my sins, and learned how awfully the human race had fallen from God, and how low all mankind, without exception, are sunken in depravity. As soon as I experienced this, I earnestly besought God day and night for forgiveness, for the Holy Spirit, for a pure heart, and for saving faith, and I felt the necessity of retirement to restrain my thoughts, and to prevent the Divine work from being hindered in me. In this retirement I forgot the turmoil of the world. In this light I regarded all vain desires and thoughts and all human works as by nature damnable in the sight of God. Fear and sorrow now seized upon my poor soul, and I thought, what shall I do to be saved? It was shown me that nothing would suffice but being born again of water and of the Spirit. Realizing that I could not be saved in any other way, I prayed still more earnestly, and it was shown me still more plainly by the Holy Ghost in my heart how sinful I was (Rom. 7), so that I stood there before the judgment of God; but the judgment of God became manifest in me, so that I judged myself, and confessed that I deserved a thousand-fold to be cast from the presence of God, and wondered that the forbearance of the Lord had not long since hurled me, poor and condemned wretch, into the lowest pit of destruction; and then too, I saw the whole world lay in sin. Feeling myself so lost, I cast myself entirely upon the mercy of God to lead me according to his holy will and pleasure, whether unto life or death, if he would only be gracious unto my poor soul for Christ's sake, and pardon my sin, and purify my heart from all uncleanness. Thus I lay at the feet of Jesus with all my heart in submission, sighing and praying night and day for his grace, and so continued for several days, until I had passed from death unto life. Then Jesus revealed himself unto my soul. Then there was great joy in heaven over me, a returning sinner. Then all my sins were forgiven me, and I was full of the Holy Ghost, and rejoiced with a joy unspeakably great. This occurred, or I experienced this joy, A. D. 1756, in the month of May. This grace caused me to despise the joy of the world, and to disregard its reproach, and kept me, thenceforth, continually with my surety, Jesus, amid many temptations not now to be mentioned, until finally I found rest for my soul. This peace and communion with God I possessed about two years, under every burden of affliction, for I had the grace to enable me, under all circumstances, to submit my will to the mercy of God. Through the grace which was in me I could govern temporal goods without danger to my soul. Upon this followed the great misery and awful fall into sin, already, alas! too well known. The devil bringing me into a greater temptation and fall than was ever known, of which Peter Schmidt was the origin and instrument. After this, by the providence of God, I was captured and cast into prison, that I might recover my reason, come to a knowledge of my great sins, and confess them before God, that thus it might awaken great wretchedness in my soul, humble me before God and man, yea, beneath all creatures, yea, that I might account myself as the poorest worm. I often thought each and every person too good to speak to me, and interest himself in me. Nevertheless I sought cordially the forgiveness of my sins in the blood of the Lamb of God, my Redeemer, who loved me and died for all my sins, and for his righteousness' sake arose, all which I heartily believe, because I experience again the witness of the Holy Spirit, which testifies unto my spirit that I am a child of God. And now, my children, beloved in the Lord, I must leave this world, and, perhaps, behold your face no more in this life. I commend you, therefore, to the protection and mercy of God! Pray without ceasing, learn and read; injure no one willingly and wilfully while you live; labor industriously and faithfully according to your ability; then, if we should meet no more in this world, we may hope to meet each other in heaven, in the world to come; which may the triune God, Father, Son, and Holy Ghost, grant to you for the sake of the crucified Jesus, Amen. Such cunning and celerity does Satan possess as to cause so great a schism and injury even among the children of God, and to lead them astray, and make them fall so suddenly against their knowledge and consent. May God preserve all persons from so great a fall, and trample Satan under foot, for Christ's sake, Amen. The grace of our Lord Jesus Christ be with you and all persons, Amen. And I beseech all persons who have been injured by me to forgive me, for Christ's sake.

"'"Written or dictated by
"'"Jacob Waeber.
"'"April 16th, 1761."'

"Dr. Hazelius' account of this tragic affair is as follows:

"'It was about this time that a number of our (German) people, living on the banks of the Saluda River, in South Carolina, being destitute of ministerial instruction, agreed to assemble from time to time for singing, prayer, the reading of the Scriptures, and mutual edification. This was as it should be, but the enemy soon sowed tares among the wheat, by introducing spiritual pride among the small flock. One man, by the name of Weaver, personated Christ, another the Holy Spirit, a certain woman, the wife of

Weaver, the Virgin Mary, and one poor fellow was doomed to represent Satan. The curiosity of the people became highly excited by the strange proceedings on Saluda River, in the neighborhood of what is now called Younginer's Ferry. Excess followed excess, until at length Weaver, representing either Christ or God, ordered, in virtue of his dignity, that Satan should be chained in a subterranean hole, and finally that he should be destroyed. For this purpose they met, placed the unfortunate man in a bed, covered him with pillows, on which some seated themselves, while others stamped with their feet on the bed until the life of the man had become extinct. The corpse was then taken out of bed, and thrown into a burning pile of wood, to be consumed to ashes. The perpetrators of this crime were taken to Charleston and tried. Weaver was found guilty, and suffered the penalty of the law on the gallows. His wife was pardoned.'

"The Rev. Christian Theus furnished Dr. Muhlenberg with a more detailed description of this sect of Weberites, as he was well acquainted with their doings, having lived about twenty-five miles from the place where the murder occurred. At a certain time he came unexpectedly into their meeting, and found Jacob Weber contending that he was God, and the said Peter Schmidt insisting that he himself was Christ, and that the unconverted members must be healed through his stripes.

"Pastor Theus opposing such blasphemy, the leaders became enraged, and threatened his life, and counselled with their rabble whether to drown or hang him. He escaped, however, from their hands, fled to the river, and fortunately found a negro with his canoe at the shore, sprang into it, was conveyed across, and thus saved his life.

"All traces of this abominable heresy have long since

been obliterated; neither are there even any descendants of Jacob Weber and Peter Schmidt to be found in the Saluda Fork. To what region of country they emigrated, or what was their subsequent history, is not known. The object of history in preserving the record of such deeds is that it might serve as a warning to all not to depart from the truth as revealed in God's word, even in their religion." * * * * *

"That Weber was sincere, his confession, which he made with eternity in view, fully proves; notwithstanding his sincerity, so great was his deception in spiritual things, that he became guilty of the most horrid blasphemy and the greatest crime known to the law."

* * * * * * * * *

"In this locality, where the Weberites had their origin, and about that period of time, A. D. 1758, according to the import of Weber's confession, the Gospel was but seldom preached, and the effects of such neglect soon manifested themselves; the people generally gave a loose rein to their passions, rioted in their wantonness, and actually believed that in doing so they were rendering service to God."

These were the people who contributed much toward bringing about the "Regulation" troubles, and here is where the largest number of German Tories was to be found during the Revolution, and on that account the whole German population of South Carolina has been charged with being of Tory inclination. But let it be remembered that the little angle between the Saluda and Broad rivers—partly in Orangeburgh District and partly in Ninety-Six District—constituted a very small part of South Carolina, and the Germans there settled constituted a very small portion of the South Carolina Germans, and they were not *all* of them Tories either.

Section 4. *The Civic Officers of the Period.*

Up to 1768, when the Province of South Carolina was divided into districts, the townships of Amelia, Orangeburgh and Saxe-Gotha formed parts of Berkeley County, as already stated, and the only civic officers in those townships were the Justices of the Peace, and the Inquirers and Collectors of taxes. After the formation of St. Matthew's Parish in 1765, representation was allowed that Parish in the Commons House of Assembly of the Province; and after the formation of Orangeburgh District in 1768, a Sheriff, a Jailer and a District Clerk of Court were added to the list of office holders. The following is a very incomplete list, made up from various sources, of the civic officers of the period:

Justices of the Peace.*

1734.
Charles Russell.†

1737.
George Haig.‡
Christian Motte.§

1747.
John Chevillette.¶

1752.
Moses Thomson°

---

*The office of justice of the peace was a far more important position in Colonial days than it has ever been since. †*S. C. Gazette*, June 7, 1734. ‡*S. C. Gazette*, July 2—9, 1737. He was also at that time a Deputy Surveyor General, as will appear by the grants of John Hearn, p. 25, Henry Salley, p. 28, and the grant made April 13, 1739, to Mrs. Mary Russell, in trust for her children.—p. 23. §*S. C. Gazette*, March 26, 1737. ¶As appears by an old original document. °*South Carolina Gazette*, 1752.

ORANGEBURG COUNTY.

Christian Minnick.*
1753.
Moses Thomson,†
Christian Minnick.‡
1754.
Moses Thomson.§
1756.

Jacob Motte.   Moses Thomson,
Tacitus Gailliard,   John Chevillette,
Christian Minnick.
1762.

Jacob Motte,   Tacitus Gaillard,
Moses Thomson,   John Chevillette,
James Mayson.
1765.‖

Moses Thomson,   Christian Minnick,
John Chevillette,   Gavin Pou,
Lewis Golson.
1768.
Thomas Bond,¶
Lewis Golson,°
Moses Thomson**
William Thomson.††

South Carolina Gazette, 1752. †*South Carolina Gazette*, Aug. 6, 1753. ‡*South Carolina Gazette*, March 26, 1753. §*South Carolina Gazette*, March 19, 1754. ‖ "In and for Amelia and Orangeburgh Townships."—From the *South Carolina Almanac*, 1765. John Govan is mentioned in the same authority as one of the justices of the peace for Granville County. He had probably removed to Granville County, for in the *Gazette* of July 18, 1768, (No. 1711—Supplement) under the caption "Provost-Marshal's Sale", appears the following notice: "On Thursday 25th of August next, will be sold, at public vendue, at the usual place in Charles-Town, All that valuable plantation or tract of 520 acres of land", &c., "whereon John Govan, Esq., deceased, lately lived, situate in Prince Williams parish, Granville-county", &c.
¶*S. C. Gazette*, May 9, 1768. °*S. C. Gazette*, April 18, May 9, July 4, Sept. 5, Oct. 10, 1768. ***S. C. Gazette*, July 11, 1768. ††*S. C. Gazette*, August 8, 1768.

1768-9.
Benjamin Farrar,*
Barnabas Arthur,*
Philip Pearson, (Saxe-Gotha.)†
Tacitus Gaillard.‡

1769-70.§

Moses Thomson,   John Chevillette,
William Hopton,   Gavin Pou,
Lewis Golson,   Christopher Rowe,
William Thomson,   William Arthur,
George Strother.

1770-71.¶

Moses Thomson,   Lewis Golson,
William Thomson,   Gavin Pou,
Christopher Rowe,   William Hopton,
John Chevillette,   George Strother,
William Arthur.

1775°

Gavin Pou,   Christopher Rowe,
Benjamin Farrar,   John Savage,
John Fairchild,   James Thomson,
Henry Felder,   Donald Bruce.

Justices of the Quorum.**

1775.

Gavin Pou,   Christopher Rowe,
Thomas Green,   Benjamin Farrar,
Moses Kirkland,   John Savage,

---

*See page 219. †*S. C. Gazette and Country Journal*, June 13, 1769.
‡The *South Carolina Gazette* of February 23rd, 1769, announced that the day before the Governor had ordered Tacitus Gaillard's name "struck out of the Commission of the Peace; and at the same time, the said *Tacitus* Gaillard, as Colonel". §For the townships of Amelia, Orangeburgh and Saxe-Gotha in Berkeley County.—The *South Carolina Gazette*, Oct. 18, 1769. ¶*South Carolina Gazette*, Oct. 18, 1770. °*S. C. Gazette*, Jan. 7, 1775. **For Orangeburgh District.

ORANGEBURG COUNTY.

David Pou,
Henry Patrick,
Joseph Kirkland,
William Tucker,
David Holmes,
Johannes Beard,
John Chestnut,
Malcolm Clark,
William Housell,
Ephriam Mitchell,
Donald Bruce,
Lewis Golson,

John Fairchild,
Thomas Young,
Samuel Rowe,*
Arthur Symkins,
John Dicks,
Michael Dickert,
Isham Clayton,
James Thompson,
Henry Felder,
William Brown,
Evan McLaurin,
William Arthur.

Inquirers and Collectors.

1758.†

Amelia and adjacent places: } William Seawright.

Orangeburgh, with the forks of Edisto river and the adjacent places: } Gavin Pou.

The Township of Saxe-Gotha and forks between the Congaree and Wateree rivers and adjacent places: } James Leslie,‡ John Lee, Thomas Kennelly,‡ Isaac Pennington.

1760.§

The Township of Amelia and adjacent places: } William Sabb.

---

*See page 218, foot note. †Stats. of S. C., Vol. IV, page 56–7. ‡On Dec. 14, 1758, an Ordinance was passed "for rectifying Mistakes in the names of two of the Inquirers, Assessors and Collectors, for the Township of Saxegotha, and the forks between the Congree and Wateree Rivers, and adjacent places, appointed by the Tax Act, passed the 19th May, 1758". James Leslie and Thomas Kennelly were by the mistake in the said Act, called "John Leslie and John Kennelly".—Stats. of S. C., Vol. IV, pages 73 and 74. §Stats. of S. C., Vol. IV, page 132.

Orangeburgh Township, with the forks of Edisto river and adjacent places:	Michael Christopher Rowe.
Saxe-Gotha Township and the fork between the Congaree and the Wateree rivers and adjacent places:	John Pearson, William Harson, William Raiford.

1764.*

For Amelia Township and adjacent places:	Major William Thomson.
Orangeburgh Township, with fork of Edisto river and adjacent places:	Gavin Pou.
Saxe-Gotha Township and the fork between the Congaree and Wateree rivers, and adjacent places:	Robert Goodin, Andrew Allison.

1765.†

Amelia Township and adjacent places:	Thomas Platt.
Orangeburgh Township, with the forks of Edisto river and adjacent places:	Gavin Pou.
Saxe-Gotha Township and the fork between the Congaree and Wateree rivers and adjacent places:	John McCord, Isaac Ross.

1766.‡

The Parish of St. Matthew:	Thomas Platt, Samuel Rowe.

---

*Stats. of S. C., Vol. IV, page 193.
†Stats. of S. C., Vol. IV, page 217.
‡Stats. of S. C., Vol. IV, page 242.

Saxe-Gotha Township and the fork between the Congaree and Wateree rivers and adjacent places: John Hamilton, John McCord.

1767.*

For the Parish of St. Matthew: John Thomson, John McNichols, Christopher Rowe.

For the Congarees: John Thomas, Thomas Corker, Jr., Thomas Green.

For both sides of Broad river: Thomas Kennedy, John Freydig.

Members of the Provincial Assembly.
1765-67.

It will be remembered that when the Parish of St. Matthew was erected in August, 1765, that two representatives in the General Assembly were allowed that parish. At an election held in October following William Thomson and Tacitus Gaillard were returned as representatives for the parish, and took their seats in the assembly that met on the 28th of the same month, and closed its session on April 12th, 1768. From the journal of that unusually long session we learn that; "His Majesty having been pleased to Repeal, the Act for establising St Matthews Parish, Major Gaillard and Collo Thomson quitted their seats in the House the 10th day of November One thousand seven Hundred and sixty-seven."

1768.

It will also be remembered that a second Act was passed, in April 1768, establishing St. Matthew's Par-

---

*Stats. of S. C., Vol. IV, page 272.

ish, and that provision was made therein for one representative in the Provincial Assembly. The *South Carolina Gazette* for Monday, September 5th, 1768, contains the following announcement:

"Wednesday last ended the general election of members to represent the inhabitants of the several parishes into which this province is divided, in the ensuing general assembly, which is to meet here on Monday the 25th instant;* when the following gentlemen were elected, viz." * * * * "For St. Matthew's. William Thomson, Esq."

1769.

The *South Carolina Gazette* for March 16th 1769. contains a list of the members elected to the General Assembly on the 7th and 8th of that month. William Thomson is named as the representative elected for St. Matthew's Parish.†

1772.

The *South Carolina and American General Gazette*, for March 31st, 1772, announced that Isaac Huger had been elected a member of the Provincial Assembly for St. Matthew's Parish.‡ The same paper for September 29th, 1772, again announced Isaac Huger as a member of the Assembly for St. Matthew's Parish.§

1773–75.

The *South Carolina and American General Gazette*. for December 29th, 1772. announced that at the late elections, Tacitus Gaillard had been returned as the representative from St. Matthew's;‖ but Mr. Gailliard was not permitted to sit easy in his seat, for the *South*

---

*Met Nov. 15, 1768. †The Assembly met on the 26th of June following. ‡The new Assembly met soon after. §The Assembly met on October 8th, following. ‖The new Assembly met on Jan. 17th, 1773.

Carolina and American General Gazette, for March 26th, 1773, announced that Isaac Huger would contest the election of Tacitus Gaillard; and the journal of the House of Representatives for Saturday, March 20th, 1773, contains the following:

"Petition of Isaac Huger Esq to set aside the Election of Tacitus Gaillard Esquire

"A Petition of Isaac Huger Esquire of Charles Town,* was presented to the House and read in the words following (   ) 'That your Petitioner with Tacitus Gaillard Esquire were candidates at the last Election of a Member to serve in the present General Assembly for the Parish of Saint Matthew That the Election was not managed and conducted agreeable to the directions of an Act of the General Assembly for ascertaining the Manner and form of Electing Members to represent the Inhabetants of this Province in the Commons House of Assembly: First that no public notice was given in Writing at the Door of the Parish Church, two Sundays before the appointed time of Election—That at two of the Clock in the Afternoon when the Box which contained the Names of the voters was produced by William Stent, one of the Church Wardens for the said Parish, two of the Seals were tore off. That many undue practices were allowed by the Church Wardens during the Election to obtain a Majority of Votes for Mr Gaillard. That several persons were refused the liberty of Voting for your Petitioner on the first day of Election, and on the second were, offered their Votes, provided they would Vote for Mr Gaillard, That many Persons under Age, some who had no property in the Parish, and several Mulatoes were allowed to Vote at the said

---
*A citizen of South Carolina was eligible for election to the Commons House from any parish or election district wherein he owned land, and Mr. Huger owned land in St. Matthew's Parish.

Election, contrary to the derections of the said Act.—
Wherefore. Your Petitioner humbly prays that the
Premises may be taken into Consideration by this
Honorable House, and on proof thereof, that the Election of the said Tacitus Gaillard Esquire may be set
aside and deemed void and of no Effect.'

"Ordered-that the Petition be referred to the Committee on Privileges and Elections. And that the said Committee have Power to send for Persons, Papers and Records." What their report was the journal does not show, but suffice it to say that Mr. Gaillard served out his term, which—by the way—lasted until September 15th 1775, when Governor Campbell prorogued the Assembly; the last Assembly under the Royal government. We may, therefore, take that date as the closing date of the colonial period in our history.

Sheriffs.
1772.
William Thomson.
1775.
John James Haig.*

Jailer of Orangeburgh District.
1775.
John Mills.†
District Clerk of Court.
1775.
James Caldwell.‡

---

* "His Honour the Lieutenant-Governor has been pleased to appoint John James Haig Esq., to be Sheriff of Orangeburgh District."—*South Carolina Gazette*, Feb. 6, 1775.

"To Be Sold
"At Orangeburgh C. H. on the 1st. Tuesday in December next."
* * * *   "Plantation", &c.   "John James Haig,
                                            "Sheriff".—*S. C.
Gazette*, Nov. 28, 1775. †*S. C. Gazette.* ‡*S. C. Gazette*, Jan. 23, 1775.

CHAPTER IV.

THE REVOLUTIONARY PERIOD.

Section 1. The Civil Affairs of the Period.

The excitement occasioned by the blockading of Boston port, by act of the British Parliament, in 1774,* caused a great number of the people of the Province of South Carolina to meet together in convention† in Charlestown, July 6th, 1774. St. Matthew's Parish was represented in that convention by Col. Tacitus Gaillard, who at that time was a member of the Commons House of Assembly (or Constitutional Assembly) for St. Matthew's Parish. (See *S. C. Gazette* for Monday, July 11, 1774.)

This convention passed a set of resolutions condemning the British Parliament for shutting up Boston port, and setting forth the rights of the American colonists; and also elected five delegates‡ to a Continental Congress, to meet in Philadelphia the first Monday in September following. This convention selected a committee of ninety-nine to act as a General Committee to correspond with the committees of the other Colonies, and to do all matters and things necessary to carry out the resolutions of the convention. It was stipulated that twenty-one of this committee should constitute a quorum and that the power of the General Committee was to continue until the next general meeting. On this committee Col. Tacitus Gaillard, Col. William Thomson and William Ancrum

---

*See *South Carolina Gazette*, June 3, 1774. †See *S. C. Gazette*, June 13, 1774,—call for meeting. ‡Henry Middleton, John Rutledge, Christopher Gadsden, Thomas Lynch and Edward Rutledge.

were appointed for St. Matthew's Parish.* At this early day St. Matthew's Parish was the only part of Orangeburgh District that was allowed representation in the Assemblies. St. Matthew's Parish, of course, included Orangeburgh Township.

The Continental Congress, which met the first Monday in September, and adjourned the 26th of October, 1774; among its other acts, formed an association to suspend importations of British goods, and the exportation of American produce, till their grievances should be redressed; and recommended to the several Colonies a strict observance of these pledges, and that the provincial conventions establish such further regulations as they might think proper for carrying the pledges into execution.

To give efficacy to the measure, adopted by the deputies at Philadelphia, it was determined by the General Committee in Charlestown, to convene a provincial congress, by electing representatives from every parish and district in South Carolina, and to submit the proceedings of the Continental Congress to their judgment. As the measures about to be adopted depended entirely on the consent of the people, a very large representation was thought advisable. The Constitutional Assembly consisted of only forty-nine, but this new representative body consisted of one hundred and eighty-four. The members of the Constitutional Assembly were universally members of the Congress, but with this difference, that in the latter capacity they could neither be prorogued nor dissolved by the royal Governor.

This first Provincial Congress met in Charlestown on the 11th, of January 1775, and took under consideration the proceedings of the Continental Congress at

---

*See *S. C. Gazette and Country Journal*, for Tuesday, July 12, 1774.

ORANGEBURG COUNTY.

Philadelphia at the close of the preceeding year. The following notice of the Provincial Congress appears in the *South Carolina Gazette* of January 23rd, 1775:*
"List of the several members of the Provincial Congress, which was held here on the 11th Instant; being the most complete Representation of all the good people throughout the Colony that ever was and perhaps ever will be obtained." Then follows a list of the members, St. Matthew's Parish, including Orangeburgh Township, being represented by:

   Col. Tacitus Gaillard,
   Col. William Thomson,
   Rev. Paul Turquand,†
   Mr. John Caldwell,
   Mr. George King,
   Mr. Simon Berwick.

The Township of Saxe-Gotha, Orangeburgh District, was represented by:

   Hon. William Henry Drayton,‡
   Hon. Barnard Elliott,‡
   William Arthur,
   Jonas Beard,
   Benjamin Farrar,
   William Tucker.

This Congress, without one dissenting voice, gave public thanks to their late deputies to the Continental Congress, approved their proceedings, and resolved to

---

*See also *S. C. Gazette and Country Journal*, Tuesday, January 17, 1775. See also Moultrie's Memoirs, Vol. I, page 17. † "Ordered, That the Rev. Mr. Turquand, a member, be desired to celebrate divine service in Provincial Congress." "Resolved, That the President do return the thanks of the Congress, to the Rev. Mr. Turquand, rector of St. Mathew's Parish, for his devout and pious performance of divine service before the Congress. And the same was done accordingly." —Moultrie's Memoirs, Vol. I, page 39. ‡Any voter who owned land in an election district was eligible to represent that district in an Assembly, whether he lived in that district or not.

carry their suggestions into execution; and to this end adopted the following resolution:* "*Resolved* that the following Gentlemen be the Committee for effectually carrying into execution the Continental Association† and for receiving and determining upon applications relative to law processes". On this Committee the following gentlemen were appointed to represent St. Matthew's Parish, which included Orangeburgh Township:

    Col. Tacitus Gaillard,
    Col. William Thomson,
    Col. John Savage,
    Rev. Paul Turquand.
    Mr. George King,
    Mr. John Caldwell,
    Mr. Simon Berwick,
    Mr. Henry Felder,
    Col. Michael Christopher Rowe,
    Mr. Lewis Golson,
    Mr. Adam Snell,
    Mr. Christopher Zahn.

And the following gentlemen were appointed for Saxe-Gotha Township, Orangeburgh District:

    Benjamin Farrar,
    Jonas Beard,
    William Tucker,
    Samuel Boykin,
    Godfrey Drier,
    Ralph Humphries.

On the 19th of April, 1775, the Battle of Lexington was fought, and the very same day a packet from

---

*See *S. C. Gazette*, Feb. 13, 1775, and Moultrie's Memoirs, Vol. I, page 43.

†The first of February, 1775, was the day fixed by the Continental Congress after which no British goods should be imported.

London reached Charlestown with intelligence subversive of the pleasing hopes of a speedy accommodation. These matters so excited the people, and affairs began to take such a serious shape that the Provincial Congress was immediately summoned by the General Committee, to meet in twenty-three days at Charlestown. "So great was the zeal of the inhabitants", says Dr. Ramsay in his History of the Revolution of South Carolina, p. 33, "and so general the alarm throughout the province, that one hundred and seventy-two members of the provincial Congress met on the day appointed, the first of June 1775, and proceeded with such assiduity, that they finished a great deal of important business in a short session of twenty-two days. Great were the objects which came before this assembly. Hitherto the only sacrifices demanded at the shrine of liberty, were a suspension of trade and business; but now the important question was agitated, whether it was better to 'live slaves or die freemen'."

On the second day of their meeting it was unanimously resolved that an association was necessary, and, accordingly, one was drawn up and signed by all of the members present, and afterwards by a large majority of the people of South Carolina.* By the terms of this association the people of South Carolina united themselves "under every tie of religion and honour", and associated "as a band in her defence against every foe". All persons who should refuse to subscribe to the association were to be considered as "inimical to the liberty of the colonies". Within three days it was resolved to raise two regiments of infantry and a regiment of rangers,* and to put the

---
*See letter of Henry Laurens to Col. Fletchall.—Collections of the South Carolina Historical Society, Vol. II, page 42.
†On June 21, 1775, the Council of Safety: "*Resolved*, That it is not

town and province in a respectable position for defence. On June 22nd this Congress adjourned.

From the *South Carolina Gazette* of September 7th, 1775, we learn that on the 7th, 8th, 28th, and 29th of August, 1775, elections were held throughout South Carolina for delegates to a "Colony Congress" to be held in Charlestown the first day of December following. St, Matthew's Parish, including the Township of Orangeburgh, elected the following delegates:

    Col. Tacitus Gaillard,
    Mr. Simon Berwick,
    Rev. Mr. Paul Turquand,
    Mr. Henry Felder,
    Mr. John Caldwell,
    Captain William Fludd.

The Township of Saxe-Gotha, Orangeburgh District, elected the following:

    Hon. Wm. Henry Drayton,
    Benjamin Farrar,
    William Arthur,
    Henry Patrick,
    Ralph Humphries,
    Dr. Jacob Richmond.

The section between the North fork of the Edisto river and the Savannah river, also a part of Orangeburgh District, elected delegates to this Congress also, but their names have not been obtained. The new Provincial Congress met, agreeably to their original appointment, on the 1st of November, 1775.*

---

necessary for the present, to raise more than fifty men per company in the Foot, and thirty men per troop of Horse, in the Regiments ordered to be raised for the service of this colony."

*A short while previous to the assembling of the Provincial Congress, Lord William Campbell, the Royal Governor, assembled the Constitutional Assembly and tried to transact business, but as most of the members of this Assembly sided with the Colonists, he could do nothing with them, and accordingly, on the 15th of September, he

"Till the year 1776, the opposition to Great-Britain was conducted on such temporary principles, that the repeal of a few acts of parliament would have immediately produced a reinstatement of British government—a dissolution of the American army—and a recommencement of the mercantile intercourse between the two countries. The refusal of Great-Britain to redress the grievances of the colonies, suggested to some bold spirits early in 1776, the necessity of going much greater lengths than was originally intended."*

* * * * * * * * *

"Public affairs were in confusion for want of a regular constitution. The impropriety of holding courts of justice under the authority of a sovereign against whom all the colony was in arms, struck every thinking person. The impossibility of governing a large community by the ties of honour, without the authority of law, was equally apparent. But notwithstanding the pressing weight of all these considerations, the formation of an independent constitution had so much the appearance of an eternal separation from a country, by a reconciliation with which many yet hoped for a return of ancient happiness, that a great part of the provincial Congress opposed the necessary measure. At the very time when they were suspended on this important debate, an express arrived from Savannah, with an act of parliament, passed December 21, 1775, confiscating American property, and throwing all the colonists out of his Majesty's protection. This turned the scale—silenced all the moderate men who were advocates for a reconciliation—and produced a majority for an independent constitution".†

* * * * * * * * *

---

dissolved the Assembly, and never afterwards issued writs for a new election.
*Ramsay.—Hist. Rev. S. C., page 81. †Ibid, page 81.

"So strong was the attachment of many to Great-Britain, which they fondly called the mother-country, that though they assented to the establishment of an independent constitution, yet it was carried, after a long debate, that it was only to exist 'till a reconciliation between Great-Britain and the colonies should take place'."*

This constitution, temporarily declaring South Carolina a free and independent republic, was adopted March 26th, 1776. "The most essential parts of this temporary constitution are contained in the following resolutions:"†

"I. That this Congress, being a full and free representation of the people of this colony, shall henceforth be deemed and called the General Assembly of South Carolina, and as such shall continue until the 21st of October next, and no longer.

"II. That the General Assembly shall, out of their own body, elect, by ballot, a legislative-council, to consist of thirteen members, (seven of whom shall be a quorum) and to continue for the same time as the general assembly.

"III. That the general assembly, and legislative-council, shall jointly, choose, by ballot, from among themselves, or from the people at large, a president and commander-in-chief, and a vice-president of the colony.

"V. That there be a privy-council, whereof the vice-president of the colony shall of course be a member and president of the privy-council, and that six other members be chosen by ballot, three by the general assembly, and three by the legislative-council; provided always, that no officer of the army or navy, in the service of the continent, or of this colony, shall be eligible.

---
*Ramsay.—Hist. Rev. S. C., page 83. †Ibid, page 89, et seq.

"VII. That the legislative authority be vested in the president and commander-in-chief, the general assembly and legislative-council.

"XI. That on the last Monday in October next, and the day following, and on the same days of every second year thereafter, members of the general assembly shall be chosen, to meet on the first Monday in December then next, and continue for two years from said last Monday in October. The general assembly to consist of the same numbers of members as this congress does, each parish and district having the same representation as at present.

"XVI. That the vice-president of the colony, and the privy-council, for the time being, shall exercise the powers of a court of chancery. And there shall be an ordinary, who shall exercise the powers heretofore exercised by that officer in this colony.

"XIX. That justices of the peace shall be nominated by the general assembly, and commissioned by the president during pleasure.

"XX. That all other judicial officers shall be chosen, by ballot, jointly by the general assembly and legislative-council.

"XXI. That the sheriffs, qualified as by law directed, shall be chosen in like manner by the general assembly and legislative-council, and commissioned by the president for two years only.

"XXII. The commissioners of the treasury, the secretary of the colony, the register of mesne conveyances, attorney-general, and powder-receiver, shall be chosen by the general assembly and legislative-council jointly, by ballot, and commissioned by the president during good behaviour; but shall be removed on the address of the general assembly and legislative-council.

"XXIII. That all field-officers in the army, and all

captains in the navy, shall be, by the general assembly and legislative-council, chosen jointly, by ballot, and commissioned by the president: and that all other officers in the army and navy shall be commissioned by the president and commander-in-chief."

In consequence of this temporary constitution the following officers were elected immediately on the adoption of the constitution:

  President, John Rutledge,
  Vice-President, Henry Laurens,
  Chief Justice, William Henry Drayton.
  Assistant Judges, Thomas Bee, John Mathews and Henry Pendleton.
  Attorney-General, Alexander Moultrie,
  Secretary, John Huger,
  Ordinary, William Burrows,
  Judge of the Admiralty, Hugh Rutledge,
  Register of Mesne Conveyances, George Sheed.

Members of the Legislative-Council:
  Charles Pinckney,
  Henry Middleton,
  Richard Richardson,
  Rawlins Lowndes,
  LeRoy Hammond,
  David Oliphant,
  Thomas Ferguson,
  Stephen Bull,
  George Gabriel Powell,
  Thomas Bee,
  Joseph Kershaw,
  Thomas Shubrick,
  William Moultrie.

Members of the Privy-Council:
  James Parsons,
  William Henry Drayton,
  John Edwards,

ORANGEBURG COUNTY.

Charles Pinckney,
Thomas Ferguson,
Rawlins Lowndes.

Pursuant to the provisions of Article XIX above quoted, justices of the peace for the several parishes and precincts of the colony were, in April, 1776, nominated by the General Assembly and commissioned by President Rutledge. The following were the justices selected for Orangeburgh District: George Ancrum, William Arthur, Jonas Beard, Samuel Boykin, Richard Brown, Donald Bruce, Peter Corbin, James Cornelley, Malcolm Clark, Isham Clayton, John Chesnut, Michael Dickert, Benjamin Farrar, John Fairchild, Lewis Golson, Tacitus Gaillard, Ralph Humphries, ——— Houschild, David Holmes, William Housell, John Kensalow, Michael Leitner, Ephriam Mikell, David Pou, Henry Patrick, James Pritchard, Samuel Rowe, M. C. Rowe, Jacob Richman, George Robinson, John Savage, Arthur Simkins, George Strawther, William Thomson, William Tucker, and Thomas Young.*

The *South Carolina and American General Gazette* for Wednesday, April 17th, 1776, states that on April 11th, the following commissioners of election were appointed by the General Assembly: For Saxe-Gotha Township, election to be held at Granby, William Arthur, Benjamin Farrar, Ralph Humphries, Jacob Richman, and Jacob Finlay. The commissioners of election for St. Matthew's were, as was the custom in all the parishes, the wardens of the parish church, and the election was held at the church.

After passing a few necessary laws, the representatives of the people closed their session on the 11th, of April, 1776. This first General Assembly, agreeably

---

*See *South Carolina and American General Gazette* for Wednesday, April 17th, 1776.

to the constitution they had framed, was dissolved on the 21st of October of the same year, and a general election for members of the Legislature was immediately held throughout the State the last Monday in October. Such was the union of the people, and so general their acquiescence in the measures adopted by their representatives, that the former members were almost universally returned. The following members were elected for Orangeburgh District:

For St. Matthew's Parish, including Orangeburgh Township: Richard Richardson,* Donald Bruce, and four others.

For Saxe-Gotha Township: Six members.

For the territory between the North Edisto and Savannah rivers: Six members.

For the lower district between Broad and Saluda rivers: Two members.

The *South Carolina and American General Gazette* for October 17th, 1776, contains the following:

"At a Court of General Sessions of the Peace, Oyer and Terminer, Assize and General Gaol Delivery, begun and holden at Orangeburgh for the District of Orangeburgh, on Monday the 20th, Day of May, 1776, before the Honorable William Henry Drayton, Esq, Chief Justice of the Colony of South Carolina.

"The ADDRESS and DECLARATION of the Grand Jury of the said District, to his Honour the Chief Justice.

---

*The *Gazette of the State of South Carolina* for April 9th, 1777: "Writs have been issued, for electing Members of the General Assembly to fill up Vacancies which have happened in the following Parishes and Districts." Among the members to be elected to fill these vacancies was one for St. Matthew's Parish, "in the room of Col. Richard Richardson, who made his election for St. James, Goose Creek". The election days were set for Tuesday and Wednesday, April 22nd and 23rd, following.

"May it please your Honour,

"Whilst engaged in an arduous but glorious Struggle for the preservation of those invaluable Rights and Liberties, which, by the Laws of Reason, and of Nature, all men have a right to possess, and without the Possession of which Life itself would be a Burthen; it was Matter of no small Grief to us that any Men should be found amongst us ready to add to the Distress of an oppressed and injured People, by endeavouring to introduce Anarchy and Confusion and thereby to light up the Flames of Civil Discord in the Bowels of this once happy Country.—We are fully convinced that those must have been the nefarious intentions, and base Hopes which induced the King's Judges to refuse the Execution of their Offices, and by so doing to put a Stop to the Administration of Justice in the Courts under their Jurisdiction; to the great Danger of the Lives, Liberties, and Properties of the good People of this Colony. But however great our Grief, we cannot say we are surprised at their Conduct—Strangers in this Land, as they are, and, induced by no Ties of Affection to this Country, or its Inhabitants, they acted as may ever be expected from the wretched Hirelings of an arbitrary and despotic Power. We trust they are the last Officers of the Kind this Colony will ever know, and hope it will be an additional Cause, for us hereafter to rejoice that we resisted, that we thereby became sensible of the true Interest of America in this, as well as many other Respects. To the base Conduct of our late Judges, among other Causes, we owe however the excellent Constitution lately established amongst us: A Constitution evidently framed for the Good, Welfare and Happiness of those who are to live under it. We declare, that as we do most heartily approve of, so we are determined with our Lives and Fortunes to support, maintain and defend it. And to that End, we will, to the utmost of our Power, endeavour to make known its Excellency to all around us, to promote and encourage Peace, Harmony and good Will among the People; and whilst we treat with the tender Hand of Pity and Compassion those few, if any, of our Brethren, who, from the Want of Information, or the artful Designs and Intrigues of wicked Men, may be found at present unfriendly to the sacred Cause in which we are now engaged, we will use our utmost Efforts to teach and instruct them what, and how many Grievances we labour under; the dutiful, humble, and we cannot help now thinking too submissive, Petitions and Remonstrances, we have vainly presented for Redress; the appeal made by our oppressors to the Sword, and driven as we are by dire necessity, the becoming and spirited Measures we have pursued and are now pursuing for a vigorous, manly, and virtuous Defence of the Liberties of ourselves and, which are still dearer to us, of our Posterity. Thus acting, we doubt not but that we shall be able to create such an Union among them, as if extended over the whole Colony, will, with the Assistance of that gracious Providence which has hitherto manifested itself in our Favour; the Goodness of our Cause, the Advantage of our Situation, our Use to Arms, and our Equality, if not Superiority in other Respects to those who are, or may be sent against us, insure us, if called to Action, both Victory and Peace.

"GREAT BRITAIN has forced us into a new Form of Government; she may continue the Sword so long unsheathed that by observing its Superiority over the old, we may be unwilling to part with it. We now have Rulers of our free Choice and Judges of our own Election; a full and equal Representation in the Government; Blessings we hope we should never lose, and which the Wisdom of the Continental Congress will enable us long to keep Possession of. In our present Situation it would be needless for us to present any Grievances to this Court: From the Joy we are in, and the Pleasures we feel in observing the Attention paid to the Interests of the Colony, at the first Session of the Assembly under the present Constitution, by the Law for the once more opening the Courts of Justice amongst us, and, the many other excellent Laws passed in that Session, we can think of none we labour under: Should there be any, we have the greatest Confidence that your Honour would pay proper Attention to them, were they pointed out, and that the Legislature will at all Times be ready to provide adequate Remedies, when they are.

"Henry Felder, (L. S.)
"George King, (L. S.)
"Michael Leitner, (L. S.)
"William Heatly, (L. S.)
"Garrit FitzPatrick, (L. S.)
"Adam Snell, (L. S.)
"Gaspar Brown, (L. S.)
"John M'Williams, (L. S.)
"Henry Rickenbacker, (L. S.)
"Henry Whetstone, (L. S.)
"Henry Crum, (L. S.)
"Godfred Drelve, (L. S.)
"Jonas Beard. (L. S.)"

From the strength of this Grand Jury report, and the ability displayed in its preparation, we are led to believe that the back country people of South Carolina were not as ignorant and illiterate as John Bach McMaster, Mason L. Weems, and some other writers would have us believe that they were at the time of the American Revolution.

The new Assembly met on the 6th of December 1776, and, in a few days thereafter, re-elected the former President and Vice-President. South Carolina was the first of the United Colonies that formed an independent constitution; but as this was done on temporary principles, the declaration of independence by the Continental Congress, which took place on the 4th of July preceding, made it necessary to remodel that temporary form of government, so as to accommodate it to that great event. The members of the Legislature, chosen in October 1776, were authorized by the people to frame a new constitution suited to the declared independence of the State. Authorized in this manner, the Legislature, in January 1777, began the important business of framing a permanent form of government. Before finally adopting this new constitution the Legislature submitted it to the people for their approval for the space of one year, so that it was not finally adopted until the spring of 1778.

The temporary constitution, ratified in March 1776, differs from that which was framed in 1777 in the following particulars: By the last, the appellation of the country was changed from colony to state, and of the chief magistrate, from president to governor. The Legislative authority was reduced from three to two branches. Instead of the Legislative-Council, to be chosen by the representatives of the people out of their own body, a senate, consisting at twenty-eight members, each upward of thirty years of age, to be elected by the people in their respective parishes and districts, was constituted a branch of the Legislature. And South Carolina was declared *absolutely* free and independent of Great Britain.

On January 16th, 1777, the Legislature passed an Act for raising taxes; and, in accordance with the 6th paragraph of the Act, appointed Inquirers and Collectors for the several parishes and districts of the State. The following were the Inquirers and Collectors appointed for Orangeburgh District: For St. Matthew's Parish, including Orangeburgh Township, Henry Felder, William Reed and Joseph Dunklin; for the district of Saxe-Gotha, George Stroul, Andrew Kaigler, and William Gieger; for the district between the Savannah river and the North fork of the Edisto river, William Robinson, James Moore, Henry Peoples and Henry Young.*

The *South Carolina and American General Gazette* for February 12th, 1778, contains the following:
"SOUTH CAROLINA,
  "ORANGEBURGH-DISTRICT.

"The Presentments of the Grand Jurors, at a Court of General Gaol Delivery, for the District of Orangeburgh, on Wednesday the 5th Day of November, 1777, before Hon. William Henry Drayton, Esq; Chief-Justice of the said State.

"I. We present as a grievance the dangerous practice of fire-hunting, and recommend that a law be passed inflicting more severe penalties than the last, upon persons guilty thereof.

"II. We present as a grievance, the want of a law, fixing some punishment on persons harboring or concealing horse and other thieves.

"III. We present as a grievance, the want of a publick general test, by which the foes may be distinguished from the friends of the American cause; and we do recommend that the abjuration oath may be made general. Lastly, We return our thanks to his Honour the Chief-Justice for his patriotic charge de-

---
*Statutes of S. C., Vol. IV, page 369.

livered to us at this sessions, and, request that these our presentments be made publick.

"Lewis Golson, Foreman, (L. S.)
"William Arthur, (L. S.)
"George King. (L. S.)
"Phillip Frierson, (L. S.)
"Gaspar Brown, (L. S.)
"Daniel Kelly, (L. S.)
"Henry Felder, (L. S.)
"Guerard FitzPatrick, (L. S.)
"David Friday, (L. S.)
"Henry Whetstone, (L. S.)
"John Harrisperger, (L. S.)
"Henry Rickenbacker, (L. S.)
"Godfrey Drehr, (L. S.)
"Adam Snell, (L. S.)"

The new constitution having been approved of by both the deliberative branches of the Legislature. and also having gained the implied consent of the people. after one year of trial, the Generol Assembly and Legislative-Council proceeded, in March 1778. to give it a final sanction in the form of a law. When it was submitted to President Rutledge he refused to sign it, because he then held office under the constitution of 1776, which made South Carolina independent of Great Britain only until an agreement could be reached with her. He therefore resigned the office of President, and Rawlins Lowndes was elected in his stead. and on the 19th of March, 1778, he gave his assent to the new constitution.

On March 28th, 1778, the Legislature passed an act for establishing a new list of jurymen for the several Districts of the State, declaring: "That the several persons whose names are inserted in the different schedules or lists hereunto annexed as jury lists for the several districts of Charlestown, Georgetown, Cheraws, Camden. Beaufort and Orangeburgh, within this State, and entitled the grand jury list, petit jury list, and the special jury list, of each of the said districts respectively, are hereby deemed and declared to be qualified and obliged to serve as jurymen for such districts respectively, according to the several jury lists in which their names are so inserted; that is to say, all persons whose names are inserted in the list of the grand jury of any of the districts aforesaid and hereunto annexed, shall be summoned, returned and obliged to serve as grand jurymen, according to law, for such districts in the grand jury list of which their names are so inserted; and all persons whose names are inserted in the petit jury list of any of the districts aforesaid and hereunto annexed, shall be summoned, returned and obliged to serve as petit jurymen for such districts in the petit jury list of which their names are so inserted; and also all persons whose names are inserted in the special jury list of any of the districts aforesaid and hereunto annexed, shall be summoned, returned and obliged to serve as talesmen on the petit jury of such district in the special jury list of which their names are so inserted, in all cases where tales are allowed by law."

The Legislature of South Carolina, on March 28th, 1778, ratified an Act for raising taxes. This act provided for the appointment of Inquirers and Collectors for the collecting of the said taxes in the various parishes and districts of the State. In the 7th paragraph of this Act these Inquirers and Collectors are named, and the following were the appointees for Orangeburgh District: For St. Matthew's Parish, including Orange Parish, lately formed, Philip Frierson, William Heatly, George Frierson and Donald Bruce; for Saxe-Gotha Township and adjacent parts, William

Arthur and Samuel Boykin; for the district between the North fork of the Edisto river and the Savannah river, William Robinson, James Moore, Henry Peoples and John Jennings.*

In 1778, James Prichard is mentioned in the *Gazette of the State of South Carolina* as sheriff of Orangeburgh District.

In the *Gazette of the State of South Carolina* for October 28th, 1778, notice is given that an election, in accordance with the new constitution, would be held the last Monday in November and the day following, Tuesday, December the first, and the following commissioners of election for Orangeburgh District were then named: For Orange Parish (late a part of St. Matthew's Parish), election to be held at Orangeburgh Court House, Henry Felder, Donald Bruce, Samuel Rowe, and John Clayton; for the district between the North fork of the Edisto river and the Savannah river; John Parkinson, James Moore, John Collins, Capt. George Robison, and Henry Peoples; for Saxe-Gotha Township; election to be held at Granby, Ralph Humphries, Jacob Richman, William Arthur, and Samuel Boykin. For St. Matthew's Parish the election was, as usual, of course, to be conducted by the parish church wardens at the church. Under the apportionment of the new constitution, Orangeburgh District was allowed the following representation: For St. Matthew's and Orange parishes combined, one senator; St. Matthew's three representatives, and Orange three; the district between the North fork of the Edisto river and the Savannah river, one senator and six representatives; Saxe-Gotha Township, one senator and six representatives. The election was scheduled

---

*Statutes of S. C., Vol. IV, page 417. Also *S. C. and American General Gazette* for April 2nd, 1778.

for the last Monday in November, 1778, and the day following.

The new Assembly met the first Monday in January 1779. As the term of office of President Lowndes had expired, and as the office of president had been abolished by the new constitution and that of governor created in its stead, the Legislature immediately elected John Rutledge governor.

The *Gazette of the State of South Carolina* for February 24th, 1779, mentions James Haig as sheriff of Orangeburgh District.

On the 9th of September, 1779, the Legislature passed an Act for raising taxes, and, under the 7th paragraph of the Act, appointed Inquirers and Collectors for the several parishes and districts of the State. The following were the Inquirers and the Collectors appointed for Orangeburgh District: For St. Matthew's Parish, Samuel Dubois, Jacob Christopher Zahn and Jared Neilson; for Orange Parish, Lewis Golson, William Hill and Henry Felder: for Saxe-Gotha Township and parts adjacent, William Arthur and Jacob Sayler; for the Fork district, John Collins, George Robison, and James Leyton Richards.*

On the 11th of September, 1779, the Legislature elected J. Wylde and P. Watters magistrates for Orangeburgh District.†

The General Assembly of South Carolina, called for, met in December, 1779, when the following representatives for Orangeburgh District appeared:‡

---

*Statutes of S. C., Vol. IV, pages 490 and 491. †See House journal for that period. ‡See the *Gazette of the State of South Carolina* for Wednesday, December 8th, 1779. These representatives were probably the ones elected in October, 1778.

Senator for the combined parishes of Orange and St. Matthew;
> Col. William Thomson.

Representatives for Orange Parish;
> Donald Bruce,
> Samuel Rowe,
> William Hill.

Representatives for St. Matthew's Parish;
> Isaac Porcher,
> Jacob Christopher Zahn,
> Samuel Dubois.

Senator for the Fork district;
> Stephen Smith.

Representatives for the Fork district;
> John Collins,
> Britton Williams,*
> Henry Hampton,
> Patrick Cain,
> James Fair.

Senator for Saxe-Gotha Township;
> John Hopton.

Representatives for Saxe-Gotha Township;
> William Arthur,
> William Gieger,†
> Ralph Humphries,‡
> Jonas Beard,
> Jacob Seyler,
> James Beams.

Senator for the lower district between Broad and Saluda rivers;
> Charles King.

---

*Hung by Tories in 1780.—Tarleton Brown's Memoirs, page 17.
†Died during the session beginning Aug. 31, 1779, and ending Feb. 12, 1780.
‡Removed from the State during the same period.

Representatives for lower district between Broad and Saluda rivers:

    Wade Hampton,
    Philemon Waters.

This Assembly adjourned February 12th, 1780; but before adjourning, it passed, on Feb. 3rd, "An Ordinance for the better defence and security of this State, during the recess of the General Assembly", which Ordinance practically vested in Governor Rutledge the powers of a dictator, as, among other things, it gave him the right, "with the advice and consent of the Privy Council", "to do all matters and things which may be judged expedient and necessary to secure the liberty, safety and happiness of this State, except taking away the life of a citizen without legal trial". Practically the same powers had been given Governor Rutledge on a previous occasion, February, 1779, when the Legislature adjourned with the State threatened by an invasion.

The fall of Charlestown, the capital, in 1780, and the subsequent overrunning of the State by the British, rendered it impracticable to hold another session of the Legislature for nearly two years. For the same reason it was not possible to hold an election for a new legislature in the fall of 1780. But, the State having been recovered from the British, towards the close of 1781, Governor Rutledge, by virtue of the extraordinary power delegated to him before the surrender of Charlestown, issued writs for new elections. These were ordered to be held in the usual places where it was practicable, and in other cases as near as safety and other circumstances would permit. By the same authority it was ordered, that at the election the votes of such, only, should be received as had never taken British protection, or who having taken it, had, notwithstanding, re-joined their countrymen on or before the twenty-seventh of September, 1781.

At this election the following were the members returned for Orangeburgh District: Orange Parish, Capt. Henry Felder, George Rennarson, and —————; St. Matthew's Parish, William Middleton, —————, and —————; the Fork district. Wm. Robison, Wm. Dunbar, John Collins, John Parkinson, ———, and ———; Saxe-Gotha Township, Jonas Beard, Michael Lietner, and four others.

This Legislature, so chosen, met January 8th, 1782. The Senate chose John Lewis Gervais, president; and the House chose Hugh Rutledge, speaker; and some days later, Governor Rutledge's term having expired, John Mathews was chosen governor; all vacancies were filled up in the different departments, and civil government was re-established, and before adjourning (Feb. 26th), the Legislature delegated to Governor Mathews the same powers, with similar limitations, that had been intrusted to Governor Rutledge in 1779 and 1780.

Section 2. The Third Regiment of South Carolina Continentals.

There are very few records to show the names of those brave men of Orangeburgh District, who went forth to battle for the independence of South Carolina and the other American colonies, but there are documents enough in evidence to show that a good part of the fighting was done by men from Orangeburgh. and that they usually had "a place in the picture near the flashing of the guns." If many of the companies and regiments to which the Orangeburgh men belonged ever had any official rolls they were not deposited in places of absolute safety, for the Carolinians recked

ORANGEBURG COUNTY. 279

not of pension bureaus that might be formed when the war should end; and many of the rolls of the organizations to which those brave men belonged, who fought for their country for their country's sake, were lost or destroyed. Many of them have been bought up since the Revolution by historical societies outside of this State, and others were destroyed during the last war. But we can recount the deeds of our heroes, even if we have not their names.

It will be remembered that in June, 1775, the Provincial Congress of South Carolina, as a safeguard, raised two regiments of infantry and one regiment of rangers. William Thomson, a member of that Congress from Orangeburgh District, was elected Lieutenant-Colonel and commander of the regiment of rangers. The officers and men of the regiment were from Orangeburgh† and the adjoining districts of Camden and Ninety-Six. The following were the officers of this regiment elected at its organization.‡ Those marked with an asterisk (*) were of Orangeburgh District:

*William Thomson, Lieut. Col.
James Mayson, Major.

1 Samuel Wise,
2 Ezekiel Polk,
3 *John Caldwell,
4 Eli Kershaw.
5 *Robert Goodwin, } Captains.
6 Moses Kirkland,
7 *Edward Richardson,
8 Thomas Woodward,
9 John Purves.

---

†Dr. Joseph Johnson says, "Traditions of the Revolution", page 90: "He" (Thomson) "being from the upper part of Orangeburg District, soon filled his regiment with many of the best riflemen in the State."
‡See Ramsay's Revolution in South Carolina, Vol. I, pages 36, 37. Also Journal of Council of Safety for June 18, 1775.—Collections S. C. Hist. Soc., Vol. II, page 24.

1. *John Lewis Peyer Imhoff,
2. *Charles Heatly,
3. Alan Cameron,†
4. Richard Winn,
5. John Donaldson,‡
6. Hugh Middleton,
7. Lewis Dutarque,
8. Francis Boykin,
9. Samuel Watson,

⎫ Lieutenants.

The commissions for these officers were signed by the Council of Safety on June 18th, 1775, and on the 21st of June, following, a commission for John Chesnut, Paymaster 3rd regiment, and nine blank commissions, all dated June 18th, for second lieutenants, were signed by the Council. The appointing of the second lieutenants was left to Col. Thomson.

On the 24th of June, 1775, Col. Thomson received, from the Council of Safety, his commission, and an order, dated June 21st, directing him to issue forthwith, orders for levying troops for his regiment; and in the Council of Safety on June 26, 1775, the following resolution was passed:

"*Resolved*, That a letter be written to Col. Thomson, directing him to station the first troop of Rangers that shall be raised, at Fort Charlotte, till further orders; that he send to Charles-Town as soon as possible, the two brass field pieces, and bayonets, that are there; and that he do take charge of all the gun-powder and military stores that shall remain there, and

---

†Cameron refused to accept the commission offered him, as will be seen by his two letters to Major Andrew Williamson, dated July 10th and July 19th, 1775, and published on page 67 of Vol. II. of Collections of S. C. Historical Society. He sympathised with the Crown.

‡Ramsay and Col. Thomson give his name as John Donaldson, but his name is given on the Journal of Council of Safety and in General DeSaussure's pamphlet as James Donaldson.

immediately transmit an exact inventory of the whole to this Council".

Orders in accordance with this resolution were then sent to Col. Thomson,* and on July 1st he transmitted them to Major Mayson to be by him put into execution; and Major Mayson was directed to place Fort Charlotte in charge of Capt. Purvis.

On the 13th of July the Council of Safety issued orders requiring Col. Thomson to make a complete return of his regiment, and issued further orders for the regiment to begin a series of movements on August the 10th; which last orders were rescinded by the Council on July 20th.

On July 14th, the Council, upon application by Col. Thomson, issued the following order, which was doubtless very agreeable to the officers and men of the Rangers:

"Pay to Col. William Thomson, to be paid by him to the Paymaster of the Regiment of Rangers, for paying the said Regiment, the sum of one thousand Pounds currency; for which this shall be your warrant.

"To *John Neufville, Peter Bacot, William Gibbes, esqs., Commissioners of the Colony Treasury.*"

From the Journal of the Council for the same day, July 14th. we extract: "The Council signed a certificate for Dr. Alexander Rogers, appointed Surgeon to the Regiment of Rangers, dated this day. upon an application by Col. Thomson."

Col. Thomson was next given orders. on July 15th, to immediately march his regiment. or such part of it as he might deem necessary for the service, to take Fort Charlotte, in case the same had not already been

---

*See his order book in Section 3 of this chapter.

secured agreeable to the order of June 26th. Upon receiving this order Col. Thomson issued orders for Captains Goodwyn, Kershaw, Richardson and Woodward to meet him at the Congarees on the following Sunday, ready to march to Fort Charlotte; but upon reaching the Congarees he met an express from Major Mayson containing the intelligence of the capture of Fort Charlotte.* Thereupon Col. Thomson went into camp at the Congarees with the four companies he had with him, issued orders for Capt. Wise to also join him at once with his company, and sent a detachment to Fort Charlotte for powder.

From his camp at "Granby near Friday's Ferry", Col. Thomson wrote a letter to the Council of Safety on July 22nd, in which he advised that some member of the Council of Safety and the Rev. William Tennent be sent among the back-country people.

It appears that when the Continental Association was carried among the settlers in the fork between the Broad and Saluda rivers, (a part of which territory was in Orangeburgh District, but the greater part of which was in Ninety-Six District) many of them refused to sign it. The Council of Safety then resolved, on July 23rd, to send William Henry Drayton and the Rev. William Tennent among them to try to persuade them into signing it. The Council also gave them the following authority: "Gentlemen—in order to give you every necessary and proper support and protection in your progress into the country, in execution of our commission of this date, you are hereby authorized to call upon all and every Officer of the Militia and Rangers for assistance, support and protection". Acting under this authority Messrs Drayton and

---

*Which was placed under the care of Capt. John Caldwell and his company.

Tennent. who had left Charleston on August 2nd, called upon Col. Thomson soon thereafter to accompany them with his regiment. The following account of their journey through Orangeburgh District, and their transactions with Col. Thomson and his regiment of rangers, is made up from Mr. Tennent's diary, several letters written by Messrs Drayton and Tennent, and various other documents:

Tennent's diary: "5th. Set out a little after 6, and by the help of Mr. Thomson's good pair of horses, passed over sixteen miles of the worst road I almost ever saw, owing to the steepness of the hills, and the gullies made by yesterday's shower of rain. Dined at Mr. Patrick's, a man of property among the Dutch, and afterwards rode with him seven miles. Arrived at Col. Chestnut's paymaster and there found Col. ——, with sundry officers of the regiment. Among others was agreeably surprised to find Dr. Charlton, from Philadelphia, a lieutenant among them. We were soon introduced to Messrs Dunn & Booth, two lawyers sent from North Carolina, prisoners, for having been busy in stirring up there in opposition to the Continent. They appear sensible and plausible men. After making known our errand to the Commanding Officer, we consulted with him and concluded to send the prisoners by a detachment to Charleston to the general committee informing them of the time of the Congress in North Carolina, to disband the Rangers for a few days, to take off the fears of the people. Sunday, August 6th. Preached in Camp at Col. ———— in the evening. Finding some disaffected among the soldiers Mr. Drayton harrangued them and was followed by myself until all seemed well satisfied, and we returned to Mr. Chestnut's 2 miles. About midnight were alarmed by an officer from the Camp, who informed us, that they had mutined and were determined to go off in the morning, we agreed to let matters rest until they ordered the Companies to come to us.

"Monday, 7th. Discovered that the Mutiny arose from some words dropped by some officers concerning their pay and duty. We dealt plainly with the Corps of Officers, and addressed the men at the head of the Regiment in such a manner as that they all went away happy".

Letter written by Drayton and Tennent:

"Congaree Store,* August 7th, 1775.
"To the Council of Safety.

"Gentlemen:—Having left Charles Town on Wednesday morning, we arrived here early on Saturday afternoon, 130 miles distant from town. In our way, we spent some hours at Col. Gaillard's,† and we flatter ourselves the visit had a good effect. It is to be hoped, he has not delivered himself in public so warmly, as he has expressed himself to us."

* * * * * * * * *

"As a first step to the particular object of our progress, upon our arrival here, we despatched notices to particular persons of influence among the Dutch, to endeavor to procure a meeting of them at the place of election as on this day. To our great mortification not one German‡ appeared, but one or two of our friends who had been industrious to procure a meeting. By them we were informed, their countrymen were so much averse to take up arms, as they imagined, against the king, least they should lose their

---

* "A few hundred yards below Granby."

†Tacitus Gaillard, who lived in Orangeburgh District, near Eutaw Springs,

‡Let it be borne in mind that these were the Saxe-Gotha and "Dutch Fork" Germans—not the Orangeburgh Germans. And even the small hopes that Drayton entertained of *these*, were redeemed afterwards.

lands; and were so possessed with an idea, that the rangers were posted here to force their signatures to the association, that they would not by any arguments be induced to come near us". * * * "However unfavorable these circumstances are, we hope you will not be alarmed at them; we yet have some hopes of success, though we confess they are but small in this quarter.

"We have engaged Col. Thomson to order a muster of two Dutch companies in this neighborhood on Wednesday next, and we have declared if the officers disobey they shall be broke. This threat was highly necessary, as the Dutch Captains had some little time ago disobeyed such an order, alledging that extra musters were warranted only by orders from the Governor. We hope this step will oblige a part of the Germans to give us a hearing; and as we flatter ourselves that our discourses to them will not be entirely lost upon them, we expect these will induce others of their countrymen to be willing to hear what we have to say. With this view, and to give such persons an opportunity of hearing us; we have engaged one Dutch clergyman to perform service at one place on Friday next, and another, at a second place on Sunday next, at both which places Mr. Drayton will be present. And in the mean time, as we know in general, that an argument relating to money matters most readily catches a Dutchman's ear, we have declared that no non-subscriber in this settlement will be allowed to purchase at, or sell to this store or Charles Town. When Mr. Drayton shall quit the Dutch settlements on Sunday next, after having had on Saturday a meeting with a large number of people of all sorts, at one McLaurin's, a store keeper, hitherto an enemy, but now, at least in appearance, a friend, he will proceed up the fork to Col. Fletchall's".

* * * * * * * * *

"Yesterday Mr. Tennent performed divine service in Camp; and in the afternoon Mr. Drayton harrangued the Rangers respecting the new and extraordinary power by which they were raised; the nature of the public disputes, and the justice of the cause in which they were engaged; the nature of their allegiance to the King and their duty to their country, their families and themselves; their duty and obligation to oppose and attack any British troops landing in this colony; their honor was awakened by contrasting their personal value and importance against the importance of the British troops; their complaints respecting provisions were entered into, and they were assured the public meant to do all that could be done for them consistently with the nature of discipline and the calamitous situation of affairs; they were informed that the public could not so much dishonor them as to imagine they had enlisted merely for pecuniary gain, but persuaded that they being actuated with a nobler motive, all men were willing to believe, that they without wishing to be at ease in every respect, as in a regular service under an established and quiet Government, did not, as they could not in honor or conscience, desire more than absolute necessaries. And that, if they thought it a hardship to go abroad to procure provisions, the Council were ready to save them that trouble by deducting a reasonable sum from their pay, and supplying them with provisions in the manner in which the foot were furnished. They had grumbled about tents, and were now informed that the British troops in America during the last war, not only generally used but preferred huts made of bushes. Finally, encomiums were passed upon the progress they had made in the art military, and it was recommended to them in the strongest terms to pay the most perfect obedience to their officers, as the only means by which they could become good soldiers, and to defend those liberties and rights which they appeared so willing to protect. Hitherto there has been but little subordination.

"To these things Mr. Tennent added assurances of the value of Congress currency which many people had endeavored to depreciate in the opinion of the soldiers, and he read and commented upon the declaration of the General Congress.

"These things being finished, we left the camp in apparent quiet satisfaction and content, the men on being discharged expressing their thanks to us. But about midnight, an officer stole from the camp (about two miles off*) and gave us the most alarming intelligence that a most dangerous mutiny had broke out in, and prevailed throughout the whole camp, in which there was no longer any command or obedience; that the men were in an uproar at the idea of a deduction of their pay, for they had in general been promised provisions above their pay, and they were determined to quit the camp this morning and disband. Col. Thomson and Capt. Kershaw lodge with us; they were willing to do any thing that was thought proper. We consulted with them upon the case, and it was thought most advisable not to take any step in the night or for either of those officers to go to the camp; but that time should be allowed for the men to cool, and for the three Captains and other officers in camp to sound the men, and learn who would be depended upon. This measure had the effect we expected, and this morning the men appeared quiet, and it became evident that the disorders arose from three or four privates of profligate dispositions,

---

* "At the Congaree Creek, below Granby".

and from improper conduct, declarations, and conversations of some officers. Capt. Woodward had incautiously at enlisting his men, made promises which proved grounds of discontent and disappointment, and yesterday had even the rashness to attempt to be spokesman to us in the hearing of the Rangers in favor of their being found above their pay; and Lieutenant Dutarque, also attempted to inveigh against the cruelty of keeping men encamped without tents. Such topics had by these officers frequently been touched upon heretofore, but we have privately given them a lecture upon the subject, and we hope as they heard us in a proper manner, that it will have a good effect. From such sources, however, it is plain the disorder of last night arose. The Rangers were this morning marched from camp to this place, where Mr. Drayton harrangued them upon the disorder of the last night, attributing it to a few disorderly persons, who in this the first instance, would by the Colonel be passed over unnoticed, in hopes such lenity would work a reformation in them. The consequences of a mutinous conduct were described as tending to expose them to the derision of their neighbors and enemies, and to cover them and the whole corps with shame, contempt, infamy and ruin, without effecting the public service; for, if they should prove unworthy of the service, they would certainly be brought to condign punishment, and other and more worthy rangers be found to supply their places. For they ought not to flatter themselves, that because some parts of this country were disaffected, that therefore they could desert and be in places of security. If any should desert they must some time be off their caution and guard, and then they would be seized, for a reward would be put upon their heads—no money would be thought too much to ferret them out wheresoever they should go;

and dead or alive they would certainly be carried to Charles Town. The situation of America was placed before them. On one side of the question stood almost infinite numbers, supported by wealth and men of learning and abilities to plan and execute measures to overcome their opponents, who, of the Americans were only a few men of little property and less knowledge and abilities to conduct affairs; and they were asked, if they could possibly think there was any safety among such men. The obligation of their oath was strongly insisted upon; and as to provisions, it was declared that the officers would endeavor to encourage people, of whom many were willing to supply the camp; in which case the soldiers should purchase as they pleased in camp, where, when there were any provisions they should not be allowed to go abroad to seek what they could find at home. They were told, they were not now to look for rewards, but that they must expect them when these troubles were over. For, as in the mean time it would be known who among them behaved with due obedience, and who conducted themselves otherwise; so, all these things in time to come would be remembered by the gentlemen below, who would in private affairs shew to the first all kinds of favors and acts of friendship whenever opportunities should offer; and they would carefully mark the latter, and discountenance and thwart them upon every occasion. This discourse we flatter ourselves had a full effect. They were called upon to say what they pleased; except three men, they were all well satisfied and contented, and showed the most perfect submission. These three were properly checked, and the worst of them severely reprimanded and spoken to in private."

* * * * * * * * *

"As well to remove the apprehensions of the Dutch

settlers as those of the interior parts, that the Rangers were posted here to force measures; and to remove every idea that we came up to issue orders to plunder and lay waste, as well as to allow the soldiers to go home to places of election, and to procure necessaries, and to shew that we place a confidence in their good behavior, we have this day broken up the camp and sent them to their respective homes under their officers, with orders to repair to a new camp in Amelia about thirty miles below this, and to join there on the 18th inst.,* at which place Maj. Mason is likewise under orders to appear at the same time with Capt. Purvis' Company. For the Major's personal presence in 96 is of disservice to the public affairs."

* * * * * * * * *

"With regards to Capt. Polk, we are at present silent, but we hope you will not delay to fill up Captain's Commissions for those two vacancies, by promoting the two eldest first Lieutenants,† as in such a case Mr. Heatly will speedily procure full compliments of recruits for   and himself. We also beg leave to inform you that a Surgeon's mate is necessary for the Rangers, although there is no provision for such a post by particular act of Congress, yet it may arise

---

*Here is a copy of one of the orders issued by Col. Thomson to his captains on this occasion: (Gibbes's Documentary History, 1855, page 127.)

"Camp at Mineral Springs, August 7th, 1775.

"Sir:—You are hereby ordered to give your men leave to go to their respective homes, and you are to order them to get their horses recruited, and themselves properly equipped, and on the 18th instant you are to rendezvous with your company in Amelia place, known by the name of Flechall's old field, where you are to camp till further orders.

"From the Honorable W. H. Drayton, or
"Your most humble servant,
"Wm. Thomson.

"To Capt. Robert Goodwyn."
†This was presently done.

from your power, as such an officer is, in our opinion and the Colonel's, necessary for the service. We beg leave to recommend Lieutenant Thomas Charlton, a man of experience and reputation in physic, and who came into the corps under an idea, that there was provision for such an appointment. He is worthy of the first post in that line in the Regiment; but being willing to serve the public in this cause, he is content with the last rank in the way of his profession."

* * * * * * * * *

"P. S. The Rangers perform their exercise at least as well as the Regulars in Charles Town", &c.

Tennent's diary: "Tuesday 8th. Spent the morning in preparing matters, to get people together in different parts of the district, crossed Congaree River and rode 5 miles to an election for the Congress, where they refused to proceed, unless we should enlighten them. We found persons had come a great way to oppose the election. Harangued the meeting in turns, until every man was convinced, and the greatest opposer signed the Association and begged pardon for the words he had spoken to the people. Returned and found that Major Mason had come. N. B. This morning about 11 o'clock sent off Lieutenant Dutarque with the prisoners to Charleston, charged with our dispatches."

Letter from Drayton to Council of Safety:

"Congaree, August 9, 1775.

"*To the Council of Safety:*

"Gentlemen:—This afternoon Mr. Tennent and Col. Richardson sat off upon their progress on the north side of Broad River. Mr. Kershaw, who came from Camden to-day, remains to continue the progress with me, through the fork between Broad and Saluda rivers."

* * * * * * * * *

"This day we procured a German audience by the means of a muster by the order of Col. Thomson, of which we informed you in our last. During our discourses, the falling tears from the audience showed that their hearts were penetrated,* and that we might hope for success. In conclusion all who were present signed the Association, except fifteen persons, who mildly desired, nay begged to consider of the affair until Friday, when they would certainly meet me at the place of divine service. They have since assured me they will subscribe. All persons joined in the election, which we judged it necessary to postpone yesterday and the day before, as no persons appeared; and as we judged we had authority so to do, as such a proceeding tended to compose the people, and bind their obedience to the measures of the Congress by giving them an opportunity of electing Representatives after they understood the nature of the dispute in which the British Empire is engaged. I expect a large meeting on Friday next, when I expect equal success; by which the whole Congaree settlement will be made parties in our proceedings. I shall then attend two larger assemblies of the people on Saturday and Sunday; and I have now no doubt of success in the Dutch settlements".†

* * * * * * * * *

"I have drawn an order upon the Council in favor of Mr. John Chesnut for four hundred and five pounds, for four horses purchased by Col. Thomson for the service of the progress".

---

* "What would I have given to have been a spectator at the Dutch crying bout, with an Hogarth's pencil in hand? one of you certainly must have been *vastly* moving, whether Tennent or yourself, we are much at a loss to know, for I find you have united the orators under the word we, and thus confounded religion and politics".—Andrew Marvell to William Henry Drayton.

†He had evidently changed his mind about the "Dutch".

Tennent's diary: "Wednesday 9th. Left here about 7, met a Company of militia and harangued them. They signed the Association and generally promised to meet Mr. Drayton in the Fork. After the meeting I gained over in private the most obstinate. Mr. Kershaw now came to us. Major James Mason came through from 96, and gave many melancholy accounts. Having agreed upon our route, we separated and I rode four miles to Mr. Beard's on the Bank of the Saluda, a romantic situation Col. Richardson accompanies me".

* * * * * * * * *

"Thursday August 10th." * * * "Reached Capt. Woodward's of the Rangers after Sun Down, an honest man who informed that his company had universally signed".

Andrew Marvell, Member of Council, to Drayton:* "I have mentioned your request respecting the vacancies in the Regulars, and the blank commissions are forwarded to Thomson by this conveyance."

Tennent's diary: "Friday, 19th. Capt. Polk now came. We find that he has laid under some mistake as to his duty".†

Col. Thomson and the five companies of Captains Wise, Kershaw, Goodwyn, Richardson and Woodward, duly met at the appointed place, "Flechall's old field", where they were soon joined by Maj. Mayson from the Congarees, and by the companies of Captains Imhoff and Heatly. From this camp Col. Thomson moved, by order of Mr. Drayton, to the "Ridge" on September 8th. In the meantime Messrs Drayton and Tennent continued their progress into the up-country, and the

---
* "Charleston, August 12th."
† He had been charged with treachery.

extracts here given from various documents, will show how the work continued:

Drayton's letter to the Council of Safety, from Lawson's Fork, August 21, 1775: "I have the honor to acknowledge receipt of your letters of 11th and 13th instant. They came to hand last night, forwarded by Col. Thomson."

* * * * * * * * *

"I believe Mr. Charleton expected to hold the lieutenant's commission together with that of surgeon's mate. I had forgot the resolution of Congress respecting one person holding two commissions; but I have acquainted Col. Thomson with the affair, who, without doubt, will transmit the explanation you expect.

"I am happy that you approve of my putting off the election at Saxe Gotha; and also that you have directed me to appoint elections for those places where none had been held. In my last of the 16th from King's Creek, I had the honor to acquaint you, that neither of the districts in the Fork, between Broad and Saluda rivers had held any election. For the lower district* I have already acquainted you with the day of election".

* * * * * * * * *

"The commissions for the volunteer companies are not come to hand, but I suppose they are with Col. Thomson, who, in all probability, will continue in his new camp until my arrival there."

* * * * * * * * *

"Things wearing so unfavorable an appearance, Colonel Richardson, Mr. Kershaw, Mr. Tennent and myself unanimously, thought it absolutely expedient, to direct Captain Polk to raise an additional troop of rangers immediately to lie on the back of these peo-

---

*The "lower district" was in Orangeburgh District.

ple. And Mr. Tennent and myself have given directions accordingly, not doubting but that the necessity of the case will induce you to approve the measure. Captain Polk came to us, appeared much concerned for his past conduct, attributing it to a mistake touching the station of the rangers, which he had thought, had been by the Congress fixed to the back country and frontiers. He has been since active in our favor as a person of influence in his part of the country on the back of Fletchall; his brother is a man of great influence in Mecklenburgh, and ready to march to our assistance when called upon; and already Fletchall looked upon Captain Polk as an acquisition to his party. Hence, to bind Captain Polk's brother, and all the friends of both to us; to quash Fletchall's expectation from the Captain, and to have a troop of rangers on the back of Fletchall's people to watch their motions, we all thought it absolutely necessary to direct the raising of this additional troop, as we apprehended you would consider Captain Polk's letter and conduct as a resignation of his commission, and that you had already disposed of it. In short, we have given Captain Polk such a lesson, which he has received with all due submission, as I believe will render him more obedient to orders, than he has been."

* * * * * * * * *

"Within twelve days, I purpose to be at Colonel Thomson's camp, where I think it will be advisable that I should remain till I shall see every spark of insurrection extinguished; but in regard to this, I shall regulate myself by your orders on the subject which I hope to receive by the time I arrive at the camp".

The following is a copy of a letter from Maj. Andrew Williamson, of the Ninety-Six militia, to Capt. Caldwell, of the 3rd regiment:

"White Hall, August 21, 1775.

"Dear Sir:—I just now received a letter from Col. Thompson and Major Mayson, dated the 10th inst., at the Congarees, informing me that they learn of a body of men going from our regiment and headed by some of the disaffected about Stephen's Creek, to attack Augusta. They desire me to give you every intelligence for the defence of Fort Charlotte, that you may be on your guard. I have heard nothing as yet of the above report, but you may depend upon it that if ever they make such an attempt they will have Fort Charlotte in their view.

"I would take the liberty to advise you, if you should hear anything of the above report—that Captain Taylor would order some of his Company to reinforce the post.

"I think it would not be amiss to send one of your men, you can put the most confidence in, to watch the motion of the disaffected about Stephen's Creek, and the Pine-a-wood House. If I learn any thing from this quarter you may depend upon me letting you know immediately—the privater this is kept the better. I this moment send an express from the Council of Safety to Mr. Hammond. Excuse me taking the liberty of dictating to you. I am, dear sir,

"Your most obedient humble servt.,
"A. Williamson.
"*Captain John Caldwell, Commandant at Fort Charlotte.*"

Extracts from a letter written by Mr. Drayton, "At Mr. Hammond's, near Augusta, Aug. 30, 1775":

"By various accounts that I received on the road yesterday afternoon, last night, and this morning, it appears to be a fact that Kirkland* is actually in arms

---

*Moses Kirkland, of the fork between Broad and Saluda rivers, who had been elected a captain in the Rangers, but had turned traitor.

to attack Augusta and Fort Charlotte. The King's men as they are called were summoned to meet yesterday at a place about twenty miles from hence; they separated last night, and I am informed they will meet again in two or three days. They have been very diligent in obtaining arms. Cunningham and Brown are of the party.

"In this situation of affairs, by virtue of your letter of the eleventh instant, I have ordered out three companies near this place to assemble immediately, and who will be joined by one hundred men from Augusta. I have ordered Major Williamson to march with three hundred men to Harden's Ford on Savannah River about thirty miles above this place. I have also ordered Col. Thomson to march his Rangers, and as near three hundred militia as he can, and take post at the Ridge; and Col. Richardson, with three hundred men, to take post near the mouth of Enoree, to be a check on Fletchall's people, in case they should show any intention of assisting Kirkland".

Mr. Tennent's diary of about the same date says: "This evening our little detachment of 200 men marched about eight miles to Foxes Creek, having news that Major Williamson was on his way to 96, and Col. Thomson in full march with the Rangers and Militia to join them".

The following is an order issued by Mr. Tennent to Capt. John Caldwell, commanding a detachment of the 3rd regiment, and some militiamen, at Fort Charlotte:

"Long Canes, September, 1775.
"*To Capt. John Caldwell, at present in Fort Charlotte:*

"Sir:—This is to direct you to employ six workmen to build platforms for fighting the cannon and small arms in the Fort you at present command, and as expeditiously as possible, to put it into the repair directed by orders from Major Mason, bearing date August 6th, 1775, now in your possession. You are to employ the men under your command to assist the workmen in the labor. You are also ordered to mount two of the best four-pounders on high wheels, that they be fit for either field or fort service, as need may require—shafts and collars being provided for them that they may be easily drawn with horses. For these you are to provide two ammunition boxes, cartridges, fuses. and all that may be needful for a march, and so fitted as to fasten on the carriages. Take great care that no man enter the Fort on any pretence, that you do not know and in whom you cannot place confidence. Be much upon your guard against surprise, especially in the night; for this purpose, as often as convenient, order out advanced sentinels and patrols. You are to clear away the standing corn to some distance from the Fort, and insist that the corn which is left be bladed and topped, nor leave any cover that may hide an enemy. In case of an alarm, and when the approach of an enemy is no longer dubious, you are to fire three cannon towards the thickest settlements as a signal; communicating timely notice of the same to the volunteer and other companies of militia that they may understand it, which companies are hereby ordered immediately to assemble and march under the command of their respective officers to your relief, or so to annoy the enemy as the service may require. And, whereas, there is a great scarcity of ammunition among the militia, and an attack from Indians is to be apprehended, you are directed to give out 150 lbs. weight of the powder, and lead in proportion, under your care to the captains of the volunteer and other militia companies in the upper part of this district, who have associated, taking a receipt from them, and directing them so to dispose it among their men, as that it may be returned upon demand when it shall be apprehended that the danger is over. But when a supply of fresh powder shall be sent up by the Council of Safety, you are to exchange the fresh powder pound for pound for the old powder that you have already given out to as many as offer the same for an exchange. You are also ordered to dismiss your horses for the present, and not hazard your men by a grass guard; but the horses are not to be sent to such a distance as that they cannot be commanded within the space of a day and a half."

From "St. Mathew's Parish, Sept. 10, 1775", Mr. Tennent wrote the following to the "*Council of Safety in Savannah*": "Being on my return from the frontiers of South Carolina, where the Honorable Mr. Drayton and myself were sent by the Council of Safety of our Province, I think it my duty to acquaint you that there exists in those parts a most dangerous conspiracy against the lives and liberties of these Colonies. Encouraged by Government and by the tories in your town and in Charlestown they have gone to great lengths. They do not hesitate to boast that they are furnished with ammunition and that even artillery are at their service any day. This I have by a trusty friend from Cunningham's mouth. I have great reason to think that they are mistaken when they boast of many thousands ready to come down at the Governor's signal—but that they have some hundreds actually enlisted, if not under pay, I make not the least doubt. That they depend upon the Cherokee nation to join their camp when it forms, and have great hopes of the Creeks, they do not pretend to keep any longer a secret. I am in possession of an affidavit by which it appears that the malcontents on the frontiers expect to gather into forts, and suffer the savages to pass on and massacre the associated inhabitants. By these circumstances, you gentlemen, will see the necessity of an immediate effort to crush the sedition, and save an effusion of innocent blood to the danger of these Provinces, and especially of the aid which you have already given to that important measure. It will be prudent to have at least one thousand five hundred, if not two thousand men, at hand when it is done; and a number not far short of that is, I hope, by this time in motion in the unhappy district."*

Drayton's letter, of Sept. 11th, from Ninety-Six, details fears of an attack by Fletchall. He says; "I immediately consulted with Major Mason, Major Williamson, and Capt. Hammond. We had a choice of three steps; to retreat towards Col. Thomson then at the Ridge—to defend Ninety-Six or to march and ambuscade the enemy." After detailing his arrangements for resisting this expected attack he goes on: "Fletchall, Brown and Cunningham have been, since the first alarm that I wrote you of, and still are endeavoring to assemble men, as they yet have no force embodied; it is plain their influence is declining, and that their people are terrified. And this last, I assure you, is a fact. They never dreamed we would take the field; they thought their boast of 4,000 would ensure their security against us. And I have well grounded information, that the assembling they are now endeavoring to make, is with a view to make terms of accommodation, so as they may be quiet and trade in Charles Town, rather than with any design of fighting. I think Cunningham had only an hundred men at the meeting which gave occasion for our

---

*The regiments of Thomson, Richardson, &c.

late alarm;* and even these, I have received certain intelligence, have no determination. In three days I shall begin to march into the heart of Fletchall's quarters with about 800 men and 6 pieces of canon. I can now, in all human probability, promise to you, that this cruel opposition will be crushed without blood spilt in battle; and if I shall be unhappily mistaken on this point—the opposition, to all human appearance, will be rooted out without risk on our side."

* * * * * * * * *

"P. S. I expect Col. Thomson will arrive here tomorrow morning."

How much of a prophet Mr. Drayton was, is shown by the fact that three days later, on September 16th, 1775, a treaty was signed at Ninety-Six, between Drayton and the Tories, whereby the Tories promised to disperse and remain neutral, and to deliver up any one of their number who should in any way violate the treaty. And it was further agreed that, "all persons who shall not consider themselves as bound by this treaty must abide by the consequences". Col. Thomson and Capt. Kershaw were present on this occasion, and signed as witnesses to the treaty.

The following is extracted from the report which Mr. Drayton sent the next day to the Council of Safety: "On Tuesday I found, that the 100 men Cunningham had on Sunday were but the first of a large party that had been summoned to meet at Neal's Mill, about ten miles over Saluda. About 3 o'clock on Tuesday afternoon, I was joined at Ninety-Six by Col. Thomson and a few of his militia. It was Wednesday before I was joined by any of Major Williamson's regiment, and it was Thursday before I was joined by

---

*This is another evidence of the fact that the Tories were few in number.

any considerable number of it. In the mean time, the enemy increased in numbers, at least as fast as I did, and by the best accounts I could depend upon, they increased faster. Fletchall joined them on Tuesday night. In the mean time, on Tuesday evening I placed all the troops in camp, about three-fourths of a mile from Ninety-Six. I caused the most exact order to be observed, even in an army composed of militia in a manner. The advanced posts are regularly and punctually kept all around the camp; and it is not only surprising, but it must be animating to the people of this country, that this army, never in service before, and now about 1,100 strong, obey punctually, keep good order in camp, are cheerful and content—even although we have had constant rains since we have been encamped. Till yesterday, this army did not exceed 900 strong, and by the best accounts I could learn, Fletchall's camp removed to about four miles on the other side Saluda, contained from 1,200 to 1,400 badly armed and under no order or command. Our people were impatient to be led against them—but as I saw if I advanced to attack, many lives must be lost, and I found I had a perfect command over our people, and could keep them together as long as I pleased—as I had every reason to think the enemy being under no command. and having no regular supplies of provision, and the weather being bad, that they could not keep long together, and that having their greatest influx, their numbers would then ebb and diminish; these considerations determined me, with the perfect approbation of Col. Thomson, Maj. Williamson and Capt. Hammond, to continue encamped, and to watch their motions. With this view, I put every thing in practice to persuade the enemy that I would persevere in this plan; and, among other devices, I sent a letter directed to Col. Richardson, in order that they should intercept it. I put forth a declaration on the 13th, which I inclose, together with the affidavit on which I grounded it. The declaration was publicly read in their camp the next day. This, together with a series of negociations, procured a deputation from their camp to me: and yesterday the deputies being in my camp, I drew up, and, with them, signed the enclosed instrument dated the 16th of September."

* * * * * * * * *

"With this treaty, the spirit of discord is gone forth among them, and there is now a great quarrel between Fletchall and Cunningham. All the people in a manner approve of Fletchall's conduct, and they are, this morning, all gone off with him. Cunningham is now left at their camp with only about 60 men, who, I suppose, will soon disperse. I am persuaded Fletchall and his people will be true, and I make no doubt but that the affair is now crushed. I have employed people to watch Cunningham, and if he offends, he will be delivered up or taken by us to be proceeded against. Kirkland stands excepted from the benefit of the treaty*—they have nothing to do with him, they disclaim all communication with him. And I continue to pursue him. It is apprehended he may get on board the man-of-war."†

* * * * * * * * *

"I mean to stay here with the rangers some days".
* * * * * "In the mean time, I shall, to-morrow, send off a company of rangers, in order to quiet the fears of the people above, but with orders not to advance anything near the Indian line".

---

*Kirkland signed the Association, accepted a captain's commission in the Colony regiment of rangers (the 3rd regiment), deserted, and afterwards endeavored to be chosen a delegate for Ninety-Six District, which he never accomplished, but finally fled the Colony.

†Which he did.

Col. Thomson left seven companies at Ninety-Six with orders to march farther back into the country, but not to go within fifteen miles of the Indian country, and after that, to repair to their homes in order to recruit themselves and their horses, and finally to join him in camp at Amelia on the 24th of October.

Nothing more now remaining for Mr. Drayton to do, he returned to Charlestown, but a portion of the armed force was left in the fork to watch the movements of the Tories; and on Nov. 2nd Col. Richardson wrote the following, from his camp near McLaurin's, to the Council of Safety: "I am now joined by Col. Thomas with about two hundred, Col. Neel as many, Col. Lyles about one hundred, together with Col. Thomson's regiments of rangers and militia, with my own, may make in the whole about 2,500; and I received, last night, accounts of Col. Polk being near with six hundred. An army, if it was a favorable time of the year might go or do anything required, which I hope we shall. I hear of their moving about, but yet have made no opposition."

Everything appearing quiet some of the troops went to their homes, but scarcely had they reached them before the troubles in Ninety-Six District broke out afresh. Capt. Robert Cuningham, a man of wealth and influence in the District, having refused to be bound by the treaty, was arrested and taken to Charlestown. Immediately his brother Patrick raised a party, and attempted to overtake the officers having him in charge, for the purpose of rescuing him. Failing in this they seized upon some powder which the Council of Safety was just then sending through their District to the Cherokee Indians, and made prisoners of the guard of twenty rangers and the officers.

The following affidavit, to be found on page 97 of

Moultrie's Memoirs, gives an accurate account of the seizure:

"South Carolina, }
"Ninety-six District. }

"Personally appeared before me, James Mayson, one of his majesty's justices of the peace, for the district aforesaid; Moses Cotter, of the Congarees, waggoner, who being duly sworn on the holy evangelist, of Almighty God, makes oath, and says, that on Tuesday morning last, at about 9 o'clock he left the Congarees, with his waggon, containing the ammunition that was delivered him in Charlestown, by the honorable the council of safety, to carry to Keowee under an escort of Col. Thomson's rangers consisting of Lieut. Col.* Charleton and Mr. Uriah Goodwin, a cadet, 2 sergeants and 18 privates, and continued on their journey there, without the least molestation or interruption, until about noon this day, when the deponent perceiving some men on horseback, ahead of the waggon, came towards him; a few minutes after, two of Patrick Cunningham's men, coming up to the deponent and asking him what he had in his waggon, the deponent answered, rum: Then up came a large body of armed men, in number, I suppose, at least one hundred and fifty, headed by Patrick Cunningham and Jacob Bowman. Cunningham ordered his men to halt, and then came up to the deponent and said, I order you to stop your waggon in his majesty's name, as I understand you have ammunition for the Indians to kill us, and I am come on purpose to take it in his majesty's name. He then ordered the deponent to take off his waggon cloth, which he refused; upon which Cunningham mounted the waggon himself, loosed the strings of the cloth,

---
*He was only a lieutenant.

and took up a keg of the powder; 'there,' said he, 'is what we are in search of.' I immediately took the keg from him and laid it in the waggon. Cunningham said, 'it is in vain for you to attempt to hinder us from taking this ammunition, as you have no arms;' then he handed out every keg to his men who were along side the waggon and prepared with bags to receive it; after they finished with the powder, he, with Messrs Griffin and Owen, and several others, took out the lead which they unfolded, cut into small pieces with their tomahawk's, and distributed it among the men. When the rangers were at some distance behind the waggon, and were riding up pretty fast, Cunningham's party said, 'there comes the liberty caps; damn their liberty caps, we will soon blow them to hell'; and such like scurrilous language. Cunningham's men, as soon as Lieut. Charleton came up with his guard, retreated behind trees on the road side, and called out to him to stop and not to advance one step further, otherwise they would blow out his brains; at the same time, a gun was fired by one of their men, but did no damage. Lieut. Charleton, with his men, were soon surrounded by the opposite party, with their rifles presented, who said, 'don't move a step; deliver up your arms, otherwise we will immediately fire upon you.' Lieut. Charleton continued moving on, when Cunningham's men marched up to him, with their rifles presented at him, and repeated, 'deliver up your arms without moving one step further, or you are a dead man:' they then took his arms, together with his men's; afterwards they tied Lieut. Charleton, Mr. Goodwin, and William Witherford, a private, by their arms.

"Lieut. Charleton seemed very much displeased at their behavior, and said 'he would rather have been shot, than used in such a manner, had he expected it;

that he did not value his own life; thought he had acted prudent by not ordering his men to fire on them, as it would be throwing away their lives, without answering any good purpose; especially as their party were so numerous, that he was sorry to see them behave in such a base manner, and that he would very willingly turn out his party against twice the number of theirs, and give them battle:' Cunningham and Bowman, some little time after asked Lieut. Charleton, 'whether if they were to unloose him he would be upon his honor, not to go off:' to which he replied, 'I scorn to run, and all your force cannot make me;' they then marched off with the ammunition, and the 'prisoners,' (as they called them,) and left the deponent, desiring him to return to the Congarees: but as soon as they were out of sight he took a horse from out the waggon and came to Ninety-six, to inform me of what had happened, and where he arrived this night about 8 o'clock. This unfortunate accident of taking the ammunition, happened 18 miles below Ninety-six.

"'Moses Cotter.

"'Sworn, before me, this } James Mayson, J. P.'"
3d of Nov. 1775.'

The news of this insurrection being laid before the Provincial Congress, that body, on the 7th of November, ordered Col. Richardson forthwith to assemble six companies of rangers, Captain Ezekiel Polk's company of volunteers, draughts of militia from Richardson's, Thomson's,* Savage's, Neel's and Thomas's regiments, and with such troops pursue such instructions as should, from time to time. by order of the Congress,

---

*At the time that Col. Thomson was made lieutenant-colonel of the Rangers, he commanded the militia regiment of Orangeburgh District. Christopher Rowe was lieutenant-colonel, and Lewis Golson major.

or the Council of Safety for the time being, be signified to him by the President.

In the meantime, Maj. Andrew Williamson had, as soon as he heard of this seizure, begun to embody the militia for the purpose of recovering the powder and lead, and of apprehending the offenders. The Council of Safety at once thanked Maj. Williamson for embodying the militia, advised him of the instructions that had been given to Col. Richardson, and directed him, with the militia under his command, to act against the insurgents with the utmost vigor.

Major Williamson lay encamped near Ninety-Six for almost two weeks, receiving the militia who came in, and waiting for the rangers. The Tories were diligent on their part, and by circulating a report to the effect that the Council of Safety had intended the ammunition which was seized, for the Indians to murder the whites with, they gained a considerable following. But notwithstanding their force, Maj. Williamson did not believe that they would dare attack him; and he continued encamped in this persuasion, until the 18th of November, when, in the evening of that day, he received certain information, that the insurgents were in full march upon him; and that they were actually crossing Saluda river in order to attack him. At this time, Major Mayson, who had been in the neighborhood with thirty-seven of the rangers, joined Major Williamson. Maj. Williamson would have marched to attack their camp in the night, but was overruled by Major Mayson and a council of war, who preferred to erect breast-works, and fortify themselves near the Ninety-Six court house and jail. It was also hoped, that by taking this position, opportunities would be furnished for reinforcements of militia, and of Col. Thomson's arriving with the remainder of his rangers. Hardly had their fortifications been erected, when the enemy appeared in force, at about eleven o'clock on the morning of the 19th of November, and taking possession of the court house and jail. they advanced troops, and completely invested the stockade fort. Maj. Williamson then dispatched an officer with a flag to Maj. Joseph Robinson and Captain Patrick Cunningham, who appeared to be the leaders, and demanded their intentions; but they refused to confer with anyone save the commanding officers. Major Mayson and Captain John Bowie were then sent out, and they were met midway between the two parties by Robinson, Cuningham and Evan McLaurin* on the part of the enemy. The Tories insisted upon an immediate surrender of arms, and a disbanding of the assembled militia. Just as Major Mayson and Capt. Bowie had returned to the fort and made their report, the Tories seized two of Williamson's men; upon which Major Williamson gave orders to rescue them and a general firing commenced from the fort, which was answered by the Tories. For two hours and a half the firing on both sides was incessant, but from that time until night, it was less severe. During the night. the fort kept up a firing to discourage any attempt on the part of the besiegers to fire the fort. On the next day (Monday), almost as heavy a fire was commenced, and continued, as had been kept up the afternoon before; and the besiegers endeavored to use mantilets which they had constructed, for the purpose of approaching the fort, to fire it; but not being able to advance them so as to cover their approaches, they were destroyed. The firing, however. only slackened

---

*None of those who had signed the treaty of Ninety-Six, on September 16th, when William Henry Drayton brought them to terms, took any open part in this affair, save McLaurin, who, with the treachery characteristic of his clan, had violated the treaty which he had signed on that occasion.

with the night, and on Tuesday it was recommenced, and continued until about sunset, when the Tories displayed a white flag from the jail, and called a parley. Strange to say, the Tories then sent a messenger to again demand a surrender. To this demand Capt. Bowie carried a negative answer, and in two hours he returned with Capt. Cuningham, who went into the fort and fully discussed the matter with the commanding officers; after which it was determined that a conference should take place the next morning. At the conference the next morning it was agreed that hostilities should cease. The following is a copy of the treaty signed upon that occasion:*

"1st. That hostilities shall immediately cease on both sides.

"2nd. That Major Williamson and Major Mayson shall march their men out of the Fort and deliver up their swivels.†

"3rd. That the Fort shall be destroyed flat without damaging the houses therein, under the inspection of Capt. Patrick Cunningham and John Bowie, Esq., and the well filled up.

"4th. That the differences between the people of this District and others disagreeing about the present public measures shall be submitted to his Excellency, our Governor, and the Council of Safety, and for that purpose that each party shall send dispatches to their superiors—that the dispatches shall be sent unsealed

---

*Gibbes's Documentary History, 1764—1776, pages 214, 215; Drayton's Memoirs, Vol. II, pages 148, 149.

†By a secret article of the treaty it was agreed that the swivels should be returned in a day or two. This mock surrender of swivels was agreed upon by the leaders to appease a large party of the besiegers, who insisted, that if the swivels were not given up, they would abide by no articles.—Drayton's Memoirs, Vol. II, page 120.

and the messenger* of each party shall pass unmolested.

"5th. That Major Robinson shall withdraw his men over Saluda, and there keep them embodied or disperse them as he pleaseth until his Excellency's orders be known.

"6th. That no person of either party shall in the meantime be molested by the other party either in going home or otherwise.

"7th. Should any reinforcements arrive to Major Williamson or Major Mayson, they also shall be bound by this cessation.

"8th. That twenty days be allowed for the return of the messengers.

"9th. That all prisoners taken by either party since the second day of this instant shall be immediately set at liberty.

"In witness whereof the parties to these articles have set their hands and seals at Ninety-six this twenty-second day of November, one thousand seven hundred and seventy-five, and in the sixteenth year of his Majesty's reign.

"Present,
"Patrick Cunningham.
"Richard Pearis.
"Andrew Pickens.
"John Bowie."

Joseph Robinson.
A. Wm. Son.
James Mayson.

On the 24th, Major Mayson directed a letter to Col. Thomson detailing an account of the siege and treaty; and on the 25th Maj. Williamson wrote Mr. Drayton

---

* "Major Robinson's messenger, or a person who pretends to be the messenger, and calls himself Floyd, has appeared before us, and declared that being drunk, he had lost all his papers at Orangeburg."
—Extract from letter of Henry Laurens to Maj. Andrew Williamson, Journal of Council, Dec. 5th, 1775, Collections S. C. Hist. Soc., Vol. III, page 48.

an account of the affair, in which he stated that Maj. Mayson with thirty-seven of the rangers, were with him;* and by the "Report of the Militia and Volunteers on duty in the Fortified Camp at Ninety-Six on Sunday the Nineteenth November, 1775, under the Command of Major Andrew Williamson, by order of the Honorable the Provincial Congress,"† it appears that Lieutenant Hugh Middleton, of the 3rd regiment, and two privates of his company were also there.

At the time Major Williamson was being besieged by the Tories at Ninety-Six, Colonel Richardson had commenced his march against them, in pursuance of the orders he had received from the Provincial Congress; and in doing so, he was directing his course towards the middle, or the upper part of Col. Fletchall's command, over Broad River. But, as soon as he was apprized of Williamson's investment, he changed his route, and proceeded by forced marches to the Congaree river, over which he crossed his troops; and on November 27th he addressed the following letter to Mr. Drayton:

"Camp near Congarees, Nov. 27th, 1775.

"Sir:—I arrived at this place last night, and take the earliest moment I can spare to write you this, as I have been very busy in getting the men's wagons, &c., over the river, which I shall scarcely complete to-morrow. The route I intended to have taken was very different from the one I at first anticipated; as when I heard of the fort at Ninety-Six being besieged, I altered my march, in order to make what speed I could to relieve them; but they had concluded articles too soon, for a possibility of my reaching them. Perhaps

---

*Gibbes's Documentary History, 1764—1776, page 216.
†Gibbes's Documentary History, 1764—1776, page 221; Drayton's Memoirs, Vol. II, page 150.

it may be said in Congress why did not Col. Thomson go and relieve them? I answer, he could not, was not able, nor had timely notice if he had been. We have yet received no accounts from there but what I herewith enclose a copy of, together with a letter from Mr. McLaurin, which was sent to-day to Col. Thomson."

* * * * * * * *

"I cannot ascertain the number of my men, as I have not, from the bustle, been able to obtain regular returns, and which, I believe, at this time, amount to about one thousand, with daily additions, and soon expect as many more." * * * * "Though we hear the opposers are very numerous and violent and desperate, yet hope in a little time to give you a more full account of our army and our opposers, who are now much elated and carry a high hand. But though much, very much, depends upon this campaign, do not be under two great apprehension for the event."

* * * * * * * * *

"P. S. After I wrote and sealed, about 12 o'clock last night we were alarmed by some of our rangers, which we had sent light to discover where Col. Thomas was, who, I heard, was on his way, in a dangerous part; they came to him about 22 miles from us, who had three prisoners. Lieut. Boykin, who commanded that light detachment of rangers, reported that Col. Thomas had stopped about dark to take a mouthful and refresh, intending then to drive on while he (Boykin) was there. Col. Thomas received a letter, informing him that Major Robinson was pursuing him with a thousand men, and would be cut off before he crossed the river. I immediately detached a party of rangers, volunteers and militia, sufficient I hope to sustain him. This evening have not yet heard; think, if proper instructions be given to look sharp for Robinson in his way to town. It would be a great matter to get him without his putting himself in your power: a good watch at Dorchester, and other places may secure him, for, I think, it will be his only refuge soon."

Whether this suggestion of placing a "good watch" at Dorchester was followed out, we know not, but certain it is that Captains Purves and Imhoff, of the Rangers, were about that time stationed at Dorchester,* and kept there for some weeks.

On November 28th Col. Thomson addressed the following letter to Henry Laurens:†

"Camp, Congaree, Nov. 28th, 1775.

"Honored Sir:—You will see by the enclosed that our party and the opposite have had an engagement, and came to a cessation of arms on the 22d; and you

---

* "Read a letter from Captain Peyer Imhoff, of the Rangers, dated Dorchester, 14th December, 1775, inclosing return."—Journal of Council of Safety, Dec. 14th, 1775.

"*Ordered*, That Capt. Peyer Imhoff be supplied with about one hundred yards of the cloth imported for the public, to clothe his company of rangers, and that he be desired to procure Doct. Chanler's accounts for attending sick rangers, properly certified, to be laid before the board."—Journal of Council of Safety, Dec. 15th, 1775.

"Read a letter from Captain John Purves, of the regiment of Rangers, dated 22nd December, 1775."

"*Ordered*, That Capt. Purves, of the Rangers upon duty at Dorchester, have leave of absence, not exceeding three weeks."

"To Capt. John Purves, the pay-bill of his company of Rangers, from 20th November to 20th December, at Dorchester,... 850 00 0."

"Capt. Peyer Imhoff, the pay-bill of his company at Dorchester, same time,......656 10 0."

"On the last two orders, the treasurers were desired to take especial care that those pay-bills be not included in other accounts—they having been issued upon an extraordinary occasion."—Journal of Council of Safety, Dec. 23rd, 1775.

†This letter had evidently not reached the President of the Council of Safety by December 2nd, for in a letter to Maj. Williamson, of that date, Mr. Laurens wrote: "As we have not heard properly, either from Col. Richardson, or Col. Thomson, we cannot account for their slow progress. When we learn their strength and plan for uniting their forces, we shall immediately give orders for such operations as we hope will prove effectual."

will perceive how dilatory they were, in giving us information of it. The moment I received it from above, I acquainted Col. Richardson with the same, who was then about eight miles distant from us, and joined me about four hours after. We immediately summoned our officers and held a consultation on the following propositions:

"1st. 'Whether according to our orders in the present situation, the cessation of arms stipulated between Col. Mayson, Major Williamson, and Mr. Bowie on our side, and Mr. Cunningham, Mr. Robinson, and others, on the part of the others, have any weight upon our operations. Carried in the negative.

"2d. 'As we have been informed of a kind of cessation of arms between the contending parties, if it be not necessary to acquaint the Congress therewith and ask their advice. Affirmative.

"3rd. 'As we have heard that troops were, or are now assembled, near Augusta, at the Cherokee Ponds, whether it may not be necessary for them to be desired to advance and meet us at some convenient place appointed, and a letter dispatched for that purpose. Affirmative.

"4th. 'Which may be the most necessary route to order our march, and the destination of the wagons now on the other side of the river.

"5th. 'Whether if they can be come at, it may not be prudent to take Cunningham, Robinson, and Pearis, in custody, though they are the persons acceding to the cessation of arms at Ninety-Six, and the best method to be pursued for that end.'

"By order of Colonel Richardson, I marched with my regiment of rangers on Monday last, with about one hundred of the draughted militia to this place. Col. Richardson gave orders for draughting two hundred men, which orders I directed the officers of my militia to distribute, but was unfortunate enough to raise but about one hundred, and those collected from three companies in my own neighborhood. When the Sergeants warned the draughted people about Orangeburgh and the Congarees, they seemed very insolent, asked which camps they were to join, and, in fact, did as much as to declare themselves King's men, as they term it. The same dissatisfaction seems to have reigned amongst a part of Col. Richardson's people. But I am persuaded, after all their murmurings, we shall have a sufficient number of men to vanquish all the disaffected people in South Carolina, and I hope Col. Richardson will have orders so to do before we break up. As I have heard several of the officers and men declare, that they would never take up arms again, unless the militia who have been draughted and do not appear, are made to suffer by fine or otherwise, and they have the liberty to subdue the enemies of America, as they observe that those who are not for America, are undoubtedly against it. Such discourses we hear spreading through our camps, and I have reason to believe is their determination.

"We have had great uneasiness amongst them, when the news arrived of the cessation of arms, and we have no other means of appeasing their disturbed minds, but by signifying that the cessation of arms was not binding on us, and so forth.

"I have some reason to believe that the late mob has privately murdered people in the woods who had been our associates. I imagine we shall march from here to-morrow, to the Forks between Broad and Saluda rivers. If any part of this you think will prove of service to the country, I beg you would show it to

the Congress; such other parts of it, beg you would treat as from a friend.
"I am, honored sir,
"Your very humble servant,
"Wm. Thomson.*

"P. S. I believe part of the disaffection among the people at Orangeburgh, proceeded part from cowardice, and part from the speeches of disappointed gentlemen in our parish. But I hope to have the liberty of putting the militia law in force against the defaulters, and that I shall see their expectations frustrated."

That "the disaffection among the people at Orangeburgh" was of short duration, is proved by subsequent events.

From his "Camp near Congarees", Col. Richardson wrote, on November 30, to Mr. Drayton: "We have now, at least one thousand men, and are still increasing, and intend entering the Fork of Broad and Saluda rivers this day."

Reaching Ninety-Six a few days later, Col. Richardson issued the following proclamation:

"South Carolina.
"Whereas, on the third day of November last past, Patrick Cunningham, Henry O'Neal, Hugh Brown, David Russe, Nathaniel Howard, Henry Green, and sundry other persons, did, in Ninety-six District, raise a dangerous insurrection and commotion, and did, near Mine Creek, in said District, felloniously take and carry away a quantity of ammunition, the property of the public, and in contempt of public authority, and did also, with further aid, and by force of

---

* "To William Goodwyn, express from Col. Thomson, £33. 00."—Journal of Council of Safety, Dec. 5th, 1775, Collections of the S. C. Hist. Soc., Vol. III, page 50.

arms, on the nineteenth, twentieth and twenty-first days of said month of November at Ninety-Six, in the District aforesaid, attack, besiege, kill and wound a number of the good people of this Colony, and in manifest violation of peace and good order, and breach of a solemn treaty entered into on the eighteenth day of September last, made and concluded between the Honorable William Henry Drayton, on the one part, and Col. Thomas Fletchall and others, on the other part, thereby becoming guilty of the atrocious crimes of robbery, murder and breach of treaty of peace. To satisfy public justice in the just punishment of all which crimes and offences, as far as the nature of the same will admit, I am now come into these parts, in the name and behalf of the Colonies to demand of the inhabitants, the delivery up of the bodies of all the principal offenders herein, together with the said ammunition and full restitution for the ravages committed, and also the arms and ammunition of all the aiders and abettors of those robbers, murderers, and disturbers of the peace and good order as aforesaid; and, in case of refusal or neglect, for the space of five days, I shall be under a necessity of taking such steps as will be found disagreeable, but which I shall certainly put in execution for the public good.

"Given under my hand this eighth day of December, 1775."

That the Council of Safety meant to spare no expense to quell the disaffection of the non-associators, the following extract from its proceedings will show:

"Upon the accounts of Mr. John Chesnut, Paymaster of the Regiment of Rangers, the order was drawn in the words following:

"Gentlemen—Please to order the above accounts and the several accounts therein referred to, to be

carefully examined; and if found free from error, pay the above mentioned sum of £9850, 7s. 8d. to Mr. Aaron Loocock, on behalf of Mr. John Chesnut, Paymaster of the Regiment of Rangers, and charge to the proper account.
"By order of the Council of Safety.
"Henry Laurens, President.
"To John Neufville, Peter Bacot, William Gibbes, esqs., Commissioners of the Colony Treasury."*

A few days after the surrender of Ninety-Six, Maj. Mayson repaired to Charlestown,† and on the 7th of December he addressed the following letter to the Council of Safety:‡

"Charlestown, 7th December 1775.

"Gentlemen,
"It is with the greatest reluctance that I presume to trouble you with a matter, which principally relates to myself. But, as its example and tendency might perhaps hereafter be of some prejudice to the cause, in which we are all engaged, if no notice was taken of it; I find myself under a necessity, of not being entirely silent on the subject.

"The few forces which were lately assembled at Ninety-Six, were drawn together by me, as well as by Major Williamson; and, though I was Lieutenant-Colonel of the same regiment of militia in which Major Williamson held his commission, and also a Major in your Regular Troops, to my surprize Major Wil-

---

*Journal of Council of Safety, December 2nd, 1775, Collections S. C. Historical Society, Vol. III, page 40.

†"Ordered, That Major Mayson have leave to visit and converse with Robert Cunningham, confined in Charles-Town jail."—Journal of Council of Safety, Dec. 6th, 1775, Collections S. C. Hist. Soc., Vol. III, page 59.

‡Drayton's Memoirs, Vol. II, page 151. "Read a letter from Major Mayson, of the Rangers, of this date."—Journal of Council of Safety, Dec. 7th, 1775.

liamson disputed the command with me—but, rather than hurt the cause, I yielded some points to him; which, I am sensible as your soldier, I shall not be justifiable in, without the greatest indulgence from you. I however think it proper to mention, that although on account of the public good I suffered his name to be inserted in the Truce before mine, yet the means of our defence was planned by me; and the whole negotiation with the disaffected party, was addressed to me.

"I thought the conduct of Major Williamson in this affair the more extraordinary, as he was a member of the very Congress, which settled these points of command; and which points, I find have been confirmed by the present Congress, as well as by the Continental Congress. But, lest hereafter the same disputes may arise, I humbly submit it to this honorable board, whether Major Williamson should not be informed, that when we act together, and hold our present commissions, I am to have the command.

"The thanks of my country, it will be my highest ambition to deserve; and, as I understand that Major Williamson is to return the thanks of Congress to the officers who were present at Ninety-Six; I shall with joy receive them, though delivered to me by an inferior officer.

"I cannot conclude without assuring you, that both Major Williamson and myself concealed our difference from all, except one or two of the officers.
"I have the honour to be,
"Gentlemen,
"With the greatest respect.
"Your most humble servant,
"Jas. Mayson."

To this letter the Council of Safety, on December 8th, addressed the following reply:*

---
*Journal of Council of Safety, Dec. 8th, 1775.

"Charles-Town, Dec. 8th, 1775.

"Sir—We have duly considered the contents of your letter, which was yesterday laid before us, and as we have received no complaint from Major Williamson, and are satisfied that each of you had the real service of the colony at heart in the late affair at Ninety-Six, we wish to avoid a minute inquiry, which in our opinion would produce no beneficial end.

"The command of the militia was, by the Congress, vested in Major Williamson, from considerations of the distance of Col. Savage, and the little probability of his heading the regiment, as well as from an information that you were at that time extremely ill, unable to take the field. It was therefore necessary to order that gentleman to call forth the militia in his district,* and to hold them in readiness to join the troops under Col. Richardson; your junction, and what afterwards happened at the fortified camp at Ninety-Six, were circumstances altogether adventitious and unexpected. Hence we are convinced, that Major Williamson, when he took the command, acted in conformity to the order of Congress, and you will perceive that those orders were not intended to overlook your merit, nor to offer you an affront. We highly applaud you, for having, after you had joined Major Williamson, yielded in any points of mere punctillio, on account of the public good. We are so sensible of your services, that with pleasure we repeat to you the thanks of this board, and desire that you will also

---

* "Mayson was Lieut. Col. of the Ninety-Six Regiment of Militia; of which Williamson was then acting as Major; but the Council of Safety did not approve of Major Mayson's commanding on the occasion, either as Lieutenant-Colonel of the regiment, or as Major of the 3d regiment of rangers; as their confidence was greater in Major Williamson; and he was more influential in that part of the country."—Drayton's Memoirs, Vol. II, page 119, foot note.

present our thanks to the officers and soldiers of the corps of rangers who were under your command.

"You are now to repair immediately to Col. Richardson's camp. We are satisfied of your zeal and attachment in the cause of the colonies, and particularly we confide that you will persevere in your endeavors to promote harmony within your sphere, and to discountenance every kind and degree of dissention, the bane of public service. We wish you health and success.

"By order of the Council of Safety.
                    "Henry Laurens, President.
"Major James Mayson."

On Dec. 12th, Col. Richardson wrote, from "Camp Great Survey, Duncan's Creek", to Henry Laurens: "The eighth instant I wrote and made public a kind of declaration, of which I herewith inclose a copy, which I hope may in some measure meet with your approbation, upon which they have come in, many of them, and delivered up their arms, all of whom, where they have not been capital offenders, I dismiss with soft words and cheerful countenances, and admonish them to use their interest with their friends and neighbors, which seems to have a good effect. Our army which is now formidable strikes terror, and the opposite party have hitherto fled before us, keeping fifteen or twenty miles distant. We often are told they will give battle, but yet have not attempted it, and do hope we shall by the measures pursuing so weaken their party that most will abandon them, and they will not be able to make head with any great body, and the salutary measures prove the best conquest. Should their behavior be otherwise we shall deal with them accordingly. We have several prisoners, amongst whom are Col. Fletchall, Capt. Richard

Pearis, Capt. Shuburg, and several others of the first magnitude. By the capture of Col. Fletchall (who was hid in a cave,* and taken by Col. Thomson and rangers, and the volunteer companies who were sent out on that and some other service) papers have fallen into my hands which the Council of Safety will be glad to see, but which I cannot venture to send by this conveyance; but shall transmit by the officer of the guard, with the prisoners, which I intend to dispatch to-morrow. Our army is about three thousand of different corps, viz: my own regiment, Col. Thomson's, and volunteer light horse. Col. Thomas, Col. Neel, Col. Polk and Lieut. Col. Martin of the North Carolina regiment, upon the continental establishment, who voluntarily stepped out on this occasion, as did Col. Thos. Polk." * * * * * "This minute, while I am writing, Capts. Plumer and Smith with thirty men surrendered themselves and arms."

On the 16th, Col. Richardson wrote, from "Camp Liberty Hill", to Mr. Laurens: "I herewith send you the persons of Col. Thos. Fletchall, Capt. Richard Pearis, Capt. Jacob Fry, Capt. George Shuburg, John McWilliams, Philip Wells, James Davis, Capt. McDavid, alias McDade, and Joseph Alexander. These being all adjudged by the officers and people here to be offenders of such a nature that from the active part they have taken, it would be dangerous for me to let either of them go." * * * * "These unhappy people are in a great panic, still flying before us, and it is told that young Pearis and others have gone to bring the Indians down, in person; if it should be the case, it could not be in a better time, and if any such intentions, should be glad the whole would come while we are here."

*Some say in the hollow of a large sycamore tree.—Drayton's Memoirs, Vol. II, page 129, foot note.

On the 22nd, Col. Richardson, from "Camp Raborn's Creek, Hollingsworth's Mill", wrote Mr. Laurens: "I thought to let you hear from us before now, but constant marching, and multiplicity of cares and business have prevented, and the more so, as I had not such things as I could wish to acquaint you with; but now, as we have got to the very extremity of the roads north-westward, take the liberty to inform you, that on Saturday last, the 16th instant, we were joined by Col. Rutherford, of Rowan, and Col. Graham, of Tryon counties, in North Carolina, with about five hundred men." * * * "On Wednesday, the 20th inst., I was joined by Maj. Andrew Williamson, Capt. Hammond, and a small party of Col. Bull's regiment, amounting in the whole to about eight hundred, so that our army is now formidable, between four and five thousand—a number most desirable to view—though we have had no occasion for more than my own regiment to have done the business. Notwithstanding, the number has a good effect, strikes terror, and shows what can be done on occasion—and, upon the whole, it may prove a happy event—we have been successful in disarming most of this unhappy people; they are coming in with fear and trembling, giving up their arms, with a sensible contrition for the errors they have been guilty of." * * * * *
"There is still a camp we cannot yet come up with, consisting of the principal aggressors, which were, by best information, camped on the Cherokee land. I detached yesterday about thirteen hundred horse and foot, about an equal number, under the command of Cols. Thomson, Martin, Rutherford, Neel, Polk, Lyles, Major Williamson, and others, commanding all volunteers, which, I flatter myself, will render us a good account, as I don't expect them in till to-morrow, or perhaps some days hence." * * * * "They

have had expectations of the Indians joining them, but by a letter from Mr. Wilkinson to Major Williamson, they will be disappointed in that, as he says all are peacable there, and the Indians well satisfied, and say the Saluda people are devils, &c." * * *
* * "We have at times got small parts of the ammunition they got, and delivered with their arms; and yesterday two barrels, say fifty pounds, and have a slight information of some more." * * *
* * * "I shall, therefore, crave your permission to discharge the North Carolinians, to make their way from hence through the upper parts by the Indian line to their own colony, which will scour that part, and Cols. Neel and Thomson through a middle direction to their different quarters." * * *
* * "The spirit of discord will so far subside, that they will hardly raise any more commotions."
* * * * * * * * *
"P. S. This minute since, or while I was writing my name, a messenger from Col. Thomson and the detachments arrived with the agreeable account, that they had surprised and taken the camp of Cunningham, &c., and taken the greatest part prisoners, with all their ammunition, guns, wagons, and utensils. P. Cunningham had escaped, and some principals, but the most are taken, &c."

"On January 2nd, 1776, Col. Richardson sent, from the Congarees, to Henry Laurens, the following report:*

"Sir:—In my last I informed you of the detachments I had sent out, and in a postscript, of my intelligence of success. Our people surrounded their camp by daylight in the morning after a long march of near

---

*"Read also a letter from Col. Richardson, dated Congarees, 2d January, 1776."—Journal of the Council of Safety, Jan. 8th, 1776.

twenty-five miles, and lying on their arms till day, they then attacked and took about one hundred and thirty prisoners, with baggage, arms, ammunition, &c., which completed the conquest of that flying party which had till then kept out of reach. They were encamped at a convenient place called the Brake of Canes on the Cherokee land; Patrick Cunningham escaped on a horse bare backed (and they say without breeches) telling every man to shift for himself.* None of our men were killed or wounded, except the son of Col. T. Polk, a fine youth, was shot through the shoulder, and was in great danger. Some five or six of the other party, I am told, were killed; happily the men were restrained or every man had died. The next day they returned to camp, the snow set in, and continued for thirty hours without intermission, which, with the hardship and fatigue the men had suffered before made them very uneasy, and seeing no more could be done they grew so uneasy it was out of my power to keep the troops together any longer. I, therefore, on Christmas-day dismissed the North Carolina troops, viz: Col. Rutherford, Col. Graham, Col. Martin and Col. Polk to all of whom, in behalf of my country, I returned my cordial and hearty thanks, &c.; the same day Colonels Neel and Thomas, and Major Williamson with proper orders to pursue such measures in their different marches, as I was convinced would be necessary for the public service. I then as I found the service pretty well done and no possibility of detaining the men longer, the snow then lying on the earth in the smoothest places at least fifteen inches deep† (most say two feet) I marched in the best manner we could downward. Eight days we

---

*He fled to Florida, where he spent a good portion of his time. (See Southern Quarterly Review for April 1847, Vol. XI, No. 22, page 484.)
†This expedition has been, by many, termed the "Snow Camp".

never set foot on the earth or had a place to lie down, till we had spaded or grabbled away the snow, from which circumstance, many are frost bitten, some very badly; and on the third day a heavy cold rain fell, together with sleet; and melted the snow and filled every creek and river with a deluge of water; but with all these difficulties we reached this place yesterday with the prisoners, whom we have used in the best manner we could—about ten Captains and a hundred and twenty of the most mischievous men (some of whom will make good soldiers); all the powder; Ninety-six and New Camp men. We retook seven kegs of gun-powder, six of which I delivered to Maj. Williamson to be sent to Mr. Wilkinson for the Cherokees; many arms have been delivered up, and I caused the men to sign an instrument of writing, which they did willingly with fear and trembling, by which they forfeit their estates, real and personal, if they ever take up arms against, or disquiet the peace and tranquility of the good people of this colony again, and to assist them if they are ever called upon. The arms taken by Maj. Williamson and those from that quarter I ordered to be stored at Fort Charlotte. which he (the Major) is to see done. Those taken by the upper regiments are to be sent down, and many lodged in the hands of the Committee to be sent to Mr. Chesnut's Store at the Congarees, and about two hundred stand I have ordered to Camden, &c." * * * *
"The prisoners I send in a boat from this place to Wilson's Ferry, under the command and guard of Capt. Thomas Sumter, who on this expedition I constituted, Adjutant-General, who has behaved very well and has been to me and the cause, of extra service; from thence Col. Thomson with the Rangers and others under him will guard them to Charleston, who, with Major Mayson and officers under them have been obliging in

behavior and alert in service, and must recommend them to your particular notice; and I must say through the whole I have been extremely happy in the mutual harmony which has subsisted." * * * * "I shall refer you to Col. Thomson and Maj. Mayson for further particulars, as I am still broke in upon every line."

On the same day Col. Richardson wrote the Council of Safety: "By Col. Thomson of the rangers, you will receive, if nothing happens, the prisoners, we thought proper to detain,* which, upon examination, find were

---

*"Charles-Town, Jan. 10th, 1776.

"Sir—We have received your several letters of the 2d and 8th instant, together with the proceedings of the Court of Inquiry in the case of Lieut. Charlton, and the general court-martial on Capt. Samuel Wise, and approve of their respective determinations—which you will signify in proper orders. We desire when you arrive at some convenient ground, at or near the Quarter-House, that you will order a halt, leaving the prisoners under proper guard, and come forward, yourself in order to attend the Board for further direction.

"By order of the Council of Safety.

"Henry Laurens, President.
"Col. Will. Thomson."

"Col. Thomson, of the Regiment of Rangers, came to town, and attended for instructions how to dispose of the prisoners sent down by Col. Richardson.

"*Ordered*, That Col. Thomson do cause the said prisoners to be conducted to Mr. Strickland to-morrow morning, and that he then attend this Council again."—Journal of Council of Safety, Jan. 10th, 1776.

"Col. Thomson and Major Ferguson of the rangers attended, with a list of the prisoners sent down by Col. Richardson, and distinguished the most culpable offenders."—Journal of Council of Safety, Jan. 11th, 1776.

"*Ordered*, That Col. Thomson do immediately attend this board; and that the prisoners from Col. Richardson do remain at, or return to, their stations at Strickland's."—Journal of Council of Safety, Jan. 12th, 1776.

"Col. Thomson reported the names of twenty of the prisoners sent down by Col. Richardson, who had voluntarily signed a paper, (which he delivered in,) being a strong assurance of their future proper behaviour.

"Whereupon, Col. Thomson was authorized by the Council to discharge them."—Journal of Council of Safety, Jan. 13th, 1776.

the most leading and active, in taking the powder at Ninety-Six, and the late camp. They were long out before taken, and have been some time since in durance, from which circumstances they of course will make but a despicable appearance, adding also, that the spirit of humility and contrition takes place of the opposite character." * * * * "I am at a loss to know how to recommend my brother Colonel, will say his behaviour has been as becomes him, and deserves your notice."

Pains have been taken to quote all of these details of these two expeditions into the back country, not only to show the part taken in them by Colonel Thomson and the 3rd regiment, but also to show that, after all, the disaffection of the people living in that section of the Districts of Orangeburgh and Ninety-Six, between the Broad and Saluda rivers, was not so serious in its consequences. We have seen how the Ninety-Six troops, assisted by only a portion of the forces from the adjoining districts, twice vanquished them with scarcely any bloodshed. We have seen them wavering from side to side, accordingly as the most plausible speeches were made them; we have seen them intimidated by a powerful force; but we have seen the final triumph of the Whigs. Col. Richardson tells us that his own regiment could "have done the business" in the second expedition, but there never was a time after that when the Ninety-Six Whigs could not handle with ease the Ninety-Six Tories. Pickens and Williams did it in the darkest days of the Revolution, and were only restrained by the British regulars—and Tories from other States thrown in, for Cruger's regiment of six hundred Tories that garrisoned Ninety-Six in 1780–81, were every one men that he had enlisted in New York and New Jersey.

The mission of Messrs Drayton and Tennent in the first expedition was of a diplomatic nature; that of Col. Thomson was both of a diplomatic and a military nature, and how he succeeded the records themselves show. In the second expedition, his excellent work is vouched for by his fellow officer, Col. Richardson, in his reports. That Col. Thomson never received a brigadier's commission in the Continental service was no fault of his. May posterity ever award him the honor that the Continental Congress failed to bestow.

We cannot refrain from adding here some extracts, anent these expeditions, from Ramsay's History of the Revolution in South Carolina, which not only concern the 3rd regiment, but the conduct of the whole people of South Carolina during the Revolution. It has been charged by partisan historians that South Carolina furnished no troops to the Continental Establishment; that troops from New England had to fight her battles for her; that the State was overrun with Tories; and that the majority of her people were lukewarm in the cause of American independence. The paragraphs from Dr. Ramsay, besides giving us a short account of the Tory uprisings of 1775, speak eloquently in refutation of these slanders. Dr. Ramsay published his history in 1785, just three years after the close of the war, while events were still fresh in the minds of men, and he had been a prominent figure in the Revolution, in South Carolina, and he therefore wrote with authority. He cannot be accused of undue partiality, for he was a native of Pennsylvania. He says, Vol. I., p. 67:

"Though there were some royalists in every part of the province, the only settlement in which they outnumbered the friends of Congress, was in the country between the Broad and Saluda rivers.* When it was determined to raise troops, the inhabitants of that part of the province could not be persuaded that the measure was necessary. Feeling themselves happy and free from present oppression, they were averse from believing that any designs, inimical to American liberty, had been adopted by the British government. Instead of signing the association, they signed papers at their general musters, declaring their unwillingness to concur in the measures recommended by Congress. The council of safety sent the hon. William-Henry Drayton, and the rev. William Tennent, into their settlement, to explain to them the nature of the dispute, and to bring them over to a co-operation with the other inhabitants. They had several publick meetings, and much eloquence was exerted to induce them to sign the association. Some were convinced and subscribed that bond of union; but the greater number could not be persuaded that there was any necessity for congresses, committees, or a military establishment. Suspicion, that bane of society, began to exert her mischievous influence. The friends of the old government doubted the authenticity of all pamphlets and newspapers, which ascribed to the British troops in Boston, or to the British government, any designs injurious to the rights of the colonists. They believed the whole to be an imposition by artful men, who wished to excite storms, that they might shew their skill in pilotage. The friends of Congress suspected the leading men of the royalists to be in the

---

* "Excepting in that part of the country included between the Broad and Saluda rivers the non-subscribers were comparatively few. In Charleston, where the general committee sat, their number amounted to about forty."—Ramsay, page 42. The Chicago paper that accused Senator Tillman of uttering a falsehood, when he said that South Carolina had "stood to the front in 1776", was evidently better acquainted with the falsehoods of the Sabines and Sumners than with the truths of the Ramsays.

pay of governor Campbell. Reports were circulated by one party, that a plan was laid to seize the commissioners sent by the council of safety; by the other, that the third provincial regiment was brought up to compel the inhabitants to sign the association. Motives and designs were reciprocally attributed to each other of the most ungenerous nature and mischievous tendency. The royalists embodied for reasons similar to those which had induced the other inhabitants to arm themselves against Great-Britain. They suspected their adversaries of an intention to dragoon them into a compliance with the measures of Congress; and they, in their turn, were suspected of a design to commence hostilities against the associators for disturbing the established royal government. Camps were formed in opposition to each other, and great pains were taken to increase their respective numbers. Moderate men employed their good offices to prevent bloodshed. After some days, the leaders on both sides met in conference. Several explications having taken place, a treaty was reciprocally agreed to, by which it was stipulated, that 'the royalists should remain in a state of neutrality.' Both parties* retired to their homes, and a temporary calm succeeded. Mr. Robert Cunningham, who had been a principal leader among the royalists, continued to encourage opposition to the popular measures, and declared that he did not consider himself as bound by the treaty. Suspicion again began to spread her poison. This declaration was construed as an evidence of a fixed intention to disturb the peace, by another insurrection. To prevent his

---

*This treaty was signed at Ninety-Six on Sept. 16, 1775, by William Henry Drayton on behalf of the Whigs, and by Thomas Fletchal, John Ford, Thomas Green, Evan McLaurin and Benjamin Wofford on behalf of the Tories. The witnesses to the agreement were William Thomson, Ely Kershaw and Francis Salvador.

attempting any thing of that kind, he was apprehended, brought to town, and committed to gaol. Patrick Cunningham instantly armed a party of his friends, and pursued, with the expectation of rescuing his brother. The party collected on this occasion seized a thousand pounds of powder, which was at that juncture passing through their settlement. This was publick property, and had been sent by the council of safety as a present to the Cherokee Indians. To inflame the minds of the people, some designing men among the royalists propagated a report, that the powder was sent to the Indians, accompanied with instructions to them, to kill every man who should refuse to sign the association.* This charge, entirely false in itself, was not believed by any of the well-informed inhabitants; nevertheless it answered the purposes of party among some of the ignorant multitude. It was confidently asserted that some private marks had been agreed on by the popular leaders and Indian chiefs, to distinguish the associators from the non-associators; the former of whom were to be spared, and the latter sacrificed. Great pains were also taken to exasperate the inhabitants against the council of safety, for furnishing the Indians with powder at a time when the white people could not be supplied with that necessary article.

"Major Williamson, who commanded the militia in

---

* "Thus Pearis swears, that he 'is assured, from what I said to the Indians, I intended to employ them against the white men, for the committee', although it is notorious, at the great store at the Congarees, that I never saw the Indians but in public, and that the speech I made to them was by an interpreter, in a crowded room, and that several copies were taken from the original draught of it, now deposited among the public papers, in which draught and copies there is no foundation for Pearis' oath and charge in this particular."—Drayton's "address to the inhabitants of the frontier settlements", Journal of Council of Safety, Dec. 6th, 1775, Collections S. C. Hist. Soc., Vol. III, pages 55, 56.

favour of Congress, went in quest of the party which had taken the publick powder, but was soon obliged to retreat before their superior numbers. The royalists, irritated by the capture of Cunningham, and flushed with success in seizing the powder, were at this time more numerous than at any other period. Major Williamson was reduced to the necessity of retreating into a stockade fort, in which he and his party were confined without any water, till, after three days, by digging they obtained a scanty supply. The royalists possessed themselves of the gaol at Ninety-Six, and from that station fired into the fort. Monsieur St. Pierre, an ingenius French gentleman who had settled there some years before, and had made considerable progress in the cultivation of vineyards, was killed by the fire of the royalists, and some others were wounded; but on the whole, very little execution was done. After some days the assailants hoisted a flag, and proposed a truce. Reciprocal permission was given to forward expresses from the royalists to the governor, and from major Williamson to the council of safety. Both parties once more dispersed, and retired to their homes.

"Domestick division at this time was particularly to be dreaded. An invasion from Great-Britain was soon expected. A British fleet and army in front, and disaffected inhabitants in rear, threatened destruction to the friends of Congress. Lord William Campbell had uniformly recommended to the royalists to remain quiet till the arrival of a British force. The advice, so well calculated to distract the views of the popular leaders, had been providentially frustrated. Similar reasons of policy to those which induced the royal governor to recommend inaction to the royalists, operated with the council of safety to crush their intestine foes before that force should arrive. Their late insurrection, in violation of the treaty of Ninety-Six, gave ground to doubt of the sincerity of their engagements to continue in a state of neutrality. From their past conduct it was feared, that, as soon as a proper opportunity should offer itself, they would throw their weight into the royal scale. It was therefore judged necessary, for the publick safety, to march an army into their settlements before that event should take place."

* * * * * * * * *

"The provincial congress did not rest their cause on reasoning alone, but enforced their measures with an army sufficiently numerous to intimidate opposition. They sent a large body of militia and new raised regulars, under the command of colonels Richardson and Thomson. They were also joined by seven hundred militia of North-Carolina, commanded by colonels Polk and Rutherford, and two hundred and twenty regulars commanded by colonel Martin. In a little time Congress had an army of several thousand men under their direction, with instructions 'to apprehend the leaders of the party which had seized the powder, and to do all other things necessary to suppress the present and prevent future insurrections'. Colonel Richardson proceeded in the execution of these orders with great moderation and propriety. A demand was made that the persons who had seized the powder should be delivered up to the justice of their country. Assurances were publickly given that no injury should be done to inoffensive persons, who would remain quietly on their plantations. The leaders of the royalists found great difficulty in persuding their followers to embody. They were cut off from all communication with governor Campbell. Unconnected with their brethren in other parts, there was no union in their measures. They were 'a rope of sand' without order and subordination, and without that enthusiasm which inspired the friends of Congress. Their leaders were destitute of political knowledge and without military experience. The unanimity of the whigs, and the great numbers which, from all sides, invaded the settlements of the royalists, disheartened them from facing their adversaries in the field of battle. They saw resistance to be vain, and that the new government had much greater energy than they had supposed. The whigs acted by system, and in concert with their brethren in the adjacent states, and were directed by a council of safety composed of the greatest and wisest men in the province. They easily carried every point—seized the leaders of the royalists—and dispersed their followers. In erecting this business they did not lose a single man, and only one of their number, major Polk, was wounded. This decided superiority gave confidence to the popular leaders, and greatly strengthened their hands. The vanquished royalists retired to their plantations; but on all occasions discovered as much obstinacy in opposing their countrymen, as their countrymen did firmness in opposing Great-Britain. Several of them, and of others who were averse from fighting, retired over the mountains, where, remote from the noise and bustle of war, they enjoyed that independence for which so many were contending. In the year 1778, when every inhabitant was called on to take an oath of allegiance to the state, many of them voluntarily abandoned their country for the barren sands of East-Florida. In the same year, when the alliance between France and the United States of America was published, others of them nominally joined the Congress. Mr. Robert Cunningham and two or three more of their leading men, were elected members of the legislature. After the reduction of Savannah, a considerable party rose a second time in favour of royal government; but they were completely routed on their way to the British encampments in Georgia.* They afterwards remained quiet till the British obtained possession of Charleston.

"Excepting these ill-concerted insurrections; no publick body in the province, prior to the British conquests in the year 1780, gave avowed evidence of their disapprobation of the popular measures."

* * * * * * * *

"Vigorous decisive measures characterized the popular party; while their opposers either acted without system, or from timid counsels which were feebly executed.

"No revolution was ever effected with greater unanimity, or with more order and regularity. The leading men in every part of the province, with very few exceptions, from the first moments of the contest, exerted themselves in the cause of their country. Their abilities and influence gave union and system to the proceedings of the people. A few persons in the colony hated republican governments, and some ignorant people in the back country were induced to believe that the whole was an artful deception, imposed upon them for interested purposes, by the gentlemen of fortune and ambition on the sea coast. But among the independent enlightened freemen of the province, who loved liberty, and had spirit to risk life and fortune in its support, there were very few to be found who took part with the royalists."

We have it, therefore, from Dr. Ramsay, an eye-witness, that the only place in South Carolina where the Tories outnumbered the Whigs, was in that little triangle between the Broad and Saluda rivers—the great-

---

*At Kettle Creek, by Col. Andrew Pickens.

er part of which was in Ninety-Six District and the lesser part in Orangeburgh District. And that little triangle constituted a very small part of South Carolina, and the people there dwelling constituted a very small portion of the population of South Carolina, and we further have it from Dr. Ramsay that they were either ignorant, or selfish, republic haters, or timid—and we might add—or criminals, and that it was not a difficult matter for the well organized Whigs to control them, as they had no organization, system or ability. We have already seen how they were thrice brought into line, the first time by Drayton's persuasion,—although he had Col. Thomson's regiment along—the second time by Richardson and Thomson, and the third time, just after the fall of Savannah in 1778.

And the fact is that nowhere else in South Carolina did the Tories attain any strength, and if the State was ever overrun by Tories it was in 1780, after the fall of Charleston, and it was not South Carolina Tories that did the overruning, but it was Clinton's overwhelming army of regulars, *assisted by Tories* direct from the Northern States; those from East Florida, who were the offscourings of the whole thirteen colonies; those of Georgia, where there were many settlers only lately from Great-Britain; and the few furnished by South Carolina. And with all of these odds against them—to say nothing of the bad management of Lincoln and Gates—the people of South Carolina were fighting their own battles and driving out and defeating the enemy at the very moment that General Greene was sent down to their assistance.

Toward the close of 1775, the Council of Safety in Charletown received intelligence of the approach of a powerful British fleet and army destined for the reduction of Charlestown. The Council immediately began to make preparations for defending the coast. With that object in view the following letter was addressed to Col. Richardson:

"Charles-Town, Dec. 30th, 1775.

"Sir—We have judged it necessary to detain your messenger Newton, upon an information which we have received by express from the Committee at George-Town, of a fleet of ships having been seen sailing southerly on Christmas evening, said to be eighteen sail, five of which are very large—the weather has ever since been boisterous and thick, in which no ship could with safety approach the land—the first clear day will probably confirm or remove our apprehensions. In the mean time we shall direct Col. Thomson to march his Regiment of Rangers immediately to Monck's Corner, and if you can prevail upon a body of volunteer foot, from 500 to 1,000 men, under proper officers, also to march to the same place, we desire you to do so. The commanding officer, upon his approach, will give notice to this board, and we will transmit the necessary orders for his further proceedings, and we shall give orders after their encampment that payments be regularly made to the troops, and rations of provision duly served to the companies. We confine our application wholly to volunteers, because we would not harrass the militia who have already been engaged in a severe service, nor call upon them out of turn but by their own consent.

"By order of the Council of Safety.

"Henry Laurens, President."

On the same day the following letter was addressed to Col. Thomson:

"Sir—If Col. Richardson from some unexpected occurrence shall not find it necessary to detain you in his army for the service of the colony, you are directed to march that part of your regiment of Rangers now with you, with all expedition to Monck's Corner, and upon your approach to that place, to give notice to this board.

"By order of the Council of Safety.

"Henry Laurens, President.

"Col. Thomson."

Col. Thomson was next placed in charge of the fort at Dorchester, as will be seen by the following extract from an order from the Council of Safety, dated January 3rd, 1776, to Col. Joseph Glover, then commanding at Dorchester: "You will, at the end of the stated time for service of the draughts now upon duty, discharge the whole, and have the command with the officer of the Regiment of Rangers."

Next we extract from the Journal of the Council of Safety for January 12th, 1776:* "Col. Huger, Col. Motte, Col. Thomson and Col. Roberts, being ordered to attend, and attending accordingly, were conferred with.

"*Ordered*, That Col. Thomson do cause a detachment of fifty or sixty of such of his rangers as are good riflemen and will volunteer to go on the service, to proceed to Sullivan's Island, immediately, for the better securing the possession thereof.

"*Ordered*, That Col. Thomson be immediately supplied with twenty-five pounds of gun-powder and one hundred pounds of lead, for the use of the said detachment."†

---

*Collections S. C. Hist. Soc., Vol. III, pages 170 and 171.

† "*Ordered*, That one quarter of a hundred more of gunpowder be issued immediately to Col. Thomson.

"*Ordered*, That fifty weight more of lead be immediately issued to Col. Thomson."—Journal of Council of Safety, Jan. 13th, 1776.

The next day the following order was sent to Col. Thomson:

"In the Council of Safety,
"Jan. 13th, 1775.

"Sir—You are to detach as many of your regiment of rangers with rifles and other good guns, in failure of rifles, as will voluntarily go,* to Sullivan's Island, under the command of Major Mayson; who must apply to Capt. Edward Blake early to-morrow for proper means of transportation; which will be provided by him.

"By order of the Council of Safety.

"Henry Laurens, President.

"Lieut. Col. Thomson."

On January 14th, "Col. Thomson of the Rangers, reported, that sixty-six rank and file, and eight officers, of his regiment, had embarked for Sullivan's Island, together with twenty-eight of the prisoners under his charge, who declared themselves willing to give all possible assistance in forwarding the works to be erected there."†

---

*In a letter, of the same date as the above, to Dr. Oliphant, Henry Laurens wrote: "The rangers are heartily disposed to the service".

†Journal of the Council of Safety, Jan. 14, 1776.

"Col. Thomson also reported the names of some other prisoners less criminal than the rest, having been misled, as objects of the council's mercy, and fit to be discharged."—Journal of the Council of Safety, Jan. 14th, 1776. Six prisoners were discharged on this recommendation.

"Col. Thomson acquainted the board, that he had brought down all such of those prisoners sent to town by Col. Richardson, as had not been already discharged, or gone to work on Sullivan's Island."—Journal of Council of Safety, Jan. 15, 1776. The last of the prisoners were thereupon discharged.

"To Col. Thomson, to pay 49 days wages of rangers employed as carpenter's on Sullivan's Island, at 15s.,......36 15 00".—Journal of Council of Safety, Jan. 29, 1776.

"To Col. Thomson, for discharging the pay allowed to prisoners from the back country, who have laboured for the public, on Sulli-

In the midst of all of these preparations for war, Col. Thomson was obliged to turn his attention to a matter of discipline in his regiment, for, from the Journal of the Council of Safety, for January 23rd, we learn that on that day Colonel Thomson "applied for a warrant to hold a general court martial", which was granted. From the Journal of the Council of Safety for January 29th we learn that William Morris was tried by this court-martial for mutiny, and that he was convicted, and sentenced by the court-martial to receive two hundred and fifty lashes and be sent a prisoner on board the ship Prosper. This sentence was approved by the Council, except as to sending Morris on board the Prosper.

At this time Col. Thomson's regiment was very much divided up. About one hundred of his men were on duty in Charlestown;* Capt. Caldwell, with his company, was stationed at Fort Charlotte;† Capt. Purvis,

---

van's Island, and are now discharged,....£118 00 0."—Journal of Council of Safety, Jan. 23, 1776.

*Journal of Council of Safety, Jan. 26, 1776.

† "To Capt. John Caldwell, the pay-bills of his company of rangers from September 26th, to 1775, Jan. 20th, 1775,.....£3525 11 8".—Journal of Council of Safety, Jan. 25, 1776.

"We desire you will augment the number of militia now on duty in Fort Charlotte to the full number of militia and rangers which are there at present, and put them under the command of an officer in whom you can confide." * * * * "When this order is carried into effect, Capt. Caldwell will withdraw the rangers and march to Charlestown; we therefore recommend it to immediate execution."

* * * * * * * * * * * * *

"Capt. Caldwell has presented to us an account for work done at the Fort by certain Carpenters, in which the charges appear to be extremely high, and the Captain has nothing to say in support of them, and declares himself a bad judge of such matters; the amount moreover is neither certified nor attested. We therefore take the liberty of enclosing it under this cover, and we desire you will cause a proper inquiry to be made, and give us the needful information."—Council of Safety to Maj. Willamson, Jan. 25, 1776.

with his company, was stationed at Dorchester;* and perhaps other detachments were serving elsewhere, but from the headings of the letters in Col. Thomson's order book we are led to conclude that his headquarters during the spring of 1776, were about the Ten Mile House. The following is a copy of one of Col. Thomson's orders during this period of preparation for a British attack:

"March 17, 1776.
"*To Capt. Robert Goodwin, Congarees.*

"Dear Sir:—I expect to see you at Nelson's Ferry by Friday next, or Saturday at farthest, with your old Company and all your new recruits. If you will call on me Thursday or Friday, I will go to Nelson's Ferry. Please to order Lieut. Liles to recruit men for Capt. Donaldson,* as he is in his Company. I hope your Company will be full very soon.

"I am, dear sir, your humble sert.,
"Wm. Thomson."

On the first of June advices were received in Charlestown that a fleet was at anchor off Charlestown bar. The next day orders were sent to the country troops to repair to the defense of Charlestown. Col. Thom-

---

"In the Council of Safety, }
Jan. 27th, 1776. {

"Sir—We desire you will order Capt. Caldwell to return to Fort Charlotte; and as soon as Major Williamson shall have put into that post as many militia men as will replace Capt. Caldwell's company, he is to march to Charles-Town, with that company, and report his arrival to the Congress or this board.
"By order,
"Henry Laurens, President.
"Col. Thomson."

*See letter to Capt. Purvis, dated Jan. 30, 1776.—Journal of Council of Safety, Jan. 31, 1776.
"Read a return of the gunpowder and other stores at Dorchester, received from Capt. Purves, dated 1st inst."—Journal of Council of Safety, Feb. 3, 1776.

son's regiment was marched down from the Ten Mile House, and the 2nd and 3rd regiments of regulars, under Colonels William Moultrie and William Thomson, respectively, were stationed on Sullivan's Island. On June 8th, Gen. Charles Lee, who commanded all the forces in and about Charlestown, issued the following order to Col. Moultrie:

"Charlestown, 8 o'clock, June 8th.

"Sir,

"As we have received information that a body of the enemy have landed, and are lodging themselves on Long-Island, and as the nature of the country is represented to me as favorable to riflemen, I must request that you immediately detach Thomson's and Sumpter's regiments; Capts. Alston's, Mayham's, and Coutirier's companies to that Island, with orders to attack, and if possible, dislodge this corps of the enemy; . . . but you must above all, take care, that their retreat across the breach from Long-Island to Sullivan's Island, is secured to them in case of necessity. For which purpose, you are desired to move down to the point, commanding the breach, two field-pieces; . . . the sooner it is done the better: . . . you are therefore to exert yourself in such a manner that the attack may be made at break of day.

"I am, sir, yours,

"To Col. Moultrie.   "Charles Lee,
                                  "Major General."

In another letter to Col. Moultrie of the same date, Gen. Lee wrote: "I have ordered a considerable reinforcement of riflemen to join Colonel Thomson, which, with the advantages of ground ought to make you totally secure."

The following is Col. Moultrie's reply to Gen. Lee:

"Sullivan's Island, June 10th, 1776.

"Sir.

"I just now received your orders for detaching Thompson and Sumpter's regiments, Allston, Mayham and Coutirier's companies. By the date of your letter it seems as if you intended this business to have been done this morning, but your letter came too late to hand for that purpose. I shall send the detachment to our advance guard, there to remain with their boats for crossing them, hid till night, then shall embark them for Long-Island, where they may be reconnoitreing till day-light." * * *

"I am, sir, your most obedient,
"William Moultrie,
"Col. 2d. regiment."

But before night Col. Moultrie received the following letter:

"June the 10th, 6 o'clock, P. M.

"Sir

"I am just returned from an excursion into the country.... As the large ships are now over the bar, and as your bridge must be finished; I would wish you would lay asside all thoughts of an expedition against Long-Island, unless your scouts bring such intelligence as almost to insure a successful stroke.

"I am, sir, yours,
"Charles Lee.

"To Col. Moultrie.
"Sullivan's Island."

In a letter to Col. Moultrie, dated the 11th, Gen. Lee wrote: "I hope the point of your Island, opposite to Long-Island is secure against the enemy lodging there." The task of guarding that point had been entrusted to Col. Thomson.

On June 16th Col. Moultrie wrote to Gen. Armstrong, who commanded at Haddrell's Point, on the mainland: "Col. Thompson is now with me, and informs me that he has taken particular notice of the movement of the enemy, he observed about 10 o'clock, 200 grenadiers, and a small battalion, (which he imagines came from Dewee to cover the landing of the rest) where they posted themselves, about one mile from our advanced guard, and waited until about seventeen hundred men were landed. They then marched off to Dewees' Island, he observed every six men carried something like a tent; they are still landing as fast as the boats can bring them. Col. Thompson begs that he may have at least his own men which are over with you (one hundred) without whom he cannot undertake to prevent their landing on this island, should they attempt it. We are all in high spirits, and will keep a good look out to prevent a surprise. Col. Thompson requests as a favor, if you have time, that you would come over and take a ride on the island to observe what a length of ground we have to defend." To this Gen. Armstrong replied, on the same day: "I shall do my utmost to comply with yours and Col. Thompson's request, respecting the residue of his regiment, no passage over, unless you can send boats in the morning." * * * * "I see no reason why you may not also reinforce Col. Thomson; nay, if they appear indeed to land on Sullivan's it must be done, and the point at the island where they may best land, prudently and vigorously defended at all events. Let the Col. know this."

On the 21st, Gen. Lee wrote to Col. Moultrie: "Those two field pieces at the very end of the point, are so exposed that I desire you will draw them off to a more secure distance from the enemy . . . in their present situation it appears to me, they may be carried off when ever the enemy think proper."

In a letter to Col. Isaac Hayne, dated June 24th, Hon. Richard Hutson relates the following incidents concerning the 3rd regiment:

"On their sending their first reconnoitering party upon Long Island, one of their men was shot by one of our Riflemen. He was dressed in red, faced with black, and had a cockade and feather in his hat and a sword by his side. By which it appears that he was an officer; but that is all we know about him. Some time after there happened an affair of a very tragi-comical nature; when they began to effect a landing on Long Island our President offered a premium of thirty guineas to any of the Riflemen who should first take one of the King's troops prisoner. Accordingly three of them went over one night for that purpose. Two of them agreed to keep together, the other determined to go by himself. In the morning by twilight the one that was alone descried the two others at a distance, and imagining that they were the King's troops, took up his gun to fire at them, thinking, I suppose, to kill one and then take the other alive; one of the others seeing his piece presented, was quicker than he was and shot him through the thigh, upon which he fell. They immediately ran up, dragged him to the boat, threw him in and pushed off, all thinking that he was one of the King's troops. They had got a considerable distance from the shore before the poor man was sufficiently recovered from his fright to speak. As soon as he spoke they discovered their mistake. He is likely to recover." * * * *

"There was a sham battle the other day between our men on Sullivan's Island, and the troops on Long Island. Some of our Riflemen had been over in order to endeavor to obtain the President's premium, and on Friday morning last, the King's troops tracked them down to the Breach between the two islands, which at low water is fordable. As soon as our guard upon Sullivan's Island discovered them, they fired upon them with a field piece, which they returned by Platoons of Musketry. They continued firing at each other in this manner across the Breach for several hours. One of our men had one of his hands blown off by our own Field-Piece, which went off while he was loading it, owing to its not having been sponged. Two others were wounded by the enemy. We have not learnt what loss they have sustained."

It was doubtless this same "sham battle" that induced Gen. Lee, on June 22nd, to write the following to Col. Moultrie:

"Sir,

"Inclosed is a letter for Col. Thompson; I send it open that you may read it; for allowing for the difference of his circumstances as a rifle officer, the spirit of the order is to extend to the whole; no vague uncertain firing either of rifles, muskets, or cannon is to be permitted." And Gen. Lee was probably referring to the three adventurers, referred to by Mr. Hutson, when he continued, in the same letter: "Soldiers running at random wherever their folly directs, is an absolute abomination not to be tolerated."

But it appears that a few days later there was another exchange of shots between Thomson's men and the enemy, for on June 27th, Mr. Hutson wrote again: "The firing yesterday was between the troops on Long Island and our advanced Guard on Sullivan's Island, across the Breach. They fired with Field Pieces, and threw several shells. The President and General Lee were down there at the time. One of the shells bursted within a few yards of the President, and he brought a piece of it up to Town with him. They did not do any execution and General Lee would suffer only two shots to be returned from an eighteen pounder which has been carried down there."

On the 27th, Gen. Lee, in a letter to Col. Moultrie, wrote: "I have ordered Gen. Armstrong to send an hundred volunteers to ease Col. Thompson's regiment of their heavy duty, for I find, that a part of Col. Horry's regiment* had most magnanimously refused to take this duty on them: We shall live I hope to thank them."

On the 28th of June the British fleet, having crossed the bar, bore down on the little fort that Colonel Moultrie occupied at the western extremity of Sullivan's Island,—but the result of the British admiral's temerity on that occasion, in bearing down upon that fort, is too well known. The battle of Fort Sullivan is American history. We have only to deal with the part taken by our own Thomson at the other end of the Island.

About the same time that the British fleet moved to attack Col. Moultrie's fort, the British army of two thousand regulars, under General Sir Henry Clinton, marched down to the western extremity of Long Island, and attempted to cross the inlet, where it is fordable at low water, over to Sullivan's Island. Clinton's army was flanked by an armed schooner and a sloop, and by a strong flotilla of armed boats from the fleet, with orders to co-operate with the army. But Col. Thomson's sharpshooters and artillerists not only drove Clinton's regulars back from the ford as often as they attempted to cross it, but swept the decks of the flotilla as often as it approached to aid the army. And after a short and decisive fight the army was defeated and driven off, and the flotilla dis-

*Militia.

persed. Clinton's forces, including the marines, numbered nearly two thousand more than Thomson's, and yet Col. Thomson had not a man killed and only one wounded.

While the fight was going on Gen. Lee sent the following letter to Col. Moultrie:
"Dear Col.

"Mr. Byrd makes reports of your conduct which does you infinite honor; they are indeed such as I expected. I have sent for more ammunition for you, and ordered a large corps of riflemen to reinforce Col. Thompson." Whether Col. Thomson received these reinforcements before, during, or after his fight, the records do not state; but Gen. Moultrie in his "Memoirs," p. 142. says that Col. Thomson's force consisted of his own regiment of 300 men, Col. Clarke with 200 North Carolina regulars, Col. Horry with 200 South Carolina troops, and the Racoon Company of 50 militia riflemen. He further says: "Col. Thompson had orders that if they could not stand the enemy they were to throw themselves into the fort"—an order which, it appears, he was not put to the necessity of obeying.

On the day after the battles, Gen. Lee wrote Col. Moultrie a letter of thanks, to which his secretary added the following postscript: "The General desires that Col. Thompson will send as soon as he can, a return of all occurrences in his part of the Island."

"On July 1st, Gen. Lee addressed a letter to Col. Moultrie to which he added the following postscript: "I must request that your garrison may be kept more vigilant than ever, and that Col. Thompson and his corps do not relax; for it is almost proverbial in war, that we are never in so great danger as when success makes us confident." But the British were satisfied with the drubbings they had received, and soon sailed away from our coast.

For his splendid victory over Clinton, the Continental Congress included Colonel Thomson's name in the general resolution of thanks to the victorious forces on this occasion.

The following is a copy of the resolution:*

"Philadelphia, July 20th, 1776.
"In Congress.

"Resolved, That the thanks of the United States of America, be given to Maj. Gen. Lee, Col. William Moultrie, Col. William Thompson, and the officers and soldiers under their commands; who, on the 28th of June last, repulsed, with so much valor, the attack which was made on the State of South-Carolina, by the fleet and army of his Britannic majesty.

"That Mr. President transmit the foregoing resolution to Maj. Gen. Lee, Col. Moultrie, and Col. Thompson.

"By order of the Congress.
"John Hancock, President."†

The six South Carolina regular regiments were now, by resolutions of the Continental Congress, passed June 18th, and July 24th, 1776, put regularly upon the Continental Establishment, and the South Carolina officers came into the Continental line as the youngest officers of their respective ranks, as will appear by the following resolution of the General Assembly of South Carolina, passed September 20th. 1776: "Resolved, that this house do acquiesce in the resolution of the continental Congress of the 18th of June, and the 24th of July last, relative to the putting the two regiments of

---
*Moultrie's Memoirs, Vol. I, page 183.
†For Col. Thomson's answer to this letter see his order book for Aug. 14, 1776.

infantry, the regiment of rangers,* the regiment of artillery, and the two regiments of riflemen, in the service of this state, upon the continental establishment."

Hildreth says, History United States, Vol. III., Chapter XXXII., p. 109, that "Congress had already† taken into Colonial pay‡ the three regiments of South Carolina, presently increased to five".

In the month of July following his victory over Clinton, Col. Thomson was called upon to furnish a detachment for an expedition against the Cherokee Indians in the upper part of South Carolina.

Upon the breaking out of hostilities, the British agents in the South instigated the Cherokee Indians to take up arms against the colonists. An Indian war commenced, and was carried on with its usual barbarity.§ The speedy departure, however, of the British fleet from the sea coast, after their unsuccessful attack on Fort Sullivan, gave an opportunity to concentrate a large force for the chastisement of the savages.

Col. Andrew Williamson,‖ of Ninety Six District, commanded the forces in this expedition. With a small force of militia he began his march on the third of July. His force being small, his progress was ne-

---

* "There are some of my officers, I am informed, who will not take Continental Commissions".—Col. Thomson to Major Morgan Conner, January 2nd, 1777.

†Toward the close of 1775.

‡It was "Colonial pay" in name only, for General Moultrie says that up to April, 1778, "the state had paid and clothed the troops, and furnished every article that was necessary for military operations from their own stores, the continent having nothing here at the time".—Memoirs, Vol. II, page 364.

§Mr. Francis Salvador stated in a letter to Mr. Drayton, dated July 18, 1776, that some of the inhabitants of the up-county were so panic stricken that they fled as low down as Orangeburgh.—Drayton's Memoirs Vol: II, page 363.

‖He was promoted colonel while on this expedition.

ORANGEBURG COUNTY. 353

cessarily slow. On the 16th he reached Dewett's Corner near the Cherokee boundary line. Here he was joined by Capt. Felix Warley, of Thomson's regiment, with a detachment of a hundred rangers, and a convoy of wagons with ammunition, arms, and stores.* The Carolinians had several sharp engagements with the Indians, but they finally defeated them; traversed their whole country; and laid waste their fields of corn; and about five hundred of the Cherokees were forced to take refuge in West Florida, where they were fed at the expense of the British government. Of this expedition Ramsay says: "None of all the expeditions before undertaken against the savages had been so successful as this first effort of the new-born commonwealth. In less than three months, viz. from the 15th of July to the 11th of October 1776 the business was completed, and the nation of the Cherokees so far subdued as to be incapable of annoying the settlements. The whole loss of the Americans in the expedition did not exceed fifty men, but in this number was that worthy citizen Mr. Francis Salvador."†

In August, 1776, Gen. Charles Lee, commanding the troops in South Carolina, undertook an expedition against the British province of East Florida. President Rutledge gave orders to Col. Thomson to send 130 men of his regiment with Gen. Lee. In consequence of this order Col. Thomson, on August 7th, issued an order to Major Mayson to take command of this detachment at Savannah. Gen. Lee's expedition

---

* "Captain Warley with this loaded convoy, marched from Charlestown to Dewett's Corner, by the road along the Congaree and Hard-Labour Creek, in fourteen days."—Drayton's Memoirs, Vol. II, page 343, foot note.

†For a sketch of this gentleman see Drayton's Memoirs, Vol. II, pages 347, 348.

left Savannah in September and marched toward St. Augustine; but two days thereafter Gen. Lee received an express from Congress ordering him to the northward with the Virginia and North Carolina troops. This put an end to the expedition, and Major Mayson returned to the Congarees with his detachment in October, and at once gave his men furloughs for thirty days, for recuperating.

On October the 6th we find, by his own order book, that Col. Thomson was in camp at the Congarees with 161 officers and privates, with the detachment that had been sent to East Florida not yet returned, though it did return a few days later.

Scarcely had the detachment under Major Mayson returned from Georgia, when Col. Thomson was ordered to send off another detachment to assist the Georgians. This detachment, consisting of two captains, three lieutenants, three sergeants and ninety-three privates, marched from the camp at Congarees on October 14th, 1776, under the command of Capt. John Caldwell, with orders from Col. Thomson to cross the Savannah just below Augusta and proceed to Fort Barrington on the Altamaha. A second detachment, of seven privates and a sergeant, under command of Lieut. Beames, marched, on October 18th, to join Capt. Caldwell, and took orders to Capt. Caldwell, instructing him to execute his orders, and then to join the regiment wherever it should then be.

On the 28th of December, a detachment under Capt. Richard Winn was ordered to Georgia to relieve Capt. Caldwell and his detachment.

The next service required of the 3rd regiment was to go to Georgia, in 1777, under General Robert Howe, who then commanded the troops in South Carolina and Georgia. Gen. Howe, in February, 1777, received intelligence from Georgia that a body of regular troops, under Col. Fuser, were marching to invade Georgia, and he immediately left Charlestown for Savannah; but the enemy soon retreated, and in March following, Generals Gadsden and Moultrie, commanding at Charlestown, requested Gen. Howe to return to that city, which he did in June following. In the meantime he wrote a letter to Gen. Moultrie, from Savannah, on March 16th, in which he said: "Thompson's are at Purisburgh, and will be ordered to march to-morrow." They were probably marched back to their homes, for we find in Col. Thomson's order book a letter, dated at "Charles Town 25th April 1777", directed to Maj. Wise, in "Camp near Nelson's Ferry", ordering him to send a detachment to Charlestown.

During the remainder of the year 1777, Col. Thomson's regiment was divided up into detachments, which performed various duties in different parts of South Carolina. One detachment, for some time, guarded the jail at Ninety-Six, another, under Capt. Lyles, was, on August 16th, ordered to capture several Tory leaders in Ninety-Six district and convey them to Charlestown jail, while other detachments were given other similar duties to perform. The regiment was encamped part of the time at Amelia and part of the time at Nelson's Ferry.

In December, 1777, the State of Georgia being much disturbed by British and Tory inroads from Florida, Gen. Howe returned to Georgia.

On April 6th, 1778, President Lowndes wrote the following letter to Gen. Moultrie:
"Sir;
"I have received letters and information from the Congarees, which give good grounds to suspect that some design is formed to disturb the tranquility

of the interior parts of this state. Several of the inhabitants have suddenly and secretly withdrawn themselves from their habitations, and have manifested, by other parts of their behavior, that some enterprise is in agitation, that may, if not timely attended to, surprise us at a disadvantage. I have ordered Colonel Beard to keep a good look out, and to raise a proper number of his militia, so as to be in readiness to oppose any sudden attempt that may be undertaken by those people called Tories. I have taken the liberty to direct him in case the matter should wear a serious aspect and require a greater force than he can readily draw from his regiment, to apply for aid and succor to Colonel Thomson, who, I believe has a detachment of his regiment near those parts, as I intended to apply to you to give the required assistance. I wish the present appearances which have given this alarm may blow over* without producing any ill consequences. Perhaps the late incursions of the Florida scouts in those parts, may have afforded an opportunity of tampering with the ill-affected, and of exciting ill humours amongst them. However this may be, it is prudent to be prepared against the worst.

"I am, &c.

"Rawlins Lowndes.
"The honorable General Moultrie."

On April 7th, Gen. Howe wrote, from Savannah, to Gen. Moultrie, wishing him "immediately to prepare, and have in readiness to march at a moment's warning, 200 men"; and in answer to this Gen. Moultrie wrote, on April 10th: "I have, agreeably, to your orders sent 150 men from Thompson's, and 50 from Sumpter's regiments in readiness to go off at a mo-

---

*They seem to have done so.

ment's warning: I hope, however, you will have no occasion for them."

Thomson's regiment seems to have been very much in demand about that time. On April 14th President Lowndes wrote to Gen. Moultrie as follows: "As it appears from the concurrent accounts of all the intelligence I have received, that the disaffected plan their hopes and expectations on being joined with a force from Florida; and that their aim is to form the junction by crossing Savannah river, a condiderable party having already taken that route, I submit to you, whether it would not be necessary and proper to post Thompson with his regiment at some convenient place on Savannah river to interrupt or prevent such a design, more especially as he would be enabled from thence, more expeditiously to remove to the immediate assistance of Georgia. The militia in all parts of the back country being in arms, and on their guard, I think no great danger is to be apprehended, unless a combined force should be effected, which must be by crossing Savannah river, the guarding of which might baffle their scheme." To this Gen. Moultrie replied on the same day: "I just now received yours, and have considered with attention what you mention with regard to posting Thompson's regiment on Savannah river, I cannot at present think it proper by any means, and I will therefore give you my reasons. That regiment consists of about one third the number of continental troops in this State (150 of them in town which we cannot do without, unless the militia will take off some of our guards) and the sending them so far from the capital would be running too great a risk, besides the harrassing the troops: should any sudden attack be made upon our sea coast, we have only the continental troops to make head until the militia can be collected, which you know will take some little time; should any attack be made on our frontier it cannot be half the consequence, and should the enemy attempt to move with an army through the back country, they must drag themselves so slowly along that before they could penetrate far we should be collected to oppose them; and should they move in small parties I think our militia quite sufficient to check their progress. I flatter myself that this bustle is not so serious as was first imagined, or I certainly should have heard from Gen. Howe ere this, to move on the troops, he had ordered to be in readiness."

But Gen. Moultrie had not long to wait on Gen. Howe for marching orders, for on the same date that he addressed his letter to President Lowndes, Gen. Howe wrote him, from Savannah, as follows: "The situation of affairs here, makes it necessary to desire that the men under marching orders, repair, with all possible expedition to Purisburgh, where they will receive directions as to their further conduct. You will take care that they are provided with every military requisite, as this state cannot furnish them. You are, however, not to delay the march of the men, for any preparations of this sort, as I am exceedingly anxious for their arrival, and shall continue to be so, till they do arrive."

* * * * * * * * *

"When I wrote you before, though I thought it eligible to prepare for the worst, yet I had hopes that things would not have been so serious; but the aspect they now wear, induces me to believe, that this state,* deplorably weak in itself, will need every support yours can give it: I am therefore under the necessity of ordering fifty men from the first regiment, and also

---

*Georgia.

thirty men from the artillery, with two field-pieces, with everything proper for action."

The occasion of these alarms was the well authenticated reports received from St. Augustine, that a British army, under Gen. Prévost, was about to invade Georgia. On April 18th Gen. Moultrie replied to Gen. Howe: "I received yours by express, last night, and shall order the first detachment off to-morrow morning; the remainder of the first regiment and the artillery will march off on Monday, under the command of Colonel Charles C. Pinckney."

On the same date Maj. J. F. Grimké, Aid-de-Camp to Gen. Howe, sent the following order to Gen. Moultrie: "I am directed by General Howe to request of you, that you would have the remaining part of the continental troops, amounting to one half the number and allowed by the president and council of your state, in immediate readiness for marching, upon receiving the general's orders."

On April 24th Gen. Moultrie answered this order: "Our first detachment* marched off a few days ago, and Colonel Charles C. Pinckney with the second, went off yesterday." * * * * "I have ordered the remainder of Thomson's and Sumpter's regiments to be ready to march on my receiving your further orders." * * * * "Our number of continental troops belonging to this state, amount to about fifteen hundred."

But Gen. Moultrie was too slow for Gen. Howe, for on the 26th, Major Grimké wrote again as follows: "I have to request your excuse if I did not deliver myself so explicitly as I was ordered to do in the last letter I wrote you by desire of Major General Howe. As I did not keep a copy, not having time to write it again,

---
*Consisting of 150 men of Thomson's regiment, under Major Wise, and 50 men of Sumter's regiment, under Lieut-Col. Henderson.

I cannot refer to the order, nor do I at present recollect in what mode of expression I delivered myself. The order, sir, that it was my intention to transmit you, should have positively declared the necessity for the immediate march of the troops, forming and remaining part of the continental battalions in the state of South Carolina. You will please, therefore, to order the troops you refer to, whom you say you have directed to be ready to march at a moment's warning, and consists of the other parts of Colonel Thomson's and Sumpter's regiments. They are to proceed to Fort Howe, by the shortest road upon the Alatamaha, without touching at Savannah." To this Gen. Moultrie replied, on May 1st: "The excuse you request should rather be asked by me, as I neglected to inform you, that your orders were very explicit, and I accordingly put them in execution, excepting for Thomson's, in lieu of which I sent the first regiment, as they are better clothed and disciplined."

The appearance in Georgia of so formidable a force had the effect of deterring Prévost from invading that State, and Gen. Howe then determined to "carry the war into Africa" by marching into East-Florida, but the country through which they passed was so barren, and the season so unfavorable that upon reaching the St. Mary's river and capturing and destroying Fort Tonyn, it was decided, on July 11th, to go no farther. Gen. Howe, with the Georgia troops, and, it appears, a portion of the South Carolina troops—among them the detachment from Thomson's regiment under Maj. Wise —returned to Savannah; while Col. Pinckney with the other South Carolina troops returned by water to Charlestown. The South Carolina troops remaining with Howe lingered out a summer season in Georgia, and when the autumn came the British army again found work for them to do.

On November 27th, Gen. Howe wrote from Zubly's Ferry to Gen. Moultrie advising him that the British were again about to invade Georgia, and requesting the assistance of more South Carolina troops. In answer to this Gen. Moultrie wrote, on the 28th: "I have sent an express to Col. Huger to expedite his march, leaving his baggage and weak men behind to come up more at leisure. I shall get Col. Henderson's battalion off I hope to-morrow; Thompson's regiment is not far from you,* they are taking the shortest rout to Purisburgh." Although Gen. Moultrie wrote "Thompson's regiment", it appears to have been only a detachment of that regiment, for Gen. Huger wrote, on December 28th, to Gen. Moultrie: "I am just now turning out my regiment with Thompson's detachment, and few of the Georgia continentals, with orders to take the field immediately"; and we find by Col. Thomson's order book that he, with the major part of his regiment, was at this time aiding the civil authorities and militia about Orangeburgh to subdue certain disturbers of the peace, and was patrolling the Edisto and Savannah rivers in order to keep out "Florida scouts" and protect the frontier settlers from Indians.

On the 29th, Gen. Howe's army was totally defeated by Col. Campbell, and Savannah fell into the hands of the British. In this fight the South Carolina troops, including Maj. Wise's detachment of the 3rd regiment, formed the right wing of Howe's army, which was commanded by Gen. Isaac Huger. In the meantime Major-General Benjamin Lincoln, a New Englander whom Congress had sent to relieve Gen. Howe, had arrived in Charlestown and assumed command there. As soon as he could collect reinforcements, he marched

---

*Where they had probably spent the summer.

for the Savannah river, arriving at Purisburgh on January 3rd, 1779,—too late to save Howe. That evening he was joined by Howe, and the next day by the South Carolina troops.

Gen. Lincoln remained at Purisburgh, with the Continental troops and some militia, having skirmishes with the enemy almost daily, until April, when he moved his army up to Black Swamp, twenty-five miles above; leaving a small force at Purisburgh. On the 20th of April Gen. Lincoln marched off up the river, leaving Gen. Moultrie with a force of 1200 men at Black Swamp. Two days later Gen. Lincoln wrote back, ordering Gen. Moultrie to send up Gen. Huger with the remaining Continental troops, excepting detachments of the 2nd and 5th regiments (numbering 220 men), to the number of 1000 men. The 3rd regiment was, therefore, with Lincoln, and shared the fortunes of his army as he marched up on the South Carolina side of the Savannah, and crossed that river and marched down on the Georgia side. The army was engaged in only a few skirmishes, it is true, but the long march through a rough, thinly settled country was more trying to the health and spirits of the men than a pitched battle would have been.

While Gen. Lincoln was marching up and down the banks of the Savannah river "inspiring the inhabitants of the country with confidence", Gen. Prévost crossed the Savannah river, on April 29th, with about 3000 men and marched for Charlestown. But Gen. Moultrie with about 250 Continentals and 1000 militia lately arrived from Orangeburgh, was between Prévost and Charlestown, and delayed his march in every possible way; all the while sending despatches to Lincoln requesting him to send reinforcements, and to return to South Carolina with his army in order to save Charlestown. Gen. Moultrie was joined at Charlestown by a considerable militia force, and by a skillfully arranged piece of deception Prévost was made to believe that the town would be surrendered; but when time enough had been gained to bring Gen. Lincoln's army, which had recrossed the Savannah and was marching to Moultrie's relief, uncomfortably near to Prévost all proposals of surrender were withdrawn. It was then too late for Prévost to attempt to storm the works around Charlestown, and he withdrew to the neighboring sea islands.

On the 20th of June, Gen. Lincoln made an unsuccessful assault on Prévost's trenches at Stono, and the next day Col. Grimké wrote a letter to Mr. J. Kean in which he stated that "the left of our line was composed of continental troops, under Gen. Huger"; and we may presume that the detachment of the 3rd regiment was there.

A few days after Lincoln's attack on his trenches at Stono, Prévost embarked his army for Beaufort, where he left a part of his force and repaired to Savannah with his main army.

About the 1st of September Count D'Estaing, with a French fleet, appeared off Charlestown bar and announced to Gen. Lincoln that he was ready to assist him to lay siege to Savannah. On September 5th Gen. Lincoln ordered all officers and soldiers to join their respective regiments. This brought Col. Thomson and all of the officers and men of the 3rd regiment to their places. On the 23rd of September, Lincoln's army joined the French, and encamped before Savannah. On the 4th and 5th of October their batteries opened on the British works, and on the 9th an assault was made, which resulted in the defeat of the allied forces. The 3rd regiment lost its major, (Samuel Wise) one Lieutenant, (Bailey) and 10 of the rank and file; while one captain, (Farrar) two lieutenants, (Gaston and DeSaussure)* two sergeants and twenty-four of the rank and file were wounded—making a total of 41 killed and wounded.†

From certain documentary evidence now before us, we are led to the conclusion that Col. Thomson and Lieut. Col. Mayson both resigned their commissions in the 3rd regiment about the beginning of the year 1780. It is on the following evidence that we base our conclusion:

Extract from a letter from Gen. Lincoln to Lieut. Col. Marion, dated Charlestown, November 25th, 1779: "I will inquire into the reason why the officers of the Third are absent, I must find some officers who belong to another corps to do duty in that Regiment."‡

Order from Major Edmund Hyrne, Deputy Adjutant General, to Lieut. Col. Peter Horry, dated February 11th, 1780: "You are this day in orders for the third Regiment, and the General desires me to inform you that your presence is immediately and absolutely necessary. We have certain intelligence of the British Troops having landed and we are just informed that sail are now off Stono."§

Letter of same date, from Major Hyrne to Lieut. Col. Peter Horry: "I am sorry to have troubled you with my letter of this date by the Express. Col. Henderson, (before the order was issued,) informed the General he had altered his mind and would accept the appointment, and he is accordingly appointed Lt. Col. of the third."‖

---

*It appears from Gen. DeSaussure's pamphlet that both of the wounded lieutenants died of their wounds.
†See *South Carolina and American General Gazette*, Oct. 29, 1779.
‡Gibbes's Documentary History, 1781 and 1782, page 4.
§Ibid, page 10.
‖Ibid, pages 10, 11.

The next service required of the 3rd regiment was to assist in the defence of Charlestown against the fleet and army which Sir Henry Clinton brought from New York against that city in February, 1780. Col. Thomson was not with the regiment during the siege. Dr. Johnson, in "Traditions of the Revolution", says that he was on detached service in Orangeburgh District; and John Lewis Gervais, Deputy Paymaster General for the Southern Department, writes, in his diary of March 10th: "Col. Thomson is forming a camp near Orangeburg, to put a stop to plunderers." Moses Young writes, in his journal of April 4th: Col. Thomson raising men—has got 20". J. L. Gervais, in a letter written from Georgetown, dated April 28th, says: "By our last advices, Gen. Caswell was, with 1000 men, near Col. Thomson. Gen. Williamson was expected last Sunday at Orangeburg, with 900 men—say 600." * * * "Col. Thomson was at Orangeburg with 200 men." * * "Major Vanderhorst, formerly in the first regiment, arrived yesterday from Colonel Thomson." And when Charlestown finally fell, one lieutenant-colonel is the only field officer* recorded as having been surrendered by the 3rd regiment—and that lieutenant-colonel was doubtless Henderson.

The reörganization of the Continental Army might have caused the resignation of Col. Thomson. Instead of having regiments with full colonels, the army was organized into 88 battalions, each commanded by a lieutenant-colonel. This was done to accord with the arrangement in the British army, and facilitated the exchange of prisoners. It is likely that this change, coupled with his long illness, caused Col. Thomson to

---

*The major of the regiment having been killed at Savannah.

resign his regular commission, and resume charge of a militia organization.

Not long after the surrender of Charlestown Col. Thomson was captured and paroled. While at home under parole he was arrested, charged with having broken his parole, and taken to Charlestown where he was confined in the basement of the old "Exchange" for some time. When he was finally released and exchanged he immediately reported to Gen. Greene, says Dr. Johnson in "Traditions of the Revolution", and was put to scouting. If he had never resigned his commission in the 3rd regiment he would, most likely, have resumed command of the remnants of that regiment after the fall of Charlestown.

Very little is known of the part taken by the 3rd regiment in the defense of Charlestown, but in order to show here what is known of the part taken by that regiment it will be necessary to again have recourse to extracts from journals and documents of that day, and histories written since:

We learn from Gen. McIntosh's journal, and from Gen. Moultrie's Memoirs, Vol. II, page 80, that Captain Goodwyn,* of the 3rd regiment, was killed by the besiegers on April 26th; and when Charlestown finally surrendered on the 12th of May, 1780, the British returns show that the 3rd regiment surrendered one lieutenant-colonel, nine captains, six lieutenants, one surgeon, one surgeon's mate, 19 sergeants, 14 drummers, and 208 of the rank and file: making a total of 259.

By the surrender of Charlestown the regiment was

---

*The roll of officers of the 3rd regiment, taken from Gen. DeSaussure's pamphlet, shows that there was a Captain Robert Goodwyn and a Lieutenant Wm. Goodwyn of this regiment, but it also shows that they both resigned May 30, 1778; but from the statements of Generals McIntosh and Moultrie we must conclude that Gen. DeSaussure was mistaken as to one of them.

practically annihilated; another regiment took its place in the Continental line while its men were on parole, and when the few survivors were exchanged they probably joined other regiments.

The following account of Col. Thomson and his regiment is taken from Johnson's Traditions of the Revolution: (p. 90 et seq.)

"COLONEL WILLIAM THOMSON.

"Colonel William Thomson commanded the third regiment, called the Rangers; he being from the upper part of Orangeburg District, soon filled his regiment with many of the best riflemen in the State, he being himself the most practiced marksman in his command. The tories in the upper country having been influenced by Sir William Campbell, the royal governor, and his agents, commenced hostilities there, and afforded the new troops a fine opportunity for exercise and for facing an enemy. The expedition was under command of General Richard Richardson,* of the militia, and was completely successful, but the cold and exposure was very severe to such soldiers. They had scarcely concluded this campaign, when news was received that Sir Henry Clinton was preparing, at New-York, a strong armament against the South. They were consequently ordered down to the sea coast, for its protection. Colonel Thomson was posted at the eastern end of Sullivan's Island, in a small battery of two guns, the brick foundation of which has lately been discovered, by the shifting of the sand. It was called the advanced guard, and was ordered to protect the island from the bayonets of Sir Henry Clinton,— his command of two thousand British regulars, being

---

*He was only a colonel at that time.

then encamped within sight, on the western extremity of Long Island.

"This gentleman was born in Pennsylvania, of Irish parents, about the year 1727, and removed with his father's family to South-Carolina, while yet a child. They settled on the west side of Congaree river, in what was called Amelia township, now known as St. Mathew's Parish, in Orangeburg District. This was at the time a frontier settlement, and young Thomson grew up 'amidst alarms and strife,' which trained his mind to deeds of enterprise and daring, and nerved his body to endure the toils and sufferings incidental to border warfare. The rifle became his favorite companion in all his excursions, and his sure reliance in danger. He planted with his father, and aided him in guiding the plough, in driving the team, and in all the other occupations of a country life.* Being sociable and friendly in his disposition, he became a favorite among his neighbors, secured their admiration by winning the prizes at every shooting match, and commanded their respect and esteem by his uniformly correct deportment.

"About the year 1763,† William Thomson married Miss Eugenia Russell, born in that neighborhood, the half sister of Colonel William Heatly. Her father was a native of Massachusetts, and born of English parents who had settled in that then Province.

"In 1769 great commotions arose in the upper parts of the State, between what were called Regulators and Schofilites. At that time no courts were established out of Charleston, and lawless depredators, living near the Indian nations, plundered the industrious, honest

---

*In an affidavit, made in January, 1761, before Andrew Brown, J. P., relative to the will of James Beames, he spoke of himself as "William Thomson, late Indian Trader in the Cherokees".

†Thursday, Aug. 14, 1755.

COLONEL WILLIAM THOMSON.

REPRODUCED FOR THE HISTORY OF ORANGEBURG COUNTY FROM AN OLD OIL PORTRAIT IN POSSESSION OF CHARLES T. HASKELL, ESQ., OF SAVANNAH, GEORGIA.

farmers, and escaped over the borders with the stolen horses and cattle. The parties aggrieved united to protect each other, soon took upon themselves to punish the aggressors, and personal feelings no doubt hurried them on into some unjustifiable acts. They called themselves Regulators; the depredators appealed to the royal governor for protection, and a silly fellow, a Colonel Schovel, was sent up for that purpose. He encouraged them to assemble in arms, and bloodshed was barely prevented by the intervention of a few more discreet persons. They took their name from that of their colonel, and having been screened by the royal authority, many of them and their descendants became royalists in the revolution, which commenced a few years after this event.

"Among the royalists of 1775, there were, no doubt, many conscientious, honest men.

"To soothe these irritations, and prevent future depredations, several additional courts were established in the upper country. one at Camden, one at Orangeburg, and one at Cambridge, in Ninety-Six, now Abbeville District. As soon as the establishments could be carried into effect, William Thomson was elected sheriff of Orangeburg District, as a man of the greatest influence, energy, and decision. He entered on the duties of his office in June, 1772, and continued to be called upon in all difficulties and in all emergencies of a public nature that subsequently occurred.

"He was elected a member of the Provincial Legislature, under the royal government, and was a member of the convention which commenced revolutionary measures, adopted a constitution. and organized the means for resisting Great Britain. When it was resolved to raise three regiments for this purpose in South Carolina, William Thomson was elected colonel of the Rangers, or third regiment, and immediately proceeded to enlist his men, under orders issued on the 17th June, 1775. Before his number was complete, and while employed in drilling his men, the royalists in Ninety-Six armed in opposition to the revolutionary government. Col. Thomson had previously been out with William Henry Drayton and the Rev. Mr. Tenant, accompanied by Colonel Joseph Kershaw, of Camden, endeavoring to conciliate and restrain the disaffected in the upper and western portions of the State. Now, that the royalists assembled in arms, and attacked Colonel Williamson, at Cambridge, forbearance ceased to be a pacific measure. Colonel Thomson marched with his command, under General Richard Richardson, captured all their officers, except Colonel Cunningham,* and crushed their hostile proceedings. This was in the winter of 1775, and such was the severity of the weather that the expedition was designated 'the snow camp.'

"Scarcely had Thomson's regiment returned from this campaign, when news arrived that the British had assembled, in New-York, a fleet and army, under General Clinton, to attack Charleston and overrun the Southern States. After this British armament had appeared off Charleston bar, but had not yet either landed their army or entered the harbor, Colonel Thomson asked for leave of absence, that he might make some arrangements on his plantation, called Belleville, about one hundred miles from the city. A furlough was granted him for only two days. He immediately mounted his horse, rode home, effected his business, and returned to the city within forty-eight hours. This is a family tradition.

"The united attack of this British army and navy on Sullivan's Island, and their total defeat, on the 28th of

---

*Patrick, captain.

June, 1776, are as well known as any part of the American history. But it is not generally known what an important part, in this defence, was performed by Colonel Thomson's command. They were posted at the eastern extremity of Sullivan's Island, in a redoubt, called 'the advanced guard,' constructed of palmetto logs, with merlins, on a brick foundation. At this point, the army under General Clinton, numbering two thousand regulars, was to make the general attack, as soon as the fleet should become engaged with Fort Sullivan. They accordingly marched from their encampment on Long Island, down to the edge of the inlet, where it was fordable, except at high water. They were flanked by an armed schooner and sloop, and by a flotilla of armed boats from the fleet, with orders to reach the landing on Sullivan's Island, and rake the platform of the redoubt, while the army crossed over the inlet and stormed the little fort, which was entirely open on the west. Colonel Thomson had but two cannon, and they were manned only by his rangers, who had never fired a great gun before this occasion. But, with small arms, they were the best marksmen in the State, and their commander, Colonel Thomson himself, was decidedly the best shot of the whole regiment.

"The flotilla advanced bravely to the concerted attack, cheered on by the army, paraded on the shore, within speaking distance of the boats. When within reach of his guns, Col. Thomson opened on them so well directed a fire that the men could not be kept at their posts; every ball raked the decks. The flotilla made repeated attempts to reach their destined point, and did come so near to it as to be within the range of grape shot. This being equally well directed, soon cleared the decks, and dispersed the flotilla.

"This attack by Clinton's regulars, on land, was well

concerted, but not well executed. They intended that it should be made at the same time with that of Sir Peter Parker's fleet on Fort Sullivan. Clinton had two thousand British infantry, exclusive of the marines and boatmen supplied from the fleet, which probably amounted to six or seven hundred more. He had, therefore, about two thousand regulars more than the whole command of Colonel Thomson, of which the Raccoon and other militia companies constituted a considerable portion. The force was sufficient to defeat Colonel Thomson, and then storm Fort Sullivan, as was intended. If Wellington had commanded instead of Clinton, he would probably have passed with more facility than he did over the river Douro, near Oporto. Clinton had the command of boats for transportation, of which Wellington had very few.

"Mr. Alexander Forrester, a near relation of the late Robert Elliott Rowand, left Charleston at the commencement of the revolution, and joined the British troops in this expedition. He said, in my presence, that he was in the schooner, and that it was impossible for any set of men to sustain so destructive a fire as the Americans poured in upon them on this occasion; that it was the destructive fire from Colonel Thomson's fort which prevented the flotilla from advancing, and not the shoals and sand bars, as was alleged; that it was the repulse of the flotilla which prevented General Clinton from fording the inlet, and not the depth of water.

"One of the opposition papers in England, the St. James' Chronicle, announces, in an epigram, a miracle on Sullivan's Island:

"'By the Red sea, the Hebrew host detained,
Through aid divine, the distant shore soon gained;
The waters fled, the deep a passage gave,
But this God wrought, a chosen race to save.

"'Though Clinton's troops have shared a different fate,
'Gainst them, poor men! not chosen sure of heaven,
The miracle reversed, is still as great—
From two feet deep, the water rose to seven.'

"Two other stations are represented on this plan*— the rear guard, of which the foundation may still be seen, as the foundation of the Episcopal Church, and the quarter guard, on or about the site of the new Moultrie House. These were spoken of by British writers, as efficient means of resisting their combined attack, but they had no opportunity of showing what they might have done; they never fired a gun. They also say, that the inlet which ran across the low land, called curlew ground, was covered by heavy cannon, mounted and pointed in the fort; but this, also, is an excuse. The annexed plan of the fort, copied from Drayton's Memoirs, will prove that not a single gun, of any description, was mounted on the eastern part of the fort. A great part of the eastern portion of the fort was unfinished, and exposed to the intended attack of Clinton's bayonets.

"The riflemen, under Colonel Thomson, were much amused with the grape shot, and the effects of shooting a pocket full of bullets into a crowd of their enemies, at every discharge; for they could not suppose that any one of their balls could ever miss its object.

"For his good conduct on this occasion, Colonel Thomson received the thanks of Governor Rutledge† and of Congress.—See vol. i., of Moultrie's Memoirs, page 183.

"Moultrie takes but little notice of Colonel Thomson's agency on this memorable occasion. The effects of his fire were not known until long after the revolu-

---

*Dr. Johnson's copy of a plan from Drayton's Memoirs.
†President Rutledge.

tion. The British officials and their ministry did not like to acknowledge it: the reputation of their navy was made to bear the disgrace of this defeat; the army was not suffered to come within gunshot of the Americans.

"American version of Sir Peter Parker's despatches to the Lords of Admiralty.

>"My lords, with your leave,
>An account I will give,
>That deserves to be written in metre;
>For the rebels and I
>Have been pretty nigh
>Faith, rather too nigh for Sir Peter.
>
>"With much labor and toil,
>Unto Sullivan's Isle,
>I came fierce as Falstaff or Pistol,
>But the Yankees,* add rat them!
>I could not get at them,
>Most terribly mauled my poor Bristol!
>
>"Bold Clinton, by land,
>Did quietly stand,
>While I made a thundering clatter;
>But the channel was deep,
>So they only could peep,
>And not venture over the water.
>
>"Devil take them, their shot
>Came so swift and so hot,
>And the cowardly dogs stood so stiff sirs,
>That I put ship about,
>And was glad to get out,
>Or they would not have left me a skiff, sirs.
>
>"But, my lords, never fear,
>Before the next year,
>Although a small island could check us,
>The continent whole,
>We will take, by my soul,
>If these cowardly Yankees will let us.

It was a happy thing for America that this flotilla

---

*The British called all Americans "Yankees", but it was a sobriquet which Southerners were never proud to acknowledge.

was so soon repulsed; had they made another attack, they might have effected a landing. Colonel Thomson had, by this time, expended all the ammunition provided for his two cannon, and would have been compelled to spike them, and rely on his infantry and small arms, to oppose the enemy in their march to Fort Sullivan. For this purpose, he had about seven hundred and fifty excellent marksmen to oppose two thousand British infantry."

* * * * * * * * *

"From this time, Colonel Thomson continued actively engaged, wherever duty or danger required his services. Under General Howe, he lingered out* a summer campaign in one of the most sickly parts of Georgia, where inaction and disease, more wasteful than war, reduced the numbers and spirits of his brave companions in arms, until the British forces, under Colonel Campbell, defeated Howe,† and overran that State. Next he served under General Lincoln, in his various endeavors to protect the Carolinas, by confining the enemy within the limits of Georgia, and, finally, to expel them, by the attack on their entrenchments at Stono. In these harrassing duties, his exposures brought on a fever, when in the neighborhood of Purisburg, and he retired for a while under furlough.

"Colonel Thomson also served under Count D'Estaing, in his well known disastrous siege of Savannah, in which it became evident, as previously demonstrated in the siege of Newport, Rhode Island, that a man high in rank at the Court of France, and high in the favor of his king, was not, intuitively, a skillful admiral or able general. It was probably lucky for the Count that he was wounded at Savannah. He had

---

*He was not with Howe in the summer of 1778.
†December 29, 1778.

something to show for his defeat—a set-off. In this unfortunate expedition, Colonel Thomson had embarked with all his family influence, with the highest hopes of success. His son, William, his three sons-in-law, and two nephews, accompanied him to Savannah, under D'Estaing; their mortification at the result was sore, indeed.

"In these battles, in the previous severe duties of the campaign, and in the subsequent exposure and sufferings of his regiment, little or no mention is made in history of the services rendered by Colonel Thomson. Justice has not been done him; probably, because he was always attached, with his light troops, to the command of some officer of high rank, to whom his services were inestimable, in scouting and skirmishing, but not reported in the line of battle. By his own men, he was designated by the sobriquet, 'Old Danger'. Even General Moultrie, when speaking of the battle of Sullivan's Island, uses the expression, 'I had seven hundred and fifty men under Colonel Thomson,' although in a detached command, about three miles off from him. Drayton, in his account of it, does not even give, on his map of Sullivan's Island, the position defended by Colonel Thomson.

"When Charleston was beleaguered by General Clinton,* Governor Rutledge was advised to withdraw from the city, that he might be better able to annoy the enemy, and cut off the aid and supplies that they might otherwise obtain from the country. For this purpose, the rangers were withdrawn from the defence of Charleston, and kept in active service in Orangeburg District. The governor's family had been previously withdrawn, like most of those who could effect it, and were residing near where Stateburg now

---

*In 1780.

stands, at the house, I believe, of Colonel William Richardson, owned and occupied by his son, the late lamented Judge J. S. Richardson. Such was the confidence of Governor Rutledge in Colonel Thomson's character, that when informed of the surrender of Charleston, he committed the care of his family to Colonel T., requesting that he would escort them with his own family to some place of safety. The governor remained in the State, with the hope of keeping up a resistance to the victorious British army. The indisposition of Mrs. Rutledge prevented their prompt removal, and thwarted this arrangement. In two or three days after the appointed time, Colonel Thomson's house was surrounded by a body of tories and British troops, and he was made a prisoner, with his son, William Russell Thomson, then about seventeen years of age.

"The father was sent down to Charleston, and confined many months in the 'Provost,' in the same damp vaults that are under the present Custom House.* He was there confined at the time of Gates' defeat. But his son was left at home, with the family, on parole. This elegant establishment was called Belleville. The British made it one of their garrisons, and stockaded it for defence. Various officers were in command of it, at different times, and of very different dispositions: some behaving with great rudeness and brutality, while others were polite, and even kind. It was the misfortune of young Thomson to displease one of the former description, who did not appear to resent it, until removed to the command of Fort Granby, opposite to Columbia. He then wrote to his successor, at Belleville, to hang young Thomson for a breach of parole, without trial or evidence. Fortunately, this offi-

---

*The old post-office.

cer was a just and humane man; his name was Stewart. He did not like the duty imposed on him, and contrived to drop the letter where it would fall into the hands of the family. Young Thomson saw that it was neck or nothing with him, and watched for an opportunity of making his escape. While standing near one of the sentinels, for this purpose, a poor, half-starved pig, belonging to the garrison, had escaped from his pen and passed close to them. Thomson had a fellow feeling for the pig, and thought that both of them might escape by the same means. He, therefore, persuaded the sentinel to catch it, and started with him in the pursuit. The pig, not being overloaded with fat or food, ran out at the sally-port, and they, whooping and holloing after him, continued the chase, until they had driven the animal out of gunshot. In the pig chase Thomson lost his hat, but he saved his neck. He soon joined Sumter's division,* where a horseman's cap was obtained, much more becoming than his old slouch. His excellent mother soon devised means for sending him a change or two of clothes, and he was free.

"Colonel Thomson was kept in close confinement until his health was much impaired. He was then permitted to return on parole to Belleville. It so happened that the officer in command was relieved in a day or two after Colonel Thomson's return. Whether from private instructions, caprice, or other motives unknown, this officer marched Colonel Thomson back with him to Charleston. He was, however, soon permitted to return to Belleville, which continued to be occupied as a British station. About this time it was attacked by the Americans, and to this day some of the bullet marks may be seen in the house. While he

---

*Brigade.

was exulting with hopes that it might be taken, and he released, he was obliged to provide for the safety of his family, by making them lie down on the floor. This attack was simultaneous with that on Fort Motte, and was only intended as a feint to prevent a junction of the two British forces, the stations being within sight of each other. The double purpose was answered; when Fort Motte was taken, Belleville was evacuated.

"On the surrender of Fort Motte, a number of tories were found among the British regulars. Most of these were of German families, who originally settled Amelia township, and built Orangeburg. The Americans were about to retaliate on them as tories, the severities inflicted on themselves as whigs. At that critical moment Col. Thomson rode over to the American camp, and knew most of these, his Dutch neighbors. He represented to Colonels Lee and Marion,* that these people had been compelled to enter the British fort, and made to labor as artificers; that they had always been harmless, and tried to keep aloof from both parties. Their release was secured. The Dutchmen, who had given themselves up for lost, now hurried off without thanking Colonel Thomson, or pausing to say 'Good by to you.' They scrambled over the breastwork instead of going through the gate, and some rolled over into the ditch, in trying to be the first out.

"In the general exchange of prisoners, effected by the address of Major Hyrne, Colonel Thomson was set at liberty, and immediately repaired to General Greene for service. From his knowledge of the country, he was particularly useful in scouting and cutting off the couriers and supplies of the enemy. In one of these

---

*General Marion.

expeditions, a very young and inexperienced recruit was sent out with a detachment, on patrol. They fell in with a superior force of the enemy, and were hotly pursued. The young man was well mounted, and a good rider, but it was the first time that ever he had faced an enemy, and when the retreat commenced at full speed, he concluded that all the detachment would be cut off. His own comrades galloping close behind him, were mistaken for the enemy, and he called out for 'quarters!' He spurred on, still crying out 'quarter! quarter! quarter!' until he was actually within his own camp. Being then stopped, and asked why he continued to cry out 'quarter! quarter!' when there was no enemy within half a mile of him, he declared that he had believed the enemy to be close upon him, and expected to be cut down at every leap of his horse.

"The whig ladies were sometimes permitted to enter Charleston, and Mrs. Thomson obtained from one of the British officers a passport for herself and little daughter, Charlotte. On her way down, she had an interview with her husband, and passed on. She made the intended purchases, and while so engaged, left her child in a room, only saying that a gentleman or two might step into the room, and she must not be frightened, he would not hurt her, but that she must keep in her bosom anything that he might place there. Accordingly while alone in the room, a gentleman entered, and looked anxiously around, then bowed to her, put a folded paper into her bosom, and went hastily out, without saying a word. The mother returned, and they left the city immediately; the father again met them, conducted them into General Greene's camp, and introduced them to the general. The little girl was asked by the general, if she had not something for him, but she, having been much amused with the novelty of every thing that she saw, had forgotten all that had passed in the room, and told him 'no.' He then asked more particularly for a paper, that had been put into her bosom, and she gave it to him. It has since transpired that General Greene had agreed with General Andrew Williamson for a particular description of the British forces in Charleston, on condition that he should be screened from confiscation and other injury. General Greene did obtain the information from Williamson, and it was probably in this way, through Colonel Thomson. The little daughter of that day, is now the venerably Mrs. Charlotte Haskill, the only survivor of Colonel Thomson's large family. He had four sons and eight daughters. Of these sons, William and Paul lived to be married; Paul had no children; William left a fine family, among whose descendants the name is preserved and cherished. The daughters, we believe, were all married, and left families.

"At the commencement of the revolution Colonel Thomson was an indigo planter, living in the enjoyment of affluence and domestic happiness. His only motive for resistance, was a sense of duty to protect the chartered rights of his country, and the rights of British subjects in America. In the course of the revolution, he lost almost everything that was movable, from his plantation. His valuable stock of horses and cattle, with his negroes, were dispersed, and most of them lost. The camp fever and small pox had been introduced into his plantation, by the British troops, and about one hundred of his people died of these dreadful disorders. But none of his negroes ever left him to join the British, notwithstanding their promises of freedom, their temptations, and their threats. One negro, named 'Abram,' had been intrusted by his master with the care of a favorite blooded horse, and the enemy heard of it. All their endeavors to obtain the horse were of no avail with Abram, and at last, from threats they proceeded to execution. He was hung up, by the neck, three several times, until senseless, but still refused to reveal the place in which he had concealed the horse. The name of Abram is gratefully spoken of by Colonel Thomson's family to this day, and his other faithful services recounted.

"When Charleston was recovered from the British. Colonel Thomson returned to his plantation, and diligently endeavored to restore his shattered fortune. He continued the cultivation of indigo, very successfully, as long as he lived. His house was ever hospitably open to all travellers; his friends and neighbors were ever generously entertained at his plentiful board. To some he was too liberal and confiding; he involved his estate by securityship to a large amount.

"He continued subject to the calls of his country, whenever his services were needed for public purposes. and again became the sheriff of Orangeburg District. He was fond of the sports of the field and of the turf, and for his enjoyment in these he kept a choice collection of hounds and horses. He enjoyed these pleasures the more, in proportion to the number of his associates, and was as much amused with their errors and mishaps, as with their success in the hunt. To him they were very exciting scenes and incidents.

"Colonel Thomson's health having declined, he travelled to the Sweet Springs of Virginia, hoping for its restoration, but he died there on the 22d of November, 1796, aged sixty-nine years."

The late Mr. Simms, in his book, "South Carolina in the Revolution", has also paid a tribute to Colonel Thomson and the 3rd. regiment, as follows:

"The resistance to the efforts of Sir Henry Clinton,

with the land army, at the east end of the Island, conducted by native riflemen, under Colonel Thompson, was such as to paralyze the enemy. This portion of the affair has been but little commented upon by our historians; yet the fire of Thompson's marksmen, with rifles, and from two small field-pieces, was such—and the British flotilla, advancing from Long Island upon the eastern end of Sullivan's, were so raked by the fire—that the men could not be kept to their guns. The decks were cleared, the flotilla dispersed, the enterprise abandoned; yet the force of Clinton consisted of 2,000 British infantry, exclusive of some 600 or 700 marines and boatmen, supplied from the fleet; while Thompson's strength lay in his two cannon, a small redoubt of palmetto logs, and 700 rifles."*

Dr. Johnson also gives, in a letter to Col. Wade Hampton, dated June 27, 1842, another account of Col. Thomson's defeat of Clinton, which, while it does not differ materially from that given in his "Traditions", adds some interesting facts. The following extracts from Dr. Johnson's letter relate to Col. Thomson and his regiment:

"Col. William Thompson, of Orangeburg District, having been appointed to the command of the 3d regiment, had his complement of men soon made up by the enlistment of some of the most expert Riflemen in the State; he himself being one of the most practiced among them. He had the finest eye that I ever saw in the head of mortal man.

"With but little experience in war, and certainly without having ever heard a cannon fired at an enemy, the 2d and 3d regiments were ordered to oppose the best appointed armament that had then been equipped against any part of the United States, not

---
*See also *Southern Quarterly Review*, 1848.

merely sent for the capture of Charleston, but for the conquest of the three Southern States." [The force that] "Col. Thompson commanded, was stationed at the eastern extremity of Sullivan's Island, called the advance guard, and ordered to protect it and fort Sullivan from the bayonets of Sir Henry Clinton's infantry, then encamped on Long Island, within sight of the redoubt. He had but two pieces of cannon and it was then first proved that the riflemen make the best gunners for artillery. The plan of attack was this; while the fleet attacked the forts, the British army was to land and storm them, if not already abandoned. An armed schooner and a flotilla of armed boats were ordered to attack Col. Thompson's redoubt, in order to cover the landing of the infantry. They did, indeed, repeatedly make the attack, but were always received by the cool, well-directed fire of the Orangeburg sharp-shooters, then for the first time firing cannon, loaded with grape shot; the flotilla was always repulsed with great loss.

"Mr. Alexander Forester, a near relation of the Rowand family, was in South Carolina at the commencement of the revolution, and like many other consciencious but mistaken men, believed that his first duty was to his king. He returned after the revolution, and told my father in my presence, that he was one of the detachment ordered to land on the eastern end of the Island; that he was in the armed schooner, and that in every attempt made to reach the position assigned to them, the destruction from Col Thompson's two cannon was so great, and their decks so repeatedly swept by grape shot, that even the seamen could not be made to work the vessel, and the landing of the British troops was thus prevented. Col. Moultrie well merited the praises bestowed on him for so ably defending the fort, called fort Moultrie, in compliment to its gallant defender: but the no less successful and important duty performed by Col. Thompson, at his station, is not generally known. They who suffered by it were the least willing to acknowledge their defeat, and ascribed their failure to other causes. In their official despatches, they said that the flotilla became embarrassed among the shoals, and the channel proved too deep for the infantry to cross over."

* * * * * * * *

"In wishing you harmony and happiness, I beg leave to offer a toast, in which I believe all will cordially unite.

"Col. William Thompson and his gallant sharpshooters of Orangeburg. as true in a fort as in a bush fight."

The following is an incomplete list of the officers of Thomson's regiment, made up from various sources:

RANK.	NAME.	APPOINTED.	REMARKS.
Colonel	Wm. Thomson	Ab: Jan. 1, 1777	
Lieut. Col.	Wm. Thomson	June 18, 1775	Promoted.
"	James Mayson	Ab: Jan. 1, 1777	
"	William Henderson	Feb. 11, 1780	
Major.*	James Mayson	June 18, 1775	Promoted.
	Samuel Wise	Ab: Jan. 1, 1777	Killed at Savannah, Oct. 9th, 1778.
Adjutant	John Esom	Ab: July 20, 1775†	
"	Charles Heatly		
Paymaster	John Chesnut	June 21, 1775‡	

*On Dec. 2, 1775, a letter was addressed by Henry Laurens, President of the Council of Safety, to "Andrew Williamson, esq., Major in Col. Thomson's Regiment at Ninety-Six". This only meant that Major Williamson was, for the time being, serving under Col. Thomson—not that he belonged to the 3rd regiment.

From the Journal of Council of Safety for Jan. 11, 1776, we extract: "Col. Thomson and Major Ferguson of the rangers attended", &c. Maj. Ferguson probably bore the same relation to Col. Thomson that Maj. Williamson did, as recited above. He was not a Major in the 3rd regiment.

†"Col. Thomson attended the Council, and represented the necessity of having an Adjutant to the Regiment under his command.

"The Council taking the said representation into consideration,

"*Resolved*, That as the Congress had not appointed an Adjutant for the Regiment of Rangers, they can only approve of Col. Thomson's choice, and agree to recommend to the next Provincial Congress to provide the pay."—Journal of Council of Safety, July 10th, 1775.

"To Col. Thomson, for pay due to John Esom, Adjutant to his regiment of rangers, ...£118 00 0".—Journal of Council of Safety, Jan. 23rd, 1776.

‡He was appointed on June 21st, but his commission was dated June 18th. See page 280.

THE HISTORY OF

RANK.	NAME.	APPOINTED.	REMARKS.
Paymaster	John James Haig*	Ab: Sept. 10, 1777	
Surgeon	Alexander Rogers	July 14, 1775	
Captain	Samuel Wise	June 18, 1775	Promoted major.
"	Ezekiel Polk	" " "	His company classed as volunteers.
"	John Caldwell†	" " "	Killed by "Bloody Bill" Cun[ingham's tories, Nov. 1781.‡
"	Ely Kershaw	" " "	
"	Robert Goodwyn§	" " "	
"	Moses Kirkland	" " "	Deserted to the enemy, 1775.
"	Edw'd Richardson	" " "	Resigned Jan. 30, 1776.¶
"	Thos. Woodward	" " "	Resigned Jan. 30, 1776.¶
"	John Purvis	" " "	
"	John Lewis Peyer Imhoff	August, 1775	
"	Charles Heatly	" "	
"	Richard Winn	Mentioned 1876	
"	John Donaldson	" "	
"	Felix Warley	" "	
"	James Warley	" "	
"	Richard Brown	October, 1776	
"	David Hopkins	"	
"	Robert Lyles	Mentioned 1777	
"	Thomas Taylor	" 1777	Resigned Oct. 1777‖
"	J. Caraway Smith	" 1778	
"	—— Maskall	" 1778	
"	William Heatly, Jr.		
"	Jesse Baker°		
"	John Buchanan°		
"	William Caldwell°		
"	Field Farrar°		
"	Alexander Keith°		Wounded at Savannah, 1779.
"	—— Keith°		
"	Thomas Marshall°		
"	Richard Pollard°		
"	Oliver Towles°		Killed by "Bloody Bill" Cuningham's tories, Nov. 1781**
Lieutenant	John Lewis Peyer Imhoff	June 18, 1775	Promoted Captain.
"	Charles Heatly	" " "	
"	Richard Winn	" " "	

"Sir—Complaints have been frequently made to us, of great inconveniences arising to the regiment and detachments of rangers, from your non-attendance in person or by a sufficient deputy. It has been alleged, that long continued sickness has rendered you incapable of performing your duty; if this be true, you ought to have appointed proper clerks, and to have acquainted us with the cause of your absence. We desire you will immediately take such measures as will tend to the public service, and prevent further complaints in your department.

"By order of the Council of Safety.

"Mr. Chesnut. Henry Laurens, President."—Journal of Council of Safety. Jan. 18th, 1776.

Journal of Council of Safety, Jan. 29, 1776: "To John Chesnut, esq., Paymaster to the rangers, for pay of the officers, and 6 companies of that regiment, up to the 20th instant,.........£11,571 12 11."

*"John James Haig is appointed Our Pay Master."—Col. Thomson to Lieut. Col. Mayson, Sept. 15th, 1777.

†He was maternal uncle of John Caldwell Calhoun.

‡O'Neall's Annals of Newberry District.

§Gen. DeSaussure says, pamphlet, page 7, that Capt. Goodwyn resigned May 30, 1778, but Gen. Lachlan McIntosh, in his journal for April 26, 1780, states that "Captain Goodwin, of 3d South-Carolina", was on that day killed in the siege of Charlestown.

¶Journal of Council of Safety, Jan. 30, 1776.

‖DeSaussure, page 10. °DeSaussure.

**O'Neall's Annals of Newberry District, page 243.

ORANGEBURG COUNTY.

RANK.	NAME.	APPOINTED.	REMARKS.
Lieutenant	John Donaldson	June 18, 1775	Promoted Captain.
"	Hugh Middleton	" " "	
"	Louis Dutarque	" " "	Resigned Jan. 30, 1776.§
"	Francis Boykin	" " "	
"	Samuel Watson	" " "	
"	Wm. Heatly, Jr.†	" 17. "	
"	David Hopkins	June, 1775	Promoted Captain.
"	Thomas Charlton	" "	
"	—— Cantey	" "	
"	David Monoghan	" "	Resigned Dec. 15, 1775.‡
"	Moses Vance	July 1, 1775	
"	—— Mitchell	1775	
"	Joseph Pledger	"	Resigned Jan. 30, 1776.§
"	—— Beames	1775 or 1776	
"	—— Crowthers	" " "	Resigned Oct. 1778.
"	—— Maskall	" " "	Promoted Captain.
"	Willam Caldwell	" " "	Promoted Captain.*
"	Charles M. Genney	Mentioned 1778	
"	—— McGinis	" "	
"	William Taggert	" "	
"	—— Hart‖	" "	Resigned Oct. 1778.
"	Wm. R. Thomson	" "	
"	—— Bailey	" 1779	Killed at Savannah, Oct. 9, 1779.
"	Louis DeSaussure	" "	Killed at Savannah, Oct. 9, 1779.
"	Robert Gaston	" "	Killed at Savannah, Oct. 8, 1779.
"	William Goodwyn*		Resigned May 30, 1778.*
"	John Lisle*		" Aug. 1779.*
"	Cato West*		" Sept. 14, 1778.*
"	Isaac Cowther*		
"	John Davis*		
"	Wm. Fitzpatrick*		
"	Benjamin Hodges*		
"	John Jones*		
"	Richard Jones*		
"	Edward Lloyd*		
"	George Liddell*		
"	William Love*		
"	Luke Mason*		
"	James Roberson*		
Ensign	Wm. R. Withers*		
Corporal	Daniel Shannon		Thomson's order book.

Section 3. *Colonel Thomson's Order Book—June 24th, 1775, to November 3rd, 1778.*

Dr. Joseph Johnson, in his "Traditions of the Revolution", page 99, states that the order books of Col. William Thomson "have been preserved by his family, and are very creditable to his officer-like conduct and

---

§Journal of Council of Safety, Jan. 30, 1776.
†Heitman's Continental Officers.
‡Journal of Council of Safety, Dec. 15, 1775.
*DeSaussure.
‖Derrill Hart, no doubt.

388   THE HISTORY OF

discretion." One of these books is now in possession of Judge A. C. Haskell, of Columbia, who has very kindly allowed it to be copied for use in this work. The book is bound in soft brown leather, is about eight by ten inches in size, contains about ninety unruled pages, very closely written in the style of script that generally prevailed at the time of the American Revolution. The following is a carefully made copy of the original:

[1]st Regiment	2nd: Regiment	Rangers:
1st: Colonel £ Mr: Gadsden : 6 per Day	Colonel 2nd: Regt: Wm: Moultrie	Lt: Colonel of Rangers Colonel Thomson
Lt: Col: Isaac Huger	Lt: Col: Isaac Motte	James Mayson Ma-
Owen Roberts, Major	Alexr: McIntosh Major	
Captains Chs: Chwt: Pinckney.... Barnard Elliott........... Francis Marion........... Wm: Cattel.............. Peter Horry............. Daniel Horry............ Adm: McDonald......... Thomas Lynch.......... Wm: Scott.............. John Barnwell.........	**Captains** Nichs: Eveleigh........... Jas: McDonald........... Isaac Harleston......... Thos: Pinckney......... Francis Huger........... Wm: Mason............. Edmd: Hyrne........... Roger Saunders......... Benj: Cattel............ Chas: Motte............	**Captains** Samuel Wise............ Ezek: Polk............. John Caldwell.......... Eli Kirshaw............ Robert Goodwyn....... Moses Kirkland........ Edwd: Richardson..... Thos: Woodward...... John Purvis...........
Lieutenants Anthony Ashby.......... James Ladsden........... John Vanderhost......... John Mouatt .... Thomas Elliott........... Wm: Oliphant............ Glyn Drayton........... Joseph Ioor.............. Robert Armstrong...... John Blake..............	**Lieutenants** Alexr: McQueen......... Jas: Perrineau........... Richard Shubrick........ Richard Fuller.......... Richd: Shingleton....... Jno: Allen Walter....... Ben: Dickenson......... Wm: Charnock.......... Thos: Lesesne.......... Thos: Moultrie..........	**Lieutenants** Jno: Lewis Pyre Inhoff Chas: Heatley.......... Allen Cameron......... Richd: Wyron Winn... John Donaldson........ Hugh Middleton....... Lewis Dutarque....... Francis Boyakin....... Samuel Watson........
Pay Master: Thos: Evance	Pay Master: Jno: Sandft: Dart	pay Master: Jno: Chesnut

Council of Safety.

Col: Pinckney } Mr: Lowndes } (Wm: Hen: Drayton) Wm: Williamson
Col: Laurens } Mr: Brewton } { Thos: Heywood   } Thos Bee
Col: Parsons } Ben: Elliott } (John Huger   ) Thos: Ferguson
                                                     Andw: Middleton

On the 24th June, I received my Commission from the above named Council of Safety with the following orders.

ORANGEBURG COUNTY.

In the Council of Safety.
21st June 1775./

To William Thomson Esq$^{r.}$
Lieut: Col: Commandant of the Regimt of Rangers or to the commanding officers for the time being.

Sir,
You are hereby directed forthwith to Issue Orders for levying in this and the adjacent Colonies proper men not exceeding thirty in each Company to serve for six months certain and not longer than three Years in the Regiment of Rangers under your command observing the Articles agreed upon in Provincial Congress, for Ordering and governing the Forces in this Colony. And it is recommended to all the good People of this and the neighboring Colonies to give you and the officers under your command all necessary aid and assistance therein.

Signed by the above Council.
True Copy.

Amelia 24th June 1775./

Sir,
Inclos'd is a Copy of orders I rec^{d} from the Council of Safty. You will observe the contents and give orders accordingly to the four upper Companies Viz: Capt^{s} Perwis, Kirkland, Caldwell, and Polk, you will also order an Encampment in the most convenient place near Reedy River and that each Captn as soon as he has enlisted Ten men to send them to the Camp in order to learn their Exercise and be in readiness with a good Horse, and Rifle, and other necessaries.

directed
To Major James Mason.

sign'd
W m Thomson
True Copy

same day gave orders to the remaining five Capts. Wise, Woodward, Kirshaw, Richardson, and Goodwyn, for their levying thirty men with speed, with orders for each Captain immediately upon raising Ten men to send the same to their Camp near Holmans.

Wm Thomson

In the Council of Safety.
Orders.
To Col: William Thomson

Charles Towne June 26th 1775

Sir,

You are hereby forthwith ordered to station at Fort Charlotte a Company of Rangers to Garrison that Post, and to take care of the Military Stores which are there deposited.

You will direct the commanding Officer of this Detachment to take an Inventory of the Military Stores he shall find in the Fort and to send to the Council of Safety an Exact Copy of it, and also an Account of the state of the works.

Order the Commanding officer, whom you send on this Service to inlist the Men at Present in Garrison to serve as Rangers if they are willing, and give Mr. Whitfield* all proper Encouragement to remain in the Fort, provided he will be subject to your order, we are very desirous of retaining him in the Service of the Colony, and therefore you might propose to him pay equal to his present allowance, which we will confirm if he accepts it, and will upon Your Recommendation of him as a proper Person appoint him to the first Vacancy in your Regiment.

You will also cause the two Brass Field Pieces, and

---

*George Whitfield, a nephew of the celebrated Rev. George Whitfield.

all the Spare Bayonets in the Fort, to be sent in a covered Waggon and by a careful Waggoner to the Council of Safety in Charles Town.

You will immediately send a copy of these Instructions to Major Mason, in order that he may not execute any thing relative to the Directions he had concerning Fort Charlotte.

We are Sir.
Your most humble serv^t

Col. Wm Thomson   By order of the Council
Henry Lawrens. President.

Colonel Wm Thomson

Amelia July 1st 1775. /
Orders:
To Major Ja^s Mason.

Sir.   Inclos'd you will find orders, I rec^d from the Council of Safety You are hereby ordered forthwith carefully to put them into Execution, direct Captⁿ Perwis to take the Command, desire You will see that he has good likely Men and good Rifles &c.

Desire You may give Captⁿ Purvis orders to see that Mr Whitfield and his Possession is not molested if he will accept the offers made him, and if it is convenient for him I would be glad to see him at my House.

I hope you will see that the four Capt^s of Rangers in your neighborhood does list good likely Rifled Men. I expect to hear from you as soon as you have executed these orders, which I make no doubt will be on sight. I intend for Town this Day week, but will be home in few Days.

Wm Thomson.

True Copy

Amelia 1st July 1775.

Sir

Yours of the 29th by Mr Swanston I received, I desire You will send some of Your Men, not less than Twelve, with one Officer, as soon as You can, I inclose You the Articles against Meeting, and the Oath to be taken by the Men when listed. Have the Meeting Act Read to Your Men, and them properly enlisted, good likely Rifles, I hope to see You have, as I know You can have choice. tell my Friend your Brother, I am oblig'd to go to Town this Day Week. as soon as I return hope to see him, in mean while hope he will endeavor to settle the Minds of the Catawbas as I am almost sure some one has been tampering with them.

True Copy.   Wm Thomson

To
Captn Eli Kirshaw.

Sir,   3rd July 1775.

Some time past I wrote to you to come down or send Your Lieutenant to receive Your commission and orders, but has not heard from You, makes me think the Letter miscarried I expect you have listed Your number of thirty before this time our Camp is near Holman's on the old Road, I shall go to Town Saturday, in the mean time beg to see you or Your Lieutenant

I remain. Sir

Your humble Servt
True Copy   W Thomson
To Captn Woodward.

In the Council of Safety, 13th July. 1775.
ordered,

That Col: William Thomson do immediately make a return to the Council of the several Companies in the Regiment of Rangers specifying the names of the officers non=commissioned officers, and Privates, the station of each Company together with a state of their Cloathing, Horses, and Ammunition.

That if the Companies are not full, he use his utmost Diligence in order to complete them- and that each Man be well mounted, armed and accoutred. On the Tenth Day of August next, Eight companies shall rendezvous at some proper Place to be appointed by the Colonel, and march by the following Routes, to wit:

Three Companies to the Southward by Orangeburgh, to the three Runs, thence down Savannah River to Purrysburg, thence to Ponpon, and downward by the High Road.

Three Companies to the Northward, by the Kings Tree, and the most Populous Parts of Waccamaw and Pedee to George Town, thence by Wambaw to Hugers Bridge, and by the Strawberry Road going up to Childsburry=Town to Biggin Bridge, Monck's Corner, and thence downward by the High Road.

Two Companies through St Stephen's Parish down to Monck's Corner thence to Edistow saw Mills, and from thence thro' the Horshoe, and Round O to Parkers Ferry, Dorchester, and thence down the High Road.

That Col: Thomson do march with the First Detachment to the Southward. That Major Mason do march with the second Detachment to the Northward.

That the senior Captⁿ on Duty march with the third Detachment of two Companies.

That the whole meet and rendezvous at some convenient Place within Ten Miles of Charles Town on the First Day of September, and that notice of the

Junction and Encampment be immediately given to the President of the Council.

That the utmost Diligence be constantly used, to train and Exercise the Regiment by Companies and otherwise as Opportunities may permit, in the use of Arms agreeable to the Manual Exercise approved of by the Council.

That strict discipline be at all times kept up in the Regiment, Companies, and Detachments... That Marauding and every degree of Injury to the Inhabitants or their property be strictly forbidden; and that exemplary Punishment be duely inflicted upon offenders against the orders of the Council and the Articles of War.

That all needful and proper Assistance be given, when required by the Parochial Committees, officers of the Colony Regiments of Foot, Magistrates and officers of the Militia who have signed the general Association; and immediate Notice transferred to the Council of such Requisitions, and services intended or performed.

That orderly Books be kept by the commanding officer of each Detachment and the whole returned, together with a State of the Regiments, at the time of their Rendezvous on the first of September to the Council.

As there are persons suspected of attempts to alienate the affections of the Inhabitants of this Colony from the Interests of America, Col: Thomson and all the officers of the Regiment of Rangers, are ordered to take proper Notice of such suspected Persons. And if it shall appear to the Colonel, or the Commanding officer of any Detachment, that the conduct or behavior of such Person or Persons are dangerous to the safety of the Colony the Colonel or such Commanding Officer of any Detachment is required to confine such Person or Persons in the District Gaol or otherwise, and report immediately to the Council of Safety.

Col: Thomson is to procure from Fort Charlotte, half a Pound of Gun=Powder per Man, and Lead in proportion, for the Eight Companies which are to march and to the Commanding Officer of Fort Charlotte, a receipt for such Powder and Lead. Strict orders to be given for the Preservation of such Powder and Lead, against all kind of Damage; and that no part be used but as occasions may require solely for the service of the Colony.

Owners and Keepers of Ferries are to charge Ferriage of the Rangers and their Horses, to the Public: Accounts thereof to be certified by the Commanding officers of Detachments, and transmitted to the Council of Safety.*

The Council of safety recommend to the Inhabitants—throughout this Colony, to treat the Regiment and Detachments of Rangers with Hospitality, and to supply them with Provision and necessaries, for their Money, at Reasonable Rates. By order of the Council of Safety.

                                          Henry Laurens
       True Copy.   President.

                Amelia 17th July 1775./

Sir,

      I herein inclose you copy of the orders received from the Council of Safety. You will please to give the three Companies in Your District orders accordingly I should be glad if you would have them all in Amelia by the sixth Day of August as I could wish to have them together four Days before they March.

---

* "To Jonas Beard, for ferriage of rangers, £34 17s 6d."—Journal of Council of Safety, Nov. 30, 1775.

You'll observe the Instructions about the Powder and Lead in Proportion and order down sufficient Quantity for the five Company's in this Neighbourhood, as perscribed in the General orders, that I may be able to make a return of the whole You may supply those three Company's with their Dividend of Powder and Lead before they come down in order to save Carriage. I make no doubt but you have comply'd with the orders concerning Fort Charlotte before this time. I should be glad to hear from You immediately.
To Wm Thomson
Major Ja^s Mason. True Copy.

Amelia 17th July 1775. /
Sir,
You are hereby required to rendezvous your Company in Amelia by the sixth of August next, in the meantime you are to be very diligent to learn them their Exercise. I hereby send you the Manual Exercise that is ordered to be learned by the Council of Safety, which You'll please to teach them except the Bayonet Exercise, and in loading, the Breech of Rifles must go to the Ground, and that You immediately make a return to me of your Company, specifying the names of the Officers, non commissioned officers, and Privates, the Station of Your Company with the State of their Cloathing, Horses, & Ammunition, if your Company is not full, use your utmost diligence to compleat it
I remain
Sir Your humble Servt
Wm Thomson

The underwritten is a Copy of Orders from the Council of Safety, which please strictly to observe.
"As there are Persons suspected of attempts to

"alienate the affections of the Inhabitants of this Col-
"ony from the Interest of America, Col: Thomson and
"all the Officers of the Regiment of Rangers are order-
"ed to take proper Notice of such suspected Persons.
"And if it shall appear to the Colonel or the Com-
"manding Officer of any Detachment that the Conduct
"and Behaviour, of any Person or Persons are danger-
"ous to the Safety of the Colony, the Colonel, or such
"commanding officer of any Detachment, is required
"to confine such Person or Persons in the District
"Gaol, or otherwise and report to the Council of safe-
"ty immediately.

The above is a copy of Letters to Capt^{us} Wise, Woodward, Goodwyn, Kirshaw and Richardson.

True Copy.

In the Council of Safety.
Charles Town, 15th July, 1775.

Ordered.

That Col: Thomson do immediately march with his whole Regiment, or such Part as may be necessary for his Service, and take possession of Fort Charlotte, if the same is not already secured agreeable to the order of the 26th of June last, after which he is to leave one Company in Garrison and follow his late orders: And that the President do forthwith transmit a Copy of this Order and write Col: Thomson on the Subject.

Sign'd

True Copy.   Pet^r. Timothy, Secretary.

10th July 1775

Sir

Please to order your Men to be in readiness to March at half a Days Warnings for perhaps I may call

upon them about Monday next to take a Tour of about Ten Days, owing to some Intelligence I just now received let Lieutenant Hopkins proceed on his Journey. forward the Express to Major Mason with all possible speed I am.
To Your hum'ble Servt
Captn Robert Goodwyn. W T.

Amelia, 10th July 1775.
Sir
I just now rec^d your friendly Letter with the orders from the Council of Safety which shall be put in execution immediately. I expected that Major Mason had executed the orders of the 26th June long before this time, as I trusted that part of the service to him with particular orders to execute it, being in his neighborhood I am very sorry the Council of Safety has to repeat their orders to me.
To W T:
Col: Hen: Lawrens.
True Copy.

19th July 1775.
Sir.
Since the Express sent You, Yesterday, I have rec^d Orders from the Council which makes it necessary to March to Fort Charlotte on Savannah River. It is hereby ordered that You, with your Company meet me on Sunday next at the Congarees in readiness for that Service.
W Th. .
Copy's of the above was sent to Capt^s Woodward, Richardson, and Kirshaw.
True Copy.

ORANGEBURG COUNTY. 399

Amelia. 19th July 1775.

Sir,
Since the Express sent you Yesterday, I have rec'd a Letter and orders of which I have sent you a Copy, I desire you will immediately transmit to me a state of the whole affair as it now stands. I shall collect four of the Lower Company's Immediately and be at the Congrees in five Days in order to March up if the needful is not done already of which I hope to be acquainted from you before that Day. I desire you will collect the four upper Company's to have them in readiness to join me when I come to Ninety six, that is if Capt. Purvis is not in the Fort already according to the first Orders, If so the express of Yesterday will acquaint You what to do with the other three Company's. I shall be extreamly sorry & surprized to find the orders of the 26th has not been put into execution by You, as I depended entirely on You, expecting to have them as absolutely executed as If I had been present. I shall add no more at present but that I expect to hear from You as above. I am
Your humble Servt
W T.
True Copy

To
Major James Mason.

For Copy of Letter and & order sent inclosed see. orders sign'd Petr Timothy & Letter. Henry Lawrens.

Granby near Fridays Ferry, the 22d July 1775

The Honourable Council of Safety.
Gentlemen,
I this evening arrived at this Place with an Intention to have March'd in the morning

with Capt? Kirshaw, Richardson, Goodwyn's & Woodward's in order to carry into Execution your orders of the 15th Instant, it was not in my Power to collect the four Cympanys together sooner Captⁿ Wise being at the greatest distance and also near a Quarter where I was inform'd several disaffected Persons live say on Thomson's & Lynch's creek's, for which reasons I only sent him your orders of the 13th Instant, & intended leaving him there in order to watch the Intentententions of these Persons, But on my way up hither, I met an express from Major Mason, to the Council of Safety and also one for my self, a copy of which I herewith send you Inclosed. I shall now Camp a few miles above this Place, with the four Company's above mentioned & dispatch an Express to Capt: Wise in the morning with orders for him to repair immediately with his Company to this Camp. I shall also send orders to Major Mason to have Fort Charlotte well guarded, If he finds it necessary with the whole of the other three Company's, or whatever part of them may be rais'd. The paymaster who is now with me, has only yet received 1000£ which I brought up from Charles Town for him, there being no more ready £500 of which shall be sent Immediately to Fort Charlotte, with a Detachment that I purpose sending there in order to get a small supply of Gunpowder, and Lead agreeable to your order of the 13th Instant being entirely without, Excepting 15lbs borrowed of Mr Kirshaw, this will be handed you by Captⁿ Woodward* who being desirous of going to Town in order to fit out himself and his Men, & as he also comes from near that Quarter where most of the disaffected lives he

---

* "The President laid before, and read to the Council, sundry papers, contained in a dispatch from Col. William Thomson, received last night by Capt. Thomas Woodward, of the Rangers."—Journal of Council of Safety, July 26th, 1775.

may be able to give some farther particulars as with regard to them.

    I am Gentlemen
     Your most obt Servt
      Wm Thomson

Sir, Your favour dated, Amelia June 27th came safe to Hand, on Sunday last the 2nd Instant. I have the honour of acquinting You by the return of the Express that we left Charles Town not sooner than the 24th of last Month, the very Day after the conclusion of the Provincial Congress, having arrived at my Place I begun immediately to enlist Men, the number of which consisting this Day in 22 well chosen, young, and well mounted Men, I shall no doubt compleat my Company, this, or the beginning of next week. But permit me Sir, to observe that our people wants time to equippe, and prepare for a march as long as such we have to perform from this place to the Camp. I hope to set out at the Head of the whole Company about the 1st of August, and Join the Camp with all possible diligence. I have the honour to be Sir
    Your most obed^t humble Servt:
      Saml Wise
Pedee the 15th July 1775.

Sir,
 Just as I was about to dispatch Mr. Sallens yesterday with the four Blank Association Papers, which you will receive in a seperate packett, certain intelligence arrived from. Fort Charlotte which render'd it proper to detain him till this morning.
 The Council of Safety alarmed by an intimation of Mr St Pierres proceed—with one Cossel, in the Fort as given by Capt: Whitefield in a letter to Mr. Gervais

& not clearly informed of the part which the Capt himself means to take, are anxious that you should carry their Orders of the 26th June into execution & immediately take possession of the Fort & all the Military & other Stores contained in it, for this end the Council made another order last night for enforcing the former, a certified Copy of which you will find here inclosed.

The Gunpowder is most particularly recommended to your care, not only to get possession of the whole, but to prevent damage waste and misapplication of any part & not a moment to be delayed.

I flatter myself with hopes that you will have anticipated the wishes of the Council, that the Fort is now in the Hands of their Officers nevertheless I have it in charge to signify their commands that if it shall be necessary You immediately attempt to surmount every difficulty by the united efforts of your whole Regiment, You at their Heads together with such assistance as our Friends & associates in that neighborhood may think proper to lend upon this momentous affair. The Council entertain hopes that Capt: Whitefield will associate in the Interest of America, in such case he will correspond with the Council, by transmitting to them a return of all the Stores at the time of his surrending to their officer which must be countersigned by that officer or Yourself if you shall find it necessary to go there.

The earnestness of the Council upon this important service impels me in conclusion of the subject again to repeat, it is their order, you take possession of the Fort and Stores without delay & also without delay you transmit a return of your proceedings including a complete Inventory.

I must also this occasion particularly refer you to the Councils orders which I delivered you Yesterday for direction in case of opposition by any person either openly or otherwise were presumptive evidence is strong. And this moment when I cannot receive the Instruction of the Council & when I dare not delay the messenger, it occurs to me that Captn Whitfield however chearfully he may shew an inclination to serve the Colony by resignation, may not be content with a subcommand ╱ if he is a man of spirit he will not╱ in such case I recommend that you advise him to come to Charles Town & apply to the Council which I add from a Zeal for the Public service as well as from a feeling for a Gentleman, in the circumstances which he will be reduced to therefore if he follows my advice & does not succeed in This application to the Council, I shall hold myself answerable to reimburse if he desires it) the expence of his extra journey in consequence of my recommendation.

I have the Honour to be president
to the Council & Sir
Your most obedt Servt:
Henry Lawrens

P S: in Council, by order, the Letter which comes inclosed with this is to be delivered to Capt Whitefield after he has signed the association otherwise not for some Days after You have taken possession of the Fort.

Col William Thomson   H L*

Null. Granby near Friday's Ferry, 22d July 177
The Honourable the Council of Safety
Gentlemen.
I have†

---

* "The Council having approved the letter, agreed with Thomas Singelton to deliver it to Col. Thomson, for forty pounds currency."— Journal of Council of Safety, July 16, 1774.

†The rest of this letter was not copied into the order book.

P: S to the Letter dated 22ᵈ July 1775 }
   to the Council of Safety.

P. S: Mr: Chesnut informs me that King Prow, with about 50 of the Catawba's are now at Camden on a friendly visit. Mr: Kirshaw & I myself are both at a loss what to do with regard to taking some of them into pay for want of Your Instructions.*

W T.

Granby near Friday's Ferry 22ᵈ July 177
Colo. Henry Lawrens,

Dʳ Sir, I herewith send you Inclosed Copy of orders I sent to Major Mason with the order of the 26ᵗʰ ulto. from the Council of safety I am sorry Major Mason, has so unfortunately lost the Gunpowder, & cannot tell why he brought it out of the Fort, perhaps the Council of Safety order'd him to do so, as he told me when on his way up from Town, that he had orders relative to Fort Charlotte, but did not

---

* "The following letter was written by the President to Joseph Kershaw, esq., laid before the Council and approved of:

"Charles-Town, July 25th, 1775.

"Sir—The Council of Safety have ordered me to acknowledge the receipt of your fovour of the 8th instant, and to return their thanks for your assiduity in treating with the old men and head warriors of the Catawba Indians.

"Your assurances that those people are hearty in our interest, and your hopes that forty or fifty of them will cheerfully enter into the service of the Colony, affords the Council additional satisfaction, and the design of uniting them to the Regiment of Rangers is a measure which they altogether approve of, but to be under the particular direction of a white man, agreeable to a resolution of the Congress in their late session.

"The Council request you to give them immediate notice when any body of the Catawbas are ready to march in order to join the Rangers, and that you will recommend a white man well qualified to lead them in scouts, and in action. Transmit your notice by the hands of such a one. The Council will give him a commission, and dispatch him with a letter to Col. Thomson, in whose camp he will meet the Indians."—Journal of Council of Safety, July 26, 1775.

inform me what they were, and kept it a secret from me, as I could wish he had done from all others. I am doubtful that the officers in that Quarter are not the persons esteem'd among their neighbors, & that they have not told the men their duty at the time of their Enlisting them, however you will be better able to Judge when you Peruse the inclosed papers, by which you will also see how Fletchall, Cunningham & Robinson has deceived and deluded the poor people, in the Fork, Between Broad & Saluda Rivers I am Clearly of opinion if some Gentlemen of the Council of Safety, or of the most noted Character together with Coll? Richardson (as many of these People formerly belonged to his Regiment) could be prevailed on to go up among them that could these unhappy disputes between Great Britain & the Colony's in a proper Light that most of them might be brought over by fair means. I do not mean Fletchall Cunningham & Robinson, if they was Cherokees Chiefs or Leaders I would venture to loose my life or send their Scalps to the Council of Safety But the poor people they have deluded, I am of opinion might yet be convinced of their Error. I think Mr Tennent would be a good hand to send up as a great many of those people are of his — Religion. I sent Lieut: David Hopkins with association Col. Fletchall, & expect him Back on Tuesday or Wednesday next, & will immediately let you know what success he had.

When I was left in Town I apply'd to the Council of Safety for a warrant for our Doctor Alexander Rogers, which I did not then get, and a Blank appointment for his Mate, I likewise apply'd to have an Adjutant appointed would be glad to know if the Council made any order for one.

      I am

       Dr Sir &c

NB

I would Just beg leave to mention that I am well informed of there being a private *eak & great resentment between Mayson, Kirkland, & this Cunningham the latter with some more of his Neighbours think they have not been taken proper notice of† I only throw out those hints for your information.

    Camp near Congaree Creek. 29 July 1775.
Gentlemen,

    My last to You was the 22nd Instant by Capt^ن Woodward since which I have rec^d the Inclosed Letter from Lieut David Hopkins who I sent with the Association from the President to Col. Fletchall,‡ You likewise have inclosed a Letter handed me last night from Capt: Wise I have rec^d a Letter from Major Mason dated the 22^d Inst: wherein he informs me of the arrival of Capt: Purvis with the Day before & that he had only Enlisted eleven Men he farther informs me that he had expected Capt: Polk within Ten Days, from whom I have never yet received any account therefore cannot inform you with regard to the state of his Company, & neither Caldwell nor Kirkland have yet made me a return of their Company's. Captains Kirshaw, Goodwyn Woodward & Richardson are now in Camp with me & have all their Companys compleat except the Latter who wants four Men yet, which I hope to get in a few

---

*Torn.

†So, after all, this "chivalrous gentleman of the old school", of whose "duty to his king" we have heard so much, was nothing but a "sorehead".

‡Letter from Henry Laurens, President of the Council of Safety, to Col. Thos. Fletchall, dated July 14th, 1775: "This letter will be presented to you by an Officer in the Colony Regiment of Rangers, who will be dispatched by Col. Thomson for that special service, and who will wait for your answer."

Days tho' I find some difficulty in raising Men, as the Enemies to the cause, take great Pains to progagate different reports that the Money they are to be Paid with will not pass &c.

The men with me are chiefly well armed with Rifles what few are wanted I expect to collect in a few Days but their Horses in General appear but low in flesh. about 50 Men are already clothed with their Regimentals & shall get the remainder ready as speedy as possible I can as I have a number of Taylors employ'd for that Purpose, but find it little difficult to procure a sufficient Quantity of low priced Blue Broad Cloth.

My Men that rides express, expects that their Expences will be paid by the publick, as their Wages will not be sufficient to support themselves & Horses, & pay traveling charges &c as I never had any Instruction in this matter shall be glad of Yours on that head.

I have order'd Major Mason, if he found that Captⁿ Caldwells company was sufficient to guard Fort Charlotte to rendezvous the other three Company's near the ridge, until I rec^d farther orders. from the moving the Gunpowder first out of the Fort to ninety six, the different accounts of Captain Kirklands behavior in that occasion, Capt: Purvis only having enlisted eleven Men, and not having any intelligence from Polk, together with the minds of the back People being so much agitated at this time that I am really at a loss in what manner to act in regard to the conduct & Behaviour of the different officers in that Quarter, shall therefore be extremely glad of your direction and am with due regard.

     Gentlemen
   Your most obed^t. Humble Servt.
       Wm Thomson

I am under the necessity of being rather troublesome to you, as the Secretary has not yet furnished me with a Copy of the resolves of the Provincial Congress.

Camp near Granby 29 July 1775.

Coll? Henry Lawrens,

Honour'd Sir, Inclos'd I send you a Copy of a Letter from the Rev.d Mr Cresswell to Major Mason which with the Letters now inclos'd to the Council of Safety will farthur inform you of the confusion in the different parts of the Frontiers of this Colony. from these & the many different accounts that I daily have from up the Country I am at a Loss to say any thing on that subject but as I know it to be my duty to have my small Regiment Trained & complete as soon as in my Power, and to have the minds of the small Part I have with me as quiet as possible, as they seem rather disatisfied at present occasioned me to solicit your Friendship in the following application.

It was agreed to in Provincial Congress that the Regiment of Rangers which I have the Honour to command was to be upon as good a Footing as the Provincial Rangers in the late Indian War, which I allow they would be at 20£ ⅌ month, provided, provisions Blanketts, Horses & Ammunition were to be purchased as reasonable as at that time, and that wild Game was as plentiful in the Back Country as they were then, & our Duty to be there, but am sorry to inform You that Goods in the Back Country are become scarce & dear, as is also Provisions of all kinds—I have four Companys of my Regiment encamp'd near the Congrees, & I find it extremely difficult to keep them from suffering for want of Provision, which causes much murmuring amongst my Men .. I am convinc'd it will not be in my Power to make my Men perfect in their Exercise, as it takes them off their duty a great part of their time providing provisions. You are sensible that our duty in the late war, was chiefly in the back - - Country were Provisions were very reasonable, and plenty of Wild Game to be met with, and we were never call'd to this place or lower down, Except when we were ordered to join the Regulars, & then we were found in Provisions at the Expense of the publick and all Detachments that were sent below this place were always found in Provisions, which I make no doubt you'll remember on recollection If you'll please to consider a few moments the expence a Person must be at at this time to maintain himself & his Horse, and furnish himself with a Rifle Gun suitable for the occasion I make no doubt but you'll find them on a much worse footing than our Rangers formerly were. If you think any step could be taken to have the privates found in Provision at the expence of the Colony am convinced it would answer a good purpose, & quiet the minds of the few I have with me that I can depend upon, and I heartily wish the first resolve of the Congress, respecting the number of Men in each Company had been carried into Execution, which number would have been easily rais'd had the Men been found in Provision, even had their pay been something less.— However, this I leave entirely to You. and shall be much oblig'd to you for your advice on the subject. And if you think it proper & Judge it a reasonable request should Esteem it a favour if you'll communicate it to the Council of Safety & use your Influence in favour of my Reg^t or if you think a petition from all the officers setting forth the Inconveniencys the Men labour under would answer a better Purpose, should be glad to be informed tho I am persuaded You can be of more service to the Reg^t than any Petition they can send down, as you are well acquainted with the Circumstances these men must be in being oblig'd to purchase Provisions at whatever prices the People where they happen to be stationed at Choses to set upon them

 I am very respectfully, Hon^d: Sir
  True Copy Your Most obed't Hble Servt
          Wm Thomson

       Charles Town 3rd Augt 1775.
Dear Sir,
   The Council of Safety having fully considered the contents of your three Letters rece'd by the Hands of Gilbert Gibson have order'd me to reply in the following Terms.

Respecting the movement of your Reg^t: under your command You are to be govern'd by their late orders untill you shall receive further Instructions. Concerning an additional allowance to Your Men, when employ'd as express messengers, the Council Concur in your opinion that somewhat more than the ordinary daily pay ought to be granted, You may be the most competent Judge in this this article & therefore you are requested to adjust & signify what will be sufficient and satisfactory, in consideration of Gibson's having been detained in Charles Town he has been allowed and paid 15 / p^r Day taking all days together, with which he is extremely well satisfied in the ordinary course—perhaps 10^s p^r Day will be full enough.

The report which has been spread in order to depreciate the value of our new paper Currency is equally nugatory and malicious. That Paper stands upon the same foundation on which all our paper Currency is establish'd, the faith and credit of the representatives of the People.

You are particularly enjoyned by the Council to be

diligent & circumspect in placing to the bottom the late conduct of Capt: Kirkland, as well with respect to the disbanding his Company, as in the affair of the Gun Powder said to have been taken from Major Mason by his contrivance. if he has been faulty take the surest evidence of facts and acquaint the Council minutely, of your discoveries on this Head, But as the Character & Honour of an officer is at stake, secrecy will be necessary in order to save both from slander if he is innocent. John Adam Summers after a conversation fair & candid on the part of the Council of Safety acknowledged his conviction of the rectitude of the measures taken by the people in opposition to Ministerial tyranny. & as a proof of his sincerity he signed the general association & promised to obtain the subscription of other Men in his Neighborhood to a paper which was delivered to him for that purpose. This Man's deportment before the Council gave no room to suspect him guilty of double dealing but should he deceive us You will soon discover it and give proper instruction* The rev.d Mr: Creswell's endeavours on the part of American Liberty are laudable & the Council request You to signify to him their sense of his Zeal & good Service.

That part of your dispatches which treats of the difficulty which the Rangers labour under in the article of Rations or daily provisions has had particular regard paid to it in Council. there is nothing before the Board of more importance than to concert proper means for keeping that Regiment compleat in number, well disciplined, & perfectly satisfied. It is therefore a matter of great concern to the Council to find that Body now expressing their discontent with terms, which each man must have been fully apprized of be-

---

*Judge O'Neall says, in his Annals of Newberry District, that Summer fought on the Whig side at the Battle of Stono.

fore he enlisted, & which the principal officers declared in Congress were sufficient for engaging as many Men, as might have been required in these circumstances what other judgment can be formed but that they are disposed to distress the Council in order to force a compliance with exorbitant demands. If after the repeated assurances given in full Congress by the Coll? & Major together with concurrent declarations of several of the Captains that upon such Pay & such conditions as were stipulated, there was no room to doubt of filling the Reg! with proper Men & in a very short space of time. If after the fair & eager Enlisting in the service upon terms previously declared & universally known murmurs are heard amongst the men, against those very terms, what rule can the Council of Safety adopt for their guide It is not likely that if the present attempt should be allowed to succeed new demands would thereby be created & somewhat else would be found wanting to pacify Men who have mark'd no limits to their desires.

If they are in earnest & mean to serve their Country the pay to the Rangers is ample & when compared to the No pay of the Militia in Charles Town who perform daily & nightly service in the same cause, it is superabundant. If they are not in Earnest, if they do not serve from Principle, 'tis impossible to know what will be satisfactory to them. It merits the attention of the Regiment of Rangers that they are paid for holding themselves in readiness to fight their own Battles, & that their fellow subjects who are to bear the principal burthen of Taxation on that account also hold themselves in readiness to join, & in the mean time receive no consideration such reflections if they are Patriots and Lovers of Liberty will stimulate them to duty & diligence. If they are void of such sentiments, how shall we depend upon them to

ORANGEBURG COUNTY. 413

Act with us as Brethern & fellow sufferers in one united struggle, against the Power which now bears hard upon the general Liberty of all America.

Upon the whole the Council of Safety admonish the officers & Men of the Reg^t: of Rangers to reflect seriously upon the cause & nature of their establishment upon the distressed state of the Colony Finances, to consider that their Brethern the Inhabitants of Charles Town & the adjacent country have chearfully embark'd in the same general service, at a vast expence to Officers & Men without any Kind of Pay or reward. And the Council have further ordered me to signify to you Sir, that they have no legal authority to allow a seperate Pay for provision to your Regimt: a fact which you cannot be ignorant of, nor can they make any alterations except such as shall be mentioned below in the appointment by the Provincial Congress, & they are of opinion that the Honour of the officers are much concerned in this case.

If the following proposition will benefit the service by saving the Men the trouble of seeking their Provision and giving more leisure for perfecting them in Military discipline. You are desired to carry it into execution Viz^t. to appoint proper Persons to provide & to Issue the necessary supplies of Provision both in Camp and upon march the expence to be deducted from the monthly Pay of the Rangers until the meeting of the next provincial Congress before whom a proper representation will be laid & their determination had thereupon. In the mean time the Council have great confidence in your discretion and integrity in the right management of this important concern, & desire to hear from you fully thereupon & and upon every other branch of public business within your department by some early opportunity. Nothing more at present need be said concerning Coll^o. Fletchall as

Mr. Drayton & the Gentlemen with him are to take up that affair. You will receive by the Bearer, of this a Packet of Articles of War which were to have gone by Mr. Drayton, & also four Copys of Extracts from the Journals of the Provincial Congress I have the honour to be Sir

      Your most obed^t Servt
       Henry Lawrens
Coll^o Thomson   President of the
       Council of Safety.

     Congrees 7th Augt 1775./
Gentleman

I herewith send you inclosed a return of the four Companys now encamped at this place. Cap^{ts} Wise, Caldwell & Purvis have not yet furnished me with the return of their Companys, and as to Kirkland and Polk, you'll see by their own Letters of their having deserted the cause as has also their officers and Men except Lieut Mitchell of Kirkland's Comp^y who I have desired to recruit more Men, & have also desired the other officers now with me to list Men in order to have the two Companys compleated again, shall be much oblig'd to You to appoint Moses Vance Lieut: instead of one of those who deserted, he has been upon duty since the first of last month and as to the other vacancies hope they will be filled up with Gentlemen who may be depended upon. for further particulars beg leave to refer you to the Letters from the Honble Wm Henry Drayton & am with due respect
      Hon^d Gentlemen
       Yrs &c
       Wm Thomson

 To the Honble the Council of Safety.
Gentlemen   Congree Store Augt 9th 1775
  Yesterday I rec^d a Letter from the Presi-

dent written by your orders and in answer to it I beg leave to inform you, that the late orders mentioned in the letter, by which I am to regulate my future movem^{ts} until further Instructions, I have not received I apprehend those late orders are those Mr. Drayton told me, he himself had drawn up by orders of the Council to be signed by the President countermanding my first intended march down the country, & directing me to remain where I was encamped & to regulate my future motions & directions from Mr. Drayton & Mr. Tennent.

These orders have never come to Hand but by Mr Drayton's representation of them and the Papers in his hands signed by the president, I have regulated myself in pursuance of directions from Mr Drayton & Mr Tennent & according to those directions, which perfectly agree with my own Judgment, I have broken up the Camp near this place and shall form a new one in Amelia on the 10th Instant.

As to the affairs of Provisions Mr Drayton has settled it I believe to the full satisfaction of the Rangers the terms are these, The officers will give all possible encouragement for People to supply the Camp with Provision & when the Troops are able to purchase Provisions in Camp they are to be restrained in the practice of going abroad to seek any. I will remember my declarations in Congress respecting the pay. Had I officers of My own Choice I should never want Men perfectly satisfied with such an allowance & even the Men now listed would have been content, but from the folly of some officers who have in a great degree been the foundation of the late almost fatal uneasiness in the Camp on Sunday night last with the particulars of which Mr. Drayton & Mr Tennent have I believe acquainted You. Mr Drayton's discourse to the Troops on this occasion has been of great service, as well as his discourse the Evening before from the Effects of which I expect a more punctual obediance than I have hitherto experienced. The Rangers now I am firmly of opinion are content, & perfectly disposed to do their duty.

Sign.ᵈ   W Thomson

In the Council of Safety.
Charles Town 20th July 1775.

Sir,

Our orders to You of the 13th Instant respecting your March to Charles Town, are hereby Countermanded, as at this Juncture the Presence of the Rangers is necessary in the interior Parts of the Country. You will therefore remain at the Post you now Occupy, unless some unforeseen cause should occasion you to remove, & for your further Proceedings, we refer You to the Honble Wm Hen: Drayton, & the Revd Wm Tennent, who are authorized to make a progress into the back Country, to examine into the present uneasiness & disturbances in those parts of the Colony.

For our sense upon your Letters, of the 22nd of July, one to the Council of Safety the other to the President, & Major Mason's Letter of the 10th of July to the Council we refer you to the Gentlemen above mentioned to be authorized to make a Progress, and we inform you that, by the Hands of Capt: Woodward we have sent the Sum of Five Thousands Pounds for the Payment of the Rangers under your command.

By order &c H. Lawrens

Col: Wm Thomson.   Copy

Charles Town 11th August 1775.

Sir,

I wrote to You the 4th Inst: by order of the Council of Safety by the Hands of G: Gibson, since which the Council have been inform'd by a private Letter that Capt: Polk & his Company of Rangers had renounced the cause of Liberty & abandoned their Duty - - affairs of such moments should be communicated by Special Messingers & with out delay, your silence would have induced the Council to suspend their belief of that report had it not been made in possitive terms by one of your officers to Mr Gervais. Great are the difficulties which the true friends of Liberty & their Country have to encounter, but we trust that by perseverance, patience & resolution every obstacle will be surmounted.

To the disagreeable tiding above mentioned we have just now received the intelligence from Savanna which you will find at large in the Copies of those Letters here inclosed— Viz: one from the Council of Safety for Georgia, dated Savanna 1st Augt: 1775./ one from the Committee at Augusta dated 6th Augt. & the other from Moses Kirkland dated 31st July to Captn Middleton to which you are particularly referred. the Council of Safety desire you will immediately consult the Hon'ble Mr Drayton if he is in your neighborhood & pursue such measures, relative to the dangerous attack threaten'd upon Augusta as shall appear most likely to suppress the Insurgents & restore peace & Quietness to our friends, Should Mr: Drayton be at any considerable distance you will act in this very important & alarming circumstance as shall seem best in your own opinion without delay - - - if our Enemies should succeed in this attempt their hands will be strength'ned & the work of suppressing them will be doubled.

You will, if it shall appear necessary apply to the Commanding officer of the Regiment of Militia & raise as many Volunteers as may be necessary to join the rangers & assure the officers & Men who may give you

their assistance that the Council of Safety will make immediate order for, paying them for the time which they may be on duty & also for their Provisions when accounts properly certified shall be sent in. In a word the Council rely upon your Zeal & good conduct in this dangerous conjuncture, when it is impossible for them to give explicit orders. and they will expect to hear from you by return of this Messenger (Philip Hill) & as frequently afterward as there shall be occasion. I am
Sir
Your Most Obed^t Servt
Henry Lawrens
President of
the Council of Safety.

You know what will be proper to be done with Captn Kirkland when practicable & safe meantime the secre'cy formerly enjoyned will be necessary.

Charles Town 13th August 1775. /
Sir,
We refer to the contents of our Letter of the 11th Inst^r which will accompany this. from the total silence of yourself and Mr Drayton upon the expected attack upon Augusta we are willing to hope, that our friends have been cautiously alarmed, nevertheless we must not loose sight of an object of such importance. We therefore Confirm our late orders & here inclose a Letter for Captn Hammond which we request you to dispatch by a special Messinger, unless some other safe & immediate opportunity shall offer. We have applied assistance in Case of need, both as an Officer of Militia & a friend to the Cause of the united Colony's Under Cover with this You will receive Eight Commissioners. Sign'd by us Viz: 1 for J L Peyer Imhoff Esqr to be a Captn of Rangers.

1 for Ch: Heatly, Esqr to be a Captn also. 1 for Moses Vance to be a Lieutenant dated the 1st July the day on which you say he entered the Service. 5 to be appointed & the Blanks to be properly filled up by you in which we trust you will consult solely the Interest of the service — this is an extraordinary measure which we have consented to in the present unsettled state of your Regiment, hoping that by a discreet distribution of these Commissions the Company's will be filled up by good Men & that the Public may reap some advantage from the vast charge which has already been incurred by that establishment, but it must not be drawn into Precedent.

We think it is now necessary to distinguish in each Company first & second Lieutenants, Seniority will be determined hereafter by the respective dates of Your Commission which in these you must vary for that purpose being careful not to antidate. When you have filled up these Commissions you will transmit to us immediately the names & dates.— We can not account for the miscarriage of our Letter which You say had not reach'd You, if our Secretary can write a Copy of it in time you will receive it under this cover.

It affords us some satisfaction to learn by Your Letter of the 9th that the remaining Rangers were Content & perfectly disposed to do their duty, we hope that disposition will be lasting, the effect of a true sense of their Duty & not the transient product of an harrangue.

You will find the Copy above mentioned under this Cover the original we believe went by the Hands of Captn Woodward & ought to be inquired for.

By order of the Council of Safety.

Henry Lawrens
President.

Coll: William Thomson.

Hon: W^m H: Drayton Esqr. Granby 10 Augt 1775.
Sir,
    Yester morning I rec^d the Inclosed Letters from Town, and immediately sett out for this place in order to forward them to You, Inclosed You have a Copy of Letter I rec^d from Coll: Lawrens, shall be glad of your advise or order on the matter, I cannot think of proceeding on any account whatsoever as long as you are continued in ye Back parts without Your order, which shall be Immediately put in Execution I expect all the Companys that had leave will meet this day in Amelia. I am to meet Captn Theius' Company tomorrow & will do all in my Power to have them to sign and settle other matters as you have desired. Sunday I shall return to Camp where I shall remain untill I hear from You. I rec^d from the Council of Safety Capt^s Commissions, for Imhoff & Heatly. 1 Lieut: for Vance, and 5 Blank Lieut: Commission I shall not dispose of any of the Blanks untill I hear from You, I rec^d from the Council of Safety Copies of three Letters from Savannah, which has alarm'd them.

I send off this day to Major Williamson to see if there is any Body of Men collected in that part, be it as it will I cannot act with Propriety without your orders as long as you are in the Back.
               Sign'd   Wm Thomson.

                       Amelia, 21st August 1775.
Captn John Lewis Peyer Imhoff.
    Sir,
        You are requested as soon as possible to Inlist 30 private Men—2 Sarjeants, and a Drummer. as soon as you have listed ten Men, you will send or fetch

them to Camp or Elsewhere if ordered. List good
Rifle Men with as good Horses a possible.
Your Humble Servt
Wm Thomson.

Mr Godfrey Drehers August 11. 1775.
Dr Sir,
Captain Shrams has not attended here today, neither has any of his Company come to us, altho this place was of the Captain's own chusing. This disobedience to Military orders ought not to go unnoticed for fear others seeing so criminal a Conduct pass with impunity, they should be encouraged to imitate a behavior that may lead to ruinous consequences. I therefore think it would be proper immediately let you let Captain Shrams know that you recall his Commission & discharge him from his command & take measure to call the company together & induce them to elect a Captain, who will receive a Commission from the Council, Your presence will greatly facilitate this work, & their chosing a Captain will naturally I hope lead them to sign the association. But do not mention this last affair to them till after they have chosen their Captain.

We have had very bad success here today & I declared that no Mills shall grind for & no dealings shall be had with any nonsubscriber.
I am Sir
Your most humble St—
W^m Hy Drayton

I am in hopes this letter will get down to you some time to night. And I shall be glad that *tomorrow* You will come up here & discharge the Captain & call the Company together, because this vigorous step being done out of hand will spread abroad immediately &

may be of good consequence in the Fork while I am there.

Sir,
   I have received the Letter you sent by the Ranger, & I most readily excuse your breaking the seal of my Letter, indeed Colonel I should have had no objection if you had read it.
   The Council of Safety mention their having sent me some blank Commissions for six Volunteer Companies. I have not received them. If you have them pray keep them till I see You.
   I find the Council have been much alarmed by the report of an attack upon Augusta. there is no foundation in it I believe, at least . . . the heads of the party I am persuaded will not attempt anything of that sort while I am in this part of the Country. I more fear an attack upon Fort Charlotte. However of this I have sent proper information & direction to the Fort & to Major Williamson.
   As I do not therefore see any occasion for any immediate movement by You, I cannot give directions for any. But I think you had best remain in your new Camp, & make the Huts snug & comfortable for the Men, and besides this, I think it advisable that you immediately build other Huts, as perhaps there may be occasion for to assemble in your Camp about 500 Militia . . In the mean time you will look out so many of the Militia who may be depended upon, & who may hold them selves, in readiness to march if they should be called upon. For these Men, will be wanted a supply of Ammunition.
   Be so good immediately & in the . . . . most private manner to send to Fort Charlotte for a moderate Quantity of Powder & Lead. I shall hold a meeting with Fletchall's People at Fords upon Enore on Wed-

nesday & after that I shall pass through ninety six, & join you with all dispatch. Above all things endeavour to have the Camp plentifully supplied with Provisions, especially if there should unfortunately be occasion to call out such a Body of Militia to join the Rangers. You will take care Colonel, that your application respecting the Militia be as private as possible.
 I have the pleasure to subscribe myself
  Sir
   Your most humble Servt
    Wm H^y Drayton.

   Lawson's fork Augt 25th 1775.
 P S. this is a paragraph in the Council of Safety's letter to me, Pray shew it to Mr: Charlton, & write the Council about it.

 "We do not understand whether you mean to ask for a Commission as Surgeons Mate for Lieutenant Charlton, in lieu of, or in addition to his Lieutenancey. If the former, altho we are not expressly authorized, yet for the good of the service we might find means to accomodate him, but you know that a double Commission would be directly contrary to a resolution of the Provincial Congress. this Article therefore must . - - - . unavoidably wait for explanation."

   White Hall. 22nd Aug^t: 1775.
Dear Gentlemen.
   I received your favour of the 10th Instant. the express to Mr: Hammond from the Council of Safety, I immediately sent to him, also at the same time wrote to Captain Caldwell advising him to be on his guard.

 I have heard nothing of any Body of Men going to attack Augusta shall acquaint Mrs Mayson that you

are well. I this day heard from Mr. Drayton directing me to reinforce Fort Charlotte with Militia, which I am now giving orders to do. and I intend immediately to throw a Quantity of Provision in. Mr. Drayton is to have a Meeting to-morrow with Fletchall's People at same Ford's, Enoree. & has some opinion that they may use violence to his person. If that should be the Case I shall endeavour to have the Militia under my Command, to march whenever he may be carried a prisoner. I have sent this day a Young Man whom I can well depend upon to be at the Meeting tomorrow. and will return immediately & inform me what is done there. Excuse haste. I am
    Dear Gentlemen
     Your most obt. humble Servt.
      A Wm. Son.

Camp Amelia Fuquett's old Field 25th Augt. 1775. /
Hon'ble Sir,

 The express sent to Mr Drayton is not yet return'd, I am now camp'd at this Place with five Companys—Capt: Wise, Kirshaw, Goodwyn, Richardson & Woodward; Capts. Imhoff and Heatly, are out recruiting as is Capt: Kirshaw in behalf of them & likewise some of the Lieutenants, I am in hopes in a short time to have their Companys Compleated. Major Mason who has been some time at the Congrees waiting for them I expect at the same time to join the Camp, from all the Intelligence I have had there was not much reason for our Friends in Georgia being so much alarm'd, the first certain accounts I had of Capt: Polk's disobedience, I recd. by a Letter from Major Mason the day before Mr. Drayton came to the Congrees, & on his arrival I deliver'd it to him. I did not chuse to write from report, where the reputation of a Gent: was at Stake. my officer, who wrote to Mr.

Gervais /yet unknown to me/ had he acquainted me, I should have had it in my power to have wrote facts. Whatever certainties might come to my Hands of consequence, either for or against the cause of Liberty, You may depend upon I shall /both as a point of my Duty & my strictest regard, for the welfare of the Country/ make immediate report of.

I have reason to believe the Nonsubscribers will be but few in a short time. I have the Promise of a Volunteer company of Sixty good Men out of Fletchall's Company near to where he lives. I have taken away the Commissioners from some of the Capt^s of my regiment of Foot, who was disobedient & disaffected.

I should be glad to know if it would be proper to fill up those places with good Men by giving them Volunteer Commissions, if not proper should be glad to know if I could be supply'd with blank Commissions from the Govr. for them I inclose You a list of Captn Wise's officers & Men. Captn Imhoff petition'd for a 2nd Lieut^s Commission, for, in the choice of which, depended the raising of Men to the number of 14 or 15. The other blank Commissions I shall not fill up untill my regiment are together, except those in the Fort, untill which time it will not be in my Power to make you a proper return of the reg^t. of Horse. The Company's now with me are Compleat, And I have the vanity to make mention, that the Men are very forward in their Military discipline I remain

Yr most obed^t Servt

Wm Thomson

NB:
Please to observe that Captn Wise himself is in No: Carolina, his Men came with Lieut: Donaldson. Captn Wise I presume will be in Camp in a few days.

The Hon'ble the Council of Safety.
 Gents.

I Yesterday returned from 96. & think it unnecessary to write of particulars, as I make no manner of doubt Mr. Drayton has already given you the same. I have left seven companies behind at 96. in order to take a Tour farther back in the Country. An alarm has been given that an Indian of the Cherokees had been killed & two wounded in Georgia which has disturbed the minds of the back Inhabitants much. And Mr. Drayton's opinion in this case concurs with my own, it is that as the Rangers were raised in defence of the Country the back settlers would think hard if they were not with them in case of danger.

We have therefore order'd them to March for some time up amongst them but not to proceed within 15 Miles of the Indian line, for fear of alarming the Indians, & in order to appease the minds of the Inhabitants in those parts After which we have given them leave of absence for a few days in order to recruit themselves & Horses, which is really requisite, when they are to meet at the Camp in Amelia which will be on the 24th Octr.

After Mr. Drayton had finish'd with Col. Fletchall, I took a ride to Fort Charlotte; & examined the whole; I think it is in very good order for defence & that there is a very good Company in it.

While I was there I had the pleasure of seeing Fort James on the Georgia side, taken possession of by some of the Georgians & Carolns at my return to 96. I met with Mr. Wilkinson from the Cherokee Nation who informed me that one of the Indians was killed & two wounded by some of the Georgia People. I immediate gave orders to Lieut Taylor of Fort Charlotte to take a party of Men with him & go in search of the Persons whom the Indians mistrusted had |killed|

committed the fact & whose names this M^r. Wilkinson mentioned to me.

Inclosed you have a General return of my Reg^t. of Rangers from the time of enlisting to the 20th Inst. which is as correct as I could possibly make it from the returns given in by the different Capt^ns Captn Wise on that same day resign'd his commission to M^r. Drayton & as he will inform you more particular on that & every other Head I think it unnecessary to add any more.

    I remain
     Gent
      Your Most Obed^t. Hble Servt
       W^m T:

Dear Sir.   Amelia 29th Septr. 1775.

 Your very kind fav^r. of the 17th Inst^r. was deliver'd to me on the road home between the Ridge & the Congarees which afforded me the greatest Pleasure.

You may depend that I shall always make a proper Distinction in my Private & Public Letters to You. Your present situation of President & Chairman I am convinc'd must be very fatigueing, & tho I cannot but think it is high time that you ought to be relieved of your burthen Yet I am afraid they will not find a Person to supercede You, who will act in both capacities & be of as much Service to the Country as you have been. I heartily wish that General Kirkland may be taken & lodged in the Barracks or Fort Johnston & that he may be severely punished for his Villainy, & am happy to hear that Fort Johnston is in our possession & that you are making every necessary Preparations for defence. I have no doubt but you have heard before this that Col Drayton has had a Meeting with Col Fletchall & some of his Head Men &

that He has in a great measure quieted him & his party. they seem to be disatisfied at first about the declaration that he had sent over to their Camp desiring them to give up their Leaders, but after a little expostulation they appeared very ready to make & sign his Treaty, which I suppose you have seen. I was informed that Cunningham & Brown were not well pleased with Fletchall for what he had done & that they had parted, not upon the best terms. However it may work a good end in time, which I heartily wish. Cole Drayton had a long talk with the Indians at the Congrees, they are very well pleased, but wishes much to have the ammunition that was promis'd them as soon as possible. Capt: Peyer imhoff I left sick at 96, but I expect to see him at the Congarees next Monday when I will present your Complim^t to him. I have given him every assistance in my Power to make up his Company & I dare say that it will be filled up in a few days. I intend going to Town some time next Week, when I will do myself the Pleasure of waiting on you to converse more fully on the news of the Country, unless I should receive new orders to the contrary from the Hon'ble the Council of Safety

I rem^n Dr Sir

Yr Most Obed^t H'ble Servt

Wm Thomson

General orders.

Gentlemen,

17 Augt 1775 Amelia

Captain Charles Heatly will shew you Your place of Encampm^t near Fuguetts old Field & the form you are to camp in.

It is hereby order'd that the Men makes good Camps to Shelter themselves from the weather.

You will order out of each Company every Day sufficient Grass Guards & Fitague Men. As soon as your Camps are Compleat, You are as usual to be very diligent in Training the Men. I am order'd on a Tour to the Beaver Dam near little Saluda, hopes to be at your Camp by Tuesday next.

To the sev!. Capt^{ns} Yr hble sev^t
of the Reg^t of Rangers. W^m T:

Amelia 17 Augt 1775

Sir,
Please to send the inclos'd to Captn Peyer imhoff. I am order'd on a Tour up Saluda, hopes to return & find you all in Camp at Fuguetts old Field, areeble to Your last orders You rec^d from me. In my absence Captn Chas. Heatley will shew You Your place of Encampment & the Form of the Camp.

As You will be the oldest Captn on the Spot you will see that the orders left with him are put in Execution. I hope to be in Camp on Tuesday I am

To Sir Yr humble Servant
Captn Eli Kirshaw. W. T.

Amelia 17 Augt 1775/

Sir,
This day I rec'd from the Council of Safety a Capt^{ns} Commission for You. On recp^t hereof you will wait on me in Amelia in order to receive the same. In the Interim & on your way, you may Enlist Men for yourself; Let them be good rifle Men with good Horses. please to fetch the date of the Commission of the 2nd Lieut. of Captn Wise, & the date of Lieut^t. Donaldson's Commission. I am

Your h'ble Servt
To W. T.
Captn Lewis Peyer Imhoff.

To the Hon'ble Henry Lawrens, President of the Hon'ble the Council of Safety.

Camp Amelia 2nd Septr 1775./

Sir,

Last night I rec^d a Letter by an Express from the Hon'ble Wm Henry Drayton ordering me to march my Regt: of Rangers immediately to the ridge, which I shall do tomorrow morning & will endeavour to march as many of my Reg^t of Foot* as I can make up agreeable to his orders

Inclosed is a Letter rec^d by said Express to the Hon'ble the Council of Safety. I remain
with great respect
Sir
Yr most hum'ble Servt
W. T.

To   Camp Amelia 2^d Septr 1775.
Lieut: Coll: Rowe & }
Major Golson .. }

Gentlemen

You are hereby ordered to meet me on Saturday next the 9th Inst^r at the Ridge, with two hundred Men well armed, out of our Regim^t of Foot, if you cant raise them as Volunteers, You must draft them, & assure them that they will receive Pay as the other Provincials in this Province from the day they leave home to they day they return. I am Gent^n
Yr humble Servt
W. T.

---

*This was the regiment of provincial militia that Col. Thomson had commanded before being selected to command the regiment of regulars known as the Rangers.

ORANGEBURG COUNTY. 431

The Hon'ble Wm Henry Drayton at Aug^{ta}
Wetherford: Exp^{ss}

Camp at the Congrees
6 Sept: 1775.

Sir,
Yesterday just when the several Companies were about marching from hence, there came an Express from Cap^{tn} Paris informing us that himself and five Cherokee Indians were stopt from coming down by Captn Hendrick & some others belonging to Fletchalls reg^t of about 10 Miles distant from the Congarees. The Companies here immediately got themselves in readiness and marched to rescue them, which they did & took Hendrick Prisoner, who is now confined in Camp, his associates made their escape a few minutes after he was taken, Captn Paris is now here with the Indians who will inform You with the Particulars. I have order'd the Companies to march early tomorrow morning for the ridge where I expect to be with them on Friday Evening & where I shall stay untill I receive your further orders. The Men that are to be drafted out of my Regim^t of Foot & the Volunteers I have order'd to meet me at the Ridge by Saturday next Your orders to Coll: Richardson I have sent, but I have not heard from him since, only that he is very much hurt from a fall* from his Indico Vatts, which

---

*The following, heretofore unpublished, letter will be of interest here:

[Direction on cover.]

On the Colony Service

To
The Honble Henry Laurens Esqr
Charles Town

Sir
I have to beg the favour of you to Communicate to the Council of Safety, that two days ago I receiv'd a line from Colo Wm Thomson, accompanied by Copy of a letter from the Hon'ble Wm Henry Dray-

I am afraid will deprive him from meeting us himself, but have not the least doubt of his complying with your Instructions the Express from the Hon'ble the Council of Safety arrived here last night with the inclosed Letter for your Honor, also two Bundles which I expect are for the Indians. Paris has just deliver'd me the Indians talk, which he desired me to forward by this same Express.

Our detention here today arrises from the Fatigue ton, wherein he desires me to March 300 men of my Regiment to Broad River & co

I had the misfortune to get a fall which renders me unable to get out of my Bed, having Broke two or three of my Ribs and am otherways much bruised. however am hopefull shall get out in some short time.

I have sent the necessary orders to Major Cantey to assemble the Regiment, and Collect the above number of men which hope will soon be carried into execution. but beg leave to represent to Council of Safety that I do not believe there are 300 loads of Powder in my Regiment, and therefore hope some speedy method will be fallen of lodging a supply to be in readiness upon any emergency that may happen; and if Possible about 200 Stand of armes, as a great number, (particularly the new Irish settlers) are distitute and many unable to provide themselves was they to be purchased for money, which at present is not the Case.

There are several Volunteer Companys assembling in different quarters of my Regiment. some of which I am informed are nearly compleat Commissions will be wanting to officer them —

As my Lieut Colo has left this Province a new arrangement of Field Officers will become necessary. to fill up by Seniority will not answer, for sundry reasons; which I hope soon to have opportunity of communicating to the Council of Safety —

   I have the Honour to be
    Sir
     Your most Humb Servt:
      Richd Richardson

St Marks —
 6th: Septmr 1775
To Henry Laurens Esqr
  President of the Council of Safety

    [Endorsement on back.]
    Collo R— Richardson
     6th. Septr 1775
    Read in Council 10th—

the Horses had yesterday. we did not return to Camp until one o Clock this morning.

    I rem!! with great Esteem
       Hon.d Sir
        Yrs &c
          W: T.

Henry Laurens Esq.r
  Camp at Congarees 6th Sept.r 1775. /

Sir,
  Since I wrote you from Camp Amelia the 2nd Inst. I received your favour of the 31st Ult.o which gives me great satisfaction. You may depend that I will as soon as possible exert myself for raising Volunteer Comp'ys & inform you of my progress therein.

  I find it impossible at present on account of our marching to make a proper return of my whole regimt. but will endeavour to do it as soon as I meet the Hon'ble M.r Drayton I had issued orders previous to the recpt. of you Letter for all returns to be dated and signed by the Commandg. offic.r of each Company but the omission of Capt.!! Wise's was owing to his not being present at the time it was given in, nor did he join the Reg.t before yesterday his reason for not joining before he says was owing to orders he received from the Hon'ble the Council of Safety.

  You may rest assured that I will to the best of my ability follow your own and Mr Drayton's Instructions & will give him all the Military aid in my Power when he shall think fit to demand it. I shall carefully review all your former instructions & give such orders with regard to the Post of Fort Charlotte & for the safety of our associated Friends at Augusta as long as I may think the most prudent at this alarming time. I am extremely obliged to you for consent-

ing to my leaving the Camps as I requested, which I
shall do, when I can with propriety do it, but at present I have not the least thoughts of it.

The reappointmt: of Captn Ez^l. Polk, I hope will be
attended with very good consequences. & that he will
endeavour to gain credid by his future behaviour. Inclos'd you will find a copy of his Letter to me which
I just received, but shall not make any reply before I
see Mr Drayton. Yesterday about noon when the several Companies were getting ready to proceed on their
march for the Ridge we rec^d an Express from Captn
Paris informg: us that one Captn Hendrick & several
others of Coll^e Fletchall's party had stop'^{d} him & 5 of
the Cherokee Indians from coming down here at about
Ten Miles distant from this, & hoped that we would
come to their Assistance, the Companies were immediately ordered to go & rescue them & take Hendricks &
his Associates Prisoners. I arrived there just about
night & took Captn Hendricks, but the others escaped
after he was taken & before any of the Companies
came up to the House they were in.

I order'd the Prisoner under a Guard to the Camp—
where he is now in confinem^t. Capt Paris with the Indians came along with us there this morning. I had a
Talk with these Indians & informed them that M^r
Drayton had desired me to conduct them to the ridge,
as he expected I should see them before he did; they
said they were tired of marching & would rather remain here untill Mr: Drayton came to them. They
gave me the talk from the Nation & desired me to
send it to him directly which I have done.

I propose marching to morrow morning early for
the Ridge where I expect to be with the Companies
on Friday Evening.

I should have done it today had not the Horses been

fatigued Yesterday. We did not return before one of the Clock this morng:
  I remⁿ with great esteem
    Yrs- &c
      W: T.

omitted..... 2ⁿᵈ Septr.   Camp Amelia
  To the Hon'ble Wᵐ Henry Drayton:
  Your orders I recᵈ late last night, shall putt them in execution Immediately. I shall march from this Camp tomorrow morning I shall do my best endeavours to take as many of the Militia with me as possible, tho I am afraid shall not be able to procure the Complimt. you mentioned. The Water's being high obliges me to go by the Congarees where I shall be detained one Day in procuring Provisions & other necessaries, as it was not in my Power to provide the same in this Place the Rivers being full the Waggons were not able to pass. I has dispᵈ your orders to Col: Richardson & your Letter to the Council of Safety.
  We have pretty certain accounts of the defeat of Gage. 9000 of his Men are said to have been slain & himself is dead of the wounds he recᵈ ... there is a Gentⁿ lately arrived at Chas: Town from Virginia with 5 Letters, whose accounts agrees exactly   I remⁿ
    Sir,
      Yr Most Obedt. Servt.
        W: T.

The Hon'ble Wᵐ Henry Drayton,
    Camp at Fairchilds Branch.
          6ᵗʰ Septr. 1775.

  Dr: Sir,
    Since I had the pleasure of writing to You under the 6ᵗʰ Inst: pʳ Mʳ Weatherford an Express to

Augusta, I rec:d your kind Lett:r of the 5th Inst: at Mr Williams about 2 o Clock this after noon on our march hither. Inclosed you will please find Capt:n Arthur's Letter to me, which I have answered desiring him that if he . . . . . . believed the report he mentions to be true that he would meet me with Capt:n Paris & the Indians at the Ridge on Sunday morn:g 10 oClock together with the Volunteers & drafted Men out of my Regm:t of Militia: I am of opinion that was I to leave the Ridge before they arrived it wou'd make them uneasy therefore I think it best to wait for them, but for further particulars refer you to Major Mayson with whom I have consulted & who will deliver this with his own Hands.

I have deliv'ed him all the Commissions for the Volunteer Companies which I rec:d from the Hon'ble the Council of Safety, to be given to You I am Sir

Y:rs &c
W:= T.

To the Hon'ble W:m H: Drayton

Camp near the ridge 10th Sep:t 1775

Sir, I rec:d Yours of the 9th Ins:t early this morning I shall strictly observe the Contents thereof. this Ins:t Capt:n Arthur and Capt Geiger with twenty Volunteers arrived here from the Congarees with whom I expected Capt:n Paris & the Indians, the alarm mentioned in Capt:n Arthur's Lett:r forwarded to you yesterday proved Groundless. Capt:n Paris endeavoured to prevail on the Indians to accompany him to the Ridge, but they rather chose to stay at the Congarees till your return, as they complain'd much as being tired as before but Paris says they seem very anxious to see You. I expect Major Golson of my Regim:t of foot with a draft of Men & the Volunteers

this day be it as it will, I shall march for Ninety six early tomorrow morning.
I am
Dr Sir,
Yr most obedt Servt
W. T.

𝄞 Lieut Caldwell

Capt. John Caldwell—12. May 1776.—Fort Lyttelton Camp near the 10 Mile house

Sir

Yours of the 7th Instant is now before me & note the contents, Your Letter by Captain Purvis did not come to my hand before the Prisoners you sent were tried, received their Sentence & pardoned by His Excellency the President The reason of their being discharged I am entirely a stranger to—I am told Capt. Purvis applied to Colonel Gadsden to deliver them their attestations & said it was by your desire—

Your first Letter did not reach me untill lately—I herewith inclose you a Roster of the officers as they now are to do Duty & Lieut Caldwell will deliver You a list of Your Men now at Head Quarters— The Pay Master will write you with regard to Your Mens Pay— I should have wrote you more fully but as Your Brother can inform You any thing farther, I shall not add, save that I am

Sir
Yours &c

His Excellency John Rutledge Esqr President & Commander in Chief of the Colony of So Carolina } in Charles Town

Camp near the Ten Mile house 7th May 1776.

Sir

Having been informed a few days ago that Mr

John Giles at Monck's Corner had some Osenburgs for Sale. I desired one of my officers to send a person there & endeavour to purchase the whole of him in order to make Hunting Shirts for my men— The person returned without doing of it & informed me that Mr Giles asked 10/ hard money & 12/6 paper Currency pr Yard—this morning I was informed he asks for the same Osnaburgs 10/ hard money & 15/ paper ⅌ yd which I think is a very great extortion—my only reason for troubling Your Excellency with this, is to beg your advice in the matter, as the distinction made between hard & paper money is of very great diservice to the Province & I hope some example will be made of such persons—

    I have the honour to be
     Your Excellency's
      Most Obed^t humb^e Serv.

His Excellency John Rutledge Esqr. in Charles Town
  Camp near the Ten mile house 1st June 1776
 Sir

  This morning early I had the other detachment of my Regiment ready to march down, but the weather proving rainy I thought it most prudent to detain them, as there are now Sick in Camp 46 Men; 40 of whom have the Flux & I am afraid many more would be laid up were they to get wet—as soon as the weather clears up Major Mayson will march down with said Detachment—I would have done myself the pleasure of waiting on Your Excell'cy last night had I not been unwell, but as soon as I am better will do it—
    I am   Your Excellency's &c

His Excellency John Rutledge Esqr   in Charles Town
          Camp on Sullivant's Island 22^d June 1776
Sir
    As I have been credibly informed that the Reg^e of Artillery at Beaufort is now nearly compleated, I take the liberty of requesting the favour of your Excellency to let the two Companies of Rangers there be relieved & ordered to join my Regiment here, could they be spared without prejudice to the Service, it would give me the greatest pleasure to have them present, as I have never once had the Reg^t together—The Men here are in the greatest spirits, the Enemy's Centinels & ours are so near to each other, that they might shake hands had we but boats & they chose to be Friendly—Two field pieces were fired by the Artillery here early this morning at a boat of armed Men which we apprehend was returning from reconnoitering last night—Could the Rangers be relieved once in two or three weeks by some other Troops it would be obliging both officers & men from whom I have had some hints to that purpose—I hope Your Excellency will not take amiss any thing I have mentioned.

His Excellency John Rutledge Esqr   Charles Town
          Camp on Sullivants Island 11th July 1776
Sir
    Lieutenant Charlton of Capt. Kirshaws Company in consequence of a Letter which he received this morning from Camden, did make application to me for leave to go there to secure his Family from a presumed insurrection of the Indians in that Quarter which I did not comply with, & He returned His Commission into my hands—I hope Your Excellency will not take it amiss in having received said Commission.
    Several of the officers & privates have received Letters from their Friends in the back Country on ac-

count of the Indians breaking out, which give them a great deal of uneasiness in regard to their families— I for my part do not think that matters are half so bad as reported to be—

I have the honour to be
Your Excellencys &c

His Excellency John Rutledge Esqr   Charles Town

Camp on Sullivants Island 11th July 1776.

Sir

I received Your Excellency's Letter just now by Mr Calvert Jun, with Keg of Gun Powder for which I have given him a Receipt I am happy to hear that Cunningham & the other Prisoners have taken the Test oath &c— & I am of the same opinion with Your Excellency that their discharge will have a good effect— The oared Barge shall be sent to Town as soon as Your Excellency shall be pleased to send Men capable of carrying her safe up as there are none in my camp fit for that purpose— I have not had any success as yet in sending the Deserters Letters to the Enemy; they now keep double the Centinels to what they formerly did, but nevertheless I expect to have them landed safe this night & I hope they will have the desired effect.

I received the Spy Glass Your Excellency has been so kind as to send me, which I shall take particular care of & return when I shall be ordered to quit this Island—

I have the honour to remain
Your Excellencys &c

His Excellency John Rutledge Esqr–   Charles Town

Camp on Sullivants Island 15th July 1776.

Sir

Your Excellencys favour I have just received

by Mr Calvert & am very sorry that the Snuff was blown in Mr Timothy's Eyes for he is very much mistaken in saying that all the Troops have left Long Island & gone on board the Transports— Yesterday Morning we perceived only one Centinel on the Breast work opposite to our when they usually planted four & this morning we did not discover any Enemy there, about 11 oClock there appeared to be some of our Friends in Arms from the main in order as I suppose to reconnoitre the Enemys Entrenchments— They no sooner appeared to the Enemy on Long Island, than they began to fire on them & fired their Field Pieces ten times, but in my opinion without doing any damage. I could wish our men had not run so far when the Enemy fired—all their Tents are still standing on the Beach & I observed just now that about 150 including Men Women & Children marching toward the East end of Long Island with their Field pieces & I think mean to embark— There are none of the Enemy left on Goat Island & their flat bottomed Boats all disappeared Yesterday; as the naval force have made a move to push off this morning, the land force in my opinion will also do the same in a few days — I should have wrote to Your Excellency before now had not I expected the Commanding Officers here whom I generally informed, would have communicated every circumstance that has happened to Your Excellency—
    I have the honour to be
        Your Excellencys Most Ob^t &c

Major James Mayson   Ninety Six
        Chas Town 7 Aug 1776
          ℔ Express

Sir
    I have this moment received orders from His Excellency the President to march 130 Men out of my

Regiment under proper officers on an Expedition into East Florida— You are therefore desired to proceed immediately to Savanna & take the Command of the Detachment which will be ready to set off from this place this Evening—You will receive further orders from General Lee at Savanna

I am Sir
Yours &Cc
W. T—

| Post |

On the Service of the united States of America

The Honorable John Hancock Esqr. President of the Hon'ble the Representatives of the thirteen United States of America in Congress, at Philadelphia	Charles Town So. Carolina 14th August 1776

Sir

    As no greater honour can be confered on a faithful Servant of the public so next to a consciousness of having done his duty nothing can afford so much pleasure to such a Servant as the thanks of the people.—

    I must confess Sir, I had not entertained the smallest expectation of such distinguished Notice as the Congress have been pleased to take of my endeavours to assist in Repelling the attempts of the Fleet & Army upon this State on the 28th of June last — I was conscious of having acted honestly in the Cause according to the best of my poor abilities & there My Ideas rested — however Sir I am not insensible of the very great honour which, for barely having done my duty, I have now received from the Congress — I beg leave to return you my particular thanks for the very polite manner in which you have transmitted their

Resolution of the 20th July in your favour of the 22nd which I have communicated to the Officers & Soldiers of my Regiment. Permit me to request Sir, you will be pleased to present my humble respect & assurances to the Congress that my Life & Fortune are devoted to the Cause of the thirteen United States of America & to the general propagation of Liberty & that while my health & Strength will permit me I shall hold myself at the Command of my Country—

I have the honour to be with great respect,
   Sir
    Your mo: obedt & mo: hum. Servt
    | Signed | Wm Thomson
     Lieut. Col. Commandr of the
     Regt. of Rangers, being the
     3rd Regt. in So.Carolina

General Robert Howe. In Charles Town
  Camp at the Congarees 6th October 1776.

Sir
  The detachment of my Regiment which went to Georgia have not yet come to Head Quarters, but I expect them here in the course of this week — There are now in Camp 161 Officers & Privates, seven of whom are sick, the remainder all fit for duty — there are numbers sick also at their homes, unable to join the Regiment at present, but I expect them as soon as they recover — I believe I shall not move from here untill towards the 1st next month, when I intend to encamp near Nielson's ferry unless I receive orders to the contrary — I have not any news this way worth Your notice — I have the honour to be
   Sir
    Yours &cc. W. T

His Excellency John Rutledge Esq? In Charles Town
    Camp at the Congarees 6th October 1776.
  Sir
    Inclosed you have a Return of the Names &
dates of the Commissions of the Officers now in my
Regiment & likewise the names of the Gentlemen who
stand next for preferment — Lieut^s Brown & Hopkins being the two first oldest Lieutenants & good
Men, I beg you will be pleased to send Commissions
for them as by the Return you will see there are two
vacancies for Captains.— There are also vacancies
for four second Lieutenants, & I shall recommend the
first four Gentlemen now on the Recruiting service
who shall raise ten men each— The bearer Capt.
Richard Winn with a detachment & 2 waggons waits
for Your Excellencys orders — You will please to observe that the first Eighteen Officers in my Regiment
Rank by number & not by the dates of their Commissions—
        I have the honour to remain
            Your Excellencys &c^c
                W. T.

General Robert Howe,   In   Charles Town
              Amelia 15th October 1776.
  Sir
    Inclosed you have a Return of the detachment
marched to Georgia, a Copy of Your Letter concerning the Expedition is sent to the Officer Commanding
said detachment with orders strictly to adhere to &
punctually to obey your directions therein contained
I have directed the officer to Cross Savanna River below Augusta & from thence to proceed to Fort Barrington on the Alatainaha. The detachment is very
badly provided with ammunition.
  I am sorry to inform you that I have been confined

eleven days with a severe fever, which has rendered me incapable of getting out of bed without help, & that a great many of the officers & Men are very sick with a disorder called the Mumps, which is very brief in Camp, besides those who were before afflicted with the fever, which occasions the Camp to be very thin both of officers & men who are fit for duty—

I remain with great respect
Sir   Yours &C:
W. T.

A Return of the Detachment of Rangers Commanded by Capt John Caldwell, which marched from Camp at the Congarees on an Expedition to Georgia. The 14th October 1776—

	Captains	Lieuts	Serjeants	Privates	Total
Marched from Camp	2	3	3	93	101
To March this Week	...	1	1	7	9
	2	4	4	100	110

General Robert Howe,   In   Charles Town
Amelia 15th October 1776

Sir,
Your orders of the 12th I this moment received by Express, I shall do all in my power to get the Batallion together, tho' I am afraid it will be some days first — the detachment that went to Georgia under Major Mayson returned only last Thursday & the Major has given them leave of absence till the 6th of November, as they are at present much scattered & a

great deal of sickness amongst them will make it difficult to collect them together & I am afraid will not be effected so soon as you may want them or I could wish for & my not being in a condition to exert myself will be some hinderance, God knows when I shall be able to leave my room, but never-theless I shall give all necessary orders to collect them as quick as possible

      I remain
       Sir
        Yours &c$^{\underline{c}}$
        W. T.

Capt. John Caldwell, on A march towards the Southward—

      Amelia 18th October 1776

Sir

 By a Letter which I received from General Howe since I wrote You last, I have reason to think the remainder of my Regiment will be ordered towards Georgia should occasion require it, but should it be otherwise, I hope as soon as You have executed Your orders there You will join me with your detachment either at the Congarees or where you shall hear the Regiment is — I have ordered Lieut. Beames to join you immediately & to take with him a sufficient number of Men to complete the detachment

 I still continue confined to my room very sick, but hope to be soon better, when I may perhaps write you further— I wish you success & a Safe return to Camp — I remain

       Sirs Yours &C^c
          W. T.

General Robert Howe   In   Charles Town
℘ Capt Warley
Amelia 1st December 1776.

Sir
Please to receive inclosed a Return of my Regiment up to this day. I am extremely sorry it was not in my power to have sent You one sooner, but some of my Captains not coming to Camp agreeable to orders was the occasion of it, however you may rest assured that in future I shall transmit you Monthly Returns——
I should have done myself the pleasure of waiting on you long before this, had not my Ill state of health prevented me, but as I find myself grow stronger daily shall endeavour to do it some time this week
I remain with great respect
Yours &C. W. T.

Captain Richard Winn —   going to Georgia
Camp near Nelson's Ferry 28th Decem 1776

Sir
You are to proceed from Camp early tomorrow morning with the detachment under your Command for Georgia, there relieve Captain Caldwell & his detachment & follow such orders as he or the Commanding officer there may give you — You are to send me a Return of Your Detachment at least once a Month, in order that I may have it in my power to render in a monthly one to the General here —
I am
Sir
Yours &C
W. T.

₽ Captain Winn.
Captain John Caldwell, at Fort Barrington In Georgia
  Camp near Nelson's Ferry 28th Decem 1777*
 Sir

  I have sent Capt. Richard Winn & 2 Subalterns with 2 Serjeants & 50 Rank & File to relieve the Detachment under Your Command with directions to follow such orders as you or the Commanding officer in Georgia may give him, after which You are to proceed with Your said Detachment to the place of Encampment here where I shall be very glad to see you — Your several Letters did not come to hand untill three days after General Howe arrived in Town & then it was the first time that I heard from you since you left the Congarees — probably you could never meet with an opportunity to write me before however be that as it may I am very glad to hear that you & the other officers were all well, I wish you & them a happy new Year & a safe arrival in Camp—

    I remain with great regard
     Sir
      Yours &C^c
      W. T.

Major Morgan Conner   In Charles Town
      Amelia 2^d January 1777
      ₽ Lieut. Maskall.
 Sir

  Please to receive under cover hereof a Monthly Return of my Regiment up to the 1st Instant, as also one for General Howe, which I beg you will deliver to him — there are some of my officers, I am informed who will not take Continental Commissions — I expect to be in Town in the course of four or five days,

---
*1776.

when I shall do my self the pleasure of waiting on You and the General—
I am with great Esteem
Sir Yours &C^c
W. T.

His Excellency John Rutledge Esqr—In Charles Town
Camp near Nelson's Ferry 19th Jany 1777.

Sir
Agreeable to the request in Your Excellency's favour of the 17th Instant which I received last night ⅌ Express, I inclose a Return of my Regiment up to this day — Your Letter to Col. Sumter was forwarded to him immediately as it came to hand, but his answer is not yet arrived — I would have wrote Your Excellency more fully by this opportunity, but as I propose being in Town in a few days, must beg leave to postpone adding any more untill I have the pleasure of seeing Your Excellency.—
I remain with much Esteem
Your Excellency's mo: hum^b Servt
W. T.

Major Samuel Wise — Camp near Nelson's Ferry
Charles Town 25th April 1777.

Sir
In consequence of orders which I just received from His Excellency the President, I hope you will immediately on the receipt hereof, order 2 Captains 4 Lieutenants, 4 Serjeants 1 Drum & 1 Fife and 100 Rank & File well mounted with Twelve Waggons to Charles Town — Capt Warley is the first officer for Duty therefore You will please order the next Captain in turn, as also the Lieutenants — endeavour to procure the Waggons without pressing if possible, but at

any rate they must be had & with the greatest expedition — Capt. Kirshaw is sick here & unfit for Duty — the Pay Master I expect will receive his Money this day & will meet the Detachment on the road & pay them —

     I am
      Sir Yr mo: humbe Servt
           W. T–

General Robert Howe – – – – – Charles Town
   Camp near Nelson's Ferry 9th June 1777
Sir
  As I was necessitated to discharge those Men belonging to my Regiment who were enlisted to serve no longer than the 1st Instant, it has been the means of reducing the Regt. to a certain number now on the Continental Establishment, which you will be made acquainted with by the inclosed Return, excepting 6 Serjeants & 45 Privates to serve upwards of Twelve Months longer who were enlisted upon the first establishment of my Regiment — My sole motive for troubling you at present, is to beg Your opinion in what I shall take the liberty of proposing & receiving your advice thereupon ——

As there seems to be not the least expectation of an Enemy shortly, I would propose sending all my officers out on the Recruiting Service & giving Furlows to all the Men in Camp for two months (save about 30 or 40) to go home, with orders to Recruit as many men as they could possibly get; this method I presume would be of infinite service in procuring Recruits, as I am well convinced that many of the men have great weight & influence in & about where they live & that this indulgence might induce others to enlist —

Lieut. Col. Mayson who is the bearer of this will in-

form you of every particular relative to the Regiment to whom I beg leave to refer you —
 I remain with great respect
 Sir
 Yr Mo: humb Sevt:
 W. T.

His Excellency John Rutledge Esqr   Charles Town
 Camp near Nelson's Ferry 9th June 1777

Sir
 I take the liberty of informing Your Excellency that I have discharged all those men belonging to my Regiment, who were enlisted to serve this State untill the 1st Instant — The Reg^t is now reduced to a certain number on the Continental Establishment & 6 Serjeants & 45 Privates enlisted on the first Establishment of My Reg^t to serve for three Years, as you will perceive by the inclosed Return———
 I am of opinion that were these men at present in Camp given Furlows to, for two months, to go home, with orders to Recruit for My Regt it would be of infinite service, as I am very certain many of them have great weight & influence in & about the neighborhood where they live & this indulgence might be of great benefit to the Recruiting service; I also purpose sending the greatest part of my officers on the same duty & I make not the least doubt of my Regiment being tolerably forward before many months—
 I shall be very happy in receiving Your Excellencys Advice & Instructions as soon as possible — the bearer Lieut Col. Mayson can give you any intelligence relative to the Regiment, in the mean time, I beg leave to add that I am with great respect
 Yr Mo: humb. Servt
 W. T——

Sir   By Major Wise please to receive a return of my Regiment you will see by it that my officers has not returned from Recruiting I do not expect them until the 1 Septr Please to let Major Wise have 200 Muskets and Bayonets Flints and Carteridges paper I intend to have Muskets and Bayonets for my men except 100 which I would have complete Rifle men with good Horses and spears I would be much obliged to you for advice in remodeling my Regiment so as to make them of most service to the State I would have waited on you before this time had it not been for a Fall from my Horse which broke my brest Bone so that as yet I am not fit to Ride as soon as the officers Comes in will wait on you then I will be able to Judge how many Muskets I shall want

    I am Sir

     Your Most Hbl Servt

      W. T

P. S I have mentioned my intentions of new modeling my Regiment to his Excellency the president hope to obtain his approbation with yours——
Amelia 13th Augt 1777 To General Robert Howe

Sir

  By Major Wise you will receive a return of my Regiment you will see by it that my [officers] are not yet returned from recruiting Please to let Major Wise have 200 Muskets and Baynets Flints and Carteridge paper If you think it proper I will have Muskets for all my men except one hundred of the most expert to be Rifle men with good Horses and Spears I should be glad to receive your approbation and advice on new modeling my Regmt to make them of the most service to the State I should have waited on you my self before this Time had it not been for a

Fall from my Horse which broke my brest Bone and am not yet able to Ride I expect all my officers in by the first of Sept then I shall be able to make proper Return and know how many Muskets I shall want

       I am   Sir
Amelia 13th Augt, 1777   Your Most Hble Servt
             W. T.

To His Excellency John Rutledge Esquir

 Sir
  Inclosed you will Receive Copy of orders I received from his Excely you will do all in your power to have them complyed with especially Capt Lyle 2 lieuts 2 Serjents & 50 men will call on you Capt Caldwell, Capt Brown 4 Lieuts 4 serjents and 100 men well guard the goal they will acquaint Col Williamson as soon as arrive at 96 of there being there Please to order all the men that is on Furlow all new recruits to Camp immediately do let any Joyn the 100 at the Goal or Capt Lyles detachmen they may if you think proper a few if there should be any up there that would rather stay and send some of them down that went from Camp Capt Caldwell Brown and Lyle will send to me their pay Bill by the first of Sept
       I am
       Sir Your Hmble Servt
         W. T-

Col James Mayson

      Augt 16th 1777
 Sir
  You will proceed to Congarees and out of the detachment that is on their March with Capt Brown take 2 Lieuts 2 serjeants and 50 Men and March them to Col Mayson and there you will exert the best measures with him to take James Lindley Richard

Pearce and John Parker and on good Evidence any that is concerned with them and send them to Charlestown under a Good Guard

       I am Sir
To   Your Hble Sevt
Capt Lyles   W: T.

    17th Augt 1777
Sir

 As soon as you arrive at Congarees with the Detachment under Your Command You will Detach off Capt Lyall 2 Lieuts 2 Serjeants and 50 men Capt Lyall has his orders where to march them then you will proceed with the remainder of your Detachment 96 where you are to Guard the Goal as soon as you arrive there you will acquaint Col And^w Williamson with your arrival and orders Please be careful to march the Men early in the morning that their March may be over before the heat of the Day I am Sir
       Your Hble Sevt
       W. T.

 I have sent 20 ℔ of my own Powder and 50 ℔ Lead And some Flints of the publicks to your Detachment You will divide with Capt Lyalls

To Capt Brown.

    23 August 1777
Sir

 Inclosed you will receive a Copy of orders I this moment received from his Excelency the President please to peruse it observe the contents and do all in your power to have them immediately comply'd with if in your power take the Command your self if not give great Charge to the Commanding officer of the Detachment to be careful of the Indians. If Mrs Mayson is not Delivered I can not expect you to go I

hope Capt Caldwell will exert himself on this occasion as I make no doubt he will let him know the Gover^{ns} orders on that head and my earnest request to have them comply'd with &c— Inclosed you have a News paper I this moment rec^d from our Major. I am much better then when I wrote to you last Please to order all the officers and men (that does not belong to the Detachment brown gave up) to repair to Camp with all convenient speed Lieut Crowders and Mascal is both very sick at Camp I am
—Sir
Yours Hble Servt
W. T.

To Colonel James Mayson
near
Ninety Six

15th September 1777

Sir
You will please order 50 horse men & 50 foot men Properly officer'd to Guard Ninety Six goal or any other service that may be required of them, all the Remainder of the Two Detachments you will order to Camp with the officers, Please to order Lieut Thomson down as I have Provided a Place in Town for him (that is School) Please send after any Deserters you hear of Belonging to our Regiment or any other of our States Regiments
I am Sir Your most Huble
W. T.

Lt Col^o James Mayson Senr.

15th September 1777—

Sir
I came yesterday from Town after being there 8 days in the hottest weather I ever felt Endeavouring to get Cloths for my men. Bought cloth a £15 ℔ yd

& Scarlet D:o a £25 ⅌ yd hope to be able to Clothe them
Compleatly as soon as Capt Hatten Arrives, who went
to France for Clothing for the Soldiers — the Assembly has Voted that the Soldiers should have 1 Coat 1
Jacote 1 ⅌ Breeches 2 Shirts 2 ⅌ Stockings 2 ⅌ Shoes
1 Black Cravat and 1 Blanket each year. I hope this
Ample Provision for Soldiers will make some that are
like to Lay cold this winter list in our Regiment—
I saw the Pay Master in Town he told me he had but
seven Returns, I am sorry to see that my request to
the officers has been treated with Disreguard I saw an
order from you on the same head as Little Noticed I
should be sorry to See in my Orderly Book any orders
that would not be a credit to them whom I so much
Esteem — John James Haig is appointed Our Pay
Master. I shall send to Town with the other Returns
as soon as they come to hand and the Money shall go
up as soon as Posible, Pray excuse me in answering
your Letters in full as I am very unwell I had the
fever Friday with heat & Fatigue Lt. Crowther has
been very sick but is recouverd & is well Mr. Richardson told me he had sent you the Papers or I Should

       I am Sir Yr Huble —
To   Sevt W. T.
Lt- Col:o James Mayson

      Camp at Orangeburgh 2 Oct:r 1778

 Sir

  In consequence of a copy of your Orders forwarded to me by Col:o Huger dated 17th September —
I joined the first Detachment under Capt F Warley
the 24th at this Place — on the 25th Capt Browns Detachment arrived at the same place from Nelsons
Ferry — On the 1st Inst: arrived Col:o Mayson with
the Remainder of my Reg:t all safe — & at 10 oclock

yesterday evening Your orders ⅌ Express of 26th Sept' came to hand which I shall immediately Comply with

    I am with Esteem
     Sir Yours &C'

P. S.
 I am sorry to acquaint you that from the behaviour of Lt Taggart to and at this place I have been under the Necessity of Putting him under arrest ——
To
 The Honble M. G. Howe

    Camp at Orangeburgh 20 N 1778
Sir
 On the Cover of M General Howes orders I Received a line from you of the 27th Ins Informing me I should Renew Orders from You & General Howe — the Latter is come to hand Perhaps the Express may have lost your orders to me as they are not as yet arrived

 The River in our Neighborhood has been Exceeding high and done as much Damage The Particulars of which I have not time at Present to Mention
     I am Sirs Yrs &C'
To
Col° Isac Huger

   Camp Orangeburgh 3d October 1778
Sir
 You are to take post with the Detachment under your Command at or near the Place where Capt Smith lately encamp'd fully empowered to remove that post to one that may keep the inhabitants & their monys secure from the inrodes & Deprodations of such unlawfull Banditty as may cross Savannah River keeping out scouting parties to Aid the Disaffected,

and Protect those citizens who are well affected in their Persons & Propertys You will use every effort in Your Power to cut off all Intercourse & Connection between the inhabitants of this State and those of East Florida, and should such persons fall into your hands, or into the hands of those under Your Command you will in that case act agreeable to the Laws of the land & articles of war You will give such aid to the Civil Authority & to the Militia as may Crush & subdue at every Hazzard Those Publick Disturbers of Peace & good order You will keep up the strictest Dicipline & take the greatest care of the arms of those Men under Your Command & see they Do not want or Destroy their Clothing and amunition Those crimes are not to Escape Your Notice or go unpunish'd you are to take great care you are not surpris'd in Your encampment having always your Arms & accoutrements Ready & well prepared fit for action

Should you Receive any Intellegence of Consequence You are immediately to Transmit it to head Quarters & I should strongly recommend that once in Ten days the parties from Capt[ns] Browns & Smiths Detachments may meet & give each other such Intelligence as may Contribute much to the advantage of the Service You are sent upon, and at the same time informing me or the Command:g officer in Camp, that I, or he may give orders accordingly You will keep an Exact Jurnal of Your proceedings which will accompany your letters in order that Government may be guarded against such applications as will be made by Persons who in Corse of Service will Complain

      I am Sir Your Most
       Obt W. T——

Orangeburgh 3ᵈ Octʳ 1778——

Sir
    Inclos'd You will please receive the Commissions of Lieutenants Hart & Thomson the Two Eldest Lieutenants in my Regiment whose Resignation is owing to the new Establish'ᵗ taking place in the army which Deprives them of Captains Rank according to the old one allso Lt Crowthers Commission who is going into Trade Capᵗˢ Brown and Hopkins with 2 Lieutˢ 4 Sergᵗˢ & 65 Rank & file March this morning for Silver Bluff on Savannah River & Captˢ Smith & Jas: Warley with the same number of officers & men for Savannah River near Mathews' Bluff with such orders to them Respectively as you have ordered —— I shall Indeavour to send the Return of the Military Stores in a few Days.
                      I am wᵗʰ great Respect
                        Sir Yours &Cc

To
His Excellency M G Howe
       Town

                Orangeburgh 3ᵈ Octʳ 1778——

Sir
    By the inclosed Roster of my Regiment you will find that I have now only ten Companies the Compᵞˢ of the Late having Distributed Captᵘˢ R Goodwyn & Maskall 1 agreeable to the new Establishment, I have sent off this Morning two Detachments consisting each of 2 Capᵗˢ 2 Subalterns 4 Sergˢ & 65 Rank & file one for Silver Bluff & the other for Matthews Bluff on Savannah.
    You will please observe that in several of the Pay Bills now sent Down that there have been many men omitted to be Return'd for, owing entirely to some off

ours being so offen Detach'd from their Companies
I am wth Great Respect
Yours &Cc

To
His Excellency
Rowlen Lownds Esqr
President & Comm^r in chief
in & for the State So Carolena

Orangeburgh 3^d Octr 1778

Sir

  This morning agreeabe to Genl. Howes Orders I sent off Two Detachments each of 2 Captains 2 Sub^{ns} 4 Sargeants & 65 Rank & file for Silver Bluff & Matthews Bluff on Savannah River. Capt Richd Brown Commands one & Capt John Carraway Smith the other — in a few day I shall make you a Monthly Return of the Regiment also a Return of the Military Stores belong to it —

To
  Col^o Isaac Huger

Camp Orangeburgh 19 Octr 1778

Sir

  Inclos'd you have a Monthly Return of my Regiment up to the 16th Instant allso a Return of the arms & accoutrements with a Return of the Stores as far as it is in my Power to make it at Present — one of the Villians who Rob'd this place is now in goal — If I am Rightly inform'd Seven More of the Same gang will never do any more Mischief — I have Likewise Inclosed the Charge against Lt Taggart. I should be glad you'd lett me know whether the Dochester guard is to be Returned from Town or from here

To   I am Sir Your Most
 Col I Huger   Humble Servt: W T

Orangeburgh 19th October 1778

Sir
    Inclos'd You have a Return of my Reg^t up to the 16th Inst: Chavis one of the Villians who was at the Robery of this place is now in goal, & If I am Rightly inform'd then Seven more of the same gang will never do, commit any more Roberys, which has Pritty well Quieted the Disturbances at Present, when I came to this place it seemed to be in great Confution it was hard Judging between Whigg & Tory, which was best

    My Orders when I came here was to Protect the Civill Power, but I could find more to Protect, on the whole thing Seem to be more Settled in these Parts than ever they were Since our Troubles First began I hope to be in Town Next Week, when I will do myself the pleasure of waiting on You & giving you further Particulars

To His Excellency   Sign'd   W. T-
    R Lowns

Amelia 23^d Octr 1778

Dear Sir
    I gladly Rec^d Yours of 20th Inst: I am Sorry to find, that heathen like Principle Still Remaining in the inhabitants of the frontiers knowing to be the beginners of all Comotions wth the Indians, Save that of 76 with Cherokees, I have sent orders to Capt Brown to furnish you wth as great a number of men, as he can spare only leaving a small guard at the Passes — & Should Capt Brown not be able to Spare you a sufficient number you will Please apply to Capt Smith at or near Matthews Bluff for 20 men having wrote to Capt Smith, that should you apply for that number to Send them immediately — I should think

myself happy in Corresponding with you when ever it may be Convenient

      I am D S Your Most
        Hmbl Servt: W T——
Geo Golphin Esqr:

      Amelia 23^d October 1778——
D. Sir

 I Rec^d Yours of the 19th Inst: wth the Return of Your Detachment, & am Exceeding glad to hear you are well —— If Mr Golphin should apply for a Guard to go to Ogeechie with him youl Please furnish him with all you can Spare leaving a sufficient number to guard the Passes — My complements to all the officers

      I am D S Yrs &Cc
C. R. Brown   W. T——

     Amelia 23^d October 1778——

Sir

 I have not had the Pleasure of hearing from you Since you left Camp, tho Expect to hear by the Pay Master —— Should Mr Golphin apply to you for any number of men not Exceeding 20 Youl Please send them Immediately My compliments to all the officers

      I am Sir Yrs &Cc
Capt Jno C Smith   W T

   Camp at Orangeburgh 21st October 1778—
Sir

 You will Proceed with the party under Your Command to Morrises Ford on North Fork of Edistoe River, when there, You will do your utmost indeavours to Cut off all Intercourse & Communication between the inhabitants of this State & those of East Florida and take up & send to me all Suspected Persons at or near your Post likewise to inform me of any Matter that is going on any where else, or any thing else that may come within Your Knowledge besides Your Post that will be of any Service or Disservice to this State — If any of the above mention'd Persons should fall into Your hands, you will send them here under a strong guard, You will Remain at or near S^d Post until further Orders

Sign'd   W T

To
    Lt Chas M Genney

Amelia 29th October 1778 —

Sir
    You wrote me some time past that the Blanketts & other Clothing the Remainder of what is Due. to the 3^d Regiment was Ready for them I have Sent a waggon for them — Please to deliver them to Corporal Daniel Shannon

I should have come to Town but hear it is very Sickly in town I shall Refir coming untill Froast Please to Send me a Bill of what you Deliver to the corporal — If there is any thing more than what I have had from you, due or that I may have a right to Receive out of the Publick Store

Please to Receive it for me and You will much oblige

Your Most Obd^t. Servt
Sign'd   W. T-

To
Jno Sandaford Dart Esqr
    Clothes Genl. for State of
        So Carolina

Amelia 3rd November 1778

Sir/
I Received Yours of the 30th this day about one O'clock with the dispatches from the Governor & Major Gen! How, I am much obliged to you for Complying with part of them in Sending the Men with Cannon; Please to Enquire amongst the Men & Know who of them has Horses within one or two days Travel of the Camps, send them for them that we may be able to comply with the other Order in Gen*r*. How*s*. Dispatches.

I should have been at Orangeburgh on Monday, but one of my Children has been Ill with the fever, which has never Intermitted this Eight days, as soon as She gets bettor I shall be at Camp.

Please to send a man with the Inclosed to Captains Brown & Smith as soon as Possible and the one to Lieut. M*c*Gines

I am
Yours &C
(True Copy)   William Thomson

To
Capt*n*. John Donaldson

Amelia 3rd November 1778

Sir
When Colonel Williamson Requires, you and The detachment (or any part of them) under Your Command You are to aid & Co operate with him.

I am Yours &C*c*
(A True Copy)   W*m* Thomson

Amelia 3rd November 1778

Sir
When Colonel Williamson Requires, you and

the detachment (or any part of them) under Your Command, you are to aid & Co operate with him.
I am
A True Copy   Yours &C:
        Sign,d   William Thomson
To
Captain John C: Smith

Amelia 3rd Novr. 1778.

Sir/
On Receipt of this You are to March The Men Under Your Command to Camp having A Guard of a Sergant & five Men in as private a place as possible, let them be men that you can depend upon, with orders to follow you to Camp in six days after you leave them, if they make no Discoveries, leave with the Sergant the same orders you received upon that Command.
I am Yours &C:
        Signed   Wm Thomson
A True Coppy
To Lieut^t McGines*

Section 4. Other Continentals from Orangeburgh District.

It has been stated that the 3rd regiment (Thomson's) of regulars contained many Orangeburgh men. The 1st regiment (Gadsden's, C. C. Pinckney's) also contained some Orangeburgh men, for Rev. C. C. Pinck-

---

*The foregoing is a copy of Colonel William Thomson's Order Book, owned, and loaned to me, by Judge A. C. Haskell. . With the exception of several pages, it was copied by me, and I certify that this is a true copy of said book.
        Susan Richardson Guignard,
Columbia, S. C.,   Member D. A. R.
  Jan. 28th, 1898.

ney, D. D., says, in his "Life of Thomas Pinckney", page 27, that as soon as Captain Thomas Pinckney was authorized to enlist men, in July, 1775: "He at once determined to fill up the ranks of his company, and went to Orangeburg to gather recruits. As soon as he had obtained the requisite number of fifty men, his military knowledge was put into requisition", &c. And again, on page 48, Dr. Pinckney says: "Recruiting formed a large part of his duty during these earlier years of the war. He had already visited Orangeburg, and enlisted three fourths of his own company in that district."*

And, in passing, it is well to relate that when General Armstrong visited the South in 1776 to inspect the Continental troops, his brigade-major (Conner) "pronounced the first South Carolina regiment the best disciplined on the continent."

When the first three regiments of regulars were formed in June, 1775, Isaac Huger, who owned a plantation in St. Mathew's Parish, and had several times represented that Parish in the Colonial Assembly, was, on June 3rd, elected lieutenant-colonel of the 1st regiment. It is likely that his influence took some Orangeburgh men into that regiment.

---

*And here it may be interesting to add that he visited Orangeburgh District several times before the war ended, for in 1779 he attended Court in Orangeburgh, and successfully defended some prisoners who had erred through ignorance of military law. And we should also judge that he had been attending court at the Motte plantation, since in the same year he was married to Miss. Elizabeth Motte. And again, after the battle of Camden, where he was wounded and captured, he repaired, under parole, to the Motte place to recuperate and be nursed.

GEN. ISAAC HUGER.
FROM AN OLD PRINT.

In addition to the four regiments raised in 1775, two regiments of riflemen were voted in February, 1776. Lieut. Col. Isaac Huger, of the 1st regiment, was made Colonel of the first regiment of rifles, which was, in July of that year, taken into the Continental service, and thenceforward known as the 5th regiment of South Carolina Continentals. It is also likely that Col. Huger* had some Orangeburgh men with him in that regiment.

Although we have not been able to find any of the rolls of any of the companies of the Continental line, we have extracted from a pension roll, dated as late as 1840, the following names of Revolutionary soldiers of the Continental Establishment from Orangeburgh District:

Orange Parish.

Leven Argrove,
Hugh Phillips,
Andrew Houser,
Erasmus Gibson.

St. Mathew's Parish.

Adam Garick.

Barnwell.

Tarleton Brown,
Jesse Griffen,
Daniel O'Dom,
Henry B. Rice.

---

*Col. Huger was appointed brigadier general January 9, 1777.

Section 5. The Local Militia.

Besides those who fought in the regular service, Orangeburgh District furnished many men to the militia branch of the service. In the early days of the war militia companies were formed in every section of the Colony. Their rolls were sent down to the Council of Safety by whom they were generally approved and their officers commissioned, and the companies assigned to regiments.

In 1775 the militia of the Province consisted of thirteen regiments, nearly every officer of which, and the large majority of the men of which, signed the Association.

The Orangeburgh District regiment had William Thomson for its colonel, Christopher Rowe for its lieutenant-colonel, and Lewis Golson for its major.* The lower district between the Broad and Saluda rivers, the greater part of which was in Orangeburgh District, had a regiment of which Robert Starke was colonel, Moses Kirkland, lieutenant-colonel, and —— Tyrrel, major. After Colonel Thomson was made colonel of the 3rd regiment of regulars (Rangers), the command of the Orangeburgh District regiment devolved upon Rowe, though Col. Thomson seems to have exercised a sort of supervision over it, and, in the back country expeditions in 1775, spoke of it as, "my regiment of militia."† And during the siege of Charlestown, and after his exchange, he probably resumed command of the regiment.

On November 21st, 1775, the Provincial Congress adopted the following resolution: "That all corps of

---

*Drayton's Memoirs, Vol. I, page 353.

†In a letter to the Council of Safety, dated Nov. 28, 1775, Col. Thomson stated that three of the militia companies existed in his immediate neighborhood.

Regulars take precedence of all corps of Militia, and that the regiments of Militia shall take precedence in the following manner: 1. Berkeley County. 2. Charles Town. 3. Granville County. 4. Colleton County. 5. Craven County, the lower part. 6. Orangeburg. 7. Craven County, the upper part. 8. Camden. 9. Ninety-Six, north of the Fish Dam Ford and between Enoree, Broad and Saluda Rivers. 10. The New Acquisition, south of the Fish Dam Ford and between Broad and Saludy Rivers, north of Enoree and between Broad and Saludy Rivers."

In the Provincial Congress on March 23rd, 1776, it was resolved: "That the fork between Saluda and Broad Rivers, be divided into three regiments, according to the division of districts by the resolve of Congress of the 9th February last; one regiment in each of the districts." The lower or "Dutch Fork", regiment was probably commanded by Col. Jonas Beard, as we find, by a letter to Gen. Moultrie, dated April 6th, 1778, mention made by President Lowndes of "Col Beard" and his regiment of militia at "the Congarees."

The militia of South Carolina were, on March 28th, 1778, divided into three brigades, commanded by Generals Stephen Bull, Richard Richardson, Sr., and Andrew Williamson, respectively. Gen. Richardson lived in the Parish of St. Mark's, which was across the Santee from Orangeburgh District, and Gen. Williamson lived in Ninety-Six District adjoining Orangeburgh District on the North, and it is therefore likely that the bulk of the militia of Orangeburgh District belonged to these brigades, though some belonged to Bull's brigade as is shown by Tarleton Brown in his "Memoirs."*

---

*By the "Return of the Different Detachments on duty at Savannah in Georgia, under the Command of Colonel Stephen Bull", we

After the fall of Charlestown, General Richardson having previously resigned,* General Bull having been paroled by the British, and General Williamson having taken British protection, Governor Rutledge commissioned Colonels Thomas Sumter, Francis Marion and Andrew Pickens as brigadiers of militia. Subsequently John Barnwell was made a brigadier of militia; and it said that Col. James Williams had just received a brigadier's commission when killed at King's Mountains.

These officers were each given, by Governor Rutledge, military jurisdiction over a certain territory. In his proclamation of August 5th, 1781, Governor Rutledge warns all persons holding any property of the enemy "to deliver it to the brigadier general of the district in which it is"; and again in his proclamation of September 27th, 1781, he stated that "the several brigadiers of militia" had been ordered to perform certain functions "within their respective districts".

It is probable that a part of Orangeburgh District—the upper and western sections—was in Pickens's militia district, and the western part, from the North Edisto to the Santee, in Sumter's militia district.

These militia brigades were very well organized and rendered valuable service, but as the militia law was quite lax, the men dispersed to their plantations at pleasure, and only assembled in times of great public danger, or when there was a chance of a fight. The result of this was that a brigade was often reduced to the size of a company. This free and easy, come and

---

learn that 1 captain, 1 lieutenant, 2 sergeants, 1 drummer and 24 privates of the New Windsor company, and 1 captain and 8 privates of the Upper Three Runs company were present at Savannah on March 15th, 1776, soon after the British attack on that place.

*He died soon after resigning.

go method of campaigning has induced many writers to apply the term "partisan militia" to the brigades of Sumter, Marion and Pickens; but is a mistake to suppose that these were Robin Hood sort of bands. They were regularly established militia brigades with Governor Rutledge's power and authority behind them. And Governor Rutledge's power and authority emanated from the State legislature, and, therefore, from the people.

But there were many militia companies that acted independently at times of the regiments and brigades to which they belonged, and without any special authority from a superior officer. There are many interesting traditions concerning several of these militia companies of Orangeburgh District.

One of them was commanded by Captain Jacob Rumph, who lived about five miles above Orangeburg village. It probably formed a part of Rowe's regiment. It is said to have marched to Savannah, in 1778, to join the American army in besieging that town, but arrived too late, the siege having been abandoned.

Mr. C. M. McMichael, of this County says that his father, Jacob McMichael,* has often related to him many of the exploits of Rumph's company which had been related to him by Lieut. Wannamaker, and says that his father has often pointed out to him the spot whereon Rumph's house stood, and also a large oak whereon he said Rumph hung many Tories. His father was a boy of 10 or 12 during the Revolution, and lived not many miles from Capt. Rumph, and he further related to Mr. McMichael that Rumph had a "bull pen" wherein he kept his prisoners.

Leaving tradition and returning to records, it is a

---

*Whose first wife was a niece of Capt. Rumph, and a daughter of Lieut. Wannamaker' of Rumph's company.

certainty that Capt Rumph still commanded a company of militia in Orangeburgh District in 1784, as will be seen by the following extract from Judge O'Neall's "Bench and Bar of South Carolina", page 341:

"November, 1784.

"Mr. Justice Heyward.

"On motion of Mr. Sheriff, ordered that Capt. Jacob Rumph do immediately send six men, out of his company, to guard the gaol for the space of seven days; and that, after the expiration of seven days, ordered that Capt. Henry Felder do relieve the aforesaid six men with six men from his company, to continue seven days; and that, after said term, Capt. Rumph shall again send the same compliment of men to relieve Capt. Felder's men, and so each to relieve the other alternately, until the prisoners now confined in gaol, and under sentence of death, be executed according to sentence, or otherwise disposed of." (From Circuit Court records.)

Below is a roll of Capt Rumph's company. It was first published in the Clayton, Alabama, *Banner*, and had, it is said, been furnished that paper by the holder of the original roll. A copy of the published roll was sent to the *Southron*, a newspaper published in Orangeburg about 1860, by the late Capt A. Govan Salley, and it was republished in the *Southron* on September 10, 1861, with the remark that the editor had "no doubt of its authenticity", and that it was "worthy of remark that after the lapse of three-quarters of a century, the names, with scarcely an exception, still exist among the present inhabitants of Orangeburg District." The writer then adds: "The following are the names of Capt Jacob Rumph's men who fought the Tories of South Carolina in 1783, Orangeburg District, commanded by Col Wm Russell Thomson."

The writer was wrong in giving the date 1783, and

he also probably mixed Wm Russell Thomson up with Wm. Thomson, his father.

Jacob Rumph, Captain

Jacob Wannamaker, 1st Lt. Lewis Golson Sergeant
John Golson, 2nd Lt. David Gisendanner, Clerk
Frederick Snell Jesse Pearson
John Cooke Jacob Amaka
Henry Whestone, (Whetstone) Jacob Hoegar, (Horger)
Peter Snell Christian Inabnet
John Moorer George Shingler
John Ditchell Anthony Robinson
Paul Stroman John Cooney, (Cooner)
Jacob Riser Jacob Stroman
Abram Miller John Deremus, (Deramus)
John Lemmerman, (Zimmerman) Jacob Cooney, (Cooner)
John Whestone, (Whetstone) Thomas Aberhart
Michael Zigler, (Zeigler) John Stroman
Peter Pound Nicholas Dill
John Ott Peter Staley
David Rumph Nicholas Rickenbacker
John Rumph Nicholas Hulong, (Herlong)
John Hoober, (Hoover) John Inabnet
John Densler, (Dantzler) John Houk
John Miller Jacob Rickenbacker
Henry Wannamaker Robert Bayley, (Baily)
John Amaka Arthur Barrot
Michael Larey, Frederick Burtz
George Ryly, (Riley) Peter Crouk, (Crook)
John Amaka Martin Grambik
John Brown John Dudley
Daniel Bowden John Rickenbacker
Wm Hall Isaac Lester

Benj. Collar, (Culler)   Henry Lester
Conrad Crider   Henry Stroman
Abram Ott   John Housliter

The company is said to have numbered seventy men, but it is evident that there are only sixty-five names on the above list.

Many thrilling stories of the exploits of Rumph's daring partisans are told by the old people of this section, but, while many of them are no doubt ill-founded, or badly mixed up with other occurrences, they are worth preserving, and perhaps future discoveries in the way of records will either confirm or destroy their truth.

The following account of some of the exploits in which Rumph's company was engaged is taken from the *Southern Cabinet* for 1840. The article is signed "J.", and was probably written by Gen. David F. Jamison, of Orangeburg, a grandson of Capt Rumph, who signed most of his articles simply "J":

"After the siege and fall of Charleston in the year 1780, and the shameful violation of the articles of treaty by the British officers, the war in South Carolina became essentially of a partisan character. The State was overrun, but not subdued. Bold spirits arose everywhere to assert their liberties, and they were frequently and instantaneously crushed by a powerful and unsparing foe, and no recollection now survives of themselves or their deeds; but not all of them thus perished. One fearful contest tradition has preserved, which I will endeavor to record—a struggle of man with his fellow man, a pursuit, a pistol shot and a death.

"Capt Jacob Rumph, (known after the Revolution better perhaps, as Gen Rumph,) of Orangeburg District, was the commander of a troop of cavalry raised in his neighborhood to protect themselves and their families, who lost no occasion of aiding their friends or annoying their enemies. They are all gone; history has not recorded their names, but few bolder spirits struck for liberty in that eventful war. Capt. Rumph was a man of prodigious size and strength, of great courage and coolness in the hour of danger, and though of a harsh and imperious disposition, no one was better fitted for the command of the hardy and intrepid men who composed his corps. They were usually dispersed at their ordinary avocations on their farms, but they united at a moment's warning from their leader.

"Not long after Charleston was taken by the British Capt. Rumph was returning with two of his wagons, which had been sent to Charleston with produce in charge of a Dutchman named Houselighter, and while slowly riding in company with his wagons on a small but strong horse, his mind gloomily brooding over the oppressed and almost hopeless condition of South Carolina, he had reached a large pond, on what is now called the old road, about seven miles below the village of Orangeburg, when he was suddenly roused by the approach of three men on horseback, whom he instantly recognized as his most deadly foes. They were well mounted, and armed like himself with sword and pistol. When the horsemen had reached the opposite side of the road to Capt. Rumph they halted for a moment and would have approached him nearer, but he, placing himself in the best posture of defence he could, called out to them: 'Gentlemen, stand off—I wish to have nothing to do with you!' The Tories, for such they were, surveyed him for an instant, and after a short conference with each other, to Capt. Rumph's great relief, rode on, and soon disappeared at the next turn of the road.

"Rumph, though he saw with no little satisfaction that the Tories had passed on, yet was too well acquainted with them to suppose for a moment that he was to get off so easily. He knew very well that the short respite they had thus given him was only that with an increased force he might become their prey with less danger to themselves. He rightly conjectured that the three who had passed him on the road were only scouts sent to apprehend him if unarmed, and who, if he had incautiously suffered them to approach him, would have shot him down while off his guard. Casting his eyes about a moment for means of escape from his wily foes, the danger of his situation became fully apparent. The three troopers he knew belonged to the corps of the sanguinary Cuningham, a part of which, he was certain, was in the neighborhood, under the command of one of his subaltern officers, and Capt. Rumph, after carefully surveying his situation, became fully conscious of his extreme danger of falling into the hands of his merciless foes. He was mounted upon a strong but slow horse, and the thought of escape on horseback was abandoned by him without hesitation. He was armed with a trusty cut and thrust sword and a brace of pistols, but it would have been madness, he well knew, to think of exposing himself to such odds as he was sure would be brought against him. There was no time to be lost. His only chance of escape at once flashed across his mind, and he immediately set about executing it. He rode his horse up to the pond already mentioned, and tied him fast to a tree. He then took off the greater part of his clothes and left them near his horse, to induce the suspicion that he had concealed himself in that pond. But that was very far from his real intention. He walked in the water near the margin of the pond until he had gained the side opposite to which he had tethered his horse, and, choosing with some caution the place at which he could best leave it, he set off at a rapid rate through the pine woods for home, a distance of some sixteen miles.

"In the meantime the three troopers, who, as Capt. Rumph truly supposed, were a party detached to seize, him if they could, returned to their main body, consisting of about twenty men under the command of Lieut. Parker, and reported the situation in which they had left Capt. Rumph. Without loss of time the party set off to overtake him. Upon their arrival at the pond they found that the wagons had proceeded but little distance from the spot which they occupied when the three Tories passed them, and Capt. Rumph's horse and clothes were in the same situation in which they had been left by him. The whole party rode up to the wagon and fiercely inquired of poor Houselighter, who was pale with terror, where Rumph was. He pointed to the pond, and they rode up to the place where the horse was tied, and when they saw his clothes and other signs of Rumph's having taken to the pond, they surrounded it on every side, and, dismounting, they entered it sword in hand, and searched every place where he could possibly have been concealed. But their search was fruitless. Rumph was far on his way towards home before those who were so eagerly thristing for his blood could satisfy themselves that he was not there. Irritated by the escape of the prey which they were so confident they had in their grasp, while one party scoured the neighboring woods in search of Capt. Rumph, the other party took charge of the wagons, and, after taking such of the horses as could be serviceable to them, they stripped the wagons of everything they could not carry away and burnt them to ashes with the remaining part of their freight. They worried poor Houselighter until he was ready to die with fear and left him.*

"Capt. Rumph reached home about sunset, with the determination to give his pursuers chance of a fight with less odds on one side, and he immediately set about collecting the scattered members of his corps. This was soon accomplished, and they, about twenty-five in number, were ready to set off in pursuit of the Tories by daylight the next morning.

"This party had proceeded for several hours on their way, and had nearly reached the spot where the wagons, of their leader had been burned the day before, and which was the scene of his perilous escape, when they were informed that the Tories, not far below, were feeding their horses near the road and were wholly unprepared for an attack. The patriots were prepared for an attack. The patriots were extremely anxious to be led to the charge. Just before their eyes were the evidences of the wanton destruction of property by the Tories, and their momories could readily supply numberless instances of their horrid barbarity, rapine and murder. They proceeded at a quickened pace along the road and soon their enemies appeared in the situation in which they had been described, with their horses carelessly feeding with their saddles on, their bridle-bits out of their mouths and their riders lying about in groups, or sleeping apart from the rest on the ground. No surprise could have been more complete. The Tories discovered their opponents at the distance of three or four hundred yards and at once prepared for fight. They soon caught their horses, bridled them and in an instant were

---

*Houselighter, who was then a mere boy, lived to a great old age, and there are several old gentlemen of this section who well remember him and his quaint Dutch expressions. He often told how Cuningham's men took his own wagon whip and flogged him severely with it.

mounted and flying in every direction. 'Save, who can', was the only word. Capt. Rumph and his troopers dashed down upon them and as the Tories scattered, everyone for himself, the patriots were obliged to single out and pursue, as they were nearly equal in number, almost every one his man. Various were the results of that fight and pursuit.

"It was the fortune of Lieut. Parker, the officer in command of the Tories, to be singled out by Lieut. Wannamaker, of Capt. Rumph's Troop. Wannamaker was a man of singular boldness and true devil-may-care sort of spirit. He was a fine horseman, and on this occasion was uncommonly well-mounted. In this respect, however, he was not superior to Parker; for after a chase of nearly two miles Wannamaker had gained but little, if any, upon Parker, but, unfortunately for the latter, after keeping well ahead for that distance, and while looking back to see if the enemy was gaining upon him, his horse carried him under a stooping tree, which struck him a violent blow upon the left shoulder as he rode under it and knocked him nearly off, and in his struggle to recover himself his saddle turned and got under the belly of his horse. In that situation he rode for some distance at an evident disadvantage, and Wannamaker began to gain upon him. Parker's horse, however, broke the girth and the saddle fell, so that Parker was again, for a while, able to keep Wannamaker at a safe distance. But it soon became apparent to Parker's great dismay, that his horse's wind was failing from being ridden without a saddle. In vain he whipped and spurred his jaded horse. Wannamaker was shortening the distance between them at every leap. Parker beheld him nearly within pistol shot, and, frightened beyond measure, he took off his hat and beat his horse on the sides with it to accelerate his speed. It succeeded for a moment, but the fagged horse had done his utmost. Wannamaker was just behind, and called out to him with presented pistol: 'Parker, halt! or I will kill you.' Parker heeded not, but continued with renewed violence his blows with his hat. Wannamaker approached nearer and called to him again, but still he rode on. Wannamaker called to him again, the third time, and offered him quarter, but the unhappy man knew that he had no right to expect that mercy which he had never given, and halted not. 'Halt, Parker!' said Wannamaker. 'I have told you the last time.' Parker rode on. Wannamaker, fearing something might occur to incline the chances against him, approached the doomed man within half a horse's length, and fired. Parker rode erect for a moment, but his hold soon relaxed—he fell backwards on his horse, rolled heavily off, and expired. J."

That "J." was mistaken in saying that history had not recorded the names of the patriotic men of Rumph's company is attested by the resurrection of the original roll, and its publication in the Alabama paper. It has several times been reprinted in South Carolina newspapers. Lieut. Wannamaker often said, after he had had time to reflect upon the matter, that he regretted having killed Parker, as he had often thought that perhaps Parker had been stunned by his contact with the tree, and could not hear him calling to him. But, on the other hand, it is quite likely that Parker preferred to die the death of a soldier than run the risk of being hung by Capt. Rumph; for traditionary accounts of Rumph say he was a perfect martinet, and seldom showed his enemies quarter.

From the traditionary accounts handed down to Mr. McMichael we also learn that it was Capt. Rumph who drove "Bloody Bill" Cuningham to his deeds of violence. The account says that Cuningham was a member of Rumph's company in the early days of the war,* and a good soldier; but that he had a brother, who was a Tory. One day this brother† was captured by Rumph's men, and Rumph, as was his custom, ordered him to be immediately hanged. William Cuningham came up and begged that his brother be spared, and said to Capt. Rumph: "If you will let him go I will guarantee that he will quit the Tories and join our company and make as good Whig as any man in the company", but Rumph was obdurate, and had the brother strung up. Cuningham quietly mounted his horse, and riding up to Capt. Rumph remarked: "From this day forth I am your deadly enemy. I have nothing against your men, but we must go different roads", and he rode off in a gallop. Capt. Rumph ordered his men to shoot him, but such was the esteem in which he had been held, and such was the sympathy for him, that not a man obeyed the order; and from that time on Cuningham was the enemy of the Whigs, and the especial enemy of Capt. Rumph. Lorenzo Sabine's work, "American Loyalists", also states that Cuningham was first a Whig and then a Tory,‡ but does not state why he changed. And a careful reading of J.'s article, above quoted, will disclose the existence of a vendetta-like hatred between Cuningham's men and Rumph.

Upon one occasion, when Rumph's men had put Cuningham's troops to flight, Lieut. Golson singled out Capt. Cuningham and gave chase. They were both riding rapidly through the woods, when suddenly Cun-

---

*He was a member of Capt. John Caldwell's company of regulars, but possibly he was attached to Rumph's command on some scouting expedition or other like service.

†As we find no record of "Bloody Bill" having a brother, it is possible that this was only a kinsman.

‡See also O'Neall's Annals of Newberry District, page 254.

ingham spurred his horse over a little ditch, and wheeling it in an instant, presented his pistol at Golson, and said: "Stop, Golson! I have nothing against you, and I don't want to kill you, nor do I want to be killed by you, but if you cross that ditch to-day one of us must die; so you had better go your way and let me go mine." Golson said afterwards that he had never seen eyes in a human head that looked as Cuningham's did on that occasion. He said it was a tigerish look—more of animal than of human being. He, however, did not further interfere with Cuningham, but returned to his company, and no one would ever have known of this incident had not Golson related it himself.

On another occasion Rumph's company come upon Cuningham's men taking their noonday naps, in fence corners, and before Cuningham awoke Rumph was upon him, and placing his sword at Cuningham's throat would have thrust it through his neck in another instant, but awaking suddenly, Cuningham, with a stroke like lightning, thrust aside the sword, sprang over the fence, and, mounting his horse, was off like an arrow, with a shower of bullets hissing all around him; but he was never touched. He seemed to bear a charmed life—he had declared a vendetta, and he lived to make his very name cause a chill of horror to those who read the story of his bloody deeds.

Upon one occasion, while Rumph's partisans were scouting in the "Upper Bull Swamp" section of Orangeburg District, they came to a deserted settlement. Rumph sent his men to hide in the swamp, near the opening in which the houses were situated, and he took Paul Stroman with him and went up to the front of the houses. When they got there they saw a tall man walking in the yard. Capt. Rumph proposed that they give him a shot, and he and Stroman fired at him, breaking one leg, but nothing daunted the man began to turn handsprings so rapidly, using his arms and the good leg, that he would have escaped had he not run (or rather turned) into the ambuscade in the swamp, where he was shot down and killed. When Capt. Rumph came up Lieut. Wannamaker asked who the man was and what he was, but no one could tell, and Lieut. Wannamaker always held that the stranger should not have been killed, as he might have been a friend and not a foe. He described him as a magnificent specimen of manhood, and said he looked like a gentleman and was well dressed.

Another story told of Rumph is that upon one occasion he was complained to by some women who had been on a trading expedition to Charlestown—doubtless before its fall—that a party of marauders had stopped their wagons below Orangeburgh and robbed them of their purchases. Rumph immediately collected some of his partisans and went in pursuit of them, and succeeded in capturing the whole party of them. He took them up to his "bull pen", and, the robbed women having identified them, he proceeded to hang them on the big oak. There was among the marauders a red-headed man named Billy Sturkie. When the rope was placed about his neck and he was about to be jerked up one of the women cried out, "Stop! that red-headed man did not take anything, but tried to keep the others from stealing". The other woman confirmed her statements, and Sturkie was turned loose, but his fright had been so great that he was only able to feebly exclaim, "You might as well a-hung me."

It seems rather peculiar that all of the best known historians of this State have totally neglected to say anything of Rumph's command, notwithstanding the fact that at least one, Dr. Joseph Johnson, knew of the existence and work of this command. In his

"Traditions of the Revolution", pages 548-50, speaking of the fight between the Tories and the Whig company, under Capt. Michael Watson, near Dean Swamp, in Orangeburgh District, he says: "Some of Watson's company, who had also taken to flight on seeing their captain fall, took possession of a farm-house near by, occupied only by a mother and her child. There was little or nothing to eat on the premises, and they now feared pursuit more than ever, believing that the woman would report them to their enemies. One of them was chosen by lot, and sent off to Orangeburg for help. Colonel Rumph came out to them as soon as possible, but, before the arrival of his company, the poor woman and child, with their unwelcome guests, were all nearly starved out."

Dr. Johnson seems to presume that the reader well knows who "Col. Rumph" was, for it is the only mention made of him in the book. He also calls him by his post-bellum title, "Colonel", yet speaks of "his company." Capt. Rumph did not attain the rank of colonel until after the war, when he was chosen colonel of a militia regiment. Some years later he attained the rank of brigadier general of militia.

Some interesting stories are told of some of the individuals of Rumph's company. One of these is about John Amaka—and, by the way, there are two John Amakas mentioned on the roll of the company, above given—who was an actual illustration of late popular song, for "One of his legs was longer than it really ought to have been"; that is to say, he had one leg shorter than the other. When the Whigs had commenced to make it unpleasant for the Tories and those of Tory sentiments, many of them left the State and went to East Florida. One day John Amaka passed by the house of George McMichael (grandfather of Mr. C. M. McMichael) and inquired of him the way to

East. Florida. Mr. McMichael told him the way, but further remarked to him, "John you can't get there on those legs of yours, so if you are going to turn Tory you had better stay here and run your chances." Amaka, however, continued on his journey, but in a day or so he bobbled back, and it seems decided to cast his fortunes with Rumph's partisans.

Paul Stroman, who lived where Mr. James H. Fowles's "Durham" place now is, has been accused of Toryism, but the traditions of his family and the appearance of his name on Rumph's roll tend to disprove the accusation. The charge was probably based on the ground that upon one occasion he, it seems, refused to obey some order of Rumph's, and it so aroused that officer's ire that he rode down to Stroman's place to arrest him. Stroman saw him coming and hid in his barn with his rifle by him. He afterwards declared that if Rumph had discovered him he (Stroman) would have shot him.

Mr. W. W. Culler, of this County, tells a good story of Capt. Rumph's wit. He relates that one night Capt. Rumph called for his grandfather, Benjamin Culler, who was a member of Rumph's company, and, with several others, they went out to waylay and capture some "outlyers". They secreted themselves in some pine brush by the road side, and after awhile a woman, the wife of one of the "outlyers", came along and began to call her husband. After calling several times she called out, "O, honey, O, honey!" At that Capt. Rumph remarked to his companions; "If that fellow is any honey, the devil was the bee."

Mr. Culler also says that his grandmother has often told him that "Bloody Bill" Cunningham had on several occasions come to her house and made her run down and kill and cook chickens for him to eat, and that she had often known, or heard, of his presence in the community.

It is related that upon one occasion Capt. Rumph had two sick members of his company staying in his house. One night he was suddenly aroused by one of his slaves, who ran in and shouted; "Run Massa de Tory comin!" Capt. Rumph quickly awakened his sleeping friends and told them to run for their lives, but one of them complained that he was too sick to run. "Then you are a dead man" shouted Capt. Rumph, and ran out of the house. Just then the Tories entered from the opposite direction, and finding the sick man, dragged him out into the yard and cut his head off with an axe.

Old James Knight, of the Limestone section, who died about forty years ago, had been a member of Cuningham's company during the Revolution, and he was often heard to tell how he escaped on one occasion when Rumph's men had put Cuningham's to flight. He said he simply lay down on his horse, threw his arms around the animal's neck, slapped his spurs to him with all his might and dashed through a thicket.

Another militia company of Orangeburgh District, which doubtless also belonged to Rowe's regiment, and of which there are many traditions, was that of Capt. Henry Felder, who has been mentioned several times heretofore in these pages as holding various civic offices, and as a member of the State Legislature, during the Revolution.

The traditions of the Felder family say that Captain Felder had his seven sons, Henry, Jacob, John, Frederick, Samuel, Abraham and Peter, in his company. It is said that John was killed during the war. He was captured with his step-mother's brother, Snell, and while the British soldiers were at dinner on the banks of the Congaree river, they attempted to escape. Snell escaped to the woods, but John jumped into the river and swam across while his hands were tied, the guard shooting at him all the while, but after he reached the opposite bank a bullet struck him in a vital place and killed him on the spot. And, strange to say, he was killed by his own gun in the hands of the guard.

The late Col. Paul S. Felder often said that when he was a young man he met an old gentleman named Rice of Barnwell District, who told him that he (Rice) had been a member of Capt. Felder's company during the Revolution, and that he was present with the company upon one occasion when they whipped a body of Tories at Holman's Bridge over the South Edisto river in Orangeburgh District.

Capt. Felder had two dwelling houses burned by the Tories during the war, and at the burning of the last one he lost his life. The following notice, in reference to the burning of the first house, appeared in the *Gazette of the State of South Carolina*, October 7th and 14th, 1778:

"WHEREAS the subscriber's house was plundered and burnt on the third inst. and all his papers either burnt or destroyed: To prevent fraudulent demands that may hereafter be made on him, he gives this public notice, that those persons who have any lawful demands on him, either in books of account, bond, note of hand or otherwise, are desired to make demand on or before the first day of january next ensuing, and receive payment: And all persons indebted to him are likewise entreated to make payment as far as may be consisent with their knowledge.

"Sept. 23, Henry Felder."

Judge O'Neall, on p. 325 of his Bench and Bar, has this to say of Capt. Henry Felder:

"This gentleman was a very active partisan in the Revolution. He brought his love of liberty from his native canton, and, like Tell, of his fatherland, he was willing to peril all, rather than submit to tyranny. He guided General Sumter in his approach to Orangeburg, and bore a part in the capture of that post.

"At or about the close of the war, the Tories surrounded his house: the gallant Swiss. by the aid of his wife and servants, who loaded his guns while he fired, killed more than twenty of his foes. His house was at last fired, and he was thus forced to fly. In attempting to escape, he was shot, and killed."

The traditionary account of the above affair, as received from the late Col. Paul S. Felder, who not only heard it from his father and other members of his family, but from the lips of an old negro servant, who, as a young man, had been an eye witness of a part of the tragedy, is as follows: One day Capt. Felder received a message from Samuel Rowe, a good Whig friend, that the Tories intended to attack his home the next day. With his sons, and his overseer, whose name was Fry, he defended his house, defeated the Tories and drove them off. As soon as they had left he sent his sons through a by-path to waylay and ambush them, but before reaching the ambush the enemy returned to the siege, and setting fire to a load of hay that was under a shed near the house they thereby set the house on fire. Capt. Felder put on some of his wife's clothes and attempted to escape, but was recognized by his boots as he jumped the yard fence and was filled with bullets. He continued his flight for several hundred yards, however, and dropped from exhaustion and loss of blood just as he reached the woods. The same negro above mentioned was cutting wood nearby and went to his master's assistance. He was not yet dead, and help being procured, he was taken to a place of safety where he lived a day or two before he died.

In the fight he is said to have killed about twenty of the Tories with the assistance of Fry, his wife and servants loading the guns, while he and Fry shot.

There are two old cannons used as corner posts in Orangeburg, that are said to have been used by him on the occasion of the siege of Orangeburgh by Sumter. However that may be, one of the guns has cut on it, "H. Felder 1781" and the other has cut on it the mark HF.

After the death of the father, his son, Henry Felder, commanded the company; and after the war this company formed a part of the District militia.*

It is also quite likely that another of these companies was commanded by Capt. John Salley. On page 12 of Tarleton Brown's Memoirs the Cowpens of "Captain Salley" are mentioned, and in a grant of land made to him shortly after the Revolution he is called "Captain John Salley." These are the only documentary evidences we have of the fact that he bore any title at all during the Revolution.

Tradition has preserved two anecdotes of Capt. Salley's Revolutionary life that are worth recording. He lived near the river swamp about half a mile from the village of Orangeburgh,† and one tradition is that whenever he slept at home a faithful old negro stood sentinel under his window, and whenever he heard the tramp of horses he jumped up and rapped on the window to warn his master. When thus warned he would slip out, and if he found that Tories were

---

*See Bench and Bar, Vol. II, page 341.

†His grave and tombstone can be seen there now, near where his dwelling stood.

abroad he would hie him to the river swamp. This was probably when he had no troops with him.

The other tradition is that he owned a very fine blooded horse which he very much feared the Tories would steal, so he carried him to his own house, the lower story of which was of brick, with a basement, or cellar. He took the horse into this basement and bricked him up in there, leaving some secret entrance through which food could be carried, and doubtless there were some sort of air holes, (Traditions never provide such things.) but, at any rate, the Tories found out the horse was there, and stole him out. This must have happened while the owner was absent, for, if he was as fond of horses as his numerous descendants are, (and he evidently was) he would have defended him with his life had he been present.

Section 5. Various Operations in South Carolina during the War; and their relation to Orangeburgh District.

From the commencement of hostilities up to Prévost's attempt on Charlestown, in May 1779, operations in South Carolina were confined to the coast and along the line of the Savannah river; with the exception of the two expeditions among the Tories of the back-country in 1775, and the expedition against the Cherokee Indians in 1776. Some account of these various operations has been given in the section on the 3rd regiment.

While Gen. Lincoln lay with his army at Purisburg, in 1779, protecting our frontier from an invasion by the British from Georgia, Governor Rutledge conceived the idea of forming a grand militia camp at Orangeburgh, as is shown by the following extract from a letter written by Gen. Moultrie to Col. Charles

ORANGEBURG COUNTY. 491

Pinckney, dated at Purisburgh, March 2nd, 1779: "I observe in a letter from the governor to general Lincoln, that he intends forming a camp at Orangeburgh, of 2,700 men, the 13th instant; and that he also intends augmenting them to 5,000. from Thomas', Lisle's, Neal's, and Williams' regiments, from the Ninety-six regiment,* without interfering with the measures necessary for defending the back country; I think all seems to be secure thereabouts."

GOV. JOHN RUTLEDGE.†

The wisdom of establishing this encampment was questioned by Col. Charles Pinckney (who was President of the Senate and a member of the Council of Safety) in a letter to Gen. Moultrie, dated March 19th, as follows: "I have received your favor of the 15th, and am glad to hear of the enemy bending their force downwards to Savannah; even though they should take a trip to our borders; especially as you say, you are of opinion we should manage them better there than where they are, which opinion I think just; this movement I think should alter the orders for our grand camp at Orangeburgh, and place it nearer the capital for fear of a coup-de-main, I think you military men call it: and perhaps may be so soon: but at present it is the ruling opinion that the other place is near enough to receive succors from, in due time, should they be wanted. I wish it may be so"; and again on March 22nd, Col. Pinckney wrote Gen. Moultrie: "His excellency has been obliged to pospone his

---

*Williamson's brigade.
†By courtesy of Everett Waddey Company, publishers Chapman's School History of South Carolina.

setting off for his camp until to-morrow noon: I am told that there are not above one thousand men in that camp; but that their number, in a few days, will be increased to double; and in due time, if orders are complied with, the given number (5,000) fixed on, may be there: be they more or less, I wish the camp had been ordered near Charlestown; and I in vain urged it should be so, but could not prevail: If you join me in opinion, I wish you would write the governor on it; for surely the present encampment at Orangeburgh, is, considering our present circumstances of expecting an attack here, much too far to give that necessary assistance that might be wanted."

On March 28th Col. Pinckney wrote Gen. Moultrie: "You wish the post you just now left, may be reinforced with militia; this, in my opinion cannot be conveniently done, otherwise than by detachments from the grand camp at Orangeburgh, under the governor, with whom no doubt, you will exchange a letter on the subject: he and his suite are now, and have been for several days past there,* and it is said his

THE BRUCE HOUSE.
FROM PHOTO BY T. H. HITCHCOCK.

*While in Orangeburgh, Governor Rutledge made his headquarters at the house of Donald Bruce, who was at that time a member of the State legislature from Orange Parish. In July, 1781, when Lord Rawdon halted for a few days in Orangeburgh on his return from the relief of Ninety-Six, he also made his headquarters in the Bruce house, but it is reasonable to suppose that his Lordship did not find as warm welcome there as did the brilliant "Dictator", the 26th chapter of "The Forayers" to the contrary notwithstanding. Many years after the Revolution, after the death of the last of the Bruces, Mr. Daniel Larey bought the house, which stood at the southeast

Camp is growing very strong, but I cannot inform you of particulars."

From his headquarters at Orangeburgh, Governor Rutledge, on April 5th, wrote to Gen. Williamson: "You will order the prisoners of war, those who are accused of sedition, now in Ninety-six goal, to be safely conducted under a sufficient guard to this place." The prisoners were ordered to Orangeburgh, "as a place of greater security", says Gen. Moultrie in his Memoirs.

Early in April Gen. Moultrie, at Gen. Lincoln's request, visited Orangeburgh to consult with Governor Rutledge. On his return to Black Swamp he wrote as follows, to Col. Pinckney: "I have the pleasure to inform you, that I returned from Orangeburgh three days ago, after a ride of two hundred and twenty miles, a very fatiguing jaunt, both to ourselves and horses, we were (Mr. Kinlock and myself) gone six days; one day we staid with the Governor, and the others in traveling. We expect Col. Simons here to-morrow, with one thousand men of all ranks: this will be a reinforcement to us that will be very acceptable. The Governor has promised more as soon as they can be collected. I was sorry to see so few" (three or four hundred) "left at Orangeburgh after this detachment marched off; though Col. Neal lay about four miles off, with two hundred and eighty men of his regiment, and was to march in that morning." And on the same day Gen. Moultrie wrote

GEN. MOULTRIE.*

---

corner of Windsor and Bull (now Dibble) Streets, and moved it down on the "Five Notch" road about two miles below Orangeburg, where it now stands. It is now the property of Mrs. Lawrence S. Wolfe. In the 26th, 29th and 32nd chapters of "The Forayers", Wm. Gilmore Simms has woven an interesting bit of romance about this historic old house. *By courtesy of Everett Waddy Company, publishers Chapman's School History of South Carolina.

as follows, to Governor Rutledge: "I have the honor to inform you, that we arrived at our camp two days ago; nothing extraordinary have happened since we left it: they are much pleased to hear of the reinforcement (1,000) you have sent, and that they are on their march; we expect them here to-morrow. I hope ere long you will send us such another."

On April 29th Lieutenant-Governor Bee wrote to Gen. Moultrie: "The Governor is again returned to Orangeburgh, from whence I hope he will be able to send to Gen. Lincoln", &c.; and on May 1st, while Prévost was on his march towards Charlestown, Gen. Moultrie wrote, from Coosohatchie, to Gen. Lincoln: "I have sent dispatches to the Gov. at Orangeburgh, and to Charlestown." That sent to Charlestown was to request two or three hundred Continentals; that to Orangeburgh, dated May 1st, was as follows: "I have here with me about 1,200 men: I wish your excellency would reinforce me speedily; and with as many field-pieces as possible." On the same day Gen. Moultrie received a letter from Lieutenant-Governor Bee saying; "Yours of the 29th April, directed to the governor came to me this morning; I have sent it forward by express to Orangeburgh, from whence, if necessary, I make no doubt you will be reinforced."

On May 2nd Gen. Lincoln wrote, from Silver Bluff, to Gen. Moultrie: "I have written to the Governor at Orangeburgh, and requested that he would reinforce you by the militia, intended for this army, and Major Grimball's artillery"; and on the same day Gen. Moultrie wrote to Gen. Lincoln, from Coosohatchie: "I have sent express to the governor at Orangeburgh, and to Charlestown, to hasten up the militia to this place." On the same day Governor Rutledge sent Gen. Moultrie a dispatch from Orangeburgh saying that he had written to the Lieutenant-Governor to

ORANGEBURG COUNTY. 495

send Horry's horse to Gen. Moultrie, &c. Lieut. Gov. Bee also wrote to Gen. Moultrie on the same day, saying that he had no doubt but that the governor would send reinforcements "as speedily as possible, from Orangeburgh"; and that the "reinforcements must be from Orangeburgh". He further stated that he had not heard from the governor since he (the governor) left town.

From Tulifiny Gen. Moultrie wrote, at "6 o'clock P. M." on May 3rd, to Governor Rutledge at Orangeburgh: "I this moment received yours; I was in hopes you would have acquainted me of a strong reinforcement marching to this place"; and again on the 4th he wrote to the Governor; "I hope your excellency will hasten your light troops to reinforce me", and to Gen. Lincoln; "I expect the governor will join me tomorrow from Orangeburgh with the Charlestown artillery; as to what militia he had I cannot inform you." On the 5th he wrote again to Gen. Lincoln: "I shall endeavor to make a stand at Ashepoo; as I will expect the governor will join me there."

On May 3rd Lieut. Gov. Bee wrote: "Twenty-two of Horry's light horse, marched this afternoon for your camp and will hurry on the party, that went to Orangeburgh with the Governor, who are just returned."

On Sunday evening Governor Rutledge wrote, from Orangeburgh, to Gen. Moultrie: "In consequence of your advice, received this afternoon; I will march with Grimball's artillery, and all the force we have here (except about 50, who must remain; and 50 more, who go as an escort to the waggons with corn, &c. for Gen. Lincoln's camp) as soon as possible, to reinforce you. I hope to get off to-morrow, and no time shall be lost on the march. You will, without doubt, take every step in your power, to procure all the reinforcements you can, and throw every obstruction in the way to annoy the enemy, and prevent their progress and ravages."

From "Edisto saw-mills, at Mr. Charles Elliot's, 12 miles below Orangeburgh", Governor Rutledge wrote, on Wednesday morning, to Gen. Moultrie: "We began our march, with what force we could bring from Orangeburgh, yesterday morning, for your camp; and shall proceed as quickly as the weather and the roads will admit. I hope to bring up, and have very close after me, 500 men (exclusive of officers) horse, foot, and artillery. I received yours dated 3d of May at 6 o'clock, about 11 last night; I hope you will be able to withstand the enemy, or stop their progress. I shall send Allston's,* and some other horse, as soon as they come up (which I expect to day,) a-head, to join you. I have sent another express for the Catawbas. I hope to see you soon."

On Thursday the Governor wrote, from the same point: "Some hours ago, on the march hither, I received yours of last night: and soon after, a letter from Major Butler; in which he says, he heard the enemy were at Ashepoo: therefore, as I think we cannot possibly assist you at Jacksonburgh (it being 24 miles from hence) I have ordered the troops here, to cross the river, (they being now on this side) and proceed, by forced marches, to Charlestown, over four-hole and Dorchester bridges, I think you had better move . . . when you do, move, down by Dorchester. You will continue to throw obstruction in the enemy's way, and advise me of these, and your motions, by ex-

---

*On page 432 of his "Memoirs", (vol. i) Gen. Moultrie says: "On my retreat from Black-swamp, Colonel Senf, feom the governor's camp, Orangeburgh, joined me at Ponpon bridge, with the racoon company, commanded by Captain John Allston, of about fifty men on horseback."

press to Charlestown; for which I am just setting off; you will give all necessary orders for destroying bridges, &c."

In his "Memoirs", under date of May 8th, Gen. Moultrie writes: "At this time there never was a country in greater confusion and consternation; and it may be easily accounted for, when 5 armies were marching through the southern parts of it, at the same time, and all for different purposes: myself retreating as fast as possible to get into town, at first with 1,200 men; but reduced to 600 before I got near the town; the British army of 3,000 men commanded by Gen. Provost in pursuit of me: and Gen. Lincoln with the American army of 4,000, marching with hasty strides to come up with the British: Gov. Rutledge from Orangeburgh, with about 600 militia; hastening to get to town lest he should be shut out; and Col. Harris, with a detachment of 250 continentals, pushing on with all possible dispatch to reinforce me; and my sending two or three expresses every day to the governor and to Gen. Lincoln, to let them know where I was; and to Charlestown frequently, to hasten their works and to prepare for an attack; in short it was nothing but a general confusion and alarm. And the militia from the north part of the country, from every parish making what haste they could to reinforce Charlestown; that I may truly say the whole country was in motion."

On the 9th and 10th the troops marched into Charlestown, and on the 10th General Moultrie issued orders making disposition of his troops on the lines. The country militia were ordered to occupy the left wing.

On the morning of 11th a detachment of the enemy appeared near the lines. They were attacked by Count Pulaski with his legion and some militia, but they were too strong for him and he lost a considerable number of his men before getting back within the lines. "Gen. Provost's whole army", writes Gen. Moultrie, "soon appeared before the town gates, at the distance of about a mile, the advance of his army being about Watson's house, in the afternoon; when I ordered the cannon at the gate to begin to fire, which stopped their progress: We continued at the lines, standing to our arms, all night, and serving out ammunition to the country militia; who only came in the day before, with the governor: we were in expectation of their attacking us that night."

On the next morning, in order to gain time for Lincoln to come up, Governor Rutledge arranged a parley with the enemy through Gen. Moultrie. After gaining the whole day it was decided, principally by Gen. Moultrie, not to surrender the town but to "fight it out", and the truce was declared at an end; and Prévost, fearing that Lincoln would be upon his rear before he could take the city, withdrew that night, filed off to the left, and went to the sea islands.

The following is the account Ramsay gives of this invasion of South Carolina by Prévost while Lincoln was up the Savannah river and Governor Rutledge encamped in Orangeburgh:*

"The series of disasters which had followed the American arms, since the landing of the British in Georgia, occasioned, among the inhabitants of South-Carolina, many well-founded apprehensions for their future safety." * * * * * * "In this time of general alarm John Rutledge, esquire, by the almost unanimous voice of his countrymen, was called to the chair of government. To him and his council was delegated, by the legislature, power 'to do every thing that appeared to him and them necessarry for the publick good.' In execution of this trust he assembled a body

---

*Revolution in South Carolina, Vol. II, pages 18 to 24.

of militia. This corps, kept in constant readiness to march whithersoever public service might require, was stationed near the centre of the state at Orangeburgh. From this militia camp colonel Simmons was detached with a thousand men to reinforce general Moultrie at Black-Swamp. The original plan of penetrating into Georgia was resumed. With this intention general Lincoln marched with the main army up the Savannah river, that he might give confidence to the country." * * * "A small force was left at Black-Swamp and Purysburgh for the purpose of defending Carolina". * * * "General Prevost availed himself of the critical time when the American army was one hundred and fifty miles up the Savannah river, and crossed over into Carolina". *
* * * * "Lieutenant-colonel Mackintosh, who commanded a few continentals at Purysburgh, not being able to oppose this force made a timely retreat. It was part of general Prevost's plan to attack general Moultrie at Black-Swamp, to effect which he made a forced march the first night after he landed on the Carolina side, but he was about three hours too late. General Moultrie had changed his quarters, and being joined by colonel Mackintosh's party took post at Tulifinny bridge, in order to prevent the incursion of the British into the state, and to keep between them and its defenceless capital." * * * *

"The position of general Moultrie at Tulifinny was by no means a safe one, for the British might easily have crossed above him, and got in his rear. A general retreat of the whole force towards Charleston was therefore thought advisable." * * * * * *
"Governor Rutledge, with the militia lately encamped at Orangeburgh, had set out to join general Moultrie at Tulifinny bridge; but, on the second day of their march, advice was received of General Moultrie's re-

treat, and that general Prevost was pushing towards Charleston. This intelligence determined the governor to march with all the force under his command to the defence of the capital." * * * * * *

"General Moultrie's retreating army, governor Rutledge's militia from Orangeburgh, and colonel Harris's detached light corps, which marched nearly forty miles a day for four days successively, all reached Charleston on the 9th and 10th of May. The arrival of such seasonable reinforcements gave hopes of a successful defence."

The following extracts concerning these movements by Moultrie, Lincoln, Rutledge and Prévost are taken from Col. Henry Lee's "Memoirs of the War in the Southern Department", (1812) pp. 82, 83: "Governor Rutledge, with the reserve militia, had established himself at Orangeburg, a central position, perfectly adapted to the convenient reception and distribution of this species of force, which is ever in a state of undulation. He was far on Prévost's left, and, like Lincoln, was hors de combat".

He goes on to describe Prévost's attack on Charlestown, and further says, pp. 83, 84: "The father of the State had removed from Orangeburg with the reserve, to throw himself into Charleston, if possible. What was before impossible, had become possible by the forty-eight hours' delay of Prevost. Rutledge joined Moultrie; and Charleston became safe".

The next important movement was the attack on Prévost at Stono. Many of the "country militia", lately brought down from Orangeburgh by Governor Rutledge, were in that engagement.

In September, 1779, when the French fleet, under Count D'Estaing, and the American army, under Gen. Lincoln, moved against the British, under Prévost, in Savannah, the militia of South Carolina were ordered to assemble near Savannah. It is said—and it is doubtless true—that some Orangeburgh militiamen fought there.

The next important event of the Revolution was the siege of Charlestown by the British under Sir Henry Clinton and Admiral Arbuthnot, from February 11th to May 12th, 1780, when the city was formally surrendered.

"The capital having surrendered", says Ramsay, "the next object with the British was to secure the general submission of the inhabitants. To this end they posted garrisons in different parts of the country." One of these posts was established at Orangeburgh. The brick court-house, which stood about where the old "Marchant House" lately stood, was fortified and a garrison placed in it. Another post was established at "Ninety-Six", and the old road now known as the "Ninety-Six" road was used by the British troops passing between the two points. Another of these posts was established at Granby, in Saxe-Gotha Township, nearly opposite where Columbia now stands, where Friday's house* was fortified and garrisoned. At a later period of the war the houses of Mrs. Rebecca Motte† and Col. William Thomson (Bellville) were also seized and fortified as British posts.

For about six weeks after the fall of Charlestown all military opposition to the progress of the British was practically suspended, but the British were not destinied to make an easy conquest of the State, for scarcely had the panic caused by the fall of Charlestown subsided before small bodies of militia arose in all parts of the State to harass the enemy, and, fortunately for the Southern States, Sir Henry Clinton

---

*Now known as the "Cayce House".
†Called "St. Joseph", afterwards known as Fort Motte.

learned that a French fleet was soon expected about New York. This induced the Commander-in-Chief to re-embark for New York early in June, with the greater part of his army. He left Lord Cornwallis as commander-in-chief in the South with about four thousand men.

As early as July 12, a part of Sumter's militia regiment defeated a body of British troops and tories under Colonel Ferguson and Captain Hucks, respectively, in the up-country. Ferguson and Hucks were both killed. Col. Sumter soon raised 600 men and in less than a month fought two more battles with the British at Rocky Mount and Hanging Rock. Col. James Williams, of Ninety-Six District, next defeated a considerable party of British and Tories at Musgrove's Mill on Aug. 18th. Various other little engagements were fought, with more or less success to the South Carolinians, during July and August.

Meantime an army of continentals and North Carolina and Virginia militia, under Major Generals De Kalb and Gates, successively, had been marching to the relief of South Carolina; reaching this State in August they were joined by various bodies of South Carolina troops, and on the 16th, was fought the Battle of Camden in which Gates's army suffered defeat and rout.

The British were very much elated over the victory at Camden, and again flattered themselves that all opposition in South Carolina was effectually subdued, but the spirit of independence was not to be crushed out in South Carolina, and the partisan organizations once more began to operate as Henry, of the Wynd, did, "on their own hook". Scores of skirmishes and and fights took place in all parts of the State—some in Orangeburgh District, already mentioned—and the South Carolina patriots had all but redeemed the State from the hands of the British when Gen. Greene arrived in the State from the North to complete the conquest.

As an example of what this partisan warfare was, some accounts of the Revolutionary experiences of Tarleton Brown, of that part of Orangeburgh District which was afterwards formed into Barnwell District, taken from his "Memoirs", will serve. He relates that when troops were first called for in 1775, a draft was ordered in his section, and that he was among those drafted; and that they were marched to Pocataligo, then under command of General Stephen Bull*, where they were stationed about seven weeks. Nothing of importance happening his company was discharged and returned to their homes. Scarely had they got there, he writes, before there was another draft for the first siege of Savannah.† He escaped draft, but was employed by William Bryant to take his place. They embarked in an open boat on the Savannah River, Capt. Moore commanding the company, and passed down the river to Savannah, which they reached in three days. He writes: "We passed some heavy and mortal shots at the enemy, which were returned with equal fierceness and more deadly effect". * * * * "We stayed at Savannah about seven weeks, and then returned to South Carolina, under the command of Gen. Bull." He then relates that having become attached to the army he enlisted in the regular service, in April 1776, at Fort Littleton, Beaufort District, commanded by Captain William Harden.‡ He next, in July 1777, left Capt. Harden and immediately joined Col. James Thompson's detachment§ on Pipe Creek, from which point he went

---

*He was only a colonel at that time.
†February, 1776.
‡State regulars—not Continentals.
§Col. James Thompson is mentioned in Gen. DeSaussure's pam-

on an expedition to Georgia under Capt. John Mumford. In this expedition Mumford was wounded and John Booth killed.

He next relates that during the final siege of Charlestown, "Captain Mumford, in attempting to make his way to the American Army, was attacked at Morris' Ford, Saltketchie, by old Ben John and his gang of Tories. In this encounter the poor fellow lost his life, and a truer patriot and braver soldier never fell. He now sleeps at the foot of a large pine, on the left hand side of the main road to Barnwell C. H., a few rods South of the bridge, just at the turn of the road from which you can see the bridge". * * *

"In conjunction with Joshua Inman and John Green, I raised a company of horse, which we called the 'Rangers,' with the view of scouting those sections of the country adjacent to the Savannah River, both in Georgia and Carolina, as occasion required."

* * * * * * * * * *

"A few months subsequent to this period, I withdrew from the 'Rangers' at Cracker's Neck, and connected myself with a company of militia keeping guard at Burton's Ferry. We exchanged shots almost every day with the British and Tories, who were on the opposite side (Georgia)." * * * * * * *

"On one occasion I was under the necessity of going home on some important business. Soon after my arrival, a company of horse passed directly in front of our residence. My first impression concerning them was that they were a reinforcement of our guard at the ferry.

---

phlet, and by the Journal of the Council of Safety, as having been commissioned as captain of the Round O company, of the Colleton County Regiment, Jan. 11, 1776. As he seems by the above to have commanded a regiment in July, 1777, he must have raised it in the meantime in the section between the Edisto and the Savannah rivers. Major Bourguoin is mentiened as of Thompson's command.

So soon as I had finished my business, I returned with all possible speed, overjoyed at the prospect of an accession to our numbers. On reaching the fort, to my astonishment, I found it completely evacuated. My reinforcement turned out to be a gang of Tories from Jackson's Branch, on the Saltkatchie, commanded by that famous old Tory, Ned Williams. When they rode up to the ferry, the guard took them to be friends, and gave them a cordial reception, congratulating themselves upon so large an addition to their force. Thus they unconsciously and ignorantly delivered themselves up to the enemy, and were taken across the river and placed in the hands of a large body of British and Tories, stationed at Harbard's store, about two miles from the ferry. The intelligence of this capture reached Col. Leroy Hammond at Augusta, who, without delay, marched down at the head of an effective force, and slew nearly the whole of the enemy, releasing and returning with the Whig captives to Augusta, from whence my father, who was one among the number taken, came safely home". Following this the writer gives some idea of the toils and perils of the Carolina Whigs in those dark days, and then he goes on to tell of an expedition into Georgia, and upon the return to South Carolina he says: "We learnt that Capt. James Roberts, who had been scouting with a company on the Edisto River, had (whilst encamping for the night, by some treachery of the Tories,) been delivered into the hands of Col. Chaney and Williams, who cruelly butchered many of his men, Capt. Roberts and the rest escaping only with their lives. For this outrage we determined to have satisfaction. So thirty-six men, myself among the number, immediately volunteered under Capt. Joseph Vince, a fine officer and a brave soldier, to pursue these scoundrels, and to avenge the blood of

our brave comrades. We overtook some of their
number in what is called the 'Fork of Edisto River,'
upon whom we visited summary and immediate justice, killing five or six. From thence we proceeded to
Captain Salley's 'Cowpens', a few miles distant. Whilst
there our commander rode, unaccompanied, to a mill
located near the house of the Pens. Here he was fired
upon by several Tories lying in ambush hard by and
seriously wounded by musket shot—in consequence of
which he was disabled from doing duty for some
time. This unfortunate circumstance interrupting
our further march, we were compelled to retrace our
steps and return to headquarters, Savannah River".

The writer next describes how a band of one hundred and fifty Tories under Chaney and Williams
murdered Adam Wood, one of his neighbors, and
burned his house; and relates that after the outrage
the Tories started towards Capt. Vince's station, on
Savannah River, and that he (Brown) suggested to
John Cave that they warn Capt. Vince of his danger,
which they did. He states that as Vince's force numbered only twenty-five it was thought best to abandon
the fort, which was accordingly done, and when the
Tories arrived they found nothing. He then goes on:
"From this point they turned towards their headquarters, on Edisto. In crossing Lower Three Runs, they
stopped at the house of a Mr. Collins, a very quiet and
inoffensive man, and far advanced in years, say about
eighty-five. Whatever may have been the sentiments
of this old gentleman, he maintained a strictly neutral position, shouldering arms on neither side; yet
those fiends of darkness dispatched him, with his head
as white as snow by the frost of many winters, for an
eternal world." He writes that he continued scouting
in both Carolina and Georgia until the fall of Charlestown; that after the fall everything looked so dark and

gloomy in South Carolina that his brother, Bartlet, and himself determined to refugee to Virginia until the outlook in Carolina should become brighter; but that they had scarcely reached Virginia when they learned that the Tories had been committing many outrages in South Carolina, "particularly in our own district. The substance of which was that McGeart and his company of Tories crossed the Savannah River from Georgia, at Summerlin's Ferry (now called Stone's Ferry), taking the course of the river, and killing every man he met who had not sworn allegiance to the King. This notorious scoundrel passed in this trip through the neighborhood where my father lived, and brutally murdered seventeen of the inhabitants, among whom were my father, Henry Best, and Moore, leaving John Cave for dead, who afterwards recovered. They burnt my father's house level with the ground, and destroyed everything he possessed— my mother and sisters escaping by fleeing to the woods, in which they concealed themselves until the vile wretches departed. But the work of death did not stop here. This atrocious deed of the sanguinary McGeart and his band was shortly succeeded by another equally, nay, doubly cruel. The British Col. Brown marched down from Augusta with an overwhelming force of Tories and Indians, and taking their stand at 'Wiggins' Hill', commenced a slaughter of the inhabitants. The news of which reached the ears of those brave and dauntless officers, Cols. McCoy and Harden, who soon hastened to the defence of the terrified Whigs, and coming upon the enemy, charged upon them and killed and routed them to a man, Col. Brown escaping to the woods. Cols. McCoy and Harden, having accomplished all that was required of them, retired from the field of action, after which Brown returned with the residue of his force and retook the 'Hill,' at which he remained until he hung five of our brave fellows—Britton Williams,* Charles Blunt, and Abraham Smith, the names of the other two not recollected—then he decamped for Augusta."

The old veteran then relates that when Bartlet and himself heard of these outrages they at once returned to South Carolina to avenge the killing of their kindred; that at "Kingstree" they found Gen. Marion and joined his brigade. Account is given of several of Marion's engagements, and then the writer once more returns to his own district. He says:

"On the first day of April, 1781, I left Gen. Marion on the Big Pee Dee River, in company with eighty others, forming a detachment under command of Cols. Harden and Baker, and Major John Cooper. The two last named officers were from Midway settlement, Georgia. There were also several other brave and energetic men who rendered themselves conspicuous in the war in our detachment, Fountain Stewart, Robert Salley, the Sharps and Goldings, from Georgia. Our route lay by the 'Four Holes'. Crossing the Edisto at Givham's Ferry, we fell in with a man who assisted Brown in hanging the five brave fellows at 'Wiggins' Hill'. We gave him his due, and left his body at the disposal of the birds and wild beasts. Pursuing our march, we came to 'Red Hill,' within about two miles of Patterson's Bridge, Saltkatchie. It was now in the night, but the moon being in full strength, and not a cloud to darken her rays, it was almost as bright as day. Near this place were stationed a body of Tories, commanded by Capt. Barton. They were desperate fellows, killing, plundering, and robbing the inhabitants without mercy or feeling. A company of men, commanded by Major Cooper, were now sent to

---

*Britton Williams had been a member of the State legislature. (See page 276.)

see what they could do with those murderers. In a few minutes after their departure we heard them fighting, which continued nearly one hour, when Cooper returned and told us he had killed the greater part of them, with but the loss of one man, John Steward, from Georgia."*

The writer then gives an account of the capture of Pocataligo by Col. Harden. The next day Col. McCoy's detachment came up and the Brown brothers joined him and turned their faces once more toward home. On their way home they chased Ned Williams and his gang of Tories into Saltkahatchie swamp. Continuing he says: "Next morning we went up to the 'Big house,' now belonging to Col. Hay, and there found those of my father's family that the Tories and Indians had left, whom we had not seen before for twelve months."

After recounting various other expeditions in which he and many of his neighbors took part he goes on to say: "Although the war had closed, the Tories were still troublesome, plundering and occasionally killing the inhabitants."

We now return to the regular army. After his de-

---

*Extract from a letter from Col. Harden to Gen. Marion:
"Camp on Saltketcher, April 18th, 1781.
"*Dear General:*
"This will be handed to you by Mr. Cannon, who will acquaint you of many particulars, which I can't mention at this present.—On Saturday, on the Four Holes, I came to a musterfield, where I took a Captain and 25 men, and paroled them, and on Sunday night got within six miles of Captain Barton, and six men to guard him. I detached Major Cooper and fifteen men who surrounded his house and ordered him to surrender, but he refused; a smart fire commenced and Major Cooper soon got the better, wounding Barton, who is since dead, and one other, killed three and took two prisoners. The Major got slightly wounded and one of his men, and lost a fine youth, Stewart, who rushed up and was shot dead."

feat and rout at Camden, in August 1780, Gen. Gates took a stand at Hillsborough, N. C., where he collected up his scattered army, but moved down to Charlotte at the end of 1780. On December 2nd, 1780, Gates was superseded by Major-General Nathanael Greene. Greene at once commenced operations. On January 17th, following, a part of Greene's force, under Gen. Daniel Morgan, won a signal victory over the British under Col. Tarleton, at Cowpens, and the Americans began at once to recover much of their lost ground. Battle after battle was fought, with more or less success to the Americans, and within one year nearly every fortified position outside of Charlestown had been either captured or so harassed as to cause an evacuation of it.

On February 19th, 1781, General Sumter crossed the Congaree in force and appeared before Fort Granby*

---

* "Camp at Friday's Ferry, Feb. 20th, 1781.

"*Dear Sir:*

"Hurry of business obliges me to be laconick. I arrived at this place yesterday morning about four o'clock. Shortly after, attacked the fort, with which I have been ever since engaged. Everything hitherto favorable, and have no doubt but I shall succeed, if not interrupted by Lord Rawdon, who, I know, will strip his post as bare of men as possible to spare, to obviate which, as far as may be in your power, it is my wish that you would be pleased to move in such a direction as to attract his attention, and thereby prevent his designs. Timely assistance in this way portends much good to this State. I have also to request that every inhabitant of this State, westward of Santee be permitted to join their respective Regiments, or rather immediately repair to my station. I desired Col. Marshall, with what men we could collect to march down, eastward of Camden, and will probably fall in with you in good time. I wish and beg that you may suppress every species of plundering, as the greatest evils to the publick, as well as individuals, are experienced thereby. You cannot be too particular. The enemy oblige the negroes they have to make frequent sallies. This circumstance alone is sufficient to rouse and fix the resentment and detestation of every American who possesses common feelings. I shall be happy to receive an account of the state of things to the East and Northward. If you can, with propriety, ad-

ORANGEBURG COUNTY.

in Orangeburgh District, and destroyed all the British stores. Lord Rawdon, then commanding the British forces in South Carolina, immediately marched from Camden to the relief of Fort Granby, upon which Gen. Sumter retired. Of this attack Simms says, p. 209: "Such was the vigor with which he pressed the fort, that his marksmen, mounted upon a temporary structure of rails, had reduced the garrison to the last straits, when they were relieved by the unexpected approach of succor under lord Rawdon, who appeared on the opposite bank of the river. Unable to contend with the superior force of the British, Sumter made a sudden retreat." Gen. Moultrie says, Memoirs, p. 273, that Gen. Sumter the next day "appeared before another British post near Col. Thompson's", which was probably "Bellville" itself.

On April 25th, the Battle of Hobkirk's Hill took place near Camden, between the forces of General Greene and Lord Rawdon.

On May 8th General Marion and Col. Henry Lee, of Virginia, (father of General Robert E. Lee) crossed the Santee, and moved up to Fort Motte, and began their approaches,† which

GEN. FRANCIS MARION*

vance Southwardly so as to co-operate, or correspond with me, it might have the best of consequences.

"I am, dear sir, with the greatest regards,
"Your most obd't humble serv't,
"Thos. Sumter.

"P. S.—I am extremely short of ammunition: if you are well-supplied, should be much obliged to you to send some into the neighborhood of Buckingham's ferry."—Letter to Gen. Marion.

*By courtesy of Everett Waddey Company, publishers Chapman's School History of South Carolina.

† "Head Quarters, Colonel's Creek, May 10th, 1781.
"General Greene has this moment received information that the

were carried on very rapidly until the 12th, when the post surrendered.* Of the siege of Fort Motte, Gen. Moultrie says, Memoirs, p. 280: "They informed Mrs. Motte, that they were afraid that they should be obliged to set fire to her house, which stood in the centre of the fort: she begged them that they would not consider her house as of any consequence in the general cause; and with great patriotism and firmness, presented them with an African bow, and quiv-

---

enemy have evacuated Camden. They moved out this morning early, after destroying the mill, the goal, and their stores, together with many private houses; what may have induced this unexpected and precipitate movement is uncertain, but the General is of opinion that the same motives which have induced Lord Rawdon to take this step will also induce the evacuation of all the outposts, which the enemy have at Ninety-Six, Augusta and on the Congaree. He begs you to take such measures as may prevent the garrison at Mott's from escaping. The army was to have moved to-morrow morning towards Friday's Ferry. I will move that way still, though by a different route and perhaps more slowly. It is uncertain which way Lord Rawdon took his route; it was either to George Town or Charles Town and most probably the latter. The General is firmly of opinion the enemy will, if they can, evacuate all their out-posts. You will therefore take such measures as you think best calculated to prevent their design.

"I am, sir, with high respect,
"Your most obd't, most humble serv't.,
"Nath. Pendleton, Aid-de-Camp."—to General Marion.

* "The 12th, Motte's fort submitted to Gen'l Marion; the garrison consisted of upward of one hundred and forty men; one hundred and twenty were British or Hessians, with seven or eight officers. The place had been invested the 8th; nor did it surrender till our troops had made their approaches regularly up to the abbatis; the redoubt was very strong, and commanded by Lieutenant M'Pherson, a very brave young officer. Great praise is due to General Marion, and the handful of militia that remained with him till the reduction of the fort. Lieut. Col. Lee's Legion, and the detachments under Major Eaton, the artillery under Capt. Finlay, and the corps of Infantry under Captains Oldham and Smith, were indefatigable in carrying on the siege. There were found, in the fort, one carronade, one hundred and forty muskets, a quantity of salt provisions, and other stores."—Extract from letter from Gen. Greene to Samuel Huntingdon, Esq., dated at "Camp at McCord's Ferry", May 14, 1781.

er of arrows, and requested they would burn the house as quick as they could. With the arrows, and skewers with combustibles tied to them fired from muskets, they soon put the house in a blaze; and the garrison commanded by Lieutenant M'Pherson* immediately surrendered at discretion. Mrs. Motte who had retired to a house at a little distance from her own, was extremely rejoiced at seeing the garrison surrender, although at the expense of her own elegant house."

"Two days after this surrender", says Gen. Moultrie, "the British quitted their post at Nelson's-ferry,† on the south side of Santee-river, about sixty miles from Charleston, blew up their works and destroyed a great part of their stores. A few days after, Fort Granby, in Granby, on Congaree-river, (which had been much harrassed by Colonel Taylor's regiment of militia) surrendered to Lieutenant Colonel Lee.‡ The garrison

---

*"Sir,
"I beg leave to return you many thanks for your politeness in transmitting to me the letters which fell into your possession at Motte's house. Lieut. M'Pherson having mentioned to me that you proposed an exchange of the garrison taken at that post, I have only to promise, that an equal number of continental officers and soldiers shall be immediately set at liberty for all such as General Greene may think proper to send to Charleston."—Extract from letter from Lord Rawdon to Gen. Greene, May 14, 1781.

†Nelson's Ferry is the point on the Santee river where the dividing line between Charlestown and Orangeburgh districts commenced.

‡Head Quarters, Congaree, May 18th, 1781.

"Sir:
"I am directed by Gen'l Greene to inform you of the surrender of Fort Granby; five pieces of iron Ordnance, nineteen officers and three hundred and twenty nine privates fell into our hands. The army will march this morning on the route to Ninety-Six. The General has directed General Sumter to continue at this post to command and organize the militia. You will be pleased to continue to harrass the enemy and to receive General Sumter's orders. You will also arrange

commanded by Major Maxwell, consisted of about three hundred and fifty men, most of them militia: in all these different forts, the Americans took a large quantity of stores. Lord Rawdon being on the south side of Santee-river, marched down immediately to the relief of Fort Granby, but after marching fourteen miles, he met officers of that garrison on their way to town as prisoners of war, and paroled to Charleston; upon which, he returned."

GEN. THOMAS SUMTER.†

On May 11th the post at Orangeburgh, consisting of seventy militia and twelve regulars surrendered to General Sumter.* There is a tradition that Sumter came into town by the "Bellville" road, and that as he reached a spot on Russell Street about in front of where the Presbyterian Church is now he stopped and planted his cannon under a large oak tree which stood there then, and which stood there for upward of

---

your Brigade with expedition, and be in readiness to co-operate with this army, should an opportunity offer.
        "I am, with great respect,
           "Your most obd't. humble servant,
                "J. Burnet, Aid-de-Camp."—to Gen. Marion.

*"On the 11th the post of Orangeburgh, defended by eighty men, under the command of a colonel and other officers, surrendered to Gen. Sumter, who, by his skill in the disposition of his Artillery and Troops, so intimidated the garrison, that the place soon submitted. We thus got possession of a very strong post, without loss either of men or time; a great quantity of provisions and other stores were found in it."—Extract from letter from Gen. Greene to Samuel Huntingdon, Esq.

†By courtesy of Everett Waddey Company, publishers Chapman's School History of South Carolina.

one hundred years after.* After firing a few shots from this position Gen. Sumter moved on down to a point on Broughton Street, about in front of the residence of the late Harpin Riggs. There he placed his artillery under another large oak, which stood there, and was still there up to about 1890. From this posi-

---

*When the same tree was cut down, the following story concerning it appeared in an Orangeburg paper:

"A LANDMARK REMOVED.—The old oak that has stood in Russell Street, and shaded that thoroughfare during its whole career, that has been one of Orangeburg's primaeval landmarks since it has been a 'burg, has at last been felled. The grand old tree has been dead for several years, but has stood in the sunshine and the storm, grand even in its decay. Standing right in the road where General Sumter marched to attack the British garrison then occupying the jail, his ancient artillery rumbling over its roots, the old oak where it voiced, could tell of historic love. Separated from its hoary comrades of the forest, it has stood in the heart of our growing town, looking and smiling upon its improvements. At last in a green old glory, it has 'departed in peace.'

"The town-council has had it hewn down, and its massy trunk, riven by explosion, has been removed. In the summer afternoon; as the reports of the blasting reverberated on the air, they seemed a funeral salute over its remains.

"So alas; must dear and grand old prejudices, smiling as if in reluctant recognition of progressive change and advancement, pass away with things and systems of the past.

"We publish below a beautiful poem, by Scribbler an occasional, and esteemed contributor:

"THE OLD OAK.

"When vengefully, the storms swept by,
With maddening roar and livid sky,
Was lit with flashings, quick and dread.
Thou'st held aloft, thy sturdy head
Like Hector, when his noble dead.
    Around him countless lay.
Defiant though the feo drove fast,
Unmoved amid the wildest blast
Thy stalwart limbs, stripped bare, and left
Of every kindred soul bereft,
And front with myriad gashings cleft,
    Yet braving up alway.

tion Gen. Sumter soon brought the garrison to terms.*
Gen. Sumter is said to have been assisted by Capt.
Henry Felder with his company of militia, and the
two old cannons now standing in Orangeburgh—one
on the northeast corner of Russell and Church Streets
and the other on the southwest corner of Russell and
Market Streets—are said to have been used by him in
the siege.

Of the events just narrated Simms says. p. 226 et
seq: "The fall of Camden† led to the rapid overthrow
of the enemy's chain of posts below, and completed
the recovery of the state to within thirty miles of the
sea. Greene, concluding after the evacuation of this
place by Rawdon, that it would be the enemy's object
to withdraw his posts on the Congaree, and concen-

> "How often have the birdlings made,
> Their home within thy plenteous shade,
> A safe retreat, till icy breath,
> Of winter wrapped in early death,
> Thy pride, and scattered far bedeath
>   Ty tendrils clinging fast.
> Changes thou'st seen, of hope and dread
> Thou'st borne, and wept thy numereus dead
> Thou'st won the fight, 'gainst many a storm,
> Yet time hath gnarled thy giant form
> And age hath fed the wasting worm,
>   And death exults at last."

* Captain Thomas Young, a Revolutionary soldier, who was still living in 1848, wrote an account of some of his experiences, and, among other things, says: "I joined a detachment of whigs, under Colonel Brandon, and scouted through the country until we reached the siege of Fort Motte. There I remained several days, when we joined a detachment, under Colonel Hampton, to take Orangeburg. The State troops out-marched us, for we had a piece of artillery to manage; we arrived the morning after them. As soon as the field-piece was brought to bear upon the house, a breach was made through the gable end—then another lower down—then about the centre, and they surrendered."

† Lord Rawdon *evacuated* Camden, on May 10th, and gradually retired into Charlestown.

trate them below the Santee, dispatched expresses to Marion and Sumter, to prepare themselves for such an event. He, himself, ordering the army to proceed by the Camden road for the Congaree, took an escort of cavalry and moved down in person to Fort Motte. At McCord's ferry he received the tidings of the capitulation of this place. Fort Motte lies above the fork, on the south side of the Congaree. The works of the British were built around the mansion house of the lady whose name it bore, and from which, in their savage recklessness of shame, the British officers had expelled her.* It was a noble mansion, of considerable value; but not of so much value as to abridge the patriotism of the high spirited owner. Defended by a strong garrison, under a resolute commander, the fortress promised to baffle for a long time the progress of the besiegers. Under these circumstances, Mrs. Motte, who had been driven for shelter to a neighboring hovel, produced an Indian bow, which, with a quiver of arrows, she presented to the American commander. 'Take these,' she said, while presenting them, 'and expel the enemy. These will enable you to fire the house'. Her earnest entreaty that this course might be adopted, prevailed with the reluctant Marion. Combustibles were fastened to the arrows, which were shot into the roof of the dwelling; and the patriotic woman rejoiced in the destruction of her property, when it secured the conquest to her countrymen."

* * * * * * * * * *

"Driven out from their place of shelter, the garrison

---

*Rev. C. C. Pinckney, her great grandson, says, "Life of Thomas Pinckney", p. 81: "While comparative peace reigned, Mrs. Motte was invited to occupy a part of the house; but when hostilities were resumed on the arrival of Greene, and Marion and Sumter and other patriotic leaders were assailing the British and their allies, Mrs. Motte was removed to her overseer's residence."

at Fort Motte was forced to surrender,* and the force under Marion was ready for operation in other quarters. A portion of it, under colonel Lee, was immediately despatched by Greene, as the van of the army, for the reduction of Fort Granby. The fall of Fort Motte increased the panic of the British, and two days after that event they evacuated their post at Nelson's ferry, blew up the fortifications, and destroyed their stores. Fort Granby, after a brief conflict, was surrendered with all its garrison, consisting of nearly four hundred men. The terms afforded by colonel Lee, were greatly complained of by the Carolinians. These terms gave to the enemy the privilege of carrying off their baggage, in which there was included an immense quantity of plunder. The approach of lord Rawdon, with all his army, is said to have hastened the operations of Lee, and to have led to the liberal concessions which he made to the garrison; but he has incurred the reproach of hastening the capitulation in order to anticipate the arrival of Sumter and the grand army. The siege had been begun some time before, by Sumter, who had left colonel Taylor with a strong party to maintain his position, while he made a sudden descent upon the enemy's post at Orangeburgh, in which he was thoroughly successful. Sumter, himself, conceived that he had suffered injury by the capitulation, in which nothing was gained but the earlier possession of a post which could not have been held many days longer, and must have fallen, without conditions, and with all its spoils, into the hands of the Americans. It was with bitter feelings that the whig militia beheld the covered wagons of the enemy, drawn by their own horses, which they

---

*Another account, with illustrations, will be found in Lossing's "Field Book of the Revolution" vol. 2, p. 477.

knew to be filled with the plunder of their farms and houses, driven away before their eyes."

The following is Lord Rawdon's account of these operations, extracted from his report to Lord Cornwallis:

"My first news, upon landing at Nelson's, was, that the post at Motte's house had fallen. It was a simple redoubt, and had been attacked formally by sap. Lieut. M'Pherson had maintained it gallantly till the house in the centre of it was set in flames by fire arrows, which obliged his men to throw themselves into the ditch, and surrender at discretion.

"But as Major M'Arthur joined me with near three hundred foot and eighty dragoons, I conceived I might, without hazarding too far, endeavor to check the enemy's operations on the Congaree. On the 14th, at night, I marched from Nelson's, and on the evening of the 15th I reached the point where the roads from Congarees and M'Cord's ferry unite. Various information was brought to me thither that Greene had passed the Congaree, at M'Cord's ferry, and had pushed down the Orangeburgh road. The accounts though none of them positive or singly satisfactory, corresponded so much, that I was led to believe them, and the matter was of such moment, that it would not admit of my pausing for more certain information; therefore, after giving the troops a little rest, I moved back to Eutaws the same night, but hearing nothing there, I pursued my march hither."*

"The British", says Gen. Moultrie, "had now lost all their posts in the three Southern States, except that at Ninety-six, one at Fort Golphan, and one at Augusta, in Georgia."†

---

*Charlestown.
†Fort Cornwallis.

The day after the taking of Granby, Gen. Greene dispatched Col. Lee with his legion to take Fort Golphin,* and to assist Gen. Pickens and Col. Clark in the taking of Fort Cornwallis; while he proceeded with his main force to Ninety-Six, before which he arrived on the 21st of May, 1781, and immediately began his approaches. The siege was continued until June 18th, when the approach of Lord Rawdon from Charlestown,† with reinforcements, compelled him to retreat across the Saluda and Broad rivers to a point above Winnsboro. The subsequent movements of the two armies are best described in the following letter, written by Adjutant-General Otho H. Williams to Maj: Pendleton, Aid-de-Camp to Gen. Greene:

"Camp Hills, Santee, July 16, 1781.
"Dear Pendleton:
"After you left us at Ninety-Six we were obliged to retrograde as far as the cross roads above Winnsborough. Lord Rawdon's return over Saluda induced the General to halt the army, and wait for intelli-

---

*Which was done by Captain Rudolph, one of Lee's officers.

† "Congaree, June 16th, 1781.
"Sir:
"The enemy are yet advancing, are some distance above Orangeburgh, their force considerable; Ninety-Six not yet taken; everything with respect to the siege going on well; time is all that is needed. I wrote to Gen'l Greene for ammunition for you, which, if he furnishes, I will have forwarded to meet you. In one day more the enemy's designs must be known, whether their object is Ninety-Six, or my party, to which they have already given much trouble in marching and counter marching. As their movements have been very singular and with uncommon caution, they are strong in horse. An express this moment from Gen'l. Greene; the post not reduced, but in a fair way. I am, sir,
"Your most obd't. humble servant,
"Thos. Sumter."—to Gen. Marion.

gence respecting his further manoeuvres, and hearing a few days after that his lordship was on his march to fort Granby, our army was ordered to march towards that place by way of Winnsborough. Before we could arrive at Congaree, Lord Rawdon retired to Orangeburgh; and as he had left a considerable part of his army at Ninety-Six, Gen. Greene detached the cavalry and light infantry to join Gen. Marion, and endeavor to intercept Col. Stewart, who was on his march from Charleston with the Third Regiment, &c., consisting of about three hundred, conveying bread, stores, &c., of which Lord Rawdon's troops were in great want. Stewart however joined his lordship at Orangeburgh; and Gen. Greene, from the information he had received, was encouraged to expect success from an attack upon the British army at that post. Accordingly he collected his troops, and called together the militia and state troops under Gen's. Sumter and Marion (Gen. Pickens being left to watch the motions of Col. Cruger). A junction of the whole formed a very respectable little army, which marched to a small branch of North Edisto,* within four miles of Orangeburgh, where we halted, and lay the 12th instant from about nine o'clock in the morning till six in the afternoon.

LORD RAWDON.

GEN. GREENE.†

"Gen. Greene reconnoitred the position of the enemy, and found it materially different from what it had been represented. The ground is broken, and natur-

---

*Turkey Hill Branch on what is now called the old Columbia road, in all probability. †By courtesy of Everett Waddey Company, publishers Chapman's School History of South Carolina.

ally strong, from the Court-house (which is two stories high and built of brick*), to a bridge four or five hundred yards distant, the only pass over the Edisto within many miles. The general had every reason to believe what he had soon afterwards confirmed, that Col. Cruger had evacuated Ninety-Six, and was on his march to join Lord Rawdon, which might possibly be done before we could force his lordship (if he could be forced at all) to a general action,—the issue of which was not certain. These considerations induced the General rather to offer than give battle. The enemy declined the opportunity, and put up with the insult. Gen. Greene, therefore, ordered our troops to retire in the afternoon to Col. Middleton's plantation, from whence we have proceeded by slow easy marches to this place, and not without leaving behind sufficient detachments to intercept their convoys from below, and to create such a diversion at Monk's Corner, Dorchester, &c., as will very probably oblige his lordship to march to their relief."

Rawdon's operations were now confined almost entirely within that extent of country which is enclosed by the Santee, the Congaree and the North Edisto. Within these limits, after the late retreat of Greene, Rawdon evidently resolved to canton his forces, but he soon found that the Americans were not to be shaken off. He was no doubt surprised when he found that Gen. Greene had not retreated a great way off, but had faced about to give him battle upon the Congaree. Having divided his force, and left one part of it at Ninety-Six under command of Col. Cruger, he felt himself unequal to an encounter, but fell back before the approaching Americans to Orangeburgh, where he was sheltered on one side by the Edisto, and on the

---

* That building was destroyed soon thereafter, or else Col. Williams mistook the jail for the Court House.

other by strong buildings, little inferior to redoubts. But even these advantages might not have saved him, had not the approach of Cruger compelled Greene to withdraw. Cruger having joined him, Lord Rawdon left the post at Orangeburgh in command of Colonel Stewart, and, with five hundred of his troops retired into Charlestown, the State troops dogging his footsteps.

Having succeeded in driving Rawdon from Camden, by striking at the posts below, Greene determined to pursue the same course to compel the evacuation of Orangeburgh. With this object in view he let loose in the country below Orangeburgh most of the State troops under Marion and Sumter. These so harassed reconnoitering parties, convoys, escorts and stragglers; so often captured or cut off supplies, and otherwise so annoyed Stewart that his situation at Orangeburgh was becoming precarious, although he had command of nearly three thousand troops.

When Stewart moved, he took post near the junction of the Congaree and Wateree rivers, but on the South side. He left a force at Orangeburgh, and Col. Lee, crossing the Congaree with his cavalry, penetrated between the main body of the British army and the post at Orangeburgh, and in sight of the latter place, drove in, dispersed and captured several of their detachments. The embarrassment produced by such operations; the great difficulty of procuring provisions; and the necessity of lessening his main army to strengthen his posts below; in order to cover his communications between Orangeburgh and Charlestown, rendered the position of Stewart still more critical.

The concentration by Greene of most of his detachments at a general rendezvous, determined the movements of Stewart. Falling back upon his re-inforcements and convoys, he took a position at Eutaw

Springs, about forty miles from Orangeburgh. He was followed by Col. Lee, who was pushed forward to watch his movements, while Gen. Pickens, with his South Carolina militia, advanced with a similar object, in the neghborhood of the enemy's post at Orangeburgh. Meantime, Greene crossed the Congaree, and moved down to Fort Motte,* where he resolved to discontinue the pursuit and await events.

This hesitation seemed to determine Stewart. Halting at Eutaw, he withdrew the garrison from Orangeburgh, and establishing it at Fairlawn Barony,† he prepared for a fight. Greene being joined by Marion, followed up, and on September 8th, 1781, the battle of Eutaw was fought.‡ Although the action was indecisive Stewart retreated towards Charlestown. And though he succeeded in escaping from his pursuers, the British power in South Carolina was completely prostrated by the battle of Eutaw.

Meanwhile intelligence reached the South that Cornwallis contemplated returning from Virginia to Carolina by land. A movement of Stewart seemed to confirm the report. Having strengthened his army he returned to Eutaw.

---

* "Near Ferguson's Swamp, Sept. 11, 1781.

"In my dispatches of the 25th of August, I informed your excellency, that we were on the march to Friday's Ferry, with the intent of forming a junction with the troops of the State and the corps of militia that were assembled, and to attack the English army, encamped near M'Leod's Ferry.

"On the 27th, upon our arrival there, I received advice that the enemy had retired. We passed the river at Howell's Ferry, and our first post was Motte's plantation, where I learnt that the enemy had stopped at Eutaw Springs, about forty miles from us."—Gen. Greene to the President of Congress.

†The plantation of Sir James Colleton, who—by the way—sided with the Americans.

‡Eutaw Springs are situated just across the line that then separated Orangeburgh and Charlestown districts.

COL. HENRY LEE.

GEN. ANDREW PICKENS.

[By permission, from Weber's History of South Carolina. Ginn & Company, Publishers.]

The advance of the British to Eutaw did not, on their part, result in any increase of vigor. They took post at Fludd's plantation, three miles above Nelson's ferry. Their force of over two thousand was so much larger than Greene's that it gave the enemy the undivided command of the country to the South of the Santee and Congaree, and westward to the Edisto. But Greene received reinforcements and within two months of the battle of Eutaw was again ready to act. Marion was ordered to operate between the Santee and Charlestown, and Sumter, with his brigade of State troops, and some companies of his militia brigade, was ordered to take post at Orangeburgh and defend the country against the loyalists from Charlestown.*

Gen. Sumter crossed the river in the beginning of November, and advanced upon the enemy. He soon fell in with a strong party of Tories under Gen. Robert Cuningham, who had advanced upon Orangeburgh, and one of his officers, a Major Morris, suffered himself to fall into an ambuscade, in which he sustained some loss. The forces of Sumter and Cuningham

---

*"Gen Sumter has orders to take post at Orangeburg, to prevent the Tories in that quarter from conveying supplies to Town, and his advance parties will penetrate as low as Dorchester; therefore you may act in conjunction with him" &c.—Extract from a letter from Gen. Greene to Gen. Marion, Nov. 5, 1781.

"Gen. Sumter is gone to take post at Orangeburg."—Greene to Marion, Nov. 11, 1781.

"Orangeburg, Nov. 23, 1781.

"Sir:

"I have some reason to think Gen. Greene don't mean to move downward until the lower posts are well explored, and the number and situation of the enemy accurately ascertained." * * * *
"The enemy in this quarter are numerous in horse, but not formidable."—Sumter to Marion.

"Would you wish to have a part of the militia of Gen. Sumter's Brigade? they are at Orangeburgh and Four Holes—please to inform me. I suppose you have heard of the General's resignation; Col. Henderson is thought of to succeed him."—Gen. Greene to Gen. Marion, March 1, 1782.

being nearly equal, operated as mutual checks upon each other. Cuningham, who had issued from Charlestown on a pillaging expedition into the upper country, was checked in his progress; while Sumter, to continue this restraint upon his enemy, and maintain himself in safety, fell back for the present, and secured himself by a carefully selected position.

About this time the news of the fall of Cornwallis at Yorktown reached South Carolina. It gave confidence to Greene and caused Stewart alarm.

On November 18th, Greene struck camp at the High Hills, and took up the line of march on the route by Simons's and McCord's ferries, through Orangeburgh, to Riddlespurger's; thence by the Indian field road to Ferguson's mill, where that road crosses the Edisto. The remainder of Greene's operations were to the South of Orangeburg District. The country from the Edisto to the Santee became thrown open in consequence, for a time, to the ravages of the enemy; and a party of Tories, under the command of William Cuningham, ("Bloody Bill.") escaped from the lower country, passed through Orangeburg District, and ascended the Saluda with a body of three hundred horse.*

By the beginning of the year 1782 the British held no posts outside of Charlestown, but they did not formally retire from that city until December 14th, 1782. In the meantime about the only warfare waged in South Carolina was that waged between Whigs and Tories. Several events of this warfare have been recorded. Two by Dr. Johnson, in his "Traditions", concern us. Of the first of these he says, p. 548:

---

*Dr. Johnson, says, p. 505: "It is supposed, that when Bill Cunningham made his bloody incursion into the up-country, in 1781, his aim was to surprise and capture Hammond." (Col. Samuel.) But on the other hand he did not surprise Hammond, but was worried by him until Gen. Pickens joined Hammond and chased Cuningham from the Saluda to Orangeburgh.

"Near the close of these troubles in South-Carolina, in May, 1782, Captain Watson* heard of a body of tories in Dean's Swamp, near Orangeburg, and, in conjunction with Captain William Butler—his friend and neighbor—it was dertermined to attack them. Watson's men were mounted militia, armed with rifles and muskets; Butler's command were cavalry, armed with pistols and cutlasses. In order to surprise the tories, the associates marched forward at sunset with great rapidity, captured a disaffected man, named Hutto or Hutton, and hurried him along with them under guard. As they approached the tory encampment, Hutton made his escape, and gave notice to the tories of Watson's approach. They immediately paraded in ambush to surprise and oppose the whigs. When Hutton's escape was reported to the two captains, Watson declared his opinion that the expedition should be abandoned, but Butler, for various reasons, thought otherwise, and they accordingly continued to advance. When they approached the edge of the swamp, two men were observed, as if endeavoring to hide themselves. Butler, Watson, and Sergeant Vardel—a very brave man—rode rapidly forward to capture them. Watson first discovered that these men were only a decoy, and, when too late, warned the others that the whole of the tories were there concealed. They arose, on being discovered, and poured on their assailants a well-directed fire, which brought down Watson, Vardel, and several others of the foremost whigs. Although sorely galled, Butler brought off the wounded men, and now found, to his mortification, that the infantry had little or no ammunition left, and that the enemy were advancing upon him with double his numbers. In this emergency, he appointed a brave young man, named John

---

*Michael Watson.

Corley, his lieutenant, and made a desperate charge on the enemy's line, so unexpectedly as to throw them into confusion. He pressed on them so hotly, mingling in their disordered ranks, and hewing them down with his broad swords, that they had not time to rally—their superior numbers only increased their confusion and destruction. Butler continued his impetuous attack, until the tories took refuge in the swamp. As the whigs returned in triumph, the gallant Vardel made an effort to rise and wave his hand in hurra, but fell immediately and expired. They buried him—where the brave are proud to lie—on the field of victory.

"Watson survived until the Americans reached Orangeburg. In that village he was buried with the honors of war, and his grave was watered with the manly tears of his fellow soldiers.

"The following incidents occurred in this expedition to Dean's Swamp. A smart young man, who had never been engaged in battle, was very anxious to become an officer in Watson's company, and very desirous of distinction. He was elected, and advanced in his command very gallantly to the attack mounted on a beautiful filly. When the enemy were discovered, he dismounted with the rest, and having hitched his horse, was advancing on foot, when the tories rose and delivered their destructive fire. Seeing the number that fell with Captain Watson, the young officer's courage suddenly evaporated from his finger ends. He turned his back, and, forgetting his horse, became more distinguished in the flight than in the fight, and never stopped until he reached home, spreading a report that the party had been ambushed and all killed but himself. The horse was saved by those who brought off the wounded. When they reached Orangeburg, finding that the owner would not return to claim her, they sold the mare, and expended the money in rum and other refreshments."

In the sketch of Captain James Ryan to be found in Johnson's "Traditions of the Revolution" the following paragraph concerns us:

"In the latter part of the year 1782, while advancing with his usual impetuosity, and perhaps too much temerity, upon a party of tories that were encamped near Orangeburg, he received a musket ball in his shoulder, which he carried to his grave. Not at all disconcerted or discouraged, although unable to proceed, he ordered, with great presence of mind, his first lieutenant, William Butler, to lead on the attack and continue the pursuit."

This warfare between Whigs and Tories did not even end with the war, though waged without the sanction of the law. But at any rate we will consider the Revolutionary war as closing in South Carolina, and in Orangeburgh District, on the day when the British vessels containing the British army sailed out of Charleston Harbor, December 14th, 1782.

> "Three hundred noble vessels
> Rose on the rising flood,
> Wherein with sullen apathy
> Embarked those men of blood."

The following list of battles fought on the soil of what is now Orangeburg County, was kindly furnished by General Edward McCrady from the manuscript of his forthcoming volume on the history of South Carolina during the Revolutionary period:

1. THOMSON'S PLANTATION, 22 and 23 February, 1781. Sumter attacks British post at, is repulsed, but next day captures wagon train and guards on way to Rawdon.

2. ORANGEBURG, 11 May, 1781. Sumter attacks British post at, and makes captures.

3. FORT MOTTE, 12 May, 1781. Taken from the British by Marion and Lee.

4. FORKS OF THE EDISTO, May, 1781. Captain Connaway Royal Militia of Orangeburg attacks Whig party, kills many and disperses rest.

5. ——————, November, 1781. Maj. Morris, Whig, is surprised and defeated by Tories under Cuningham.

6. ——————, 27 November, 1781. Colonel Richard Hampton is surprised and defeated by Tories under Cuningham.

7. DEAN SWAMP, May, 1782. Captains Watson and Butler attack Tories. Led into ambush. Watson and Vardell killed, Butler defeated.

Section 6. *The Germans and Scotch of Orangeburgh in the Revolution.*

The German people who resided in Orangeburgh District have never received justice in regard to their conduct during the Revolution, at the hands of any of our historians, and for that reason outside historians have been free to declare that the large German settlements in South Carolina were of Tory sentiments.

On this subject Lorenzo Sabine in his work, "American Loyalists", says, speaking of the conduct of South Carolina in the Revolution: "The population, composed as it was, of emigrants from Switzerland, Germany, France, Ireland, and the northern colonies of America, and their descendants, was, of course, deficient in the necessary degree of homogeneity, or sameness of nature, to insure any considerable unanimity of political sentiment." After giving the above as one of the principal reasons why the people of South Carolina were not true to the cause of Independence, Sabine continued by making many *assertions* to the effect that South Carolina's conduct was reproachful, but proved nothing.

In his admirable pamphlet, "South Carolina in the Revolution", Mr. Simms refutes many of the slanders of Sabine, but even he has fallen into the error, that so many other historians had fallen into, in regard to the conduct of the German and Scotch elements of our population. Mr. Simms says on p. 17 of his pamphlet: "The Scotch, a people remarkable for their loyalty, were naturally with Great Britain. The German population found no arguments equal to the conclusive fact that George the Third was a Prince of Hanover." Again on p. 71 he says: "Her numerical force was lessened by the Scotch, German and Quaker settlements of the interior all of which were loyalists."

Dr. Joseph Johnson, in "Traditions of the Revolution", pp. 101-2, makes the same error. He says: "The Germans in South Carolina generally refused to take part in the revolution, either for or against the government, saying that the King was of German descent, and that they did not understand the dispute."

Quotations from other historians might be cited, but these will suffice.

Now, the bulk of the German people of South Carolina lived in the districts of Orangeburgh and Ninety-Six—that part of Ninety-Six now embraced by Newberry and Saluda counties.

This work does not concern the conduct of the Ninety-Six Germans, but extensive research as to the conduct of the Orangeburgh Germans, shows that among them were some of the truest Whigs in South Carolina, and we must insist that only a very small percentage of them were Tories, outlaws or neutrals.

A careful examination of the Giessendanner Record, given in the second chapter of this work, will disclose the names of the German families of Orangeburgh

District. A comparison of those names with those to be found on various Revolutionary documents will show that prominent representatives of almost every one of those families were ardent Whigs, and as the same men had been leaders among their fellow-countrymen before the Revolution began, it is reasonable to suppose that their leadership was still followed during the Revolution, especially when we consider that as a race the Germans are particularly given to sticking together and following their leaders when in a foreign country. We see illustrations of that before our very eyes almost daily.

Again we have seen that at least two strong military organizations existed among the German Whigs in the immediate vicinity of Orangeburgh village, and the only roll extant (so far as we know) of one of those companies contains about sixty German names out of a total membership of sixty-five. That there were other German soldiers fighting in other branches of the service it is reasonable to suppose; else why should Governor Rutledge have selected Orangeburgh, as his headquarters in 1779, and as the place of rendezvous of the militia, if it was not a Whig stronghold? And from the letter of Col. Charles Pinckney to Gen. Moultrie, of March 2nd, 1779, (p. 491.) we infer that Governor Rutledge expected to raise 2,700 men in the vicinity of Orangeburgh, and with four Ninety-Six militia regiments added, he expected to have a force of 5,000. We have shown that from his camp at Orangeburgh he detached, on the 13th of April, 1779, Col. Simons with a thousand men to Gen. Moultrie at Black Swamp, and yet retained a force of six or seven hundred men. We have also seen that after sending out several detachments, amounting to one or two hundred men in all, he joined Gen. Moultrie in Charlestown with about 600 militia.

ORANGEBURG COUNTY. 533

From the proofs already furnished, it is quite certain that Orangeburgh District furnished a large militia force during the Revolution, and as a large percentage of the inhabitants of the District were Germans, then a large percentage of the militia of the District must necessarily have been Germans. And of the large militia force assembled in 1779, by Governor Rutledge, right in the heart of this, the principal German settlement in South Carolina, surely a good proportion of it must have been from the country around, and as a very large majority of the people around there were German people, then a fair proportion of the Orangeburgh militia with Governor Rutledge must have been Germans. We have likewise seen that many of the regulars in Thomson's regiment were from Orangeburgh, and many of these were necessarily Germans also. The same thing may be said of the company of fifty men recruited by Capt. Thomas Pinckney in Orangeburgh in July, 1775. And here it may be proper to ask why Capt. Pinckney went among the Germans to recruit if they were opposed to the Revolution, and how it happened that he secured three fourths of his men from among them? And in Col. Rowe's regiment; and in Col. Beard's militia regiment; and in those three militia companies mentioned by Col. Thomson as existing in his immediate neighborhood; and in that militia company commanded by Capt. John Salley, there must have been some Germans. And of the four Continental veterans of Orange Parish who drew pensions from the United States government in 1840, two were Germans, while the only one of St. Matthew's Parish was a German.

General Knox, who was Secretary of War under President Washington, reported that during the Revolution South Carolina had furnished 35,507 enlistments to the Continental service. When we consider that the maximum white population of South Carolina for that period was only about 90,000* this seems incredible. But as the war lasted seven years, and as the longest term of enlistment was for three years† and after that had expired, for six months or longer, or for the war, many had a chance to serve out a first enlistment and then re-enlist; a thing which they must undoubtedly have done. Again it must be taken into consideration that a small boy at the beginning of the war was old enough to enlist long before the end of the war. South Carolina furnished fifteen regiments to

---

*When the six regiments of South Carolina regulars were first raised in 1775–76, the men enlisted therein were enlisted for three years, so that when, in 1776, these six regiments were taken into the Continental service they were already engaged for three years, although the Continental Establishment only required enlistments for six months at a time. This is one reason why Massachusetts could furnish 67,907 to South Carolina's 35,507. The New England States enlisted their regular troops for six months. The following note from page xviii of Drayton's Memoirs (vol. i.) will be of interest in this connection:

"When the Congress began to consider of a Continental army, they were for leaving the army in Massachusetts, as belonging to the Colony, which they were willing to pay—and besides, to raise a Continental one. But the N Delegates said, this army has stood the brunt—you are willing to pay them—why deprive them of rank? Well, they were made continentals. The regulations came on next; the British, were proposed. No, said they, they have signed other articles; and will you impose others upon them? And, this was yielded. The term, was next; the six months the New-Englanders has enlisted for, was thought too short: no, said they, the war will be over in that time—besides, will you make these men serve longer, than they have agreed for? Well, then, they were answered, rescind the resolve for making them continentals. No. And thus it was, that the ruinous policy of short enlistments obtained.—*This from J. Rutledge.*"

†In 1774, the population of South Carolina was estimated by the Continental Congress at 225,000; but that included the negroes, and negroes did not, strictly speaking, count as *population* (but as property) in that day—a Republican "Committee on Elections" was, a thing, at that time, yet to be created.

the Continental service, and besides, she was never with less than three militia brigades of her own—sometimes five. So that with her Continentals, militia, State troops, (which sometimes acted as Continentals,) old men, women and children very few of her population of 90,000 were left for Tories or neutrals. Consequently, very few of the large number of Germans in Orangeburgh could possibly have been elsewhere than with the Whigs.

Eighteen men were appointed on the "Committee for carrying into execution the Continental Association" for Orangeburgh District in February, 1775; and of this number Henry Felder, Lewis Golson, Adam Snell, Christopher Zahn and Godfrey Drier were undoubtedly Germans, while several other names on the list have a German sound. Surely if *all* of the Germans were opposed to the Revolution, five Germans would not have been put on a committee of eighteen from one district alone. And again, in August of that same year, of the six members of the State legislature returned for St. Matthew's Parish, one, Henry Felder, was a German. Of the thirty-six justices of the peace for Orangeburgh District, appointed in 1776, five, perhaps more, were Germans. And on that grand jury, which in May, 1776, made such an able and eloquent presentment to Chief-Justice Drayton, the German names Felder, Leitner, Snell, Rickenbacker, Whetstone, Crum and Drehr appear. Henry Felder was the foreman, and it is probable that he wrote the presentment which speaks nothing but the loftiest words of Whig patriotism. Henry Felder was probably educated in Zürich before he left that place, and was doubtless well able to write such a paper, since we have it as a traditionary joke that "whenever he got up in the legislature to present a bill it became a law before he sat down", from which we infer that he must have been a John T. Morgan in his day and time. (And there are those who seem to believe that the ability to say a great deal is really ability.) And if handwriting is any test of education then Henry Rickenbacker, of the same jury, must have been educated, for he wrote a beautiful hand, almost like copy plate. There were doubtless many well educated Germans among the Orangeburgh settlers. Their pastor, Rev. Giessendanner, was characterized as "a man of learning, piety and knowledge in the Holy Scriptures", and his book clearly shows that he was at least a man of learning.

But to return to their immediate share in the Revolution. On the list of tax collectors for 1777, for Orangeburgh District, were the German names Felder, Stroul, Kaigler and Geiger. And on the Orangeburgh grand jury, that in 1778, presented as a grievance, "the want of a publick general test by which the foes may be distinguished from the friends of the American cause", and recommended that "the abjuration oath be made general", we find the German names Lewis Golson (foreman), Felder, Whetstone, Harrisperger, Rickenbacker, Drehr and Snell. Surely a loyalist, or a neutral who "did not understand the dispute", would not, in the first place, have been on the grand jury, or have signed such a presentment.

And so on, throughout the war, we find a large percentage of the civic officers of the district, Germans. Much to the same effect might be said of the Germans elsewhere in South Carolina, but this essay deals only with Orangeburgh District.

Now, while the Cuninghams, Evan McLaurin, Moses Kirkland, John Stuart, Joseph Robinson, and other Scotch settlers of the "back country" were Tories, by no means *all* of the Scotch settlers of South Carolina were Tories. In fact the Tory element in South Carolina was confined to no special race or creed; they were representatives of every nationality then settled in America, and they were usually either the latest arrivals, or the scum of the ante-Revolutionary society; while the majority of them were the "driftwood" of the NORTHERN colonies.

But in Orangeburgh Township there were several true and tried Scotchmen whose names were scarcely ever absent from the council rolls of the State during the Revolution. Among these were Col. Christopher Rowe, Henry Rowe, Samuel Rowe, and Donald Bruce the latter of whom had, up to 1774, been a merchant in Charlestown; though we are told that it was among the Scotch merchants of Charlestown that the most dangerous Tory sentiments were to be found. And even he has been unintentionally misrepresented by that earnest and painstaking historian, Wm. Gilmore Simms, who speaks, in "The Forayers", of the "widow Bruce" as a loyalist. The fact is there was no widow Bruce until ten years after the close of the war, and her husband was not only a member of the State legislature for several years during the Revolution, but likewise belonged to the Whig army, as was shown by an old letter, written by him during the war, lately in the possession of one of his descendants.

In the dark days just subsequent to the fall of Charlestown the tories of Ninety-Six District, backed by the British army, committed all manner of crimes; murdering, plundering, burning and riding rough shod over the people, while at the same time the people of Orangeburgh District were enjoying comparative quiet, and all because the Tory sentiment was not so strong in that district, and because the post at Ninety-Six was more strongly garrisoned by British regulars than that at Orangeburgh.

Again, when "Bloody Bill" Cuningham made his

famous raid into the back country in November, 1781, while Gen. Pickens was busy with the Ninety-Six militia in the lower country, he found little opposition, save in Orangeburgh District, where the brave Rumph proved his match and perhaps a little more than his match. In fact, Cuningham's luck seemed to forsake him whenever he reached Orangeburgh, and, to crown all, his favorite charger, "Ringtail", a blooded mare presented to him by his kinsman, Capt. Patrick Cuningham, died on a roadside near Orangeburgh while Cuningham was on, probably, his last trip to Charlestown, whence he soon after embarked for Nassau, where he spent the remainder of his days. a pensioner of the British government and a wretched example of the South Carolina Loyalist.

> "He left a name at which the world grew pale,
> To point a moral or adorn a tale."

The Cuninghams were the most conspicuous Tories in South Carolina. They were people of affluence, wealth and influence. They were Scotch people. They lived in a community composed largely of Scotch and German people. They used their best endeavors to influence their neighbors against the revolutionists; but they were unsuccessful, and two of them died alone in a foreign land.

The number of South Carolina Tories—whether Scotch, or German, or English, or Irish, or Hebrew—has been greatly exagerated. It is time to call a halt. It is time to seek the truth.

ORANGEBURG COUNTY. 539

INDEX

Abbeville District, 369.
Abecklin, Kilian, 96, 108.
Aberly, Anne, 167, 180.
Aberly, Catharine Margaret, 167.
Aberly, John, 120, 159, 167, 180.
Acadia, 33.
Acker, Magdelin, 99, 101.
Acker, Johannes, 100.
Acker, Susannah, 98.
"Adventure", Barque, 34.
Aiken County, 9, 17.
Alamance, the battle of, 118.
Albany, 236.
Alder, Anna, 210.
Alder, Conrad, 95, 108, 210.
Aldridge, Agnes, 167.
Aldridge, Sarah, 167.
Aldridge, William, 167.
Aldridge, Zachariah, 167.
Alexander, Joseph, 323.
Allison, Andrew, 250.
Alston, Capt., 344-5.
Altamaha, 334, 360.
Amaker, Anna, 114, 125.
Amaker, Hans, 214.
Amaker, Johannes, 105, 116.
Amaker, John, Jr., 136, 137, 147, 217.
Amaker, John, Revolutionary soldier, 473, 484-5.
Amaker, name, 31.
Amelia Chapel, 68, 170, 172-3, 175-81, 183-6, 190-3.
Amelia, the Princess, 2.
Amelia Township, 2, 3, 9, 10, 23-4, 33-4, 45-6, 63-4, 70, 74, 95, 97, 100, 111-19, 121-4, 126, 128, 130, 145, 147-8, 153, 155, 158, 162, 163, 165, 168, 171, 179, 198, 218, 219, 226, 228-9, 237, 246-50, 290, 368.
America, 33, 42-3, 72-3, 76, 88, 230, 236, 286, 289, 316, 336, 381, 402.

"American Loyalists", 530.
"American Lutheran Church". 238.
Amherst, Gen., 235.
Ancrum, George, 265.
Ancrum, William, 255.
Anding, Anna Barbara, 180.
Anding, John, 120, 137, 143, 159, 167, 168, 180.
Anding, John Nicholas, 167.
Anding, Margaret, 159, 167-8, 180.
Anding, Veronica, 143, 214.
Andrews, Robert, 112.
"Annals of Newberry District", 386, 411, 481.
Anne, the Princess, 35.
Annis, Jacob, 161.
Anson Street, 91.
Anthony, Rev. J. B., 83.
Appenzel, Canton, 36, 52.
Arant, Mrs., 67-8.
Argrove, Leven, 467.
Armstrong, Gen., 345-6, 349, 466.
Armstrong, Robert, 388.
Arthur, Barnabas, 217, 248.
Arthur, Capt., 436.
Arthur, William, 12, 248-9, 257, 260, 265, 272-6.
Ashby, Anthony, 388.
Ashly River, 89.
Astor Library, 78.
Atkinson, John, 97.
Augusta, 2, 36, 296-7, 315, 354, 417-8, 422-3.
Ax, Catharine, 136.
Bachman, Rev. John, D. D., 92.
Bachrden, Margretta, 99, 101.
Bacon's Bridge, 89.
Bacot, Peter, 281, 319.
Baden, 70, 80.
Badenhop, J., 27.
Bailey, Lieut., 363, 387.

Baird, Eugenia, 162.
Baird, James, 162.
Baker, Capt. Jesse, 386.
Baker, John, 145.
Baldrick, James, 230.
Baldridge, Margaret, 180.
Baldridge, Mary, 180.
Baldridge, Richard, 180.
Ballentine, Eleanor, 147.
Ballentine, Eugenia, 147.
Ballentine, Katherine, 178.
Ballentine, William, 144, 147, 155, 156.
Ballew, Thomas, 115.
Balmarin, Magdaline, 98.
Balziger, George, 184.
Balziger, Hans (1), 104, 125, 129, 136, 140, 152, 157, 202.
Balziger, Hans (2), 150.
Balziger, Mary, 125, 129, 136, 152, 157.
Balziger, name, 31.
Bamberg County, 9.
Bamrick, Thomas, 163.
Barbadoes, 34.
Barber, Elizabeth, 125.
Barber, Thomas, 125.
Barber, name, 32.
Barker, Elizabeth, 122, 131, 138, 158.
Barker, Elizabeth, daughter of former, 131.
Barker, James, 124.
Barker, John, 122.
Barker, Thomas (1), 122, 131, 138, 158.
Barker, Thomas (2), 158.
Barker, name, 32.
Barklow, Richard, 230.
Barnwell County, 9, 17, 90, 219.
Barnwell District, 15, 16, 87, 220, 467.
Barnwell, Gen. John, 388, 470.
Barr, John George, 30, 199, 200, 215.
Barr, Margaret, 161.

Barrie, Elizabeth, 117-8, 130, 138.
Barrie, William, 31, 114, 117, 126, 130, 135, 138, 198.
Barrin, Anna Catharina, 154, 176.
Barrin, Anna Margaret, 138, 168, 173.
Barrin, Eva Catharina, 119, 138, 144.
Barry, Michael, 101.
Barwick, Edward, 119, 153, 156.
Barwick, Margaret, 153, 156.
Barwick, Mary, 153.
Barwick, Thomas, 159.
Baumgartner, Conrad, 192.
Beames, James, 276, 368.
Beames, Lieut., 354, 387, 446.
Beard, Jane, 176.
Beard, Jonas, 249, 257, 258, 265, 269, 276, 278, 293, 356, 395, 469.
Beaufort District, 13.
Beaufort, 363, 439.
Beaver Creek, 3, 13, 213.
Beck, Jacob, 117.
Beck, John Peter, 145, 155.
Beck, Margaret (1), 145, 173.
Beck, Margaret (2), 173.
Beck, Mary (2), 145.
Beck, Samuel Bly, 145, 173.
Bee, Thomas, 11, 264, 388.
Bellville, 64, 377, 379.
Beltzer, Margaret, 102.
Bently, James, 139.
Bently, Susannah, 139.
Berkeley County, 1, 2, 3, 7, 18, 22, 28, 29, 111, 116-7, 120, 246, 248.
Berkeley, Election District of, 16, 17.
Berne, Canton, 30, 35, 79, 195.
Bernheim, Rev. G. D., 39, 61, 64, 70, 75, 88, 89, 91, 92, 238.
Berry, James, 159.
Berry, Mary Anne, 159.
Berry, William, 111, 124.
Berry, William, son of James, 159.
Berwick, Simon, 257-8, 260.

INDEX

Beystein, 94.
Biddys, M., 108.
Biegelmann, Anna Elizabeth, 103.
Bieman, John Jacob, 71.
Biggin, Bridge, 393.
Binsky, Martin, 112, 114, 116.
Black Swamp, 362.
Blake, Capt. Edward, 341.
Blake, John, 388.
Bodening, Margretta, 100.
Bollerin, Margretta, 99.
Bolzius, Pastor, 46, 49, 58, 83-6, 88.
Bond, Thomas, 228, 247.
Bonnell, William, 131.
Bonnetheau, Peter, 231.
Booser, Ulrick, 161.
Booth, Bellinder, 133.
Booth, Elizabeth, 133.
Booth, William, 133.
Bossart, Ann, 30, 199.
Bossart, Henry, 175, 218.
Bossart (Bussart), Jacob, 30, 190, 199.
Boston, 255, 331.
Bowers, William, 170.
Bowie, Capt. John, 309-11, 315.
Bowman, Barbara, 126, 133.
Bowman, George, 136.
Bowman, Jacob, 126, 133, 192.
Bowman, Jacob, Tory captain, 305, 307.
Boy, Alexander, 186.
Boy, Anne, 186.
Boy, Mary Elizabeth, 186.
Boykin, Francis, 280, 313, 387-8.
Boykin, Samuel, 256, 265, 274.
Brady, Edward, 116, 176.
Brady, Edward (2), 176.
Brady. Rachel, 176.
Brant, Mrs., 99.
Bress, Anna, 146
Bress, Jacob, 146.
Bress, Mary Elizabeth, 146.
Brewton, Miles, 388.

Brick, Margaret, 110.
Brickel, Adam, 218.
Brier Creek, 90, 219.
Bright, name, 32.
Bright, Samuel, 112-13, 122.
Brimstone, Jonathan, 110.
Bringolt, Margaret, 98.
Brood, Mary, 100.
Broughton, Lieutenant-Governor, 2, 27, 70, 74, 75.
Broughton Street, 11, 65.
Brown, Andrew, 368.
Brown, Bartilot, 182.
Brown, Bartlet, 90.
Brown, Benjamin, 182.
Brown, Capt., 77, 78, 79.
Brown, Caspar, 132, 139, 140, 163, 172-3, 269, 272.
Brown, Hugh, 297, 300, 317, 428.
Brown, Katharine, 182.
Brown, name, 32.
Brown. Patrick, 231.
Brown, Richard, 265, 386, 444, 453, 459, 460, 461.
Brown, Tarleton, 90, 467, 503-509.
Brown, Tarleton, "Memoirs", of 90, 219, 220, 276, 469.
Brown, William, 160, 249.
Brown, William, son of Bartilot, 182.
Bruce, Donald, 248-9, 265-6, 273-4, 276, 492.
Bruderer, John, 99, 101.
Bruel, Jacob, 98.
Bruel, Margaret, 98.
Brunner, Eve Mary, 166, 178, 190, 212.
Brunner, Jacob, 190.
Brunner, John, 178, 212.
Brunner, Margaret, 120.
Brunner, Rudolph, 120.
Brunner, Ulrick (1), 166, 178, 190, 192, 212.
Brunner, Ulrick (2), 166.
Brunson (Brunzon), Abraham, 127.

INDEX

Brunson, Alexander, 128.
Brunson, Barbara, 113, 125.
Brunson, Elizabeth, 191.
Brunson, Elizabeth (2), 156.
Brunson, G. W., 24.
Brunson, Isaac, 125.
Brunson, Jacob, 113, 125.
Brunson, James, 191.
Brunson, John, 128, 156.
Brunson, Jonathan, 127, 167.
Brunson, Martha, 127, 167.
Brunson, Martha, (2), 166.
Brunson, Mary, 167.
Brunson (Brunzon), name, 31.
Brunson, Peter, 152.
Brunson, Rachel, (1), 128, 156.
Brunson, Rachel, (2), 128.
Brunson, Rebecca, 167.
Brunson, Samuel, 167.
Brunson, Sarah, 152.
Brunson, Sirrah, 128.
Brunson, Susannah, 166.
Brunson, William, 152.
Brunson, William, son of John, 156.
Buchanan, Capt. John, 386.
Buester, Anna, 99.
Buester, Ulrick, 99.
Bull, John, Provincial Secretary, 7.
Bull, Lieutenant–Governor William, 2, 6, 37, 54.
Bull, or Phul, Peter, 227.
Bull, Gen. Stephen, 264, 324, 469.
Bullinger, 36.
Bull Swamp Road, 11, 65.
Bunch, Elizabeth, 132.
Bunch, Gideon, 134.
Bunch, Mary, 132.
Bunch, Mary, daughter of Paul, 132.
Bunch, name, 32.
Bunch, Naomy, 119, 132.
Bunch, Paul, 109, 132.
Buph, Joseph, 104.
Burdell, Elizabeth, wife of John, 129, 139, 163, 178.
Burdell, Elizabeth, daughter of John, 129.
Burdell, John, 4, 8, 116-17, 129-30, 139, 163, 170, 178.
Burdell, John (2), 139.
Burdell, Susannah, 178.
Burdell, Thomas, 163.
Burckhard, Barbara, 137, 147, 156.
Burckhard, Frederick, 137.
Burgin, Anna, 95.
Burns, Katherine, 168.
Burns, Peter, 168.
Burrows, William, 264.
Burton's Ferry, 90, 219.
Buser, Ann, 107.
Bush, Magdalene, 96.
Busk, Johannes, 131.
Busk, Mary, 131.
Busk, Richard, 131.
Bustrin, Anna, 95.
Butcher, Isabel, 110.
Butler, A. P., 69.
Butler, Capt. William, 527-8.
Cabarrus County, N. C., 118.
Cain, Patrick, 276.
Caldwell, James, 230, 254.
Caldwell, John, 8, 257-8, 260, 279, 282, 295-7, 342-3, 354, 386, 388-9, 406-7, 414, 423, 437, 445, 448, 453, 481.
Caldwell, William, 386-7, 437.
Calhoun, John C., 386.
Calhoun County ("in future"), 9.
Callyhon, Mary, 110.
Calvert, Mr., 440-41.
Calvin, John, 36, 44.
Cambridge, 369-70.
Camden, 291, 327, 369, 370.
Camden District, 279.
Cameron, Alan, 280, 388.
Cammel, Mary, 131, 147.
Cammel, Mrs., 100.
Cammel, W., 100.
Cammel, William, 112.
Campbell, Archibald, 111, 139.

INDEX

Campbell, Charles Fouquett, 139.
Campbell, Col., 361, 375.
Campbell, Eugenia, 139.
Campbell, Governor William, 254, 260, 332, 334-5, 367.
Campbell, Mr., 65.
Canada, 236.
Canadian Indians, 234.
Cantey, Josiah, 179.
Cantey, Josiah, son of William, 191.
Cantey, Lieut., 387.
Cantey, Maj., 432.
Cantey, Rebecca, 191.
Cantey, William, 152, 191.
Cape, James, 132.
Carmichael, James, 11.
Carney, Arthur, 183.
Carney, James, 183.
Carney, Mary, 112, 183.
Carney, Samuel, 183, 193.
Carney, William, 193.
Cars, James, 98.
Carse, Eugenia, 95, 108.
Carse, Faithy, 95, 108.
Cartaret County, 1.
Carter, Benjamin, 95, 97, 100, 108.
Carter, Elizabeth, 123-4, 143.
Carter, Henry, 123-4, 133, 147-8, 163.
Carter, James, 123-4, 143.
Carter, John, 124.
Carter, Joseph, 133.
Carter, Mary (1), 123-4, 133, 147, 163.
Carter, Mary (2), 123.
Carter, Mary (3), 133.
Carter, name, 32.
Carter, Rachel, 163.
Carter, Rebecca, 100.
Carter, Robert, 148.
Carter, Sarah, 97.
Carter, Susannah, 143.
Caswell, Gen., 365.
Catawba Indians, 21, 40, 431.
Catawba Nation, 234.

Cattel, Benjamin, 388.
Cattel, William, 388.
Cattle Creek, 38.
Chambers, Joseph, 158.
Chanler, Dr., 314.
Charles Edward, the "Young Pretender", 32.
Charleston Library, 218.
Charleston Presbytery, 39, 57.
Charleston road, the old, 11, 225.
Charlton, Lieut. Thomas, 283, 291, 294, 305-7, 328, 387, 423.
Charnock, Wm., 388.
Chatterton, Ann, 149.
Chatterton, John, 149.
Chatterton, Mark, 149.
Chavis, robber, 461.
Cheavy, Ann, 123.
Cheavy, name, 32.
Cheavy, Sarah, 123.
Cheavy, Thomas, 123.
Cherokee Indians, 18, 19, 20, 21, 40, 86, 88, 304, 327, 333, 352-3, 461.
Cherokee Nation, 19, 20, 234, 299, 324, 326.
Cherokee Ponds, 315.
Cherokee war, 88, 232-3, 235-7.
Chestnut, John, 249, 265, 280, 283, 292, 327, 385-6, 388, 404.
Cheves, name, 23.
Chevilette, Col. John, 4, 32, 98, 102, 106, 111-12, 117, 119, 181, 214, 233, 237, 246-7.
Chevilette, John (2), 32.
Childsbury-Town, 393.
Church of the Redeemer, 64-5, 68-9, 91, 96, 199.
Clarke, Col., 350.
Clark, Malcolm, 249, 265.
Clarry, Joseph, 133.
Clatworthy, James, 120.
Clausand, George Henry, 105.
Clausand, Leopold, 105.
Clausand, W. A., 105.
Clayton, Abraham, 175.

INDEX

Clayton, Anne, 180, 187, 193.
Clayton, Isham, 119, 158, 167, 175, 180, 187, 193, 226, 249, 265.
Clayton, Isham, son of Isham, 193.
Clayton, Isham, son of John, 153.
Clayton, James, son of Isham, 180.
Clayton, James, son of John, 167.
Clayton, Jane, 189.
Clayton (Cleaton), John, 11, 107, 125, 133, 137, 153, 167, 175, 184, 189, 274.
Clayton, John (2), 133.
Clayton, Sarah (1), 125, 133, 137, 153, 167, 175, 189.
Clayton, Sarah (2), 125.
Clayton, William.
Clements, Andrew, 123.
Clements, Gabriel, 123.
Clements, Rebecca, 123.
Clements, name, 32.
Clement, William, 110.
Clemmons, Joseph, 184.
Clemmons, Lucretia, 184.
Clemmons, Sarah, 184.
Clinton, Sir Henry, 338, 349, 351, 365, 367, 370-72, 376, 382.
Colleton County, 1. 25, 26, 27, 119.
Collins, John, 191, 274-6, 278.
Collins, Joseph, 191.
Columbia, 14, 18, 21, 25, 36, 50, 377.
Concord, N. C., 118.
Congaree garrison, 22, 70.
Congaree Indians, 21, 40, 41.
Congarees, 18, 19, 20, 21, 40, 80, 82, 85, 87-8, 122-3, 231-2, 234-6, 251, 282, 291, 296, 305, 307, 312, 314, 316-7, 325, 327, 333-4, 343, 354-5, 408.
Congaree Township, 2, 69, 74, 84.
Conner, Maj. Morgan, 352, 448.
Cook, Anna, 178.
Cook, Anna (2), 178.

Cook, James, 8.
Cook, Joseph, 178, 218.
Cooper, Catharina, 186.
Cooper, Elizabeth, 134.
Cooper, Joseph, 109, 126, 129, 134, 136, 164, 186.
Cooper, Margaret, 126, 129, 134, 164, 186.
Cooper, Rachel, 164.
Cooper, Sarah, 125-6, 131, 134, 139, 153, 261.
Cooper, William, (1), 112, 125, 126, 131, 134-5, 139, 153.
Cooper, William (2), 126.
Corbin, Peter, 230, 265.
Corker, Thomas, 231.
Corker, Thomas, Jr., 251.
Cornelley, James, 265.
Cornwell, Billander, 190.
Cornwell, George, 190.
Cornwell, Mary, 190.
Cornwell, Peter, 190.
"Corpus Evangelicum", 82.
Cossett, Justice, 231.
Cotter, Moses, 305, 307.
Coullett, Christopher, 4.
Courtonne, James, 137, 181.
Courtonne, Jerome, 193.
Courtonne, Thomas, 115.
Coutonne, Anne, 181.
Couton, Joseph, 141.
Couton, Mary, 141.
Coutier (Cuttier), Anna Maria, or Mary, 104, 128, 149, 156, 164, 182, 185.
Coutier, Joseph, 96, 109, 128, 149, 156, 164, 185.
Coutier, Joseph, Jr., 182.
Couturier, Capt., 344-5.
Cowther, Isaac, 387.
Cox, Ann, 115, 132.
Craven County, 1, 23, 174, 204.
Crell, Stephen, 33, 235.
Cresswell, Rev. Mr., 408, 411.
Crider, (Kryter, Kreyter, Kreuter), Anne, 154.

INDEX 545

Crider, Barbara, 122, 214.
Crider, Conrad, 189, 215.
Crider, Johannes, 170.
Crider, Joseph, (1), 102, 103, 105-6, 108, 115, 142-3, 154, 170, 197, 206.
Crider, Joseph (2), 103.
Crider, Sarah, 197.
Crider, Susannah, 103, 105, 143, 154, 170, 189.
Crider, Susannah (2), 105.
Crommelich, Catharina Margaret, 136.
Crommelich, Margaret, 136.
Crommelich, Thomas, 136.
Crossby, Elizabeth, 187.
Crossby, James, 187.
Crowthers, Lieut., 387, 459.
Crum, (Crumme, Crummy) Anne, 193.
Crum, Barbara, 174.
Crum, Elizabeth, 182, 186-7.
Crum, Elijah, 187.
Crum, Henry, 114, 116, 118, 134, 145, 158, 174, 186-7, 193, 269.
Crum, Henry (2), 158.
Crum, John Herman, 182, 186-7.
Crum, Magdalene, 145, 158, 174, 186, 193.
Crum, Mary, 182.
Crum, Peter Herman, 145.
Crum, Rachel, 186.
Crum, Sarah, 193.
Cryer, Elizabeth, 142, 191.
Cryer, Lidia, 142.
Cryer, Thomas, 114, 142, 191.
Cryer, Thomas (2), 191.
Culler (Koller, Kohler, Collar), Anna, 186-7.
Culler, Benedict (1), 99, 102, 108, 115, 162, 189, 210, 223, 224.
Culler, Benedict (2), or Benjamin, 102, 222.
Culler, Elizabeth, 162.
Culler, John Ulrick, 189, 210.
Culler, Magdalena, 102, 104, 162, 189, 210.

Culler, Margaret, 99, 174, 175.
Culler, W. W., 222-3, 485.
Cuningham, "Bloody Bill", 386, 476, 480-82, 485, 526.
Curtis, Frances, 132, 178.
Curtis, Jane, 178.
Curtis, Moses, 218.
Curtis, Priscilla, 132.
Curtis, Thomas, 132, 178.
Danly, Anne, 159.
Danly, James (1), 150, 159.
Danly, James (2), 150.
Danly, John, 159.
Danly, Mary, 150, 159.
Danly, Rose, 150.
Dann, Elizabeth, 172.
Dann, Mary, 172.
Dann, William, 172.
Danner, Barbara, 101.
Danner, Hans, 97, 100, 101.
Danner, Jacob, 101.
Danner, John, 96.
Dantzler, Anna, 192.
Dantzler, Anna Margaret, 177, 186.
Dantzler, Appollonia, 177, 192-3.
Dantzler, Barbara, 181, 215.
Dantzler, Hans Henry, 177, 215.
Dantzler, Hans Ulrick, 164-5, 177.
Dantzler, Henry, 165, 177, 192-3, 215.
Dantzler, John, 215.
Dantzler, Margaret, 165, 177.
Dantzler, Ottinaries, 215.
Dargan, Ann, 118, 153.
Dargan, Dorcas, 153.
Dargan, Elizabeth, 191.
Dargan, John, 153, 158.
Dargan, Katherine, 169, 172.
Dargan, Timothy, 4, 148, 172.
Darlsley, Edward, 20.
Darweta, Ann Magaret, 142.
Dattwyler, Anna, 105, 110.
Dauge, Indian agent, 20.
Davis, Elizabeth, 98, 109.
Davis, James, 323.

Davis, John, 191, 387.
Davis, Salome, 103.
Davis, Samuel (1), 103, 107, 113, 125.
Davis, Samuel (2), 103.
Dayton, Ralph, 20.
Dean, James, 110.
Dean Swamp, 221, 528.
Densmore, Margaret, 174.
Densmore, Samuel, 174, 183.
Deramus, Anne, wife of John, 126.
Deramus, Anne, wife of Joseph, 131, 147, 152, 165, 170, 175, 184, 192.
Deramus, Catharina, 131.
Deramus, Joseph, 108, 131, 147, 152, 165, 170, 184, 187, 192.
Deramus, John, 126.
Deramus, Mary Cartharina, 152.
Deruraseux, Daniel, 110.
DeSaussure, Lieut., 364, 387.
DeWitt, Joseph, 174.
DeWitt, Mary, 174.
DeWitt, William, 182.
DeWitt, William, son of Joseph, 174.
Dickert, Michael, 249, 265.
Dicks, John, 249.
Diebuebdin, Agnes, 98, 106.
Diedrick, Anna, 101, 120, 132, 154.
Diedrick, Anna Maria Margretta, 100.
Diedrick, Barbara, 95, 99, 108.
Diedrick, Hans (John), Jr., 28, 96.
Diedrick, Johannes, 100.
Diedrick, John, 30, 95, 96, 98, 209.
Diedrick, Margaret, 175.
Diel, Anna, 96, 99, 108.
Diel, Catharina, 125, 214.
Dill, Catharine, 200.
Dill, Nicholas, 164, 215.
Dirr (Durr), Anna Maria, 94, 133.
Dirr, Hans Ulrick, 165.
Dirr, Jacob, 119.

Dirr, Katharine, 180.
Dirr, Margaret, 178.
Dirr, Mary, 136, 144, 152, 165.
Dirr, Nicolas, 94, 128, 133, 136, 143, 144, 152, 165, 202, 213.
Dirr, Peter, 178, 180.
Dirr, Theodor, 136.
Dolch, Johannes, 98.
Domin, Hans, 96.
Donaldson, John, 280, 243, 386-88, 425, 429, 464.
Drechsler, George, 180.
Dreher (Dreyer, Drier, Drehr), Godfrey, 227, 237, 258, 269, 272.
Dubois, Samuel, 275-6, 278.
Duboy, Mary, 188.
Dukes, A. L., 24.
Dukes (Duke), Barbara, 155, 175, 189.
Dukes, George Alexander, 155.
Dukes, John H., 24.
Dukes, Joseph, 155, 175.
Dukes, Joseph, 114, 127, 136, 138, 189.
Dukes, Margaret, 127, 138.
Dukes, Rebecca, 189.
Dukes, Sarah, 138.
Dukes, Susannah, 175.
Dukes, Thomas, 127.
Dukes, William, 34.
Dunklin, Joseph, 271.
DuPuis, Abraham, 173, 204.
DuPuis, John Jacob, 173.
DuPuis, Susannah, 173, 204-5.
Durberville, Mary, 171.
Durberville, William, 171.
"Durham", 485.
Dutarque, Louis, 280, 288, 291, 387-8.
Eberhardt, Anna Maria, 103, 129.
Eberhardt, Benjamin, 150.
Eberhardt, Dorcas, 150.
Eberhardt, Isabel, 150.
Eberhardt, I. P. H., 103.
Eberhardt, Jacob, 129.
Eberhardt, Mary (1), 147, 184.

INDEX 547

Eberhardt, Mary (2), 147.
Eberhardt, Thomas, 103, 129.
Eberhardt, William, 184.
Eberly, Anna (1), 102, 141.
Eberly, Anna (2), 102.
Eberly, John, 102, 110, 116, 141.
Eberly, Susannah, 141.
Ebert, Anne, 136.
Ebert, Gotlieb, 114, 136.
Edisto Township, 2, 25, 27, 28.
Edwards, John, 264.
Edwards, Thomas, 156.
Efird (Aifred), Benjamin, 159.
Efird, Dorcas, 159.
Efird, John, 159.
Egly, Barbara, 143, 148.
Egly, Martin, 168, 171, 189.
Egly, Zibilla Catharina, 171, 189.
Elders, John, 128, 132, 207.
Elders, Sarah, 207.
Elerson, Elizabeth, 116, 137.
Elerson, James, 116.
Elliott, Barnard, 100, 257, 388.
Ellison, Frances, 137.
Ellison, Joseph, 137.
Ellison, Robert, 137.
Ernst, Anna Barbara, 112, 214.
Ernst, Anthony, 107.
Ernst, George Adam, 108, 112.
Erwin, name, 90.
Esom, John, 38'.
Eutaw Springs, 284, 524.
Evance, Thomas, 388.
Evans, John, 20.
Evans, Joseph, 159,
Evans, Josiah, 119, 152.
Evans, Martha, 122, 124, 152.
Evans, Mary, 159.
Evans, Powel, 122.
Evans, William (1), 122, 124, 125.
Evans, William, 122.
Even, Dina, 110.
Everleigh, Nicholas, 388.
Evinger, Adam, 152, 176.
Evinger, Ann Margaret, 152, 176.
Evinger, George Lewis, 176.

Evinger, Joseph, 152.
Fair, James, 276.
Fairchild, John, 97, 218, 227, 228, 248, 249, 265.
Fairy, Christina, 132.
Fairy, James, 132.
Fairy, John, 107, 114, 132.
Farles, Thomas, 182.
Farrar, Benjamin, 8, 219, 248, 257, 258, 260, 265.
Farrar, Capt. Field, 364, 386.
Faure, Anne, 167.
Faure, Patience, 103.
Faure, Peter, 130, 133, 135, 138, 166, 167, 180, 187.
Faure, Sarah, 130, 133, 138, 167.
Faust, Ann Mary, 101, 102, 214.
Faust, Burril, 159.
Faust, Caspar, 159, 211.
Faust, Christian, 101.
Faust, Eugenia, 103.
Faust, Henry, 101, 102.
Faust, Henry (2), 102.
Faust, Jacob, 215.
Faust, John, 186, 215.
Faust, Naomy, 159.
Felder, Abraham, 170.
Felder, Frederick, 141.
Felder, Henry or Hans Henry, 30, 105, 107, 114, 118, 119, 130, 131, 133, 136, 141, 145, 151, 155-6, 158, 160, 170-71, 177, 182, 185, 188-9, 193, 215, 248-9, 258, 272.
Felder, Henry (2), 11, 105, 472, 486-89.
Felder, John, 130.
Felder, Mary Eiizabeth, 105, 130, 131, 136, 141, 145, 151, 155, 160, 161, 170, 177, 182, 185, 215.
Felder, Col. Paul S., 487.
Felder, Peter, 185.
Felder, Samuel, 155.
Ferstner, Ann Mary, 130.
Ferstner (Festner), John Henry, 128.

Ferstner, Joseph, 126, 128, 139, 145, 172.
Ferstner, Mary, 128, 139.
Fichtner, Elizabeth, 115.
Fichtner, Margaret, 119, 143.
Fichtner, Theodoris, 136, 163, 183.
Finlay, Jacob, 265.
First Baptist Church, 65.
Fitch, John, 110.
Fitz, John, 103.
Fitzpatrick, Agnesia, 128, 144, 165, 177, 181, 192.
Fitzpatrick, Garret, 128, 133, 142, 144, 165, 177, 181, 192, 269, 272.
Fitzpatrick, Garret (2), 144, 165.
Fitzpatrick, Helena, 192.
Fitzpatrick, Jacob, 177.
Fitzpatrick, Mary, 193.
Fitzpatrick, William, 128, 387.
Fludd, Frances, 186.
Fludd, James, 186.
Fludd (Flood), Katherine, 179, 186.
Fludd, Margaret, 119.
Fludd, Mary, 186.
Fludd (Flood), Sarah, 111.
Fludd, William, 4, 8, 186, 260.
Fluhbacker, Veronica, 96.
Flutt, George, 110.
Fort Motte, 24, 379.
Fort St. John's, 21.
Fort Sullivan, 349, 352, 371, 372, 375.
Fort, Thomas, 103.
Fouquett, Ann Mary, 128, 180.
Fouquett, Marion, 154, 169.
Fouquett, John, 128, 139, 154, 169, 180.
Fowles, Jas. H., 485.
Fox, George, 172.
Fox, Jane, 154.
Fox, Mary, 130, 154.
Fox, Rebecca, 130.
Fox, Samuel, 130, 154.
Fox, Willoughby, 130, 150, 172, 174.

Frances, Elizabeth, 132.
Frank, Jacob, 111.
Fraser, Alexander, 140.
Fraser, Mary, 140.
Frauenfaederin, Anna, 98, 100.
Frederick, Andrew, 11, 38, 151, 161, 178, 188.
Frederick, Hans Peter, 161.
Frederick, Jacob, 178.
Frederick, Margaret, 161, 178, 188 (Maria).
Freeman, George, 230,
Friday (Fridig, Freydigs, Friger), David, 237, 272.
Friday, Hans George, 126, 195.
Friday, Hans, 96.
Friday, Henry, 98.
Friday, Jacob, 98.
Friday, Jacob, Jr., 207, 237.
Friday, J. P. H., 95.
Friday, Johannes, son of John, Jr., 140.
Friday, John, Sr., 112, 117, 126, 136, 140, 151, 152, 207, 209, 214.
Friday, John, Jr., 30, 112, 115, 117, 129, 133, 136, 147, 152-3, 157, 160, 167, 170, 173, 195, 199, 200, 213, 251.
Friday, Margretta, 99.
Friday, Martin, 225, 234.
Friday, Mary Elizabeth, 173, 200.
Friday, Susannah, 126, 136, 140, 147, 152, 153, 157, 160, 173, 195, 200.
Friday, Verona, 99.
Frierson, George, 273.
Frierson, Philip, 272, 273.
Fritchman, Elizabeth, 113.
Fritchman, John, 112. 124, 149, 153, 157, 163.
Fritchman, M., 109.
Frittstein, John, 99.
Fritz, Elizabeth, 122.
Fritz, Naomy (1), 122.
Fritz, Naomy (2), 122.
Fritz, Nicolas, 122.

INDEX

Frogat, Adin, 97, 113, 123.
Frolich, Adam, 156, 171, 207.
Frolich, Barbara, 156, 171, 177, 179, 207.
Frolich, Barbara (2), 171, 207.
Frolich, Henry, 156.
Fry, Caspar, 71.
Fry. Catharine, 115.
Fund (Pfund), Ann, 108.
Fund, Barbara, 30, 107, 131.
Fund, Catharina, 107.
Fund, Jacob, 184, 189.
Fund, Mary, 189.
Funtzius (Funtius, Pfuntius), Catharina, 139, 154, 180.
Funtzius, Elizabeth, 170.
Funtzius, Zibilla, 142.
Fuster, Barbara, 94.
Fuster, Elizabeth, 107.
Fuster, Johannes, 94, 96.
Fuster, John, 107.
Fuster, Salome, 107.
Fuster, Sirrah, 107.
Futchman, Michael, 213.
Gaillard, Tacitus, 3, 4, 6, 8, 233, 247-8, 251-5, 257-8, 260, 265, 284.
Gallier, John Casper, 70.
Gallman, Henry, 33, 111, 226-7, 234.
Gallman, John, 226, 234.
Gandy, Samuel, 110.
Gant, Joseph, 181.
Gant, Rachel, 163.
Gant, Rebecca, 109.
Gardner, John, 132.
Garick, Adam, 467.
Garick (Carick), George Ulrick, 134.
Gartman, Barbara, 97, 108.
Gaston, Lieut. Robert, 364, 387.
Gatz, George, 107.
Geiger, Abraham, 71, 82-3.
Geiger, Ann Barbara, 107.
Geiger, Capt., 436.
Geiger, Herrman, 71, 111, 122, 233-4.

Geiger, John, 235.
Geiger, John, Casper, 71.
Geiger. John Conrade, 227.
Geiger, John Jacob, 71, 107, 141.
Geiger, Margaret, 141, 166.
Geiger, William, 271, 276.
Geltzer, Daniel, 101.
Genney, Lieut. C. M., 387, 463.
Gibbes's Pond, 224, 225.
Gibson, Edward, 98, 109.
Gibson, Elizabeth, 159-60.
Gibson, Erasmus, 467.
Gibson, Eugenia, 150.
Gibson, Gilbert, 159, 410, 416.
Gibson, Hopert, 122.
Gibson, John, 119, 154, 171, 174.
Gibson, Josias, 122.
Gibson, Margaret, 171, 174.
Gibson, Martha, 171.
Gibson, Mary, 122.
Gibson, Sarah, 159.
Giegelman, Ann Elizabeth, 122, 126-7, 141, 165, 169, 174, 184.
Giegelman, Anne Margaret, 190.
Giegelman, Hans (John), 107, 126, 127, 141, 150, 162, 165, 169, 173-4, 184.
Giegelman, Jacob, 126, 150, 169, 174, 184, 190.
Giegelman, Jacob (2), 190.
Giegelman, Mary Elizabeth, 174.
Giessendanner, Agnes, 103, 106, 114, 124, 213.
Giessendanner, Anna, 187.
Giessendanner, Ann, 194.
Giessendanner, Barbara, wife of Rev. John, 101, 104-6, 129, 134, 140, 156, 162, 171, 183, 185, 187-8, 190-91, 200, 206, 214.
Giessendanner, Barbara, wife of Henry (1), 102.
Giessendanner, Daniel, 194.
Giessendanner, Elizabeth, sister of Rev. John, 60.
Giessendanner, Elizabeth, daughter of Henry (1), 102, 120, 191.

Giessendanner, Elizabeth, daughter of Henry (2), 194.
Giessendanner, Elizabeth, daughter of Daniel, 194.
Giessendanner, Elizabeth, wife of Henry (2), 194.
Giessendanner, George (1), 60, 98, 105, 126, 145, 160, 177, 213, 215.
Giessendanner, George, Jr., 105-6, 113, 114, 124-6, 128.
Giessendanner, George, son of Rev. John, 206.
Giessendanner, Henry (1), 102.
Giessendanner, Henry (2), son of Rev. John, 59, 91-2, 101, 120, 194, 224.
Giessendanner, Jacob, 30, 98, 103-5, 115, 119, 129-30, 141, 156-7, 161-2, 166, 178, 185, 209-10, 215, 233.
Giessendanner, Johannes, 104.
Giessendanner, Rev. John Ulrick, 30, 35, 39, 41, 43-4, 46, 47-8, 56, 58, 62, 83, 92-5.
Giessendanner, Rev. John (John Ulrick, Ulrick), 23, 30, 31, 35-7, 39, 41, 44-5, 48-50, 53-60, 62-3, 65-8, 83, 91-3, 95, 104-6, 110-11, 156-7, 162, 165, 168, 171, 182-3, 185, 187-94, 197, 200, 206, 213, 216, 226, 233, 237.
Giessendanner record, the, 29-32, 34-5, 41, 43-4, 47, 59, 60, 63, 65-7, 83, 88-9, 91-216, 237.
Giessendanner, Susannah Barbara, 129, 138, 145, 150, 160, 163-4, 166, 170, 174.
Giessendanner, Susannah, daughter of Rev. John, 134, 200.
Giessendanner, Susannah (2), daughter of Rev. John 156.
Giessendanner, Ursula, 115, 214.
Giles, John, 438.
Gill, James, 231.
Gill, Mary, 150.
Ginnoway, Ann, 123.

Gisburne Parish, 29.
Gleaton, Isaac, 127.
Glover, Judge T. W., 64, 229.
Golson, Elizabeth, 160, 173, 181, 183, 217.
Golson, John Caspar, 160.
Golson, John Lewis, 183.
Golson, Lewis, 115-16, 154, 160, 172-3, 181, 183, 190, 217-18, 226, 247-9. 258, 265, 272, 275, 307, 430, 436, 468.
Golson, Lewis (2), 473, 481-2.
Godfrey, Mary, 110.
Golphin, George, 462.
Good, Elizabeth, 123.
Goodby, Sirrah, 109.
Goodwyn, Robert, 250, 279, 282, 290, 293, 305, 343, 366, 386, 388, 390, 397-8, 400, 406, 424.
Goodwyn, Uriah, 12, 305-6.
Goodwyn, William, 317, 366, 387.
Gossling, Anne, 181.
Gossling, Elizabeth (1), 125.
Gossling, Elizabeth (2), 125.
Gossling, George, 125.
Gossling, Robert, 113, 123, 125, 138, 181.
Gould, or Cloud, Mrs. Mary, 234-5.
Govan, Andrew (1), 8, 33, 174, 182, 187.
Govan, Donald, 32.
Govan, Eliza, 32.
Govan, John, 4, 33, 247.
Govan, Rachel, 182, 187.
Gramling, Mrs. Caroline, 66.
Granby, 265, 274, 282, 284, 287, 510.
Grant, Frances, 185.
Grant, James, 185.
Grant, Rebecca, 185.
Gray, William, 110.
Gredig, Julius, 71.
Greene, Gen., 366, 381, 510-526.
Green, Henry, 317.
Green, Thomas, 248, 251, 332.
Greiter, Joseph, 96.

INDEX 551

Griffen, Absalom, 135.
Griffen, Agnes, 135, 139.
Griffen, Choice, 135.
Griffen, Jesse, 467.
Griffen, John, 135, 139.
Griffen, Mary, 139.
Griffith (Grieffous, Griffous, Griffice), Abraham, 174.
Griffith, Ann Margaret, 127.
Griffith, Ann, 103, 123, 127-9, 142, 148, 158, 166, 197.
Griffith, Catharine, 197.
Griffith, David, 111.
Griffith, John, 149.
Griffith, Joseph, 103, 111-13, 123, 127-8, 132-4, 139, 149, 153-4, 164, 167, 172, 174, 186, 198.
Griffith, Margaret, 103, 134, 139, 149, 154, 164, 167, 174, 186, 198.
Griffith, Mary (1), 123, 133.
Griffith, Mary (2), 123.
Griffith, Peter, 97, 103, 108, 111, 127, 129, 134, 142. 148-9, 158, 160, 166, 172, 197.
Griffith, Samuel, 103.
Griffith, William, 134, 198.
Grimm, Susannah, 108.
Grimlock, Thomas, 147.
Grissert, Kilian, 185.
Grossman, John, 116.
Guignard, Susan Richardson, 465.
Gumble, Thomas, 140.
Guphill, Ann, 191.
Guphill, Edward, 191.
Guphill, Elizabeth, 191.
Guphill, William, 191.
Gusseand, John, 105.
Gussert, Killian, 211.
Hagin, Anna Maria, 110.
Hagood, Gen. Johnson, 90.
Haig, Elizabeth, 63, 122-3.
Haig, George, 23, 25, 28-9.
Haig, James, 275.
Haig, John James, 254, 386, 456.
Haigler, Joanna, 155, 175.
Haigler, Jacob, 155, 175.

Haigler (Hegler), John Frederick, 155.
Hails, Eleanor, 148.
Hails, Robert, 148.
Hails, Thomas, 148, 171.
Hainsworth, Elizabeth, 193.
Hainsworth, Maria, 193.
Hainsworth, Richard, 193.
Hales, George, 230-31, 233, 246.
Hall, David, 117-19, 143.
Hamilton, John, 96-7, 107, 251.
Hamilton, Mary, 186.
Hampton, Henry, 276.
Hampton, Wade, 277.
Handasyd, John, 150.
Handshy, Mary, 96, 108.
Hannicke, Caspar Andrery, 144
Hannicke, John Christopher, 144.
Hannicke, Sophia Elizabeth, 144.
Hardman, Sirrah. 127.
Harley, James. 66.
Harris, Mary, 105.
Harris (Harrys), William, 100.
Harris, William (2), 100.
Harris, William (3), 105.
Harrisperger, Anne Mary, 165.
Harrisperger, Barbara, 175.
Harrisperger, Elizabeth, 136, 139-40, 146, 153, 165, 173, 178.
Harrisperger, John, 113, 125, 131, 135-7, 139-40, 146, 153, 157, 163, 165, 173, 177-78, 183, 202, 205-6, 272.
Harrisperger, Rudolph, 149, 157, 161, 165, 166, 205.
Harson, William, 220.
Hart, Derrill, 387, 459.
Hart, Sarah, 138, 171.
Hart, Stephen, 171.
Hart, William, 113, 138, 171.
Hartel, Anne, 159.
Hartel, Henry, 159.
Hartzog, Anna Maria, 183.
Hartzog, Anne Mary, 163, 168.
Hartzog, Barnard, 119, 157, 163, 168.

INDEX

Hartzog, Eve Elizabeth, 146, 184, 215.
Hartzog, George, 290.
Hartzog, John Theodore, 163.
Hartzog, Mary Barbara, 190.
Hartzog, Mary, 193.
Hartzog, Tobias, 193.
Hasford, Abraham, 127, 152, 164, 167, 175.
Hasford, Barbara, 99, 100.
Hasford, Elizabeth, 98, 109.
Hasford, Joseph, 96, 98.
Hasford, Richard, 95-7, 100, 108.
Haskell, A. C., 388, 465.
Haskell, Mrs. Charlotte, 381.
Hatcher, Ann, 124.
Hatcher, Barbara, 28.
Hatcher, Frances, 149.
Hatcher, Mary, 149.
Hatcher, Rachel, 118.
Hatcher, Seth, 32, 124, 132, 149, 177, 202.
Hatcher, Seth (2), 177.
Hatcher, Sirrah, 107.
Hatcher, Susannah, 124, 149, 177.
Hauscig, Henry, 99, 100-1.
Hauscig, Margaretta, 99, 100.
Hawskin, Mrs., 178.
Hayge, Charite, 19, 20.
Haym (Heym), Barbara, 97, 104, 108, 129.
Haym, Henry, 30, 102, 112-13, 129, 144, 156, 207, 211, 214.
Hayner, Eve Elizabeth, 158, 168, 173, 176, 184.
Hayner, John George, 119, 158, 162, 168, 173, 176, 184.
Hayner, John George (2), 168.
Hayner, Margaret, 176.
Hay, Mary, 150.
Hay, William, 150.
Hearn, John, 24-28, 55, 96-7, 246.
Heartley, Henry, 33.
Heatly, Andrew, 193.
Heatly, Charles (1), 20, 22-3, 232, 246.

Heatly, Charles (2), 121, 230, 281, 290, 293, 385, 386, 388, 417, 424, 428-9.
Heatly, Elizabeth, 153.
Heatly, James William (William, Jr.) 128, 386-7.
Heatly, Mary, wife of Charles, 22.
Heatly, Mary, daughter of William, 137.
Heatly, Mary Elizabeth, 121, 128, 130, 137, 143, 153, 180-81, 184. 193.
Heatly, Rachel, 181.
Heatly, Richard, 22.
Heatly, William, 4, 8, 22, 33, 63, 121, 128, 130, 137, 143, 148, 153, 180-81, 184, 193, 230, 269, 273, 368.
Heckler, Anna Mary, 116.
Heinein, Barbara, 98.
Heller, Ann, 145.
Heller, Esther, 145.
Heller, John, 115, 129-30, 145, 148, 157.
Hent, David, 79.
Hepperditzel, Susannah, 32, 98, 106.
Hergersperger, Anna Barbara, 95, 108.
Herlong (Herlan), Jacob (1), 143, 165, 173, 185-6, 203.
Herlong, Jacob (2), 143.
Herlong, Johannes, 185-6.
Herlong, Mary Catharina, 203.
Herlong, Mary Susannah, 143, 165, 173, 186, 203.
Herlong, Susannah, 165.
Hertel, Henry, 33.
Herter (Hirter), Eve Catharina, 158, 178.
Herter, John Nicholas, 215.
Hessy (Hesse), Anna Catharina, 102, 154, 162, 187.
Hessy, Catharina, 130, 140-41, 145, 148, 152, 181, 195.
Hessy, Christina, 111.

INDEX 553

Hessy, Elizabeth, 203, 214.
Hessy, George, 102, 119, 144, 153-4, 162, 187.
Hessy, Hans George Henry, 97, 108, 111, 130, 132, 140-41, 145, 148, 152, 181, 195, 213.
Hessy, Henry, 203.
Hessy, Jacob, 148.
Hessy, Johann Nicolas, 130, 195.
Hessy, John, 102.
Hessy, Joseph, 187.
Hessy (Hessig), Margaret, 100.
Hickie, Margaret, 123.
Hickie, Rachel, 163.
Hickie, Rachel (2), 181.
Hickie, Rebecca, 123, 181.
Hickie, William, 109, 123, 163, 181.
Hickie, William (2), 163.
Hill, Ann, 117.
Hill, Sarah, 117.
Hill, William, 275-6.
Hirsch, Veronica, 215.
Hodge, Sarah, 159.
Hodge, Thomas, 159.
Hodge, Thomas (2), 159.
Hodges, Benjamin, 387.
Hoeffertin, Barbara, 98.
Hoff, Frederick, 173, 188.
Hoggin, Verena, 115.
Hoggs, Anna, 168, 182.
Hoggs, Frederick, 168, 182.
Holman, Conrad, 123, 126, 132-5, 139, 144-5, 147, 169-70, 172-3, 183, 227, 237.
Holman, Mary Ann, 123, 126, 132-5, 139, 144-5, 169-70, 172-3, 183.
Holman, Mary Ann (2), 139.
Holmes, Ann, 110.
Holmes, David, 249, 265.
Holmes, Solomon, 122-3.
Honig, Barbara, 99, 101.
Hook, Barbara, 105.
Hook, Magdalene, 105.
Hook, Peter, 105.
Hope, Frances, 169.
Hope, John, 169.

Hope, Sarah, 169.
Hopkins, David, 386-7, 398, 405-6, 44, 459.
Hopton, William, 248.
Horger, Barbara, 102.
Horger, Catharine, married Henry Stroman, 99, 107.
Horger, Catharina (wife of Henry, Jr.), 169, 176, 190.
Horger, Catharina (2), 176.
Horger, Henry, 30, 169, 211.
Horger, Henry (2), 104, 115, 169, 176, 190.
Horger, Jacob, 105, 124, 169, 181, 215.
Horger, John, 157.
Horger, John, son of Jacob, 181.
Horger, Lovisia, 105, 124, 181, 215.
Horger, Magdalene, 104, 113.
Horger, Maria Magdalene, 169.
Horger, Peter, 97, 99, 100, 101.
Hormutt, Elizabeth, 116.
Hossleiter, Ann Margaret, 145, 161, 185, 203.
Hossleiter, Christina, 215.
Hossleiter, Hans Emanuel, 145, 203.
Hossleiter, Hans Paul, 185.
Hossleiter, John Martin, 145, 161, 185, 203.
Hossleiter, John Michael, 161, 478.
Housell, William, 249, 265.
Houser, Andrew, 467.
Houser, Elias, 227.
Howell, Malachy, 159.
Howell, Race, 159.
Howell, Thomas, 159.
Howell, William, 204.
Huber, Agnes, 185, 215.
Huber, Anna Barbara, 139, 144, 153, 161, 170, 175, 180.
Huber, Christian, 200.
Huber, Dorothea, 94.
Huber, Elizabeth, 142, 144, 205.
Huber, Hans, 98, 200, 204, 214.

Huber, Johannes, 94.
Huber, John Conrad, 144.
Huber, John Frederick (Fredrick), 112, 116, 119, 131, 139, 141, 143, 144, 151, 153, 161, 170, 173, 175, 180, 183, 185, 187, 191.
Huber, Joseph, 103, 114, 142, 144, 152, 188, 205, 214.
Huber, Juliana, 144.
Huber, Magdalena, 110.
Huber, Magdalene, 109.
Huber, Margaret, 188.
Huber, Rosina, 144.
Huber, Susannah, 105, 214, 214.
Hudson, Samuel, 109.
Hueden, Barbara, 98.
Huger, Isaac, 252-3, 340, 361-3, 388, 456, 466-7.
Hugin, Anna, 98.
Hugin, Theodore, 98.
Hugg, Anna, 151, 154, 156, 162.
Hugg, Barbara, 59, 101, 105.
Hugg, Magdalene, 143, 203, 214.
Hugg, Peter, 30, 105, 124, 194, 203.
Humphries, Ralph, 258, 260, 265, 274, 276.
Hungerpiller, Bernhard David, 138.
Hungerpiller, Catharina Margaret, 154.
Hungerpiller, Christina Barbara, 138, 155, 164, 173, 188.
Hungerpiller, Conrad, 138, 154, 164, 168, 173, 178, 181.
Hungerpiller, Elizabeth, 138, 154, 173, 178.
Hungerpiller, Hans Barnard, 155.
Hungerpiller, John Jacob, 138, 155, 157, 164, 173, 188.
Hungerpiller, John Jacob, son of Conrad, 173.
Hungerpiller, Zibilla Catharina, 138.
Hutto, Anna, wife of Charles, 104, 139, 143, 157-8, 175, 178, 190-92, 197.
Hutto, Anna, married Peter Grieffous, 108.
Hutto, Charles, 104, 108, 113, 127, 139, 143, 157-8, 174-5, 178, 189-92, 197.
Hutto, Charles (2), 158.
Hutto, Henry, 135.
Hutto, Jacob, 158, 164, 170, 183, 189, 190, 215.
Hotto, Isaac (1), 102, 116, 125, 127, 129, 131, 135, 148, 160, 167, 175, 197, 215.
Hutto, Isaac (2), 127, 175.
Hutto, John Henry, 139.
Hutto, Margaret Barbara, 127, 135, 143, 154.
Hutto, Margaret, 190, 215.
Hutto, Martin, 154.
Hutto, Mary Catharina, 116, 129, 131.
Hutto, Peter, 103, 108, 127, 135, 143, 154.
Hutto, Sirrah, 108.
Hutto, Susannah, 197.
Hutto, Ulrick, son of Charles, 191.
Hyde, Ann, 150.
Imboden, Catharina, 144.
Imboden, Hans, 144, 189.
Imboden, Margaret (1), 189.
Imboden, Margaret (2), 189.
Imdoden, Peter, 218.
Imboden, Ulrick, 144.
Imdorff, Hans, 30, 96-7, 101, 104, 107, 128, 143, 145, 149, 158, 160, 204, 214.
Imdorff, Magdalena, 30, 102, 128, 143, 149, 158, 204, 214.
Imhoff, J. L. P., 280, 293, 314, 386, 388, 418, 420, 424-5, 428-9.
Inabinet, Andrew, 108, 114, 125, 195, 208.
Inabinet, Baldhazar, 104.
Inabinet, Christian, 121.
Inabinet, John, 97, 104, 108, 121, 125-6, 129, 136, 143, 155, 160, 169, 170, 177, 214.

INDEX

Inabinet, Margaret, 102, 104, 121, 129, 143, 160. 169-70, 177.
Inabinet, Margaret (2), 143.
Inabinet, Maria, 125, 215.
Inabinet, Mary, 114, 121, 125, 187, 214.
Inabinet, Mary, wife of Andrew, 208.
Inabinet, Mary, daughter of Andrew, 208.
Inabinet, Peter, 177.
Inabinet, Samuel, 129.
Ininjlin, Agnes, 98.
Izlar (Yssler), Jacob, 179.
Jackson, Agnes, 193.
Jackson, Anne, 170.
Jackson, David, 112, 129, 139, 170.
Jackson, David (2), 170.
Jackson, John, 129.
Jackson, Joseph, 131.
Jackson, Lydia, 139.
Jackson, Mary, 129, 131, 139, 170.
Jackson, Miles, 97, 109.
Jackson, Richard, 150.
Jackson, Thomas, 97.
James, Francis, 153.
James, Mary, 153.
James, Patty, 153.
Jamison, Dr. V. de V., 38.
Jamison, Capt. V. de V., 68.
Jamison, Gen. D. F., 59, 68, 475.
Jenkins, Ann, 114.
Jennings, Barbara, 122, 124, 130, 137, 141, 143, 152, 164, 166, 174, 185-7, 213.
Jennings, Elizabeth, 105, 129, 137, 152-3, 164.
Jennings, or Zanini, Gideon, 31, 195, 202, 214.
Jennings, Gideon (2), 137.
Jennings, John, 31, 96, 105, 120, 122, 124, 130, 134, 137, 141, 143, 152, 164, 166, 174, 185-7, 274.
Jennings, Margaret, 164.
Jennings, Phillip, 31, 98, 105, 109, 129, 137, 152-3, 156, 164, 188.

Jennings, Ursetta, 109.
Jennings, or Zanini, Ursula, 31, 202.
Johnson, Hannah, 189.
Johnson, John, 193.
Johnson, Jonathan, 189.
Jones, Anne, 165, 184.
Jones, Elizabeth, 133.
Jones, Esther, 104, 113, 123.
Jones, Eugenia (1), 103, 105.
Jones, Eugenia (2), 103.
Jones, Hannah, 103.
Jones, Henry, 104.
Jones, John (1), 100, 103-4, 113, 123.
Jones, John, son of John, 100.
Jones, John, son of Thomas, 105.
Jones, Joseph, 103.
Jones, Mary, 123.
Jones, Samuel P., 64.
Jones, Thomas, 98, 103, 105, 109.
Jones, Thomas (2), 103.
Jordon, Henry, 166, 188.
Jordon, Mary, 166.
Jordon, Mary (2), 166.
Joyner, Agnes, 132, 191.
Joyner, Charles, 135.
Joyner, Elizabeth, 132.
Joyner, Faithful, 132.
Joyner, John, Jr., 119.
Joyner, John, son of John and Miles, 131.
Joyner, Joseph, 97, 109, 131-2.
Joyner, Mary Ann, 155.
Joyner, Mary, 98, 109.
Joyner, Miles, 131.
Joyner, Nathan, 98, 109, 135, 155.
Joyner, Samuel, 132.
Joyner, Thomas, 95, 108, 132.
Joyner, Winifred, 132, 135, 155.
Jubb, Ann Margaret, 166.
Jubb, Elizabeth, 140.
Jubb, Eva Catharina, 127, 140, 149, 166, 189.
Jubb, John, 107, 127, 140, 149, 166, 189.

Jubb, Susannah, 189.
Jubb, William, 127,
Justus, Valentia, 97.
Kaigler, Andrew, 271.
Kannady, John, 110.
Kaun, Henry, 137.
Kays, Anna, 178.
Kays, Elizabeth, 215.
Kays, John, 137, 153.
Kearn, Jacob, 161.
Keller, Ann Mary, 147.
Keller, Christopher, 147.
Keller, Mathias, 96, 102, 108.
Kelly, Daniel, 230, 272.
Kelly, Gersham, 230.
Kelly, John, 146.
Kelly, Margaret, 146.
Kelly, Samuel, 228.
Kemmler, Anna Margaret, 192-3.
Kemmler, Anna Maria, 167.
Kemmler, Ann Mary, 147.
Kemmler, Christopher, 147.
Kemmler, Hans Henry, 165.
Kemmler, Hans Michael, 147.
Kemmler, Henry, 167.
Kemmler, Margaret, 165, 181, 192-3.
Kemmler, Martin, 165, 181, 192-3.
Kennelly, Thomas, 249.
Kern, Catharina Elizabeth, 141, 151, 157, 160, 164, 175.
Kern, Elizabeth Barbara, 160.
Kern, John Frederick, 175.
Kern, Lewis, 116, 141, 151, 154, 157, 160, 164, 175.
Kern, Mary Elizabeth, 141.
Kershaw, Eli, 279, 287, 293, 301, 332, 386, 388, 390, 392, 397-8, 400, 406, 424, 439, 450.
Kesebirnger, Anna B , 95.
Kesselringer, Anna Barbara, 100.
Keyser, Eva Catharina, 119.
King, George, 257-8, 269, 272.
King, Mary, 111.
Kinsler, (Kuntzler, Kensalow), Caspar, 71.

Kinsler, Conrad, 71.
Kinsler, John, 265.
Kinsman, Samuel, 21.
Kirchner, Ann, 141.
Kirchner, Eberhardt, 141.
Kirrel, Christopher, 147.
Kirrel, Mary Margaret (Magdalene), 147.
Kirrel, Michael, 147.
Kitchen, Barbara, 210.
Kitchin, Charles, 109.
Kitchin, John, 107.
Kitelman, John, 206.
Kitelman, Mary Catharina, 206.
Knight, James, 486.
Knobel, Elizabeth, 143, 152, 168, 183.
Knobel, George Frederick, 115, 143, 152, 168, 183.
Knobel, John Martin, 168.
Knobel, Margaret Barbara, 143.
Knobel, Maria Regina, 152.
Koch (Cook), Ann, 127, 137, 198.
Koch, Hans Heinrich, 127, 198.
Koch, Johannes, 137.
Koch, Joseph, 127, 137, 144, 198.
Koch, Maria (1), 102.
Koch, Maria (2), 102.
Kock, Regula, 105, 108.
Koenig, Margaret, 100, 145.
Koone, Anna, 145.
Koone, Henry, 145.
Koone, Margaret, 145.
Kooner, (Kuhner, Kuhnen, Kurner, Koonen, Cooner), Anna Catharina, 146, 156, 179.
Kooner, Anna, 175, 215.
Kooner, Anna, wife of Jacob, Sr., 138, 157.
Kooner, Anne, daughter of Francis, 162.
Kooner, Barbara, 205.
Kooner, Catharina, 122, 134, 157, 165, 175, 184, 187-8, 202, 211.
Kooner, Francis, 98, 103, 141, 149, 151, 154, 162, 175, 184-5, 187-8, 203, 211, 214.

INDEX

Kooner, George Jacob, '116, 146, 156, 179.
Kooner, Hans George, 184.
Kooner, Hans Jacob, 134, 202, 138.
Kooner, Jacob, Sr., 30, 97, 104, 149, 151, 157, 196, 201.
Kooner, Jacob (2), 110, 134, 148, 157, 162, 165, 175, 184, 187-8, 202, 214.
Kooner, Jacob, son of Francis, 151, 203.
Kooner (Kooney), Jacob, 120, 217.
Kooner, Margaret, 157.
Kooner, Martin, 30, 98, 109-10, 202, 205, 207.
Kooner, Mary, 151, 154, 162, 184, 185, 187, 203.
Kooner, Regina, 196, 214.
Kotgen, Christina Barbara, 104.
Kotgen, Christina, 104.
Kotgen, George, 104.
Kramer, Christina, 159.
Kramer, Lewis, 159.
Kramer, Peter, 159.
Kranich, Anne Mary, 162.
Kranich, John Peter, 162.
Kranick, John Valentia, 116, 162, 174.
Kranick (Cronich), Valentine, 218.
Krichen, Regina, 99, 101.
Kubler, George, 218.
Kuhn, Anna Barbara, 195.
Kuhn, Anna Maria, 153, 164, 172, 175, 188.
Kuhn, Caspar, 112-13, 153, 164, 172-3, 175, 188, 195.
Kuhn, Jacob, 95.
Kuhn, John Adam, 153.
Kuhn, John Conrad, 164.
Kuhn, John Lewis, 172.
Laehryig, Margretta, 100.
Laessig, Anna Barbara, 100.
Lammons, Francis, 110.
Lammon, Robert, 113.
Lane, John, 159.

Lane, Mary, 159.
Lane, Sarah, 159.
Lap, Elizabeth, 123, 133.
La Puis, Abraham, 144.
La Puis, Abraham (2), 144.
La Puis, Susannah, 144.
Larey (Larry), Daniel, 91.
Larey, Magdalena, 104.
Larey, Margaret, 107, 129, 136-7, 158.
Larey, Margaret (2), 122.
Larey, Margaret (3), 197.
Larey, Mrs. Mary, 91, 120.
Larey, Michael, 97, 108, 114, 116, 124, 127, 133, 147, 156, 170, 172, 197, 208, 214.
Larey, Michael (2), 133.
Larey, Nicholas, 122.
Larey, Peter, 129, 134, 136-7, 151, 158.
Larey, Regel, Regula, or Rachel, 104-5, 122, 124, 127, 133, 147, 156, 172, 197.
Larkins, Margaret, 119.
Larrywecht, Ann Catharina, 116.
Lebennder, Ann Catharina, 139.
Lebennder, Appollonia, 139, 161, 173.
Lebennder, Barnard, 139, 161, 169-70, 173.
Lebennder, John, 173.
Lebennder, Mary Elizabeth, 161.
Lee, Col. Henry, 379, 511, 518, 523-4.
Lee, John, 249.
Leitner, Michael, 237, 265, 268, 278.
Leslie, James, 249.
Leviston, Esther, 150.
Leviston, Hugh, 150.
Lewis, David, 156.
Lewis, Esther, 156.
Lewis, James, 113, 156.
Leysaht, Johannes, 140.
Leysaht, John William, 115-16, 134-5, 138-40.

Leysaht, Ursula. 134, 140, 188.
Linder, Daniel, 117, 152, 166-7, 182.
Linder, Daniel (2), 152.
Linder, Elizabeth, 100, 166.
Linder, Lewis, 30, 100, 114, 116, 120, 140-1, 151-2, 159, 206.
Linder, Mary, 114.
Linder, Mary Magdalene, 140-41, 152.
Linder, Samuel, 166.
Linder, Sarah, 152, 166-7, 182.
Linder, Susannah, 182.
Linsey (Lindsay), Barnard, 182.
Linsey, Charles, 182.
Linsey, Martha, 182.
Little, William, 194.
Liver, Jacob, 111.
Lloyd, John, 118-19, 130, 137, 143, 162, 172, 181, 185, 193, 218, 233.
Lloyd, Joseph, 162.
Lloyd, Rachel, 130, 137, 143, 162, 172, 181, 185, 193.
Lloyd, Rachel Elizabeth, 130.
Logan, John, 137, 141.
Looser, John Conrad, 147.
Looser, Mary, 134.
Looser, Mary Magdalene, 134, 147.
Looser, Michael, 134, 147.
Lovelies, Anne, 171.
Lovelies, Elizabeth, 171.
Lovelies, Sarah, 171.
Lovelies, Thomas, 171.
Lucas, John, 60, 61, 63-4, 66, 68-9, 91-2, 96, 193, 199.
Lyons, Barbara, 104.
Lyons, Joseph, 97, 108.
Lywick, Thomas, 172.
Mackey, Elizabeth, 117, 135.
Marion, Gen. Francis, 511-13.
Markis, Joseph, 112.
Markly, Ann, 110.
Markly, Anna Maria, 102.
Markly, Rosina, 130, 145.
Martin, Priscilla, 142.

Martin, William, 63, 97, 114, 131, 142, 155.
Maskall, Lieut. (Capt.), 386-7, 448.
Maxwell, Margaret, 109.
McCarthey, Jeremiah, 181.
McCarthey, Rachel, 181.
McCarthey, Randal, 181.
McColloch, George, 177.
McColloch, John, 177.
McColloch, Lydia, 177.
McCord, Alexander, 117.
McCord, Charles, 140, 185.
McCord, David, 185.
McCord, John, 23, 112, 114, 118-19, 121, 130, 143, 169, 185, 250-51.
McCord, Mary, 143.
McCord, Russell P., 40.
McCord, Sophinisba, 130, 143, 169, 185.
McCoy, Hugh, 196.
McCrady, Gen. Edward, 529.
McFarlen, Elizabeth, 168.
McFashon, Thomas, 122.
McGinis, Lieut., 387, 464-5.
McGowan, Margaret, 171, 179.
McGowan, Mary, 171, 176.
McGowan, John, 171, 179.
McGrae, Edward (1), 122.
McGrae, Edward (2), 122.
McGrae, Obedience, 122.
McGrue, Alexander, 140, 150, 159.
McGrue, Margaret, 140, 150, 159.
McGrue, Mary, 140.
McGrue, William, 140.
McIntire, Ann, 147.
McIntire, Duncan, 147, 165.
McLennen, Ann Margaret, 117, 139.
McMichael, C. M., 471, 480.
McMichael, George, 484-5.
McMichael, Jack, 222.
McMichael, Jacob, 471.
McNichols, Catharina, 148.
McNichols, Elizabeth, 148, 171.
McNichols, Elizabeth (2), 171.

INDEX 559

McNichols, George, 179.
McNichol, John, 8, 251.
McNichols, Margaret, 153.
McNichols, William, 148, 171, 176, 180.
McQueen, Alexander, 388.
McWilliams, John, 269, 223.
Mecket, William, 113.
Meekel, Anna, 129, 142, 149.
Meekel, Hans Henry, 129.
Meekel, William, 129, 142, 149.
Meetze, Rev. J. Y., 89.
Megrew, Eugenia, 109.
Mell, Anna Catharina, 215.
Mell, Henry, 116-17, 139, 155, 172, 174.
Mell, Mary Catharina, 155, 172, 174.
Mercier, Elizabeth, 63, 140, 149, 159, 163, 226, 231, 237.
Mercier, Margaret, 140.
Mercier, Peter, 140, 233.
Merkly, David, 126, 130.
Merrimans, James, 96.
Merryan, Francis, 110.
Michill, Flowers, 110.
Middepen, 221.
Middleton, Charles, 12, 159.
Middleton, Hannah, 111.
Middleton, Hugh, 280, 312, 387-8.
Middleton, John, 109.
Middleton, William, 278.
Mikell, Ephriam, 265.
Miller, Angelia, 151.
Miller, Anna, 178.
Miller, Catharina (1), 136.
Miller, Catharina (2), 136.
Miller, Christopher, 116, 151.
Miller, Emanuel, 114, 136, 146, 154, 178, 208.
Miller, Jacob, 20.
Miller, John, 115, 136, 178.
Miller, John, son of Emanuel, 136.
Miller, John Frederick, 151.
Miller, Magdalene, 154.
Miller, Mary, 136, 154, 178.

Millhouse, John, 228.
Millis, Anne, 172.
Millis, Eugenia, 156.
Millis, Fanny, 178.
Millis, John (1), 156, 172, 178.
Millis, John (2), 156.
Millis, Thomas, 172.
Mills, John, 254.
Milner, Benjamin, 158.
Milner, Dorcas, 158, 191.
Mineor, Emanuel, 118.
Minnick, Christian, 4, 113, 135, 153, 217, 227, 233, 237, 247.
Minnick, Rebecca, 135, 138, 153.
Minnick's Bridge, 226.
Mintz, Anna Barbara 136, 151, 167, 183-4, 209.
Mintz, Hans Jacob, 183-4.
Mintz, Johann Caspar, 136.
Mintz, John, 143.
Mintz, John Caspar, 136, 151, 167, 183-4, 209.
Mintz, John George Melchior, 167, 207.
Mintz, John Jacob, 151, 209.
Mitchell, Ephriam, 249.
Mitchell, John, 170, 193, 204.
Mitchell, Lieut., 387, 414.
Mitchell, Phibbe, 170, 204.
Mitchell, Rebecca, 184.
Mitchell, William, 158, 184.
Mitchell, William (2), 170, 204.
Monheim, Catharina, 158.
Monheim, Christopher, 115, 155, 158, 199.
Monheim, Eve Catharina, 158.
Montier, Lewis, 96, 108.
Moor, Mary, 109.
Moore, Col. James, 19.
Moore, James, 271, 274.
Moorer, Dorothy, 194.
Moorer, Frederick, 186.
Moorer, John, 150.
Moorer, John Henry, 169.
Moorer, Magdalene, 145, 150, 169, 186.

Moorer, Peter, Sr., 11, 30, 98, 150, 162, 208.
Moorer, Peter, Jr., 103, 107, 113, 145, 150, 169, 186, 188, 191, 194.
Morff, Barbara, 113.
Morff, Christiana, 193.
Morff, Felix, 129, 214.
Morff, Hans Ulrick, 113, 129.
Morff, Jacob, 111, 181, 193.
Morff, Margaret, 129.
Morris, William, 342.
Morrison, Catharina, 128.
Morrison, John, 128, 147, 165.
Morrison, Mary (1), 128, 147.
Morrison, Mary (2), 147.
Morys, Thomas, 96.
Motte, Maj. Christian, 24, 35-6, 47, 53, 57, 94, 246-7.
Motte, Elizabeth, 466.
Motte, Jacob, 247.
Motte, Rebecca, 24.
Moultrie, Gen. William, 490—500.
Murphy, Grace, 123.
Murphy, Hugh, 123.
Murphy, Mary, 123.
Murphy, Rebecca, 95, 108.
Murray, Isabel, 192.
Murray, Margaret, 192.
Murray, Thomas, 192.
Murrowe, William, 66.
Myers (Meyer, Myer), Anna Barbara, 94.
Myers, Ann Margaret, 151, 155, 193, 215.
Myers, Ann, 142.
Myers, Catherine, 96, 107.
Myers, Christian, 94.
Myers, Elizabeth, 146.
Myers, Henry, 95.
Myers, Johannes, 94.
Myers, John, 30, 94, 142, 151, 155, 175, 181, 186, 192.
Myers, John (2), 99.
Myers, John Frederick, 155, 175.
Myers, John Jacob, 95, 99, 100.
Myers, Margaret, 142, 175, 186, 192.

Negely, Anna, 30, 154, 178, 205, 214.
Negely, Barbara, 154, 158.
Negely, Caspar, 125, 143, 160, 214.
Negely, Catharina, 110.
Negely, Hans, 127, 134, 142, 154.
Negely, Margaret, 97, 102, 108.
Negely, Mary, 108.
Negely, Peter, 134, 142, 144.
Nelson, Jared, 3, 275.
Netman, Lewis, 170, 180.
Newton, James, 218.
Newton, Jane, 180.
Newton, John. 230.
Newton, Rachel, 180.
Newton, Thomas, 230.
Nicks, Edward, 171.
Nicks, James, 183.
Nicks, Judith, 183.
Nicks, Samuel, 183.
Noe, Margaret, 167-8.
Noe, Nicholas, 167-8.
Nuffer, Christina, 146.
Nuffer, Christopher, 146.
O'Dom, Daniel, 467.
Ofill, Elizabeth, 158.
Ofill, John, 119, 158.
Ofill, John (2), 158.
Ofill, William, 158.
O'Hearn, John, 132.
O'Hearn, Morris, 132.
O'Hearn, Phibbe, 132.
Oisins, Lucretia, 174.
Oisins, Lydia, 174.
Oisins, Mary, 174.
Oisins, Thomas, 174.
Oliver, John, 4.
Oliver, Mary, 126.
Oliver, Peter, 126, 156.
Oliver, Thomas, 126.
O'Neal, Frederick, 150.
Orange, William, Prince of, 2, 35.
Orangeburgh, Siege of, 514.
Ott (Oth), Barbara, wife of Melchior, 208.
Ott, Barbara, wife of Ulrick, 191.

INDEX 561

Ott, Caspar, 112, 115, 142, 157, 162, 172, 187.
Ott, Elizabeth, 191.
Ott, Esther, 115, 127.
Ott, Hans George, 157.
Ott, Jacob, 113, 115, 119, 129, 157, 166, 178, 182, 192.
Ott, Jacob (2), 157.
Ott, John, 181, 186-7, 190-91, 198.
Ott, John Frederick, 112.
Ott, Margaret, 157, 178, 182, 192.
Ott, Margaret (2), 142.
Ott, Maria, 172.
Ott, Mary, 142, 157, 162, 172, 187.
Ott, Mary Elizabeth, 187.
Ott, Melchior, 30, 98, 107, 142, 201, 205, 208.
Ott, Ulrick, 186, 191, 211.
Otto, Anna, 97, 123.
Otto, Isaac, 97, 123.
Ottow, Maria Catharina, 123.
Owen, Thomas, 228.
Ox, John Frederick, 144.
Parker, Lieut., 477, 479.
Parkinson, John, 12, 274, 278.
Parks, John, 159.
Parler, Sadrick, 230.
Partridge, Ann, 149-50.
Partridge, Martha Ann, 149-50.
Partridge, Nathaniel, 149-50.
Partridge, Nathaniel (2), 150.
Patrick, Frances, 161.
Patrick, Henry, 249, 260, 265.
Patrick, John, 126.
Patrick, Lewis, 161, 163, 171, 184.
Patrick, Lewis, son of Lewis, 184.
Patrick, Lewis, son of Luke, 154, 202.
Patrick, Luke, 114, 126, 133-4, 154, 161, 163, 166, 168, 171, 202, 205.
Patrick, Luke (2), 134.
Patrick, Mary, 126, 134, 154, 168, 171, 202.
Patrick, Paul, 161.
Patton, N., 110.

Pearson, John, 96-7, 100, 107, 150, 250.
Pearson, Martha, 150.
Pearson, Mary, 97, 150.
Pearson, Philip, 218, 248.
Peck, Brigitta, 147.
Peck, Jacob, 144, 147.
Pendarvis, Abraham, 147.
Pendarvis, Arketta, 105.
Pendarvis, Benjamin, 131.
Pendarvis, Brand, 98-9, 101, 105, 109, 121, 127, 130-31, 133, 152, 154, 165, 188.
Pendarvis, Hannah, 146, 151-2, 166, 168, 188.
Pendarvis, James, 96, 107.
Pendarvis, Joseph, 188.
Pendarvis, Sarah, 151-2.
Pendarvis, Sertina, 127, 131, 152, 154.
Pendarvis, Thomas, 146, 151-2, 166, 168, 188.
Pendarvis, Ursula, 103, 105.
Pendarvis, William, 125, 127-8, 165-6, 184.
Pennington, Isaac, 249.
Peoples, Henry, 271, 274.
Peterman, Catharina, 117.
Petri, Anna, 106.
Petri, Johann, 106.
Petri, Matthias, 106.
Petri, Zibilla Catharina, 138.
Phillips, Hugh, 467
Pickens, Gen. Andrew, 524.
Pickings, Anna, 112, 158.
Pickings, Martha, 110.
Pickings, N., 110.
Pickings, Samuel, 110, 119, 158.
Pieren, Magdalene, 96, 107.
Pinckney, Thomas, 465-6.
Platt, Barbara, 142, 157, 160, 174, 190.
Platt, Elizabeth, 142.
Platt, James, 190.
Platt, Jane, 175, 185.
Platt, Jane (2), 185.

Platt, John, 142, 157, 160, 174, 190.
Platt, Mary, 157.
Platt, Patty, 174.
Platt, Thomas, 4, 8, 175, 185, 250.
Platt, William, 175.
Porcher, Isaac, 276.
Porter, Jacob, 103.
Potts, Ann, 123.
Potts, Barbara, 123.
Potts, Isabel, 122.
Potts, John, 123.
Pou, David, 249, 265.
Pou, Gavin, 4, 8, 33, 100, 129, 131, 134, 141, 149, 152, 156, 160, 186, 227, 247—250.
Pou, George (1), 103.
Pou, John, 120.
Pou, Margaret, 129, 134, 141, 149, 152, 156, 160, 186.
Pou, Mary, 129.
Pou, Philip, 156.
Pou, Robert (1), 100.
Pou, Robert (2), 141.
Pou, William, 186.
Poutchmouth, Frederica, 134.
Poutchmouth, Magdalena, 134.
Poutchmouth, Martin, 134, 140.
Poutchmouth, Mary, 140.
Powell, Anne, 176, 191.
Powell, Deborah, 191.
Powell, Elizabeth, 114.
Powell, John, 191.
Powell, Martha, daughter of Thomas and Sarah, 124.
Powell, Martha, daughter of Thomas and Anne, 176.
Powell, Sarah, 124, 176.
Powell, Thomas, 176, 191.
Powell, Thomas, 122, 124-5.
Powell, William, 116.
Powell, Winnifred, 124.
Pritchard, James, 265, 274.
Pruncén, Jacob, 94.
Puckridge, Anne, 165.
Puckridge, Catharina, 126, 131, 165-6, 184.
Puckridge, Elizabeth, 126.
Puckridge, John, 184.
Puckridge, Thomas, 107, 126, 131, 165-6, 184.
Puhl, Philip, 226.
Purvis, Capt. John, 279.
Raber (Reber), Anna Angelia, 124, 126, 146, 151, 160, 194.
Raber, Anna Magdalena, 194.
Raber, Ulrick, 115-16, 124, 126, 140, 146, 151, 160, 194.
Raiford, Mary, 107.
Raiford, William, 250.
Railly, Ann, 133.
Railly, Ann, wife of Thomas, 142.
Railly, John, 133.
Railly, Patrick, 133.
Railly, Thomas, 142.
Ratford, Joseph, 95, 108.
Ratford, Mary, 155.
Rawdon, Lord, 511-523.
Rawlins, Robert, 117.
Reece, Evan, 205.
Reece, Marget, 123.
Reed, William, 271.
Regulators, 218-19.
Reich, Elizabeth, 102-3.
Reich, Louis, 102-3.
Reichart, Christian, 117.
Reichman, Henry, 102.
Reigchig, Elizabeth, 100.
Rennarson, George, 12, 278.
Rice, Elizabeth, 119.
Rice, Henry B., 467.
Richard, Elizabeth, 110.
Richards, James Leyton, 275.
Richardson, Ezekiah Cantey, 179.
Richardson, Mrs. N., 179.
Richardson, Miss N., 179.
Richardson, Col. (General) Richard, 174, 179, 264, 266, 291-370, 405-6, 424, 431, 469.
Richardson, Richard, Jr., 179.
Richmond, Dr. Jacob, 260, 265, 274.
Rickenbacker, Ann, widow of

INDEX

Henry (1), 108.
Rickenbacker, Anna, wife of Henry (2), 102, 104, 125-6, 135, 140, 155, 165, 172.
Rickenbacker, Anne Catharina, 164.
Rickenbacker, Elizabeth, daughter of Henry (2), 140.
Rickenbacker, Henry (1), 28, 95.
Rickenbacker, Henry (2), 11, 96, 99, 108, 115, 117, 125-6, 135, 140, 154-5, 164-5, 172, 177, 190, 200, 210, 214, 227, 237, 269, 272.
Rickenbacker, Henry (3), 99.
Rickenbacker, Jacob (1), 104.
Rickenbacker, Jacob (2), 66-7.
Rickenbacker, Johannes, 125.
Riemensperger, Hans Jacob, 74, 87.
Riley, Elizabeth, 131.
Riley, Miles, 112, 114, 131.
Rintz, Hans George, 146.
Roach, Nash, 32.
Roberts, Charlotte, 192.
Roberts, Elizabeth, 189.
Roberts, John, 192.
Roberts, John Jacob, 192.
Roberts, Mary, 189.
Roberts, Reuben, 189.
Roberts, Reuben (2), 189.
Roberts, Solomon, 189.
Robinson, Anna, 125, 130, 133, 201.
Robinson, Antony, 133.
Robinson, George, 12, 230, 265.
Robinson, John, 11, 110.
Robinson, Joseph, 96, 98-9, 121, 125, 130, 133, 194, 201.
Robinson, Joseph (2), 222.
Robinson, Mary, 215.
Robinson, William, 100, 222, 271, 274, 278.
Robison, Capt. George, 274-5.
Rohrig, Anna, 101.
Rose, Ann, 105.
Ross, Isaac, 250.
Roth, Agnes, 205.

Roth, Ann, wife of Peter, 30, 127, 196, 198.
Roth, Ann, married William Mecket, 113.
Roth, Catharine, 177, 179, 180, 188.
Roth, Catharine Elizabeth, 181, 213.
Roth, Christian, 101, 134, 143, 160, 177, 192.
Roth, Christian (2), 160.
Roth, Elizabeth, 100, 103, 106, 128, 143, 160 177, 192, 214.
Roth, Elizabeth (2), 177.
Roth, Hans, 97, 143.
Roth, Hans George, 160.
Roth, Jacob, 105, 107, 115, 129, 160, 177.
Roth, John, Jr., 170-71.
Roth, John Ulrick, 127, 198.
Roth, Lewis, 141, 152, 160, 165, 173, 176, 181, 213.
Roth, Maria Christiana, 101.
Roth, Mary Barbara, 141, 160, 165, 173, 176, 181, 213.
Roth, Peter, 30, 114-15, 127, 145, 157, 165, 190, 196, 198, 203, 205.
Roth, Ulrick, 127, 129, 142-3, 147, 149, 177, 179, 180, 188.
Rowe, Anna, wife of Henry, 99, 101, 182.
Rowe, Christopher, or Michael Christopher, 4, 8, 33, 67, 99, 100-106, 111-17, 119, 129-30, 133-5, 137, 139-41, 143-4, 147, 151-2, 154, 165-6, 187, 190, 193, 196, 213, 227-8, 237, 248-9, 250-51, 258, 265, 307, 430, 468.
Rowe, Christopher, son of Henry, 182.
Rowe, Donald (2), 66-7.
Rowe, Henry, 33, 158, 182.
Rowe, Capt. John C., 66-7.
Rowe, Margaret, 103, 106, 129-30, 133-35, 139-40, 143, 151-2, 165, 193, 196.
Rowe, Maria, 129, 196.

INDEX

Rowe, Peter, 66-7.
Rowe, Rachel, or Regina Barbara, 99, 101, 164, 166, 171, 215.
Rowe, Samuel, 8, 33, 218, 249-50, 265, 274, 276, 488.
Rowe, Dr. William, 66.
Rumph, Abraham (1), 150.
Rumph, Abraham (2), 150, 201.
Rumph, Ann, wife of Jacob (1), 125-6, 130, 133, 150-51, 157, 162, 170, 188, 201, 214.
Rumph, Anna, daughter of Jacob (1), 125.
Rumph, Anne, daughter of David (1), 168.
Rumph, Catherine, 96, 107.
Rumph, David (1), 100, 124-5, 127, 130-31, 146, 168.
Rumph, David, son of David (1), 124.
Rumph, David, son of Jacob (1), 188.
Rumph, Elizabeth, daughter of David (1), 59, 120.
Rumph, Jacob (1), 105, 110, 124-6, 130, 133, 137, 148, 150-51, 157, 162, 170, 184, 188, 190, 201, 218, 226, 237.
Rumph, Jacob, son of Jacob (1), 133, 471-86.
Rumph, Mary, wife of David (1), 124 (Ann), 125, 130, 146, 168.
Rumph, Mary, daughter of David (1), 130.
Rumph, Sarah, 146.
Rumph, Susannah, 170.
Rumph's company roll, 473-4.
Runtgenauer, David, 30, 138, 199.
Rupp, Adam, 184.
Rupp, Anna Barbara, 184.
Rupp, Eva Catharina, 184.
Rush, Mary, 120.
Russell, Ann, 63, 158, 162, 169.
Russell, Capt. Charles, 20, 22-3, 232, 246.

Russell, Charles (2), 63, 113, 117-18, 121, 130, 133, 158, 162, 169.
Russell, Charles (3), 158.
Russell, Eugenia, 23, 119, 128, 130, 147, 153, 368.
Russell, Hans George, 142, 160.
Russell, John, 113, 128, 131, 169, 185.
Russell, Joseph, 94, 162, 172.
Russell, Margaret, 94.
Russell, Mary, 23, 63, 68, 113, 121, 123-4, 126, 132, 198, 246.
Russell, Mary Margaret, 142.
Russell, Rosina, 142, 160.
Russell, Salome, 160.
Russell, Sophinisba, 23, 113, 121.
Rutledge, John, 490-500.
Ryan, Capt. James, 529.
Sabb, Ann, 184.
Sabb, Deborah, 154, 184.
Sabb, Thomas, 8, 226.
Sabb, William, 154, 184, 193, 226, 249.
Salley, Mrs. A. S., Sr., 68.
Salley, Anne, 138.
Salley, Ann Elizabeth, 168.
Salley (Zaley, Sally), Henry, Sr., 28, 184, 246.
Salley, Henry, Jr., 110, 135, 138, 154, 172, 184, 211.
Salley, John, Sr., 29, 168, 218, 221, 489-90, 533.
Salley, John, Jr., 29.
Salley, Magdalene, 138, 158, 211.
Salley, Margaret, 158.
Salley, Martin, 137-8, 154, 168, 182.
Salley (Sahly), Mary (Ann Maria), 96, 109.
Salley, N., 184.
Salley, Robert, 508.
Salley, Sarah, 182.
Salley, Susannah, 168, 182.
Sandel (Sondel), Catharina Margaret, 188.
Sandel, Elizabeth, 179.
Sandel, George Henry, 156.

INDEX

Sandel, John Peter, 156, 161.
Sandel, Magdalene, 151, 156, 161, 179, 188.
Sandel, Peter, 151, 179, 187-8.
Sanger (Zangin, Zangerin), Barbara (Ann Barbara), 98, 102, 107.
Sanger, Simon, 94, 97, 98.
Santee Jack, 40.
Savage, John, 248, 258, 265.
Saylor, Jacob, 275-6.
Schmidt, Peter, 81, 87, 239, 242, 244-5.
Schwartz, Christian, 96-7, 114.
Schwartz, Elizabeth, 114.
Schwartz, Joseph, 97.
Schwartz, Mary, 96, 108.
Schwartz, Susannah, 97, 109.
Schwerdt, Joseph Abraham, 98, 109.
Scytes, Archibald, 190.
Scytes, Charles, 190.
Scytes, Henry, 189.
Scytes, James, 189.
Scytes, Lucy, 190.
Scytes, Mary, 189.
Scytes, William, 189.
Seawright, Esther, 140.
Seawright, Robert, 112.
Seawright, William, 140, 213, 226, 249.
Sellider, Capt. Daniel, 234.
Shalling, Elizabeth, 71.
Shalling, John, 71.
Shannon, Abigail, 96, 109.
Shannon, Corporal Daniel, 187, 463.
Shaumloffel, Anna Margaret, 97, 107.
Shaumloffel, Anna Maria, 157.
Shaumloffel, John, 94, 115, 127, 183, 207.
Shaumloffel, Lovisia, 107.
Shaumloffel, Mary Elizabeth, 102, 107.
Shaw, Ann, 110.
Shilling, Anna, 172.

Shilling, Ann Margaret, 166, 172, 189.
Shilling, John, 150.
Shilling, John Henry (Henry), 117, 138, 140, 154, 166, 172, 189.
Shilling, John Jacob, 189.
Shindler, Rev. R. D., 68.
Shlappy, Hans George, 109.
Shoemaker, Dorothy, 134, 170.
Shoemaker, Frederick Purly, 211.
Shoemaker, Margaret, 142.
Shoemaker, Margaret Catharina, 142.
Shoemaker, Valentine, 134, 142, 170.
Shoeman, Anna Barbara, 180.
Shoeman, Barbara, 180.
Shoeman, Peter, 178-80.
Shoolegre, Anne, 170.
Shoolegre, James, 170.
Shoolegre, John James, 170.
Shroder, Christina Dorothea, 146.
Shroder, Dorothea, 146.
Shroder, John Frederick, 146.
Shuler, Ann Elizabeth, 107.
Shuler, Ann Margaret, 127, 149.
Shuler, Appollonia, 106.
Shuler, Catharina, married Jacob Wannamaker, 96 (Susan), 107.
Shuler, Catharina, daughter of John Nicholas, 154.
Shuler, Catharine, wife of Hans George, Sr., 135.
Shuler, Catharina Margaret, 97, 108.
Shuler, Daniel, 186, 190.
Shuler, Daniel, son of John Nicholas, 186.
Shuler, Eve Catherine, 107.
Shuler, George, 127, 149, 161, 214.
Shuler, Hans George, Sr., 127, 135.
Shuler, John Frederick, 141.
Shuler, John Henry, 171.
Shuler, John Nicholas, 115, 151, 154, 171, 186.

Shuler, Margaret, 107.
Shuler, Margaret Barbara, 108.
Shuler, Nicholas, 102, 113, 122, 130, 133, 141, 146, 187, 237.
Shuler, N., 109.
Shuler, Susannah, 96, 108.
Shuler, Verena, 133, 141, 151, 154, 171, 186-7.
Siddal (Siceceals), William, 99, 101.
Simms, Wm. Gilmore, 33, 233, 382.
Simms, Mrs. Wm. Gilmore, 32.
Simmons, Ann Catharina, 139, 189, 193.
Simmons, John, 107, 139, 161.
Simons, Col. Maurice, 493.
Sims, William, 191.
Sistrunk (Serstrunk), Henry, 33.
Smid, Fullix, 79.
Smith, Anna, 186.
Smith, Ann Margaret, 142.
Smith, Ann Mary, 142.
Smith, Brigitta, 117, 140, 144.
Smith, Jno. Carraway, 386, 459-60, 465.
Smith, Melchior, 151, 167, 175, 230.
Smith, Michael, 142, 151.
Smith, Stephen, 276.
Smith, William, 96, 109.
Smitzer, Mary Elizabeth, 117.
Snell (Schnell), Adam, 104, 109, 119, 124, 129, 131, 136, 149, 153, 155, 163, 169, 176, 178, 188, 204, 210, 258, 269, 272.
Snell, Anna Catharina, 176.
Snell, Ann Barbara, 214.
Snell, Ann Margaret, 148-9, 200.
Snell, Barbara, 104, 136, 149, 201.
Snell, Barnard, 109, 115, 129, 136, 153, 173, 226.
Snell, Catharina Magdalene, 104.
Snell, Catharine, 168, 176, 207.
Snell, Catherine (2), 168.
Snell, Christian, 136.
Snell, Elias, 30, 94, 97, 109, 125, 131, 134, 139, 148-9, 153, 163, 165, 173, 200, 208.
Snell, Elizabeth, 124, 153, 210.
Snell, Elizabeth Barbara, 139.
Snell, Henry, 94-5, 99, 101, 104, 117, 119, 126, 149, 168, 176, 201, 207.
Snell, Henry, Jr., 117, 146, 149, 155, 168, 176, 187.
Snell, Jacob, son of Adam, 188.
Snell, Johannes, 104.
Snell, Johannes, son of Adam, 131.
Snell, John, 163.
Snell, John Adam, 149.
Snell, John Frederick, 187.
Snell, John Peter, 155.
Snell, Juliana, 146, 149, 155, 168, 176, 187.
Snell, Magdalene, 169, 173.
Snell, Margaret, 104, 124, 129, 131, 149, 155, 169, 176, 178, 188, 204.
Snell, Margaret (2), 129.
Snell, Maria Magdalena, 215.
Snell, Mary Catharina, 131, 134, 139, 148-9, 163, 165, 173, 200.
Snell, Sarah, 178.
Snell, Susannah Elizabeth, 129, 136, 153, 173.
Snellgrove, Edward Freeman, 99, 101.
Snellgrove, Freeman, 99, 100-1, 114, 122.
Snellgrove, N., 109.
Snelling, Henry, 123, 150.
Snelling, Sirrah, 122-3, 150.
Snyder (Shnyder, Sknyder, Shyder), Ann Margaret, 153, 163, 189.
Snyder, Daniel, 110, 145.
Snyder, Elizabeth, 145.
Snyder, John, 145.
Snyder, Mary Barbara, 115.
Snyder, Mary Margaret, 135, 149, 213.
Snyder, Michael, 237.

INDEX

Souderecker, Elizabeth, 98, 109.
Souderecker, John, 97.
Spencer, Edward, 66.
Spring, Bartholome, 102.
Spring, Hans, 225.
Spring, Johannes, 95, 201.
Spring, Magdalena, 95, 99, 108.
Spring, Margaret, wife of Bartholome, 102.
Spring, Margaret, wife of John 201.
Spurlock, Benjamin, 117.
Stack, Anthony, 79.
Starley, John, 218.
Stauber, Jacob, 30, 112, 194, 214.
Staley (Stehely), Christopher, 114.
Staley, Elizabeth, 115.
Staley, John, 170, 178, 186, 190.
Staley, Maria, 125.
Staley, Mary, widow, 142, 154, 214.
Staley, Mary, married Caspar Oth, 115, 214.
Staley, Peter, 172-3.
Starke, Robert, 468.
Stean, Chris, 97.
Stent, William, 253.
Stephen, Margaret, 116.
Sterling, Henry, 18, 34, 39.
Stetzel, George, 98.
Stetzel, Johannes, 98.
Stetzel, Maria Linden, 98.
Steventir, Ebenbard, 218.
Stewart, Ann, 155.
Stewart, John, 225.
Stewart, Robert, 155.
St. John's fort, 232.
Stoudenmeyer, Anna, 131.
Stoudenmeyer, Maria Catharina, 131.
Stoudenmeyer, Martin, 131.
Stroman (Strowmann, Strowman, Straumann), Anna Margaret, 102, 130, 204.
Stroman, Anna Margaret (2), 183.
Stroman, Barbara, 94, 102.
Stroman, Catharina, 99, 106, 126, 144, 148, 165, 195.
Stroman, Catharina (2), 126.
Stroman, Eva Catharina, 183.
Stroman, Hans Henry, 99.
Stroman, Hans Jacob, 195.
Stroman, Henry, 97-9, 106-7, 112, 126, 144, 148, 165, 195, 199, 214-15.
Stroman, Jacob, son of Henry, 165.
Stroman, John Jacob (1), 97-8, 101, 107, 121, 130, 183, 204.
Stroman, John, 148, 473.
Stroman, Maria Elizabeth, 101, 176, 187, 215.
Stroman, Paul, 473, 482, 485.
Strother, Catharina, 155, 179.
Strother, Catharine (1), 191.
Strother, Catharine (2), 191.
Strother, Charles, 174.
Strother, George, 248, 265.
Strother, Jeremiah, 155, 179.
Strother, Joseph, 155.
Strother, Moses, 179.
Strother, William, 191.
Stroul, George, 271.
Strubel, Elizabeth, 164.
Strubel, Frederick, 164, 171.
Strubel, Mary Catharina, 164.
Strutzenecker, John, 28.
Sturkie (Stareky, Stereky), Anna, 187.
Sturkie, Ann, 142.
Sturkie, Anne, wife of John Caspar, 164.
Sturkie, Elizabeth, 142, 151, 198, 204.
Sturkie, Henry, 142, 151, 156, 198, 203-4.
Sturkie, Henry (2), 198.
Sturkie, John, 187.
Sturkie, John Caspar, 160, 164.
Sturkie, Margaret, 136, 187.
Sturkie, Ulrick, 136, 160, 187.
Sturkie, Ulrick, Jr., 151.
Sturkie, Ulrick, son of Henry, 151.

Sullivan, John, 109, 124, 138.
Sullivan, Mary (2), 138.
Sullivant, Margaret, 124.
Sullivant, Mary, 124, 138.
Sumter, Gen. Thomas, 510, 514-16, 518, 525.
Suther, Elizabeth, 135-8, 141, 149, 156, 162, 191.
Suther, Elizabeth (2), 191.
Suther, Jacob, 162.
Suther, Johann Henry, 135.
Suther, Samuel, 113, 117-18, 120, 129, 131, 133, 135-8, 141, 149, 155-6, 160-62, 190-91.
Switman, John, 218.
Switman, Richard, 218.
Syfrett (Srefret, Sigfritt), Margaret, 136, 140.
Syfrett, Mary Ann, 140.
Syfrett, Mary Margaret, 140.
Syfrett, Matthew, 136, 140.
Symkins, Arthur, 249, 265.
Taggart, Lieut. William, 387, 457, 460.
Tapp, Ann Barbara, 108.
Tapp, Anna Magdalena, 170.
Tapp, Christian, 95.
Tapp, John Julius, 95, 101, 108.
Tash, Barbara (1), 137.
Tash, Barbara (2), 137.
Tash, William, 137.
Tate, Alexander, 148, 172.
Tate, Elizabeth, 123.
Tate, Isabel, 148, 172.
Tate, Margaret, 148.
Taylor, Anne, 174.
Taylor, Elizabeth, 170.
Taylor, James, 117, 170.
Taylor, Rev. J. W., 66, 68.
Taylor, Mrs. J. W., 67.
Taylor, John, 174.
Teat, Elias, 100.
Tennison, Alexander, 163.
Tennison, John, 163.
Tennison, Judith, 163.
Theiler, Elizabeth, 175.

Theiler, Rudolph, 175.
Themboro, Elizabeth, 179.
Themboro, Swen, 179.
Theus, Capt., 420.
Theus, Rev. Christian, 74, 80-83, 85-7, 109, 244.
Theus, Simon, 116-17.
Thieren, Jacob, 99.
Thomas, John, 174, 251.
Thomson, Charlotte, 380.
Thomson, Eugenia, 162, 169, 172, 380.
Thomson, Eugenia (2), 162.
Thomson, James, 248-9.
Thomson, Jane, 176, 185.
Thomson, John, 176, 180, 182, 251.
Thomson, Mary, daughter of Col. William, 172.
Thomson, Mary, wife of William, 176.
Thomson, Moses (Colonel), 4, 23, 63, 115, 117, 125, 137, 147, 155, 168; 176, 183, 185, 192, 215, 227, 232, 236-7, 246-8.
Thomson, Moses, Jr., 162, 185.
Thomson, Rebecca, 128, 137.
Thomson, Sarah, 176, 180, 192.
Thomson, Sarah (2), 176.
Thomson, William, 176.
Thomson, William (Colonel), 4, 8, 12, 23, 114-15, 119, 128, 132, 137, 153, 162, 169, 172, 185, 218, 227, 229, 232, 237, 247-8, 250-52, 254-5, 257-8, 265, 276, 278-465, 468.
Thomson, William Russell, 376, 387, 459, 472.
Thore, Frederick, 168.
Thornton, Elizabeth, 166, 171, 172.
Thornton, Joseph, 166, 171-2.
Thwartz, Christian, 107.
Thys, Cornelius, 181.
Tilly, Elizabeth, 178, 182, 186.
Tilly, George, 161.
Tilly, James, Sr., 117, 119, 121, 135, 152, 161, 166, 196, 199, 233.
Tilly, James, Jr., 119.

INDEX

Tilly, Joseph, 121.
Tilly, Marget, 121, 135, 161, 196.
Tilly, Susannah, 182.
Tilly, William, 135.
Tittily, Mary Elizabeth, 144.
Tittily, Rosina, 130.
Tittleby, John (1), 126, 130, 144, 147.
Tittleby, John (2), 126.
Tittleby, Regania, 126, 130, 134, 144.
Tommen, Veronica, 106.
Tondel, John, 143.
Tondel, John Peter, 143.
Tondel, Magdalene, 143.
Toomer, Jacob, 149.
Treadwell, Mrs. M. B., 91.
Tshudy (now Judy), Anna, 108, 115.
Tshudy, Anna, daughter of Jacob, 190.
Tshudy, Dorothy, 175, 190.
Tshudy, Elizabeth, 123.
Tshudy, Jacob, 139, 157, 175, 190.
Tshudy, Margaret, 175.
Tshudy, Martin, 115.
Tshudy, Mary Catharina, 175, 177.
Tshudy, Mary, 215.
Tucker, William, 230, 249, 157-8, 265.
Turkey Hill, 38.
Turquand, Rev. Paul, 62-4, 68, 257-8, 260.
Twiddie, Elizabeth, 163, 169, 192.
Twiddie, Robert, 163, 169, 192.
Twyther, Jacob, 28.
Tyner, Ann Margaret, 167.
Tyrrel, Major, 468.
Ulmer, Anne Mary, 119, 127, 133, 141, 144, 148.
Ulmer, Barbara, 215.
Ulmer, Eva Maria, 127.
Ulmer, Frederick, 141, 183.
Ulmer, George Adam, 146.
Ulmer, Hans, 168.

Ulmer, John Frederick, 115, 146, 148, 155, 162, 178, 213.
Ulmer, John Jacob, 178.
Ulmer, John Lewis, 213.
Ulmer, Lewis, 178.
Ulmer, Mary Barbara, 146, 162, 178.
Ulmer, Mary Catharina, 144.
Ulmer, Mary Magdalene, 162.
Ulmer, Verena Maria, 133.
Ulmer, Warner, 119, 127, 133, 144, 213.
Ulrick, Anna Catharina, 146.
Ulrick, Catharina, 146, 161.
Ulrick, George, 146, 161, 188, 211.
Ulrick, Nicholas, 161.
Ulrick, Susannah Barbara, 188.
Usman, Hans George, 161.
Usman, Magdalene, 161.
Usman, Mary Catharina, 161.
Utsey (Yutsey, Jutsig), Conrad, 113, 117, 153, 163, 190.
Utsey, Daniel, 180.
Utsey, Elizabeth, 153.
Utsey, Magdalene, 153, 163, 190.
Utsey, Margaret, 109.
Utsey, Mary Regina Philippina, 122, 206.
Utsey, Regina, 99, 101, 105.
Utsey, Valentine, 112-13, 176, 206.
Vance, Elizabeth, 148, 180.
Vance, George, 137.
Vance, Moses, 387, 414, 419, 420.
Vance, Sarah, 137.
Vance, William, 137.
Vardel, Sergeant, 527-8.
Volckart, Agnes, 185.
Volckart, Esther, 185.
Volckart, Henry, 185.
Waber, Anna Maria, 146, 164.
Waber, Catharina, 183, 192.
Waber, Elizabeth, 146, 157, 161, 163-4, 171, 183.
Waber, Elizabeth Barbara, daughter of John, 171.

570 INDEX

Waber, Elizabeth Barbara, daughter of George, 183.
Waber, George, or Hans George, 183, 192.
Waber, Hannah, 164.
Waber, John, 146, 155, 157, 160-1, 163-4, 171.
Waber, Maria Barbara, wife of Nicholas, Jr., 164, 171, 183, 192.
Waber, Maria Barbara, daughter of George, 192.
Waber, Mary Catharina, 157.
Waber, Mary Elizabeth, 146.
Waber, Nicholas, Sr., 146, 164.
Waber, Nicholas, Jr., 146, 164, 171, 183, 192.
Wagner, Philip, 188.
Walling, Mary, 155.
Walling, Robert, 155.
Walling, William, 155.
Wannamaker, Anna, 170, 192.
Wannamaker, Anna (2), 192.
Wannamaker, Anne, 135, 212.
Wannamaker, Catherine (Ann Catharine), 104, 135, 176, 212.
Wannamaker, Henry (1), son of Jacob and Catharine, 104.
Wannamaker, Henry (2), son of Jacob and Anna, 170.
Wannamaker, Jacob (1), 96-7, 101, 104, 107, 135, 170, 176, 192, 212.
Wannamaker, Jacob (2), 471, 479.
Wannamaker, Mary Magdalene, 176, 212.
Wannamaker, William, 101, 192.
Warley, Capt. Felix, 353, 386, 456.
Warley, Capt. James, or Joseph, 386, 459.
Warnedow, Anna, 178.
Warnedow, John, 103.
Warnedow, Leonard (1), 103, 108, 125, 131, 148, 164, 178.
Warnedow, Leonard (2), 125.
Warnedow, Sarah, 103, 125, 131, 148, 164, 178.

Warnedow, Sarah, daughter of Leonard, 131.
Warnedow, Thomas, 164.
Warner, Magdalene, 117, 124, 129, 133.
Warren, Elizabeth, 110.
Waters, Philemon, 275, 277.
Watson, Jane, 183.
Watson, Mary, 183.
Watson, Capt. Michael, 484, 527-8.
Watson, Nathaniel, 183.
Weanright, William, 110.
Weber heresy, 86, 238.
Weber, Jacob, 81, 87, 238-40, 243-5.
Wechter, George, 112.
Wechter, Magdalene, 112.
Wedlin, Anne Mary, 116.
Weekly, Elizabeth, 112, 125.
Weekly, Thomas, 100, 125.
Weekly, William, 100.
Weigne, Anna, 215.
Whetstone, Adam, 217.
Whetstone, Anna, 99, 100-1, 145.
Whetstone, Anne Margaret, 161.
Whetstone, Barbara, 142, 145.
Whetstone, Dorothea, 103.
Whetstone, Eleanor, 128.
Whetstone, Henry, 113, 121, 127-8, 142, 145, 218, 237, 269, 272.
Whetstone, Johannes, 98-9, 100-1, 228, 145, 210.
Whetstone, John, Jr., 88, 99-100, 210.
Whetstone, Margaret, 98.
Whideman (Wideman), Anna, 151, 161, 168, 175, 177, 191.
Whideman, Jacob (1), 142, 145, 149, 151, 161, 168, 175, 177, 191.
Whideman, Jacob (2), 161.
Whideman, Johannes, 191.
Whisenbunt (Yssenhut), Abraham, 105, 124-5, 127, 133, 136, 143, 151, 169-70, 173, 177, 184.
Whisenhunt, Abraham (2), 105.
Whisenhunt, Ann, 107.
Whisenhunt, Isaac, 136.

INDEX 571

Whisenhunt, Jacob, 136.
Whisenhunt, Johannes, 124.
Whisenhunt, John, 169.
Whisenhunt, Maria, 151.
Whisenhunt, Mary, 105, 124, 136, 143, 151, 169, 173, 177, 184.
White, Bryan, 168.
White, Katherine, 168.
White, Katherine (2), 168.
Whiteford (Whitford), Mary, 123-4, 126, 133, 138, 145, 148, 155, 163, 173.
Whiteford, Rachel, 116.
Whiteford (Whitford), Robert, 96, 125-6, 133, 138, 145, 148.
Whitman, Catharina Barbara, 144, 199.
Whitman, Mary Ann, 144, 161.
Whitman, Mary Catharina, 161.
Whitman, Stephen, 144, 161, 199.
Whitten, Robert, 4, 8.
Wild, Thomas, 11.
Williams, Britton, 276, 508.
Williams, Hannah, 110.
Willis, Adam, 172.
Willis, John, 139.
Willis, Regina, wife of Adam, 172.
Willis, Regina, wife of John, 139.
Windlee, Ann Margaret, 146-7.
Windlee, David Frederick, 146.
Windlee, John, 146.
Winigum, Amy, 169.
Wise, Christopher, 229.
Witham, Solomon, 110.
Witt, John Adam, 152.
Witt, Regina, 152.
Wolfe (Woolf, Wolff, Wolf), Ann, 103, 132, 134, 196.
Wolfe, Ann Apollonia, 122, 132, 141, 152, 169, 187, 212, 214.
Wolfe, Ann Apollonia (2), 122.
Wolfe, Elizabeth, 128, 149, 202, 212.
Wolfe, Hannah, 149, 156, 158.
Wolfe, Jacob, Sr., 96, 106, 122, 132, 134, 141, 152, 169, 187, 189, 227.

Wolfe, Jacob, Jr., 11.
Wolfe, Jacob, son of John, 149, 202.
Wolfe, Johannes, 114, 128, 149, 162, 176, 202, 212.
Wolfe, John (of Saxe-Gotha Township), 79.
Wolfe, John (of Orangeburgh), 103, 126, 151, 166, 169, 174, 196.
Wolfe, John Lewis, 100 (Lucy), 186.
Wolfe, Lucas, 98, 105, 129.
Wolfe, Mary Elizabeth, 132.
Wolfe, Nessa, 95.
Wolfe, Peter, 128, 202.
Wolfe, Regina, 187, 212.
Wolfe, Samuel, 169.
Wolfe, Sertina, 100.
Wolfe, Thomas, 103.
Wolfe, Zibilla, 30, 208, 214.
Wood, Benjamin, 151.
Wood, George Riggs, 172.
Wood, Jonathan Riggs, 160.
Wood, Jonathan, 163.
Wood, John, 105.
Wood, Joseph, 120, 138, 151, 163, 182, 217.
Wood, Joseph (2), 138.
Wood, Martha, 138, 151, 163, 182.
Wood, Mary, 171-2.
Wood, Olivia, 110.
Wood, Peter, 160, 171-2.
Wood, Solomon, 218.
Wright, Samuel, 98.
Wurtz (Wuester, Wurtzer, Wartzer), Henry, 28, 30, 96-7, 100-3, 106, 114-15, 119, 120, 136, 144, 158, 162, 185, 206, 210.
Wurtz, Verena, 103-4, 136, 144, 162, 185, 214.
Wylde, J., 275.
Wymer, Anne, 165, 203, 208.
Wymer, Anne Margaret, 165, 203.
Wymer, Jacob, 165, 187, 203.
Wymer, John Jacob, 120, 208.
Ygly, Barbara, 157.

Ygly, Catharina, 107.
Yonn, Anna, 182.
Yonn, Anna Barbara, 209.
Yonn, Christina, 138, 166, 168, 184, 189, 209.
Yonn, Nicholas, 138, 166, 168, 178, 184, 186, 189, 209.
Yonn, Nicholas (2), 209.
Yonn, Simon, 175, 190.
Yonn, Susannah, 135, 157.
York, Agnesia W., 103.
York, Christian, 97, 108.
York, Lewis, 97, 103.
Young, Anna Barbara, 215.
Young, Ann, 153, 166, 186,
Young, Henry, 117, 153, 166, 186, 230, 271.
Young, Henry (2), 166.
Young, Mary, 140, 166.
Young, Mary (2), 166.
Young, Rebecca, 94, 153.
Young, Sirrah, 113.
Young, Thomas, 186, 249, 265.
Young, William, 8, 30, 94, 113, 114, 140, 166.
Young, William (2), 140.
Zahn, Christopher, 258, 275-6.
Zauberbuhler, Bartholomew, 36, 37, 50-1, 54-6, 58-9.
Zeigler, Angelia, 116.
Zeigler, Anne Mary, 142, 146, 155, 157, 173, 188, 199.
Zeigler, Bernard, 116, 138, 142, 146, 155, 157, 173, 178, 188, 193, 199.
Zeigler, Eva Catharina, 188.
Zeigler, Hans Caspar, 173.
Zeigler, John Jacob, 157.
Zeigler, Zibilla, 142, 199.
Zellwegerin, Rosina, 110.
Zimmerman, Martin, 184.
Zorn, Anne Katharine, 180.
Zorn, Catharina, 107.
Zorn, Henry, 177, 180, 184, 193.
Zorn, Magdalene, 114.
Zorn, Nicholas, 161, 177, 180.
Zorn, Susannah Elizabeth, 177, 180.
Zubly, Rev. Dr., 46.

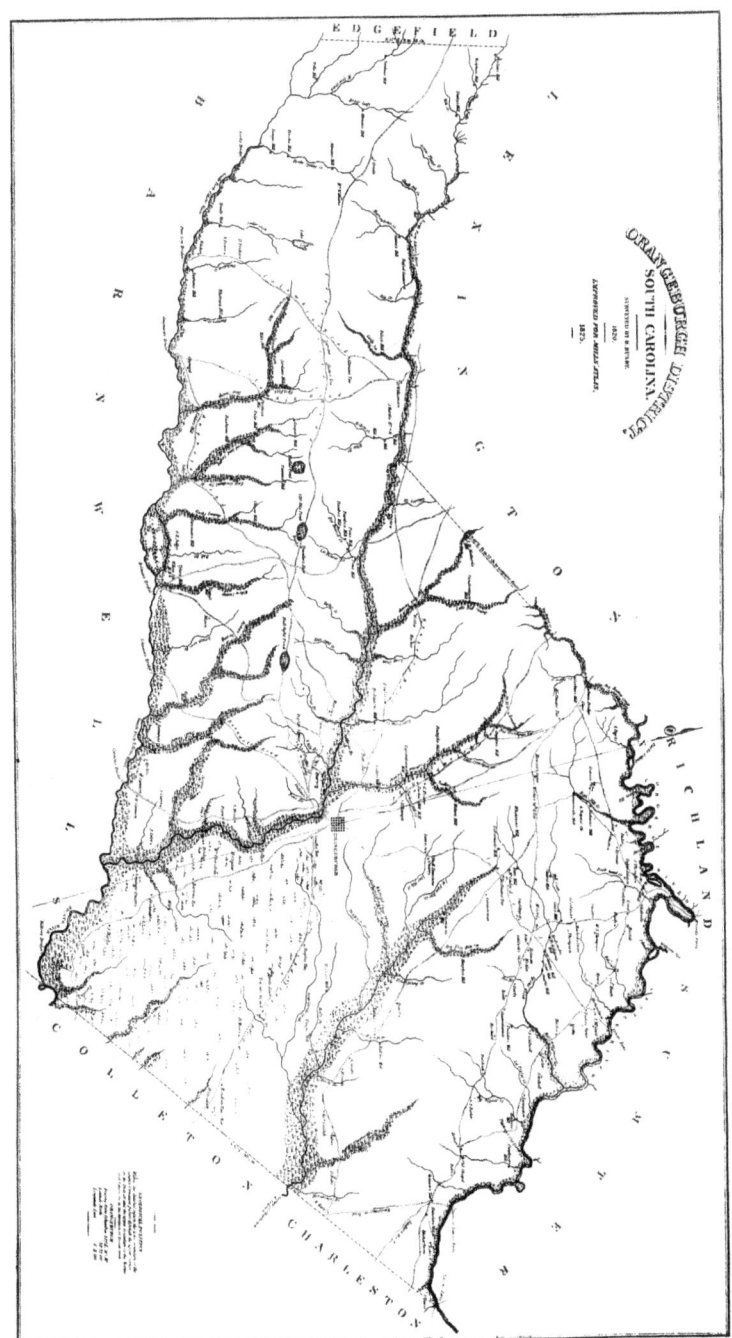

www.ingramcontent.com/pod-product-compliance
Lightning Source LLC
Chambersburg PA
CBHW070004010526
44117CB00011B/1423